The Marketing Research Process

5th edition

THE MARKETING RESEARCH PROCESS

5th edition

Len Tiu Wright and Margaret Crimp

FINANCIAL TIMES
Prentice Hall

An imprint of **Pearson Education**

Harlow, England · London · New York · Reading, Massachusetts · San Francisco · Toronto · Don Mills, Ontario · Sydney
Tokyo · Singapore · Hong Kong · Seoul · Taipei · Cape Town · Madrid · Mexico City · Amsterdam · Munich · Paris · Milan

Pearson Education Limited
Edinburgh Gate
Harlow
Essex CM20 2JE
England

and Associated Companies around the world

Visit us on the World Wide Web at:
http://www.pearsoneduc.com

First published 1981
Fourth edition 1995
Fifth edition 2000

ISBN 0130-11753-6

British Library Cataloguing-in-Publication Data
A catalogue record for this book is available from the British Library

Library of Congress Cataloging-in-Publication Data

Wright, Len Tiu.
    The marketing research process / Len Tiu Wright and Margaret Crimp.--5th ed.
        p. cm.
    Includes bibliographical references and index.
    ISBN 0-13-011753-6
        1. Marketing research. I. Crimp, Margaret. II. Title.
HF5415.2.W75 2000
658.8'3--dc21   99-051903

10 9 8 7 6 5 4 3 2
04 03 02

Typeset in 9.5/12 pt Stone Serif by 30
Printed and bound in Great Britain by Ashford Colour Press Ltd, Gosport, Hants.

Contents

Contents

14 Qualitative research *Mary Goodyear*   373

15 The international marketing research process *Caroline Noon*   401

Preface

This fifth edition maintains the style of the previous editions in focusing on the marketing research process, the essence of the book. It not only updates previous editions, but also includes much that is new in terms of material and authors. The fifth edition takes on the objective, in its entirety, of explaining how the concept of locating and satisfying customer needs, while meeting supplier goals profitably, is undertaken amidst the continuing dynamism of changes in markets and the diversity of industries. This objective can be fulfilled by the discipline or rigour of the marketing research process. Consideration has been given to the effects of changes in the marketing research environment as the 1990s drew to a close and a new millennium started.

This fifth edition takes on the challenge with many updates and new case studies. It not only provides updates, but breaks further from the earlier editions by addressing the concerns of readers. The research process, explained in the fourth edition, is clarified further. The fifth edition is no longer restricted to the view of the research process as 'stages' implicit in the progression of the chapters in the first, second and third editions. In the fifth edition the research process is one that is stimulated by influences in the external environment, and it is a lively one. True, the stages of a process itself – locating a need in the market, conducting exploratory research, putting up a research proposal, and a research design – will seem a descriptive process. While they remind us of the importance of research which is subject to disciplined and systematic procedures, research by its very nature, is embryonic. This is why the insights which the practitioners bring to the book are valuable in showing the realities of research within companies. Each new research study brings with it its own problems and new ways of looking at problem-solving and opportunities. The environment in which it is undertaken is subject to a lot of changes and it is dynamic. Another major strength of the book is that the principles and techniques in the research process itself, from the design procedures and sampling to data collection and analysis, in effect provide both the content and armoury needed for new researchers in both academic and practitioner circles.

Those familiar with the previous editions will notice the additions of new authors for chapters and case studies, some of which are suitable for seminar discussion or presentation purposes. There is also more international material – with the inclusion of published figures and their discussion about the international research industry, and Chapter 15 is devoted to international marketing research.

One of the intentions, apart from being an instructive textbook for market research and marketing courses, is to take the reader through an exploratory, informative and, I hope, an enjoyable journey. Explanations of research and the research processes are supported by the authoritative work and expertise of authors who are at the forefront of their professions, for which, see *Notes on contributors*.

I hope the book proves to be compulsive reading, not just for the purposes of studying and passing institute and university examinations. The words 'informative' and 'a good read' are what I hope readers of the book will perceive the fifth edition to be.

There are facts and pertinent discussion. For example, there is a historical, original account and contemporary overview of market research with examples of organisations and types of research work, and descriptions of what research companies are doing in their specialist applications of qualitative and quantitative research. The impact of multimedia technologies in research work for the media is reflected in the use of technology to assist monitoring, customer interviewing and feedback to clients. There is a need for marketing information systems in an environment that has seen many changes in the past 40 years, with the development of the Internet in particular. The facts and discussion in the fifth edition set the scene for readers to appreciate what I have called the 'three Ds: Discipline, Dynamism and Diversity' of the marketing research process. The fusion of academic and practitioner perspectives is one of the major strengths of the book. The contributions of experts in their respective fields benefit the book and there are those who have helped with material and contacts even though they have not written chapters. Contributors' names are presented in the *Acknowledgements*.

Chapter 15 on international marketing research highlights the disciplined conduct and diversity of outlooks needed for international research processes. At the outset, ideas are 'progressed' about how the research process feeds through in pretesting, acceptances of consumer and cultural nuances, to advertising and the media and onto institutional buyers of research. So the outcomes lead directly into marketing activities as client organisations make use of marketing research to develop products for their own needs.

In summary, this book is a contribution to the discipline of marketing research with in-depth analysis and new ideas from the efforts of all the contributors concerned.

Readership

This fifth edition with its specialist contributions is suitable as a textbook on undergraduate degree courses and university foundation courses at Master's level in Business Studies. The organisation of the book improves its applicability to core market research courses and modularised option modules.

It is also suitable for diploma and certificate courses where marketing, international marketing and marketing research are taught and examined at professional institutes as many elements of the marketing mix and research strategies for domestic and international markets are related.

Both academics and practitioners will, I hope, find the insights in the book to be intellectually stimulating and the contents of practical benefit.

Acknowledgements

This section enables me to pay tribute to the individuals and organisations who have helped along the way.

The quality of the book is due to the tireless efforts of those who participated in the writing of it and others who parted with their information so that readers in the wider world could benefit from the use of that information: thanks are due to the AQRP, the Advertising Association, ESOMAR, Granada Mediasales, Nielsen, NRS, MRS, BARB and RAJAR. I am also indebted to Michael Waterson (NTC Publications), David Barr (MRS), Steve Martin (BMRA), Ian McClellan (Outdoor Advertising Association), Philip Mason (The Royal Mail) and Philip Spink (the Advertising Association).

Credit is due to the late Margaret Crimp whose contributions from the first, second and third editions helped to lay a sound foundation upon which to build the fourth and fifth editions.

My thanks go to the individuals whose names appear in the order in which their chapters are printed in the book: E. John Davis (sampling and Appendix 3); Mike Hussey (spreadsheets); Martin Evans (geodemographics and biographics); Rory Morgan (modelling techniques); Ken Clarke (business-to-business research); Mary Goodyear (qualitative research); Caroline Noon (international marketing research); and John Bound (Appendix 2).

I am grateful for the contributions of specialist sections from Miriam Catterall (qualitative work), Mark Davies (semantic differential) and the Taylor Nelson Sofrès Plc team: Brian Roberts (BARB audience measurement research), Sue Homeyard (CATI) and Caroline Shefras (field interviewing and CAPI). Christopher Goard and Carol George's help in locating contributors are acknowledged with thanks.

I am very appreciative of the efforts of the individuals concerned in developing the teaching case material from C. and M.D. Vignali and D. Vrontis, M. Kirkup *et al.*, and K. Clarke.

Finally, my thanks to all the individuals and the organisations whose information has been cited in the fifth edition and whose names are too numerous to mention in a short Acknowledgements section.

Len Tiu Wright
Keele University
July 1999

Notes on contributors

John Bound

John Bound was a marketing researcher in fast-moving consumer goods manufacture and taught Marketing at the University of Strathclyde. Since then he has been a visiting researcher at the London Business School and currently the South Bank University. He has been a member of the Councils of the Royal Statistical Society and of the Market Research Society. He has presented papers to the conferences of the MRS and of ESOMAR, and in 1992 with Professor Andrew Ehrenberg read a paper to the Royal Statistical Society.

Ken Clarke

Ken Clarke has been in research for many years. On leaving Merton College Oxford with a degree in PPE, he joined BMRB for some seven years before moving to Unilever. There he variously held positions as a Market Research Manager, Marketing Services Manager, Marketing Manager, and Sales and Marketing Director. Since leaving Unilever he held a board appointment with a food company, in which he had responsibility for a multiple retail operation, before joining Millward Brown over 10 years ago.

Within Unilever he chaired the Unilever Committee of Research Managers for many years, and also headed up special studies in the econometric assessment of advertising effects, promotional methodology, etc. He is a member of the MRS, and has organised a number of their courses on subjects ranging from product testing to marketing. He has also played a leading role in the education programme of the Society, including the running of its main education vehicle, the annual Summer School.

He has delivered and published papers at the MRS annual conferences and at conferences organised by ESOMAR, and has contributed to specialist journals on marketing and advertising research.

Margaret Crimp

Margaret Crimp passed away in 1993. Her background had been as a research executive, account executive and account director for three large London advertising agencies. She taught marketing research at Ealing College of Higher Education, City of London Polytechnic and Hatfield Polytechnic and on occasions, had reviewed articles for the Market Research Society.

E. John Davis

John Davis has worked in marketing and market research since 1951 with Gillette, British Overseas Airways Corporation (BOAC), Television Audience Measurement, BMRB and J. Walter Thompson. In 1974 he joined Henley Management College as Director of Marketing Studies and since retirement in 1987 has remained active in education and consultancy. He has written three books and numerous papers on the quantitative aspects of marketing. He was awarded the MRS Gold Medal for his work on test marketing.

Martin Evans

Martin Evans is Royal Mail/Mail Marketing Professor of Marketing and Director of the Bristol Business School Research Unit in Marketing. Previously he held professorial posts at the Universities of Portsmouth and Glamorgan and other academic positions at Cardiff Business School and Newcastle Polytechnic. His industrial experience was with Hawker Siddeley and then as a consultant to a variety of organisations for over 25 years. He has published over 100 papers plus eight books, mostly in the areas of marketing research and information, consumer behaviour and direct marketing. He founded the Direct Marketing Research Consortium which is a grouping of collaborative researchers at the Universities of Cardiff, Glamorgan and Portsmouth.

Mary Goodyear

Mary Goodyear is President of MBL Group Developments Ltd, having been Chairman and Chief Executive of one of the Group's operating companies, Market Behaviour Limited.

After taking a degree in Psychology with Philosophy, she helped develop the then newly-fledged British qualitative research sector in the mid-1960s.

For the next three decades much of her time was spent overseas on project work and in training local suppliers in qualitative methodologies. She pioneered the qualitative sector in India, West Africa, the Caribbean and the Middle East.

She is a Fellow of the MRS, having been an active member for 30 years, writing articles, giving papers and running seminars. She is on the Editorial Advisory Board of the JMRS and of the newly formed *Qualitative Market Research Journal*.

She has been closely involved with ESOMAR's expansion beyond Europe. Between 1992 and 1994 she was the first woman and the first qualitative researcher President of the Society.

Mike Hussey

Mike Hussey teaches marketing research at Aston Business School when he is not moonlighting as a service quality consultant or jobbing statistician.

He is co-editor (with Graham Hooley) of the research text *Quantitative Methods in Marketing* as well as being author of a couple of children's books.

Apart from service quality, his research interests include the role of marketing within the gambling industry and the application of Bayesian methods to marketing models.

Rory P. Morgan

Rory Morgan began his career in market research in 1972 when he joined Research Bureau Ltd, a leading custom research agency based in London, which subsequently became the founding member of the Research International Group of world-wide companies. With an initial background in biological sciences and experimental psychology from London University, he has worked since then in a variety of roles within that organisation and has been involved in projects spanning numerous product areas in both consumer and business markets. He has had considerable experience of international research and his career has included a period of working in RI's East African subsidiary based in Nairobi.

His particular specialisms include the areas of computer modelling techniques, multivariate analysis (including market segmentation) and pricing research. In these subjects he has delivered papers in Europe and North America, in addition to contributing to various textbooks and learning aids. His previous role was as a Board Director of Research International UK and Managing Director of RI Technical Systems Ltd, the subsidiary responsible for developing and supporting advanced research techniques, particularly those involving computer applications. He is currently the Research and Development Director for the entire group of world-wide companies.

He has guided a large number of projects involving the use of forecasting models in a wide range of areas including transportation, manufacturing, service industries and government bodies.

Caroline Noon

Caroline Noon has worked in international market research for 13 years, and is now a Director at the Research Business International specialising in international, qualitative research. Caroline has updated the international marketing research chapter previously written for the fourth edition by **Carol Coutts**, one of the founders of the Research Business International and its previous Chairman, who is now retired.

Len Tiu Wright

Currently, Len Tiu Wright is a Senior Lecturer in Marketing in the Management Department at Keele University. She has been employed in marketing in a variety of industries and has a PhD in Industrial and Business Studies. She has lectured overseas and in the UK. Her last two appointments were at the Universities of Loughborough and Birmingham. Her overseas researches in Japan, Asia, Europe and the United States have been the subject of publications in American, British and European refereed journals. She is the Editor of *Qualitative Market Research – An International Journal* and the Internet Editor of the *Marketing Intelligence and Planning Journal*. Her main interests are in marketing research, international marketing and international management.

List of tables, figures and boxes

1 An introduction to marketing research

What is marketing research and why is it an important discipline? In this chapter we define marketing research, the integrative nature of research within marketing and the importance of research in the solution of marketing opportunities and problems. The background to the development of marketing research is given in terms of a historical perspective, which illustrates its evolution within the marketing discipline. This is followed by descriptions of different types of research, from product to customer research. The nature, scope and importance of the market research industry today will be illustrated from the contexts of the types of research activities and methods employed by firms in the industry.

1.1 The importance of marketing research

As modern-day consumers we are aware of the proliferation of product and brand choices available to us. When we walk into any large retail store we can see the many and various examples of products on sale. Many of these are the results of market research activity where investigations into changing tastes and fashion have enabled companies to make informed choices about what new products to introduce. This in turn can lead to greater customer choice at the point of sale. As an example, the *Financial Times*[1] has estimated that 1000 new consumer products reach British supermarket shelves each month. So marketing research serves an important purpose. First, it provides needed information to suppliers about customer demand for their products and services. Second, it serves customers by providing opportunities for their views and needs to be taken into account.

Moreover, modern methods of manufacturing and production, storage, transportation, electronic stock ordering and customer payment systems have helped to speed up the processes of market transactions (goods and payments) between suppliers and their customers. Modern-day marketing research, in an increasingly competitive and sophisticated environment, has to find ways of getting in touch with industrial customers and the populations in consumer markets which are increasingly supported by advances in telecommunications such as cable and satellite. The advent of the Internet and supplier web sites, together with new hardware and software to support computerised multimedia technological advances are also revolutionising the transactional processes between suppliers and their customers.

As organisations fight for market shares in mature and declining markets, they intensify their research and development for new products and new markets, so the uncovering of marketing intelligence from research activities becomes of vital importance. Knowledge is power, but only if it can be used effectively. Research is an innovative and high risk activity when developing new and complex products for the marketplace where there are pressures to justify large returns on capital investment and increases in production.

With new markets emerging, new sources of competition have also emerged and businesses, through new telecommunications and computing technologies, transcend national boundaries in their fight for sales. We can take as examples the leading mobile phone companies Vodaphone and Cellnet, and in the Internet sector, book and magazine retailing over the Internet.

However, in the introduction of new products, services and new technologies, developments are normally accompanied by substantial increases in the financial capital required to produce and nurture them. There are greater penalties for mistakes when business failures are accompanied by bigger increases in capital requirements and larger job losses. Within these contexts, marketing research has to operate in a world which is dynamic and where technologies and their products are ever evolving.

Marketing research, therefore, reports on trends, the nature of demand and competition, and the phenomenon of change in the marketplace. The processes of research isolate the key elements of that change and explain them in relation to the activities of an organisation and vis-à-vis its competition. Marketing research performs an advisory role to managers by making recommendations from the pursuit, acquisition and analyses of information.

The optimisation of the integration of research results into the decision-making process is reflected in the mission statement of the European Society for Opinion and Marketing Research (ESOMAR), which is based in the Netherlands, and was founded in 1948, 'to promote the use of opinion and market research for improving decision making in business and society worldwide'.[2]

Generally speaking, the more open or easier to enter a market is for competitors, the greater the risk they pose to the organisations already established in selling to that market. So marketing research is needed, not just in new markets for the established organisations, but also to finely tune or to refine new decisions which have to be taken in old markets. Some organisations may subscribe to the 'follow the market leader' mentality. Others may dispense with this, preferring to uncover new market opportunities and seek to fulfil their customer needs while at the same time reaping the profits for this. Managers, nowadays, cannot afford to be ill informed about market conditions. Decisions taken about markets and customers can be the subject of very critical analysis at board level meetings so managers and their directors will seek better quality decision-making to justify their responsibilities and expenditures. Thus, marketing research has penetrated the culture of thinking from the corporate level to the shop floor.

Marketing research has become an established discipline, employing many people, with a direct impact on the lives of those who work in it or who are the industrial customers or individual consumers of the products of the research. The term 'marketing research' covers the processes by which information on customers and their product needs and usage is systematically gathered and analysed by research suppliers on behalf of their clients, hence the title of this book, *The Marketing Research Process*.

1.2 Marketing research defined

Two definitions by the Market Research Society (MRS) and the American Marketing Association (AMA) are useful in clarifying what marketing research is. In the past there used to be some confusion as to the use of the terms 'market research' and 'marketing research'. Market research was the term given to the different types of research carried out by individual researchers and companies, while marketing research came to symbolise the wider implications of the use of research in the systematic processes of the gathering and evaluation of data. However, it can be seen from the MRS and AMA definitions that it is now widely accepted that the terms are interchangeable in the nature and scope of the work carried out and in dealing with information about customers and the marketplace.

Market research is defined by the Market Research Society within the wide context of covering all kinds of data gathering and examination dealing with market and social investigations.

> Research is the collection and analysis of data from a sample of individuals or organisations relating to their characteristics, behaviour, attitudes, opinions or possessions. It includes all forms of marketing and social research such as consumer and industrial surveys, psychological investigations, observational and panel studies.[3]

The American Marketing Association also looks towards marketing research in its functional forms with the specification of responsibilities and tasks, its relevance to marketing problems and opportunities, and the processes involved in feeding back the products of the research.

> Marketing research is the function which links the consumer, customer, and public to the market through information – information used to identify and define marketing opportunities and problems; generate, refine, and evaluate marketing actions; monitor marketing performance; and improve understanding of marketing as a process. Marketing research specifies the information required to address these issues; designs the method for collecting information; manages and implements the data collection process; analyzes the results; and communicates the findings and their implications ... Marketing research is the systematic gathering, recording and analyzing of data about problems relating to the marketing of goods and services.[4]

The linkage function to the market through information and the generation of activities and outputs underlies its fundamental importance, as expressed in the AMA description.

The word *systematic* means that marketing research is not about a hit and miss collection of observations about the marketplace. The orderly and methodical approach to the collection of data is important. Research has to be designed so that it achieves the objectives set for it in the first place, e.g. in the client's brief or the initial research proposal. The *gathering* and *recording* of data in the research design needs to be methodical. It is vital that irregularities are ironed out so that the research findings can be treated as impartial and can be validated or supported by evidence in a constructive way. Otherwise the research outcomes will be 'without foundation'.

The activities covered in these definitions outline much of the **marketing research process**. The primary contribution of the marketing research process is the acquisition and analysis of information pertinent to managerial decision-making in the appraisal of markets. As more organisations embrace the marketing concept with its focus on organisational resources and activities to satisfy the needs and wants of customers, so the scope for marketing research increases. When market conditions change, as with the application of technology in the evolution of products and their servicing requirements, these changes will influence customer demand as we have seen, for example, in the increasing uptake of hand-held mobile phones in the marketplace. Changes in markets and with customers, therefore, hold important implications for the market research industry and its clients.

1.3 Synopsis of the marketing research process

Figure 1.1 sets out the framework for the marketing research process. Within this framework there are activities associated with each of the stages. It should be borne in mind that the activities are shown in 'stages' as a guide. Different individuals and organisations will vary the ways in which their marketing research processes are conducted. Some might want to dispense with the exploratory research when there is thought to be sufficient information to formulate the research proposal and to invite market research agencies to compete or to tender for their work. Others might choose to spend more time consulting with their market research suppliers and to give these suppliers a relatively free hand in the research design. Still others might buy in ad hoc or one-off research to add to the ongoing efforts of the organisations in gathering marketing intelligence and their marketing planning.

Define the problem

A typical starting point for the research process is the problem definition stage which sets out what choices an organisation is faced with in its marketing activities in a particular situation and what it wants to achieve or to solve.

Companies which have periodic and systematic formal marketing audits will have updated qualitative and quantitative assessments of their internal organisational and external business environments (for descriptions of marketing audits see McDonald[5]). A SWOT (strengths, weaknesses, opportunities and threats) analysis can supplement the audit to determine the organisational strengths and weaknesses of the organisation commissioning the research and to identify opportunities and threats to its business from external environmental forces (e.g. political, economic and social forces).

A review of whether past marketing objectives have been met can be determined from an assessment of organisational activities which will assist companies in setting out their new agendas for research, such as the commissioning of market surveys, and to set out new research objectives.

Exploratory research can be used to clarify the problem areas for research. As an example, initial qualitative research as a precursor to an expensive full-scale quantitative survey can be undertaken if a company wants to undertake a risk assessment about whether resources for the survey should be spent and whether the original marketing objectives need modifying.

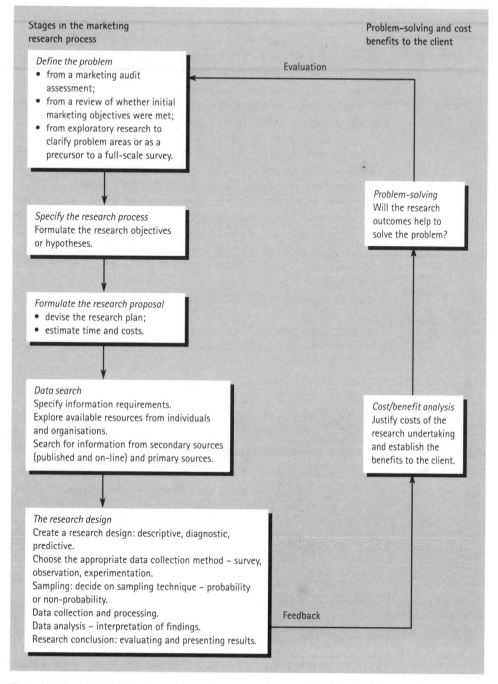

Stages in the marketing research process

Define the problem
- from a marketing audit assessment;
- from a review of whether initial marketing objectives were met;
- from exploratory research to clarify problem areas or as a precursor to a full-scale survey.

Specify the research process
Formulate the research objectives or hypotheses.

Formulate the research proposal
- devise the research plan;
- estimate time and costs.

Data search
Specify information requirements.
Explore available resources from individuals and organisations.
Search for information from secondary sources (published and on-line) and primary sources.

The research design
Create a research design: descriptive, diagnostic, predictive.
Choose the appropriate data collection method – survey, observation, experimentation.
Sampling: decide on sampling technique – probability or non-probability.
Data collection and processing.
Data analysis – interpretation of findings.
Research conclusion: evaluating and presenting results.

Problem-solving and cost benefits to the client

Evaluation

Problem-solving
Will the research outcomes help to solve the problem?

Cost/benefit analysis
Justify costs of the research undertaking and establish the benefits to the client.

Feedback

Fig 1.1 The marketing research process

Specify the research process

Problem definition does not necessarily have to be about identifying threats to a company's business and how to resolve these threats. A company can be faced with how to plan its growth because of the desire to diversify into new products or new markets or to acquire new brands and new distribution outlets by merging with or acquiring other companies. Such changes to a company's marketing efforts or operational status will require new studies of its market to be carried out since previous information may become inadequate or inappropriate in the changed circumstances. In this context, new research objectives will have to be set. These should be clear, measurable and achievable.

An example of a research objective can be to establish whether there is an opportunity for a new brand in a particular product field. Research investigations can then be carried out on a brand name for a product and the associations which potential customers can make towards the brand image. The brand image can then be developed in advertisements and in all the other communications associated with the product, including its packaging for the market.

Hypothesis testing starts with a hypothesis in a null form, which means formulating a statement that a population parameter has a particular value or set of values. If, for example, the managers of a cinema pondered on the problem of attracting larger audiences to its film shows and wanted to start with an investigation of its target market, they would need to know what the mean age of its cinema-goers was.

If the managers thought that the mean age of its cinema-goers was 23 years old, the null hypothesis (H_0) would be: H_0: $\mu = 23$.

The managers would then set out to test whether this hypothesis can be accepted, or if rejected, what alternative hypothesis can be accepted.

In simple terms, the major purposes of marketing research are to find the information for marketing decisions and the solutions to marketing problems. So the necessary questions at the outset are:

'Do we need this piece of research?'
'Will the value of the research more than pay for itself?'
'What is the type of research to be carried out?'
'When should this piece of research be done and concluded?'
'Who are the people who will carry it out?'
'What additional resources are required to carry out the research?'

The research proposal

If the answers are 'yes' to the first two questions above, then the **research proposal** should have some answers to the last four questions.

The research proposal will contain an outline of the research requirements. It contains the 'blueprint' for the proposed creation of a systematic and logical research activity which will include time and cost inputs and the equipment and computing software when required. The research proposal is more like a guide so that both parties, the research agency and the client, know where they stand and what they have agreed to in principle. In the course of conducting research it could transpire that more resources are needed at different stages. In general, researchers should aim to keep the costs of research within the budgeted constraints, though in practice this might not always be possible.

The people responsible for bidding for the work from the client need to take account of client personalities and objectives in presenting their proposals, both to convince the client and to win the contract for the research proposal to be put into practice.

Careful planning in the initial stages of the research process will be of benefit in guiding decision-makers in problem-solving. This will lessen any difficulties between the research agency and the client, and the risks involved if business decisions do not work out as planned.

Data search

Having made the decisions about why the information is being sought in the first place, the data search stage is important in determining what information critical to the problem at hand may exist within the organisation and outside it.

Secondary and primary sources of information are investigated. These are explained in Chapter 2.

The research design

The **research design** consists of choosing the survey method to be adopted, the sampling technique, data collection, data analysis, interpretation and evaluation of findings and the presentation of research work to the client organisation. The research design stages constitute an important part of the research activity.

The research design stages are explained at the beginning of Chapter 3, which also introduces a discussion of data collection methods. Chapter 2 details the types of information and methods used. The process of sampling and its techniques is explained in Chapter 4. Having decided on the sample, researchers need to approach the sample populations. The different techniques in asking questions are presented in Chapter 5 on questionnaire design. Chapter 6, on the use of spreadsheets in marketing research, explains the different types of spreadsheets and their applications which aid the procedures, analysis and presentation of results.

The Halfords case study at the end of Chapter 10 shows the research design process at work and the types of activities carried out.

Cost/benefit analysis

Did the outcomes justify the expenditure and time devoted by both parties, the client and the research supplier? The costs and benefits of the research to the client company must be determined to see whether the research outcomes have significantly aided the client company or organisation in its problem-solving.

It is important to provide constructive feedback to the client. If the client organisation is kept aware of research developments periodically and the research is carried out according to client expectations, as agreed in the research brief with the research supplier, then the supplier will have an easier task of convincing the client of the merits of the research and of accepting the research recommendations.

Problem-solving

Was the client satisfied with the outcomes? In other words, did the outcomes aid in problem-solving or solve the problem?

Evaluation of the research outcomes is an important part in helping to assess whether the financial and human resources used have met the expectations of the decision-makers from the client organisation. If the research activities have been useful in helping them in various ways, e.g. meeting the objectives for problem-solving: reformulation of marketing plans and strategies; adaptation of their marketing campaigns for segmentation, product differentiation and positioning purposes in the effective application of the elements in their marketing mixes, then the whole research process will have been invaluable.

There are different time factors involved in evaluating such work, as the outcomes expected (through systematic research work) and unexpected (such as greater competitive activity or changing customer demand) may not be immediate. For example, sales promotions are easier to measure than mass advertising because customer returns of money-off coupons from labels and customer enquiries can be attributed to particular types of promotions. However, the effectiveness of advertising can be notoriously difficult to measure and its effects may be more long lasting or shorter than predicted. People advertise because increased advertising should normally have an effect of raising sales, but the outcomes may not be as hoped for.

The monitoring function is also important because it is aimed at reducing uncertainty when plans are being made (whether these relate to the marketing operation as a whole or to individual components, as in advertising) and keeping an account of performance after the plans have been implemented.

1.4 Historical perspectives of marketing and market research

As the new century begins it is worth taking a look back to see how far marketing research has come. Its growth has been closely bound to the development of the marketing discipline.

1.4.1 Marketing concepts and relevance to marketing research

In the early days when mass markets were developing, consumers had less choice concerning the finer points of the products they could buy. Marketing research was in its infancy. As one of the early pioneers in the car industry, Henry Ford, demonstrated, when he mass produced his Model T black car, his customers bought the standardised model, in the absence of choice. When consumer demands and markets were increasing firms could concentrate on finding ways to expand production and getting their goods to their customers. The period 1900 to the latter part of the 1920s came to be known as the production era in marketing, when mass-produced low-cost products were made widely available.

By the mid-1930s industrial incomes were rising. Production-oriented management aimed increasing volumes of consumer products at growing and attractive markets. As more firms were attracted into markets, competition grew.

By the 1930s and the 1940s there were problems with distribution associated with uneven variations in the quality of infrastructure facilities within domestic markets and in the getting of goods to export markets. Less attention was given to the sensitive adaptation to consumer needs. By the 1940s increasing competition and greater consumer choice were contributory factors to the evolution of the product and selling concepts in the development of marketing. Both concepts started the shift towards consumer orientation and hence to interest in advertising and consumer research. The **product concept** implied that consumers favoured products with the best features, performance and quality. So more effort was given to researching and advertising such aspects.

Those who held to the **selling concept** were of the opinion that consumers would not necessarily buy if left to themselves so aggressiveness in selling and pro- motional activities were called for. To induce such transactional exchanges firms were prepared to introduce more attractive sales incentives or persistent hard- selling efforts in order to persuade potential customers to part with their money. However, the concept was still oriented to what the firm wanted to sell rather than to what a customer wanted to buy.

One should not see these concepts as relegated only to the specific periods in which they were deemed fashionable. The 1950s and 1960s saw periods of economic growth in the western economies of the world. For example, the Conservative Party slogan in the 1959 UK general election was 'You've never had it so good!' As a later example, in the 1970s and very early 1980s the general world-wide recession in traditional manufacturing industries such as shipbuild- ing, textiles and machine tools meant that many firms went in for cost-cutting measures including rationalisation of product lines, redundancies and lower prices to undercut competitors, cutting back on the size of marketing depart- ments and emphasising their selling efforts. Firms which did the latter exhibited a marked sales orientation.

This period also saw a trimming down of the size of market research depart- ments, and rather than having the expense of employing people, work was contracted out to external research suppliers or agencies whenever there were spe- cific jobs to be done. Research agencies often found themselves dealing with their corporate clients' brand and marketing managers rather than in-house market research managers.[6] Dealing with other managers meant that the research data supplied was only a part of the overall information used by the clients, whereas in- house market research managers would have made far more use of or placed greater importance on the research data supplied. Companies which survived the recession were seen to be 'leaner and fitter' because they put the focus on product innovation, performance, and quality. They combined the best aspects of the prod- uct concept with a strong orientation to following the marketing concept. The latter part of the 1980s to the present time has seen a sustained period of growth for the market research industry.[7]

The 1980s also saw a period of privatisation of nationalised industries in a number of industrialised countries, e.g. the UK, France and Italy.[8] Governments were prime spenders on research and advertising to sound out public opinion and to inform their publics about privatisation issues in order to encourage people into buying shares in these newly privatised industries.

The **marketing concept**, as a business philosophy today, has been an enduring one for organisations, which has emphasised the satisfaction of customer needs and good customer care. Organisations implementing the marketing concept would 'integrate marketing activities in determining and satisfying the needs and wants of target markets more efficiently than competitors and profitably to achieve organisational goals'.[9] Since the marketing concept has the external focus on consumers, marketing research has, therefore, evolved in importance by uncovering the needs of target markets and feeding the information back to client organisations. Both the disciplines of marketing and marketing research have grown in their relevance to businesses and consumers at large, for example in the growth of external consultancies for firms, in-house training, market research qualifications[10] and inclusion in the syllabuses of business studies courses in universities and colleges.[11]

1.4.2 Contributions of individuals and institutions

Marketing research has also shared another similarity with the evolution of marketing as an academic and practical discipline in the early part of the twentieth century. To appreciate this it is useful to look at some of the early work pioneered by individuals and institutions. Some of this occurred through the interest of individuals studying the food industry, primarily in agricultural production, the use of equipment or implements and the marketing of commodities. Charles Coolidge Parlin, sometimes referred to as the 'father of marketing research', was one of those who conducted a survey of the farm implement market which he produced in 1911. His publication of an extensive study into the textile market in 1912 formed the basis of sales estimations in US city department stores. His activities in the systematic gathering and production of market surveys had an impact on the emerging market research industry. Parlin was also known for his work with the Curtis Publishing Company as its commercial research division manager.

Robert Bartels[12] has drawn attention to the contributions of the early US pioneers from the universities of Wisconsin and Harvard and the mid-western universities of Minnesota, Michigan, Illinois and Ohio. For example, L.D.H. Weld who worked at the University of Minnesota in 1912 before moving to the College of Agriculture, researched the course of butter and eggs to market, their pricing and distribution channels through wholesalers, jobbers and retailers. He also carried out market research work for firms such as Swift & Co. and was a founder member of the early National Association of Teachers in Marketing.

One of the early pioneers at Wisconsin, Benjamin Hibbard, undertook a limited study of grain marketing in 1902 after noticing that farmers in northern Iowa had sold their produce at very low prices, which when sold on by others fetched higher augmented prices. Interestingly, US grain production has been the focus of a market survey by an advertising agency, N.W. Ayer and Son, in 1879. Hibbard became responsible for marketing studies and research at the University of Wisconsin in 1913 and organised the first course in the cooperative marketing of agricultural products. Hibbard and his contemporaries, who held various positions at Wisconsin University, helped to pioneer the establishment of marketing as a science in their research and publications. For example: Theodore Macklin (*Efficient Marketing for Agriculture*, 1921); Paul Nystrom (*Retail Selling and Store Management*, 1911 and *Economics of Consumption*, 1929); Ralph Butler (*Selling and Buying, 1911* which changed to *Marketing*, 1912); Floyd Vaughan (*Marketing and Advertising*, 1928). Nystrom became a commercial research manager at the US Rubber Company in 1915 and director of the Retail Research Association and the Associated Merchandising Corporation from 1921 to 1927. Butler's book on marketing was attributed as the first book with the title of 'Marketing'.

Those who held positions at the University of Harvard, such as Paul Cherington, A.W. Shaw, Melvin Copeland and Neil H. Borden, also contributed to the development of the principles of marketing and research. For example, Cherington was best known for his book *Advertising as a Business Force* published in 1912, which was followed by *The Elements of Marketing* in 1920, and A.W. Shaw for *An Approach to Business Problems*, in 1916. Shaw sought a concept for the unformulated and undescribed evolutionary activity of marketing as the matter of 'process in motion' and began to apply the discipline of business practice to it. In his work with the firm of L.D. Walker which manufactured office equipment, Shaw had observed that business procedures and their uniformity could be used to improve functions in marketing.

Copeland's contacts with Dean Gay who lectured on 'the merchant in the economic history of England' led him to develop and pioneer the notion of using 'cases' in teaching from 1912. Rather than lectures, discussion with students would be through case studies. Copeland became director of the Bureau of Business Research in 1916 and took charge of the studies of operating expenses in wholesale and retail trades. Neil Borden completed his MBA work in 1922 at Harvard and remained for a while as a 'case collector' who also taught marketing under Professor Copeland. His publications include *Problems in Advertising* in 1927 and his well-known article on *The Concept of the Marketing Mix*.[13] The latter was a phrase borrowed from James Culliton's study, in 1948, of manufacturers' marketing costs, where the business executive was described as a 'mixer of ingredients'. The Harvard School's principal contributions in these early years were in the compilation, analyses and publications of marketing problems.

The Kellogg company and the Campbell Soup company were amongst the early users of market surveys in investigating consumption habits, advertising and readership. The first systematic readership survey was attributed to R. Eastman, an advertising executive for Kellogg, in 1911.[14] He went on to establish his Eastman Research Bureau in 1916. Daniel Starch of the Readership Survey Organization pioneered a system of 'Starch Scores' in advertisement recall. The names of George Gallup and Tom Harrison became synonymous with public opinion polling. Gallup was attributed as the first to record a readership's interest in a newspaper in 1928. His name is still regularly called to mind in the media's use of the Gallup Polls at general elections. The Gallup Organization is Britain's longest established survey and polling company, founded in 1937. It is a wholly-owned subsidiary of the Gallup Organization of Princeton, New Jersey, USA.[15] Mass Observation, founded by Harrison, also pioneered observational studies and is well known for its public opinion polling. Research firms such as Nielsen pioneered the use and development of store retail audits in Britain and the USA. RSL-Research Services Ltd was formed in 1946 in Britain and is known for its high-technology processing, data collection and fast data delivery systems to clients. It launched the UK's first national CAPI (computer-assisted personal interviewing) network in 1990 using laptop computers for in-home interviewing and revolutionised the UK omnibus market with CAPIBUS. In 1974 CAPIBUS Europe was introduced to cover five major European markets.[16]

Qualitative research, according to Bill Schlackman,[17] started out as motivational research with its roots in psychology, and owed credit for its initial popularisation to Dr Ernest Dichter in the USA. Schlackman, who has been widely credited with introducing qualitative research in the United Kingdom in the 1960s, saw motivational research lose its title to become 'qualitative research', which he thought was a more accurate description. Mass Observation was also an early pioneer in this field.

In Britain, as on the continent, much pioneering work came from social reformers and early consumer groups which undertook limited social and market studies in efforts to persuade their governments, the influential ruling classes and business corporations that there were cases for reform. Social class divisions with their impact on poverty amongst the working classes, the limited provision of education, poor living conditions and low welfare standards were items for reform on their agendas. Governments, in expanding their public sector commitments, set up more national corporations such as those overseeing broadcasting and public transport.[18] After the Second World War the expanding public and private sectors provided more work for market research agencies.

1.5 The market research industry

1.5.1 Size and scope of world research activity

The size of the world research market has grown to be worth more than 10.4 billion Euros in 1997, as estimated by ESOMAR.[19] (At 1999 rates, one Euro was equal to 67 pence in sterling, US$1.1 and Yen 1.4 approximately). The 15 European Union member countries accounted for a sales turnover of over 4.314 million Euros, against a total European figure of 4.688 million. The sales turnover figures for the United States was estimated at 3.900m, Japan at 875m and the rest of the world 972m.

In 1997 in market share terms, the European Union accounted for 41% and the United States for 37% of the world market. Within Europe itself, in terms of sales turnover, the United Kingdom has led the way with a 25% lead, Germany 22%, France 16%, Italy 7%, Spain 5%, Netherlands 4%, Sweden 4%, Switzerland 2%, Belgium 2% and Austria 2%.

A lot of market research work is now international in scope. ESOMAR has estimated that 18% was work commissioned from abroad. In 1997 amongst 'the top ten research groups world-wide' (see Table 1.1), which accounted for 43% of world turnover, were companies that were also amongst the top ten in the European Union (ACNielsen, Cognizant Corporation, Kantar Group, GFK, Sofrès Group, Infratest/Burke, IPSOS Group, Taylor Nelson AGB, NOP Information Group Ltd, PMSI, respectively in rank order by turnover size).

Takeovers and mergers have resulted in some large research groupings which are able to offer a wide range of expertise and specialised services to clients, supported by innovations in the information technology field such as: data gathering; processing; and speed of delivery of the results to clients throughout the world. Research International (RI), Millward Brown International and the MRB Group belong to the Kantar Group. Taylor Nelson, which acquired Audits of Great Britain (AGB), also acquired the Sofrès Group in December 1997 to become Taylor Nelson Sofrès, thus becoming the top company by size of sales turnover in the UK market.

Client organisations buy research data from different types of market research suppliers, and they commission research work in a variety of ways. As an example,

Table 1.1 Top ten research groups world-wide

Research group	Turnover in Euros (million)
ACNielsen Corporation	1,227
Cognizant Corporation	1,181
Kantar Group	476
Information Resources Incorporated	402
Sofrès Group	288
GFK	265
IPSOS Group	179
NFO Worldwide Incorporated	168
Westat	161
Infratest/Burke	153

syndicated continuous panel services and other large-scale, shared-cost surveys will typically be bought from one of the member companies belonging to the new British Market Research Association (BMRA).

In 1998 the BMRA was formed from the amalgamation of the Association of Market Survey Organisations (AMSO) and the Association of British Market Research Companies (ABMRC), a trade body for small to medium-sized agencies.[20]

1.5.2 Agencies' sales turnover, domestic and international rankings

AMSO was founded in 1964 in the United Kingdom and grew to become the largest research companies trade organisation with 70% of total UK market research revenues. In 1992, the largest companies in AMSO had turnovers exceeding £5 million, as shown in their Annual Report 1993.[21] For instance, in 1992, AMSO members earned £239.3 million from domestic research (8.1% up on 1991 earnings) and £53.7 million from overseas research (11.3% up on 1991 earnings). By 1997 former AMSO companies accounted for £502m and those of ABMRC for £190m. On average for both, the increase year on year has been around 11%. Member companies now belong to the BMRA which constitutes the major part of the UK research industry. Many of their employees are also members of the Market Research Society (MRS).

Table 1.2 shows the 1997 sales turnover of 16 leading market research companies together with the percentage change in turnover compared with the previous year (1996 figures in brackets). The table does not reflect all market research companies, but it serves to highlight the earnings of such agencies in Britain and overseas, as indicated by their international rank order. At the time of writing league tables for the BMRA were not yet available.

1.5.3 Demand for research

As shown in Table 1.3, research commissioned by organisations in the majority of sectors showed an increase from 1995 to 1996. The fast moving consumer goods (fmcg) sector for food and non-alcoholic drinks continued to provide the strongest

Table 1.2 Former AMSO companies 'league table for 1997'

Rank order by turnover	1997 sales turnover in £ millions (increase/ decrease over 1996)	Domestic ranking in 1996	International ranking in 1996
Taylor Nelson Sofrès	87.3 (10.6%)	1	n/a
[Taylor Nelson AGB	–	1	3]
NOP Research Group Ltd	67.4 (7.8%)	2	4
Research International Ltd	52.3 (4.1%)	4	1
Millward Brown International Plc	47.9 (7.2%)	3	2
BMRB International	29.1 (15.1%)	5	13
RSL-Research Services Ltd	25.6 (3.4%)	6	5
The Research Business International	18.7 (12.7%)	7	19
MORI (Market & Opinion Research Int.)	18.2 (10.2%)	10	6
MBL Group Plc	15.1 (13.5%)	9	9
Infratest Burke Group	14.0 (12.1%)	17	15
IRI Infoscan Ltd	13.8 (24.5%)	8	–
Martin Hamblin Group	11.2 (5.3%)	13	8
Simon Godfrey Associates Ltd	8.5 (20.9%)	25	11
ISIS Research Plc	6.6 (15.9%)	37	7
Pegram Walters Group	5.9 (11.8%)	20	16
The Gallup Organization Ltd	5.8 (20.5%)	19	21

Source: Adapted from The Newsletter of the BMRA, no.1, July 1998, p. 8 and AMSO Annual Report 1997, p. 7.

Table 1.3 Areas researched by former AMSO companies

Commissioned research from client sectors	1996 revenue in £ millions (% change compared to 1995)	
Food and non-alcoholic drinks	61.3	(+12%)
Media	39.6	(+9%)
Public services & utilities	35.0	(+9%)
Financial services	31.5	(+10%)
Pharmaceutical companies	30.3	(+9%)
Health and beauty	29.4	(+12%)
Vehicles	27.5	(+6%)
Business and industrial	25.9	(+17%)
Retailers	25.9	(+40%)
Government and public bodies	20.8	(+13%)
Household products	16.4	(–2%)
Alcoholic drinks	16.2	(–2%)
Travel and tourism	14.2	(+1%)
Advertising agencies	10.1	(+4%)
Oil	5.8	(+50%)
Household durables and hardware	5.1	(–3%)
Tobacco	2.7	(–2%)
Other direct clients	41.3	(+7%)
Other AMSO companies (mainly sub-contracted fieldwork)	7.4	

Source: AMSO Annual Report 1997, p. 9. Reprinted with permission.

source of revenue for AMSO members at £61.3 million in 1996, an increase of 12% on 1995. In 1992 this figure was around £47.4 million, which shows the sustained importance of the fmcg sector.

Whilst some marketing research companies provide a wide range of services, particularly the larger ones, others specialise in particular marketing applications, for example in product, packaging, pricing or communications research. A client organisation may choose to plan its own research programme and then buy fieldwork from a specialist market research company. In the past the data may then have come back to the client organisation as computer printouts from an agency specialising in electronic data processing. Translating the data into a report and recommendations was then the sole responsibility of the client organisation. Today's clients expect a fast turnaround in service using the latest computing technologies.

The two data collection methods most commonly used in qualitative research are depth interviews and group discussions. These are also used in industrial and other 'non-domestic' enquiries where the interviewer is often seeking information from an expert. This has not changed significantly since 1994. The personal interview method is most commonly carried out in the UK and in Europe, in contrast to the United States where telephone interviews are widely used. Around 13.5 million interviews are carried out each year in the UK by AMSO members and the data collection methods are shown in Table 1.4.

Table 1.4 Interviewing methods by value

Method	%
Personal interview	43.1
Telephone interview	18.3
Hall test	11.2
Group discussion	9.9
Self completion/post	8.0
Depth interviews	4.0
Street interviews	2.6
Mystery shopping	2.2

Source: Adapted from the *AMSO Annual Report 1997*, p. 9. Reprinted with permission.

Current services offered by research agencies are set out in the Market Research Society (MRS) *Yearbook* 1999. The yearbook, updated annually, is a wide-ranging and essential source of information about the market research industry. It can be seen that all the large companies include syndicated services in their product line. These make a major contribution to turnover (as shown in Table 1.2), contributing to the leading performance of companies such as TN Sofrès and ACNielsen.

Data collected during the course of retail audits, consumer panels (see Table 1.5) tracking studies and omnibus surveys (all of which feature in this book) constitute rich databases. In-house computer terminals linked to a host bureau's mainframe computer, make it possible for a client organisation to access a number of databases.

Table 1.5 Continuous research

	£ millions
Audits and panels	70
Advertising and brand tracking	48
Customer satisfaction	36
Media	22
Others	11

Source: Adapted from the *AMSO Annual Report 1997*, p. 9.

1.5.4 Rights and responsibilities: ensuring quality standards in marketing research

What are the rules, mutual rights and responsibilities governing the undertaking of marketing research? These are important considerations which are fundamental for the health of the industry and for disseminating guidance to maintain respected professional standards.

The ICC (International Chambers of Commerce)/ESOMAR Code of Marketing and Social Research Practice[22] sets out two general statements:

- Marketing research must always be carried out objectively and in accordance with established scientific principles.
- Marketing research must always conform to the national and international legislation which applies in those countries involved in a given research project.

The rights of respondents and the mutual responsibilities of researchers, their agencies and their clients are set out in this international code of conduct. In the UK, the key principles of the MRS's Code of Conduct[23] also define and embody the key responsibilities of the research agencies to informants (respondents), to clients and to the general public and business community:

- **Research** is defined as 'the collection and analysis of data from a sample of individuals or organisations relating to their characteristics, behaviour, attitudes, opinions or possessions. It includes all forms of marketing and social research such as consumer and industrial surveys, psychological investigations, observational and panel studies'.
- A **respondent** is 'any individual or organisation from whom any information is sought by the researcher for the purpose of a marketing or social research project. This includes those approached for research purposes whether or not substantive information is obtained from them and includes those who decline to participate or withdraw at any stage from the research'.
- An **agency** is 'any individual or organisation, department or division, including any belonging to the same organisation as the client which is responsible for, or acts as, a supplier on all or part of a research project'.
- A **client** is 'any individual or organisation, department or division, including any belonging to the same organisation as the research agency which is responsible for commissioning a research project'.

The growth of the marketing research industry has attracted new entrants into the market, eased by the fact that any individual can set up as a research agency to bid for work from firms. The MRS is funding a 'Marketing Market Research Initiative' in collaboration with representatives from the BMRA and AURA (Association of Users of Research Agencies) to 'promote the benefits of quality market research to businesses and the public, differentiating genuine research from other forms of so-called research and malpractice'.[24]

Special research interests provide opportunities for external liaisons between professional associations. For example, the Research Development Foundation (RDF) sponsored by the MRS has a primary cross-industry focus for research and strategic thinking on research.

The importance of raising standards in qualitative research work is also reflected in the key activities of the Association of Qualitative Research Practitioners (AQRP).[25] Much of AQRP's activities are in training and education. AQRP is also involved in establishing best practice guidelines with the MRQSA (Market Research Quality Standards Association) and in aiding the development of the qualitative section of the MRS Code of Conduct. An important part of the code of conduct is shown in Chapter 2, Box 2.3.

1.5.5 Qualifications and jobs in marketing research

Market research is taught as a major module in its own right and also forms part of marketing and international marketing modules in university business schools in the UK and internationally.

Details of both the Diploma and Certificate entry requirements for the MRS qualifications, the syllabus contents and examination details are available direct from the Market Research Society in London or from its approved centre at the Leicester Business School, DeMontfort University.[26] Over 12% of the MRS total membership and a third of new members are diploma holders. For anyone study-ing or working in market research, the publications of the MRS are given in Appendix 4. The Direct Marketing Association, with links to the Bristol Business School at the University of the West of England (UWE), has also done much to foster the development of direct marketing and research activities in the UK with client companies and the academic community.

Most of those who work in market research are members of the various professional bodies such as the Market Research Society, which was founded in 1947 and has over 7,000 members. However, the Industrial Marketing Research Association (IMRA) in the UK ceased to exist by 1998. Others belong to, for example, the Association of Qualitative Research Practitioners and the European Society for Opinion and Market Research. There are other professional bodies in closely related research areas. The United States has the largest market research industry in the world.

Types of data collection methods used by suppliers of research and marketing information include computer-aided research, continuous consumer panel, execu-tive interviewing, face-to-face interviews, hall tests, observation, omnibus, postal panels surveys, qualitative methods, retail audits, telephone interviews, and view-ing facilities for in-door experiments and focus group discussions. The tables in this chapter detailing the names of companies and their research activities demon-strate the health of this vibrant sector. From interviewers to market research executives, managers and directors of research, those in the research industry represent the variety and large numbers of jobs, the many specialist skills, the transferable expertise across continents and the contributions to the foreign exchange earnings of the countries they represent.

1.6 Major types of research

The scope of marketing research is therefore considerable. The major types of research are shown in Figure 1.2 and are dealt with in more detail in Chapter 2.

Fig 1.2 Major research types

1.7 Divisions of research: quantitative and qualitative

There are, generally speaking, two main groups of market researchers, those who use the methods of quantitative research and those who conduct qualitative research. There are others who use both types, so the distinctions between the two groups can be blurred, and rightly so. There are merits in both approaches and they should be seen to be mutually supportive rather than exclusive. Since quantitative research has the advantage of reliability in numbers, that is, aiming to produce the statistical evidence for a study, qualitative research can sometimes have a bad press because of its informality and exploratory nature. However, there is richness in qualitative studies which throws much light on the way respondents think, feel and behave, as opposed to the quantitative analysis of people subjected to being measured in terms of, for example, the sampling error and sophisticated statistical calculations.

The market for qualitative research in the UK and internationally is buoyant. The major qualitative method used in the UK is still focus group discussions, though the claim for Germany was 73% for qualitative interviews and for Austria 91% for individual in-depth interviews. Group discussions are still a dominant method in Russia, the Czech Republic, Ireland, Denmark, Greece and Italy.[27]

Quantitative research is carried out to investigate 'how many' people have 'similar characteristics and views'. When there are large numbers of people to be studied, it is more cost effective to carry out a quantitative survey to collect the data, often by questionnaires which can be posted, faxed or sent to respondents by computer. The broadest example of the collection of data is the tradition of having full-scale census surveys which are quantifiable, to collect information for governments all over the world, particularly within the developed economies, to aid their planning and forecasting.

Quantitative research tends to focus on 'what is now', that is, what respondents intuitively know and have the facts of, including 'what respondents have done'. So it can be akin to a snapshot. Its strength lies in the way the science of mathematical analysis and modelling can be used to explain marketing phenomena by showing the key constructs, their interrelationships and their relative strengths within these interrelationships. Marketers can base their decisions on statistically proven facts with known margins of error.

Quantitative data can be easier and cheaper to collect by post, telephone or computer-aided interviewing systems than qualitative data which would be costly for the same number of people.

However, quantitative research has been criticised for 'scraping the surface of people's attitudes and feelings'. The complexity of the human soul is lost through the counting of numbers. The advantage of qualitative research is that it guards against 'the sin of omission', that is, the failure to research a topic in greater detail through probing and understanding of respondents' attitudes, motivation and behaviour. Qualitative research attempts to go deeper, beyond historical facts and surface comments, in order to get to the real underlying causes of behaviour. Many factors and influences affect people in their everyday lives so that qualitative research to seek out and to understand the complexities surrounding the underlying causes of behaviour can sometimes be more appropriate than quantitative research methods.

The two approaches, quantitative and qualitative, should be seen as mutually supportive, since there are core strengths in both approaches in benefiting the problem-solving and decision-making processes for clients.

Qualitative research is discussed in detail in Chapter 14, which explains the sound foundations, principles and practices upon which this type of research has been built. It puts the context of qualitative research clearly into perspective. Chapter 15, on international marketing research, has a short section dealing with qualitative research as it applies internationally.

REFERENCES

1. *Financial Times* (1995), 'Not so much choice, please', 30 November, p. 26.

2. ESOMAR (1998), *ESOMAR Annual Study on the Market Research Industry*, p. 4.

3. Market Research Society (1998), *Code of Conduct*, April , p. 4.

4. *Marketing News* (1985), 'AMA board approves new marketing definitions', 1 March, p. 1 and (1987), 'New marketing research definitions approved', 2 January, pp. 1, 14.

5. McDonald M. (from 1992 to the most recent editions), *Marketing Plans: How to prepare them, How to use them*, Butterworth Heinemann, Oxford.

6. Bates B. (1996), 'Quality will mark the route to deeper client relationships', *Research Plus*, March, pp. 9, 14.

7. AMSO (1997), *Annual Report*.

8. *Economist* (1997), 'Italian shares – the price of privatisation', 3–9 May, p. 96.

9. Kotler P. (1997), *Marketing Management*, 9th edition, Prentice Hall, pp. 17–19.

10. MRS (1998), *Training courses and industry qualifications*.

11. De Montfort University (1999), 'Market Research Centre: Foundation and Certificate Programme'.

12. Bartels R. (1970), 'Influences on development of marketing thought, 1900–1923' in Bartels R. (ed.) *Marketing Theory and Metatheory*, Irwin, pp. 108–25.

13. Borden N. (1964), 'The concept of the marketing mix', *Journal of Advertising Research*, June, pp. 2–7.

14. Chisnall P. (1997), *Marketing Research*, McGraw Hill, p. 8.

15. AMSO (1997), *Annual Report*, p. 17.

16. AMSO (1997), *Annual Report*, p. 29.

17. Schlackman B. (1999), 'The history of UK qualitative research, according to Bill Schlackman', *The AQRP Directory and Handbook of Qualitative Research 1989–1999*, p. 16.

18. *Economist* (1993), 'The Britain audit: Government', pp. 26, 29.

19. ESOMAR (1998), *ESOMAR Annual Study on the Market Research Industry 1997*, pp. 1–4.

20. *BMRA Bulletin: The Newsletter of the British Market Research Association* (1998), no. 1, July, pp. 1, 8.

21. AMSO (1997), *Annual Report*, pp. 7–29.

22. MRS (1998), *Code of Conduct*, 'ICC/ESOMAR Code of Marketing and Social Research Practice', April, p. 11.

23. MRS (1998), *Code of Conduct*, 'Code definitions', April, pp. 4–5.

24. MRS (1998), *The Members' Handbook*, p. 20.

25. AQRP (1999), *The Directory and Handbook of Qualitative Research 1998–1999*.

26. De Montfort University (1999), 'Market Research Centre: Foundation and Certificate Programme'.

27. AQRP (1998), *In Brief*, 'All eyes on international', July/August, p. 2.

FURTHER READING

Qualitative Market Research – An International Journal, an MCB University Press Publication, 60/62 Toller Lane, Bradford, West Yorkshire BD8 9BY. Tel: +44(0)1274 777700, Fax: +44(0)1274 785200.

QUESTIONS

1. Explain the popularity of marketing research. What changes in the environment have facilitated the growth of the market research industry?
2. What responsibilities do marketing researchers have to: (a) their clients and (b) their respondents? Discuss the ways in which the various market research associations can ensure that these responsibilities are met and that quality standards can be maintained.
3. What is the marketing research process? Discuss the importance of the various stages within the research process.

2 Exploring the market and data search

The exploratory phase sets the stage for an organisation to explore the level and topics of relevance to its assumptions about its market and the marketing environment. Exploratory research is appropriate for asking questions of:

- experts – consulting with experts relevant to the market which is being explored;
- the trade (suppliers, wholesalers, distributors, retailers) – making approaches to the market by sounding out interest at an early stage;
- customers – collecting information on needs and wants relevant to the research problem;

and feeding back the information to the client in order to clarify and set research goals and formulate the brief. The researcher then sets up the most appropriate research design to achieve the agreed goals. See Figure 2.1.

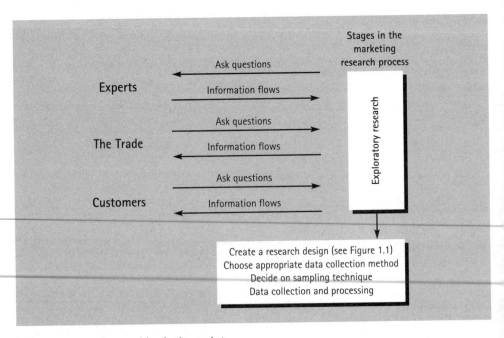

Fig 2.1 Exploratory research: consulting in the market

2.1 Consulting people in the market

If a company is considering entry into a new product field, the research planner may feel the need to seek expert advice. Much depends on how thoroughly he or she has been briefed.

Consulting an expert

Experts are those people with specialist knowledge and expertise who, by virtue of their occupations or the positions they hold at work, can be consulted about the research problem in question or who can, if willing, impart information, for the purposes of the research. The expert may be a senior member on the board of a corporation, a vice-president of marketing and sales, a well-known entrepreneur, a chemist or engineer in a research and development (R&D) department, a recognised authority on the subject by occupation, writings and teachings or a member of a professional or trade association and so on.

Consulting the trade

Suppliers, wholesalers, distributors and retailers in the same or related trade all hold information pertaining to their own customers and their own operating requirements. There is a need to find out first hand from the trade what the responses to past product or service failures and successes have been that have a direct bearing on the research problem. Other areas such as the necessary transportation of goods by road, rail, sea or air and the provision of insurance and credit facilities required might also entail initial investigation. In brief, initial investigations could raise more questions or find answers to whether the trade was enthusiastic or not in carrying a new product, whether goods could be easily deliverable to customers and what provision of credit facilities would be available to help consumers to 'buy'.

Consulting customers

In a consumer market there is a clear distinction between seeking the advice of experts and seeking to add to the secondary data statistics by encouraging individuals in the market to talk, either alone in face-to-face interviews or in focus groups. In industrial markets the distinction between 'experts' and 'buyers' is muddied by the industrial buying process. The industrial buyer is often buying at the behest of company experts. Indeed, determining just who makes the buying decision presents a problem when designing industrial marketing research surveys (who should be asked the questions?).

If the market is reasonably well documented, the search so far will have told us what demographic variables are likely to affect the behaviour of consumers in domestic markets with regard to the product field. We will have a good idea whether age is a critical variable, or whether social class, having or not having children, living in the north compared with living in the south, going out to work or being a housewife full-time, and so on, are important criteria.

Again, one should take account of the distinction between 'who buys' and 'who uses' in this market when deciding about what sort of consumers to consult.

Electric razors and male toiletries are often bought by women for men, but who determines the kind of holiday the family takes, the model of family car, or the kind of bicycle a child shall have?

We need to know as much as possible about consumers or industrial users in the market because we are going to encourage a limited number of people to talk freely and at length about their behaviour in the product field, their attitudes towards what is available in the way of products (or services), their needs and wants.

A decision-making unit (DMU) in an industrial establishment typically consists of a buyer or initiator, a user, a specifier and a budget holder. For a household a decision-making unit is the head of household or the members of the household who normally undertake the control of the buying process for the specific product in question.

People are 'contactable' as individuals. However, it may be necessary to contact more than one person within an organisation, because the senior buyer within the DMU, other buyers, managers as budget-holders and engineers can all influence what is ultimately bought. These people are visited and interviewed at work premises. Consumers can be brought together in focus groups of about eight, for example, a number small enough to encourage general discussion and large enough to make it likely that such a group would have a good variety of ideas. This kind of research, which seeks to illuminate the motivation behind consumer behaviour, is described as qualitative, as compared with the quantitative type of research study, designed to produce statistical data.

The importance of informed assumptions

It is unlikely that all exploratory avenues will be followed in any one piece of exploratory research. The objective, which can be reached by a variety of routes and with a limited number of interviews in the market, is to gain sufficient certainty about the following in order to design a cost-effective research study:

- the structure of the population to be sampled, whether this is to be a number of individuals, households, firms or retail outlets;
- the topics that are relevant to the marketing problem.

We need to be sufficiently well informed about the population to be able to design a sample which takes account of those variables likely to lead to marketing action, for example:

If AB class behaves in a markedly different way from C1 in this market, then we are going to have to ensure that our sample includes enough ABs for us to have confidence in the representativeness of the AB results.

If AB and C1 behave in much the same way, then making separate provision for AB would be wasteful. But we must avoid the risk of getting results in and finding we want to make recommendations about AB as a separate group, but cannot (or ought not!).

2.2 Why the exploratory stage is important

The exploratory stage is important because it is necessary for an organisation to establish what is already on record about the market of interest and the kind of product envisaged for it. Most markets are well documented because there is a wealth of information, both statistical and literary, stored in public archives and data banks and the libraries of large commercial organisations and trade associations, while the Internet and on-line information systems make it possible to access the data without long and laborious searches through journals, published reports and newspapers.

However, the problem is that the available data may not focus closely enough on the product market in question and the decision may be taken to commission an ad hoc survey. Once a problem or an opportunity has been identified in the market, exploratory research, which is usually small-scale research, is needed to define the exact nature of the problem or opportunity and the environment in which either one or the other has occurred. Its small-scale nature means that qualitative research lends itself to the exploratory stage of the research process. Qualitative research enables researchers to probe deeper in exploring ideas and clues with small samples of experts, specialists, industry leaders and customers to allow a high degree of flexibility, especially in obtaining valuable unpublished primary data and secondary data publications not readily available outside the membership of professional and trade bodies.

So it is important that information on customers and conditions in the marketplace should be gathered and evaluated. Normally the collection and feedback of information is an ongoing necessity for companies and is carried out by their marketing departments and sales forces. Organisational data such as accounts and orders plus feedback from sales representatives is a useful source of market intelligence, especially in industrial markets where there is a heavier reliance on personal selling rather than on mass advertising.

However, information derived from organisations' existing sales records and their own representatives' reports will not in itself be enough to enable the organisation to focus effectively on the following:

- the behaviour, attitudes and needs of the consumers in its market;
- the behaviour, attitudes and needs of the intermediaries on whom it relies to make its goods available to consumers;
- the activities of competitors and the response of consumers and intermediaries to these activities.

This is because, whilst the managers of an organisation can control their own marketing mixes, there are forces in the external environment, as listed in Figure 2.2, over which they have little control. Managers can vary the price, product, promotion and place (distribution) elements in their marketing mixes, but changes in the marketplace will occur as old customers drop out and new ones enter due to changes in circumstances such as consumption and purchasing patterns. The marketing research process is critical here because information about customers and conditions in the marketplace is changing – markets are dynamic – and continual updates are necessary.

For example, even though large financial institutions such as banks have their own extensive customer databases, they still need ad hoc market research from time to time to give them feedback about the advertising and promotion of their existing products and their corporate image, and to enable them to develop new products tailored to target market segments.

When Midland Bank launched a 24-hour, 365-day banking facility through its subsidiary, First Direct in 1989, it established the UK's first person-to-person, tele-banking service. Exploratory market research to find out what customers wanted from such a service included the use of postal questionnaires which were sent to employed professional men and women on the bank's database. The findings contributed to helping the bank design a more efficient, convenient and better value facility to conduct its savings, mortgages, loan accounts and payment systems for First Direct customers over the age of 18. The market research and data generation and analysis which followed helped the bank to successfully establish a new market niche and at the same time to satisfy customer perceptions about its advertised corporate image, 'the listening bank'. Its 1997 advertising campaigns reinforced the image of this slogan.

2.3 Explanations about consumer and organisational markets

What organisational contacts can be utilised to gather information? Both consumer and industrial goods companies can use freelance sales representatives working on a commission-only basis and spread over a wide area, increasingly in more than one country. The advantages of this are that these individuals are not employees and the costs of using them are reduced. However, training needs and expertise vary and in industrial markets particularly, it is crucial to have commissioned sales engineers and consultants with the right expertise. In consumer markets, companies will also be in direct contact with these individuals if they use mail order or direct door-to-door selling methods, e.g. Avon Cosmetics and Great Universal Stores. For many products sold to mass markets, retail intermediaries are used.

Companies can sell direct to retail organisations, such as the large superstores which control the outlets where their products are bought. They can also sell via wholesalers or voluntary groups of wholesalers, such as the Mace and Spar food chains in the UK, which break bulk and pass goods onto their members' outlets.

By using feedback from all these intermediary contacts in their supply, distribution and retailing facilities, companies gather vital socio-economic and demographic information about their customers to improve their own marketing and sales functions. They also gather vital information about the way their products are bought and used, and what their customers think of them and their goods.

Consumer goods

Consumer goods may belong to the category of those that are used up quickly, or fairly quickly, such as ice-cream, detergents and toothpaste, in which case they are **fast-moving consumer goods**. Or they may be more durable and infrequently bought, such as motor cars, washing machines and power tools for DIY, and thus classified as **consumer durables**. For fast-moving consumer goods repeat purchases are a very important consideration as well as ensuring the products are tried by a large number of buyers.

Industrial goods

Industrial goods fall into three categories:

1. Materials, e.g. timber, and parts, e.g. timing devices.
2. Capital items, e.g. generators.
3. Supplies, e.g. lubricants, and services, e.g. advertising and transport.

Businesses are interested in the frequency with which goods are bought when planning research in industrial markets. Success in marketing goods in categories (1) and (3) depends on repeat purchase as well as penetration, while items in category (2) are infrequently bought by any one customer.

The nature of derived demand is such that in an industrial market the ultimate consumer may be some stages away, but there are industrial markets in which the ultimate consumer is close at hand. Therefore, companies need to study the behaviour of consumers who are end-users as well as the behaviour of their major industrial customers. The effective demand for turning devices is influenced by the dynamics of demand for motor cars, cooking stoves or washing machines, all of which incorporate timing devices in their mechanisms.

Non-profit-making organisations such as universities, local authorities and government corporations, major charities, nationalised monopolies and consumer watchdog bodies such as the Consumers' Association also need to have information concerning their markets and how their products and services are received by their customers. Consumer perceptions of quality of service and value for money affect the levels of their voluntary donations to charities, or in the cases of taxpayers, the number of election votes cast for political parties. Public accountability, therefore, involves non-profit-making organisations in making quality assessments of what they provide; for example, the Conservative Government's Citizens Charter of 1993 and the Labour Government's quality and accountability initiatives in 1999 in the education and health service sectors.

Trade associations such as the UK Motor Industry Trade Association and the USA's Machine Tool Technologies Association carry out regular surveys on their industries for their members. The Confederation of British Industry takes soundings from its members and publishes annual updates on business confidence which are printed in the media. Both profit and non-profit-making organisations require feedback from their customers, members or their publics, so marketing research is important in helping them improve upon their levels of provision of products and services.

In exploratory research, in order to describe the varying habits and attitudes of different groups in the population, such as different age groups, it is necessary to break the sample down. A minority group may look like being of particular interest. The sample design must provide for the collection of data from a sufficient number of consumers in this group. Statistical data is required about the population in order to design the sample.

Similarly, in order to design the questionnaire, or any other data-collection instrument, it is necessary to have explored consumer behaviour and attitudes with regard to the type of products and brands available and the context in which these are used, such as motoring, clothes washing, do-it-yourself, and so on.

Survey design

The designer of the survey risks two sins:

- **the sin of omission** – not treating a topic in sufficient detail, or failing to include sufficient respondents in a group which has marketing significance;
- **the sin of commission** – collecting data which proves to be immaterial or cannot be acted on, or breaking the sample down to a wasteful extent.

It would, for example, be wasteful to provide for a breakdown of the sample into four social classes where two would be sufficient, as in many fast-moving product fields. Companies do not have the means to cover the entire national population, that is, to conduct a census. In any case, a well-constructed sample can bring in results which are as relevant to a company's needs.

The answers gathered from exploratory research will affect the design of the questionnaire, the time taken to answer it (or fill it in), the complexity of data processing and the cost of the survey. Here again, the sins of omission and commission should be avoided. Take the following example:

Qualitative work has given us a list of statements expressing motorists' attitudes towards driving a car. We want to quantify these attitudes by putting them to a sample of motorists. Do we need to distinguish between how the motorist feels about driving the car when going to work, ferrying children to school, taking grandparents for a run; or is it sufficient for our purpose to establish how the motorist feels about driving in general?

We need to be careful about what information requirements should be included in the design of a questionnaire for a cost-effective survey.

Exploratory research will indicate what available data is needed relating to the following:

- the parameters of the survey population;
- the ideas held by this population about the product field;
- ideas about the brands available in the product field.

In order to define the parameters of the survey population quantifiable data is required relating to geographic, demographic and socio-economic variables. For example, in industrial markets data is required about the location, concentration and dispersion of organisational establishments, their economic activity, size and composition. Likewise in consumer markets, data is needed about the location, types of dwelling and the composition of households with reference to income, occupation, age, sex, race, education and religion. A sample based upon a representation of the population to be surveyed can then be constructed.

The attitudes held by a sample of the population about a given product field, for example, fast-moving consumer goods can be investigated. It is essential to obtain qualitative data about the perceptions, motivations and purchasing behaviour of the family and industrial decision-making units. Data can also be gathered concerning the types, costs and numbers of products bought or consumed. The main qualitative research techniques of observation, depth interviews and focus groups are explained in this chapter. Exploratory research uses each or all of these methods. Exploratory research is limited by the goal of preliminary investigation, whereas a full-scale research design following on from the initial exploratory phase would involve a qualitative study with bigger representative samples and a longer, more costly investigation.

In order to clarify and define problem areas and the research objectives, ideas about manufacturers' brands available in industrial and consumer markets can be investigated through:

- analysis of customer purchases;
- behaviour, use of and attitudes of customers to specific brands;
- susceptibility of customers to advertising, personal selling, discounts or sales promotions, their level of complexity in buying decisions;
- customer patronage of outlets selling the particular branded products.

Market research firms are brought in to design market experiments and to build marketing models to test the frequency with which products are bought (as explained in the pre-testing and pricing research discussed in Chapters 9 and 11).

2.4 Interrelationships: causes and effects

The research planner undertakes exploratory research to investigate a fertile opportunity. Information has to be obtained so as to arrive at a set of assumptions which can be employed to build the model upon which the research design will be based. Within the model (see Figure 2.2) assumptions are made about the factors relevant

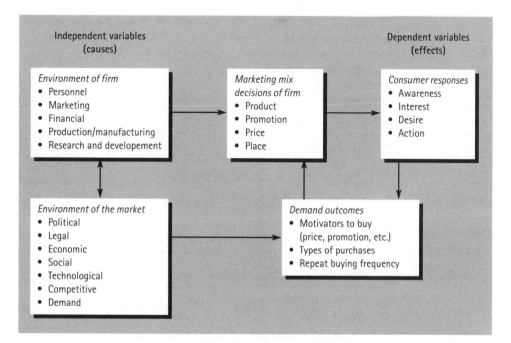

Fig 2.2 Model of the decision-making processes within the marketing system

to a given situation and the relationships of the variables. It is apparent that the more thorough the explanation and the better the quality of the information obtained, the firmer the assumptions will be.

The model depicted illustrates the interrelationships between the independent variables (causes) and the dependent variables (effects). It also identifies the marketing mix decisions (controllable responses) and factors in the marketing environment (uncontrollable influences) which determine buyers' decisions. The information needed by marketing managers is obtainable from internal company records, marketing intelligence and marketing research.

2.5 Understanding interrelationships in the marketing environment

External forces beyond the control of a company include the following:

- economic trends
- government action
- changes in the law
- technological developments
- social and cultural changes
- demographic changes
- competitors' activities
- physical terrain, geographical spread of population and climatic changes.

These are sometimes listed as political, economic, social and technological, from which the convenient mnemonic PEST may be derived.

The health of an organisation largely depends on the capacity of its management to interpret the needs, attitudes and behaviour of its consumer and industrial buyers who make up its markets. Moreover, in a mixed economy the capacity of a company to raise funds by public subscription to finance its activities is dependent on investors' confidence in its present market performance and its future business projections. By using marketing research to diagnose the needs and wants of its customers, the management of the organisation can alter its marketing mixes and thereby manipulate its interrelationships in response to reports on changes in the marketing environment, which can have good, indifferent or determined effects on its business. If 'research' and 'marketing' are fully integrated, radical and unexpected changes of plan can be avoided.

The challenge, then, for a firm is to recognise the potential effects of these external forces and to interpret their impact on its business. This helps a firm to be more proactive, that is, to anticipate customer requirements and to focus its marketing efforts more effectively in the marketplace, as opposed to being reactive to market developments. The reactive approach can mean a firm losing its competitive advantage to an aggressive competitor which is forging ahead to gain market share at its expense.

Causes and effects need to be examined because the effects of the interrelationships of the different variables and their resulting complexities affect market demand and organisational performances. Marketing research has essential roles to play in providing managers with vital information which will help them to focus their marketing planning efforts and understand the environmental forces which influence their company's target markets.

2.6 Key roles of marketing research

Marketing research performs several key roles within the marketing system. These roles are descriptive, diagnostic and predictive.

- **Descriptive research** provides historic and current data on consumer and organisational markets and their marketing environments. For example, descriptive data is provided on the market size and sales turnover of firms, emerging technologies, competitor profiles and changes in market environments, such as periodic publications on the machine tool industry by government and industry bodies.

- **Diagnostic research** gives new insights into problem-solving such as cause and effect relationships on the impact of marketing strategies and their marketing mixes on target markets. For example, manufacturers of food and drink products commission market research agencies to assess the effectiveness of their promotional campaigns on their consumers or they can buy into omnibus surveys. Consumer attitudes, lifestyle needs, purchasing behaviour and disposable incomes are researched.

- **Predictive research** seeks to identify new opportunities in the marketplace and research is used to forecast the outcomes for marketing decisions. For example, predictive research into new customer requirements can be undertaken for new products and services developed for the health and fitness, electronic video games and cellular telecommunications markets to name but a few. New industries with emerging technologies require a reorientation and refinement of market analysis modelling and research techniques.

2.7 Sources of information: primary and secondary

In a well-documented industrialised society it is difficult to envisage a market about which there is no information available in addition to a company's own records. Figure 2.3 illustrates sources of information.

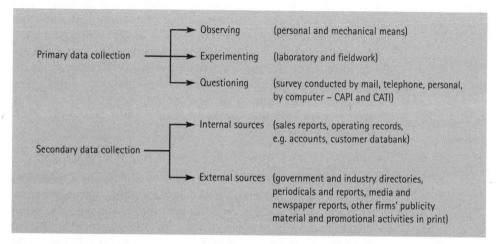

Fig 2.3 Data collection methods

Available information is called **secondary data**, while that derived from a new research study is called **primary data**. Since search of secondary data takes place before the collection of primary data, use of these terms can be confusing.

Secondary or desk research builds upon previous records and information. It employs the wealth of data held in libraries and in the government departments dealing with the collection of information for work done in a particular country. For example, in the UK, the Department of Trade and Industry's Companies House in London or Cardiff and the London Statistics and Market Intelligence Library can be visited by the public for data search. Professional and trade bodies also hold publications; in the UK the Institute of Direct Marketing (IDM) and the Market Research Society have their own libraries. For a list of company sources and publications see Appendix 1.

There are advantages in conducting secondary research:

1. It avoids repeating work that may already have been carried out by others.
2. It is unobtrusive research and non-reactive, quietly undertaken without alerting competitors.
3. It is impersonal and so is relatively inexpensive compared with primary or field research and can be undertaken without leaving one's own premises by going on-line. Some free and easy to access web sites are discussed in Sections 2.15.1–2.15.3. Some are free and very easy to access.
4. It takes place before the collection of primary data in order to assess the availability of information and to arrive at the assumptions or hypothesis for primary research. Qualitative data is more difficult to locate than statistics which are regularly collected and published by government departments, e.g. population trends, inflation and growth rates. Library catalogues facilitate location of archived material, trade directories and company publications.
5. Sources can be evaluated and gaps identified in the literature so that study proposals can be economically validated. Published data is used to support opinions and statements so accountability is not usually a problem.
6. Whole industries and not just one's own organisation can be compared in global terms.
7. Confidentiality is not usually a problem provided permission to publish has been obtained from copyright holders.
8. What is already published becomes historical. So historical trends are provided in the literature and comparisons can be made to 'what is current or now'. For example, from documentation of past company experiences, statements, data relating to their products, marketing programmes, personnel and accounts.

   Periodic publications – usually monthly, quarterly or annually – provide a snapshot of historical data. Publications which are ad hoc (meaning to this end or purpose), e.g. Mintel's specialist reports on the machine tool or the footwear industries, are useful if one is investigating these particular industries, and if the publications are updated.

However, it is also important to collect primary data because:

1. It is gathered to help solve a specific problem when information is needed to make decisions. External secondary data publications have been developed by other people according to different criteria and purposes and may, therefore, contain much information which is mostly unrelated to the job at hand for the researcher. So there is insufficient data on the topic being investigated.

2. Secondary data may also be irrelevant to the problem-solving process if the data on the topic has not been updated.
3. Some decisions, e.g. for a new product innovation or a new type of service, cannot be based on secondary data as the product attributes have to be assessed in the light of current customer responses.
4. Even when there is some availability of secondary data about an industry it may not be in-depth enough, so that it would be necessary to conduct a field study to come up with conclusive measures about particular segments of a market. As validation with the targeted market segments can be made 'at source' it allows for greater accuracy of information.

Examples of secondary data searches include:

- examining internal organisational sources, e.g. organisational records;
- finding available external publications, including statistics from government and syndicated sources.

Examples of primary data searches include:

- consulting experts who have specialist knowledge about a particular industry;
- monitoring behavioural patterns with or without the respondents' knowledge in observational studies;
- consulting people in the market by holding focus group discussions and by conducting 'depth' interviews;
- buying into an omnibus survey, as one of several firms contributing questions for survey research.

2.8 Secondary data sources

Internal sources can be divided into two categories: first, the company's operating records, and second, research previously carried out by the company which forms part of its records.

Company operating records

These will cover subjects ranging from the cost of raw materials for a manufacturing company to sales of the company's output. Ex-works, transport costs, sales costs, advertising and other promotional expenditures are marketing costs to be set against sales revenue. Packaging and warehousing costs may also be regarded as marketing costs.

Whether or not the operating records are kept in such a way that they can be used to allocate marketing costs to specific branded products, and to help to monitor marketing performance, indicates whether the company is truly focused on the market. Records of this kind were originally designed to enable accountants to account for costs incurred, and for sales managers or sales directors to control the sales force.

The detail and analysis needed for these purposes are not the same as that needed by a marketing director or brand manager striving to predict the contribution to profit likely to be made by a particular branded product or service.

Previous research conducted

If a company does not have an extensive customer database its own sales figures will not tell:

- how large each customer is by way of organisational size in terms of market capitalisation, number of employees and sales turnover;
- what the amount of business that competitors have with the company's customers is;.
- how much the company could maximise is sales targets with potential customers.

However, before researching secondary data the reports from sales representatives and from staff belonging to technical and professional bodies can convey intelligence about competitive activity. This provides a starting point. If this is not enough the search is extended to include data deriving from sources outside the company.

The advantage of secondary data is the amount of published and therefore non-confidential material available. Much internal data held by organisations includes confidential material. This relates to documents concerning company property, personnel, meetings, plans, financial statements, research and development, production, and transactional details of clients, suppliers, distributors, debtors, creditors and investors. Bought-in secondary data to supplement managerial knowledge about customers, competitors and developments in their industries can greatly enhance an organisation's ability to make marketing decisions.

External secondary data on information already collected by individuals and organisations specific to their purpose are usually available in the form of reports, books and periodicals. For example, libraries take out subscriptions for government and industry publications and these are made accessible and free to library users. Such sources can be quoted (for extensive quoting, permission is normally sought as a matter of courtesy) and they are used as 'authorities' to sanction or support research objectives and recommendations.

In consumer markets it is helpful if sales records can be related to television areas such as Central or London Weekend Television even if the company is not a television advertiser. Large companies tend to be television advertisers and the data generated by syndicated services (retail audits and consumer panels) is generally presented in this way. So are the statistics relating to readership of newspapers and magazines.

In the case of industrial markets, sales are best recorded by standard region for comparison with the wealth of information published by the Government Statistical Service (GSS).

The focus on an industrial market is sharper if sales and costs are recorded by the use to which the industrial consumer is putting the product. If this happens to equate with a standard industrial classification, the figures derived from internal records can be related to a wide and international range of statistical data. Such data can be derived from sources such as the International Monetary Fund (IMF), and the UK's Central Statistical Office publications, e.g. exports and balance of payments statistics.

Trade directories such as the Kompass and Keynote publications in the UK generally group names of companies under the titles of product output and industry sectors. The operating records of a company contain customer details, and the inclusion of a customer database would show further details of customers' personnel, output, sales turnover and market performance if such a company had been trading with these customers for some years, collected data on them and updated its records about them, as well as keeping an eye on competitors.

2.8.1 Government statistics

The most prolific source of secondary data is the Government Statistical Service (see Appendix 1). The new Office for National Statistics (ONS) in Southport, UK was formed by the merger of the Office of Population Censuses and Surveys (OPCS) and the Central Statistical Office (CSO).

As government statistics are collected for the purpose of government, they do not always fit a particular marketing purpose, but every effort is made to meet business requirements. Additional data is often made available on request.

A list of GSS publications is available from the address given in Appendix 1. The MRS *Yearbook* includes a useful review of GSS output by department. Two offices are of particular interest to market researchers: the Business Statistics Office of the Department of Trade and Industry and the Office for National Statistics.

The BSO processes returns made by samples of industrial establishments, retailers and suppliers of services and these are published in a series of regularly updated *Business Monitors*. There is a production series, a service and distributive series and a miscellaneous series. The last covers a range of subjects such as motor vehicle registrations, cinemas, finance and overseas travel. The monitors are published monthly and quarterly.

The validity of these published statistics depends on the care with which businesses make their returns. The anonymity of businesses supplying data is carefully safeguarded, and the BSO does not tell companies who their competitors are.

The work of the ONS is particularly relevant to the planning of surveys because it is concerned with the size and distribution of the UK population by age and social grade, with the way in which the population is housed and the amenities it has or does not have, including telephones and a range of durable goods. The last census was taken in 1991. Census data, together with other 'lifestyle' statistics collected by the ONS, constitutes the computer input of geodemographic systems such as Experian's MOSAIC described in Chapter 8. The ONS carries out two continuous surveys which illuminate social trends: the Family Expenditure Survey and the General Household Survey.

The CSO databank holds macro-economic statistical data. This is more immediately relevant to researchers concerned with industrial products and services than to those in fast-moving consumer markets.

Box 2.1 shows an approach to 'government statistics' to help the student engaged on exploratory research for a marketing project.

> **Box 2.1 Exploratory research for a marketing project**
>
> 1. Write for *Government Statistics*: *A Brief Guide to Sources* which may be free from the Office for National Statistics.
> 2. Consult the *Guide to Official Statistics*, published annually by the CSO.
> 3. Consult the cumulative and recent list of government publications.
> 4. Familiarise yourself with the *Monthly Digest of Statistics*, *Economic Trends* and *Population Trends* (quarterly).
> 5. Take note of the classifications used for population, production and distribution.
> 6. If there is a Government Bookshop near you, visit it.
> 7. If you are in London, make use of the Statistics and Market Intelligence Library.
>
> See Appendix 1 for the addresses of the CSO, the Government Bookshops and the Market Intelligence Library.

2.8.2 Industry publications

Secondary data is also published by banks, stockbrokers, trade and professional associations, media owners, local authorities and government agencies. Appendix 1 contains a list of addresses.

It would be tedious to discuss these sources individually. It might be helpful, however, to mention the MCB University Press marketing journals and NTC publications, e.g. annual yearbooks and pocket books on advertising and consumer statistics. *Retail Business* (Economist Publications) and *Mintel* are both published monthly. The annuals and journals summarise data from government and trade sources relating to a wide range of markets. They can be found in some libraries with a marketing section. Appendix 4 lists publications by the Market Research Society. It is possible to avoid library research by subscribing to commercial on-line systems such as that provided by Mintel.

2.8.3 Syndicated sources: retail audits and consumer panels

Another source of secondary information is the trend data supplied by the research agencies who regularly operate retail audits and consumer panels. A panel is drawn from a representative sample of consumers maintained by a research supplier over a specified time so that panellists' behaviour and shopping trends can be monitored. There is much rich historical trend data collected in this way.

Buying such syndicated research enables comparisons to be made between one's own company's estimates of sales and those of competitors and the industry as a whole. For example, one of the indicators for evaluating a company's performance is 'brand share'.

The traditional retail audit records sales to consumers through a panel of retail outlets (auditing being a method of data collection). The estimate of consumer sales arrived at is as follows:

| Opening stock for period (checked last audit) | + | Net deliveries since last audit | – | Stock held at present audit | = | Sales to consumers during period |

As well as estimating consumer sales, the retail audit monitors the distributive, selling and merchandising programmes associated with brands in the product field. The number of brands recorded in the reports bought by subscribers depends on their individual requirements and on the amounts subscribed above a minimum: i.e. the size of the 'all others' category varies. In the UK Nielsen, Retail Audits and Stats MR are substantial operators in the retail field. Electronic point of sale (EPOS) obviates the need for most manual point of sale auditing, for example automatic services such as Nielsen's Scantrack can take over. Scantrack reduces the reporting interval from bi-monthly to monthly.

The recording of the passage of goods along the distributive channels generally rests upon the electronic scanning of the bar codes on the labels of products. Nielsen's syndicated Scantrack service is based on a panel of retail outlets with checkouts equipped to read bar codes so that the information is captured electronically. There has been considerable development in the application of electronic methods in the research industry. For example, every time a product is registered as sold from a store within a retail chain, another product is ordered electronically and automatically to replace it from a central warehousing facility. Payment transactions have also been speeded up encouraging the burgeoning use of credit cards, cash cards, store loyalty cards, and so on.

A consumer panel generates useful information about the characteristics of those who buy and about their buying habits. Most panels relate to products purchased frequently but panel data relating to a wide range of durables is available, e.g. the Taylor Nelson AGB's SuperPanel launched in 1991. Fast-moving purchases are recorded by means of an electronic capture device which scans the panel member's bar codes on the products from the grocery shopping.

It is important to realise that once information has been collected and is published, e.g. survey reports sold to clients such as retailers, financial institutions and academic libraries, such data collected via audits and panels becomes 'secondary data'.

We need to distinguish between three types of consumer panels:

1. The household panel – a regular record of housewives' food purchases through the year.
2. The individual panel – a record of purchases including consumer goods, leisure pursuits and holidays by individuals for their own use.
3. A special-interest panel – such as the Motorists' Diary Panel, for example, devoted to the recording of petrol and engine oil purchases, plus information on accessories, servicing and car insurance.

The range of data available from consumer panels relating to repeat-purchase products is summarised as follows:

- trends in the total volume and value of consumer purchases in the product field;

- demographic characteristics of those buying in the product field, such as age, social class, size of family;

- buying behaviour in the product field: average amount bought and frequency of buying. Since this data records individual purchasing of individual brands, i.e. the data is 'dis-aggregated', repeat-purchase and loyalty patterns can be established.

All this information can be recorded within television areas, e.g. BARB areas discussed in Chapter 1, and by the type of retail outlet at which purchases were made, and seasonal patterns can be seen.

But data derived from consumer purchasing panels does not answer either of the following:

- how products and brands are used;
- how buyers perceive brands in a product field.

For both retail audits and consumer panels 'back data' may be available if the company is not already subscribing. This previously collected trend data can, therefore, be taken into account in exploratory research. The range of this data will relate to the requirements of subscribers, but important product fields and major brands in those fields will have been covered.

The first purpose of audits and panels is to monitor the effect of marketing programmes, while the accumulated trend data constitutes an important input to diagnostic predictive models (see Chapter 11). The British Market Research Bureau's (BMRB's) Target Group Index (TGI) serves a strategic planning purpose. The TGI annual reports, based on a sample of 25,000 adults, relate individual product-field and brand purchases to media 'consumption'. The 86-page questionnaire (placed by interviewers for self-completion) covers 4,500 brands in 500 product and service fields, as well as the respondent's media habits and attitudes. Questions are also asked about attitudes towards, for example, drink, diet and health, home and do-it-yourself items; and a lifestyle system called Outlook, useful for segmenting markets, is based on the answers.

Data gathered from consumer panels by research companies provides current information about the lifestyles, needs and wants of consumers. This is related to the products consumed or used and the media watched, read or listened to. This product/media data is normally location-specific, e.g. by recording the consumers' postcodes to identify where they live. The method of using the postcode address file is explained towards the end of Chapter 3. In fact postcodes are of necessity collected by direct marketing agencies to target their selected consumer groups with mail. The term 'junk mail' is used by people who do not want to receive such mail and who might view it as an intrusion on their privacy. It is also possible to relate personal consumer data to the traditional ACORN classification of residential neighbourhoods based on the census of population and related to lifestyle indicators, such as how many families each have two or three cars and take two or more holidays abroad a year. ACORN is explained in Chapter 8.

TN Sofrès consumer panels and the BMRB's Target Group Index generate very substantial databases from panel research. So given an adequate research budget, it is possible that exploratory research can locate much information on most markets in considerable detail.

2.8.4 Buying omnibus surveys

Secondary data captured in previous omnibus surveys can be bought to contribute information about the needs of markets in exploratory research. The MRS's monthly newsletter carries a regular feature in which research suppliers advertise their omnibus surveys. Each research supplier draws the sample, administers the questionnaire and processes the data reports results. Or a research buyer takes space in the questionnaire and pays according to the number of questions asked and the statistical breakdowns required.

The number of questions one can include in an omnibus questionnaire is limited, but sufficient to establish basic market characteristics. The market may be the subject of a specialist omnibus. There are, for example, motoring omnibuses and baby market omnibuses as well as the more general omnibus surveys based on a sample of all the adults in Great Britain, or on a sample of all the households.

There are also omnibus surveys relating to the European Union, 'all-Ireland', Scotland, Hong Kong, the Middle East and Malaysia, to pick an arbitrary selection from one issue of the MRS newsletter. The samples are specified and carefully drawn. The omnibus survey is an important item in the research supplier's range of products. The surveys are conducted at regular intervals and are relied on for a regular contribution to revenue.

An omnibus survey would, for example, be a good way of establishing what sort of people are in the DIY market, their DIY equipment and their most recent DIY job done. A shared questionnaire is likely to range over a number of subjects so that it is difficult to engage the respondent's attention in more than a superficial way. This does not apply quite so much to the specialist omnibus, but the questionnaire still represents the interests of a number of sponsors.

The development of computer-assisted telephone interviewing (CATI) makes it possible to capture and process omnibus data very quickly, e.g. 'Questions by Friday noon, results by Monday'.

2.9 Use of camera recordings and observational studies in exploratory work

In this section observation as a research method is considered.

Videos of customer behaviour provide material for observational studies. The 1990s have seen an increasing use of closed circuit television (CCTV) in large stores and shopping centres in major industrialised countries and surveillance cameras on roads and motorways. While used to deter offences from being committed, they also provide a view of how people shop and how they behave.

If the product field is unfamiliar to the person concerned with conducting the exploratory research it may be advisable for him or her to go out and observe, for example, the following:

- how motorists behave on the forecourt of a filling station;
- how housewives buy bread;
- how retailers shop in a cash-and-carry wholesaler's;
- how customers behave in a DIY centre.

How videos are used depends on the nature of the product and the planner's experience as a consumer.

The rationale behind observational studies is that we can learn more about the consumption of products and services by observing and talking with consumers in their 'natural' context or environment. As noted by Miriam Catterall, of the University of Ulster, observation studies have gained considerably in popularity amongst researchers and their clients. They are often referred to as ethnographic studies and draw from the expertise and experience of anthropologists. Because so much of our consuming behaviour is habitual, it can be difficult to recall and articulate all the details even in expertly moderated focus groups or depth interviews. The minutiae of consuming and the relationships between consuming events are often difficult for consumers to recount simply because they become taken for granted and are not seen as important or significant. For example, an advertising agency, BBH gave people Polaroid and conventional cameras to use and asked them to bring back some photographs. By contrast with the self-conscious poses in the 35 mm camera photographs, the Polaroid pictures demonstrated a lack of self-consciousness and exhibitionism. This research demonstrated how people use Polaroid cameras in more dramatic and visual ways than could have been obtained from a focus group discussion.

2.10 Exploring the market: depth interviews and group discussions

Individual, intensive 'depth' interviews and group discussions are the two most commonly used qualitative research methods. It would be possible to conduct a sufficient number of lengthy, unstructured interviews to draw statistical conclusions, and indeed this is sometimes done. The more cost-effective approach, however, is to do enough qualitative work to reveal most, if not all, of the ways in which consumers behave in the market and the attitudes they hold. Then to use this rich data to design a quantitative study of a sample large enough to allow conclusions to be drawn or to conduct enough depth interviews and group discussions in a qualitative study.

In industrial and other non-domestic markets, where information is often being sought from experts and a formal questionnaire can be out of place, individual, intensive or depth interviews are frequently used, as are group discussions.

The depth interview and group discussion are both clinical methods. Depth interviews in market research are shallower compared with the interviewing techniques used in psychotherapy. 'Extended' or 'intensive' are better descriptions, but 'depth' is still in common use. Individual, depth or intensive interviews are used when the subject might prove embarrassing or when it is necessary to avoid interaction between group members. The interview may be *non-directive* or *semi-structured*. In the first case the interviewer, having established a relaxed atmosphere, leaves the respondent free to come up with an experience, attitude, need or idea that bears on the subject which, at the exploratory state, is likely to be broadly defined as, for example, 'feeding the family'. For a semi-structured interview, the interviewer is equipped with an agenda or checklist designed to ensure that specific aspects of interest are covered.

Group discussions have cost and time advantages. A group of consumers with an interest in common, such as motoring, child-rearing, taking holidays or DIY, can develop a synergy so that more ideas are discussed over a shorter time than would emerge from the same number of depth interviews, however skilful the interviewer at establishing rapport. The type of group most commonly used is described here. Groups based on syndicated and brainstorming techniques are more appropriate to new-product development.

The number and make-up of the groups depends on the variability in the consumer market shown by the secondary data search. If the market is not sufficiently well documented a limited number of questions in an omnibus survey will establish the main variables.

Any variable which is known to be significant is allowed for in the design of the groups, not forgetting regional differences. The groups can either be alike in some ways (homogeneous) or unlike (heterogeneous) types. A mixture of types in each group could reveal a greater variety of experience and ideas. It could also have the opposite effect. In many product and service markets, social grade is no longer a discriminator where buying behaviour is concerned, but in the UK it is still usual to distinguish between middle class (ABC1) and working class (C2DE) when designing groups; see Chapter 13 for details on social class classification.

Discussions are tape-recorded and often filmed so that body language can be observed. (If participants are not told about this recording beforehand, their permission to use tape and film must be sought after the session. This is in the MRS Code of Conduct.)

Risk of bias

Group discussions are recorded on tape and later transcribed. Statements expressing habits, attitudes and wants are listed verbatim. The lists are cut up into individual statements and the statements are sorted into piles. Then the discussion is summarised, using the respondents' own words as far as possible.

In qualitative work of this kind there is clearly a risk that the results may be biased:

- group members may not be representative of the market;
- the interviewer may influence the course of the discussion;
- the content analysis may not truly represent the experience and attitudes of the group;
- the report writer may impose a doctrinaire psychological interpretation on the content.

In exploratory research qualitative methods are often used extensively in the search for product and advertising ideas and in the development of concepts. In later stages for the full-scale research the methods of interviewing and focus groups can generate rich data about customer types. A comparison of these methods is given in Box 2.2.

Box 2.2 Depth interviews and focus group methods

Depth interviews

A single depth interview can last over an hour and generate 20 pages of data in the form of an interview manuscript. In other words, a small number of these interviews will be very time consuming and therefore expensive to conduct and will generate a large volume of data for analysis. Too many interviews can simply result in data overload and encourage an analysis that skims the data so that the richness in the detail can be lost. What makes the depth interview so valuable is the richness of the data it generates and a close and intensive study of this data will usually reveal insights and ideas that would be difficult, if not impossible, to obtain from quantitative surveys or panel studies. Apart from depth interviews a wide range of data collection methods, such as accompanied shopping trips, can be used.

The one-to-one qualitative or depth interview is particularly useful when the researcher needs to consult with experts in a particular field, such as buyers and users of business software. The open-ended nature of these interviews makes them particularly suitable for gathering information on the ways that individuals make decisions or for listening to extensive individual experiential accounts of using products and services. Depth interviews are also used with consumers, but can be perceived as rather intimidating for individual respondents. In this respect focus groups offer respondents a little more security and comfort due to the numbers involved and they are less likely to feel the focus is on them as individuals. For this reason, many qualitative researchers prefer to undertake paired depths with consumers. This means the researcher interviews two respondents together, usually two friends, and the ensuing interview becomes more like a discussion between the three parties involved.

Focus groups

Focus groups are an increasingly popular method of consulting consumers and are used by a wide range of organisations, such as manufacturers of consumer and industrial products, local authorities and political parties. The focus group is a research interview with a group of respondents (participants) who discuss the research topic under the direction of a moderator. Usually market research interviews involve an interviewer asking questions and each individual respondent providing answers. The focus group involves discussion between participants and the role of the moderator is to facilitate this discussion by ensuring that all participants have opportunities to express their views and that the discussion remains on the research topic. The presence of other participants means that the atmosphere in focus groups tends to be more informal and relaxed than in one-to-one interviews. As they listen to the opinions and experiences of others, group participants are able to identify the degree to which what they are hearing fits their situation. By comparing and contrasting the views of others, participants can become more explicit about their own views. Thus researchers argue that the data generated from focus groups is more than the sum of the views of the individual participants.

Focus groups usually consist of around eight participants who are specially recruited on the basis of some shared characteristics or experiences. For example, the participants may be recruited for the focus group on the basis that they are all Ford Fiesta drivers, readers of *The Times* newspaper, buyers of office stationery, or have experience of diabetes. On recruitment, participants are issued with invitations to a discussion venue.

The venue may be the recruiter's own home or, increasingly, a special focus group facility. Focus group facilities are laid out like living rooms and are equipped with high quality audio and video equipment that records the discussion. The discussion room is equipped with a one-way mirror and representatives from the client company and the advertising agency can sit in a room concealed behind the mirror and observe the discussion. Client companies value the opportunities this provides to view and listen to the ways that consumers discuss their products and advertising.

The focus group discussion will usually last around an hour and a half and, afterwards, the moderator and the representatives from the client company will take some time to consider and agree the key themes or points to emerge from the discussion. Later the discussions are transcribed from the audio or videotapes and the researcher will analyse each transcript for emerging themes and compare these with the themes from other group transcripts. The researcher will usually analyse a transcript in conjunction with listening to the audiotapes or viewing the videotapes. This is because the way that something is said (emotional or sarcastic tone) and the non-verbal behaviour (grimaces or smiles) can be just as important in interpretation as the content of what is said. On completion of the analysis, the researcher will debrief the client. Normally this takes the form of an oral presentation, which provides opportunities for the client company representatives to clarify and discuss the findings and their implications with the researcher.

There is considerable variation in focus group research and indeed, the focus group has become a generic term for a range of approaches that vary depending on the purpose of the research project. Focus groups are most frequently employed to sound out consumer attitudes and opinions or to obtain feedback on a company's goods and services. However, they are also used in more proactive ways to generate new ideas for products, services and advertising. A company interested in ideas about the ways that its brand could develop in the future may organise a series of focus groups with key market influencers such as fashion designers, magazine editors and web site designers. The company might also commission some extended groups with consumers. Extended groups can last up to four hours and participants may be asked to engage in a number of projective techniques. For example, in order to generate new ideas for advertising group participants might be asked to role-play. Participants could be asked to think themselves into the role of a new range of fresh cream cakes and to persuade reluctant consumers to purchase and eat them.

On other occasions clients might be invited to participate in the focus group along with the consumers of their products and services, so that they can share information and ideas, say, about telephone banking or local authority leisure services. Many market researchers are using focus groups in combination with other data collection methods. The moderator and the group participants may visit some local supermarkets to view the shelf displays of breakfast cereals and, afterwards, return to the focus group facility to discuss what they have seen.

Although the focus group is the most widely used data collection technique in qualitative market research, many other techniques are used. Consumers may be given video cameras or audio recorders and asked to record a video or audio diary of some event such as a shopping trip or a night out. Market researchers may observe consumers in situ, say in a pub, and later discuss their consumption with them individually or in groups. The researcher may accompany a number of consumers on a visit to a bank and encourage them to articulate their decisions, experiences and opinions as these arise during the visit.

Continued

The value of using these qualitative research methods

There is little doubt that different researchers bring different theoretical and conceptual frameworks to the interpretation of qualitative market research data and, as a result, there is no guarantee that two different researchers will interpret this data in exactly the same way. Qualitative researchers and their clients do not see this as a disadvantage. On the contrary, they argue that this diversity in the conceptual frameworks and approaches mirrors conditions in the marketplace. Increasingly brand and marketing managers refer to their marketplaces as post-modern. Post-modern markets are characterised by diversity, fragmentation and contradiction, for example, markets are increasingly globalised and, at the same time, increasingly localised (Brown, 1996).

This means that many clients and researchers accept that there is no single truth lying out there waiting to be discovered by somebody. As a result, multiple interpretations of qualitative research data are something to be valued and, because of this, many researchers and their clients make a case for multidisciplinary teams of researchers working on a qualitative project. Researchers with backgrounds in anthropology, sociology, literary theory, semiotics and psychology will, individually and collectively, generate a rich range of insights and ideas from qualitative data. It is these insights and ideas that the clients of qualitative market research are buying when they commission qualitative research projects.

There are benefits from this diversity and the ways that imaginative and thorough analysis of qualitative data can contribute to marketing decisions, as shown by the 'Guinness egg' research (Broadbent and Cooper, 1987) and the 'it's good to talk' research (Alexander *et al.*, 1995). Both resulted in the development of very successful advertising campaigns for Guinness and BT respectively. Furthermore, each team of researchers, from CRAM and Semiotic Solutions, brought different theoretical perspectives to the analysis of the qualitative data.

Ethical concerns

Data collection techniques in qualitative research involve close and extended contact with respondents. For this reason it is important that researchers and their clients follow certain ethical standards. Researchers need to inform focus group participants if they are to be observed and the discussion is to be recorded. The Market Research Society publishes a set of guidelines for qualitative research (MRS, 1998).

References

Alexander, M., Burt, M., and Collinson, A. (1995), 'Big talk, small talk, BT's strategic use of semiotics in planning its current advertising', *Journal of the Market Research Society*, vol. 37, no. 2, pp.91-102.

Broadbent, K. and Cooper, P. (1987), 'Research is good for you', *Marketing Intelligence and Planning*, vol. 5, no. 1, pp.3–9.

Brown, S. (1996), *Postmodern Marketing*, Routledge, London.

Market Research Society (1998), *Qualitative Research Guidelines*.

Source: Miriam Catterall (1999), University of Ulster, Northern Ireland.

The validity of focus groups depends on recruiting suitable participants with a relevant choice of stimuli to allow them to formulate and express their own thoughts and discuss their motivations within the groups.

2.11 Impact of information technology

Computers and the availability of specialist office automation software systems can considerably improve the planning utility of a company's internal records. Database organisers, electronic work flow management forms, public bulletin boards, scheduling facilities, video-conferencing systems, and electronic mail, the Internet and web-based services, have all helped to revolutionise the working environment.

Market research personnel, increasingly faced with developments in information technology, have to keep pace with the need to access data on-line at computer terminals from secondary sources at diverse company locations. Early office automation has progressed from word processing to far more complex products such as 'groupware',[1] where information can be scanned onto disks and where retrieval viewing on computer screens can be carried out in seconds.

The market for groupware (a combination of products covering the main office requirements of finding, using and communicating information) in products, consulting and training continues to rise.

2.12 Acquisition and examination of research data

Computerisation has speeded up enormously the gathering, examination, storage and retrieval of research data. While the cost of computer hardware has decreased, there has been a proliferation of hardware and business software applications. The *Financial Times* series of surveys on information technology, published in spring 1999, is highly recommended reading, for current content about product and services usage (for example, the 'millennium bug' issue[2]) new developments with organisations and forecast assumptions about the future.

Major innovations will be described as this book follows the marketing research process, but the following are some examples of the impact of information technology on the market research industry:

- The use of interactive TV/telephone/cable/satellite technologies has ushered in the development of interactive optical media, videotext, ceefax, teletext, video phone, multimedia home banking and shopping by video link, enabling customers and companies to make contact with each other in addition to the traditional ordering systems by post and telephone. Market researchers have to make the effort to keep up with developments in telecommunications and information technologies as they affect both their clients and their clients' customers in these industries as well as the speed, accuracy and handling of the market researchers' information.

- Computer-assisted telephone interviewing (CATI) and push-button handsets (peoplemeters) are effective examples illustrating how widespread access to the telephone and television has enhanced the gathering and recording of market research data. Instead of encircling code numbers manually on a questionnaire, the use of CATI means that the interviewer reads the question shown on a computer monitor over the telephone and the respondent's pre-coded answers are keyed straight into the computer. Peoplemeters capture the television viewing habits of individuals in a household, saving the individual viewer on a panel from the need to keep a diary, thus reducing error and accelerating data capture.

- Bar coding of products with electronic point of sale (EPOS) systems means that retailers are able to record on a daily basis the products (and their value) sold through their checkouts. By using the cash register to enter the value and by passing the barcoded product over the scanner at the checkout, the retail sales assistant is feeding information to a control computer. This records the sale for stock-checking and calculation of the customer's bill with the change given for cash transactions released automatically. Taylor Nelson Audits of Great Britain and Nielsen make use of electronic data capture of coded products sold across scanners in major grocery outlets which are then matched to consumer purchasing panels. Their work provides key insights into the seasonality of purchases, competition between companies and their products, the effects of changes in prices, costs and promotions, and customer traffic density in-stores.

- The computer makes it possible to relate together data from diverse sources. Using the postcodes recorded on computer files, it is possible to 'flush out' and locate consumer targets in a market. Electronic data processing has made possible the rapid scrutiny of relationships between the many population variables, for example, census data (the last UK census was in 1991).

- Customer database planning is driving the way in which companies market and service their products. For example, financial services institutions have the benefit of possessing their own databases containing highly detailed information personal to their existing customers. In addition organisations can also subscribe to commercial databases, e.g. the Target Group Index to help them identify customer characteristics from the most profitable market segments, and prospect for new customers with similar characteristics. Companies subscribing to the TGI's services buy in the information they need relating to their own markets.

- The computer's capacity to handle calculations and relationships between data types enhances the superimposition of geodemographic classifications. These are geographical locations combined with population characteristics and lifestyle categorisations of customers. Such classifications are regularly updated and widely available from databases held by media owners, market research companies and software bureau providers. For example, geodemographic systems are produced by CACI's ACORN (a classification of residential neighbourhoods), PinPoint's FINPIN, CDMS SuperProfiles and Experian's MOSAIC, a topic treated in more detail in Chapter 12.

The benefits of information technology can be summarised thus:

- **Efficiency**. Making more efficient use of the valuable resource in customer data for storage, electronic retrieval and updating of customer information; matching customers' purposes to a company's products and cross-selling related products to these customers.

- **Problem-solving**. Enhancing a faster response time to demand, handling of orders and resolving customer and supplier problems.

- **Improved marketing**. Facilitating the improved positioning of products to customer targets to enhance short-term sales and profits.

- **Competitive advantage**. Achieving this in the long term through the integration and control of critical information relating to the customer interface with an organisation's operations to make it easier and speedier for customers to do business with it and vice versa.

2.13 Benefits of having a marketing information system

Organisations need to study their information needs, and design suitable marketing information procedures or systems in order to organise the flow of information to their people.

> The effectiveness of the marketing plan depends on the quality of information received and acted upon by marketing managers.
>
> A marketing information system (MIS) will require human and equipment resources, and procedures to provide analysis and distribution of reliable and up-to-date information to marketing managers.

To carry out their responsibilities effectively, marketing managers can draw on information which has been accumulated and updated from internal organisational records, marketing research and marketing intelligence sources. Most organisations have computerised databases on their customers and their markets. Computerisation has greatly increased the speed of data collection, analysis and distribution and many organisations have in place some form of marketing information system which is accessible by computer.

Marketing activities have to be consistently monitored and controlled. Because of the uncontrollable elements in the marketing environment (see Figure 2.4) every organisation should be aware that surprises can occur and it may be appropriate to have contingency plans should competitors decide to take offensive action against an organisation's marketing activities. For example, if a firm is planning a new sales drive with a sales promotion incentive, say, a free sachet with every product purchased, its major competitor could go on the offensive. The competitor could reduce its price for a specified period on a brand of product which is in direct competition with the firm's product. This could spoil the promotional effort by the firm.

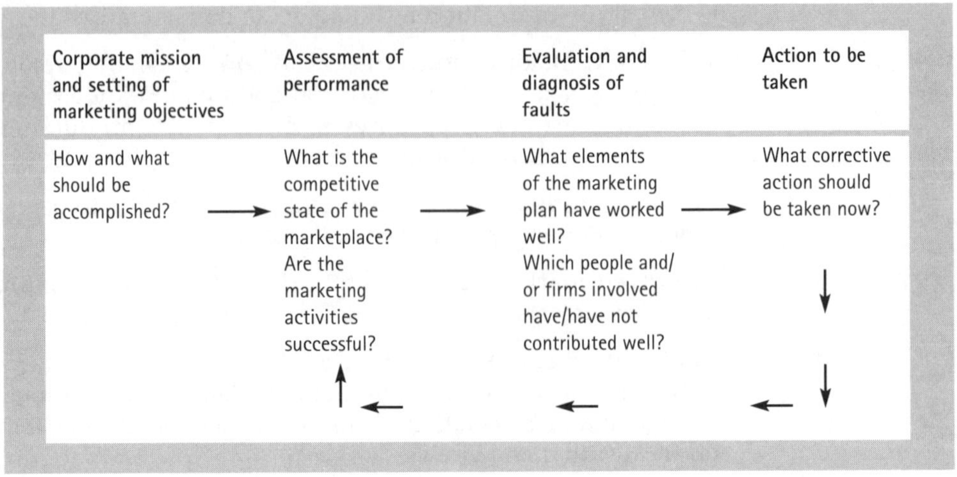

Corporate mission and setting of marketing objectives	Assessment of performance	Evaluation and diagnosis of faults	Action to be taken
How and what should be accomplished? →	What is the competitive state of the marketplace? → Are the marketing activities successful? ↑ ←	What elements of the marketing plan have worked well? → Which people and/ or firms involved have/have not contributed well? ←	What corrective action should be taken now? ↓ ← ↓

Fig 2.4 Nature of the control process and the information requirements

A broad description of a company-wide information system has been given by Mülbacher *et al*.:[3]

a structure, such as data files, reports, analytical tools and PCs, a network relating these elements to each other and information processes through which internal and external information is gathered, evaluated, processed and distributed among all the decision-makers in the company.

Control of marketing activities applies at all levels in organisations from the senior management to the line and staff positions, so information relevant to the jobs at hand needs to flow to the key personnel concerned. Marketing is formally carried out by people involved in market research and analysis, product and brand management, sales, advertising, promotion and those overseeing the totality of the marketing function. There are well-defined tasks and responsibilities for each of these jobs which carry responsibilities for managing programmes and resources.

A marketing information system is required to help managers do their task more effectively because information is needed in order to:

- control annual, medium and long-range planning functions to assess whether the planned results have been achieved;

- control costs to determine the impact of marketing expenditures;

- control the profitability of products, sales territories, order sizes, distribution channels and market segments;

- assess whether the organisation in its strategy is making the best use of its human, financial and technological assets to achieve its best opportunities with reference to the marketplace and the state of competition.

In order to satisfy customer and organisational objectives, information for organisational planning is required about customers and changes in market conditions. Such changes can have good, indifferent or bad effects on an organisation's

---

The marketing environment

Macro-environmental forces (listed under the mnemonic PEST):

Political/legal – What is the effect on an organisation's business of laws and regulations enacted by national, European and overseas governments to control, e.g. product safety, worker employment and pollution on a company's home and export sales?

Economic – What will be the effects of consumer spending power on company sales, profits and business confidence to re-invest?

Sociodemographic/cultural – What changes and trends in the size and structure of the population affect customers' lifestyles and consumption habits? What attitudes of national, regional, ethnic minority and political pressure groups will affect business?

Technological/ecological – What changes in research & development, manufacturing processes, product substitutes and new product development have occurred? What are the costs and availability of raw material resources and energy for an organisation's business?

Market forces:

Customers – What are customer needs and what are the buyer behaviour processes? What customer segments exist and what are their sizes, locations and growth prospects?

Competitors – What are the objectives, resources, strengths and weaknesses, strategies and market shares of major competitors competing for sales volume and market share?

Intermediaries – What wholesalers/stockists/distributors/dealers/retailers in the channels of distribution are needed to bring the producers' products to the customers? What are the costs and types of physical (transportation) functions and finance provision?

Suppliers – What are the availability and cost of supplies to an organisation's production processes? What key trends are occurring with suppliers and how may the supplier effort be integrated with an organisation's lead times in production?

↓

Information flows

↓

The marketing information system

- Is the market research conducted (whether an overview of or limited to certain studies of the marketing environment above) sufficient and reliable for an organisation to plan its marketing efforts?
- Are the marketing intelligence reports taking account of information received and disseminated in the marketplace of an accurate and timely nature?

↓

Processed information flows

↓

Marketing planning

Corporate mission – Statement of market-oriented goals in the light of the evaluation and adoption of the information above for the corporate well-being of an organisation.

Marketing objectives – Setting of achievable objectives given organisational resources.

Marketing strategy – Adoption of appropriate strategies to achieve such objectives. Use of marketing mix tactics to develop product, pricing, promotion and distribution policies to reach customer target segments and to position products effectively in the marketplace.

Fig 2.5 MIS and information flow requirements

business. By analysing such information, market researchers can help marketing managers alter their organisation's strategies and plan marketing mixes in response to market intelligence reports on changes within the marketing environment. If information requirements and marketing are fully integrated, radical and unexpected changes of plans can be avoided. Figure 2.5 presents an example of the information flow requirements for organisational planning.

The comprehensive and periodic account of the marketing environment and the organisation's resources and competences is called the **marketing audit**. The marketing audit presents an overview of an organisation's historical and current situation. It has the following important components:

- an examination of the macro and market forces in the marketing environment;
- an analysis of goals, resources, efficiencies, strengths and weaknesses of an organisation and its competitive environment;
- an analysis of existing marketing strategies, plans and control;
- an evaluation of successes or failures in the implementation of the marketing effort.

It is therefore crucial for an organisation to have relevant and accurate information and computerised databases on the marketplace, which are constantly updated, so that it can work out timely and effective changes in its marketing plans in order to adapt to the marketing environment. A computerised marketing information system and its databases will help in information storage, updating, and retrieval in planning functions.

A marketing plan should include the following elements:

- a summary of the proposed plan to present an overview for management;

- an examination of background data from secondary and primary sources so that relevant information can be extracted on markets, e.g. competitors, products and market sizes;

- a SWOT analysis of an organisation's abilities to develop and protect its market situation;

- identification of objectives to increase sales volume, market share and profits;

- a statement of strategy to show how the objectives can be achieved, that is, a statement of who does what, when and by what methods;

- a forecast of expected costs and revenues from implementing the plan;

- an indication of the control and evaluation procedures necessary to monitor the progress and to provide feedback on the effectiveness of the plan.

2.14 A historical perspective of the Internet

The Internet, or the 'information superhighway', had its origins in the Cold War from US military-funded projects. The Advanced Research Projects Agency (ARPA), now known as DARPA, is a branch of the US Department of Defense. In the 1960s it funded research at universities and corporations including the Massachusetts Institute of Technology (MIT) and the RAND Corporation to develop a method of communication by computers.[4] ARPAnet made its star debut in 1972 at the International Conference on Computers and Communications, Washington D.C. Terminals at more than 40 different locations were able to find the ARPAnet IMP (Interface Message Processor). After the introduction of this revolutionary technology, private sector manufacturers and vendors also took an interest and by 1973 distant host terminals were connected over telephone lines with a satellite link to Hawaii. Developers at DARPA worked on a new protocol, TCP/IP (Transmission Control Protocol/Internet Protocol) which would handle large numbers of users and this came into existence by the middle of the 1970s. 1 January 1983 has been seen as the official beginning of the Internet when all of ARPAnet was switched to using TCP. There were also many other developments within universities and companies, e.g. to develop Csnet (Computer Science Network) and BITNET (Because It's Time Network), but these are too extensive to mention here. It is sufficient to say that the Internet as we know it today has come a long way from its beginnings in a relatively short space of 30 to 40 years. The potential for commercial applications, including marketing research, to be exploited on the Internet, represents 'the tip of an iceberg', to borrow a phrase.

The **Internet** is a network of computers linked together. A graphic or text browser is used to access a large network of interlinked documents. Once plugged into this system a person can have access to discussion groups, bulletin boards, and so on on other people's web sites. So even when one part of a network is down or switched off other parts still operate. The Internet, therefore, operates around the clock and 'never sleeps'. So availability to link into the Internet is constant.

Companies have found the Internet to be a useful, non-personal promotional tool judging by the numbers of well-known multinationals who have web sites, for example, IBM, Procter & Gamble, Ford, General Electric and Kraft.

The Internet has been extremely successful, if measured by the number of users, and increasingly in growth terms, projected to rise to over 200 million users in the year 2000. As an example of its growth, Table 2.1 shows the number of on-line shoppers in three European countries and a projected increase.

Table 2.1 On-line shoppers in Europe

	Current on-line shoppers	Potential on-line shoppers (next six months)
UK	0.5m	1.8m
Germany	0.61m	0.8m
France	0.26m	0.65m

Base: All current Internet users
Source: Jameson, R. (1998), *MRS Research*, June, p. 54.

2.15 Using the Internet

This section explains the different applications available when using the Internet.

The World Wide Web

The **World Wide Web (WWW)** can be described as a collection of sites on the Internet. Companies and individuals can design their own sites to provide a form of inexpensive and easily accessible information about themselves, their products and services. Some charge for access to their information and provide passwords to those who pay. Others give freely of their information, see Section 2.15.2. Since there is so much free information that can be easily accessed the popularity of the Internet with personal computer users has increased. Market research data collection is aided electronically without having to leave one's office to search for information.

The Web has a network of hypertext links which connect its pages, and by following these links the user travels easily from one document to another. Web search engines, such as Yahoo!, Excite or Infoseek, connect users to other organisations' and individuals' web sites. Web browsers, such as Microsoft's Internet Explorer, Mosaic or Netscape, allow users to gain access to major sites. Once on the sites, internal search engines facilitate searches by using key words, such as 'marketing research' or 'consumer marketing'. The user is then linked directly to a number of relevant documents. Examples of web sites are given in Sections 2.15.1 to 2.15.3.

The cybermall

Web sites can be linked together in a 'virtual market', the **cybermall**, a concept built from the shopping mall or precinct in a neighbourhood. A cybermall consists of cyberstores selling similar products or a wide range of different products. Compared to the traditional methods of physical distribution and advertising, firms can now display their wares cheaply and conveniently in cybermalls or on their own custom-designed web sites, thanks to the Internet.

The intranet

For internal communications within their own organisations, firms can also use an **intranet** based upon groupware technology on a similar open format to the Internet. When organisations increase in size communications can become difficult. Intranets enhance coordination between different departments by allowing an open format to be used where 'shareware information' is made easily accessible to those working within the organisation.

Electronic mail

For external and internal use, electronic mail or **email** as it is popularly known, works on the same principle as a post office service. Messages and document attachments are sent to recipients' mailboxes using a mail server system such as Pegasus, Telnet or Simeon. The messages are then 'downloaded', that is, shown on computer screens/monitors to be read and replied to. Both messages and attachments can be saved to folders.

Email takes the form of an electronic postal service that never shuts. So messages can be sent to any individual with an email address anywhere in the world at any time. It is very fast, reduces mailing costs and importantly as well, reduces paper consumption. Customers can be put on 'mailing lists' and firms can just as easily send out information to groups as they can to individuals.

The **Usenet** news system is an electronic service which distributes news at different levels, for local consumption or world-wide distribution. Users can contact newsgroups to research or ask questions on any topic, e.g. on a range of medical treatments. Users of newsgroups range from absolute beginners to god-like experts. Http://www.dejanews.com is one address to use for accessing newsgroups.

Table 2.2 provides a comparison of the methods which market researchers can use with their selected respondent samples.

The broad range of web sites available is too numerous to cite here. However, the following selected examples give a flavour of the breadth of information that can be obtained. There are examples of web sites from academic, government and industry sources. These are presented in the following section (as adapted from the Internet News in the *Marketing Intelligence and Planning Journal*).[5]

Table 2.2 Comparison of web-based research with other research methods

Research methods	Advantages	Disadvantages
Phone	Direct and immediate contact. Good control of sample. High population penetration.	Calls are expensive at peak and overseas rates. Intrusive into privacy.
Post	Cheap. Cost effective for large surveys.	Impersonal and slow to get results. Sample bias occurs when questionnaires sent are not returned.
CAPI and CATI	Introduction of visual stimuli. Automated data collection. Fast, accurate, cheap. Capable of handling multivariate data and analysis by computer.	Expensive to set up. IT support required. Greater staff training.
Email	Cheap, fast and easy to use. No international restrictions. Sound and vision can be mixed. Convenient for people to reply. Versatile – different types of questions can be asked. No interviewer bias.	Incomplete directories of names and poor lists can make the sampling frame a poor one. Problems of junk mail and unrepresentative samples.
Web sites	Similar advantages to email. Greater detail can be put on sites. Attractive visual moving images and sound creation. New users can be registered to gain new customer lists.	Respondents select themselves so little control over sample by researchers. Penetration of population limited to respondents who have computers. Reliance on people to find and visit a web site.

2.15.1 Examples of academic web sites in the UK

Most universities now have web sites with specific details pertaining to their own organisations, for example the different types of departments, how to apply for admission, contact names of staff, leisure and sporting facilities, types of accommodation and some areas of local interest for newcomers. The University of Birmingham (http://www.bham.ac.uk) falls into this category. Students are now able to visit university web sites at home and abroad without the tedium of having to wait for information by post.

Some university web sites such as the Centre for Learning and Teaching at Nottingham Trent University (http://www.celt.ntu.ac.uk) have produced web resource packs with links to a variety of academic training and development bodies. For example, the Keele teaching network, Sheffield 'Open University', CEDIR (Centre for Educational Development and Interactive Resources), distance learning at Hull, Lancaster and Heriot-Watt universities. There are details of externally funded projects, video-conferencing, deliberations on learning and assessment resources. Information like this is useful for people who want to know about the provision of courses, grants, contacts and networking between academics in the teaching areas.

Strathclyde University has a very useful site (http://www.strath.ac.uk). Access to its Internet Resources page (/resources.html) gives a guide to:

- general resources – a reference shelf to guides, directories, references and publishers' lists; subject services by university faculties and departments; government information in the UK, Europe, USA and world-wide;

- UK higher education – includes details of the National Committee of Inquiry into higher education, the Dearing Report, research information and administrative bodies as well as various UK information projects;

- other web servers and summary listing by location. The subject launchpads, by the title of Pinakes, include attractive colourful boxes itemising specific categories such as EdWeb (educational reform and information technology), GEM (gateway to educational materials, educational resources), NISS Directory of Networked Resources and the WWW Virtual Library;

- network guides – to network resource tools;

- 'search the Internet' – includes searches via other Internet search engines. Search guides provide guidance on search programmes and strategies. Examples of major search programmes offered by this site are: AltaVista, Electric Monk, Excite, Google, Goto.com, Hotbot, Infoseek, LookSmart, Lycos, Northern Light, Search.com and Webcrawler.

2.15.2 Examples of UK government and industry web sites

Reed Business Information, part of the publishing giant, the Reed Elsevier Group, is a business partner of the Department of Trade and Industry's (DTI's) 'Information Society Initiative'. The DTI's British Exports Interactive site, developed by Reed, is at http://www.british.exports.com, and has information for exporters. Reed Business Information also publishes an established directory, *Kompass British Exports*. The company is based at East Grinstead, UK.

British Exports Interactive focuses on international trade between British exporters and overseas firms. The site makes the following claims:

- to be the world's most advanced product search system with an unrivalled product classification system on more than 42,000 product and service categories;

- product sourcing is made easy by having five languages – English, French, German, Spanish and Italian – 'the only site to offer full product translations';

- as completely free of charge 'the most comprehensive database of UK exporters on the Internet' providing access to over 90,000 UK exporting companies;

- an association with UUNet Pipex, the world's largest Internet service provider, and the National Westminster Bank, enabling direct purchases from firms listed on the site. Electronic commerce a growth area;

- a discussion forum and contacts with firms world-wide;

- agency opportunities with a database of UK companies wishing to appoint overseas agents.

There is a banking and finance section (/docreed/general/banking.htm) which includes information about the Bank of England and the four large UK banking groups. These topics are listed under UK Equities Direct, MoneyWorld, PCQuote, Sharelink and the Universal Currency Convertor.

The (/docreed/general/goverment.htm) section provides information on the departments and agencies of the British government, such as the Environment Agency and the Office for National Statistics. Business link offices, contacts and services for the Department of Trade and Industry are also offered.

Another organisation, Advertising Age (at http://adage.com) has information including the top 100 research companies, the 100 leading media companies and 100 leading national advertisements in different media, for example, the top 200 brands and global markets.

2.15.3 Examples of overseas governmental agency and industry association web sites

To give a flavour of the numerous sites available, some well-known governmental web sites abroad include the powerful US Food and Drug Administration, at http://www.fda.gov/default.htm, which controls the examination and licensing of new drugs and food products. The US Department of Commerce has an easy to remember web address, http://www.doc.gov/. The European Union's site is at http://www.europa.eu.int/index-en.htm, while the International Monetary Fund has its site address at http://www.ipc.org/external/. The World Intellectual Property Organization has its address at http://www.wipo.org/eng/newindex/index.htm. An example of a trade association site is the one at http://www.aeanet.org/ for the American Electronics Association.

2.16 A Code of Practice

The issue of customer confidentiality has to be treated sensitively to avoid infringing the rights and privacy of individuals and organisations. Members of the Market Research Society are expected to abide by the **MRS Code of Conduct**[6] which provides an ethical basis by which the privacy of members of the public and the confidentiality of organisations are respected. See Box 2.3.

Box 2.3 The MRS Code of Conduct

This Code of Conduct was agreed by the Market Research Society to be operative from January 1997. It is an amended version of a self-regulatory code that has been in existence since 1954.

The Code of Conduct is designed to support all those engaged in marketing or social research in maintaining professional standards throughout the industry. ... Assurance that research is conducted in an ethical manner is needed to create confidence in, and to encourage co-operation among the business community, the general public and others.

Relationship with the Data Protection Act

Adherence to the Code of Conduct will help to ensure that research is conducted in accordance with the principles of data protection encompassed by the Data Protection Act. It is a requirement of membership of these bodies that researchers must ensure that their conduct follows the letter and spirit of the principles of Data Protection from the Act. *These eight principles are*:

The First Principle

The information to be contained in personal data shall be obtained, and personal data shall be processed, fairly and lawfully.

The Second Principle

Personal data shall be held only for one or more specified and lawful purposes.

The Third Principle

Personal data held for any purpose or purposes shall not be used or disclosed in any manner incompatible with that purpose or those purposes.

The Fourth Principle

Personal data held for any purpose or purposes shall be adequate, relevant and not excessive in relation to that purpose or those purposes.

The Fifth Principle

Personal data shall be accurate and, where necessary, kept up-to-date.

The Sixth Principle

Personal data held for any purpose or purposes shall not be kept for longer than is necessary for that purpose or those purposes.

The Seventh Principle

An individual shall be entitled

(a)   at reasonable intervals and without undue delay or expense –
      (i) to be informed by any Data User whether he/she hold personal data of which that individual is the subject;
      and
      (ii) to access any such data held by a Data User; and
(b)   where appropriate, to have such data corrected or erased.

The Eighth Principle

Appropriate security measures shall be taken against unauthorised access to, or alteration, disclosure or destruction of personal data and against accidental loss or destruction of personal data.

From time to time guidance notes applying to the Eight Principles are published by the Data Protection Registry – Guideline 4 is of particular relevance to market research and fair obtaining of data.

Members should note that as from 1990, there is now an exclusive Method 2 Purpose for registering systems used for holding and processing any applicable data under the heading of Confidential Survey Research. Members using this new Purpose will need to write in the exact wording shown below in the appropriate place on the Registration form. Confidential Survey Research is defined as:

'Academic, Market or other Survey Research including the collection and analysis of personal data, with no disclosure of identifiable personal details about survey respondents to any third party (including any client for the research) and no use of the personal data for anything other than statistical and research purposes.'

Full details of how to register or re-register under this new Purpose are available from the MRS. Members should note that registration under the Method 2 purpose 'Confidential Survey Research' will exempt a company from its obligation to fulfil the Seventh Principle.

In order to help members keep within the Data Protection Act, a Guide to Good Practice is also available from the MRS.

Relationship with other Codes

This code is compatible with the Codes of AMSO (Association of Market Survey Organisations), and the ICC/ESOMAR International Code of Marketing and Social Research Practice.

Source: MRS Code of Conduct, 1998. Reprinted with permission.

The Code of Conduct is important because market research depends on the collection and storage of personal information provided by individuals which is protected by the Data Protection Act of 1984. This Act relates to 'any file of personal data capable of being processed automatically' – 'personal' meaning any information relating to a living individual which allows you to identify that 'individual'. Further, a 'data user' is anyone who controls the contents and use of personal data. It is as well for the MR industry that the habit of protecting the individual's privacy is well ingrained. In fact the Act is more beneficial to the industry than harmful, for it makes it more difficult for bogus organisations to sell under the guise of conducting research.

2.17 Conclusion

This chapter assumes company interest in a particular market and considers how this market may be explored. The time spent on the preliminary investigations reviewed here will depend on the company's familiarity with the market. The Internet and web-based sites have revitalised secondary data investigation.

There is a wealth of published and syndicated data available for the initial secondary research. This data, together with qualitative work in the early stages of research, may fit a company's particular objective so well that there is no need for further data collection. However, what is more likely is that the data, while illuminating about the general characteristics of the market and the distributive channels serving it, is not focused sufficiently closely on the habits, attitudes and requirements of the market. Exploratory research puts firms in a better position to define research objectives and to design primary research, tailored to those objectives.

Secondary and primary data collection methods have been explained to show how they are used for major qualitative and quantitative studies.

In the following chapters we will consider the research methods and sampling.

REFERENCES

1. The *Financial Times*, (1994), Survey: 'Software at work', 10 March, p.12.

2. The *Financial Times*, (1999), Survey: 'The Millennium "bomb" is already ticking', 2 December, p. 1.

3. Mülbacher, H. Dahringer, L. and Leihs, H. (1999), *International Marketing: a global perspective*, Thomson Business Press, USA, p. 423.

4. Ruthfield S, (1999), 'The Internet's history and development', http://www.acm.org/crossroads/xrds2-1/net-history.html, in *Crossroads: The ACM's first electronic publication*.

5. Wright L.T. (1999), 'Internet news', *Marketing Intelligence and Planning Journal*, MCB University Press, vol. 17, no. 2, pp. 120; no. 3, pp. 169–70.

6. *Market Research Society* (1994; 1998), *Code of Conduct*, January and April respectively, pp. 3–8.

QUESTIONS

You are employed in the research department of a chain of food stores with national (but rather uneven) distribution.

1. You have been asked to report on developments in the market for wine consumed in the home. How would you tackle this problem?

2. Write a report drawing on the sources you have consulted (the consumer market for wine is well documented).

3. How would you proceed if you were asked to report to management on the distribution of wine to the retail trade in Great Britain?

3 Research design procedure and choices

Initial exploratory research can be very useful in guiding management in the right direction as to whether to proceed with, for example, a major research project, or a product launch or in giving sufficient clues to arrive at informed assumptions about how a customer group or market sector might react. Managers may decide that the results yielded are sufficiently conclusive so that there is no need for a quantitative or qualitative research project to be undertaken. However, it should be noted that exploratory qualitative research at the outset is particularly useful, for example, when it contributes to inputs in the design of an expensive large-scale quantitative survey by helping to reduce risks in decision-making, thereby saving time, costs and uncertainty at the start.

In this chapter we are assuming that the initial exploratory research has shown that we need to carry out the whole research project because:

- the exploratory research has put us in a position to formulate hypotheses about the characteristics of the population we are interested in;

- the extent to which these characteristics of habit and attitude held by the target groups we are interested in, is open to question;

- answers to such questions will enable managers to make important decisions in solving their problems such as how to price, distribute and promote a new product launch or to reposition an existing product in a way that will optimise sales.

This chapter is designed to give a general view of the decisions that have to be made, and the choices of research procedure available, when markets are described. Sample design and data-collection methods are considered. (For explanations of the fundamental methods in sampling, see Chapter 4.) The use of the computer in data collection and processing is illustrated in the CATI and CAPI examples from TN Sofrès. The Halfords case study at the end of Chapter 10 serves to highlight the stages of the research design within the marketing research process.

3.1 Stages in the survey procedure

The order of events from the review of marketing objectives to the provision for monitoring performance is illustrated in Figure 3.1. The diagram shows an example of the functional responsibilities and tasks which provide the resources for the implementation of each stage by the client organisation (C) and the external research supplier (S).

Even though a client organisation will have internal inputs from its own marketing and marketing research functions, it may feel that it needs the specialisms of an external market research agency to supply it with the necessary information and direction. The client might also feel that secrecy, in the case of new product development, e.g. for the new model of a car, is necessary to guard against competitors' interest, so the work is subcontracted out to be conducted anonymously. Companies need to guard their reputations – the object of corporate advertising and careful nurturing of publicity and public relations efforts – so that much research work carried out tends not to be public knowledge. In an omnibus survey where respondents can answer one comprehensive questionnaire there are a number of companies that take part. These companies within the 'syndicated research effort' will pay the research agency concerned for the replies and analysis of those parts of the questionnaire which relate to them. The advantages of taking part in a syndicated omnibus survey are anonymity, regular updating (monthly, quarterly, etc.) and lower costs compared to the cost of hiring an agency to conduct the work on an individual basis. The information added to a company's market intelligence efforts and sales records could be enough to formulate clear objectives for a particular project and to obviate the need for exploratory research.

Different firms will have different resources and organisational structures so they will vary in their inputs into the marketing research processes. Accordingly, what is shown in Figure 3.1 is intended only as a guide.

As indicated in the Key in Figure 3.1, the supplier of research is the external research agency commissioned or brought in by the client organisation to conduct the research effort on its behalf.

The stages are explained below.

Stage 1

Marketing objectives are fully discussed with those responsible for designing research and the discussion includes consideration of possible courses of action before the research plan is made. The supplier may be a research agency offering a range of services or an organisation specialising in one research function, e.g. data collection or data processing. The client company may feel confident that it already has enough knowledge and information about its targeted market segments to bypass Stage 2 and proceed directly to Stage 3 (research design work carried out by the supplier).

However, exploratory research in Stage 2 can be of benefit to the client company when it is thought necessary to gather initial data helpful in making decisions about the appropriateness of objectives and courses of action in the design of the research project.

Stage 2

The figure illustrates a procedure which provides for second thoughts about the nature of the marketing problem after exploratory research has been carried out. If research had been ordered without due discussion of marketing objectives and possible courses of marketing action, the client organisation would not be in a position to judge whether the research problem could be better defined.

Research objectives are not a repetition of marketing objectives. The marketing objective might be, for example, to enter the market for accelerated freeze-dried convenience foods and the marketing problem the definition of the launch range. The research objectives will then be to establish clearly the demographic characteristics of those using the main categories of convenience food, to define their attitudes towards products they had tried, how they had prepared them, when they had used them, and whether existing competitive options available fell short of requirements.

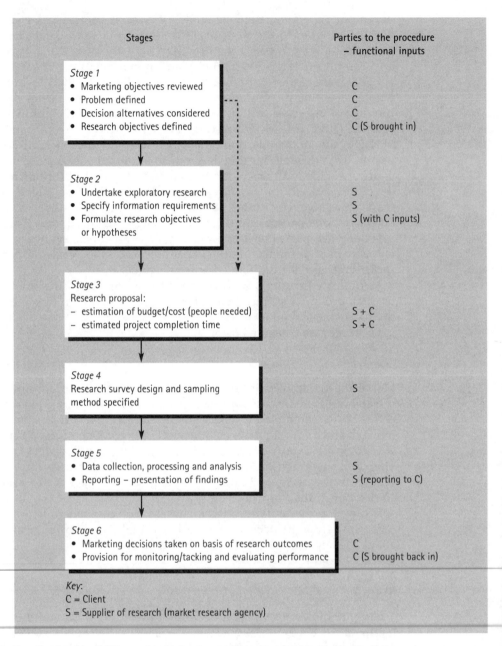

Fig 3.1 Functional responsibilities and tasks for stages within the marketing research process

Stage 3

The research proposal specifies when, where and by whom the survey is being carried out. It summarises the research proposal, specifies the method of data collection, sampling procedure and how the data is going to be analysed, and estimates the personnel, time and cost involved.

The client needs to be informed about budget estimates and whether costs significantly exceed the agreed projections from Stage 4 onwards.

The going rate for qualitative research has been put at £1,500–£2,000 per group for one and a half hours' work, with consumer groups of around 6–8 participants.[1] Big price fluctuations are not normal. Projects vary in the time taken and in whether full reports are wanted by the client organisations. For a typical straight-forward consumer project (4–8 groups), the time taken could be up to two weeks for each piece of the work required, such as recruitment, fieldwork, analysis and interpretation, debriefing (one week) and the preparation and presentation of the report (if required).

Stage 4

The research design and sampling procedure are described. The possible choices are reviewed later in this chapter. Cost is, of course, an important constraint. The research agency (as the supplier) has the responsibility to create its research design, based on choice of data-collection and sampling methods, and to keep within the agreed time and cost constraints with the client organisation.

Pilot work consists of trying out the proposed design – the questionnaire or other recording device it is proposed to use, together with the selection of respondents for questioning, or observing. It is not the same thing as exploratory research. Exploratory research helps to determine the research design whereas pilot work tests the design and helps to determine costs. For example, in the early days of pet-food marketing, a research agency underestimated the cost of fieldwork. Pet owners like to talk about their pets and, in the event, interviews took longer than had been anticipated. If sufficient pilot calls had been made, this problem could have been averted.

Stage 5

In large consumer surveys it is unusual for a client organisation to carry out its own fieldwork to collect data. Using a research agency helps to ensure that competitors are not alerted to a company's intentions to develop a competitive new product.

In a large organisation with significant marketing and marketing research functions, the research agency will present the analysis of its findings to managers in these departments who will in turn feed back the findings to senior managers through the organisation's management hierarchy. A small to medium-sized company may not have established marketing research and marketing departments. Marketing intelligence reports in these firms could be dispersed and held by various individuals or groups, say, in sales, distribution, production and finance. In such cases, it is likely that the marketing or sales directors and managing directors would commission the survey work from the research agency and the agency would report directly to these senior managers.

Stage 6

Marketing decisions can be made building upon the recommendations of the research agency and the company's capabilities. Implementation of these marketing decisions needs to be accompanied by some mechanism or provision for monitoring the effects of these decisions. For example, a car manufacturer or a financial services institution may be spending heavily on an advertising campaign to promote a particular product to a specific market segment. The impact of this advertising campaign needs to be evaluated and assessed for its effectiveness in reaching sales and profit projections. To facilitate a good working relationship the supplier should keep the client informed of progress or any significant developments that might have an effect on the research outcomes.

Box 3.1 presents a checklist guide to good working practice for the supplier in his or her provision to the client.

Box 3.1 Reporting and presenting: agency provision to client

Reporting

C. 10. By the time a survey is completed the agency shall have provided the client with: A copy of the questionnaire (or, in the case of multi-client surveys, the relevant part of a questionnaire) or similar document.

Any relevant extract from interviewers' instructions.

Relevant details of:

(a) its objectives;

(b) its universe – actual if different from intended;

(c) size and nature of sample – achieved and intended;

(d) any weighting methods used;

(e) where relevant, weighted and unweighted bases (clearly distinguished) for all major conventional tables;

(f) where relevant, statement of response rates and discussion of any possible bias due to non-response;

(g) method(s) by which information was collected;

(h) general nature of any informant incentives offered;

(i) the dates, and geographical coverage of, fieldwork and, on prior request from the client, a detailed list of the sampling points used and the times of day and/or days of the week when fieldwork was carried out;

(j) fieldforce(s) involved at any stage;

(k) sub-contractors used for major parts of the research;

(l) in qualitative work – method of recruitment;

(m) in desk research – method of recruitment;

(n) identified inaccuracies in any of the information collected (beyond those which may be reasonably inferred from the methodological details specified above), which might materially affect the validity of the information reported and/or inferences which may draw from it.

Presenting

C.11. When presenting results, members shall endeavour to make a clear distinction between the results themselves and their own interpretation of the data and recommendations.

Source: The Market Research Society, *The Members' Handbook 1998*, p. 39. Reprinted with permission.

3.2 Parties to the procedure

The extent to which research work is 'put out' varies. At one extreme, the client's marketing department may collaborate with an outside research agency at the exploratory stage, then commission the agency to cover all stages from research design to presentation of findings. Or the department may merely commission fieldwork and electronic data processing – handing over the questionnaire, specifying the sample and receiving computer printouts of the analysis.

At the other extreme, a small firm may not have the marketing and marketing research skills nor the facilities to carry out the research processes, such as field trials or observations of focus group discussions. In this case the firm will hand over the entire project to a research supplier.

Interpretation of the findings will be a joint operation so that the significance of the findings is fully (management) and properly (marketing research) exploited.

What do both parties reasonably expect from this relationship? Box 3.2 presents another useful checklist from the Market Research Society as a guide to the commissioning of market research for both parties: the company commissioning the research and the market research agency as the supplier.

Box 3.2 A guide to the commissioning of survey research

This guide has a very simple purpose. It is intended to help potential buyers of survey research in the selection and briefing of a supplier. Many organisations which undertake a considerable amount of survey research divide this work among a number of suppliers. There is no one supplier which is the best for every project, and selecting a supplier for a particular piece of research is not a simple matter.

Notes of this kind can only be broad guidelines to the sort of things that should be considered when selecting a supplier. The two sections which follow attempt to set out a check-list of things that should be covered in your contract.

1. **What the supplier can expect from you** lists things which you should do to ensure that you give the supplier the opportunity to contribute fully in the resolution of your problem.

2. **What you can expect from the supplier – general** lists the areas that should be considered in evaluating the overall competence and standing of the supplier and thus should be used in deciding whether or not to approach the supplier on a specific problem.

3. **What you can expect from the supplier – specific** is intended to cover the points a supplier should include in his specific proposals and upon which final decisions in the choice of a supplier should be made.

1. What the supplier can expect from you

(a) A statement of the research problem, preferably in the form of a written brief.

(b) A setting of the problem in its general background and context, in some cases, users may be able to define their overall problem within its generalised context but not have the experience to define it in research terms.

(c) An opportunity to meet and discuss the problem and its background.

Continued

(d) An indication of the sorts of decisions that are likely to be influenced by the research results and the uses to which the results are to be put (e.g. whether publication is envisaged).

(e) A broad indication of the budget available for the research project.

A research supplier cannot be expected to provide satisfactory and comprehensive research proposals in the absence of the above; it is therefore in your interests to supply them. There are three other things a supplier can reasonably expect, though of themselves they will not necessarily affect the quality of research proposals.

(f) That you should only approach suppliers on a formal basis when there is a reasonable probability that the project under commission will actually be commissioned.

(g) If it is the type of project which you feel should be the subject of tenders, that you should restrict the suppliers you approach to a reasonable number (say 2–4), and inform them that they are in a competitive situation.

(h) If you should submit a project to tender in this way, the suppliers can reasonably expect an opportunity to meet you to discuss your reaction to the approach suggested in their research proposals before you make your final choice of supplier.

Suppliers will often spend a considerable amount of time in the preparation of research proposals. It is desirable that this practice should continue but this will only be the case if suppliers perceive their investment has some chance of paying-off.

2. What you can expect from the supplier – general

The first check-list details the criteria which can be used to assess the supplier's general level of competence and will help in the decision as to whether, in principle, a particular supplier will suit your requirements.

(a) Evidence of the background and quality of his/her research executives.

(b) Details of any specialists (psychologists, statisticians) employed full-time and/or on a consultancy basis.

(c) Evidence of experience that may be relevant to your particular situation; work on similar kinds of problems; work within the same market; experience of using relevant research techniques.

(d) Details of the field operation; selection and training of interviewers; level of supervision; checks on quality and accuracy.

(e) Details of editing, coding, and purchasing operations; quality and training of staff supervision of these functions; checks on quality and accuracy.

(f) Details of analysis and tabulation; computers and machinery used; restrictions on numbers and types of tabulations.

(g) Details of normal standard of reporting; the style and content of reports.

(h) Details of accounting and legal aspects; normal billing procedures.

3. What you can expect from the supplier – specific

This second check-list sets out the specific points you can expect a supplier to include in its proposals for a particular project.

(a) Demonstration, in its statement of the research objectives and of the scope of the inquiry, that the supplier understands your problem.

(b) Detailed descriptions of the research design including:

  i) A statement of the scope and nature of any preliminary desk research, qualitative work, or pilot studies.

  ii) For any quantitative study a statement of: the data collection technique (how the information is to be obtained); the universe to be sampled (who is to be interviewed); the size of the sample (how many are to be interviewed); the method of sample selection (how the individuals are to be selected).

(c) A statement of the cost of the project and a clear indication of the assumptions on which it is based and what is included, e.g. assumptions made about length of interview; assumptions made about degree of executive involvement; whether personal briefing of interviewers is included; number of copies of report envisaged; approximate number of tabulations envisaged; whether there will be a written interpretation of the tabulations; whether visual presentation of results is included.

(d) A reasonably detailed timetable for the project and reasonably firm reporting date.

(e) A statement of the specific executive(s) responsible for the project.

Source: Extract reprinted from the *Market Research Yearbook*, 1998 with permission.

Clearly, within a two-way relationship there must be a good element of cooperation. However, managers in client organisations may not wish to give too much internal marketing information to a research agency. Reasons for this can include:

- the desire not to influence or to prejudice the outcomes of the agency's work;
- the desire for the agency to uncover new information through its own work to add to the marketing intelligence effort;
- some information regarded as confidential may be difficult or time consuming to separate out from reports to give to the agency;
- the agency may take on work for another company which is a competitor once its work for the client organisation is finished.

The attitudes of both parties to the research, the resources available for conducting the research, the cost-benefit implications and the potential usefulness of the research findings are relevant considerations to take into account in the appraisal of whether a marketing research project should be conducted.

Research agencies need to generate results to demonstrate the financial values of their research outcomes which can be clearly communicated to their clients. However, clients also need to involve researchers in their decision-making processes and provide them with adequate funds to do the job if clients are to do their part in ensuring a successful outcome to their research effort.

3.3 Design choices

Research design has been mentioned within the context of the description of the marketing research process in Chapter 1. The data-collection and sampling methods in this section will be the product of the choices set out in Table 3.1. Selection of the data-collection and sampling procedures will, of course, depend on the research objectives and the funds available for research from the sponsoring company. In this chapter we are focusing on the use of surveys to describe markets but we might have decided to take a qualitative rather than a quantitative approach. Qualitative work is invaluable, indeed essential, at the exploratory stage. We must not underrate its importance, for the qualitative approach is widely used in the search for new product ideas to formulate new brands, and to create and develop advertising campaigns.[2] However, when market description is going to affect marketing decisions involving substantial expenditures, findings from quantitative surveys based on statistically significant numbers of cases carry more conviction than those based on small numbers of cases, even though the data yielded by the few is likely to be richer in ideas and detail than that collected in a large-scale survey.

It is possible to have the best of both approaches: to collect the ideas at the exploratory stage and then to design a survey which quantifies the significant ones.

The design of questionnaires, including the risk of interviewer bias, is discussed in Chapter 5. As we shall see, interviewers play a critical part in the selection of respondents for quota sampling, a method widely used in survey research. The rest of this chapter concentrates on the methods used in primary data collection and sampling within the research design. Secondary data collection, including the use of the Internet, is explained in Chapter 2.

Table 3.1 Design choices

Primary data collection		
I Observing	II Questioning	III Experimenting
(A) Personal diary	(A) By personal interview and CAPI	(A) Laboratory
(B) Instrumental	(B) By telephone and CATI	(B) Field
(C) Electronic	(C) By post	

Sampling	
I Probability (random)	II Purposive (non-random)
(A) Simple random	(A) Convenience
(B) Systematic random	(B) Judgement
(C) Stratified – proportionate and disproportionate	(C) Quota
(D) Cluster (area) sampling	
(E) Multi-stage sampling drawn with pps* and random location	

* probability proportionate to size of population

There are two major ways of collecting survey data:

- by secondary data collection – using existing material published in paper or electronic form;
- by primary data collection – observing behaviour, questioning respondents and experimenting.

In practice, the distinction between the two methods is by no means cut and dried.

3.3.1 Secondary data

The use of secondary data has been discussed in Chapter 2 and sources of information and publications are provided in Appendices 1 and 4 at the end of the book. It is important for researchers to be able to use existing material where relevant to their research purposes in terms of managing time effectively, saving costs (there is no point in reinventing the wheel) and validation of effort, through cross-checking with best practice elsewhere or ensuring that the work done is up to the standards of the industry.

There have been considerable developments in computer-aided interviewing since the mid-1980s. Companies have built up substantial businesses based on data captured in computer-driven self-completion interviews.

For smaller agencies with fewer financial resources, logistical and cost factors are likely to confine computer-assisted interviewing to shared-cost operations for some time to come. It is in the syndicated areas such as omnibus surveys where the big research money is made. For example, in the mid-1990s the Netherlands Gallup poll operated a consumer panel in which the respondent was provided with a home computer with a disk drive, a modem and a diskette with an interview and communications program.

3.3.2 Primary data collection

I Observing

In this section we shall look at some examples for personal diary, instrumental and electronic equipment for observation in market research.

(A) Personal diary

Personal diaries are used for a wide variety of marketing purposes. Historically, they have long been the means by which consumer purchases were recorded, before the widespread use of computers to gather in-store data for market research. Nowadays, most are so designed that the respondent is only required to mark coded positions and the data is re-electronically 'mark-sensed' when the diary is returned to the research company. But as the choices being offered to consumers proliferate – manufacturers' brands, retailers' 'own labels', generic products, varieties within brands, special offers – it is easy for the wrong position in the diary to be marked or for a purchase to be overlooked.

Human observation is also used in comparison shopping. Retailers are as interested in comparing consumer prices as are consumers themselves. The John Lewis Partnership's claim to be never knowingly undersold is supported by observation research of this kind. 'Mystery shoppers' acting for a particular organisation, e.g. a brewery, can be sent to pubs and country inns to observe the quality of drinks and services offered. They record their observations unobtrusively. The *Michelin Guides* to restaurants are another example of observation.

Distribution checks are also used to observe retail selling prices. The observations may be made by the marketing company or by a research agency offering trade research services to a manufacturer wishing to check on the offers made by wholesalers and retailers for competing manufacturers' products or for its own product range. The distribution checks may be made regularly to yield trend data or on an ad hoc basis. This use of observation is cheaper than the continuous audit based on a panel and it gives a marketing company the chance to conceal its interest from the retail trade, but the data yield is limited to what can be seen at the point of sale.

(B) Instrumental

As an example of observing, from time to time motorists may be held up while traffic is funnelled past an observation post. The post is manned by observers with recording instruments, e.g. voice recorders and clipboards. The passage of all vehicles is recorded and every nth vehicle is stopped. The driver of the nth vehicle is asked where he or she has come from, where they are going to and the purpose of their journey. Other questions might be included to find out more about the motorist's reasons, for example whether it is a one-off journey for a special occasion or a routine trip.

This example illustrates the strength and limitation of observing as a method of data collection. The strength is its objectivity. Given that the recording instrument is in good working order and that traffic is sufficiently slowed for the necessary observations to be made (e.g. commercial vehicles, passenger cars, etc.), risk of bias is reduced to a minimum. The data is not influenced by how questions are asked or by the respondent's capacity to answer. But the weakness of the data is that it will tell us nothing about the purpose or frequency of journeys unless a sample of, say, commercial vehicles and cars is stopped and questions are asked.

It is sometimes claimed that data derived from observation is more objective than that derived from questioning. This holds true if the data is automatically recorded by instruments, provided the sample being observed is representative of the population concerned.

In the television audience research carried out by TN AGB for the Broadcasters' Audience Research Board (BARB), meters attached to panellists' sets automatically record whether the set is switched on and which station is being received. (This electronic form of audience measurement research is dealt with in more detail in Chapter 13.) But in order to know the size of the television audience it is necessary for individual viewers to record their presence in front of the set. People-meters (instrumental press-button handsets with key pads) have taken the place of diaries for this purpose. It is, of course, less onerous for the viewer to press a button at the start and at the finish of a viewing session. The risk of human error is reduced, but not eliminated, and the passage of the data from viewer to databank is accelerated by computer technologies.

When observations are being made by people, reliability of the record will be affected by whether the observer has anything else to do at the time. When self-service was first introduced to the petrol station forecourt the behaviour of motorists was observed to see if they had difficulty in following the instructions on the pump. The behaviour of those being observed may be affected by the fact that they are being watched, however discreetly. When the observer is disguised, say as a forecourt attendant, he is liable to be distracted from the business of recording observations.

Hidden cameras get round this difficulty, but the rules of the Market Research Society require that the subject be informed before use is made of data collected in this way. However, cameras placed in retail stores ostensibly to deter shoplifters and to provide security also record shopping behaviour.

(C) Electronic

Electronic closed circuit television (CCTV), which has been growing in use in the 1980s and 1990s ostensibly to monitor crime within shops and shopping precincts, is a rich source of videotaped evidence to help shop managers, store owners and local authorities or local government personnel view the behaviour of shoppers and through traffic, as well as to plan for the layout and development of their sites to draw in more shoppers.

Observation and recording of the passage of goods along the distributive channel now generally rests on the electronic scanning of bar codes. As we have seen, Nielsen's syndicated Scantrack service is based on a panel of retail outlets with checkouts equipped to read bar codes so that data may be recorded electronically instead of by manual audit. There has been considerable development in the application of electronic methods outside this country, and major research suppliers, such as TN Sofrès, Millward Brown and Nielsen, operate internationally.

Instead of keeping diaries, there are two approaches that can be used. In the first case, an interviewer keys in the panellist's answers to a structured questionnaire, while in the second, the panellist is equipped by the research company with a modem, together with an electronic device to read the bar codes as the shopping is being unpacked. The modem connects the domestic telephone to the company's mainframe computer and the data is transmitted as the bar codes are read. So data about consumer purchases can be collected in the home environment.

Article numbering, bar coding and laser scanning have revolutionised the collection of sales data. The use of electronic point of sale provides research data from a variety of sales outlets, for example, the regular scanning of records and cassettes carried out by Gallup for the music industry record charts.

The laser scanning of consumer sales is related to the work of the European Article Numbering (EAN) Association. The essential nature of EAN is that each article has a number assigned to it which is unique, universally recognised and can be shown in a form readable by machines as well as humans. The basic EAN was originally 13 digits in length. The digits in the bar codes read by the scanners represented the country of origin, manufacturer's code, product code and the checkout till code for individual items.

Box 3.3 shows a comparison of the use of retail audits and consumer panels. Features of the retail audit and consumer panel are as follows:

Box 3.3 Data yield: retail audit and consumer panel compared

Retail audit	Consumer panel
Consumer sales and brand shares:	Consumer purchases and brand shares:
Units	Units
Sterling	Sterling
Average per shop handling	Brand penetration
	Consumer typology
	Demographic characteristics
	Psychographic characteristics
	Buying behaviour
	x amount bought
	x loyalty/switching
Retailer purchases	Where purchase made
Units (not sterling)	Type of outlet
Brand shares	
Source of delivery	
Direct/via depot/other	
Retailer stocks and brand shares	
Units	
Average per shop handling	
Stock cover	
Days, weeks, months	
Prices	Prices
Average retail selling prices at time of audit	Average purchase price
Promotion	Promotion
Display at point of sale	Offers associated purchases
Special offers	Advertising
	Media consumption by panel-members
	(e.g. MEAL data, see Chapter 13)
By type of retail outlet	
By ITV (Independent Television) area	By ITV area

- The retail audit is based on samples of retail outlets which represent the volume of business going through different categories of outlet. The sample for each Nielsen index (grocery, home improvement, health and beauty services) represents the range of outlets relevant to the products covered by the industry.

- The consumer panel will represent either private households with data collection via the housewife, or individuals. In addition to panels representing consumers in general, there are a number of specialist panels.

- The retail audit is a demanding but straightforward operation:

  Opening stock + Deliveries − Closing stock = Sales

  'Opening stock' was left for sale at the close of the last audit; 'deliveries' means stock coming in since the last audit. The formula is simple, but the procedure is infinitely detailed.

- The consumer panel data is derived either electronically via scanners or from an audit of household stores. The panel is made up of individuals from selected categories of consumers, to respond to the research questions asked relating to their purchases and repeat buying patterns, and their non-purchase intentions.

- The retail audit is valuable in the experimental situation because, in addition to recording retail sales and brand shares, it monitors distribution achieved and signals the danger of running out of stock.

The rapid availability of marketing information made possible by EPOS has to be set against the fact that collection of the data depends on retail cooperation and efficiency at the checkout and on the smooth running of the computer installation. Laser scanning of article numbers at the point of sale makes it possible to report consumer purchases in a short space of time, by brand within product field and by variety within brand (size, price, flavour, etc.). Article numbering (AN) has facilitated the attribution of variable costs to individual company brands. AN also makes it possible to allocate shares of production, warehousing, transport and selling costs to specific sizes, scents, flavours and types of packaging within brands. Allocation of advertising costs, often a substantial variable cost, can also be straightforward provided the company's sales areas can be related to the ITV areas used in media planning and provided that not more than one brand or brand variety is included in the campaign.

Thus, the use of observation as a method of data collection has been stimulated by developments in the electronics field. 'Mechanical' methods are used in the development of pack designs, the pre-testing of advertisements and in the measurement of television viewing. Electronic methods using EPOS have helped retailers to gain competitive advantage, for example by using store loyalty cards.

Loyalty cards have proliferated, and the information held in computerised databases has enabled the organisations who give them out to gather large amounts of data daily on their customers in-store, without the need to depend on consumer panellists' information or the traditional retail audits. They are a common form of incentive in developed countries that are given out by large supermarkets and petrol stations, for example, to encourage customers to continue to shop with a particular organisation. The more purchases one makes over the course of time, the more points one accumulates on one's card. The accumulated points can then be exchanged for goods at the petrol station or in a retail store, or taken off the bill to reduce the cost of one's shopping basket. In the UK, from research about their customers to the accumulation of large customer bases and databanks, with the help of strong brands and low costs, the large supermarkets have been able to diversify into other areas, such as financial services.[3]

II Questioning

Questions can be asked of respondents in a personal interview, by telephone or through the post. As we shall see with the descriptions of CATI and CAPI that follow, the computer has facilitated the ease and speed by which the data is accumulated and processed.

The choice of which method to use depends on the following:

- the subject of the survey;
- the nature of the survey population;
- the research budget.

Surveys vary in the ease with which the required type of respondent may be contacted and in the length and complexity of the questionnaire. In deciding between personal, telephone and postal interview the criterion is the cost of each satisfactorily completed questionnaire. This must, of course, be estimated in advance, the estimate being based on the prior experience of the research agency or of the marketing company and on the results of exploratory or pilot work.

(A) By personal interview and CAPI

Face-to-face interviewing is still the most commonly used method of collecting survey data in the UK (see Chapter 1, Table 1.4), whereas in the United States telephone interviewing has largely taken over. Research suppliers in Britain have conducted 13.5 million interviews each year of which approximately 16% are telephone and 54% are personal interviews.[4] But personal interviewing is labour-intensive and costly. During the 1990s economic pressures and intensification of competition have stimulated marketing companies to demand faster and cheaper data. The development of computer-assisted personal interviewing has helped research suppliers to meet this demand as has the use of computers to enhance the role of market research[5] and extend analysis.[6]

The CAPI method using a computerised system is demonstrated in Box 3.4. The information comes from Specialist Field Resources, part of the TN Sofrès Group which ranks as one of the largest research companies world-wide (see Chapter 1, Table 1.1).

Box 3.4 Computer-assisted personal interviewing (CAPI): pen CAPI and the Field Management System

Introduction

CAPI has been an integral part of Market Research for some years now, but Specialist Field Resources Ltd (SFR), a wholly owned subsidiary of Taylor Nelson Sofrès plc, has taken it a stage further by investing in and using the latest state of the art technology in order to provide their clients with the ultimate CAPI service.

As well as the standard benefits of CAPI, such as the administration of complex questionnaires, speedy transmission of despatch and return of interview data for immediate processing, there are innovative and unique elements such as written, open-ended responses and detailed sample and quota control management. These have been accomplished by the selection of pen technology hardware, the use of tried and tested software tailored to the needs of interviewers and clients alike, as well as an in-home designed and developed Field Management System (FMS) to ensure thorough monitoring of the fieldforce.

Each of these elements are described in more detail below:

Hardware – CAPI

The machine opted for is the Fujitsu Stylistic 500, a powerful (486,50 MHz), light-weight computer with small and easy to change batteries and an in-house purpose designed carrying case. So CAPI surveys can be conducted both in the street and on the doorstep.

The most critical element is the pen interface which allows answers to be recorded by touching the screen with a 'pen' and writing answers in the space allotted on the screen. This close resemblance to pen and paper methods enhances the accuracy of the responses recorded and allows an uninterrupted interview flow.

The system introduced, thereby utilises the benefits of CAPI whilst retaining the personal contact element of the face to face interview and the vast experience built up by interviewers over the years. By making it easier and more natural for interviewers to record their answers, it enables them to concentrate on the interview process itself and the relationship with the respondent. This leads to greater respondent interaction, better input and fewer abandoned interviews.

Software – CAPI

1. *Questionnaire*

    The software used is a tried and tested program developed by a European Market Research organisation, NIPO. It produces an easy to administer questionnaire by offering user-friendly menus and flexible scripting.

    Some of the features include: item/code control (i.e. exclusion of previously selected codes), automatic randomisation or inversion of lists, logic setting, randomised selection of question sets, as well as control of multi or single choice responses.

    An experienced team of scripters combines this with other software, such as Visual Basic programs to produce user-friendly grids and complex USA lists which despatch location specific information where applicable. Recently, TN Sofrès has introduced the OPTIMA brand to CAPI as well.

2. *Other*

    The software allows precise control of sampling by the issuing of address lists to the interviewers. This allows SFR to look at all contacts made by interviewers and calculate response rates for each survey. In addition, quotas are also electronically despatched and monitored via the Fujitsu.

    As well as removing the need for postal despatch of questionnaires, address lists and quota cards, showcards and interviewer instructions are also contained within the questionnaire.

    With the added facility of forcing a test interview to be conducted before fieldwork can take place, each stage to fully cover how a Market Research interview should be conducted, is thought through.

Continued

The Field Management System (FMS)

The FMS, a computerised interlink system, calculates all quotas for any given survey and then distributes this amongst each assignment. This is electronically despatched to the interviewers via a 'quo-file' which is updated as the interviewers complete their interviews.

All information is sent back to Head Office daily and is read into the FMS. From this, all quotas set and achieved and achieved rates against target, are looked at. By having access to this information so speedily, any change in requirements can be acted upon immediately.

Individual interview times are stored, as are find times, and these are then calculated for an individual average and then compared with the National and Regional Average. As well as this, the number of trips conducted, number of 'phone numbers recorded' and detailed non-response information to view all contact details and response rates, can all be looked at.

CAPI back-checks can be done as soon as an interview has been completed and polled back to Head Office. The necessary information is read into the FMS and a team of back-checkers input all telephone back-check results straight into the FMS as well. The status and grade of each assignment is automatically calculated and details transmitted to our Regional Managers. This, combined with the wealth of information gathered from Progress, allows Specialist Field Resources to maintain standards of high quality data.

Summary

SFR's vision was to systemise the way ad hoc surveys were run and then to link all the different areas of field management to be accessed by all through one computer system. With the advent of CAPI, SFR could streamline the organisation of surveys and prevent the duplication of tasks that were a way of old working practices, thereby improving efficiency, costs and speed. CAPI opens up a whole new way of looking at what an interviewer has done with a wealth of information.

Source: C. Shefras (1999), 'Field Management System', Specialist Field Resources Ltd, Taylor Nelson Sofrès.

For a questionnaire of any length or complexity, satisfactory completion is most likely to be achieved in a personal interview. In overseas research in the United States and Japan, personal interviews with senior managers solicited important data that was not easily obtainable by post or telephone, because the personal approach established a valued point of contact.[7]

Given proper training, an interviewer has the opportunity to establish rapport with a respondent and to achieve this without biasing answers to questions. In addition, the face-to-face interview offers the opportunity to show supporting material, such as cards listing all possible answers to multi-choice questions or scales to help respondents rate how strongly they feel about a subject. It is possible to include open-ended questions which demand verbatim written answers. Computer-assisted telephone interviewing does not lend itself to open-ended questions.

CAPI has helped to build in safeguards to ensure veracity and reliability in the responses returned by interviewers. Hence the standards of professionalism and benefits to interviewers working in the field and to the company are enhanced, as shown in Box 3.5.

Box 3.5 SFR's Field Management System

Specialist Field Resources (SFR) currently have approximately 700 interviewers who aim to give the Field Management System 3 days work per week to cover 1,400 days per week.

There are eight Regional Divisions managed by six employed Regional Managers and an internal operation of 26 employees to manage Field, CAPI, Despatch, Booking In, Quality Control and Invoices.

Background to the System: allocations

From the overall Job Set Up, we move to what this means on a Regional and Interviewer level. The total number of interviews required by the rate per day gives the number of assignments necessary to reach the target. The Field Management System creates these assignments, each made up of a data file containing the target number of interviews, the quota levels and the address attached via Sampling. These are allocated by entering the Interviewer Number booked to work.

These allocations are 'exported' to the Central System where the scripted question-naire is also placed and these are then linked by a unique I.D. number. Each interviewer's machine has its own I.D. (identification) number and when they communicate via modem, they will pick up from the Central System all allocations related to them.

The aim of the Progress Module is to have all this information every morning to feed back to the Executive and Client. 'Problem' jobs can now be dealt with in an efficient and smooth manner.

Field Management covers a wide area in terms of job type and content:

1. *Helpline* – to assist interviewers and keep track of stock.

2. *Interviewer Database* – all interviewer details, transfer of previous information – who, where, what they did and training details.

3. *Job Set Up/Sampling* – entering all the overall details of the survey i.e. sampling method, payments, schedule, workload, number of interviewers, quota details and assignments, etc. Therefore, if an Executive requires address-supplied surveys, the addresses from the sampling system are obtained and feed into the Field Management System.

4. *Progress/Booking In* – Interviewers communicate every day and all successful inter-views are polled back to the Central System. This, along with other information, is automatically sent to the Field Management System.

5. *Quality Control* – Backchecking based on back-checked IQCS standards and SFR's own list. Backchecking of interviewer data stored in an Interviewer's work history, along with every type of survey they have worked on and a grade for how they have done, so viewing of what's done and how well could then be seen.

6. *Automation of Interviewers' Pay* – interviewers electronically send back their pay claims via their computers, checks are run electronically within the FMS to match what was achieved against what was set-up and what is claimed, then automatic send to payroll.

Continued

> 7. *Regional Managers* – The circle is not complete, unless regional managers have access to the Field Management System and can obtain the same information as at Head Office. They can then give their input and still maintain personal contact with the interviewers, collecting progress and making bookings 'as normal'.
>
> *Source*: C. Shefras (1999), 'Field Management System', Specialist Field Resources Ltd, Taylor Nelson Sofrès.

(B) By telephone and CATI

Before the development of computer-assisted telephone interviewing conducted from a central location, the telephone offered little, if any, advantage in cost and time over face-to-face interviewing. The developing popularity of telephone interviewing is due to the following:

- the immediate demand for information. CATI now makes it possible to collect, analyse and despatch research findings within a day;

- the spread of telephone ownership. There is a high proportion of adults available on the telephone in the home even with the increasing popularity of hand-held mobile phones;[8]

- increases in fieldwork costs and the reluctance of interviewers to work in certain areas and in the evening;

- the improved and more cost-effective control of fieldwork when telephone interviewing is centrally located;

- the opportunity to record and process results as questions are answered. The interviewers reads the questions and enters the respondent's selection of the multiple-choice answers;

- the ability to avoid clustering in nationwide surveys;

- where fast-moving packaged goods are concerned, buying habits are much the same for those without as for those with telephones.

With telephone interviewing, the demands of structured questionnaires with pre-coded answers do not lend themselves to long questionnaires. Ideally a telephone interview should not last longer than 15 minutes. Questions asked should not be too complicated, and they should be designed to be quickly introduced and understood by respondents.

The MRDF findings described in Box 3.6 were based on carefully matched samples and defined population differences and still have important design implications for face-to-face and telephone interviewing for researchers today. Indications are that respondents find face-to-face personal contact a more rewarding experience.

Box 3.6 The use of telephone interviewing

Back in 1987 the UK's Market Research Society's Development Fund (MRDF) published research on the use of telephone interviewing and telephone availability. Analyses and answers to the question 'Have you your own telephone?' put to adults aged 15 and over in the National Readership Survey (a meticulously designed probability sample representative of the adult population of the United Kingdom) showed the following:

The telephone was readily available to A, B and C social grades, but a sample drawn from telephone directories would not give due weight to D and E grades:

Social grade	A	B	C1	C2	D	E	Total
Adults %	98	96	94	85	74	55	82

Telephone penetration varied by region:

	ITV regions (adults %)		
Highest	London (88)	Southern (87)	Anglia (86)
Lowest	Lancashire, Yorkshire, Tyne Tees (all 78)		Border (74)

Source: MRDF Research Projects (1986), 'Comparing telephone and face to face interviews'; and (1987), 'Telephone availability', MRS, UK.

When the MRDF research was conducted in the mid-1980s there were four television channels and 12 ITC regions in the UK. The pace of technological change in this market has been rapid. By 1993, there were 30 TV channels with the entry of satellite and cable television networks and 14 ITV regions.[9] Nowadays there are many more channels available to viewers. Many more homes have telephones and some telephone companies are merging with cable TV companies to develop multimedia technologies, see Chapter 13.

It is clear that to represent the general population by a sample available and willing to respond on the telephone involves weighting not only by region, sex and age (a common practice whether the sample be a probability or a purposive one) but also by social grade, to ensure due representation of the habits and attitudes in the population sample.

The telephone is a useful means of reaching business respondents. Here the problem is one of deciding who should be asked the questions. Who makes the decisions? The professional buyer? The managing director? The chief chemist? A committee? The telephone has a useful screening function and it is also used to put straightforward questions, but in more searching business enquiries a telephone call will precede an interview. The renting out of lists of decision-makers derived from databases can create the risk of an 'irritant factor' when key decision-makers find themselves being contacted too often.

The convenient storage and rapid retrieval of data now possible encourages companies to make marketing use of the telephone, for example to stimulate customer interest in goods and services. Companies have to weigh the benefits of improved direct responses and prompt evaluation using computerised methods such as CATI against the start-up costs involved. The rewards are potentially greater with larger samples for CATI than with traditional telephone interviews. Research comparisons of live and automated surveys[10] have looked at the productivity of human interviewers against automated techniques. The indications are that while start-up costs of automated techniques are higher, productivity can also be higher with the larger samples. There is a danger of overkill, particularly when the target is a non-domestic one.

Sugging (in which the voice on the telephone pretends at first to be conducting a research enquiry) is a dubious form of telemarketing frowned on by telemarketers as well as market researchers.

Electronic and telephone connections in trade centres, for example at large purpose-built exhibition centres in Birmingham and Wembley, London, have meant that data at trade shows can be gathered by electronic means by market researchers. With direct computer interviewing, on-site computerised interviewing stations or rooms can be set up with several PCs which link via telecommunications equipment into a mainframe computer.

In the USA interviewers can key in their responses at computer keyboards in shopping malls in response to questions shown on computer screens. Trend data and omnibus surveys can be updated with the use of CATI and self-administered computerised interviewing. However, they are not cost effective for small samples.

Box 3.7 contains an explanation of why CATI is used, in this case by Audience Selection, part of TN Sofrès.

Box 3.7 Computer-assisted telephone interviewing (CATI)

The advantages of CATI are:

1. Sample management i.e. excellent for sequential sampling, tight quotas, limited sample universe, instant sample status reports during fieldwork.

2. Overall quality e.g. all filtering and routing are automatically conducted by the computer, ensuring standardisation and consistency. This also frees the interviewer to concentrate on the interview with the respondent, rather than worrying about which questions should be asked etc.
   Supervisor has immediate access to view and listen in to interviews. Also repeat waves of interviewing – e.g. a tracking study, will be entirely consistent.

3. Statistical validity enabling random allocation of sample plus management of available telephone numbers helping to reducing non-response.

4. Speed of data delivery which means that data is available at the touch of a button – ideal for when results are required immediately subsequent to interviewing.

5. Cost saving where interviewers tend to be more productive when using CATI and where the need for printing and punching questionnaires is also eliminated.

In the past the main constraints against using CATI were:

1. If the questionnaire contains predominantly open questions.
2. Where the sample is not easily available on disk/tape ready for insertion into the CATI system.
3. Where the costs for keying in a sample escalates the final price of a project.

The technology which links into the CATI system is a fairly recent innovation, for example with automated dialling, whereby the telephone number is selected and dialled by computer.

Nowadays, the benefits of CATI are very much taken for granted. Audience Selection uses CATI for all telephone interviewing work. This includes the omnibus survey (PhoneBus) as well as ad hoc projects, domestic and international.

PhoneBus is a fast U.K. consumer omnibus study. It is run every weekend. Questions are input on a Friday morning, interviewing takes place over the weekend and results are out to the client by Monday lunchtime.

Almost all sample is available in electronic format which means that it can be loaded directly into the CATI system with very little additional work.

The main technological advances within the CATI software used are predominantly to be found in the ease of which sample can be manipulated and filtered for greater interviewer productivity and survey management. For example, the supervisor in charge of a survey can make on the spot decisions as to how to maximise the sample for greatest efficiency through a few simple computer commands. Previously, this would have been done by a specialised department and there would have been a time lapse which impacted upon survey deadlines, in addition to the additional cost through lack of interviewer productivity while waiting.

Source: Homeyard, S. (1999), 'CATI', Audience Selection, TN Sofrès.

(C) By post

The response rate achieved by a postal survey is likely to be low (30–40%), unless the survey population consists of members of a special interest group: e.g. new car buyers, members of the Royal Horticultural Society, or of the Wire-haired Dachshund Owners Association. Here we can expect a better than average response to a postal questionnaire, provided the questionnaire is about new cars, gardening or wire-haired dachshunds.

For a subject of more general interest, mailing questionnaires may prove more expensive than anticipated. It is necessary to take into account the following considerations when comparing costs with personal interviewing:

- the number of completed questionnaires returned;
- the cost of follow-up letters and other inducements to stimulate response, e.g. a ball-point pen to fill in the questionnaire;
- the cost of reply-paid envelopes;
- possibly the need for some personal interviews, for the responses may add up to what appears to be a biased sample.

Nowadays with the growth of direct marketing, the use of direct mail to inform selected respondents with extras such as a free promotion and a questionnaire to fill in, are becoming commonplace, so that the expression 'junk mail' becomes true when respondents receive mail they do not wish to have. The use of postal questionnaires as a form of conducting impersonal research, where the researcher saves on the time and cost of meeting the respondents face-to-face, is made more difficult by having to compete with the direct marketing activities of others. Today, mailed questionnaires have to compete with an ever-increasing volume of direct mail.

A postal questionnaire has the advantage of being read from beginning to end when respondents answer questions. There are, of course, occasions when a family or household response is required and the postal questionnaire gives all members a chance to join in. It may be necessary for documents to be consulted in order to answer the questions: for example, to consult the registration document (or 'log book') in an enquiry about motor cars.

There may be a case for combining data collection methods. If the questionnaire is long, or if the respondent is being asked to keep a diary record, a questionnaire or a diary may be placed during a personal interview. The introductory interview will add to the research costs but it is likely to secure a higher response rate, so that cost per satisfactorily completed interview might be improved.

III Experimenting

The direct contrast between laboratory and field experiments is that laboratory experiments take place within internally controlled environments (humidity, heat, light or darkness can all be set and controlled) and field experiments are conducted externally in market environments. Pre-market lab and field tests are explained further in Chapters 8 and 10 in the development of products and services. As an aside, interesting examples of a non-commercial type concerning both field and laboratory research into the psyche of individuals have been presented in publications by Horne *et al.*[11] in the research into the sleep pattern of adults.

(A) Laboratory

Most market research work is done in the field with the realism generated by relating causal relationships to external settings. Field experiments therefore have a stronger claim to external validation compared to laboratory experiments which have strong internal validation (through a closer study of selected dependent and independent variables under controlled conditions). Research data gathered from laboratory experiments would use experimental and control groups to study the compared behaviour, of, for example, a specific calorie-controlled slimmers' diet amongst young adults, over a specified time period under controlled conditions. Field experiments include test market studies, for example, manipulating individual elements of the marketing mix (price, promotion, place and product). The experimental treatment could be conducted within selected retail stores within certain regions of the country, such as testing the impact of special offers and sales promotions. Alternatively the whole marketing mix could be tested in a limited way when a test product is launched.

The advantages of laboratory experiments over field experiments can be seen in the following:

1. There can be obstacles to external validity in field experiments when variables in the marketing environment are beyond the control of the market researchers conducting the experiment. For example, competitors may intensify their fight for market share in the same market as the product types under trial.

2. In a laboratory test it is possible to ensure that the new treatment is introduced to experimental and control groups in exactly the same way. Or it can be introduced to the experimental group only (results are then compared to a monitored control group which does not receive the same treatment). This is not always the case with field experiments: for example, in an experiment at the point of sale the positioning of items (packs/merchandising material) may well be altered unwittingly during the course of the experiment so that experimental and control groups do not receive exactly the same treatment.

3. It is sometimes difficult to isolate the effect on sales of one particular element in the mix as distinct from the effect of others. For example, measurement of the effect on sales of an increase in advertising weight may be contaminated by differences in the merchandising performance of sales representatives, one area being better served by the salesperson than another.

4. There is a risk of 'hothousing', particularly in the case of an experimental launch when reputations are at stake and there is the temptation to show too much management interest, and when sales representatives become unduly zealous to earn higher commissions.

5. The financial commitment is greater in a field than in a lab-type experiment. Anxiety to show a return encourages hothousing and may cause the experiment to be stopped too soon. When it looks as if an experiment is proving successful, considerations of 'opportunity cost' may prompt too rapid an extension of the experiment to the wider market.

(B) Field

Before going into the field it is necessary that the following preconditions have been met:

- objectives must be formulated and criteria set against which results are to be judged;
- the ultimate objective will usually be increased profit contribution but the immediate objective is likely to be seen in terms of sales;
- it must be decided where the experiment is to take place, on what scale and for how long;
- a research programme must be set in motion designed to monitor happenings in the market as well as to measure effects of the experiment.

It is possible in a well-designed experiment to ensure that obstacles to a valid result are anticipated and so allowed for. Given an adequate budget, the research programme will monitor competitive, and own, activity at the point of sale. A marketing intelligence system can be organised to ensure that environmental happenings are noted. Use of a control group, essential in field experiments, and, where possible, replication of the experiment, make it possible to calculate margins of error and show how precisely results may be interpreted. See Appendix 3, 'Statistical tests'.

Most experiments in the field relate to individual elements in the mix or to relationships between elements, as explained in the following:

- Experiments related to an established brand are likely to be focused on individual elements in the mix concerning price/packaging/advertising/sales promotion, and so on, or on the relationship between just two elements of the mix. This could be the effect on profit contribution of different ratios of advertising to sales/promotional expenditure, not forgetting that, once a brand is established, manipulation of elements in the mix takes place in the context of the image created by its marketing history.

- For a new introduction the experimental treatment in the field is likely to be the whole mix, but the experimental launch may be preceded by a pilot launch with the product packaged, named and priced. This is designed to ensure a smooth transaction from the production line through the distribution channel to the consumer.

- Some elements in the mix lend themselves to field experimentation on a limited scale, whereas others demand a more extended environment. The effect of a change in pack design can be assessed by comparing sales achieved in two matched and comparatively small groups of retail outlets. To measure the effect on sales of a change in the level of advertising expenditure may involve comparison between sales achievement in two television areas.

Before setting up a field test, we need to have considered the criterion against which the effect of the treatment is to be judged.

It is desirable that the possible benefit to be derived from the manipulation of mix elements should be estimated in advance for two reasons:

1. Account has to be taken of two kinds of cost: out-of-pocket costs and (given success) opportunity costs.

2. In order to determine the size of the matched samples we are going to use we need to know not only what proportion of those in the market are likely to respond to the treatment but also the precision with which results are to be considered. The results will be estimates. That is, what margin of error can be accepted around the estimates? (See Appendix 3.)

These considerations determine the scale of the experiment: in how many retail outlets to put the experimental pack (see Box 3.8); through how many doors to put the promotional offer; how many people to ask questions on product awareness and performance, and so on. In the United States there are many small television stations serving local markets. It is comparatively easy to represent regional differences and to match experimental and control areas.

Box 3.8 shows how store tests and retail audits can be used to measure the results of media impact on customers. Retail audit, consumer panel or both types of data source are used to monitor brand shares. In a test area it may well be necessary to enlarge the regular, ongoing samples of retail outlets or of consumers, or to set up special ad hoc ones. It depends on the choice and size of the test area. In addition, the usual reporting interval may be shortened, but the data-collection procedures are standard. In an experimental design, the type of commercials watched on television by consumer panels made up of housewives (panellists) can be related to the data obtained from laser scanning of their purchases at the point of sale checkouts. The panellists are given code numbers and these are recorded when they scan their purchases at the particular store checkouts within the test area. The data can be retrieved by the research agency via modems linking the panellists' domestic telephones to a central computer.

Earnings from work conducted in retail audits and consumer panel research represent very important sources of revenues. For example, the AC Nielsen Corporation with total revenues of US$1,392m in 1997 has long been at the forefront of retail measurement (continuous tracking of consumer purchases at the point of sale through scanning technology and in-store audits) and consumer panel research (detailing information on purchases made by house members, as well as their retail shopping patterns and demographic profiles). Such measurement and research contributed $989m and $92m, respectively, to its 1997 global earnings.[12]

Box 3.8 Measuring media impact on customers using store tests and retail audits

When an in-store experiment is being designed store tests and retail audits will show the following:

- whether it is necessary to include more than one type of retail outlet in the test;
- whether it is necessary to take account of regional differences in selecting test stores;
- whether one or more retail organisations are of critical importance.

It may well be that one particular type of outlet (say, supermarkets) is so important that the experiment can usefully be confined to this type of store; and to one dominating trade customer (say Tesco, the current UK supermarket leader in sales turnover).

Locations in which to stage the experiment are more likely to be made available if the negotiations are carried on with one retail organisation. In order to measure the effect of sales, the level of sales have to be recorded both before and after the test, and over a period of time. In addition, administration of the treatment must be controlled. In other words, the experiment depends on the cooperation of head office and of the managers of the selected stores.

There is a statistical reason for basing the experiment on one particular store group, where this is practicable: the selected stores are more likely to be 'alike'. This reduces error deriving from extraneous variation.

In an area test, a retail audit or consumer panel is likely to be used to log brand shares, both before and after the treatment is applied. Certain elements in the mix lend themselves to 'in-store' testing whilst manipulations of pack and point of sale promotion is applicable for an in-store design.

In the in-store design we measure the effect of the promotional treatment by recording sales *for a period before and a period after* the offer is made to consumers. In the design based on consumer interviews, we use intermediate measures. We seek to establish levels of awareness of the offer, changes in use of the brand and changes of attitude towards it, but we cannot interview the same respondent before and then again after the offer has been made about awareness, use and attitude. The respondent would learn from the first interview and be more likely to notice and act on the offer.

We can use an after-only design and seek to establish past as well as present behaviour at the 'after' interview, or, more likely, use a larger number of respondents in matched groups, interviewing one group before the offer is made and the other after.

The first procedure would need three groups overall – one for each offer and one control group – while the second would require at least five, preferably six (since the control group may learn) and we have made no allowance for regional differences. Simulation of the shopping context would be a cheaper and less time-consuming procedure and it would be possible to ensure that the arrangement of brands and displays remained under control.

To measure effects we need to record observations taken *before, during and after introduction of the experimental treatment.*

Continued

The period of time to be allowed for in planning and costing a field experiment is influenced by three factors:

- how long to allow for the experimental treatment to begin eliciting a response (penetration);
- how quickly brand loyalty and switching patterns can be expected to develop (repeat purchase);
- the degree of precision required in the estimate of effects.

In the case of an experimental launch the speed with which penetration is achieved will depend on the nature of the product, the creative effectiveness of the advertising campaign, together with the success in achieving retail distribution of the tested product and its 'stand-out' at the point of sale.

The success of the product is reflected in its sales achievement and sales are usually reported in terms of brand shares. The research programme for a field experiment may provide for the collection of data about other marketing factors such as:

- the level of distribution achieved;
- awareness of advertising and response to an offer from customers.

The critical measurement is likely to be a sales measurement.

Ex-factory sales, however well recorded, suffer from three important limitations as a data source for experimentation in the field:

1. They do not tell us how competitive brands are performing in the experimental and control areas.
2. The 'pipeline' between the factory gate and the checkout makes it difficult to separate effects due to changes in sales from those due to changes in stocks.
3. It is difficult to isolate the volume and value of sales ex-factory attributable to the experimental and control areas.

These limitations may be overcome but subscription to a continuous retail audit and consumer panel service is common practice. Retail buying power is increasingly concentrated so that securing effective distribution depends on the decisions of a few stores. Therefore the five large UK supermarket chains: Tesco, Sainsbury, Asda, Gateway and Safeway have much consumer data of their own.

Generally speaking, to arrive at a valid estimate it is necessary to remain in the field for nine to 12 months. There is, therefore, a need for procedures which get closer to the verdict of the market than is possible in the hidden lab-type experiment. The lab-type experiment depends on such intermediate measures as intention to buy. What is wanted is a sales or brand-share measure without exposure to competitors and retailers.

Sales predictions, given various levels of marketing costs, e.g. for promotions, will most certainly have been made at stages on the road to the market. It will be decided beforehand that, for the proposed mix of marketing expenditure, a specified sales minimum must be achievable at the breakeven level and above to cover all costs and make the contribution to profit.

A real-life simulation adds to research costs, and to avoid the learning effect, the design would need to be a monadic one with groups of testers matched. An experimental design can get as close as possible to real life under the following conditions:

- advertising and pack are 'finished' – they may not be final but they appear to be so;
- the pack is of a size it is intended to market;
- the intended consumer in a product test trial tries the product where it would normally be used, say in a kitchen, bathroom, garage or workshop;
- sufficient time is allowed for a thorough trial by all those in the sample who represent the ones likely to buy the product;
- the brand is introduced as being on the market elsewhere.

In addition to asking questions about the 'likelihood of buying', other questions can be asked about the product, the kind of people who would use it, how the product would be used and the acceptable price levels at which respondents would buy, both at the concept stage (i.e. before it has been manufactured and tried) and afterwards at the test launch of the product.

Box 3.9 provides an analysis of the factors to consider when undertaking consumer panel research in the field.

Box 3.9 How to evaluate syndicated panels

Syndicated representative panels

Clients buying syndicated data from research suppliers need to consider the relevance and usefulness of an ongoing panel, designed to measure the size of markets, segments, brand shares and trends. The following factors need to be considered:

- panel coverage
- product pipeline
- panel pick-up
- panel representativeness
- mortality rate of panel members
- client service.

The first issue is to determine the precise definition of the population that the panel covers. Does it cover all segments of the market? A panel of individuals, for instance, may exclude children under 16 who could represent a significant share of sales and future trends. Consumer panels obviously do not cover purchases by organisations. However, a toiletries company may have a percentage of, say, its soap sales accounted for by this sector. This is a point to bear in mind when a client carries out periodic checks on the accuracy of syndicated panel data by trying to reconcile their own ex-factory absolute levels of sales and sales trends with those shown by a panel. Such reconciliation analyses also have to take into account the effect of pipeline delays and 'pick-up'.

'Pipeline delay' is the time it takes from products being dispatched through 'middle-men' such as wholesalers or even retailers to reaching the destination population that is being monitored on a panel (retailers or households/individuals). For perishables this may only be hours or days but for non-perishables the pipeline can be weeks or months.

Continued

'Pick-up' is the proportion of sales or purchases made by a panel member that the panel-measuring instrument successfully detects. In the latter case, this will need to be built into reconciliation analyses. Some product categories suffer relatively poor pick-up levels. Crisps, soft drinks and confectionery, for instance, often 'disappear' on the journey home from a shopping trip and so may be underrepresented when it comes to the moment of recording in a household diary or in-home bar scanner. Other factors that affect pick-up levels can include poor respondent recall, respondent human error, respondent fatigue and, of course, a poor measuring instrument. Pick-up levels can be as low as 20–30% in some categories and near perfect in others. Low pick-up is a particular problem if it is not even across different segments of the sample and these segments behave differently on the variables under study.

Two courses of action can be taken to deal with poor pick-up levels:

- to try to improve them;
- to weight the data to get an approximation of the real level of sales or purchases.

Weights may be derived by comparing ex-factories of clients with projections based on the panel. Ways of improving the pick-up level might include giving monetary incentives to respondents and/or improving the measuring instrument.

One research agency improved its pick-up of consumer purchases on a diary panel by using more specific prompts. Instead of asking what skin care products the respondent had bought it listed the different types: hand care, body care, face care, sun care and subcategories, e.g. moisturiser, cleanser, toner, etc. In such cases, it is obvious any trend in the data will be disrupted and so it is prudent to introduce the change on only, say, half of the sample (selected randomly or purposively to be matched) to see what the level of improved pick-up is by contrasting it to the 'control' panel. Once the effect of the change is known, it can be introduced to the rest of the panel and the data weighted to maintain trend analysis.

Another concern about panel members is whether they are representative on important characteristics, e.g. for consumers (sociodemographic data) or for firms (standard industrial classification or SIC size) and whether they behave normally once on the panel. While consumer demographics and 'firmagraphics' are relatively easily checked against population parameters and company sales turnover, some things are less easily checked such as values, lifestyles or personalities.

As regards whether behaviour is normal or not, some precautions may be necessary. On some panels, some respondents may 'posture' or be slow to act in the initial stages of being a panel member. The other concern is what effect being questioned has on later behaviour. Clearly it would be unwise to mix brand awareness and image questions with purchase questions as the former could 'educate' or 'condition' and so change future buying and usage behaviour. In Europe, there are panels of householders and individuals appearing where any client can buy questions on an Omnibus principle (Netherlands research agencies have pioneered these). Clearly, conditioning could be an issue but one can argue that the problem of conditioning may be overstated. This might be a bias one might live with when the exercise requires broad fixes rather than great accuracy.

The issue of how long panel members stay on a panel, the mortality rate, can be critical if brand switching and brand loyalty are major concerns. Some panels suffer from a high drop-out rate. If the turnover of panel members is high it can reduce both the effective sample size for long-term analysis and cast doubts about how representative the base might be for such analyses.

Finally, client service and cost are often major concerns where a panel operation has no competition. In many countries this is a very real problem. Monopoly is not the best basis for quality and good value. One tactic clients of syndicated panels may adopt is the formation of a 'user group' to exert pressure for better service and more reasonable fees.

Syndicated non-representative panels

There are some panel operations that are designed to provide qualitative insights rather than quantitative fixes or trend data on markets and brands. One such method, Sensitivity Panels, involves group discussions with participants who have been 'trained' to perform optimally (see Schlackman, 1987) . The group formation process and experience of projective and enabling techniques are covered in preliminary group meetings. Once the group is formed and used to performing together, live projects are introduced. The 'training' should lead to more productive group sessions, though whether the respondents are still 'typical' may be debatable. Clients may consider such panels for checking out a new product at various stages of its development prior to launch. Of course, some client organisations such as Cheesbrough Ponds have run their own qualitative panels composed of a convenience sample of family members and friends of staff in order to test early concepts or new product variants. The aim is to learn as much as possible and screen out 'disasters' before committing to more expensive forms of research. Such data is clearly not syndicated.

Reference

Schlackman, W. (1987) 'A discussion of the use of sensitivity panels in market research: the use of trained respondents in qualitative studies', *Journal of the Market Research Society*, vol. 26 no. 3 pp. 191–208.

Source: Nancarrow, C. (1999), Bristol Business School, UWE

3.3.3 Categorising variables

In marketing research we often consider attributes and variables. Attributes, such as being able to drive a motor car, are either present or not present whereas variables, such as the amounts spent on petrol, have a range of values. For example, variables can be reduced to means or averages and attributes to proportions or percentages.

The dichotomous (binary) variable is the simplest category of variable denoting the presence or absence of some attribute, e.g. attitude towards a product (good/bad) or intention (will vote 70%, won't vote 30%). Polytomous variables have more than two categories using a range, e.g. rating scales (excellent, good, moderate, bad, worse) and age (under 10, 11–17, 18–24, 25–40, 41–59, 60+). Survey variables can be categorised or classified into mutually exclusive groups for examination rather than be further measured on a continuous scale. Exogenous variables which are quantifiable on continuous scales are not categorised, for example those measured on a mileage clock or a centigrade/Fahrenheit scale.[13]

The numbers of observations (attributes) sorted into each category of a variable can be shown in a frequency distribution. A joint frequency count representing the combination of two or more categorised variables can be represented in a cross-tabulation. The simplest form of a cross-tabulation or contingency table is conventionally represented by a 2×2, $r \times c$ table showing the rows (categories of the predictor variables) and columns (categories of the dependent variable). Applying the chi-square tests a multiway table (categorising multivariate data) can generate estimated expected counts for each cell so that comparisons can be made between them and the corresponding observed counts for the goodness of model fit. The chi-square test is suitable when it is desirable to establish a significant difference between one distribution and another where the expected values in all cells of the tables are greater than 0.5.

Methods of analysis and statistical tests of data are explained further in Chapter 4 and Appendix 3. Representation of data in table format is shown in Appendix 2 and in spreadsheet format in Chapter 6.

3.3.4 The sampling process

The purpose of this section is to explain the sampling terms and to show the different types of sampling methods available. The choice of which method to use will be influenced by the researcher's preferences and their background training in data analysis. It is, however, important that the choice of sampling method should be made according to its suitability to the type of research project and the particular requirements of data for problem-solving.

This section continues the discussion about the choices available. The next chapter is a layperson's comprehensive guide to sampling which presents basic sampling techniques with examples.

The process of sampling is illustrated in Figure 3.2.

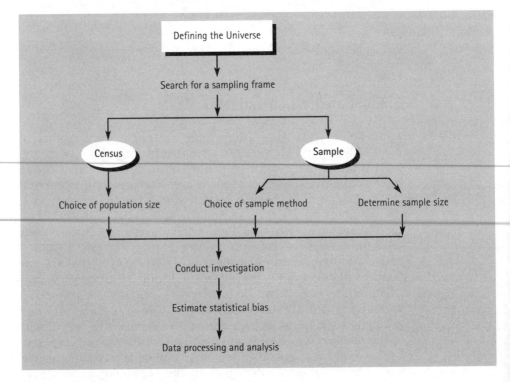

Fig 3.2 Census or sample

The **Universe** represents the complete set of elements with a given characteristic in common.

A **census** is a survey which draws from every member of the population. As we shall see below this is not practical for many market research studies.

A **sample** draws data from a selected portion of the population. While this is a common method of gathering survey information it can lead to uncertainties in the data since we lose something when we sample. To be truly representative the sample requires the same spread of characteristics as present in the census.

Random error results when the sample is not truly representative of the population from which it is drawn. This can decrease if sample size is increased or if proper sampling techniques are used.

Statistical bias occurs when there are discrepancies in responses, such as when the same respondent gives varying answers if asked at different times or prompted in different ways, or from low rates of responses from varied contact methods (postal/telephone/interview) which distort the results. There are other factors which can produce bias, e.g. seasonal factors which distort results by creating fluctuations in consumer demand. So estimation of statistical bias is necessary, for example in informing a client of factors that need to be taken into account which could have an effect or bearing on the results.

A Glossary of sampling terms is given towards the end of this book.

Whatever the type of design, the objective of probability or random sampling is to draw or select individuals from the population in such a way that the sample represents the population being surveyed, whether this is of consumers, retail outlets, industries or organisations. This type of sampling is one in which every element has a known probability of selection. We can 'quota' the sample by choosing only a few variables which relate to each element that has been picked.

We want to ensure that the sample is large enough to pick up variations in behaviour and attitude which are relevant to our marketing plans, and to be reassured that these variations appear in much the same proportions in the sample as in the survey population. (The expression 'in much the same proportions' is used because the statistics derived from the samples are estimates.) We can be pretty sure that a properly designed and managed survey will yield a sample estimate which reflects population values but we cannot be 100% sure. We can see why later on this chapter.

The techniques for probability sampling in survey research provide two particular advantages in that:

- human judgement does not enter into the selection or rejection of respondents;
- it is possible to measure the extent to which values in the population may vary from the estimates yielded by the sample.

Taking a census or a sample

National censuses present a different scenario. Most organisations large or small do not have the financial and manpower resources to conduct censuses for their own use, nor do they necessarily want to. For instance, multinational companies such as Procter & Gamble produce many different types of adult consumer goods ranging from toothpaste, soap, detergent, deodorants and coffee to baby products such as disposable nappies. Within each product range, the company will have different brands, as for detergents (Ivory, Snow, Dreft, Tide, Joy and Bold). Market research may only be required at any one time, say for one brand of detergent bought by a small sample of a population rather than for the whole product range.

More importantly, most organisations do not possess the legal authority to enforce participation in market surveys, unlike agencies of government, for example, in the requirements for the household returns collected for the UK population census in 1991 or company accounts and statements for the Central Statistical Office and Companies House. There exists much published, validated and accessible data, some free, some accessible to members only, available to organisations and individuals (see Appendix 1 for secondary sources and Appendix 4 for associations' publications). Thus researchers do not need to reinvent the wheel if they can use published information which has some relevance to their survey populations.

Secondary information can be of use in sampling design, for example in giving a general indication of population size, characteristics and locations. The market researcher undertakes sampling because detailed data on the characteristics, nature of demand and behavioural patterns of survey populations specific to a particular market for an organisation's products is not available. So the data needs to be collected for problem-solving and marketing planning.

The researcher does not need to draw on large proportions of the population in the sample provided that the sample size and the method by which it was drawn (given the nature of the population) can be validated. Samples of 2,000 or less are commonly used to represent a population of approximately 50 million adults in Britain. Sampling, therefore, constitutes a cost-effective and efficient method in survey research.

In any survey of a population, unless a census is conducted, random (probability) sampling or some form of clustering is essential. Consumer research is usually based upon sample survey techniques. However, in industrial research it is possible within an organisation or a small locality to use a census approach.

A **census survey** of employees, for example, can be undertaken in a small or a large industrial organisation where all employees are given the opportunity to express their feelings and preferences. This is important when it concerns changes in normal working practices or work facilities supplied.

The census method has benefits in that:

- all employees are seen to have been consulted in the interest of good labour relations;

- employees feel included by senior managers in the decision-making processes of the organisation;

- criticism is avoided of why some employees might have been chosen for a survey and others not (e.g. to avoid infringing Equal Opportunities legislation);

- contributory or root causes to problems, anxieties and complications in human relationships can be made more apparent;

- importantly, unlike consumer research, commitment from the highest management levels drives the research programme itself to ensure a successful response outcome.

As an alternative, a **sample survey** can be constructed using a mixed approach to include a sample of employees from the big departments and a census of those from the smaller departments. Weighting of the resulting data might be necessary to make it representative of the survey population.

The five main data-collection techniques for quantitative surveys with employees can be summarised as:

- individual self-completion;
- group session self-completion;
- face-to-face interviewer administered;
- telephone interviewer administered;
- computer (email, questionnaire on a web site when there are subsidiary companies at different locations).

Validity of the sample estimates depends on the following:

- size of the sample in relation to the variability in the population where the subject of the survey is concerned. If habits and attitudes were uniform throughout the population, the responses of one individual would suffice;

- the care with which the sample has been drawn. However random error usually exists in all sample data;

- there being an adequate number of respondents in any one group which is to be considered in isolation;

- avoidance of 'non-sampling errors' when the data is being collected and analysed, errors such as 'interviewer bias' and use of ambiguous questions.

Examples of sampling in industrial and consumer surveys

There are, of course, very many possible samples in any population. In consumer surveys, can we be confident that the sample we happen to have drawn is a representative one? We cannot. But we can take individual sample estimates and establish what the relationship between sample estimate and population value is likely to be. See Chapter 4 which explains the bases for sampling and methods used.

Take telephone interviewing, for example. A substantial proportion of consumers selected and approached may refuse. But some of those drawn from a company's sales records may be unavailable for interview, or they may refuse to be interviewed. The sample we achieve may be unbalanced when compared with the population as known. 'Weighting' aims to rectify this. The procedure is described by Ehrenberg thus:

> If an unstratified sample of 10 has given us 6 boys and 4 girls and we know that boys and girls are 50:50 in the population, the results in each stratum can be 'weighted' to bring the sample into line with the population proportion (e.g. by multiplying all the girls' readings by 1.5). This kind of 'posterior' stratification is usually less effective than prior stratification. The weighted portion of the sample has an undue effect on sampling errors (e.g. an untypical girl would count for 50% more than an untypical boy).[14]

Weighting by region, sex and age is standard procedure in a sample drawn from the general public. In the case of telephone surveys 'telephone-accessible weighting' is used. The surveys are up-weighted (together with the oldest and youngest age groups). Ehrenberg's caveat is relevant here. The MRDF's methodological survey, *Comparing telephone and face-to-face interviews*, found that those with a telephone may behave differently from those without. Today's accessibility to households for sampling in telephone surveys is hampered by the wider spread of unlisted telephone numbers (ex-directory), the use of answering machines (answerphones) and increasing purchases of hand-held mobile phones.

In purposive sample designs, research agencies can find data derived from reliable sources, such as the Government Statistical Service, to stratify the population before individuals are drawn or selected for interviewing.

In consumer markets the individual purchaser has, with rare exceptions, little effect on total sales. In industrial markets, where one or two firms may dominate, these dominating firms must be included in the sample if sampling estimates are to reflect the behaviour and attitudes of the industry as a whole. In any non-domestic market there is going to be sufficient variation in the demand of different-sized establishments for it to be desirable to design a sample which attaches due weight to variations in size.

Box 3.10 illustrates a situation in which 79.2% of establishments account for only 13.3% of gross output while 1.4% account for 40.7 per cent. The 84 establishments which constitute the 1.4% make a contribution to gross output out of all proportion to their numbers. Let us assume that we decide to draw a sample in which the 84 are self-selecting and all size categories are represented in proportion to their contribution to gross output. The constitution of the sample is illustrated in the box.

Box 3.10 An example of the constitution of a sample

Employees N	Establishments N	%	Gross output %	Sample n	%
1–99	4,532	79.2	13.3	27	13
100–199	452	7.4	8.1	16	8
200–499	459	8.0	17.7	37	18
500–999	281	3.1	14.0	29	14
1,000–1,499	50	0.9	6.2	13	6
1,500+	84	1.4	40.7	84	41
Total	5,858	100.0	100.0	206	100

There is a wealth of statistical information available about the structure of manufacturing, distributive and service industries. The standard industrial classifications (SIC) used by the Government Statistical Service are broad, but around 30 SIC orders are sub-divided into nearly 200 headings and some of these are further divided into sub-divisions. The closeness with which the SIC definitions fit marketing requirements varies. The mass industrial market will embrace a number of classifications. But the official statistics usually make it possible to define a non-domestic population in terms such as those used in this example.

The official statistics enable us to set quotas, and the chances are that we will decide to proceed on a purposive basis, using names of establishments derived from internal records, directories and business associates to fill the quotas.

To draw a probability sample we would need to acquire a complete list of establishments: a sampling frame. It is clearly desirable that we should be able to assign firms to strata before we draw: to stratify after drawing is likely to be wasteful of effort, time and money.

Sampling frame shortcomings

In order to draw a sample at random we need a list which is complete, up to date and without repetition of items. Box 3.11 shows a number of publications from organisational sources that could be used as sampling frames, more useful for quota sampling, but likely to be inadequate for a probability sample for the reasons mentioned.

Box 3.11 Non-domestic sources

The *financial directories* such as the *Stock Exchange Yearbook* and Dun and Bradstreet, define the overall worth of an enterprise but may not record separately that part of the enterprise in which we are interested. They may give no indication of the geographical location, size or activity of individual plants.

The *Kompass directory* relates enterprises to standard industrial classifications, but subsidiaries may be omitted and information relating to financial standing and to size may be inadequate for the purpose of stratification.

Trade directories vary in their effectiveness. Omissions within and duplications between directories occur.

Trade associations are not necessarily supported by important and large enterprises.

The classified *Yellow Pages directories* and phone books listing business enterprises are invaluable when it comes to making contact with establishments selected for the sample, but they do not include information about the size of establishments. To use the yellow pages file as a sampling frame necessitates telephone screening.

Records built up over time from representatives' reports, the financial press, industry and trade association sources together with previous research are valuable sources of marketing information. But they are unlikely to be sufficiently complete for a probability sample.

Knowing the size structure of a market, and being able to relate establishments to the size structure, are crucial to sound estimates of market size.

It is possible to project from sample estimates to the real world with confidence in the results if the following conditions are met:

- the market in question fits the SIC classification system;
- there is a complete, up-to-date and unduplicated listing of establishments available;
- the source of information has been located within establishments;
- unambiguous answers have been given to survey questions.

There are usually a good many 'ifs' and 'buts' attached to the projections, so much so that, particularly in a market extending over several industrial classifications, e.g. heating and ventilating equipment, there may well be a case for the sequential approach:

1. Decide what returns, for instance in terms of return on investment or contribution to profit, are required to make the venture viable.
2. Translate this into minimum demand for the product or service.
3. Estimate its potential popularity in terms of market share, taking account of viable marketing expenditure.
4. Sample the market until sufficient potential has been located.

I Probability (random) sampling

(A) Simple random sampling

In **simple random sampling** every member of the population should have an equal or known chance of being selected. It is important to get as close to the population values as possible if the sample is to represent the population from which it is drawn.

Each individual on a list is identified by means of a number and numbers are drawn at random until the sample has been filled. This is a simple random sample. For example, a telephone directory can provide a convenient sampling frame. Every seventh name can be picked out of the directory on a simple random basis. If the survey population is of any size, we may decide to adopt a systematic procedure – systematic random sampling.

(B) Systematic random sampling

Let us assume we need to draw 500 individuals from a survey population of 5,000: the sample members will amount to 1/10 of the survey population. We draw the first numbered individual at random, say this is the individual numbered 5. We then program a computer to generate the names of the individuals numbered 15, 25, 35 and so on until the sample is filled, i.e. to add 10 four hundred and ninety-nine times.

This is a **systematic sample** and this drawing technique is generally used in probability sampling. We have to be sure that the names are recorded on the sampling frame in a sufficiently random order, and that there is no periodicity in the listing. Application of the fixed interval to a list recorded in a hierarchical way, say the army list, could produce a biased sample.

When the survey population is large and widely dispersed a probability sample will commonly be drawn in more than one stage – this is multi-stage sampling.

It would be possible to draw a sample of, say, 3,000 adults from the adult population in the UK in one stage but:

- the sample members might be found to live at addresses scattered throughout the UK without regard to region or population density;
- dispersal of calls would make it difficult to organise fieldwork and supervise investigators;
- scattered calls would add to the time taken to complete the fieldwork and so to the cost of the survey.

(C) Stratified sampling – proportionate and disproportionate

In **stratified random sampling** the population is divided into strata or segments which are mutually exclusive groups, e.g. on the basis of sex or age. A random sample is then drawn from each of these groups.

Stratified random sampling contains proportionate and disproportionate sampling techniques. The samples chosen by using either of these techniques prevent the occurrence of a skewed sample which does not give a fair representation of the population.

Simple random sampling does not allow for an adequate representation of members from 'each group' since the population members may be made up of diverse groups of varying sizes, e.g. religions, ethnic groups, student classes (see Box 3.12). In stratified random sampling, the chosen sample will contain units from each stratum or segment of the population. The units can be selected from each stratum (or segment) 'proportionate' to the total numbers in the stratum or related to the 'disproportionate' i.e. varied sizes of the units within the stratum. This has the result of enabling a quota to be selected within each stratum.

Box 3.12 Reducing sampling error in stratified sampling

In a simple random sample all the individuals in the population go into the draw and the sample is drawn in one stage.

If we stratify the population and draw a simple random sample from each stratum, we reduce the sampling error. If we sampled a population of university undergraduate students without prior stratification we might, by chance, draw too many engineers and too few business studies students, or too many full-time students and too few part-time ones.

In a survey relating to courses we might need to be sure that engineering and business studies were duly represented, while for a survey about amenities we might want to ensure that the attitudes and behaviour of part-time students carried due weight. There is here a clear case for stratification, whether we are considering courses or amenities.

We can use a probability design when student records enable us to assign students to strata. If we draw in more than one stage, with probability proportionate to size of population, we increase the sampling error. The multi-stager procedure has the effect of clustering the members of the population included in the sample. Clustering has a stronger effect on sampling error than stratifying.

One cost-effective procedure is to divide the population into geographic groupings (geographic stratification) which take account of region and population density and to draw the sample in more than one stage. We might, for example, draw a sample of constituencies within geographical regions at the first stage, and then of electors from the electoral registers for the selected polling districts at the second stage.

A sample is drawn in more than one stage in order to cluster calls. This improves administrative efficiency and reduces fieldwork costs, but if calls are unduly clustered we may end up with a sample which does not represent the variety in the population as a whole.

(D) Cluster (area) sampling

A **cluster (area) sample** is taken when the population can be divided into mutually exclusive groups, e.g. geographical region, so that a random sample of the groups can be selected.

The decision as to how may constituencies to draw and then how many polling districts to select, is based on informed judgement. If we were using the postcode file as a sampling frame we would have to decide how many postcode areas, and sectors within areas, to draw.

It is common practice for research agencies to use a master sample of first-stage units for all their survey work. The field force will be recruited and supervised in randomly drawn constituencies, administrative districts or postcode areas representative of the distribution and environmental circumstances of the population as a whole. Fieldwork might, for example in the UK, be concentrated in 200 out of over 630 voting constituencies. Samples will be drawn in these constituencies as required. A random procedure may be used up to and including the selection of respondents, or up to and including the selection of sampling points, as in random-location sampling.

In random-location sampling the final selection of respondents is also based on quotas. In probability sampling, the randomly drawn individual must be interviewed. A 100% response is difficult, if not impossible, to achieve, but at least three calls must be made at the householder's address, and sometimes interviewers are instructed to make more than three. The cost of call-backs is added to the cost of drawing respondents from a sampling frame. The fieldwork for a national survey is likely to cost twice as much when probability methods are used throughout the drawing of the sample.

(E) Multi-stage sampling – drawn with probability proportionate to size (PPS)

The PPS procedure is associated with **multi-stage sampling**. For example, let us assume that the first-stage sampling unit is the constituency. The 633 parliamentary constituencies in Britain (excluding the 17 in Northern Ireland) are first stratified by region using the Independent Television Commission's ITV regions. The order in which the constituencies are listed within regions is important because we are going to draw the first constituency at random and then take a systematic interval.

Every individual in the population must have had a chance of being included in the sample when we get to the end of the drawing process, but first of all we want to ensure that the regional distribution of constituencies, together with their varying population densities, are duly represented in the sample.

Using the electoral register as a sampling frame

The electoral register contains the names and addresses of all subjects aged 18 and over who are entitled to vote and who have been registered to vote. In the UK the returns are made in October and the register is published in February of the following year. From the marketing point of view the main weakness of the register as a sampling frame is the fact that it excludes young adults and immigrants. Box 3.13 shows a procedure for selecting electors for interviewing from one electoral district.

Box 3.13 Selecting a sample from the electoral register

Let us assume that we are making five personal calls, i.e. visits to households in a polling district. There are 845 electors listed on the register (sampling frame) and numbered 1 to 845 ($N/n = 845/5 = 169$).

We draw a number at random between 1 and 169. Let us say this is 100. By adding the sampling interval onto the random start we draw the following respondents:

100	Marks, Ann M., 10 Bran End Road
269	Low, James W., The Brambles, Spinney Lane
369	Fellows, Jean B., 40 Garden Fields
469	Crisp, Elizabeth M., Mill Cottage, Rosemary Lane
569	Humphreys, Christopher A., 12 High Street

As demonstrated in Box 3.14, a group of electoral districts can represent a convenient representation of data for the PPS exercise.

Box 3.14 An example of drawing random numbers using the PPS procedure

$N/n = 40$ million/200,000

A country of 40 million electors is conveniently divided by a sampling interval of 200,000 people. This is a notional figure based on statistical experience.

We draw random numbers within each sampling interval i.e. 200,000 to 400,000 to 600,000 and so on.

A random draw gives us 135,000 with consequent draws of 325,000 and 535,000.

The sampling interval using 200,000 is added on 199 times.

At a second stage wards or polling districts may be listed, their electorates accumulated and a second draw made using PPS (Box 3.15). For even finer detail, one could use postal districts.

Box 3.15 Making a second draw

Let us assume that we are drawing a sample of 3,000 people using a master sample of 200 constituencies. The varying sizes of the constituencies have been allowed for in the PPS procedure so we have to make 15 calls in each constituency. The extent to which we cluster the calls will depend on the subject of the survey and the extent to which habits and attitudes vary where this subject is concerned. We could, for example, draw five names from each of three polling registers or three names from each of five registers to get our 15 per constituency. Here again, variation in the size of polling districts will have been taken into account in the PPS drawing procedure.

There is less risk of undue clustering if respondents are selected at the second stage, that is, after the constituencies have been drawn, but this could still produce a rather widely dispersed sample.

Savings in cost and improved supervision have to be weighed against undue clustering of sampling locations. But there have been other costs, too. Box 3.16 illustrates some examples from the results of the 1970, 1987, 1992 and 1997 general elections in the UK, when there were big surprises.

Box 3.16 Examples of variability in opinion polling and lessons that can be learnt

The 1970, 1987 and 1992 election results did not match the predicted outcomes.

- In 1970 most of the national opinion polls predicted a Labour Party victory but the victor was the Conservative Party led by Edward Heath. One reason given by the pollsters for this surprise was that the national polls had completed their findings at the weekend before the start of polling day. There was a late turnout of voters in support of the Conservatives which affected the results.[15]

- In 1987, the BBC commissioned a *Newsnight* panel of voters in marginal constituencies and an eve-of-election survey from Gallup. A 'poll of polls' was taken, which averaged the results of the national opinion polls throughout the election campaigns.

  The BBC's prediction of 26 seats and ITN's (Independent Television) prediction of 68 seats for the Conservative Party were far lower than the actual majority of 102 seats won by Margaret Thatcher and her party.[16]

- In 1992, out of 50 national published polls, 39 suggested the likelihood of a hung parliament (if the results were converted into seats), 8 predicted a Labour victory and 3 predicted a Conservative victory. Three exit polls (the ICM poll for Sky television, *Today* newspaper and the *Sun* newspaper; the NOP poll for the BBC; and the Harris poll for ITN) were indicative of hung parliaments.[17] In the event, the Conservative Party under John Major was returned to office.

- In the 1997 general election the Conservatives and the Labour Party had different polls taken which were contradictory and in some respects constituted no more than a public relations exercise on television and in the newspapers.

By now, though, the research agencies conducting the polls had learnt from experience and refined their methods. The majority of the polls were correct forecasts of a Labour win. However, there were errors in the sizes forecast for the majority of the win. No one had predicted such a big landslide victory for Labour when overnight the political landscape was changed. The Labour Party took 43.2% (nearly two-thirds of the seats in the House of Commons), the Conservatives received 30.7% (thereby ending 18 years of Conservative government) and the Liberal Democrats got 16.8% of the vote.[18]

Even with well-designed samples, there is an inherent difficulty in measuring public opinion despite any seemingly unpopular record of the political party in power. Nowhere is this fickle nature shown more than with electoral samples where the voting intentions of the electorate can change right up to the time they cast their votes. Big and late swings from one party to another, particularly in key marginal constituencies can, as Box 3.16 shows, lead to a different political outcome. For some background on the British system of opinion polling, see Worcester,[19a&b] the nature of constituency polling by Waller,[20] improving polling techniques by Sparrow,[21] and developing a methodology for exit polls, Moon and McGregor.[22]

The MRS enquiry[23] into the performance of opinion polls in the 1992 general election found that 60% of the difference between the final polls and the election outcome could have been accounted for by three factors:

- late changes in voting intentions;
- failure to reveal voting intentions amongst disproportionately Conservative supporters;
- a small impact from the deregulation of voters.

The Economist[24] pointed to two serious sources of error uncovered in the MRS report: the 'spiral of silence' where those thinking that their party was not fashionable, refused to tell the pollsters that they would vote for it, and sample quotas designed from old social class definitions.

Secret ballot questionnaires are now used by some market researchers to avoid the problem of respondents refusing to disclose voting intentions for an unfashionable party. The European elections in June 1994 to elect members for the European Parliament presented an opportunity for market researchers to get their predictions in their polls close to the outcomes through adjusting results to check their representations with past elections, and also for the UK 1997 general election.

The predictive nature of opinion polling at the constituency level was regarded as 'very patchy' by Waller since people were interviewed in certain areas at certain times in the days, weeks or months prior to the day of voting. Even the eve-of-election polls (on the evening immediately preceding the day of voting) could be affected by the last minute differential turnout of party supporters. Sample sizes for constituency polling need to be large (1,000 respondents if possible). Moon and McGregor's support for the accuracy of exit polls[25] was that such last minute differential turnout could be circumvented by interviewing electors at polling stations from the time the polls open to the time they close.

Such methods were adopted by Harris for ITN and the BBC's exit polls. NOP's sampling strategy was to aim for maximum coverage of the maximum variability. Variability in this respect refers to variations between polling districts, between hours of the day, and times of the day between polling districts. Since polling takes place in polling stations, these stations would be the primary sampling units (PSUs) chosen for exit polls, rather than the polling districts.

In cluster sampling, the alternative choices of PSUs are:

1. a random selection of population size with a constant sampling interval so that bigger PSUs could generate more interviews; or
2. PSUs proportionate to population size with a varied sampling interval to produce the same number of interviews in each PSU.

Since population sizes between polling districts vary greatly, the first choice would be uneconomic if a constant sampling interval set large enough to generate the required number of interviews for large constituencies produced only a few interviews for the smallest polling districts. Moon and McGregor recommend the selection of PSUs with a probability proportionate to size and a varying sampling interval, i.e. (2). PPS selection would be achieved in pre-election polls by 'the simple means of listing population size against each unit in the stratified list, accumulating population down the list and then applying a constant sampling interval'. For exit polls consideration of the functions of time and place are required so that each polling station could have '15 calls in each stratified list – one for each hour of voting' (Moon and McGregor, 1992).

In summary, there are many complex factors at work affecting voters in choosing which political party to support. Take the example below from the *Economist* in 1997,[26] with reference to the first round of voting on 25 May 1997 in the general election in France, when the ruling centre-right combination party lost more votes than expected to a loose alliance of Socialists, Communists and other leftwingers:

a close result is not the same as a debacle – and that against the predictions of all the opinion polls was what happened in the first round on May 25th.

It is not surprising that despite systematic methodological endeavours, the outcomes can be different from the predictions when complex forces are at work and when research predictions can become more of an art than a science.

II Purposive (non–random) sampling

This is also referred to as 'judgemental' or 'non-probability' sampling where every member of the population does not have an equal chance or known probability of being picked. Exploratory research often uses judgemental sampling, for example in selecting opinion leaders or 'captains of industry', i.e. chief executives of firms who are significant in directing and influencing the course of events in their firms.

Qualitative research normally uses non-probability methods while quantitative research uses probability sampling.

Non-probability (non-random) sampling usually includes the three common forms of convenience sampling, judgemental sampling and quota sampling. These will be considered in turn.

(A) Convenience sampling

As this name suggests, a **convenience sample** is picked on the basis of convenience, for example companies can use their employees to evaluate new products or prototypes developed by their R&D departments. Universities and colleges can carry out market research surveys based on convenience samples of students and visitors to their campuses.[27]

Convenience sampling lends itself to exploratory research where consumer information can be obtained fairly quickly, inexpensively and effectively from convenient population samples which are accessible and close to hand. The rationale is to select the most accessible members of the population from which to conveniently draw the sample. Unless the members of the population are reasonably uniform, e.g. in expectations, sociodemographic make-up, and so on, there can be problems of representativeness. In such cases a judgemental sample would be a better method.

(B) Judgement sampling

Judgement sampling is used in both purposive and probability sampling. We have already seen that judgement enters into multi-stage probability sampling; it fits as well as into purposive designs. The description 'judgement' is particularly applicable to industrial and trade research sampling.

In industrial and trade research we are concerned to sample output or sales turnover. Our base for sample design is output or turnover and not the number of establishments or shops in a particular industry or trade.

For example, there are a vast number of retail outlets selling food in the UK, but the leading food stores which have control of the national supermarket chains are few: Asda, Gateway, Safeway, Sainsbury and Tesco, in alphabetical order. When we consult secondary data sources at the design stage, we soon realise that in many fields there are a few concerns so large that, if they were excluded from the sample in a probability draw, sample estimates would be unlikely to represent values in the real industrial or trade world. So any survey of the manufacturers of paints should include the large ICI paints and any survey of the grocery trade should include Tesco as the current supermarket leader. This is judgement sampling, as these firms represent the members of the population who are good prospects from which to draw accurate data.

In this circumstance our sample design is:

Census of dominating firms + Sample of the rest

If no one concern is so dominant that it must be included in the sample, we are likely to find that a comparatively small proportion of the industrial or trade population we are surveying (say 20%) does a substantial proportion of the business (say 80%): the '80–20' rule. Stratification by volume or value is accordingly an important factor in the design of industrial or trade surveys.

The official statistics provide information about the structure of industries and trades, but firms return this information on the understanding that names are not published. Fitting names to strata requires skilful judgement in the use of secondary sources.

Where it is possible to establish a complete list of firms within a stratum a probability design is theoretically possible, but purposive selection of firms within the stratum is the more general practice. Survey design calls for the exercise of judgement.

(C) Quota sampling

In marketing research it is common practice to use **quota samples**. A prescribed number of members of the population are found in each of several categories or quotas. Quota samples are widely used in marketing research because cost-benefit analysis favours their use.

For example, in developed countries a good deal is known about the structure of populations whether these are from consumer, trade, industrial or public sector organisations and the records are regularly updated. Governments collect and publish statistics, as do professional, industrial and trade associations (see Appendix 1). A quota sample can take into account the wealth of this statistical data by making the most of updated socioeconomic variables (class, age, sex) from the census and the National Readership Survey, with monthly or even weekly sampling points, which can be regularly carried out and updated from these sources, when possible.

An example of selection of a sample quota from the UK adult population is shown in Table 4.4 in Chapter 4. An interviewer's daily assignment may be anything from ten to 20 calls on consumers in their homes, depending on the nature of the survey. (Length of questionnaire is critical.)

Television is the most popular advertising medium, as we see later in Chapter 13. So we could use the Independent Television Commission's television areas in order to obtain a stratification of the population by region. We can stratify the population by social class group and by age group. These sociodemographic variables are used for market segmentation purposes. However, classifying people according to social classes has always been one of the most dubious areas of market research investigation, but is also one of the most widely used classification systems. Along with age, the use of social class is generally seen as a control in the selection of requirements for quota sampling.

Quota samples are often controlled by social class and by age because other relevant data is classified in this way, an important example being the continuous surveys on which media planning is based. (See Chapter 13.) But other controls may be relevant, such as size of family and whether a housewife works outside the home. In a survey relating to convenience foods or to durables the interviewer is likely to be required to collect data from a laid-down proportion of 'gainfully occupied' housewives (such as 22% of housewives working full-time, and 21% working part-time).

In other words, the selection of respondents is purposive. They are chosen to fit a quota designed to mirror relevant characteristics in the population. They are not drawn from the population by a random procedure. This is the essential difference between purposive (non-random) and probability (random) sampling.

These decisions depend on the nature of the product field or service being surveyed and the extent to which exploratory research indicates that behaviour and attitudes vary by social class and age. For most fast-moving packaged goods, class is a weak discriminator and a breakdown of the sample by three social class groups – middle class, skilled worker and unskilled group – could even be sufficient for planning and control.

A quota sample can be as reliable as a probability sample in practice when the following requirements are met:

- up-to-date statistics relating to the structure of the population are available for cross-checking;
- the quota is set in such a way that important population characteristics are interrelated, such as age and social class, age and size of family or age and adults working outside the home;

- classification questions are carefully designed so that, for example, the occupation of the head of the household is established with some certainty;
- the interviewer's choice of location is restricted. This is not always possible, but where the decision as to which door to knock is taken out of the interviewer's hands, the main criticism of quota sampling is removed;
- the selection of respondents features in the interviewer's training programme.

3.4 The postcode address file (PAF) as a sampling frame

In probability (random) sampling, the procedure of drawing a sample in more than one stage with PPS is applied to the postcode units in the same way as to parliamentary or local government units, or as with constituencies and wards and polling districts. These different units are best explained by taking a typical postcode, e.g. LE11 3TU.

The first half of the postcode (LE11) is the outward code which indicates to the accepting office where mail is to be directed and the second half (3TU) is the inward code for the sorting office near to the point of delivery so that letters and parcels can be correctly delivered.

LE	11	3	TU
Postcode area (i.e. Leicestershire)	Postcode district	Postcode sector	Postcode unit

The introduction of postcodes dates back to 1857 when Sir Rowland Hill split London into postal areas, e.g. NW and SW. Following this, cities such as Birmingham and Sheffield introduced postal districts up to 1932. Numbers were added to the initials during the First World War. In the 1950s, automatic sorting systems were introduced – as well as the alphanumeric coding format.[28] The UK was fully coded by 1974, followed by the coding of Guernsey, Jersey and the Isle of Man by the early half of the 1990s, see Table 3.2. There are 180,000 large users each with their own postcodes and the Royal Mail computerised postcode address file (PAF) can be purchased on standard computer media, that is, compact disk, floppy disk and magnetic tape.

Table 3.2 Postcode figures

Postcode areas	122
Postcode districts	2,807
Postcode sectors	9,114
Postcode units	1.6 million
Addresses	24.5 million
Delivery points per code	15 (av.)
Large user codes	180,000 with 50 items per day
Guernsey	fully coded
Jersey	fully coded
Isle of Man	fully coded

Source: Mason, P. (1999), 'Postcodes', The Royal Mail Postcode Centre, UK.

The PAF system provides an up-to-date database resource for use by other organisations to check and add to their databases, for example:

- geodemographic profiling by market researchers;
- postcode mapping software for transport companies;
- geographic information for service centres and major retailers to select profitable locations for new service and retail outlets;
- property coding for crime prevention;
- credit referencing for insurance companies for assessing risk and insurance premiums;
- hospital billing using National Health Service area codes;
- direct responses promotion and sales targeting by firms to other businesses and to households.

It will be readily appreciated that, with the postcode file as a sampling frame, it is possible to draw a national sample in more than one stage: stratifying by postcode areas, treating districts and sectors as first- and second-stage units, and arriving at a sample of postcodes (i.e. groups of on average 17 homes) at the third stage, the draw at the first and second stages being made with probability proportionate to the number of addresses in each district or sector.

The postcode file is used by Taylor Nelson Audits of Great Britain as a frame for their syndicated home audit of consumer durables, based on a large sample of households, 30,000 of which are audited quarterly (the sample has to be large because durables are infrequently bought). TN AGB draws in two stages, having stratified by postcode area, drawing sectors at the first stage and postcodes at the second. Their interest is in households. To use the postcode as a frame for adults it would be necessary to list all the individuals at selected postcodes and then draw the required number of respondents or to interview every adult at each of the 17 addresses covered on average by each selected postcode. A more efficient method would be to select postcodes at random and then select respondents to fit a quota relevant to the subject of the survey, i.e. to use a random-location design.

3.5 Conclusion

Use of a probability procedure to draw a sample of individuals, householders, firms or other 'units of enquiry' has two advantages: it makes it possible to measure sampling error when translating sample estimates into population values; and it ensures that human likes and dislikes do not influence the selection or rejection of units for the sample.

It is possible to cluster calls while ensuring that every item in the population has a known chance of inclusion in the sample. Drawing in more than one stage with PPS reduces fieldwork costs and makes for improved supervision, but this procedure, as we have seen, is a complicated and lengthy one. When it is used to draw a master sample the procedure is likely to be cost effective in consumer markets and there are certain non-domestic markets of a 'mass' nature offering opportunities for the use of a master sample drawn in more than one stage with PPS.

Drawing in more than one stage makes it possible to concentrate the sampling frame for the final draw, for example to draw from a comparatively small number of registers. This concentration is particularly valuable where non-domestic surveys are concerned, because sampling frames do not come ready-made in non-domestic markets; it is usually necessary to construct them. The advantages to be derived from probability sampling are dearly bought. In non-domestic surveys it is usually necessary to compromise and in consumer survey work there is a cost-effective case for drawing sampling locations at random and then setting quotas relevant to the nature of the enquiry.

In survey research cost-effective allocation of often scarce resources depends on certain factors. For instance, there should be close collaboration between those who are commissioning the research and those responsible for its design and execution, both while the research proposal is being developed and when the findings are interpreted. It is relevant to estimate what proportion of questionnaires (or other means of collecting data, such as diaries) are likely to be satisfactorily completed before deciding whether to contact respondents in a personal interview, over the telephone or through the post. Quota samples can be used when the parameters of the survey population are well documented, provided sampling points are specified and the selection of respondents is controlled and there is proper provision for the training and supervision of the field force. To use a probability sample when a quota sample would be suitable is to incur opportunity costs. This means that, to use the opportunity within the research budget to enlarge the sample can mean not carrying out further research in other areas.

In research design, primary and secondary data collection methods along with probability and purposive sampling should be considered carefully in the initial consideration of the choice of research methods.

REFERENCES

1. Imms, M. (1998–99), 'Making it work: briefing agencies', *The AQRP Directory and Handbook of Qualitative Research*, p.25.

2. Berkowitz, E., Kerin, A., Hartley, S. and Williams, R. (1998), *Marketing*, Irwin, USA.

3. *Financial Times* (1998), 'Banking in the aisles', Weekend, 16–17 May, p.11.

4. AMSO (1993), *Annual Report*, p.5.

5. Whitten, P. (1991), 'Using IT to enhance the roles of market research', *Journal of the Market Research Society*, vol.33, no.2, pp.113–32.

6. Freeman, P. (1991), 'Using computers to extend analysis and reduce data', *Journal of the Market Research Society*, vol.33, no.2, pp.127–36.

7. Wright, L. (1996), 'Exploring the in-depth interview as a qualitative research technique with American and Japanese firms', *Marketing Intelligence and Planning Journal*, vol. 14, no. 6, pp.59–64.

8. *Economist* (1998), 'Economic indicators', 28 March, p.136.

9. *Economist* (1993), 'Bad show', 6 Nov., p.30.

10. Havice, M. and Banks, M. (1991), 'Live and automated telephone surveys. A comparison of human interviewers and an automated technique', *Journal of the Market Research Society*, vol.32, no.2, pp.91–102.

11. Horne, J., Pankhurst, F., Reyner, L., Hume, K. and Diamond, D. (1994), 'A field study of sleep disturbance: effects of aircraft noise and other factors on 5,742 nights of actimetrically monitored sleep in a large subject sample', *American Sleep Disorders Association and Sleep Research Society Journal*, 17 (2) pp.146–59. and Marjee, V. and Horne, J. (1994), 'Boredom effects on sleepness/alertness in the early afternoon vs. early evening and interactions with warm ambient temperature', *British Journal of Psychology*, 25 Jan., pp.1–17.

12. AC Nielsen (1997), *1997 Company Accounts*, pp.24–5.

13. Bagozzi, R, (1997), *Advanced Methods of Marketing Research*, Blackwell Publishers, USA, Chapter 3.

14. Ehrenberg, A. (1975), *Data Reduction Analysing and Interpreting Statistical Data*, Wiley, p.291.

15. Waller, R. (1992), 'Constituency polling in Britain', *MRS 1992 Conference Papers*, 18–20 March, pp.63–82.

16. Moon, N. and McGregor, R. (1992), 'Exit polls – developing a technique', *Journal of the Market Research Society*, July, vol.34, no.3, pp.57–68.

17. Hutton, P. (1992), 'Industry issues: after the poll is over...', *MRS Newsletter*, May, pp.12–13.

18. *Economist*, (1997), 'Britain: still undecided', 26 April, p.27.

19a. Worcester, R. (1992), 'Opinion polls in British General Elections', *MRS 1992 Conference Papers*, 18–20 March, pp.51–61.

19b. See also Worcester, R (1991), *A Guide to the History and Methodology of Political Opinion Polling*, Blackwell.

20. Waller, R. (1992).

21. Sparrow, A. (1993), 'Improving polling techniques following the 1992 General Election', *Journal of the Market Research Society*, vol.35, no.1, pp.79–89.

22. Moon, N. and McGregor, R. (1992).

23. *MRS Newsletter* (1992), 'MRS Inquiry into the performance of opinion polls in the General Election', July, p.1.

24. *Economist* (1994), 'Opinion polls', 9 July, p.35.

25. Moon, N. and McGregor, R. (1992).

26. *Economist* (1997), 'Those mutinous French', 31 May, p.35.

27. Wright, L. (1991), 'Research in concert', *Marketing Education Group Conference Proceedings*, University of Cardiff, July, pp.1386–404.

28. The Royal Mail, (1994), *The Complete Guide to Postcodes*.

QUESTIONS

1. 'The design of a survey, besides requiring a certain amount of technical knowledge, is a prolonged and arduous intellectual exercise.' Discuss the merits of this statement.

2. Faced with the following assignments, what method of data collection would you propose in each case? List the main topics of interest and explain your choice of method.

   (a) A survey of voting intentions at a general election.

   (b) A survey to establish where and in what way gardening tools are selected by the population of an expanding town served by a variety of traditional and modern retail outlets.

   (c) A survey of 'buying intentions' of car accessories to be conducted with new car buyers.

   (d) A survey designed to show the regional differences in the use of equipment by commercial laundrettes.

3. A company marketing a premium brand of cooking oil has to decide whether to adopt a revolutionary new bottle closure. The closure, which acts as a pourer, is more efficient and hygienic than those in general use. However, its adoption would increase the price of the brand to consumers by at least 3p a bottle, irrespective of size. (The current prices are 110p for 1 litre and 68p for the 1/2 litre size.)

   The marketing director is anxious to get in first with the new closure but has to show what effects its adoption would have on profit contribution. A research agency is asked to establish the effect on consumer sales of price increases of 3p and 5p on both sizes. The research budget is 'flexible' but a time limit of two months is set.

   The research agency is told that the company's brand is the leading premium brand in most parts of the country, but the consumption of premium cooking oil is higher in the south than in the north.

   (a) Does the research agency need a more extensive brief? What sources of information and data collection methods could it use?

   (b) Specify the research design you would recommend to arrive at a viable conclusion for the firm in the two months' time available. Explain your choice of design.

   (c) Assume adoption of the new bottle closure and a decision in favour of a rolling launch with television advertising demonstrating the convenience and efficiency of the closure.

   How would you monitor consumer acceptance of the change? (Media planning is discussed in Chapter 13.)

4 Sampling

E. John Davis

4.1 Introduction to sampling

The basic ideas of sampling are simple. If a representative sample can be drawn from a defined population of people or organisations, and measurements taken, then it should be possible to make inferences about the way those measurements apply to the whole population. The simplicity of the basic ideas should not, however, be allowed to hide the fact that applying the concepts and theory in practice can lead to some very complex designs and delicate decisions.

A major text on sample design one can run to over 700 pages, and on wider issues of survey research to almost 500 pages, of which over 150 may specifically be devoted to sample design. The most that can be attempted here is to provide an understanding of the basic ideas and concepts of sampling, the broad principles of their application in a market or social research setting and, together with Appendix 3, some of the basic calculations to enable proper interpretation of the data collected. In practice market research companies engaged in quantitative work will have access to specialist statisticians who through their knowledge and experience can ensure that sample designs and the interpretation of results match professional standards and are appropriate to each investigation. Beyond that the reader here should be able to appreciate the problems of sampling, realise when professional advice is needed, and communicate with professional statisticians about the objectives, problems, and expectations surrounding a research project.

Some of the earliest experiments with sampling procedures were undertaken by governments faced with problems of extracting data quickly from a census, where there was the advantage that results from systematic samples of every nth return could eventually be compared with the full analysis of all the census returns. Later developments were concerned with the rapid analysis of data in problem areas such as unemployment.

Commercial applications of sampling in market research began to appear in the 1920s, with both ad hoc surveys and continuing panels of stores or consumers. There was rapid development after the Second World War, with specialised survey research units being set up in the London School of Economics and the University of Michigan among others. Development work was also taking place within the commercial market research companies, separately or in conjunction with university units, and in the area of political or opinion polling. Since the middle of the twentieth century the availability of computing power has simplified the routine analysis of survey material and permitted the wider use of more complex weighting and analytical methods. While this has led to a general raising of standards and the provision of results more quickly and more focused on client problems, the uncritical use of 'black box' computer programs can sometimes lead researchers to lose sight of the underlying assumptions on which the statistical validity of their results are based.

This chapter will be concerned with the basic ideas of sampling and statistical inference, and hence the extent to which data obtained from samples can be trusted to provide information about their parent populations.

4.2 Defining the population to be studied

The object of study in virtually all market or social surveys is a defined population of people, establishments, organisations or things. Examples of defined populations include:

- all women living in a defined geographic area who, at the time of the survey, are 20 years of age or more and under 35, with two or more children under five years of age living with them;

- all sub-post offices in a defined postal area;

- all retail companies in a country with ten or more branches;

- all passenger vehicles currently licensed for private use in an area, and originally registered before 1 January 1997;

- all state primary schools within a specified administrative area;

- all children attending state primary schools within a specified administrative area.

From these examples it becomes clear that the definition of a 'population' needs to be quite clear about the qualifications for inclusion, often involving age, sex and geographic location for people, and similar characteristics for other categories. In practice there may well be a need for further definition of some of the terms used in these examples, e.g. 'private', 'primary'.

Where a survey is being done to update previous work, then it is logical to use the definition used before, to make it easier to compare the new results with the old. Then any notes made at the time of the previous survey will be invaluable in setting up the new in as comparable a way as possible. When setting up a new survey which may be repeated in the future it is then important to ensure that details of the planned sampling scheme and of experience with it in practice are recorded to ensure future comparability.

The last two examples emphasise the difference which may arise when dealing with individuals within groups. Whether schools or scholars are to be the object of the investigation will lead to different sampling schemes. In a non-human area, as for example when surveying the incidence of disease in a wooded area, whether the units of investigation are to be trees or leaves leads to different sampling procedures.

One source of confusion sometimes in industrial or business-to-business research is the difference between an organisation and an establishment. In business research an organisation is a partnership or a company with some legal standing, and which counts as one when considering its corporate activities. An establishment is a single unit, whether part of a larger organisation or not, such as a sub-post office, a licensed restaurant, a factory or depot. If the establishment is the only one in an organisation, then it may well be classified both as an organisation and an establishment. At the other end of the spectrum, care needs to be taken when dealing with subsidiary companies within a conglomerate. Under appropriate circumstance charities, local education authorities, voluntary organisations and so forth may be classed as organisations, with individual branches, schools, or whatever as the establishments.

With people surveys it is equally important to decide whether the research is concerned with individuals, households or some other unit, and to be clear about the distinction between a family, a household and people living at an address.

It is essential that a clear definition of the population to be covered in any survey is laid down at the start, so that there can be no doubt or confusion by anyone involved about whether a particular 'unit' is included or not.

4.3 A sample or a census?

In some cases the defined population will contain only a few members, such as 'all members of the UK House of Commons' or 'all fully paid-up members of the Nonesuch Flower Club'. Here it may be possible to carry out a census, contacting each and every member for their views or whatever. The results may still not cover all members as some will decide not to complete a questionnaire, agree to an interview, or to vote, but at least they were all equally included in the plan for the vote or research.

With these small populations, particularly where close contact between the individuals is a factor, there may be a good case for a census including all eligible members, for diplomatic reasons. Taking a sample of half the members of a club or association may lead to such antagonism among those not included that the acceptance of any results is put in doubt. 'Ownership' of the results by the membership may then call for more interviews than necessary to achieve the objectives of the survey and get the findings accepted.

4.4 The basis of sampling

In most cases the definition of the population to be studied includes many more units than can possibly be contacted – perhaps because of cost, time or other valid reasons. Hence the need to restrict the research to only a fraction or a sample of the defined population, so we end up with two groups, the sample we have contacted and know about through the information they have given us about their attitudes, activities, etc., and the rest about whom we have to infer their general or average characteristics from the sample results. Hence if valid inferences about the whole population are to be drawn from the information obtained from the sample, then the sample must be selected and analysed in ways which yield unbiased results which can be accepted as representative of the whole, within assessable limits.

In its purest form this means that the research sample should be selected in ways which ensure that each and every member of the defined population has a known

– usually equal – chance of being included in the sample. When all members have an equal probability of selection, then the process of selection is known as **simple random sampling**. The selection process will be free from any human judgement or other intervention, and is normally based on sets of 'random numbers' generated by computer programs. These operate in much the same way as ERNIE (Electronic Random Number Indicator Equipment) in selecting winners of the UK premium bond prize draw each month.

The beauty of the technique of simple random sampling lies in the links between the methodology, the size of the sample, and the margin of error or uncertainty which should be attached to the results. (The term 'error' is used here in its scientific meaning, of inexactitude in our results because we do not have full knowledge of a situation.) When dealing with large defined populations, such as people qualified to vote in government elections, we normally have a small group in the sample, and a very large group outside it. This raises the problem of how large a sample should be in order to adequately represent the shades of opinion, beliefs, habits, and so forth of the defined population. Clearly a very small sample, say of only ten people, has little chance of correctly reflecting the potential variations in a large population. A sample of 20 should be slightly more useful, but only when we reach levels of 100 or more, and preferably 1,000 or more, can we hope to estimate the characteristics of our defined population with any reasonable degree of accuracy or precision. Common belief and statistical theory here run in parallel although this is not always the case. Fortunately statistics known as the **variance**, the **standard deviation** and the **standard error** can be calculated from the sample data itself which indicate just what range of uncertainty we must allow for in making projections or inferences about the whole of the defined population from the sample.

4.5 Calculation of the variance, standard deviation and standard error

In the arithmetic concerned with sample statistics the following symbols are commonly used:

N is the number of people or other units in the defined population

n is the number of people or other units in our sample

F is the sampling fraction $= \dfrac{n}{N}$

x_i denotes the measurement, scaled value or coded attribute for the ith member of the sample, where the series of x_i will start at x_1 and run to x_n, for the last unit.

Then the arithmetic mean of the sample, denoted by $\bar{x}$, can be found in the usual way by adding all the values x_i together and dividing by n. In symbols:

$$\bar{x} = \frac{1}{n} \cdot \Sigma x_i$$

where Σ indicates the sum of all values of x_i.

This average or mean value, denoted by $\bar{x}$ could be average shoe size, average number of employees, average attitudes on a scale from 1 to 7, or whatever. Given a good sample, it is to be expected that the (unknown) mean of the whole population will be somewhat similar to that of the sample. The question is how similar?

In an extreme case where all units in the population were the same, then the mean of even a small sample would give a precise estimate of the population mean. In most cases, however, the need for a sample survey stems from the variability in the population, and some measure of the reliability of the estimated mean is needed.

The 'shape' or the pattern of the measures under investigation is important in determining the extent to which a sample will reflect the characteristics of the whole, and these patterns can be graphed as in Figure 4.1. The values of the variable are shown along the horizontal or x-axis, while the frequency with which each value occurs is plotted against the vertical or y-axis. For many variables such as heights of adult men the bell-shaped pattern emerges, with a high degree of symmetry around the arithmetic mean in the centre. The mode and the median, two other measures of where a distribution is centred, also occur at the centre of the symmetrical bell-shaped curve. The other dimension, the spread around the mean, is given by the standard deviation of the measure, which in turn is the square root of the variance. It should be noted that a graph showing the heights of both men and women adults together would be a combination of two curves, based around the two differing mean values. For some purposes, such as planning production of unisex T-shirts, results for the combined distribution might be useful, but in most cases such different distributions would be best investigated separately.

The variance, abbreviated to Var or V, which is a measure of the spread of a distribution about its mean, is computed by taking the differences between each of the individual values of x_i and the mean $\bar{x}$, squaring them, and taking the average.[1] In symbols this becomes:

$$V = \frac{1}{n} \cdot \Sigma(x_i - \bar{x})^2$$

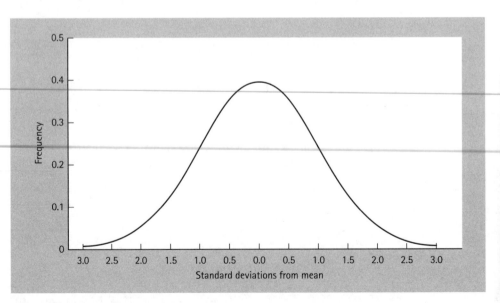

Fig 4.1 The bell-shaped, or normal curve

The square root of the variance links back to the bell-shaped curve which is often referred to as the 'normal' curve. This square root is sometimes called the root mean square deviation, showing how it has been derived, but more commonly the shorter title of the standard deviation is used. This is defined in symbols as:

$$sd = \sqrt{V} = \sqrt{\frac{1}{n} \cdot \Sigma(x_i - \bar{x})^2}$$

An estimate of the range of error or uncertainty attaching to the sample mean is called the standard error of the mean and is the sd of the sample divided by the square root of n, the sample size.

$$se = \frac{sd}{\sqrt{n}}$$

The benefit of the standard error is that it is also linked back to the bell-shaped curve, so that it is possible to make the following broad statements relating the sample mean to the unknown but true population mean:

- In 95% of cases the population mean will lie within ±1.96 se of the sample mean.
- In 99% of cases the population mean will lie within ±2.58 se of the sample mean.

Other ranges of error can be calculated from statistical tables, or may be thrown up by computer programs written for survey analysis, but these two are in common use and are often known as the 95% limits or the 99% limits respectively.

In the particular case where only two answers are possible to a question, such as being male or female, if the alternatives are coded 0 and 1 and these values put through the calculations above, a simple formula emerges for dealing with either proportions or percentages.

If p is the proportion of people/units with a particular attribute, opinion or whatever

and q is the proportion of people/units not having that attribute, opinion or whatever so that $p+q=1$ (or $p\%+q\%=100\%$)

then the standard error of the proportion p is given by:

$$se = \sqrt{\frac{p \times q}{n}}$$

As long as they are used consistently, either proportions or percentages can be used in the calculation, and the effective result is the same.

Given a simple random sample of 1,000 voters who split 40–60 in their voting intentions, then using the formula the se of the estimates can be calculated as follows:

$$se = \sqrt{\frac{40 \times 60}{1000}}$$

$$= \sqrt{\frac{2400}{1000}}$$

$$= \sqrt{2.4}$$

$$= \pm 1.55\%$$

Taking 1.96 times this figure of ±1.55% then translates into the 95% limits of about ±3%, the figure often quoted in the press and on TV for such surveys to indicate the range within which such results can be 'trusted'. In practice the factor of 1.96 is usually rounded to 2.0, and a factor of 2.5 used as a working approximation at the 99% level.

Two things should be noted about these calculations of the standard errors. The first is that the size of the sample, n, appears in the denominator, but under the square root sign. This means that although the range of error around the sample mean becomes less as the size of the sample is increased, the range only falls in proportion to the square root of n. Hence to reduce the range of error by half, n must be increased four-fold, and so on. To reduce the standard error in the calculations above by half to give 95% limits of around 1.5% would need a sample of four times the size, putting n at 4,000 respondents. Hence the cost of reducing the margins of error rises rapidly with n, but the precision rises only with $\sqrt{n}$.

The second point is that the numbers in the population outside our sample do not normally have any effect on how precise our estimate of the mean may be.

A sample of 1,000 people from 40m voters nationally
or 1,000 people from 120,000 voters in a constituency
or 1,000 people from 40,000 voters in a ward,
will all provide means with virtually the same degree of precision in estimating the relevant population mean.

In each case we are making an estimate for several thousand people about whom we have no current information, on the basis of our 1,000 sample. In each case we only have information from $2\frac{1}{2}$% of the people at most and are inferring that the other $97\frac{1}{2}$% or more of the population will follow the same patterns. This is an area in which some people have difficulty in accepting that the size of the population being sampled normally has no influence on the precision achieved with a given sample size. With large populations, say more than 20 times the sample size, it is the numbers about whom we have information which govern the precision of the results, and not the numbers outside the sample.

However, if we are dealing with a much smaller population, of say 3,000 people in a polling district, and take a sample of 1,000, then we have a gain in precision because we are only making an estimate relating to the other 2,000 people. We have information from one-third of the population and are only estimating for the other two-thirds. We can take advantage of this to calculate a narrower range of error in the results, because there is no error in one-third of our inference. The calculation involves the finite population correction factor,

$$\sqrt{(1 - n/N)} \text{ or } \sqrt{(N - n)/N}$$

which allows for the fraction of the population n/N, about which information has been collected. This can be inserted into the calculation of the standard error:

$$se = \sqrt{\frac{40 \times 60}{1000} \times \frac{3000 - 2000}{3000}}$$

With a sample of 1,000 from a population of 40m voters the finite correction factor has a value of 0.999975, which is virtually 1.0 and can be ignored. With a sample of 1,000 from a population of 40,000 the value becomes 0.975 which can still be approximated to 1 for most purposes, but for the sample of 1,000 from

3,000 people, the factor becomes 0.667 which should not be ignored. However, since the factor is also under the square root sign its ultimate effect is to reduce the range of error around the sample mean by its square root, in this case to about 82% of the crude value. Clearly as the size of a sample is increased and approaches the population level, then the factor approaches zero and the standard deviation about the sample mean tends to vanish – as would be expected in a census.

4.6 Calculation of sample size

The formulae relating sample size and standard deviation to the uncertainty surrounding the population mean can be used in reverse, to calculate the size of sample needed to meet a required level of precision, given some knowledge or assumptions about the variance or the standard deviation of the population. The formula is:

$$n = \frac{z^2.\mathrm{sd}^2}{d^2}$$

where: n is the sample size required to meet the conditions,

z is the factor to give an agreed percentage confidence level, e.g. 1.96 for 95% limits,

sd is the standard deviation of the population, estimated from previous surveys, experience, gut feel or whatever,

$\pm d$ is the permitted range of uncertainty, or the acceptable confidence interval.

(For percentage calculations sd^2 is replaced by $p \times q$)

This formula depends on the standard deviation being either known from previous work, or estimated. When dealing with percentages, as in an opinion poll, either an estimated result can be used in the formula or the default values of $p = q = 50\%$, which give a maximum value for n, and thus a safe result.

In practice the formula is seldom used to determine total sample size since in most cases analysis by subgroups is anticipated, such as by age of respondent, region and so forth. Here the requirements for precision within each subgroup become important, and the size of the smallest subgroup is an important figure in determining total sample size and any weighting system. The required subgroup sample sizes are then added together to give the total sample size. In many cases the available budget has more influence in limiting sample size than statistical limits of reliability.

4.7 Taking a simple random sample

Simple random sampling is the core technique in sampling. The basic theory is built round the process, and it is the standard against which variants of sampling methodology are assessed for efficiency. The word 'random' used in a statistical or sampling context means that the selection has been due to chance and chance alone. However, in other contexts outside statistics the word has a less precise meaning, and is applied to selection processes where some intervention, wittingly or unwittingly, takes place. In many texts, particularly from overseas, the words 'probability sampling' are used instead of 'random sampling', but the meanings are the same. In either definition selection of a unit is simply due to chance and nothing more or less. The converse, non-random or non-probability sampling is applied to situations where units have been selected by other means, because they fit certain patterns, have particular attributes, and so forth. Hence quota sampling and other forms of purposive sampling discussed below are examples of non-random or non-probability sampling.

In simple random sampling a sample is drawn from a defined population solely by chance. In essence each member of the population has the same chance of selection as any other, and the process is free from any human intervention. Normally a list or 'sampling frame' is needed, in which the people or other units can be numbered from 1 to N, the population size, and then random numbers selected from a list or through the use of a computer program. For small populations, such as members of a club or association such methods are quite practicable, and lead to very simple, straightforward methods of analysis, which is a further benefit.

However, given a much larger population in a defined area, e.g. all persons between 18 and 65 in the UK, while a similar method of selection would be possible, it may not be very practicable. For a mail survey with one standard postal rate across the country such sampling would be feasible; a telephone survey would be possible but the scatter might well add to the cost; and for interviewing face-to-face the travelling costs would be prohibitive. However, for smaller populations, such as members of a profession, or of clubs or associations where such lists already exist and the numbers run only to thousands rather than millions, the method can often be used. It then has the simplicity and transparency to be accepted by (most) members.

4.8 Systematic random sampling

Even with small populations the process of drawing random numbers and linking them to specified units in the sampling frame is laborious, and a short-cut method known as systematic random sampling is normally used. In this all members of the population to be sampled are listed – as is the case if electoral lists are used as a basis for selecting voters for a survey of voting intentions. The total number of all the entries listed is then divided by the number of individuals to be selected for the sample, to give the 'sampling interval', say g. A starting number of g or less is selected at random, say h, and this identifies the first person to be chosen as the hth one on the list. From then on each person falling at intervals of g, i.e. at positions $h+g$, $h+2g$, $h+3g$ and so on, is selected until the end of the list is reached, and the appropriate number of people should have been selected.

The units in a systematic sample will still be randomly selected, provided that there is no periodic element in the construction of the list and some check should be carried out. For example, if a list of recently married couples always shows the groom's name first, then any even sampling interval will produce a string of contacts all of one sex, which one depending on whether an odd or even starting number was used. Some housing estates are laid out geometrically, so that houses are in terraces of a given number, which may then be linked to the sampling interval, and so forth. Generally though, given a list which is free from such problems the formulae given above will still apply to the results without any modification. However, these methods of simple random sampling suffer from some severe practical limitations when used for face-to-face surveys in the field.

4.9 Field requirements for valid random samples

Selection of a random sample of people or other sampling units results in a list of contacts to be made. Attempts to contact these units will not always be successful, as some will refuse an interview, and some will not be contacted at all, having moved, died, closed or whatever. Rules need to be laid down to deal with these situations in ways which will not impair the integrity of the sampling process. A simple device for dealing with those no longer eligible for inclusion is to draw more units from the lists as spares, to be used when contacts have died or closed and this is generally acceptable. Sometimes it is acceptable for the same procedure to be used for those who have simply moved to another area, but this may reduce the representation of the more mobile elements in the community. An alternative in this situation is to accept the incomers as substitutes, with provision for selecting the individual to be interviewed when necessary.

Problems arise, however, when dealing with people who cannot be contacted, through refusal or not being at home at the times of calls. Normal practice is to make three attempts at contact, using any information which can be gleaned from other members of the household, and making appointments if possible. Even so some people will not have been contacted, and the problem of making good the numbers may arise. Using any extra names selected will lift the numbers, but hide the problem that substitutes, by being available and willing to be interviewed, may be different from those not available, or unwilling. Other methods of allowing for non-contacts have been suggested, usually asking each contact how often they have been at home on other days at the time of the call. Weights can then be given to those at home less often to allow for those who have been missed. However, the methods only become important for surveys in which the final respondents have been selected by a full random process, such as those used for government surveys which need to be as near perfect as possible.[2]

One commonly used practical way round the problem is to draw a sample of sufficient size to give the required numbers of valid contacts, using past experience of non-response as a guide. This then may lead to drawing, say, 2,400 names in order to achieve 2,000 interviews. Linked with this should be an analysis of the results of calling on these selected people at the 2,400 addresses. This might take the form of Table 4.1.

This analysis could be continued to show the proportions interviewed at the first, second or third attempts, but the main point is that the ways in which the sample has fallen short of the original selection are shown as a first step in the analysis, so that readers can see the pattern of the gap and can make their own reservations.

This method of using substitutes or additional names does of course assume that those not contacted will conform broadly to the patterns of those who have been

Table 4.1 Analysis of responses to a random survey

Original number listed		2400	100%
Died, too ill to interview	64		2.7
Moved away	157		6.5
Refused to be interviewed	85		3.5
No contact after 3 calls	57		2.4
Total not interviewed		363	15.1
Rejected at editing stages		27	1.1
Valid interviews included in analyses		2010	83.8

included in the survey, and this assumption needs to be challenged when considering the results of any survey. Steps can often be taken to minimise such bias, including the weighting schemes mentioned above, but the details are beyond the scope of this introduction. They generally revolve round analysing those who were away from home more often, those who were only contacted at the second or third call, and so forth, and using the results in some form of corrective weighting.

While random sampling methods can be used in mail surveys, the generally lower level of response, sometimes as low as 3% and seldom above 30%, makes any attempts to allow for non-response somewhat over the top. There may still, however, be merit in logging the date when each questionnaire was received back, so that analysis can be made by promptness of return. This can show changes in responses with the passage of time which can sometimes be used in interpreting the data and making more informed allowance for non-response.

4.10 Variations on simple random sampling

The major problem with simple random sampling as described above is the resultant scatter of the units selected. A sample of 1,000 units selected at random across a country will naturally fall more heavily in the major centres of population, but even here the amount of time needed in travelling between contacts is normally prohibitive. With uniform postal charges across a country then scatter has no effect on mailing costs, but there may still be costs involved in consulting a sampling frame, however constructed, stretching across the whole country. Local authority rating or taxing lists, which are frequently used as sampling frames in business-to-business surveys, are only held locally, and consultation means travelling to the lists. Other business listings, such as yellow pages, cover business contacts well, are available to purchase and hold centrally and do not suffer from the same problems, but ordinary telephone directories do not provide full cover of private subscribers. Commercially available lists may provide a base for the extraction of an adequate sampling frame and thus overcome some selection problems, but still leave a wide scatter.

4.11 Cluster sampling

To overcome the cost and logistic problems associated with simple random sampling the processes of cluster sampling have been developed. Before going into detail it is useful to make a distinction between the **unit of enquiry** and the **sampling unit**. In simple random sampling they are the same thing, as enquiry units are selected directly from some suitable listing. However, it is possible to take a sample of identifiable groups, as in parliamentary constituencies, as **first-stage sampling units**, and then to select the people to be contacted as **second-stage sampling units** within each first-stage unit. When dealing with a large population running into several millions, there may be advantages in taking more than two stages in the selection process, and in the UK electoral constituencies may be taken as first-stage units, with wards or polling districts then selected within each constituency as second-stage units, and individuals then selected within the ward or polling area, as third-stage units. Provided that appropriate methodology is followed the result will still be a properly selected sample of the planned size, but the units of enquiry are now clustered in a number of second-stage units, all within selected first-stage units.

A survey of 2,000 adults (suitably defined) covering the UK could now consist of groups of, say, ten individuals in each of two wards in each of 100 parliamentary constituencies. If the constituencies, and the wards within each, are selected with appropriate probabilities, and adults in each ward selected by simple or systematic random sampling, then calculations of the mean and variance of the whole sample, or parts of it, can still be made. All other things being equal, these calculations will lead to unbiased estimates of the parameters.

If all constituencies were the same size, and each ward within a constituency the same size, then clusters of equal size could be drawn in each second-stage area, making administration and analysis straightforward. However, there are problems when the populations of both constituencies and wards can vary considerably, often by a factor of 2 or more. The technique which permits the development of unbiased samples from a motley collection of first- and second-stage units is selection with 'probability proportional to size' or PPS sampling. Large units have a greater chance of selection than small, but at the final stage all clusters can be the same size while all units of enquiry in the population will have had an equal chance of selection for the final sample.

Apart from constituencies and wards other units may be used for selection with PPS, given some hierarchical structure and the necessary counts for each unit. Hence post or zip codes can be used, given broader sorting office codes, area codes, and on down to local delivery areas. Local government records may be used, with local authorities as the first-stage units, wards or parishes then become the second-stage units, before final selection of the enquiry units. The structure must be logical, complete, and counted, but if satisfactory conditions exist, convenience may become a major factor in deciding which hierarchy of first- and second-stage units to use for a survey.

4.12 Selection with probability proportional to size

The procedure is to list all the eligible first-stage units of the type chosen for use in the survey, such as parliamentary constituencies, local administration areas, postal districts and so on, with their respective numbers in the population to be sampled, and then to calculate the cumulative total populations down to each entry in the list (see Table 4.2). A sampling interval is calculated by dividing the total population in these first-stage units by the number of units to be selected, virtually as described above with systematic random sampling. Similarly, a starting point is selected within the sampling interval, and the sequence of selection points developed as before, e.g. h, $h+g$, $h+2g$, ... The process is both quick and efficient, but the precision of the results may be enhanced by methods described later under stratification.

The same process is applied to the second-stage units, such as wards, parishes, sub-code areas and so on, within each selected first-stage area. These second-stage units are listed with their populations within each selected first-stage unit, the cumulated figures are calculated, and an interval and a starting point selected to give the required number of second-stage units. (Normally more than one second-stage unit will be selected in each first-stage unit in order to give some indication of the variability between second-stage units, but if only one is to be selected the random starting number is selected which is less that the total cumulated population, giving the single selection needed.)

From within each selected second-stage unit, whatever its population, the same number of individuals is selected for the sample. A simple calculation now shows that the final probability of selection of each individual in the total population to be sampled is the same:

Table 4.2 Drawing sampling units with PPS

Constituency	% Cons. to total Cons. + Lab. votes[a]	Electorates[b]	Electorates accumulated[c]	
Sutton Coldfield	81.3	71,410	71,410	
Edgbaston	56.6	53,041	124,451	1st number drawn at
Hall Green	54.6	60,091	184,542	random is 135,000
Yardley	49.7	54,749	239,291	
Northfield	49.3	70,533	309,824	2nd number drawn
Selly Oak	47.9	70,150	379,974	is 325,000
Erdington	42.7	52,398	432,372	
Perry Barr	40.7	72,161	504,533	3rd number drawn
Hodge Hill	40.4	57,651	562,184	is 535,000
Sparkbrook	27.9	51,677	613,861	
Ladywood	27.8	56,970	670,831	
Small Heath	27.7	55,213	726,044	

Notes
[a] These are listed in order of the percentage of Conservative to the total of Conservative and Labour votes cast at the 1991 general election.
[b] This is the total number of adults eligible to vote in each constituency.
[c] The three constituencies selected with probability proportionate to their electoral populations are Hall Green, Selly Oak and Hodge Hill.

Let N be the total population being sampled.

Let n_i be the population in the ith first-stage unit selected.

Let n_j be the population in the jth second-stage unit selected.

Let k be the number to be sampled in each selected second-stage unit, to form a cluster.

Then the probability of selection of the ith first-stage unit is $\dfrac{n_i}{N}$

The probability of selection of the jth second-stage unit within the ith FS unit is $\dfrac{n_j}{n_i}$

The probability of selection of an individual within the jth SS unit is $\dfrac{k}{n_j}$

Hence, the overall probability of an individual being selected is:

$$\frac{n_i}{N} \times \frac{n_j}{n_i} \times \frac{k}{n_j} = \frac{k}{N}$$

The beauty of this method is that it allows for the final selection of equal-sized clusters, despite the first- and second-stage units being of different sizes, while ensuring equal probabilities of selection for the individuals. This leads to considerable administrative and cost benefits in the field.

There is a price to pay for these benefits. In selecting a sample of, say, 2,000 individuals from a large population the contacts will be widely scattered, and there will be only minimal correlation between the measurements, attitudes or whatever, of the individuals. In taking clusters of, say, 20 people from each of 100 sampling points, then there may well be some correlation between the 20, and they will tend to be more like each other and like others within the geographic boundary than with the population at large. Twenty people drawn from a small town in the north of a country will probably be more similar to each other in many ways than they are to people, even in a similar type of community, in the south. In political polling in particular, local areas will tend to show more homogeneity in voting than the country as a whole. The results obtained from these people are no longer statistically independent from each other, which is an assumption underlying the theory of sampling error.

The averages or means of results obtained will still be the best estimates available, but the simple calculation of the standard errors of the means will be underestimates, as clustering usually reduces the effective size of the sample. The correlation between individuals in a cluster, known as the 'intra-class correlation', may range from virtually nothing where there is little local resemblance between individuals, to 1 where there is perfect resemblance, at least so far as the characteristics being researched are concerned. In this latter case, a cluster of k individuals will provide no more information than a single individual from that cluster, and the effective sample size is reduced accordingly. The range of the intra-class coefficient is between 0 and 1, and the appropriate value, denoted by ρ (rho), is inserted into the following formula to assess what is known as the design factor:

Design factor = $[1 + (K - 1)\rho]$

where K is the cluster size.

The range of error for a clustered sample will be unaffected where there is no intra-class correlation and $\rho = 0$, and the design factor will be 1. However, when ρ takes a positive value and is multiplied by $(K - 1)$, even a small level of correlation and a fairly normal cluster size of 20 units will rapidly increase the range of error over that for a simple random sample. At a low level of only $\rho = 0.1$ and $K = 20$, the level is almost doubled. While the detailed calculations of ρ can be done to allow for the correlation within sampling units this can be complex and is seldom undertaken in normal market research work. Instead a rule of thumb is applied, and the theoretical range of error is increased by a factor of 2 or more.

One side effect deriving from cluster sampling is the use of master samples by some major research organisations. There are clear administrative advantages if a field force can be kept uniformly employed, and without undue travelling expenses. If then a master sample of perhaps 100 or more first-stage units is randomly selected, and interviewers recruited in each of them, the administration is greatly simplified, and with no great loss of rigour. For each large-scale survey it is still possible to draw an independent sample of second-stage units, with appropriate methods then used to locate enquiry units. For smaller surveys separate samples of first-stage units can be drawn from the master sample.

Some precautions need to be taken to maintain the validity of the survey results. In some smaller first-stage units there may be wear-out, as there may be in some smaller second-stage units, but with regular replacement of a fraction of the first-stage units the problems can be minimised. Against this, a more stable field force can then be employed and trained to high standards in the expectation of longer-term employment, a factor which links well with professional recognition and accreditation schemes for interviewers.

Such master samples are often behind the details given in the press about opinion polls, e.g. 1,200 voters were interviewed in 103 constituencies between 15 and 18 March or whatever.

4.13 Stratification

It is sometimes possible to improve on the precision of a simple random sample of any given size by stratifying the population before selecting the sample. It is not unusual, for example, for attitudes or behavioural patterns to vary from one part of a country to another, or between the sexes or age groups, in food consumption, use of leisure, voting intentions, and so forth. In statistical terms the population may not be homogeneous, or showing the same mix across the area.

In a random sample one factor which will itself be subject to sampling error will be the proportions of the different parts of the population included. In a sample of 1,000 from some defined population with roughly equal numbers of two types within it, such as males and females, the percentage of each type found in the sample would have a range of error attached of ±3%, and the percentage of either sex could range from around 47% to 53%. If now some attributes under study, such as smoking habits, vary between the sexes, then any overall estimate of the incidence of smoking will be affected by this error in the proportions of the two sexes. Similar sources of error will occur when the proportions of the sample falling into different geographic regions are allowed to vary within the total sample, and again stratification will help to reduce the overall sampling error. Factors such as numbers of employees or turnover, SIC codes and so forth can be used in industrial surveys.

The basic method is to stratify the population to be sampled, or to regard the whole as a set of parts or strata, and virtually to take separate samples within each stratum. In this way the allocation of interviews between strata is controlled, and the source of variation removed from the overall results, but without any loss of random selection within strata. However, once the mechanism is in place to draw the separate samples the way is open to use different sampling fractions in each area, with appropriate weighting at the analysis stage to restore the balance between strata.

In most surveys apart from analyses covering all groups in the population there is a need for breakdowns by area, age, sex, status, size of firm, SIC code, and so forth, and proportions of these groups in the population may not give adequate subgroups for analysis in an economically acceptable sample. Frequently analyses are required separately for small segments, such as small TV areas where experiments have been carried out, mothers with children under five, or other small target groups. In administrative surveys special attention may be focused on groups with special needs, or specific age groups; in business-to-business surveys the attitudes or buying patterns of a small number of heavy users may be of more importance than larger numbers of lesser users. In any of these situations, and many more, stratification and the use of weighting techniques will make better use of available resources than the basic simple random sampling approach.

Weighting is a simple process now with the available computing power, but at one time it led to laborious hand calculations. It can be combined with stratification and different sampling fractions to ensure that the user's requirements for analyses in small segments do not lead to wasteful over-sampling of larger segments or strata. In many investigations it may be expected that the Pareto curve applies, in which 20% or so of the population being surveyed account for 80% or so of activity, whether buying consumer goods, or in business-to-business situations. For example, in many business surveys the distribution of firms by size is very skew. See Figure 4.2.

With perhaps 80% of businesses in the small category and only 20% medium or large, any sampling scheme with equal sampling fractions across the industry would end up with 80% of the sample being small, and only 20% being large. This

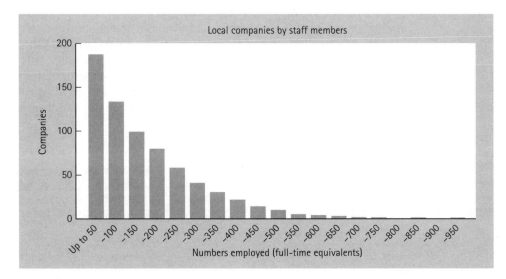

Fig 4.2 An example of a skewed distribution

is usually a waste of resources, as a much lower proportion of the small companies would normally be sufficient to discover what was needed about them, while a census of large companies might not be inappropriate. Hence where possible prior identification of the characteristics of companies, and stratification by size, and selection within strata with differential sampling fractions would increase the amount of information gained considerably. In some cases a census may be appropriate among the major units, such as major chemical companies, while normal sampling methods are used in other strata.

In order to provide unbiased results over the whole population, the means and variances from each stratum need to be combined in a way which brings them back to their due proportions in the population. This is usually the reciprocal of the sampling fraction, so that where a stratum has been subject to a census, as with the large firms, they are included at face value (subject possibly to some weighting to allow for non-response) while small firms, which have been sampled, say on a one in ten basis, have their results lifted by a factor of 10. Appropriate combination of the results – within the scope of modern survey analysis packages – leads to unbiased calculations of means and so forth, for the whole population or for each stratum within it.

Stratification is possible before selection in many cases, and particularly in surveys of organisations, where lists are available or can be compiled from directories, company records and so on, containing not only the names and addresses of units in the population to be covered, but also indications of size (turnover, number of employees, etc.). Then stratification by size is not difficult, even if only into large, medium, small on some acceptable criteria as indicated above. An example of where it may be highly logical to attempt to carry out a census among the biggest units, to sample one in four of the middle group, and perhaps only one in 16 of the smallest units is shown in Table 4.3. The sampling fractions in the table were calculated to give sufficient numbers for broad analysis in each stratum, subject to budgetary constraints. The precise lines of stratification in any survey will depend on the nature of the enquiry, and the calculation of the sampling fractions will depend on the numbers needed to provide confidence in the results.

This simple example illustrates the process, but in a major survey the sample design would have been based on analyses of the variability of the units across the range, and the allocation of resources to minimise the overall sample variance. The calculations can become complex and are beyond the scope of this chapter.

The overall pattern of means, percentages, and so forth, combining all strata is then obtained by weighting each stratum by the reciprocal of the sampling fraction – in this case by 16 for the small units, by 4 for the middle group, and by 1 for

Table 4.3 Sampling from a skew distribution

Unit size	Number of firms	Numbers employed	Sampling fraction	Sample	Raw weight
Small units	807	3,000	1 in 16	50	16
Medium units	140	7,000	1 in 4	35	4
Large units	12	15,000	census	12	1

the large units. These raw weights may need to be modified in the light of the responses obtained, and the methods adopted for dealing with non-response. The weighting can be done either at unit level or after the results from each stratum have been calculated. With the availability of computing power weighting at unit level is normal, allowing easy analysis across as well as within strata. Calculation of the standard deviation is slightly more complicated as the variances (sd^2) for each stratum need to be used, but are weighted in the same way, and the square root of the resulting sample variance gives the value of the standard deviation.

In many cases it is not possible to gather sufficient information to permit any useful stratification of the population before drawing the sample, but it may still be useful and possible to carry out some stratification after the survey is completed. This is not normally as effective as prior stratification, but it can be useful where category data is available, as from government statistics, but no data is readily available on the individual firms. The benefits can be the same as for pre-stratification, but are likely to be diluted.

A form of stratification which can be used together with any systematic selection process such as PPS, merely involves putting the sampling units into some order before starting selection. This helps to ensure that there is a good spread of the sample through the population. Hence a typical overall design may start with stratification by region, such as administrative regions, marketing regions (TV areas, sales regions, etc.), with first-stage units such as constituencies within each then arranged in order of income per head, consumption patterns, percentage voting for a particular party, or whatever measures may be available which are considered relevant in a particular enquiry. Within each first-stage unit the subareas can be similarly ordered according to some logical measurement. In all this the advantages of using widely recognised units lies in the availability of both official and private statistics for the areas concerned. Among the useful sources are the geodemographic analyses based on census data, showing population characteristics by polling districts, census enumeration districts or postal codes. Suppliers, availability and details of material vary from country to country, but can easily be obtained from research or sponsoring organisations.

In a survey covering Western Europe, for example, there would certainly be stratification by country, with each country being in effect sampled separately. Identification and selection of both first-stage and second-stage units could then be different for each country depending on local structure and statistical data, but clearly for comparative purposes the more uniform the process across national boundaries, the easier it will be to make valid comparisons from the results. First-stage units could be based on European parliamentary constituencies, within which administrative areas could be ordered by degree of urbanisation, ranging from fully urbanised through to fully rural.

As the extent of stratification is increased, and the number of layers in the selection is increased, so the complexity of the calculations to deal with different sampling fractions and to build up the various levels of subtotals inevitably increases, and so does the complexity of tabulation. With modern computers this in itself need not pose a problem, but complexity in itself may open the way for errors in planning or executing the sample design.

4.14 Effects of clustering and stratification on errors and the precision of results

As we have seen, the clustering of contacts tends to lead to decreased precision in the results for any given sample size because of correlation between individuals within clusters. Conversely stratification in sample design will normally have a beneficial effect on the precision of results by ensuring that data from different components of the sample is being collected and analysed in their proper proportions. Both effects are variable, with large numbers of small clusters having less effect than small numbers of large clusters. Equally, a limited amount of stratification will normally enhance the precision of results, but benefits can be lost if the process is taken to extremes.

In practice a well-designed sample can be analysed cell by cell to provide an estimate of the variance, and thus the standard error to be applied to results.[3] These results can then be compared with the theoretical precision to be expected from an unstratified simple random sample of the same size from the same population, to give an estimate of the overall gain or loss in precision. This can then be set against the relative costs of the two types of sample to provide a cost-benefit comparison. Such calculations can only be carried out after the event but where a survey is a repeat of earlier work then previous results can be valuable for planning purposes. Where no such history is available rules of thumb developed from experience of similar surveys may be applied in the planning stages to gauge whether proposed designs will match the criteria set down for the survey.

4.15 Validation of the achieved sample

Having designed the sample and carried out the fieldwork the first step in analysing the data should be to compare the composition of the achieved sample with census or other reputable data as a check on the validity of the sample. The achieved sample should of course match the population from which it was drawn on any criteria used for stratification purposes, but there are normally many other factors that can be used for comparisons, such as age, marital status, household composition, and so forth, for people, and patterns of turnover, numbers employed, numbers of branches, and so forth, for business units. The expectation is that, taking account of weighting systems built into the initial sample design, the sample will show the same composition as the population within an acceptable range of error.

Basically the sample is broken down into cells, each defined according to the criteria being used. Hence for a sample of housewives (however defined) a breakdown by four age groups, six areas of the country, five household types would produce 15 cells if simple analyses were done, or 120 cells if full cross-tabulations were carried out. The proportions of the sample in each cell could then be compared with census data to check the overall structure, and to gain insights of where any departures from published data were being generated.

Should the sample characteristics not match those of the population within acceptable limits the reasons should be sought. Possible bias in some aspect of the operation is always a first hypothesis to be investigated, partly for future reference, but more immediately to indicate where the problem lies, and to provide a logical basis for rectification. Rectification normally takes the form of weighting the data to bring the composition of the weighted sample back towards the population pattern, and although this can be done blind, without any knowledge of how the problem arose in the first place, this can be dangerous. Post-hoc weighting can be effective, but justification for the weighting and confidence in the results will only come from a proper investigation of possible causes. Inevitably, however, sooner or later any researcher may come across the survey which simply by chance falls outside normal expectations of matching the population. Judgement is then needed in deciding on the action to be taken – but again this usually comes back to some form of weighting of the available data. Discarding suspect data is a possibility, giving the rejected items an effective weight of zero, but again discarding suspect data can become a dangerous game unless carried out according to some carefully framed rules.

4.16 Quota sampling

Since the first test of a newly-drawn sample will be its fit against available statistics of its parent population, could not the sampling process be aimed directly at making the appropriate numbers of interviews in each cell? Why make the effort to select people at random, find them at home or at work, with the travelling involved plus call-backs and so forth, if in the end the requirement is simply to get the right numbers of people in each cell? Can valid research be carried out simply through looking for people who fit into the categories in the first place?

The answer lies in 'quota sampling', which provides a simple direct method of contacting a collection of people, as defined by the population to be surveyed, with much less effort and cost than random sampling methods. In its simplest form, a sample of first-stage units is drawn as for random sampling, and second-stage units may also be drawn, using selection with probability proportional to size in each case to justify the use of equal size quotas. Selection of the people to be interviewed is then made by the interviewer, according to a set of instructions which will detail where to work and the numbers of different types of people to be interviewed. The numbers of interviews to be included in each quota will usually be linked back to the expected numbers of interviews which can be conducted in the interviewer's working day. Thus, assuming that for a particular survey an interviewer can expect to complete 20 interviews in a day, quotas will be set on that basis for simple administrative and economic reasons.

The simplest form of quota is the non-interlocking form in which only totals by characteristic are set. For an adult (ages 18–69 years) survey a quota might appear thus:

Sex	No.	Age	No.
Male	10	18–24	3
Female	10	25–39	7
		40–59	7
		60–69	3

One problem with quota sampling is the latitude it can give to interviewers in their selection of contacts, and with this very simple form of quota it would be possible for interviewers to 'fill their quota' with young women and old men.

To avoid such distortion, interlocking quotas are normally used, with at least separate age requirements for males and females, and even further complications. These measures will clearly tighten up the fit between the sample and the population, but if the complexity of the quota is taken too far then it may be quite impossible to meet all the requirements in some areas, and sufficiently difficult in others, so encouraging some blurring at the boundaries. Table 4.4 shows an example of a sample quota taking a spread of four age groups and tree social-class groups for personal interviews.

The use of street interviewing linked to quota sampling clearly raises problems about the probabilities of various groups being contacted. People in full-time employment may be less likely than some others to be on the streets during working hours, and even when they are they may be too pressed for time to be interviewed – going to or from work, and at meal breaks. Conversely those not in employment are more likely to be out at other times, and hence controls may be added to quotas about the numbers to be contacted who are 'gainfully employed' on a full-time basis, part-time, or not at all. Even the weather can affect probabilities of being contacted, as those who do not need to go out may not do so in cold or wet weather – those not in employment, not having to take children to school, not owning a dog!

A further complication in street interviewing is the motor car. Interviewing in car parks increases the probability of contacting motorists; keeping to pedestrian areas may swing probabilities the other way.

Beyond that there may be problems of interviewing people in moving populations, whether shoppers, travellers or whatever. Given flows of people, such as into or out of a building, bus or train station, airport, for example, arrangements can often be made to place interviewers at appropriate points to collect information. However, to ensure that an unbiased sample is contacted care is needed in both the location of interviewers and the monitoring of the flow. Even with a single entry/exit situation the flows on either side of the opening may be self-segregating. People arriving at the location from different directions may have different characteristics, perhaps having arrived on foot, by private car, taxi or public transport. People leaving the location may form separate streams for taxis, bus stops, business centres, shopping, and so on. Hence the point at which an interviewer stands may affect the types of people presenting themselves for selection, with clear opportunities for bias to come in. There may be further complications when a location has

Table 4.4 An interlocking sample quota

Social class	Age				
	15–24	25–44	45–64	65+	Total
ABC1	7	13	11	7	38
C2	6	10	9	6	31
DE	6	10	9	6	31
Total	19	33	29	19	100

a number of access points, as with some London underground stations, where different exits lead to quite different living/working/shopping environments.

Once the location of interviewers has been decided (with the consent of the owners/occupiers where appropriate) attention should be given to recording the flow of people. Given, say, a five-minute interview, and allowing time for selection of the next contact, rest breaks and so on, a rate of striking of perhaps eight interviews an hour might be reasonable. If now the flow of people varies through the day, from, say, a peak rate of 500 an hour down to 50 an hour, then the probability of a person being selected by an interviewer at a peak time would be only 8 in 500, giving a sampling fraction of around 1 in 60. Given the same rate of interviewing at slack periods, the sampling fraction can rise to around 1 in 6. The differences can be allowed for by weighting at the analysis stage, but the differences must be quantified for appropriate weights to be applied. It is necessary then for the time of each interview to be noted (a fairly general requirement anyway) but data is also needed on flows, and usually this is done by having interviewers work in pairs or teams, with one member recording the traffic count through time, and the others conducting interviews. In some locations other, usually electronic, means of recording traffic flows may be available, but it is normally wise to arrange for the specific data required for weighting the survey results to be obtained during the interviewing slots. Making good any deficiencies in the data afterwards can be difficult, and lack of good data may jeopardise the results.

In attempts to overcome the problems associated with interviewer selection, controls other than straight quotas have been developed, mostly based on a 'random walk' or 'postman's walk'. Here first- and second-stage units are selected normally, but followed by the selection of one or more points or addresses in each second-stage unit. The typical instruction to interviewers would then be to stand outside (facing, back towards) the given address, turn right, take the first turning to the left, then first right, and so on, knocking at every house with a number ending in a given digit. Quotas can be set on characteristics such as sex, age or gainful employment, but those relating to any form of status are not usually used because of the constraint already imposed by the random walk. In this way some of the control over contacts is taken back from the interviewer, and it is comparatively easy to run validation checks on routes and house numbers. Provision has of course to be made for flats, institutions, rural areas, dead ends, and so on, but every method of sampling has its problems as well as its merits.

Where the household is the unit of enquiry, and where any responsible contact can be accepted, there are no problems beyond making some contact. Where interviews are to be made with the housewife (properly defined) or some specified person (such as the oldest child over five years of age and under 18 at the time of the call) determination of who is to be interviewed at an address is normally straightforward. Where the process is being used to contact a sample of individuals, however, unbiased procedures are required for selecting the individual within a household. This is a problem of sampling generally, and is discussed below in the section on sampling frames.

4.17 Non-response in non-random sampling

Given the lists of contacts drawn in random sampling it is not difficult to calculate a response rate, and to account for those not contacted. With quota and some other forms of non-random sampling, as no prior list is used there is no automatic way of assessing a response rate, but it is still useful to collect whatever information is available, even if only as a basis for trying to improve future performance.

It should be normal practice to use some form of reporting which provides a record of those contacts attempted but which failed. Interviewers are supplied with contact sheets in which basic and observable details are noted of people spoken to but not interviewed, sometimes linked to a few filter questions to establish whether the contact is eligible for the survey. Hence a distinction can be made between those filtered out and those opting out of further discussion. Even so there is only a fuzzy line between those who may see an interviewer approaching and take avoiding action, and those with whom some more positive contact was made before refusal. While any analysis of the data will be limited, it can indicate potential problems with the response rate, and it may be useful in identifying potential sources of bias, in making comparisons between interviewer achievement, and in providing a basis for improving techniques.

4.18 Purposive sampling

Quota sampling is one form of purposive sampling which is widely used and approved for many purposes. However, purposive sampling also has its uses where very small numbers are involved, such as in selecting people for discussion or focus groups, and in many areas of business research. In appropriate circumstances well-conducted purposive sampling is both cost effective and acceptable.

In such small-scale enquiries, perhaps involving only a dozen or so contacts, it is not expected that the 'sample' will be statistically representative of the whole, but that it should yield qualitative results reasonably free from selection bias. In a recent investigation the views of fund managers were needed about attitudes to certain forms of investment. A large-scale survey was ruled out on problems of timing, and also of cost. A small survey with a randomly drawn sample among managers of all eligible funds would lead to the bulk of the contacts being from small operations, since the Pareto 80/20 rule was evident, with 20% of funds accounting for over 80% of the money. However, simply taking the top echelon of fund managers gave a sample of managers who:

- were pleased to be included once the basis of selection had been explained;
- were able to speak with authority about the topic;
- controlled between them a large slice of the investments in that market;
- were sure enough of their positions to agree to be interviewed.

The result was that through a dozen or so interviews with people who were purposively selected because of their knowledge and position, data needed for decisions was collected, and with a high degree of belief that it was valid in its context.

For purposive sampling to be accepted as a valid method in a research project it must be carried out with the same due diligence as for any other form of sampling. The population must be defined, and rules established for the selection of respondents. Three criteria are important in maintaining the integrity of the research:

- the planned basis of selection must be properly adhered to and described in any report on the research;
- another worker at another time should be able to reproduce the method of selection to achieve comparable results;
- the process of selection must be transparent, logical and appropriate.

A sample of friends in the industry is not likely to meet these criteria. Even where sample design and selection is carried out with due diligence, such research is essentially qualitative in nature, and calculations of even a simple kind should be avoided. Better to say 'six out of the twelve contacts ...' rather even than 'half of those interviewed ...' which may soon be reported as 50%, a figure which cannot be ethically supported on a sample of such size.

4.19 Sampling frames

Sampling frames have been mentioned at several points in this chapter, and it is now useful to cover them in more detail.

Technically any process of random sampling depends on there being a listing in some form of all eligible members of the defined population. However, lists can vary greatly in their coverage and integrity, and even for simple lists such as members of a club a number of questions need to be asked before it can safely be used:

- Does the qualification for inclusion in the list match the definition of the population to be sampled? Or if the list is wider than the defined population, can eligible members be identified, e.g. are those in different grades of membership identified?

- Is the list up-to-date? For UK electoral registers which are often used in sampling the date for inclusion in the list is 10 October of each year, and the lists are published in February of the following year. Hence the lists are six months old when published and 18 months old before they are replaced. The age qualification for inclusion as a voter is 18, but the lists also contain names of those who will become eligible to vote during the life of the register.

- Is the list complete? The electoral registers do not cover the whole adult population, as there are some people who do not have the vote. Further, there are people who do not want to appear on the register. The coverage will vary from country to country, depending on local legislation, custom and so on.

- Is the list free from duplication? This can be a problem with trade lists, often compiled from a range of sources, with companies being included more than once, or under more than one category. It also applies where establishments are listed but a sample of organisations is being sought.

Commercial lists are usually compiled for mailing purposes and not for sampling purposes. Nevertheless they can be useful as starting points in the development of a sampling frame, but subject to stringent editing to pass this set of requirements. Other lists, too, may need editing before being used as sampling frames, such as where a list covers but does not match the defined population. In some cases procedures can be applied in the office to edit a list, but in other cases editing has to be done in the field after contact is made.

If a sample of households is required from a list of individuals, such as the UK electoral registers, then straight random selection will lead to over-selection of larger households, as they have more entries in the lists than small ones. However, a sample of households can be drawn if the lists are, or can be, arranged in address order, simply by selecting a household only if the individual on whom the random number falls is the first name at the address. Alternatively a filter can be employed, so that all households selected with only one entry are retained, only one in two of addresses with two entries, one in three of those with three entries, and so on.

The converse problem of randomly selecting individuals where addresses have been sampled either from rating lists or through random walks, is normally dealt with in the field. First a list is made of those at the contact address who fit the defined population. Various procedures are then used to select the individual to be interviewed, ranging from taking the person with the most recent or next birthday through to complex procedures involving tables of random numbers and the sequence of interviews. Those planning the survey should remember that any such selection procedure may need to be applied by a weary interviewer standing on a wet and windy doorstep, trying to retain the interest and cooperation of a member of the household, while deciding who should be interviewed.

In planning how to adapt a listing which is not ideal for use as a sampling frame, the principles of random sampling need to be kept in mind, and the potential effects of any procedures on the probabilities with which individuals are being included or rejected should be traced through. There are usually more ways of introducing bias into the results through faulty selection than there are ways of drawing an unbiased sample.

The random walk and its associated procedures of listing people at the selected addresses is close to several procedures used in surveys among people or business units. These processes may begin with the selection of defined but small geographic areas as first-stage units. These may be city blocks or abstract areas such as squares on a map grid, and the choice may be influenced by population density and town plans. Lists are prepared of all eligible units within each randomly selected first-stage unit, which becomes the sampling frame, and selections then made of dwellings, commercial units or whatever. Some city plans lend themselves more to block sampling than others, and some forms of sample can be effectively drawn using the abstract geometric blocks, including, for example, low density establishments such as petrol stations. While farms could be sampled in this way care must be taken with the individual probabilities of selection, and there are normally good lists of many types of rural holdings giving useful details of area, types of farming, stock levels, and so on as aids to stratification and selection.

For telephone interviewing there are special problems, starting with the high proportions of ex-directory subscribers in many localities. The situation is better with business surveys as the Yellow Pages cover all business telephone subscribers, but firms operating across a number of categories will have multiple entries, for example in the marketing area there are categories for market research and analysis, marketing and advertising consultants, sales promotion consultants, telemarketing, and information services.

Where enquiries are being undertaken within clearly specified groups, such as among members of a profession or a club, phone numbers should be available from those commissioning the research (but care may be needed under data protection acts in some countries). In the immediate area of marketing and statistical bodies, the lists of members of the Market Research Society show affiliations and phone numbers; that for the Marketing Society gives only a member's affiliation; ESOMAR shows names, affiliation, phone numbers, fax and email; the list of Fellows of The Royal Statistical Society shows affiliations, addresses, phone and fax numbers and email addresses, and while Fellows may suppress any or all of these details if they wish, few appear to do so. For many surveys there is no need to use telephone listings or directories as sampling frames, even though they may be needed as sources of phone numbers for those selected. Thus the use of lists as sources of information may be quite distinct from their use as sampling frames. Much the same considerations apply to the use of fax machines as a method of contact in surveys.

For large-scale telephone surveys the services of specialist research units is usually needed, where advantage can be taken of sophisticated equipment to monitor calls and provide rapid analysis through computer-assisted telephone interviewing. These organisations also have their own ways of designing sampling schemes which will meet clients' requirements. More generally for all forms of survey, lists are now available commercially covering a wide range of activities, buying habits, current ownership and intentions to purchase durable goods, and so on. A questionnaire from one such commercial organisation which arrived while this section was being written contains over 60 separate questions, some to be answered for oneself and a partner, or the family. Those who participate are offered products or services, inclusion in lotteries and draws. The results are certainly of interest to those sponsoring the surveys, including those planning surveys in particular areas, but since some people may be deterred by the time required to complete the questionnaire, due diligence is required in testing such lists against the criteria for accepting a sampling frame for further research.

When attempting to reach specialised segments of the population, e.g. mothers of babies under six months old, use can often be made of omnibus surveys to provide a list of contacts. The sampling frame which is then developed is as good as the omnibus survey from which it is derived. Alternatively organisations exist which collate data on births, engagements, marriages and deaths from local and national papers, and make it available commercially. Again with due diligence, such sources may provide sampling frames for survey work, but normally the lists tend to be used more for the distribution of samples of products or of information, as may be appropriate.

The use of the Internet as a means of making contact in a survey is subject to much the same considerations as telephone surveys. While the penetration of the net is still far below that of the telephone, most companies of any size already have links to the net, as well as web sites. Surveys among companies involved directly in IT or other high-tech areas have been successful in achieving good response rates from among key people, but junk email may blur the picture, as it can do with ordinary mail. Under appropriate circumstances the method can provide for sound samples from known populations, with the immediacy of fax or phone, and the opportunity for the contact to find data and consider their answers before replying.

135

4.20 Conclusion

It is unfortunate that sampling error is the only component of survey error which can be easily (although not always appropriately) calculated, particularly for opinion polls or other research reported mainly in proportions or percentages. Overall survey error includes errors or bias arising from faulty definition of the population to be surveyed, perhaps including numbers of people who do not have the knowledge or experience to give valid answers to the questions raised; faulty selection of respondents; faulty questionnaire design or questions; faulty editing, coding or analysis of responses, and so on. Occasionally such sources of error come to the surface, notably after elections when the results of previous surveys are compared (often unfairly, as they are measuring different things).

While the emphasis in this chapter has been on the design of sampling procedures, even among the readership of a market research text there will be comparatively few who ever get to design a sample for real use – beyond student projects or examination questions. This is not to say that such knowledge is not necessary for a practising researcher, but simply that for most researchers the knowledge is used as a basis for assessing surveys conducted by others, whether for marketing purposes, as indicators of public opinion or other matters. Hence it is perhaps not inappropriate to end this chapter with some questions which should be asked in relation to any survey which one is asked to take on board for either professional or personal reasons.

The main questions are:

- What is the definition of the population covered by the survey?
- How large was the sample and how was it selected?
- Who carried out the fieldwork/telephoning/mailing?
- When was the fieldwork done?
- Who carried out the analysis?
- Who commissioned/paid for the survey?
- What was the objective?
- How do the results stack up against related research?

With satisfactory answers to these questions it should be possible to sort sheep from goats, surveys aimed at discovering 'the truth' from those aimed at supporting a point of view, those done with due diligence and those which have perhaps fallen short in some ways.

NOTES

1. Kish, L. *Survey Sampling*, Wiley. (1965)

2. Moser, C. A. and Kalton, G. (1971) *Survey methods in social science investigation*, Heinneman.

3. Strictly where the variance is calculated from the sample values the divisor should be reduced to $n - 1$, but given sample sizes of 30 or more units the refinement is usually ignored, as it is here for simplicity.

4. The methods based on finding out times when people were at home or out were developed in the 1940s and 1950s when crime was less evident than now, and less exception would be taken to questions which could reveal when property was left unoccupied.

5. This is subject to the requirement that at least two second-stage units have been drawn from each first-stage unit, and so on, to enable assessments of variability within each stage to be included in calculations of the overall variance, and thus standard errors.

FURTHER READING

Dent, T. (1992), 'How to design for a more reliable customer sample', *Business Marketing*, 17(2), pp.73–6.

Ehrenberg, A. (1975), *Data Reduction Analysing and Interpreting Statistical Data*, Wiley, p.291.

Henry, G. (1990), *Practical Sampling*, Sage.

Malhotra, N. (1999), *Marketing Research*, third edition, Prentice Hall.

Moon, N. and McGregor, R. (1992), 'Exit polls – developing a technique', *Journal of the Market Research Society*, July, vol.34, no.3, pp. 57–68.

Semon, T. (1994), 'Save a few bucks on sample size, risk millions in opportunity loss', *Marketing News*, 28(1), p.19.

Worcester, R, (1992), 'Opinion polls in British General Elections', *MRS 1992 Conference Papers*, 18–20 March, pp.51–61.

Worcester, R. (1991), *A Guide to the History and Methodology of Political Opinion Polling*, Blackwell.

QUESTIONS

1. (a) You have been asked to conduct a survey into the cinema-going habits of the adult population between 18 and 70 years of age. Outline the methods you would use in collecting the information and in designing the sample of people to be contacted.
   (b) You have been asked to conduct a survey into the frequency with which cinema-goers between 18 and 70 years of age visit a cinema. Outline the methods you would use in collecting the information and designing the sample of people to be contacted.
2. A local supplier of stationery and office equipment has asked you to conduct a survey among office managers within a 30-mile radius of his showroom, and which will involve showing photographs and samples. Outline the methods you would recommend, and the sources you would consult in designing a sampling frame. What questions would you need to ask your client as a basis for your planning?

5 Questionnaire design

Questionnaire design is of key importance in both qualitative and quantitative research. In the former, as the case example at the end of this chapter helps to illustrate, even small samples can be investigated using semi-structured (or in other cases, unstructured) questionnaires to elicit answers and to probe deeper into interviewees' responses. The questionnaire in quantitative research is used as a survey instrument with larger samples, normally containing structured questions for ease of coding and statistical analysis.

This chapter focuses on 'question and answer' as a means of finding out about the habits, awareness and attitudes of consumers relating to the products and services available to them, and their needs which these products and services are designed to meet. The chapter proceeds from a general discussion of types of questionnaire and kinds of question to a detailed examination of the stages in the development of a questionnaire and consideration of the questions themselves: 'the art of asking questions'.[1] The case study at the end of the chapter includes exhibits of the questionnaires used.

Methodological research funded by the Market Research Society suggests that more than half of the questions asked in surveys of the adult or housewife populations are attitude questions. These are discussed in Section 5.7. There are certain techniques in common use for measuring attitudes and they are best considered in isolation, but, for a survey, attitude questions are likely to be introduced into the questionnaire as and where relevant to questions of behaviour and awareness.

Back in 1993, the MRS produced a booklet backed by ABMRC and AMSO aimed at achieving consistency in approach in the conduct of face-to-face interviews.[2] The booklet provides answers to the questions that are most often asked with samples of the 'interviewer identity card' and the 'Market Research Mark'. The MRS Freefone service verifies for respondents that the research company carrying out interviews with them is a genuine market research agency operating under MRS or related associations' codes of conduct.

5.1 Asking questions for attitude and product usage studies

The questionnaire is a very useful, flexible and far-reaching tool for the market researcher who can use it to obtain important information on:

- **consumer behaviour**: what consumers buy, where they buy and how they use what they buy;

- **consumer awareness**: how aware consumers are of available services, brands, product characteristics and the claims made for them by their manufacturers;

- **consumer attitudes**: how consumers view the relevant activity (e.g. motoring, clothes washing, shaving) and the types of products and services available for pursuing the activity.

An attitude is a learned predisposition to respond in a consistently favourable or unfavourable manner with respect to a given object. An opinion is the expression of an underlying attitude. An individual might hold the attitude that smoking is anti-social and express the opinion that people who smoke in non-smoking railway carriages should be put out at the next station. A smoker might still feel the inclination to smoke and to maintain the right to do so, even in non-smoking railway carriages. The distinction between an opinion and an attitude is a fine one and the terms are often treated as interchangeable.

Attitudes are the product of experience (what has happened to the respondent), awareness (what has been noticed and learnt) and volition (what is wanted or willed). Attitudes are recorded to help explain behaviour so that informed assumptions may be made about future behaviour. (For techniques used to elicit and measure attitudes, see Section 5.4.3).

The questionnaire is an indispensable tool for the market researcher to research attitudes and solicit facts, since the results are critical to the research outcome. The questionnaire is a common form of collecting information on markets. Markets can be described and analysed in detail so that opportunities can be taken, company performance assessed and competitors' activities tracked.

So why do we not just ask consumers what they are going to do? One reason is that people will not necessarily disclose their real intentions if, say, the product they want is perceived to be the 'unfashionable' one at the time.

Studies are undertaken on consumer attitudes and product usage because it is important to understand what is happening in the product markets. It is also important for organisations to have these insights in order to identify new opportunities which arise.

To aid management decision-making, ad hoc or one-off studies can be undertaken on consumer attitudes and product usage. These are designed to aid the making of a specific and immediate decision because it is important for managers to understand what is happening in their markets at a particular point in time.

If we lack trend data we can arrive at hypotheses concerning future behaviour as follows:

1. First, by asking questions about present experience of the product or service: about what is being bought, used, owned or done now.

2. Then by asking questions about past experience in order to determine whether present behaviour is habitual. Questions about intentions, such as intentions to buy or to invest capital, can usefully be asked if sufficient data has been collected over time to establish relationships between intentions as expressed and past actions.

3. Lastly, answers to awareness and attitude questions, taken together with answers to the behavioural ones, help us to decide what the respondents' future behaviour is likely to be. It is important for managers to develop these insights so that future behaviour may be anticipated and new opportunities identified.

5.2 Questionnaire types

In an industrial society, the prevalence of the use of the questionnaire method means that it is difficult for people to avoid participating in questionnaires about themselves, for example, in applications for financial services products such as mortgages and insurance policies or to take part in direct marketing mailshots linked to sales promotions. Most people become familiar with the notion of questionnaires before they have reached adulthood, having disclosed information on themselves in applications, for example, to study at educational establishments or for membership of sports and travel clubs.

The questionnaires put forth by organisations and individuals vary between two basic types. At one extreme, they are fully structured with closed questions, while at the other extreme they are completely unstructured with open-ended questions. A compromise is the semi-structured questionnaire which incorporates a mix of the two.

Structured questionnaire

The order in which questions are asked, together with their wording, is laid down. The interviewer must not alter or explain questions. Many questions are closed and the possible answers to most questions are pre-coded so that all the interviewer has to do is to draw a circle round a code number or tick a box. (See Section 5.3.5.)

Unstructured questionnaire

Most of the questions are open-ended. The interviewer is free to change the order of asking questions and to explain them. The questionnaire may take the form of a checklist for discussion. The unstructured questionnaire is used in depth interviews, group discussions and in non-domestic surveys. The interview can be respondent-led, particularly if the interviewee is an expert in the field, so that their observations and expertise can be taken account of.

Semi-structured questionnaire

This usually constitutes a mixture of closed or fixed-response questions, quick response ranking or rating scales for measuring attitudes, organisational and product attitudes, and open-ended questions or spaces for respondents to fill in their comments. Semi-structured questionnaires are useful in enabling the interviewer to 'stage-manage' the interview by making sure that all questions are covered with room for the interviewee (respondent) to add comments to the specific questions already asked.

Closed questions

The respondent chooses between possible answers to a question. This may take the form of 'yes' or 'no' answers with a tick in the relevant box. A good example is the data collection for the government's household census in 1991. This was by questionnaire containing a long and detailed list of closed questions to elicit demographic data on heads of households and their families. Answering of the questionnaire was compulsory. The questionnaires were distributed and collected door-to-door by temporary workers who could give assistance to any householder who had difficulty in answering the questionnaire, because of low levels of literacy, for instance.

In a closed question, the question is **dichotomous** (either/or) if there are only two possible answers (apart from a 'don't know' or 'no preference'). If there are more than two possible answers, apart from 'don't know', the question is **multichotomous**. Answers to questions can be given by ticking the yes/no boxes or by ringing the correct answers or code number. For example:

Dichotomous
    Is your mower:
    a rotary mower?   (code no.)
    a cylinder mower?   (code no.)
    (The mower has to be one or the other)

Multichotomous
    Is your mower driven by petrol?   (code no.)
    Mains electricity?   (code no.)
    Battery?   (code no.)
    Human effort, unaided?   (code no.)

Coding

A numerical code is allocated to each type of response to facilitate data processing. All possible answers may be listed and coded in advance of the interview and, in surveys of any size, this is done wherever possible. When responses cannot be allocated to a range of possible answers, coding takes place after the interview. (See Section 5.3.5.)

Open-ended questions

The respondent is left free to answer in his or her own words and the interviewer is required either to write down the answers verbatim, or to allocate the reply to a range of possible answers set out and coded on the questionnaire. Verbatim answers demand subsequent coding. Answers to the question 'Would you tell me why you chose a rotary mower?' might receive 'open' treatment.

Direct questions

The respondent is asked about his or her own behaviour without equivocation, as in the questions given above.

Indirect questions

The respondent's own behaviour or attitude is inferred from answers to questions about the behaviour or attitudes of other people: 'Why do you think people have pets?' or 'Why, would you say, do people go to church?' (Respondents reluctant to give true answers can also be overcome by using a projective technique such as 'sentence completion' or 'word association', see Section 5.4.3.)

Electronic data processing

EDP puts a premium on questionnaire structuring, which has in the past been counterproductive, impeding instead of facilitating data collection – both the interviewer and the respondent have suffered from the computer revolution. The practice of recording answers on grids and scales, which are easy to analyse, causes boredom and frustration in the interview situation, unless the subject is absolutely riveting.[3]

By making the processing of data so fast and effortless EDP removes or weakens obstacles to the lengthy questionnaire. Using the computer to feed in and to analyse data is now a common and to some an essential part of the research effort. Both computer-assisted telephone interviewing (CATI) and computer-assisted personal interviewing (CAPI) have integrated the interviewing and electronic data processing functions. Computer hardware and software have been made more accessible due to lower costs and better designed user-friendly programs such as the Statistical Package for the Social Sciences (SPSS). SPSS was originally created in the 1960s for use with mainframe computers but has been adapted subsequently as a statistical and data analysis package available for use with UNIX, OS/2 Macintosh, MS-DOS and Microsoft Windows.

5.3 Design of a structured questionnaire

We are going to consider the stages in the development of a structured questionnaire from the formulation of research objectives during exploratory research (as discussed in Chapter 2) to the pilot test in which the proposed questionnaire is tried out on members of the survey population. (The proposed sampling method may be tried out at the same time.) The Red Rose case study at the end of this chapter is an illustration of these research processes.

Figure 5.1 illustrates the stages which are considered in the following sections:

5.3.1 Formulation of hypotheses
5.3.2 Topics of interest
5.3.3 Survey methods
5.3.4 Levels of generality
5.3.5 Plan of tabulations
5.3.6 Ordering of topics
5.3.7 Treatment of topics
5.3.8 Questionnaire layout
5.3.9 Pilot testing.

By the time we come to design the questionnaire we should know what topics are relevant to the decision-making task and from what population the sample is to be drawn. We ought to have arrived at tentative ideas (hypotheses) about behaviour and attitudes in the market, and we should be clear as to the conclusions we are going to need to be able to draw, depending on whether our hypotheses are accepted or rejected.

In order to do this we have to decide the following:

1. In what detail we need to ask questions about the survey topics – the level of generality (see Section 5.3.4).
2. How we are going to relate answers to respondents – the plan of tabulations (see Section 5.3.5).

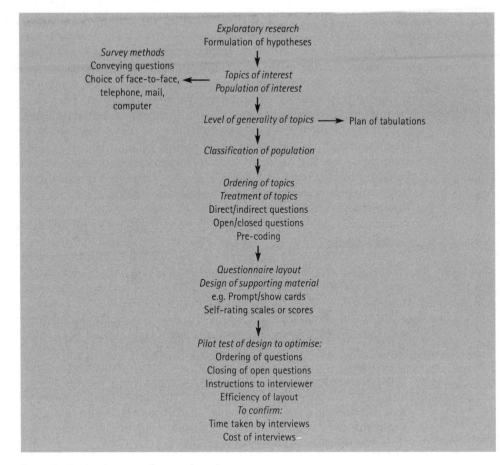

Fig 5.1 Stages in the development of a questionnaire

5.3.1 Formulation of hypotheses or research objectives

We are not prejudging the answers even if we anticipate the conclusions. We are just making sure that when the time comes to draw conclusions, the data available is in sufficient detail for us to be able to accept or reject our conjectures about the market we are describing. The intellectual effort involved is illustrated in the case study at the end of this chapter.

5.3.2 Topics of interest

The research effort can be to describe a particular market from the viewpoint of a consumer. The objectives can be set around the identification of market opportunities or the solving of a specific problem, optimising the positioning of a brand or making recommendations for a marketing mix approach to target markets.

Topics can be examined, such as consumer awareness of a product or a specific brand, sources and frequency of brand purchase and use, prices paid and quantities consumed, attitudes and needs of consumers using the brand.

5.3.3 Qualitative and quantitative approaches to survey methods

Qualitative research usually involves a small number of sample units of individuals or groups because the qualitative approach is used to explore problems in depth and to identify root and contributing causes. Inferences can then be made about a range of respondents' experiences and their opinions. The cause and effect relationships in data generated can be inferred. So the qualitative approach is necessarily inductive and respondents are usually chosen on the basis of purposive (non-probability) sampling.[4] By its nature, qualitative research lends itself to face-to-face in-depth interviews undertaken in respondents' houses or in their work environments. Semi-structured and non-structured questionnaires are normally used to engage respondents with exploration of their feelings, opinions and interest about specific issues or products.

Quantitative research provides a statistically valid picture. Larger numbers of sample units are chosen using probability sampling. Quantitative research can also be conducted by re-interviewing samples, for example, from a pool of known cooperative respondents using random-digit dialling by telephone with interviewing via a CATI system.[5] Results can be correlated and statistically quoted with cost-benefit analysis supplied. Quantitative research is thus more applicable to self-completion postal questionnaires and electronic data collection methods such as CATI and CAPI. Structured questions are normally used. Short structured questionnaires are used in conjunction with shopping centre interviewers or hall tests, consumer panels and in-house tests, where consumers can try out a sample of products before completion of questionnaires.

There is some evidence that with the main types of survey methods – personal interviewers, telephone interviewers and postal self-completion questionnaires – the inclusion of some monetary incentive or product promotion will increase response rates.[6]

5.3.4 Levels of generality

Decisions are made not only about the topics to be included in the questionnaire but also about the detail in which they should be covered. We must be careful not to leave some critical aspect out. Relevant information collected on topics of interest also needs to be related to consumers in terms of socio-economic and demographic profiles and attitude observations. This information can be usefully applied to segment markets for targeting new products, representing brands or other marketing promotion initiatives.

In designing the questionnaire it is also necessary to take into account the way in which the survey population can be broken down. When it comes to making decisions, which groups are going to be critical? The sample should be designed to yield enough individuals in each critical group for us to be confident that they represent this group in the population. On the other hand, each interview costs money. The group's behaviour and attitudes must be relevant to the decisions we anticipate having to make. The best way of deciding which classifications are relevant is to take each survey topic in turn and to consider the importance of each group in the survey population in relation to it. A detailed picture of the kinds of decisions that have to be made by the research planner at this stage is given in the case study at the end of this chapter.

5.3.5 Plan of tabulations

The topics have been listed in the required detail and the population has been classified into relevant groups, as shown in Figure 5.1. This is a good point at which to plan the tabulations, bearing in mind that too much detail is as counter-productive as too little. We need to take each topic in turn and to decide which groups in the survey population warrant individual attention when it comes to discussing this topic.

The agreed classification of respondents may usefully be applied to every answer, but this is not invariably the case and we are likely to want to consider other groupings, such as those whose answers to the questionnaire show them to be alike in their behaviour.

Taking the example of the Red Rose case, it goes without saying that we are going to put questions about the work culture and expectations of service delivery.

How the data is going to be analysed and used for measurement needs to be decided upon before the questionnaire is written, because the wording of the questionnaire must make it crystal clear whose answer is required to each question. This applies when an interviewer is putting the questions in a personal or telephone interview, and when the questionnaire has been mailed to a respondent for self-completion. Decisions about the tabulations also affect sample size. Particularly crucial for the calculation of sample size is the decision on whether to break down the behavioural groupings by a demographic classification. Where 'feelings about the company' are concerned we might hypothesise that the workforce's attitude towards 'senior managers' is enough to warrant a breakdown in communications.

It may be helpful, when considering tabulations, to set up a matrix with topics in detail down the side and standard demographic and other groupings across the top. The plan of tabulations can then be seen at a glance and we will have ensured that nothing of importance is left out. The code frame should include a description of the question and a description of who should be answering it.[7] For a more detailed treatment of this subject see Appendix 2, and for the data reduction approach to survey analysis, see Collins (1992).[8]

5.3.6 Ordering of topics

It is good common practice to follow these principles:

- Open with one or two general, bland questions which the respondent is expected to find easy to answer.

- Explore present behaviour in the market before delving into the past, i.e. focus on what is being done, used, bought, eaten now before asking about earlier experience.

- Record behaviour before putting attitude questions. Answering behaviour questions concentrates the respondent's mind on the topic in question so that he or she is ready to express an opinion about it or to take up a position on a self-rating scale.

- Take topics in a logical order so that the respondent is not confused.

- Withhold topics that might be embarrassing until the personal or telephone interview is under way or, in the case of a mailed questionnaire, until the respondent's interest may have been aroused by the earlier questions.

- Be prepared to try more than one place in the questionnaire for the 'difficult' topic, at the pilot stage.

- Try to avoid boring sequences in the questionnaire, e.g. a run of multi-choice questions or too many rating scales one after the other.

- In a personal or telephone interview, make sure that the topics are ordered in such a way that ideas influencing answers to later questions are not put into the respondent's head. The mailed questionnaire is likely, if filled in, to have been read right through first.

Classification questions are often embarrassing or difficult, but they can be left until the end in the case of a probability sample, for the respondent drawn at random must be interviewed. In the case of a quota sample, some classification questions need to be asked at the outset because it is necessary to establish that the respondent fits into the quota set.

In a postal survey classification questions can be put at the end of the question-naire. They are unlikely to be as disturbing as they would be in an interview because the respondent is not always asked to fill in his or her name and address.

'Show cards' are often used to take the embarrassment out of age and income questions because the respondent can be asked to point at the slot they fit into. For example:

'Would you show me your age last birthday on this card?'

| 15–24 | 25–44 | 45–64 | 65+ |

In the case of a mailed questionnaire the respondent ticks the appropriate box, while in a telephone interview age and income brackets, if used, must be kept few and broad.

It is clearly desirable that questions designed to classify respondents should, as far as possible, be standardised so that the results of surveys can be compared. The Market Research Society set up a working party back in 1971 'to consider whether the use of standard questions in survey research should be encouraged, and if so to put forward recommendations'. The recommendations still relevant today are based on research agency practice and are summarised in *Standardised Questions: A Review for Market Research Executives* (1984).[9]

5.3.7 Treatment of topics

We are going to consider the actual wording of questions in Section 5.4, but before writing the questionnaire, we need to decide whether we should treat the topics in an 'open' or 'closed' way, and in a 'direct' or 'indirect' way.

In the survey research there is a practical case for pre-coding, and also for closing as many questions as possible. The respondent is given a choice of answers plus 'don't know'. The interviewer has merely to ring the code number alongside the respondent's choice of answer. Too many closed questions may bore the respondent but interviews and data processing take less time than they would if the questions were open and the answers had to be put into coding categories after the interview. Also the closed pre-coded question is more likely to yield valid data: there are fewer opportunities for lapses of memory on the part of the respondent and for the incorrect recording of answers by the interviewer.

Box 5.1 Example: car accessories

Open: 'What extras and/or accessories were already fitted when you bought your car?'

(The respondent tries to remember, perhaps goes out to look at the car. The interviewer writes down items as they occur to the respondent.)

Closed: 'Which of these extras and/or accessories were already fitted when you bought your car?' [SHOW CARD]

	Col. 9
Wing mirrors	1
Seat belts	2
Radio/tape recorder	3
Heater	4
Head rests	5
Fog lamps	6
Reversing lights	7

We need to distinguish between questions which are pre-coded and closed (as in Box 5.1) and questions which are pre-coded but put to the respondents as if open. In both cases the respondent answers and the interviewer rings the relevant code number, but in the first case all possible answers are put to the respondent and memory is stimulated.

There is evidence that respondents react differently to the two types of question as if they are being asked to perform two different answering tasks. In the open situation the respondent is required to generate and define items relevant to the question. In the closed situation he or she has to choose or judge between relevant items already selected. It has been shown when the same question is put to matched samples of respondents, responses vary with the approach used.

The importance of this finding depends on the nature of the question being asked. In the car accessories example the respondent is being asked a strictly factual question and the closed question is clearly more likely to produce a true answer than an open one. When attitudinal or 'why' questions are being asked, there is room for doubt. This is illustrated in Belson's comparison of open-ended and checklist questioning systems (Box 5.2).[10]

Box 5.2 Belson's comparison of open-ended and checklist questioning systems

During survey work in five different product fields an experimental 'why' question was asked. The five samples were split so that half received the experimental question open and the other half, closed. Half were required to volunteer reasons for liking, disliking or using, as the case might be; the other half were given a list of reasons to study. The items on this checklist were derived from 'preliminary open-ended research'.

Example

1,521 interviews with 'bath additive' users in Great Britain dealing with reasons for using a bath additive.

The checklist system

'You've said you have used … (READ OUT ALL RESPONDENT CLAIMS TO BATH ADDITIVES USED) in your bath. I would like to know all your reasons for using this/these.'
PAUSE
'Here is a list of possible reasons.'
PASS CARD AND SAY:
'Please go through it and call out all that apply in your case'.
WAIT FOR RESPONDENT TO FINISH WITH THE LIST.
WHEN HE/SHE HANDS IT BACK, SAY:
'What other reasons do you have for using this/these bath additives?'

The open-ended system

'You've said you have used … (READ OUT ALL RESPONDENT CLAIMS TO BATH ADDITIVES USED) in your bath. Please tell me all your reasons for using this/these'. (PROBE FULLY, USING PROBES SUCH AS: 'What else?'/'What other reasons?'/'Uhuh', followed by a waiting silence).

Findings

The five samples yielded six experimental treatments (one sample was asked first about things liked and then about things disliked). The following findings are based on all six sets of data.

- The checklist stimulated a substantially higher overall level of response.
- Checklist respondents offered fewer 'other reasons', suggesting that the use of the checklist has a dampening effect upon the volunteering of any further items.
- The frequency with which individual reasons were given by the two halves of the samples varied (from 0.93 to 0.02), i.e. rank order is not stable between the two systems.
- Reasons only quoted once during the preliminary research scored frequently when on the checklist, e.g.

From bath additive study	Checklist	Open-ended
% endorsing/volunteering each reason:	(760 cases)	(741 cases)
To ease my feet	22.1	5.4
It has a clean smell	9.3	0.1

The checklist questioning system stimulates memory and it may put into words the ideas which the respondent was not conscious of having or it may introduce new ideas. The checklist also draws attention to items which the respondent might not have considered worth mentioning when asked an open-ended question. That is, the two questioning methods cannot be assumed to produce the same result. Full advantage is taken of electronic data processing when questions are closed and pre-coded. In survey work it is common practice to use the open-ended system at the exploratory stage and then to reduce the list of items and close.

We need to remember that the two questioning methods are likely to produce different data sets and that, when we reduce the list by discarding less frequently mentioned items, we are making the assumption that ideas voiced infrequently are less important in determining behaviour than those voiced frequently.

In order to pre-code questions it is necessary to anticipate the possible answers. For standard classification questions (such as age, class, sex) or regular items such as 'don't know', 'no preference', 'anything else'/'any other', pre-coding is a straightforward matter. But in order to pre-code answers to most survey questions, prior knowledge of this range of possible answers is needed. Exploratory research will have suggested what answers are to be expected and the pilot test will confirm the completeness of the list, provided an 'anything else?' is included and respondents are given time to think whether or not there is 'anything else'. A questionnaire consisting entirely of 'closed' questions is boring for both respondent and interviewer. Open questions break the monotony. But when designing a survey to describe a market as many questions as possible should be pre-coded and open questions necessitating handwritten answers kept to a minimum.

If a closed question means choosing between more than three possible answers, it can be best to list the choices on a show-card. This assumes a personal interview. On a mailed questionnaire the choices would be set out alongside the printed question. If a topic proves to be 'difficult' or embarrassing at the exploratory stage, we may decide to approach it indirectly when it comes to formulating survey questions. In survey research we need the comfort of numbers, so our treatment of the subject must be a quantifiable one.

A quantifiable questioning technique used by Research International is the Cognitive Response Analysis (CRA). This elicits spontaneous reactions to a commercial, as well as an understanding of how involving the commercial is for the viewers. According to worded instructions, viewers are required to write down all their spontaneous thoughts, ideas and reactions to an advertisement. They are then asked to rate each of their thoughts on a scale ranging from positive to negative. These responses are then analysed for self-relevance and positive or negative associations. While the responses are quantifiable, the technique is said to retain 'the benefit of qualitative elicitation … it adds a unique extra dimension to conventional pre-testing methods'.[11]

5.3.8 Questionnaire layout

Apart from the questions relating to the survey topics, we have to provide for the following:

- identification of the job by means of a reference number;
- identification of each individual questionnaire by means of a reference number;

- identification of the interviewer in the case of a personal interview;
- introductory remarks;
- classification of respondents, plus, in some personal interviews, the respondent's name and address.

The job may be one of many being handled by a research agency. In addition, it may be necessary to identify the filed data long after the job is finished. In the case of a personal or telephone interview it is good practice to check a proportion of calls. Alternatively, quality may be controlled by comparing the answers recorded by one interviewer with those recorded overall.

The MRS Quality Control Scheme now has a membership of 50 companies supplying research. These companies all operate above, or at least to, the standards laid down by the Scheme. All have been visited by QCS inspectors, who have required access to all their documentation relating to training supervision, quality control and the office procedures and records that are kept by each company. At the end of the inspection companies have compiled a short summary describing their field-work operation.

An example of an interview can start with the following:

'Good morning/afternoon/evening.'

SHOW INTERVIEWER BUSINESS CARD

'I am from Researchplan. We are conducting a survey on do-it-yourself activity and the sort of jobs people do around the home, and would be grateful for your help.'

In a personal interview, a card (complete with the interviewer's photograph) introduces the interviewer (provided the research supplier is a member of the MRS Quality Control Scheme), but it is still important to explain to the respondent why their privacy is being invaded. This applies whether the data is being collected face-to-face, over the telephone or by mail. In a structured survey the words used will be standard so that each respondent is introduced to the subject of the survey in the same way. These introductory remarks often appear at the beginning of the questionnaire, but if the questionnaire is mailed the introductory remarks are more likely to be the subject of a covering letter.

We discussed the placing of the classification questions and the ordering of topics in Section 5.3.6. Here we are concerned with the effect of the layout of the questionnaire on the respondent in the case of a mailed questionnaire and on the interviewer in the case of face-to-face and telephone enquiries.

It is important that the layout of the questionnaire should distinguish questions from instructions. It is good practice to use upper and lower case letters for questions and capital letters for instructions. There should also be no doubt as to who is to answer the question, for example:

ASK THOSE WHO WENT BY AIR
'Did you get there on time?'

or, for a mailed questionnaire:

'If you went by air...'

The extract from a questionnaire shown in Box 5.3 illustrates the following ground rules:

- Questions are best clearly separated from answers in the layout of the questionnaire.

- The route through the questionnaire should be immediately clear (see Q1 'SKIP to Q3').

- The interviewer must be told whether to read out the pre-coded answers (compare Q2 and Q.4). By reading out the answers as coded the interviewer stimulates the respondent's memory. If some memories are stimulated and others not, bias is introduced.

- The interviewer must be told when to show a card (the instruction at Q4 might have been SHOW CARD instead of READ OUT).

Box 5.3 The art of asking questions

In this example we assume that the first four columns are allocated to classification data.

Col. 5

Q1 Do you own an electric drill?

Yes	1	
No	2	SKIP to Q3

Col. 6

We assume 'Researchplan' is a member of the Quality Control Scheme.

Q2 What brand or make of drill
do you own at the moment?

Black & Decker	1
Wolf (and so on)	2
Other	8

Col. 7

Q3 Do you use a drill in your day-to-day work?

Yes	1
No	2

IF NOT A DRILL OWNER NOR A USER
AT WORK, CLOSE INTERVIEW

Col. 8

Q4 About how often do you use some
sort of power drill?

READ OUT

Less than once a week	1
At least once a week	2
At least every two weeks	3
About once a month	4
Less than once a month	5

Finally, in an open-ended, uncoded question ample space must be left for taking down the respondent's answer in his or her own words.

5.3.9 Pilot testing

Pre-testing a questionnaire is an important part of the research effort.[12] When designing a new questionnaire, it is best to pre-test it to gauge anticipated reactions from a sampled population, to check for ambiguities in the questions and level of understanding of the questions from the respondents, and to help in the elimination of bias. The initial choice of respondents has to be carefully selected so that it can incorporate fair representation of the target population to be surveyed. Careful screening avoids the time and cost of mistakes and enhances the accuracy of the findings.

5.4 The art of asking questions

Here we would overload the text if we attempted to do more than set out some generally accepted principles, together with examples. The content of the questionnaire is determined by the research objectives as laid down in a research proposal, and the way in which the questions are put will be influenced by the following:

- the nature of the survey population;
- the method chosen to convey the questions to the survey population.

There is interaction between those two factors. If our research objective were to predict demand for private motor cars, we might well decide to focus our enquiry on the behaviour and attitudes of new car buyers and to send questionnaires through the post because the subject is of particular interest to this survey population. We would need to define 'new' and to take account of new cars other than outright 'company' cars, whose funding is aided by employers. It would also be desirable to repeat a survey of this kind at regular intervals to establish trends.

Having determined the topics to be covered and in what detail individual topics should be investigated, we need to ask ourselves the following:

- Has the respondent got the information?
- Will the respondent understand the question?
- Is the respondent likely to give a true answer?

5.4.1 Has the respondent got the information?

It is easy to assume that the respondent has had the experience necessary to give a valid answer to your question. You can ask a respondent 'Which do you prefer for cooking, gas or electricity?' and he or she may well answer 'gas', having had no experience of electricity. He or she may use solid fuel, or may not cook at all.

Or the respondent may give you an opinion about packaged tours without having been on one. On the whole, respondents feel they ought to have an opinion. They also, on the whole, aim to please the interviewer by having an opinion to give in return for the question. The respondent may not have the information because he or she is not the right person to ask, for example they may not know how their house is insured, or the professional buyer, or purchasing officer, may not know why a particular piece of laboratory equipment is being used.

It is good practice to find out about a respondent's actual experience of a product or service before putting questions about how it is used or regarded.

5.4.2 Will the respondent understand the question?

At the pilot stage we may find that a commonly used word is variously interpreted. Everyday words like 'lunch', 'dinner' and 'tea' can be ambiguous. 'Tea' may be confused with 'supper', 'dinner' may be a midday meal or an evening one, and 'lunch' may be a 'bite' or a sit-down meal. If you want to find out how and when bacon is used, it is safer to pin the questions to 'midday meal', 'evening meal' and 'main meal'. Words such as 'generally', 'regularly' and 'usually' are a common source of ambiguity. Faced with a question about what they generally/regularly/usually do respondents either describe their recent behaviour or answer in terms of the way in which they like to think of themselves as behaving.

An unfamiliar word in a question either leads to misunderstanding or puts the interviewer into the undesirable position of having to interpret the question. Words such as 'faculty', 'facility', 'amenity', 'coverage' are not helpful in an everyday context, though they would be appropriate if the respondents were academics, insurance brokers, hoteliers or media planners.

It is easy, but of course wrong, to ask two questions in one, for example,

'Do you think Tide gets clothes clean without injuring the fabric?'

or to ramble on, so that the thread of the question is lost:

'Do you buy your dog any dog treats – by dog treats I mean any item that is outside the dog's normal diet, is consumable at one occasion (i.e. excluding rubber toys) and is not fresh food, such as human biscuits or fresh bones?'

Instead of trying to define 'dog treats' in the question it would be better, as recommended, to list all the items regarded as dog treats on the questionnaire or a show card.

5.4.3 Is the respondent likely to give a true answer?

Given that the respondent has the information and understands the question, what are the chances of the question eliciting a true answer? And, since all people are different, will they always respond to the same questions in the same way? Some respondents may not be as fluent or as accommodating as other people.

There are three outstanding hazards:

1. The respondent may find it difficult to verbalise.
2. The respondent's memory may be defective.
3. The respondent may be reluctant, or unwilling, to answer the question.

The respondent may find it difficult to verbalise

The respondent has an answer to give but cannot find the right words, or the respondent is slow and the interviewer records 'don't know' and moves on to the next question. This hazard is avoided when questions are closed and the respondent has merely to choose between possible answers. If the question is open but pre-coded, the interviewer may be tempted to read out the code answer categories to hurry the interview along. This is not desirable!

The respondent's memory may be defective

Memory varies from one individual to another, and with the importance of the event. Questions about their new car are more likely to get true answers than questions about the brand of motor oil last bought. There are three practical measures that can help respondents to remember:

1. Recall can be aided by means of a checklist.
2. The respondent may be asked to keep a diary.
3. A recording mechanism may be installed, for example, the set meter used in TV monitoring.

The diary and the mechanical device properly belong to observation as a means of collecting data. The checklist is a questionnaire component, which we have met in the form of the closed question.

By showing a card or reading out a list we are stimulating memory and we have to be definite about what and how to ask to avoid confusion with the respondent or introducing interviewer bias. If we ask a respondent what electrical appliances he has in his house we might get an incomplete answer, such as forgetting to mention the power drill in the garage. However, if the respondent is shown a list of appliances, and provided that the list is complete, the answer stands a good chance of being true. If we need to know what comes to mind unprompted, we can always ask the open question first (unaided recall) and then use the show card.

The respondent may be reluctant, or unwilling, to answer the question

We all have ideas as to what is expected of us by other people. We all have a self-image which we aim to preserve. We do not want to give ourselves away or show ourselves in a poor light. Oppenheim[12] quotes five barriers to true answers:

1. The barrier of **awareness**: 'people are frequently unaware of their own motives and attitudes'.

2. The barrier of **irrationality**: 'our society places a high premium on sensible, rational and logical behaviour'.

3. The barrier of **inadmissibility**.

4. The barrier of **self-incrimination**. These two are aspects of the same problem, the problem of reconciling our everyday behaviour and attitudes with those we consider desirable (3) and those we consider acceptable (4). For example, some respondents may fancy themselves as being able to drink large quantities of liquor but be wary of revealing their actual alcohol consumption.

5. The barrier of **politeness**: 'people often prefer not to say negative, unpleasant or critical things'. The respondent may fear repercussion from others in control, for example their superiors at work, or be motivated by kindness 'as the interviewer is only doing his/her job', or by a desire to get the interview over with as quickly as possible.

One way of getting people to talk is to use semi-structured questionnaires which enable the researcher to ask a combination of structured questions (where responses can be easily coded numerically as for yes/no answers) and open-ended questions (where respondents are led on to express their ideas and feelings). The latter is essentially 'qualitative'.

Oppenheim's barriers are, perhaps, more critical in social than in marketing research, but research at the exploratory stage may alert us to a sensitive area in our survey.

Projective techniques have been developed by clinical psychologists to enable their patients to express motivations which come up against Oppenheim's barriers. Projective techniques are sometimes used in marketing research to uncover motivations behind the opinions expressed about products and services and the communications designed to advertise them. Applications of these techniques in qualitative research are shown in Chapter 14, Box 14.4. The more commonly used techniques are as follows:

- **Sentence completion**. The respondent is asked to complete a series of sentences without 'stopping to think'.

- **Word association**. Here the stimulus is a word and the respondent is asked to give the first word that comes into his or her head. It might be 'cholesterol' in response to the prompt word 'butter'.

- **Thematic apperception test (TAT)**. The respondent is shown illustrations of critical situations and is asked to describe what is going on.

- **Cartoon test.** This is similar to the TAT except that the characters have balloons coming out of their mouths or heads and one balloon is waiting for the respondent to fill it in.

In each case the respondent is being given an ambiguous stimulus. The stimulus is meaningful to the psychologist but not to the respondent who is being given opportunities to express his or her own behaviour and attitudes without self-censorship. Interpretation of the data collected can also be ambiguous. This also applies to the responses to 'third person' questions. The respondent, on being asked 'Why do you think people …', may well give what he or she believes to be the behaviour or views of 'people', and fail to project their own.

5.5 Asking questions about attitudes

We have defined attitude as:

'a learned predisposition to respond in a consistently favourable or unfavourable manner with respect to a given object'

and opinion as:

'the expression of an underlying attitude'.

We said that the distinction between 'attitude' and 'opinion' was a fine one. In this section we do not attempt to draw the distinction, using 'attitude' throughout, as in common practice.

Respondents hold attitudes about general subjects, or 'attitude objects', such as motoring, and about specific objects such as a Range Rover. Where specific objects are concerned attitudes can be held about physical or functional properties, such as acceleration and petrol consumption or subjective and emotional ones about the kind of lifestyle suggested by Range Rover ownership. Attitudes are the product of the respondent's experience to date: what he or she has become aware of, and what he or she has come to want. They are influenced by the respondent's view of what society regards as desirable, and this influence depends on the extent to which they are inclined to conform.

We ask respondents about the attitudes they hold to help us predict their future behaviour in the market. In making predictions we should be careful to relate the attitudes expressed to the respondent's present and past behaviour.

5.6 Establishing the 'universe of content'

When we ask an attitude question we sample a 'universe of content': the body of ideas held by the relevant population about the attitude object, say driving or running a car. Depth interviews or group discussions during exploratory research will have generated a variety of statements about products or services in the market we are investigating and the contexts in which they are used. We can be reasonably sure that we have spanned the dimensions of the attitude when we no longer meet fresh ideas about the attitude object, but we cannot be entirely sure.

In order to quantify the results of this qualitative work we need to arrive at a list of statements representing the universe of content. If exploratory research has been adequately thorough we have the following in the transcribed recordings of depth interviews and/or group discussions:

- the ideas held about the attitude object by the population we are going to survey;
- the expressions used by the population when talking about these ideas.

The same basic idea may be expressed in different ways by different respondents and the compilation of an attitude battery requires considerable skill. Decisions have to be made about the order in which ideas (or topics) are put, and the number and variety of attitude statements associated with each topic. It is important to recognise that, among the statements listed, some are likely to be more important to the respondent than others. A respondent might agree strongly with both of the following statements:

'Convenience foods are a necessity to the modern housewife.'
'Convenience foods make it possible to give more time to the family.'

However, the second statement might count for more than the first with the respondent concerned. It is also important to bear in mind the fact that, in agreeing with a statement that 'Convenience foods are a necessity to the modern housewife', the respondent may be either expressing a belief ('I accept this as a true statement') or making an evaluation ('I identify with this point of view').

5.7 Choosing the type of scale

We now have to decide in what form to administer the attitude statements to the respondent. At the simplest we put the statement, in words or in writing, and ask the respondent whether he or she 'agrees' or 'disagrees' with it, or neither:

'Convenience foods are a necessity	Agree	1
to the modern housewife'	Disagree	2
	Neither agree nor disagree	3
	Don't know	4

This is a normal scale. We sum the responses by adding up the number in each of the four categories and for each statement, comparing the 'agree', 'disagree', 'neither' and 'don't know' numbers. We could, of course, compare the individual statement scores with the scores for the battery as a whole.

To establish the relative importance in rank order of the attitude statements we might construct an ordinal scale. If we were investigating attitudes towards biological detergents we might, for example, ask respondents to rank statements such as 'remove stains', 'saves time', 'no need to soak', 'gets clothes cleaner', 'the modern way', in order of importance. To summarise the responses we would allocate a number to each rank. Given five items to be ranked, the first/top position scores five, the second scores four and so on down to the fifth which scores one. The ordinal scale lacks sensitivity. However, the rank order gives no indication of the intensity with which attributes are viewed. The attribute ranked first may, for example, be far and away first for the respondent who may not find much to choose between the rest. This limitation also applies to the nominal scale. We have no indication of how strongly those who reply 'agree' do agree, nor how strongly those who reply 'disagree' do so. In order to get an indication of the strength or weakness with which an attitude is held, we need to construct rating scales. We are going to consider two commonly used types of rating scale:

- Likert summated rating scale;
- Osgood semantic differential scale.

5.7.1 The Likert scale

Using this scale a statement is put to the respondent and the respondent is asked 'Please tell me how much you agree or disagree with ...' It is common practice to give the respondent the choice of five positions (1–5) on the scale ranging from 'strongly agree' to 'strongly disagree'. To avoid responses converging on the middle ground around '3', that is, neither, some people may prefer a seven-point or a ten-point scale to have more response. The scale may be put to the respondent in the form of words printed on a show card, for example:

Agree strongly
Agree slightly
Neither agree nor disagree
Disagree slightly
Disagree strongly

For a postal survey the approach would, of course, need to be modified ('Here are some of the things ...'). Whether in a personal interview or through the mail, respondents rate themselves; these are self-rating scales. As an alternative, a diagrammatic rating scale based on the Likert approach is as follows:

Strongly agree	Slightly agree	Neither agree nor disagree	Slightly disagree	Strongly disagree
0	0	0	0	0

The statement is read out by the interviewer, or written on the questionnaire in the postal survey. The respondent is invited to point at the position that expresses his or her feeling in response to the statement, or to tick in the appropriate position in the case of a postal survey. In a personal interview the interviewer has the scale with them to show to the respondent. It is a form of show card.

The words used to denote varying strength or weakness of attitude are not immutably those quoted so far. A Likert-type scale might range from 'true to untrue' or from 'a very important reason for ...' to 'an unimportant reason for ...'.

The responses are analysed by allocating weights to scale positions. Given five scale positions we might allocate 5 to 'strongly agree', 3 for the mid-position, 1 for 'strongly disagree', or vice versa: it does not matter provided we are consistent. If the scale battery includes both positive and negative attitude statements, as most do, we have to make sure that 'strongly agree' for a negative statement rates 1 and not 5.

We can extend the scale from 1 to 7, or further, so that 1 would be 'strongly agree' and 7 'strongly disagree'. This would give a wider scope to respondents to make their choices and would reduce the tendency for respondents to avoid having to make up their minds.

We want to be able to compare the sample's total response to individual statements with its response to the battery as a whole, remembering that the statements have been chosen to span the dimensions of this attitude object, i.e. to represent 'the universe of content'. We also want to be able to compare the summed scores of individual statements, to see how responses to statements correlate.

5.7.2 The Osgood semantic differential scale

Likert-type scales are commonly used to investigate general subjects such as motoring, do-it-yourself, clothes washing. They are used to rate agreement/disagreement with the specific attributes of individual models of motor car, makes of power drill, or brands of detergent. But in practice, scales of the semantic differential type are found to be easier to administer and more meaningful to respondents when it comes to rating responses to statements about the specific attributes of named products and services, say a product or service designed to have certain desirable attributes. We want to find out whether or not and how strongly, these desirable attributes are associated with our product as compared with the competition.

Let us assume that our product is a Rover motor car and that we want to investigate attitudes towards power, styling, driver's image, petrol consumption and reliability in relation to our make/model and others in the market.

Following Osgood and his colleagues we might construct the following double-ended scales:

Good acceleration	0 0 0 0 0 0 0	Poor acceleration
Up-to-date styling	0 0 0 0 0 0 0	Out-of-date styling
Thrusting driver	0 0 0 0 0 0 0	Sluggish driver
Extravagant consumption	0 0 0 0 0 0 0	Unreliable

The respondent is asked to rate each model in turn on these attitude dimensions. It is important that the order in which the cars are named, whether by the interviewer or on a postal questionnaire, is rotated so that the Rover car is not always considered first. Semantic scales can be either mono-polar (e.g. sweet ... not sweet) or bi-polar (e.g. sweet ... sour). With bi-polar scales it is important that the two poles should be perceived as opposites by the survey population.

An example of a semantic differential scale using a scoring system is given in Box 5.4.

Box 5.4 Applications of the semantic differential scale

Developed by Charles Osgood, the semantic differential scale is a popular attitude scaling technique for measuring the preferences of a marketable object, such as brands, stores, other organisations (corporate brands) or people (e.g. political parties). The most common form is based on a number of seven-point scales anchored at each end by one of two bi-polar adjectives or phrases.

For example, recent shoppers at a supermarket might be asked to rate the following criteria to build up a store profile and aggregate analysis for individual customers. Note that the adjectives are randomly assigned as positive or negative to one side of the scale. This discourages respondents from answering on autopilot without concentration, thus avoiding the tendency to allocate the same score to each criterion. Sometimes the frequency of responses in the middle option appears high, which may be interpreted as a number of respondents reluctant to provide strong views either way. It is then difficult to discriminate between these and others who genuinely feel neutral. This difficulty can

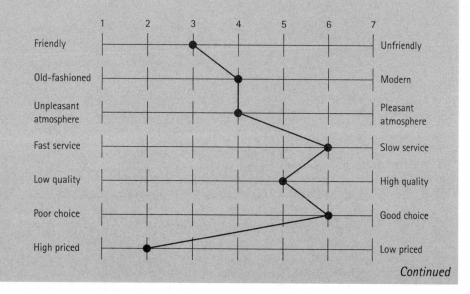

Continued

be tackled by resorting to an even number of option responses, as with the stapel scale described later. It should be acknowledged that if an even number of option responses is used, some respondents, genuinely holding neutral feelings, are forced to give an alternative and inaccurate response. The choice of scale and format of options therefore needs careful thought, as with any attitudinal scale.

A **store profile** would examine the mean or median values assigned to each adjective pair for the supermarket. Store management is then able to determine their strengths and weaknesses. Better still, if the store is rated against a relevant frame of reference, such as its main competitor, this provides management with relative strengths and weaknesses. This is commercially more meaningful to management because they can now understand how different they are from their competitors, according to their customers. For example, the consumer ratings from the mean score profile above shows that the store scores well on choice and quality, but is considered expensive, with a slow service.

A **customer profile analysis**, sometimes referred to as **aggregate analysis**, involves the summation of all the ratings across all adjective pairs for each individual. For example, the consumer ratings from the figure below show that the store scores an aggregate of 23 on service quality of its contact staff, from a maximum of 42 (6 criteria, multiplied by 7 alternative scores per criterion), which would suggest there is room for improvement in terms of staff training. Assuming more favourable ratings are allocated higher scores from 7 (most favourable) to 1 (least favourable), the score of 23 is calculated as 3+5+5+4+3+3. Note that in the case of the last criterion (difficulty in understanding) the score has been reversed (from 5 to 3) because the respondent score represents a negative attitude. If the aggregate score of this consumer was similar to the average customer score, then action should be taken for improvement.

Compared to Store X, Store Y has staff who are:

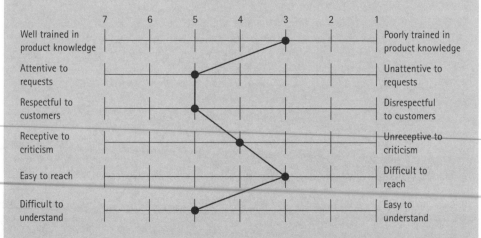

A number of issues should be considered when designing semantic differential scales. First, it is important to fine-tune the wording of the adjectives or phrases that are to be used for measurement. Adjectives used at either end of the scale should be *exact* opposites. If they are not, respondents are restricted in their choice of responses which will induce bias in the responses towards one side of a scale.

Second, as is often the case, management may be interested in assessing the relative strengths and weaknesses over a range of brands on a manifold range of criteria. To reduce the prospects of a lengthy questionnaire which may affect response rates, steps can be taken to reduce the repetition of similar questions for each and every brand.

An **upgraded semantic differential scale** involves the scoring of two or more brands on the same scale (Stem and Noazen, 1985). Thus in the above examples, several stores might be rated across each scale to save on space. Another improved format, the **numerical comparative scale** (Golden, Albaum and Zimmer, 1987), involves the respondents recording the category number that best fits their response against each scale, as shown below:

				Store 1	Store 2	Store 3
Unfriendly	1 2 3 4 5 6 7	Friendly		4	2	2
Old-fashioned	1 2 3 4 5 6 7	Modern		1	6	2
Unpleasant atmosphere	1 2 3 4 5 6 7	Pleasant atmosphere		5	4	5
Fast service	1 2 3 4 5 6 7	Slow service		2	4	1
Low quality	1 2 3 4 5 6 7	High quality		3	2	4

Interpreting these results, each store brand has its own strengths and weaknesses. For example, Store 1 has a fast service but relatively low quality, and this may or may not be influenced by an old-fashioned image. Having an old-fashioned image may or may not be a strength, depending on the customer aspirations and the type of merchandise sold. For stores selling antiques and real ale, it might be a strength, for computers it would be the opposite. Store 3 has an even faster service, but may be over-compromising on being unfriendly. It would appear that all stores could improve on quality.

Research in service quality and performance (Cronin and Taylor, 1992; Mattsson, 1992) suggests more information can be gleaned if such ratings are compared to an expectation or an ideal standard, as a benchmark of quality. This should be continuously assessed to track and meet changing customer tastes and perceptions.

Some critics have suggested that the semantic differential scale can only measure ordinal, not interval data, because the weights assigned to the scales are arbitrary.

A variant of the semantic differential scale is the **stapel scale**. This is a unipolar rating scale, and values may range from +3 to –3 or +5 to –5 to represent criteria, such as, say, friendliness, quality, value for money, and so on. The advantage of this technique lies in its simplicity, insofar as adjectives need not be pre-tested or fine-tuned to ensure precise bipolarity.

Further reading

Cronin, J.J. and Taylor, S.A. (1992), 'Measuring service quality: a reexamination and extension', *Journal of Marketing*, 56, pp.55–68.

Golden, L.L., Albaum, G. and Zimmer, M. (1987), 'The numerical comparative scale', *Journal of Retailing* (Winter), pp.393–410.

Mattsson, J. (1992), 'A service quality model based on an ideal value standard', *International Journal of Service Industry Management*, 3,3, pp.18–33.

Stem, D.E. and Noazen, S. 'Effects of number of objects and scale positions on graphic position scale reliability', in R.F. Lusch (1985), *AMA Educator's Proceedings*, AMA, Chicago, pp.370–2.

Source: Mark Davies (1998), *The Semantic Differential Scale*, Loughborough University Business School, Leicestershire.

5.7.3 Kelly's 'personal constructs'

A structured depth interview procedure using 'cards' based on Kelly's theory of personal constructs can help respondents to express their views about individual brands, products and models:

- The product (or service) field is represented by names on cards, photographs of models or of packs, or by the packs themselves, depending on what stimulus is most appropriate.

- The respondent is handed a pack of cards and is asked to discard any brand, name or model that is unfamiliar.

- The retained cards are shuffled by the interviewer who deals three to the respondent.

- The respondent is asked to say one way in which two of the brands or models named on the cards are the same and yet different from the third.

The answer is the respondent's personal construct and it can be used to form a semantic scale. For example, faced with cards showing three shampoos, a respondent might make one of the following responses:

'These two are scented, that one isn't' (monopolar semantic scale);
'These two are for greasy hair, that one's for dry hair' (bipolar scale).

The shuffling and dealing of triads goes on until 'the respondent can no longer think of any reason why two items are different from the third'. The procedure is fully described by Sampson in the *Consumer Market Research Handbook*.[13]

5.7.4 Some further considerations

It has been found that too many scale positions confuse respondents and demand too much of their capacity to discriminate. However, we need at least five because there is a tendency to avoid the extreme scale positions, especially the negative ones.

Giving the respondent an even number of scale positions to choose from forces choice. There is no middle position to accommodate uncertainty. Opinions vary as to whether this is a desirable practice or not. When choice is forced, a more clear-cut verdict 'for' or 'against' is delivered but this may be dangerously misleading.

If a product or service is liked, the respondent may automatically rate it high on all attributes (the halo effect) and, in the course of scoring his or her own attitude on a large number of attitude scales, the respondent may get into the habit of going for the same position on the scale. This tendency is less likely if favourable (positive) and unfavourable (negative) statements are interspersed.

When attaching weights to responses to attitude statements it is important to discriminate between favourable and unfavourable statements and to maintain a consistent direction. This is illustrated by Green and Tull.[14] See Box 5.5.

Box 5.5 Example: consumer attitudes towards the advertising industry

Item 1: Advertising contributes very importantly to America's industrial prosperity.

Item 2: Advertising merely inflates the prices I must pay for products without giving me any information.

Item 3: Advertising does inform the public and is worth the cost.

Item 4: The American public would be better off with no advertising at all.

Item 5: Advertising old products is a waste of the consumer's dollar.

Item 6: I wouldn't mind if all advertising were stopped.

Item 7: I wish there was more advertising than exists now.

Three of these scale items (or attitude statements) are favourable towards the advertising industry (1, 3 and 7), and four are unfavourable (2, 4, 5 and 6).

A Likert-type scale is used:

Strongly approve   Approve   Undecided   Disapprove   Strongly disapprove

and each subject (or respondent) underscores 'the description that most suits his/her feeling' towards each statement.

Green and Tull use the following weights:

+2   +1   0   −1   −2

(The procedure is the same if weights running from 5 for 'strongly approve' down to 1 for 'strongly disapprove' are used.)

For items classified as favourable these weights are used without modification. For items classified as unfavourable, the order of the weights is reversed so as to maintain a consistent direction.

Application of the weights is illustrated in the following example, based on the responses of one subject to the seven items:

Item	Response	Weight
1	Strongly approve	+2
2	Disapprove	+1
3	Approve	+1
4	Strongly disapprove	+2
5	Disapprove	+1
6	Strongly disapprove	+2
7	Strongly approve	+2
	Total score	11

As a matter of interest, it is assumed by Green and Tull that these seven items are taken from a scale battery of 100 items.

The data derived from weighted responses to rating scales is used as the basis for sophisticated statistical analyses.

It is important to remember the following:

- the scale positions and the weights attached to them are arbitrarily fixed;
- with the scales in common use in marketing research, distance between positions appears equal but for the respondent this is not necessarily the case. A distance in strength of feeling between 'approve' and 'strongly approve' may well be different from the distance between 'disapprove' and 'strongly disapprove', but responses are weighted as if the distances were equal.

The rating scales in common use give us useful assessments of the way in which consumers respond to attitude statements about products and services and the needs these are designed to meet. The statistical data derived from rating scales enables us to make comparisons and draw useful conclusions, but it is not, strictly speaking, a measurement.

5.8 Conclusion

The questioning techniques discussed in this chapter may be applied to a wide range of descriptive surveys, from a simple recording of products, services and brands in current use to the collection of data about how these were acquired, how they are used, why they are used, why they were chosen and how far they go to meet the needs as perceived by the respondents.

Asking questions remains the most fruitful way of collecting statistical data about consumer behaviour. From an examination of the relationships between habits, awareness, attitudes and needs revealed in answers to questions it is possible to arrive at a sufficiently robust understanding of consumer behaviour to formulate hypotheses as to 'what might happen next', or 'what might happen if'.

REFERENCES

1. Payne, S. (1951), *The Art of Asking Questions*, Princeton University Press. The classic text on this subject. Excerpts are quoted in J. Seibert and G. Willis (eds) (1970), *Marketing Research*, Penguin, Harmondsworth.

2. *Magazine of the Market Research Society* (1993), 'A very clear "Thank you"...' July, no. 326, p.3.

3. Fabridge, V. (1980), 'Introduction to Fieldwork and Data Processing', supp. to the *MRS Newsletter*, no.177 (Dec.).

4. Sykes, W. (1991), 'Taking stock: issues from the literature on validity and reliability in qualitative research', *Journal of the Market Research Society*, Jan., vol.33, no.1, pp.3–12.

5. Hahle, G. (1992), 'Examining the validity of re-interviewing respondents for quantitative surveys', *JMRS*, April, vol. 34, no.2, pp. 99–117.

6. Brennan, M., Hoek, J. and Astridge, C. (1991), 'The effects of monetary incentives on the responses rate and cost effectiveness of a mail survey', *JMRS*, July, vol.33, no.3, pp.229–41.

7. Market Research Society (1987), *Guide to Good Coding Practice*.

8. Collins, M. (1992) 'The data reduction approach to survey analysis', *JMRS*, April, vol. 34, no.2, pp.149–62.

9. Wolfe, A. (ed.) (1984), *Standardised Questions*: *A Review for Market Research Executives*, 2nd edn, The Market Research Society, London.

10. Belson, W. (1982), 'A comparison of open-ended and check-list questioning systems', MRS Conference Papers.

11. Reynolds, N., Diamantopoulos, A. and Schlegelmilch, B. (1993), 'Predicting in questionnaire design: a review of the literature and suggestions for further research', *JMRS*, April, vol.35, no.2, pp.171–82.

12. Oppenheim, A. (1970), *Questionnaire Design and Attitude Measurement*, Heinemann Educational Books, London.

13. Sampson, P. (1986), 'Qualitative research and motivation' in R. Worcester and J. Downham (eds), *Consumer Market Research Handbook*, 3rd edn, Elsevier Press, Amsterdam.

14. Green, P. and Tull D.S. (1988), *Research for Marketing Decisions*, Prentice Hall, Englewood Cliffs NJ.

FURTHER READING

Belson, W. (1986), *Validity in Survey Research*, Gower, London.

Collins, M. and Courtenay, G. (1984), 'The effect of survey form on survey data', MRS Conference Papers.

Parasuraman, A. (1991), *Marketing Research*, Addison-Wesley, Reading MA, Chapters 10 and 11.

QUESTIONS

Imagine that you are designing a questionnaire for a face-to-face usage and attitude survey of the in-home wine-drinking habits of the population (British, Dutch, American, French, etc.).

1. (a) Define the population of interest (the survey population) and prescribe population breakdowns, taking account of the statistical data quoted.
   (b) Draft classification questions and pre-code them.

2. List topics of interest and construct a flow chart to illustrate the ordering of topics and the route taken through the questionnaire by the interviewer.

3. Draft the questionnaire including introductory comments and instructions to the interviewer.

4. Pre-code answers wherever possible.

Users of table wine (base all adults)

Heavy users	3–5 bottles a month	7.5
Medium users	1–2 bottles a month	20.0
Light users	Less than 1 bottle a month	29.5
All users		57.0
Non-users		43.0

Demographic profile (base all users)
For an example of social grade classification, see Chapter 13, Table 1.2

Men	47.4	15–24	18.7	AB	23.9
Women	52.6	25–34	21.2	C1	27.2
		35–44	18.5	C2	29.0
		45–54	14.5	D	14.1
		55–64	13.3	E	5.8
		65 +	13.8		

CASE STUDY 5.1

Red Rose: An investigation into service excellence in the building industry[†]

Introduction

Red Rose Building Services is a small company, geographically positioned in Darwen, a small town in the north west of England. The organisation was founded in 1988 and from small beginnings has expanded, employing a total of 90 workers. There seems to be no organisational structure and management tend to be laissez-faire in their management style.

There are two managers who control the business, Mr Mark Holden (Manager A) and Mr Mick Anderson (Manager B), two young men in their early thirties, with a great deal of practical experience, but no real business or academic qualifications. The management of the company are at present contemplating down-sizing the firm, because they have described the business as being 'totally out of control'. The workforce is not multiskilled to perform a variety of jobs, which in this industry range from drylining, plastering and studding to taping abilities. Workers perform jobs in pairs, but do not tend to adopt a team approach to activities. Many of the workers also have a problem with punctuality and reliability, which are considered important characteristics contributing towards service quality within this industry. Management have indicated that they lack the theoretical business knowledge to run the business effectively. Surprisingly, the company is still making huge annual profits.

[†]This case study was contributed by C. Vignali (Manchester Metropolitan University), M.D. Vignali (Croydon College) and D. Vrontis (Manchester Metropolitan University).

Red Rose's target market is 100% industry and the firm's client base consists of a total of 23 clients, for whom they provide services including, primarily, the drylining and plastering of newly built homes. Manager A has indicated that relationships within the business need improving dramatically, but has no real idea where to begin. Management/client relationships vary, but on the whole there are only a handful that can be considered good and that is because such clients have been with Red Rose from its early beginnings and are thus slightly more understanding with problems such as unreliability. The relationships between the workers and clients is somewhat different and clients in the industry have described the lay people as having attitudinal problems as well as foul language. Manager A thankfully emphasises that the only strong relationships within the firm are between the managers of Red Rose and suppliers such as Keyline, British Gypsum and Lafarge. These suppliers constantly maintain their end of the bargain, supplying raw materials such as plaster board on time as and when required. There is something of an irony, however, in the relationship being defined as good. It is only recently that Red Rose received a court summons from Keyline because Red Rose had failed to pay for goods supplied by Keyline in March of this year.

Management at Red Rose work from one office, where a receptionist is employed to deal with documentary information such as the filing of invoices and completion of wages forms. The receptionist is also responsible for answering the telephone and recording important messages. Manager A has indicated that the receptionist is useless as she is only 17 and would prefer to spend her time reading magazines, rather than concentrating on her job. Because of this, both Manager A and Manager B are constantly amending invoices which have been filed in the wrong place and wage forms which have been completed incorrectly. The firm also employs a surveyor, who is responsible for pricing up all the work on behalf of the clients.

Red Rose's main competitors have been described as other drylining companies offering services in close proximity. It has been emphasised by the interviewee, however, that there is no real need to compete in this industry, because there will always be work which needs completing for the larger firms.

In terms of implementing human resource policies, the firm spends little time selecting workers, and although some training is conducted, no budget, time or commitment is invested in people. Manager A believes that this would be far too costly and probably too demanding. Workers join and leave the firm on a regular basis, so it would also be a waste of money. All workers are subcontracted, so Manager A has indicated that each is their own boss. In other words, if they have just been paid for a job, they might not turn up for work for two days, even if Red Rose is desperate for workers.

Red Rose is a firm driven solely by money. After a general conversation with both managers, it is clear that making money is the organisation's prime objective. The firm is by no means marketing orientated. The only promotion the firm conducts, is to send a one-page letter out to various construction firms, informing them about Red Rose's services. When asked about service quality, Manager A indicated that 'doing a good job' was all that mattered in providing a service offering that would keep clients happy. The essence of providing 'a good job' does not seem to be understood by both managers.

In the construction industry, although service providers do not regularly come face-to-face with the clients, some contact is made and there is regular interaction over the telephone. The client is still receiving an experience, so the attitude and level of knowledge

Continued

conveyed over the telephone still creates a perceived impression of the service firm in the mind of the receiver. The level of interaction between service provider and client is thus highly relevant in imparting a professional approach to the client. Although interpersonal skills over the telephone may not be as important in the construction industry as in banking, for example, delivering high levels of service still depends on a willing attitude and a certain degree of integrity. Therefore, creating an appropriate environment where an effective human resource policy can be implemented successfully is as important in helping a firm to succeed in the construction industry as it is in the retail sector or banking. For Red Rose to prosper its managers and workforce needed to understand what the essence of delivering the appropriate service quality meant.

Exploratory research using an initial interview

This was carried out to establish the objectives and criteria of research. Through an exploratory initial interview conducted with both managers the context of the problems facing the firm was established:

1. The service offering provided by Red Rose is not up to standard. One of the major objectives of the firm is to raise prices, because in relation to their competitors, Red Rose's prices are much cheaper. However, if the service offering is not up to standard, the organisation may need to concentrate first on improving service quality

2. There is a need to focus on how service quality can be achieved through implementing human resource policies effectively. Again, this goes back to a complete re-evaluation of the organisation's overall structure and culture, so that people can be managed in an environment which promotes motivation and commitment.

3. There is a need to diversify, e.g. into painting. This is another area the firm may need to reconsider. Diversification is a useful strategy for broadening a market base, but it may be necessary to concentrate first on the core business activities and to become more sophisticated in their approach to the service offering, before looking for expansion possibilities. This goal in itself is a contradiction to Manager A's stated wish to downsize the firm. It is a reflection of a poor theoretical understanding of business.

The management at Red Rose are convinced that there is no real need to compete in this industry, particularly if the construction industry is booming. However, Manager B indicated that their key to success is to be able to offer cheap prices to their customers. This is because Red Rose have managed to form strong relationships with some of the major suppliers: Lafarge and British Gypsum. Materials can thus be bought at a cheaper price. By working on slightly lower profit margins, the firm is able to offer competitive prices to some of its main clients, including Wimpey and Barratt. If a major organisational goal is to increase prices, the service offering would probably become much more important. Kotler (1997) indicates that when a product has a premium price, the consumer's expectations in terms of added benefits also increases. It is thus possible to assume that the firm is successful at the moment because its service offering is priced cheaply, so any flaws in the quality of that service are more easily accepted, the cheap price compensating for any delays in the completion of works. However, once a firm begins to charge higher prices, it is evident that its clients' expectations will rise also (Gronroos, 1991).

While there are some good relationships with clients, there are also many problematic ones. In the interview, Manager A indicated that the number of client complaints is enormous, one of the main reasons being that Red Rose cannot always supply men when there is a demand. This issue overlaps with the point that the firm has few multiskilled workers. An interesting comment made was that Red Rose is due to take Armstrong's Homes, one of its main clients, to court in the near future. Armstrong's have failed to make their outstanding payments for work conducted by Red Rose Services. It seems apparent that in this industry, both the supplier and buyer of a service have a duty of care for the relationship to be classified as being 'good'. When this matter was investigated further, by probing the interviewee, it became apparent that Armstrong's had failed to pay because of their great dissatisfaction in the service experience they had obtained. Their argument was one which clarifies the lack of appropriate people management within this industry (Keynote, 1995). Armstrong's were unhappy with the way they had been spoken to by the workers on site, the 'shabbiness' of the workmanship and the fact that it had taken an extra three weeks to complete a site, because of unreliable and inexperienced lay people. The point of the matter here emphasises the unsophisticated service offering adopted by the firm and the organisation's lack of customer orientation.

The insights gained from the exploratory discussion illustrate that the organisation is extremely money orientated, which tends to be a general trend in the industry. The firm also tends to review many of its business activities on a short-term basis. There is no strategic plan that considers important issues which may need to be looked at in order to improve the company's service offering.

Specific objectives

From the exploratory research, specific objectives were devised to direct the investigation. These were:

1. To evaluate which component of service quality, technical or functional, is regarded as being more important to customers in the building industry and to examine if, and if so how, this affects the way the workforce is managed.

2. To evaluate management of quality in order to compare and contrast the service which is actually being delivered against the service being received by customers. It is thus necessary to examine first of all the level of importance management place on the criteria for assessing service quality.

3. To examine the organisational culture of the proposed company for study in order to evaluate the positive or negative effects the organisational set-up has on business performance and to determine whether this has an impact on the quality of service being offered to customers.

4. To examine whether service excellence is linked to the level of workforce commitment using a semi-structured questionnaire to establish their attitudes about certain aspects of their work and whether some of the key aspects to obtaining organisational commitment are being met.

Reasons for adopting the semi-structured approach

Semi-structured interviews differ from focused methods such as structured interviews in that questions are normally specified, but the interviewer is freer to probe beyond the answers in a manner which would appear prejudicial to the aims of standardisation and comparability. Qualitative information about the topic can then be recorded by the

Continued

interviewer, who can seek both clarification and elaboration on the answers given. It is primarily for this reason that semi-structured interviews have been chosen as a research method for this study. They will allow more latitude to probe beyond the answers and thus enter into a new dialogue with the interviewee. These types of interviews are also said to allow people to answer more on their own terms than in a standardised interview, while still providing a greater structure for comparability. May (1997) emphasises that the investigator must also be able to record the nature of the interview and the way in which the questions were asked.

The important factor, as with all types of research methods, is how the information obtained will be analysed. The section below on data analysis will investigate this issue in greater detail.

The first semi-structured interview

The first semi-structured interview has been used to establish the context of the firm and the questions can be found in Exhibit 5.1. The purpose of conducting this initial interview was to find out some generic details about the company in terms of its basic annual turnover, a competitor analysis, the firm's predominant target market, the main clients, how many employees make up the workforce, some general views on management's perception of the relationships within the firm and attitudes towards certain human resource policies.

The initial exploratory interview is important because it gives guidance on how to structure questions for the rest of the research to be conducted. For example, Red Rose employs 90 workers and the business caters for 23 different clients in the construction industry. This information is vital as it is necessary to know whether the workforce is of a sufficient sample size to conduct a questionnaire.

Exhibit 5.1 Establishing the context of the firm

1 When was your organisation founded? How many offices exist and can you explain any major developments in terms of business processes that you have experienced?

2 Can you indicate approximately how much the firm turns over each year and how does this compare with your major competitors?

3 Can you explain who your major competitors are, and how do you aim to compete effectively?

4 Can you define your target market?
   Probe: Do you cater for the general public and industry and if so, what in percentage terms is the distribution of labour?

5 Does the workforce primarily work on empty premises?

6 How many major contracts do you have and how would you define your relationship with these clients?

7 How many workers do you have and could you explain
   (i)   how they work together?
   (ii) how they are managed?

8 Do you subcontract?

9 How do you recruit and select?
   Probe: What criteria do you use to select your subcontractors?

10 Do you think training and development is important and if so, do you contribute in terms of time and resources?

11 Finally, can you discuss how you market yourself as a firm and explain how you ensure a quality service is delivered?

The main research investigation was conducted using two semi-structured questionnaires, one with top management (Exhibit 5.2) and the other one with the workforce (Exhibit 5.3).

The semi-structured interview geared towards top management

The interview questions are found in Exhibit 5.2. The purpose of repeating the interview with each manager on a one-to-one basis is to obtain another perspective on the business and to compare and contrast answers. This will also give some idea of how efficient communication is within the firm and whether top management (the two senior managers) have contrasting views of how the workforce should be managed.

Th questions were designed to find out what the perceived present structure and culture of the firm was, relationships and management of people within the firm, lines of communication and empowerment. According to May (1997) question wording is of the utmost importance if the results are to be of value. Questions should not be too general or insufficiently specific. It is also important to use the simplest language possible to convey the meaning of the question, bearing in mind the intended audience. This is important, particularly in this context, because management will be unfamiliar with many of the academic terms, such as 'empowerment'.

Exhibit 5.2 Semi-structured interview geared towards top management

Organisational structure/culture

1 Can you explain what you see your role as manager involving?

2 If you were to describe yourself as a manager, what characteristics would you use to describe yourself?

3 Could you please describe a normal day's work.

4 Is there a large amount of pressure/stress involved with your duties and if so why?

5 What are your main expectations of the workforce?

6 Who would you say has the most responsibility in the firm? Or is it shared? Do you delegate any responsibility?

7 How would you describe your relationship with the workforce?

8 Can you give examples of types of decisions you might have to make while doing a day's work?

9 Would you say your organisation takes a team-orientated approach to business activities?

Relationships

10 Can you explain your relationships with some of your clients? Give examples of good and bad ones and the reasons why they are good/bad.

Communications

11 Can you describe how you communicate to one another in the firm?

People management

12 What criteria do you use to select appropriate workers within your firm?

13 Do you consider training to be important to overall business performance?
   Probe: Does the firm train, budget, assess training progress?

14 Can you describe how you manage your workforce?

Continued

Empowerment

15   What do you think are the main needs of your workforce and what motivates them?

Service quality

16   Can you describe what you think offering a good service involves?

17   Do you get any complaints and if so who deals with them?

The semi-structured questionnaire geared towards the workforce

May (1997) states that questionnaires are useful for measuring facts, attitudes or behaviour through questions that respondents can understand. A questionnaire was developed (Exhibit 5.3) aimed at finding out what the workforce attitudes are and what their specific needs or desires towards work were.

Exhibit 5.3: Semi-structured questionnaire geared towards workforce attitudes

1   What do you consider to be the most important thing for making sure you provide a good service?

   (a)   Being reliable, i.e. ensuring you turn up to do the job on a regular basis.

   (b)   Being consistent in your workmanship, i.e. making sure that you do a good job, for every site you complete.

   (c)   Being flexible, i.e. being able to do a variety of jobs, plastering, dabbing, studding, etc.

   (d)   All of the above.

   (e)   Being friendly and pleasant to the client.

2   What do you think are the two most important characteristics of your job?

   (a)   Workmanship, i.e. how skilful you are at doing your job.

   (b)   Punctuality, i.e. making sure you turn up to the job on time.

   (c)   Both of the above.

   (d)   The ability to do a variety of jobs, i.e. being able to dryline, dab and tape.

   (e)   Being reliable, skilful and punctual.

3   Do you think being pleasant and having a good attitude when dealing with the client is important in this job?

   (a) Yes, definitely   (b) Sometimes   (c) Not really   (d) Definitely not

4   Are you happy at work?

   (a) Yes   (b) Not really   (c) Sometimes   (d) No   (e) Not sure

5   Are you supervised at work regularly?

   (a) Yes   (b) No   (c) Sometimes

6   How would you describe management's leadership style?

   (a) Domineering   (b) Distant   (c) Team orientated   (d) Too friendly and lax

7   Do you come into contact with management regularly?

   (a) Yes   (b) No   (c) Sometimes/Depends

8   How would you describe your relationship with management?

   (a) Excellent   (b) Very good   (c) Good   (d) Satisfactory   (e) Poor

9   Do you feel your job is relatively secure?

   (a) Yes   (b) No   (c) Not sure

10 When was the last time you had a chat with your managers about your performance at work, i.e. how well you are doing or whether you've made any mistakes?

   (a) In the last 3 months

   (b) In the last 6 months

   (c) In the last year

   (d) In the last 3 years

   (e) Never

11 Would you like to be promoted, if there was the option, to maybe a supervisor?

   (a) Yes   (b) No   (c) Not sure

12 Are you attending any training courses at present?

   (a) Yes   (b) No   (c) Possibly in the future   (d) Definitely in the future

13 Have you received or will you receive any training on the job?

   (a) Yes   (b) No   (c) Not sure   (d) Probably

14 Does Red Rose offer any of the following?

   (a) Money incentives

   (b) Rewards if you do a good job

   (c) Pension schemes

   (d) Most of the above

   (e) None of the above

15 Are you happy with your pay?

   (a) Yes   (b) No   (c) Not really

16 Are you given any responsibility in your job?

   (a) Yes   (b) No   (c) Sometimes

17 Does this responsibility give you stress?

   (a) Yes   (b) No   (c) Sometimes   (d) Other (i.e. not applicable)

18 Are you rewarded for this responsibility in any way?

   (a) Yes   (b) No   (c) Other (i.e. not applicable)

19 Does the responsibility make you feel important?

   (a) Yes   (b) No   (c) Other (i.e. not applicable)

20 How loyal and committed are you to Red Rose?

   a) Extremely loyal

   b) Very loyal

   c) Fairly loyal

   d) Would leave if another job was offered (same pay)

   e) No comment

Data analysis methods

It is important to establish how the entire research is to be analysed and evaluated as this will form the basis for providing suitable conclusions (May, 1997). In the first instance, the semi-structured interviews were recorded and the transcripts were used as a starting point for the evaluation of the findings. While being attractive, recording has advantages and disadvantages. These can be categorised in terms of interaction and

Continued

transcription and interpretation. Transcription is a long process and a one-hour tape can take eight or nine hours to transcribe fully, depending upon one's typing ability (Feagin, 1991). However, tape recording can assist interpretation as it allows the interviewer to concentrate on the conversation and record the non-verbal gestures of the interviewee during the interview. It is then necessary to employ techniques which can make some analytic sense of raw data. Conventional methods of achieving this involve the coding of open-ended replies in order to permit comparison.

Coding has been defined as:

> the general term for conceptualising data; thus, coding includes raising questions and giving provisional answers about categories and about their relations. (Strauss, 1988, pp.20–1)

The way in which data is categorised will depend upon the aims of the research and theoretical interests. In relation to this study, the broad aim is an investigation into service excellence in the construction industry and how this can be achieved through well-integrated human resource policies. It will therefore be necessary to understand key categories associated with this aim, such as organisational structure, culture, management styles, decision-making, commitment, empowerment, communication and attitudes towards training and development and general people management, and code the responses obtained from the research in order to compare and contrast different levels of analysis obtained through the interview process.

In terms of analysing the questionnaires about the workforce attitudes the same methods were used as above.

Findings from the semi-structured interviews

Both managers share the entire responsibility for the business, and both regard the management role as one which primarily involves organising the workforce.

Comparing the two managers throughout the interviews, it is apparent that each tends to adopt a different style. Manager B believes that taking an interest in workers should be a priority, as this 'makes them work harder'. On the other hand, Manager A believes he is approachable, but gives many orders to ensure jobs are completed on time. Manager B has mentioned adopting a friendly appropriate approach when dealing with workers. He does, however, indicate that although this approach may be suitable in the short term, it doesn't always work in the long term.

Red Rose is still working within the idea of being cost-led, but the findings from both questionnaires suggest that the management and workforce understand the benefits of being services-orientated. It is more a case of the environmental circumstances, such as the firm's structure, underlying culture and lack of effective people management, which is prohibiting the achievement of a high quality service offering to clients.

Another delay in enabling the firm to deliver service excellence is that the building industry is prone to recession. With most firms experiencing a period of limited growth, there had been a serious cut back in training and development, resulting in a workforce that was predominantly underskilled. Manager A commented that before the recession there was no real need to compete, since there was plenty of work. He stated that it is in times of hardship that the need to compete on service becomes much more important. In fact, the recession has made many small firms realise that being completely services-orientated is of primary importance, in contrast to the traditional view of being cost-led and simply having the ability to provide labour.

The findings show that although the prime goals and objectives of Red Rose justify the comments made by Mintel (1996), in that the emphasis is primarily based upon offering a competitive price and being able to provide labour in relation to demand, there was no indication to suggest that the firm is committed to designing effective training programmes or a culture which will create a more highly committed and motivated workforce. First of all, this attainment is perhaps unachievable given the current structural format adopted by Red Rose. The evidence from the findings suggests that the firm is out of control, since it operates on a web basis. The fact that the firm now incorporates too many members for the present structure means that communication is ineffective within the company, and communication is known to be vital in obtaining workforce commitment.

Red Rose is driven by a culture which is concerned with dealing with the immediate, rather than having a strategic approach which incorporates a mission to a commitment to employee development and being totally service-orientated. The findings prove that the reason for this is again due to the firm's inappropriate structure, and thus the need to deal with the immediate, since there is no control over business activities. The evidence has suggested that management do understand the need for an improved service offering, yet are in a position where their ability to provide this offering is impossible, due mainly to the prevailing structure and culture.

In terms of management style, there is an inconsistent approach being adopted by Managers A and B. The literature discusses the importance of creating an appropriate climate which promotes employee commitment. Part of this creation involves a culture which involves all members striving towards a similar goal. The evidence has suggested that first of all there is no strategic mission and secondly, workers are treated differently by each manager. Manager B's approach is described as being 'very friendly' and quite 'laissez-faire'. Manager A, in contrast, adopts a more authoritative and dictative role, which perhaps has the effect of causing confusion amongst workers as to which approach is right or wrong. The findings have illustrated that neither approach is effective, and again the reason for this is because there are no systems installed that effectively identify the needs of workers and that support and attempt to meet these needs successfully.

For instance, in terms of technical quality – this being the skills of workers – research was conducted to assess the attitudes of workforce members. It is evident that there is a gap between what management feel the needs of workers to be and the actual responses given by workforce members. An evaluation of the semi-structured interviews revealed that management are solely driven by money. The findings suggest that this to a certain extent is true; 80% of workers are not happy with their pay, which is perhaps another reason for low motivation within the firm. The research did indicate, however, that 10% were not interested in advancement prospects, 37% were interested, and 53% were unsure. This illustrates that the majority of workers are, or might be, interested in developing themselves, but are not being given the opportunity. Other factors prohibiting motivation and commitment are centred around the lack of incentives and the fact that a majority felt their jobs were insecure and that they were not being provided with enough help and support in terms of developing their skills. Hence, when asked about how loyal they were to Red Rose, only 7% indicated that they were extremely loyal.

Continued

Conclusion

Workers felt unhappy because they were given heavy workloads without an increase in responsibility, this being defined by the workers as ensuring they were reliable, constantly available to provide high quality workmanship, yet are not rewarded for their efforts, or supported by management in terms of their training. As a consequence, 73% of workers believed there was a great deal of stress involved with their work.

Another issue prohibiting service excellence within this industry were the ineffective relationships between all stakeholders involved with the company. The findings illustrated that the management/worker relationship on the surface tends to be decent; 50% of workers felt they had a satisfactory relationship. However, 73% felt that management were either domineering or distant in their approach. The fact that the research illustrated that the majority of workers were dissatisfied at work for one reason or another, illustrates again the lack of an appropriate structure, culture and commitment towards various human resource policies to improve the situation.

Relationships between the clients and workers are thus poor, because employees are unreliable, they have a punctuality problem and an attitude problem and clients on the whole are dissatisfied with the service performance. This was highlighted throughout the semi-structured interviews.

This case study serves to highlight the usefulness of semi-structured questionnaires to probe, via the personal interviewing technique, into the attitudes, motivations and behaviour of managers and the workforce concerning the delivery of service quality.

References

Feagin, J.R. (1991), *A Case for Case Study*, University of North Carolina Press, Chapel Hill.

Gronroos, C. (1991), 'The marketing strategy continuum: towards a marketing concept for the 1990s', *Management Decision*, pp. 7–13.

Keynote (1995), *The Home Building Industry*, Keynote Publishers, London.

Kotler, P. (1997), *Marketing Management*, Prentice Hall.

May, T. (1997), *Social Research: Issues Methods and Process*, Open University Press.

Mintel (1996), *Homes and Housing*, Special Report, Market Intelligence, London.

Strauss, A., (1988), *Qualitative Analysis for Social Scientists*, Cambridge University Press, Cambridge.

Questions

1. Do you think the exploratory research carried out established the objectives and criteria of the research?
2. Do you agree with the research plan undertaken by the researchers or do you think there is a better way they could plan their empirical research and collect data? Discuss.
3. Critically evaluate and judge the data analysis methods. What alternative method would you propose?

6 Spreadsheets in marketing research

The essential electronic toolkit

Mike Hussey

The year 1999 marked the twenty-first anniversary of the spreadsheet.

6.1 Introduction

Despite the rumour that the first manual spreadsheet was used by the East India Company in the later half of the eighteenth century, there can be little doubt that the electronic spreadsheet was invented in 1978 by Daniel Brinklin, an MBA student at Harvard. He is reported to have developed a 5-column by 20-row prototype in order to obtain an improved 'solution' to a case study.

During the summer of 1978 Brinklin was joined by Bob Frankston and Daniel Flystra, who not only improved the program coding but introduced marketing expertise into the partnership. Software Arts was formed in the same year and by 1979, when Brinklin had completed his degree, VisiCalc was launched at $100 per head. The novel software was aimed at the Apple II computer and the effect was immediate – many people bought computers simply to be able to run the spreadsheet package. In total, about 1 million copies of VisiCalc were sold.

Unfortunately, VisiCalc was slow to respond to the introduction of the IBM PC with its Intel chip. Lotus 1-2-3, developed by Mitch Kapor, quickly became the industry standard. Amongst other things it introduced the cell referencing system that is used today and added a graphics facility. By 1985 Lotus had bought Software Arts and discontinued VisiCalc.

Excel was launched for the Apple Macintosh 512K in 1985. With a proper graphics interface, true pull-down menus and a 'point and click' mouse it became the natural flagship product when Microsoft unveiled its original Windows environment in 1987. Excel remained the only Windows spreadsheet until 1992 .

Today there are three well-known spreadsheet programs, Microsoft Excel, Quattro Pro and Lotus 1-2-3. Excel is the clear market leader.

In a UK survey on end-user computing, Hirst[1] first drew attention to the large number of marketing managers and directors using spreadsheets for data analysis, sales forecasting and for developing their own decision support systems. Further empirical evidence for the extensive use of the electronic spreadsheet in marketing is shown in Table 6.1. The figures relate to the uses of PCs within the marketing departments of a sample of 437 European companies. Besides noting the very high incidence of spreadsheet use it can be observed that the categories of survey analysis,

Table 6.1 Uses of computers in marketing

Use	Sample % (n=437)
Word processing	94
Spreadsheets	88
Databases	87
Survey analysis	49
Analysing data	61
Sales forecasting	52
Market modelling	26
Marketing information systems/DSS	44

Source: Hussey and Hooley, 1994[2].

database analysis, sales forecasting and market modelling all fall within the subject area of marketing research.

More detailed information on the software used by marketing research companies when carrying out work for clients can be seen in Table 6.2. When the overall figure of 82% for spreadsheet usage amongst the 240 members of the European Society for Opinion and Market Research (ESOMAR) is examined more closely, it can be seen that the larger companies, i.e. those employing upwards of 50 people, actually recorded an incidence of 96% for spreadsheet usage when working for clients.

More specific applications range from the use of spreadsheets in competitive sales intelligence[3] through the computation of customer lifetime value[4] to target marketing applications.[5 and 6] Davirs[7] even describes how a spreadsheet might be used to improve service quality to customers by noting that BMW provide their customers with a template in order to enable them to evaluate fuel economy.

From the above evidence it is clear that the spreadsheet plays a major role in the analysis of both marketing and marketing research data.

Before moving on it is perhaps useful to note that Gorski and Ingram[8] suggest that a good market analysis system needs three basic components: a data input

Table 6.2 Software used when carrying out work for clients by marketing research companies

Use	Sample % (n=240)
Spreadsheets	82
Databases	70
Survey analysis packages	80
CATI	50
Specialist modelling software	38
MIS	20

Source: Hussey and Hooley, 1995.

facility, data manipulation techniques and good data output capabilities. Contemporary spreadsheets more than meet these three criteria.

6.2 The electronic scratchpad

Just using the spreadsheet as a calculation aid can be a major benefit at the start of the marketing research process. Working out field interview costs, hourly rates for telephone calling and travel expenses all need to be carefully evaluated if a research agency is to be sure of making a viable profit.

One of the first decisions that a marketing research company has to make is whether or not to pitch for a particular contract. This will depend on, amongst other things, the value of the work, the likelihood of getting the contract, the cost of preparing the presentation and likely profit levels.

Figure 6.1 gives an example of a possible input screen for a project evaluation exercise. In essence it requires research directors to enter a number of subjective probabilities about the likely outcome of the project bid as well as likelihoods of profit levels.

The output screen, Figure 6.2, displays simulated profit statistics indicating that the chance of making a profit is 71.6% and the expected profit from the project is £33.9K.

In this example the spreadsheet function RAND() has been used to provide a simulated solution. A simple probability calculation would have given the exact probability of making a profit as 72% but it would have been more tedious to evaluate the precise expected profit figure of £34.5K. What's more, any change in probability inputs could lead to a revised calculation structure.

Any research manager who is not a probability whiz or who has limited time could find the above application to be useful to discover that if the likelihood of

Presentation evaluation

Cost of presentation (£K) =	30
Probability of winning contract =	0.8
Value of contract (£K) =	260

Profit probabilities, if presentation successful

Profit % of contract value	Probability
0	0.00
10	0.10
20	0.20
30	0.30
40	0.30
50	0.10

Fig 6.1 Input screen for evaluating the chances of a successful project pitch

Profit simulation	
Maximum profit (£K)	100
Minimum profit (£K)	–30
Average profit (£K)	33.9
Probability of profit	0.716

Fig 6.2 Output screen for evaluating the chances of a successful project pitch

obtaining the contract is reduced to 0.5 (50%) – then the probability of making an overall profit falls to 45% with an expected profit figure of just £10.3K.

A more realistic scenario in which the chance of winning the pitch is reduced to a mere 20% with reduced pitching cost of £10K, yields an overall profit probability of 18% and associated overall profit figure of £6.1K.

In the light of the above figures it seems only reasonable that clients be encouraged to further support the practice of meeting at least part of the presentation costs.

Another question that is often raised in the early stages of a research project is 'How large should the sample be?'

Most practitioners know that this depends on a number of variables, the most important of which is the size of the client's budget. There is, however, an academic formula that can be found in most marketing research textbooks that can easily be programmed into a spreadsheet in order to carry out 'what if' analyses

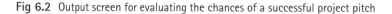

Question – 'How would you vote if there were an election tomorrow?'	Poll	%	Adj %	
				Sampling error on Conservative vote (%) = 2.5
Conservative	597	40.2	42.4	
Labour	575	38.7	40.8	
Liberal/SDP	178	12.0	12.6	Sample size required for an accuracy (%)
Nationalist	43	2.9	3.1	level = 2
Other	16	1.1	1.1	and a 95% confidence
Don't knows*	76	5.1	100.0	coeff. = 2345
Total sample size	1485	100.0		
*Includes 'will not vote' and 'refused'				

Fig 6.3 Using a spreadsheet to provide a 'working' report

against sampling costs. This tends to be rather depressing as the cost of obtaining the required degree of accuracy becomes prohibitively expensive.

An alternative approach, and one that uses the strength of the spreadsheet, is to provide the client with a working spreadsheet model as part of the report. Figure 6.3 gives an example of a working report, in this case the results of an opinion poll question. Once the sample has been conducted, of course, it is not possible to alter the sample size or results. However, we might wish to carry out 'what if' scenarios on what might have happened with different voting frequencies and accuracy levels. Optimum sample size for given confidence levels and accuracy can also be displayed, although the formula may need adjusting for samples from smaller populations.

6.3 Survey analysis

Some proprietary survey software packages such as SNAP5, SphinxSurvey or PinPoint offer questionnaire design facilities. Whilst this is possible but not entirely practical using spreadsheet packages, a few lines of Visual Basic code can transform the electronic spreadsheet into a useful vehicle for CATI studies.

Again, most proprietary survey and statistical packages mimic the spreadsheet in respect of direct data entry – with variables or questions being represented as columns and respondents as spreadsheet rows.

Where products like Excel and Lotus 1-2-3 score over the professional survey analysis packages is in their flexibility of data analysis. This makes them an excellent device for combining survey analysis with different modelling approaches. Table 6.3 lists the main data analysis techniques used by European marketing research companies when carrying out work for their clients.

It is only comparatively recently, however, that the pivot table capability has been introduced into Excel, thus making the most popular bivariate analysis technique, cross-tabulation, readily available. Indeed, some commentators[9] have suggested that it was the introduction of the pivot-table wizard that has made Excel a serious marketing research tool.

Table 6.3 Use of data analysis techniques by marketing research companies

ESOMAR sample (n =182)	%	Bivariate techniques	%	Multivariate techniques	%
Univariate techniques					
Frequency counts	8	Correlation	60	Multiple regression	4
Graphical	8	Cross-tabulation	88	Cluster analysis	6
Summary statistics	8	Two-variable	37	Factor analysis	6
		ARIMA modelling	3	Discriminant analysis	3
		Exponential smoothing	11	Conjoint analysis	3
		Correspondence	44	Log-linear analysis	9
				MDS	1
				AID	1
				LISREL	4

Source: Hussey and Hooley, 1994.

Tables 6.4 and 6.5 describe a small training survey database, COXDATA, extracted from a much larger investigation by Tony Cox.

Figure 6.4 illustrates how frequency tables and cross-tabulations can be constructed by dragging field variable buttons to the relevant row/column destinations. Table 6.6 demonstrates the effect of selecting the 'Market' field for the row variable and the 'Activity' field for the column variable.

Table 6.4 Column headings: COXDATA

Column	Heading	Meaning
A	COMP_ID	Identification number of responding company
B	ACTIVITY	Main area of company activity (manufacturing, retailing, wholesaling, services)
C	MARKET	Type of market company predominantly works in (durables, FMCG, industrial goods, capital goods, industrial services, cons. serv.)
D	EMPLOY	Approximate number of employees worldwide
E	APPROACH	Company's approach to marketing (product-led, sales-driven, marketing focus)
F	RESEARCH	How often company carries out market research (never, ad hoc, continuous)
G	STRAT–5	Company's strategic focus over past five years (good short-term profits, long-term market position gain)
H	STRAT+5	Company's strategic focus for next five years (good short-term profits, long-term market position gain)
I	IMPROFIT	On a scale (1=most important, 5=least important) please rank the following five factors in regard to their importance for your company as a basis for measuring performance
J	IMPSALES	
K	IMPSHARE	
L	IMPROI	
M	IMPCASH	
N	ROI(%)	Return on investment

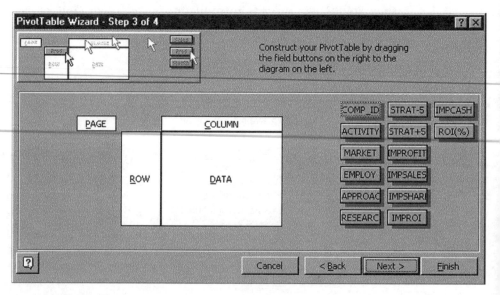

Fig 6.4 Excel's PivotTable Wizard

Table 6.5 COXDATA survey results

COMP ID	ACTIVITY	MARKET	EMPLOY	APPROACH	RESEARCH	STRAT-5	STRAT+5	IMPROFIT	IMPSALES	IMPSHARE	IMPROI	IMPCASH	ROI(%)
1	Manufacture	Durables	70	Market	Continuous	Position	Position	3	4	5	1	2	32
2	Service	IServices	30	Market	Never	Position	Position	3	3	3	3	3	22
3	Retail	FMCG	700	Selling	Ad Hoc	Profit	Position	1	2	2	3	4	20
4	Service	IServices	35	Market	Never	Profit	Position	1	3	3	2	1	5
5	Service	Capital G	200	Product	Ad Hoc	Position	Profit	3	1	5	2	4	-12
6	Manufacture	FMCG	50	Market	Continuous	Position	Position	2	4	1	3	5	40
7	Manufacture	Industrial G	2400	Market	Ad Hoc	Profit	Position	1	4	5	2	3	20
8	Service	FMCG	520	Market	Ad Hoc	Profit	Position	2	1	3	2	2	17
9	Manufacture	FMCG	500	Market	Continuous	Profit	Position	1	4	5	3	2	7
10	Manufacture	FMCG	100	Market	Ad Hoc	Profit	Position	1	2	5	3	4	8
11	Manufacture	Capital G	180	Market	Ad Hoc	Profit	Position	1	3	2	4	5	11
12	Service	CServices	1000	Selling	Ad Hoc	Profit	Position	5	4	3	3	3	4
13	Manufacture	Durables	32	Market	Never	Position	Position	1	1	4	2	3	6
14	Manufacture	Capital G	100	Market	Continuous	Position	Position	2	1	5	4	3	100
15	Service	IServices	60	Selling	Ad Hoc	Profit	Position	2	4	5	1	2	60
16	Service	FMCG	10000	Market	Continuous	Position	Position	5	2	1	4	3	21
17	Manufacture	Durables	200	Market	Ad Hoc	Profit	Position	1	3	3	2	1	-20
18	Manufacture	Industrial G	650	Selling	Never	Profit	Position	1	4	5	2	3	45
19	Manufacture	FMCG	80	Market	Never	Position	Position	2	1	1	2	5	13
20	Service	CServices	150	Market	Ad Hoc	Position	Position	1	2	3	5	4	4
21	Service	CServices	150	Market	Continuous	Profit	Position	1	4	3	2	5	34
22	Manufacture	Industrial G	35000	Market	Ad Hoc	Position	Position	3	5	4	2	1	14
23	Manufacture	Capital G	180	Market	Continuous	Profit	Position	2	4	5	1	3	18

Table 6.6 Example of a cross-tabulation table from a company strategy survey

Count of ACTIVITY	ACTIVITY				
MARKET	Manufacture	Retail	Service	Wholesale	Grand total
Capital G	5	0	1	0	6
GServices	0	1	7	0	8
Durables	4	0	0	1	5
FMCG	6	4	2	0	12
Industrial G	10	2	1	3	16
IServices	1	0	11	1	13
Grand total	26	7	22	5	60

Tables can be further modified by using filters, different percentage breakdowns, averages, standard deviations, subtotals, maximum and minimum values, and so on. Although Excel will also calculate significance levels using the chi-square statistic, it has to be admitted that currently this is a rather clumsy process.

Clearly, the extensive chart galleries available in modern spreadsheets provide an excellent platform for providing clients with graphical output. Using the COX-DATA example, Excel's chart wizard only needs a few key presses to produce Figure 6.5, a bar chart summarising the importance rankings for different companies' profit objectives.

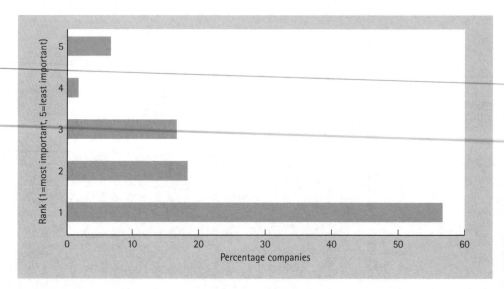

Fig 6.5 Importance of profit (ranking)

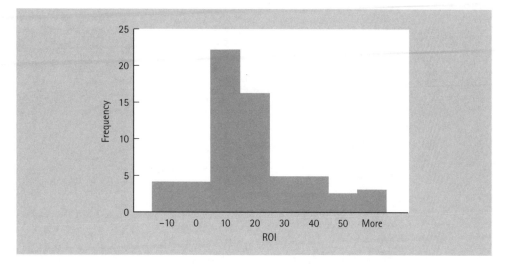

Fig 6.6 Continuous data (ROI)

Chart wizard is adequate for charting discrete data but, what about a graphing of a continuous variable such as rate of return or ROI? Here it's first necessary to set up suitable intervals using Excel's histogram option and then use Excel chart facilities on the resulting frequency distribution, as shown in Figure 6.6.

It is often necessary to provide a graphical description of multivariate data. Here the radar chart can be particularly useful. Although evaluating the averages of ranked data is not an example of best practice, Figure 6.7 portrays the mean ranks for each of the five importance scales for both the consumer services and industrial goods segments. This proves to be a handy device for highlighting similarities and extreme differences.

Of course many clients will wish to be given some idea of the relative weightings of the five importance factors. By constructing frequency counts for each of the five importance factors and then applying a differential scoring system (e.g. 5 for each of the most important rankings down to 1 for each of the least important), a total weight can be calculated for each variable. Figure 6.8 illustrates the relative importance of the five rankings.

The third most popular univariate technique noted in Table 6.3 is summary statistics. Excel provides a good range of basic measures under the descriptive statistics choice which is located in the tools menu under the data analysis option. Table 6.7 displays the results for the ROI data.

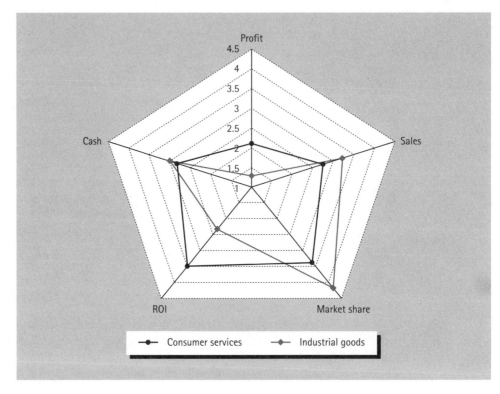

Fig 6.7 Example of radar chart for multivariate display

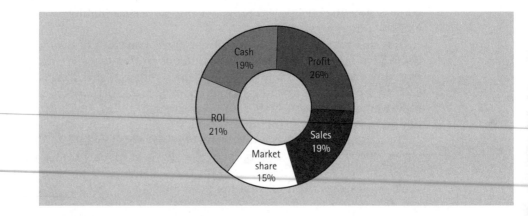

Fig 6.8 Importance ratings

Table 6.7 Summary statistics for return on investment (ROI)

	ROI(%)
Mean	14.08
Standard error	2.63
Median	10.5
Mode	5
Standard deviation	20.37
Sample variance	414.82
Kurtosis	5.45
Skewness	1.79
Range	120
Minimum	−20
Maximum	100
Sum	845
Count	60
Largest(1)	100
Smallest(1)	−20

6.4 Significance tests

As far as significance tests for data are concerned, spreadsheets like Excel have in-built function wizards for carrying out t-tests and z-tests as well as calculating correlation statistics and evaluating probabilities from the better-known distributions. The data analysis module boasts basic multivariate regression analysis as well as forecasting techniques such as exponential smoothing and two-way analysis of variance. Several recent texts[10] give comprehensive coverage of these applications. Table 6.8 shows an example of output from a paired comparison t-test.

In order to perform more sophisticated data analyses it may be necessary to resort to programming bespoke algorithms in Visual Basic. However, it will probably turn out to be much more economical to purchase an add-in such as xlSTAT described in the next section.

Table 6.8 Example of output from paired comparison t-test

	IMPSALES	IMPSHARE
Mean	2.917	3.567
Variance	1.603	2.216
Observations	60	60
Pearson correlation	0.394	
Hypothesised mean Difference	0	
Df	59	
t stat	−3.296	
P(T<=t) one-tail	0.001	
t Critical one-tail	1.671	
P(T<=t) two-tail	0.002	
t critical two-tail	2.001	

6.5 Multivariate analysis

Over the past few years convenient and powerful Excel add-ins like xlSTAT, created by Thierry Fahmy, have greatly added to the range of data analyses that can be carried out using spreadsheets. Techniques available include ANOVA, ANCOVA, cluster analysis, correspondence analysis, discriminant analysis, factor analysis, multiple regression, multidimensional scaling, PCA and binary response models.

As a short example consider Table 6.9 which represents distance measures between city centre pubs. The figures in the table represent respondents' 'averaged' judgements about the similarity of the public houses. A score of 1 registers a view that the two pubs under consideration are virtually identical while a score of 9 reflects the opinion that the two establishments being compared could not be more different.

With only a few key strokes an MDS map can be obtained as shown in Figure 6.9. It goes without saying that the axes' labels or dimensions need to be inferred by the user.

Table 6.9 Distance measures between eight city pubs

	Crown	Union	Bull	Lodge	Mill	Turks	Queens	Castle
Crown	1	5	6	9	5	6	5	8
Union	5	1	2	4	1	6	4	5
Bull	6	2	1	5	2	5	4	6
Lodge	9	4	5	1	5	8	9	2
Mill	5	1	2	5	1	5	6	5
Turks	6	6	5	8	5	1	3	9
Queens	5	4	4	9	6	3	1	8
Castle	8	5	6	2	5	9	8	1

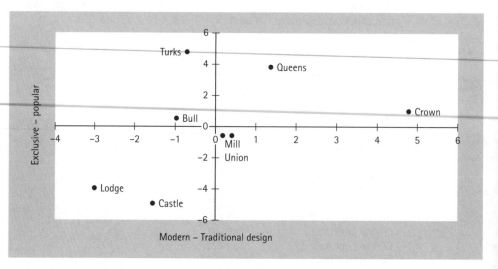

Fig 6.9 MDS diagram for city pubs

6.6 Modelling

The simplest but perhaps most useful form of spreadsheet modelling involves little more than using standard templates in order to evaluate marketing decisions in well-known areas such as optimal pricing strategies,[11] profit maximisation and sales response evaluations in direct marketing, Ozimek (1993).

The optimising power of the spreadsheet is one of its many features that are often overlooked even by experienced users. Figure 6.10 shows how straightforward it is to specify a problem involving the maximisation of a profit function subject to constraints on advertising, cost and retail price. In this case the form of the advertising-sales response function was sufficiently complex to prevent solution by the classical methods of differential calculus but the 'solver' returned the level of advertising expenditure needed to maximise profit (ADVERT = 2.47) in a fraction of a second.

One of the principal strengths of spreadsheet packages is their ability to combine survey data entry and model development within the same application. Collecting service quality data using the SERVQUAL instrument is a case in point. Once the data has been entered, the weighted and unweighted SERVQUAL measures can be calculated, tested for significance between segments and the results charted. Any doubts about the importance weightings can easily be explored using sensitivity analysis.

Lilien[12] provides what is probably the best exposition on the topic of using spreadsheets in marketing modelling. His examples – available on disk – range from stochastic consumer choice models through salesforce sizing to new product development applications. The following illustration, adapted from Lilien's brand-switching Markov model, demonstrates the range of possibilities available for analysis when the survey database and modelling capability are combined in the same application.

Survey data was first collected for four brands of motor insurance purchased for each of two consecutive years. Once the survey data had been entered into the spreadsheet, it was possible for the pivot-table wizard to construct Table 6.10.

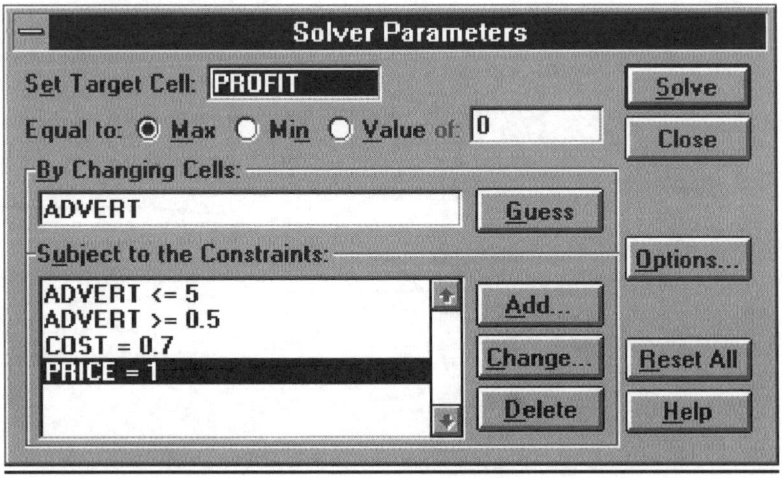

Fig 6.10 Using Solver to maximise profit subject to cost, price and advertising constraints

Table 6.10 Brand-switching example

Count of year 1	Year 2				
Year 1	Brand A	Brand B	Brand C	Brand D	Grand total
Brand A	97	58	25	24	204
Brand B	20	69	14	3	106
Brand C	4	13	33	17	67
Brand D	5	6	11	38	60
Grand total	126	146	83	82	437

Initial marketing share figures were obtained from secondary sources and, adopting the Markov assumption of constant brand-switching probabilities, it was desired to compute the equilibrium market share of the four brands.

This can be accomplished in four easy stages:

1. First reduce Table 6.10 to a joint probability table. (Divide entries in the main body of the table by the overall total.)
2. Convert the joint probability table to a conditional probability table by dividing cell values by row totals.
3. Combine the initial market share data with the conditional probability table using matrix multiplication in order to obtain estimated market shares for year 3.
4. Use the spreadsheet 'copy' command in order to replicate this process for several more years.

Chart the results. Sample output is shown in Figure 6.11.

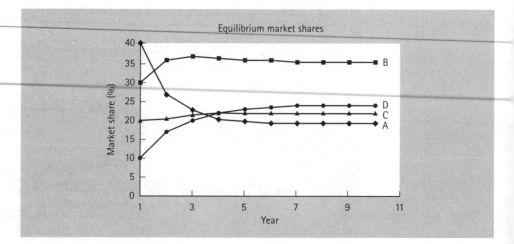

Fig 6.11 Brand-switching equilibrium

It is, of course, a fairly severe assumption to suppose that brand switching rates always remain constant. Perhaps a more realistic situation would be one in which they vary over time – and this is where simulation comes in.

Despite the very powerful and sophisticated data modelling methods such as LISREL and Monte Carlo Markov Chains that are now available on desktop PCs, many marketing models have too complex a structure to make them amenable to traditional analysis techniques. By using the spreadsheet's random number generator, however, it is often comparatively straightforward to obtain a simulated solution to any problem.

Armed with values obtained from the RAND function which can then be modified according to the inverse transform theorem, spreadsheets will provide not only a simulated solution to the problem in question but also an associated error distribution.

Being able to inspect the shape of an error distribution is popular with both students and professional marketers who intuitively feel more comfortable seeing a range of possible outcomes rather than a single value – even if the single parameter is accompanied by t-statistics and significance levels.

Simulation is another area where it probably pays to purchase a decent add-in. Figure 6.12 shows the output from the popular spreadsheet simulation package Crystal Ball. It displays simulated income generated by a property renting agency and is based on a survey of current tenants' and future potential tenants' intentions. By selecting the appropriate options, analysts are able to interpret the model with a view to discovering how changes in variable inputs will affect output probabilities.

Packages such as Crystal Ball can also make an excellent learning and teaching aid. Explaining how customer buying might follow a binomial distribution is not always easily digested, even by the more numerically gifted. This is because the purchase parameter varies according to beta distribution with the result that the unconditional purchase distribution follows the beta-binomial. However, if the process can be demonstrated to work by using graphical aids such as those shown in Figure 6.13 – the results become that much more acceptable.

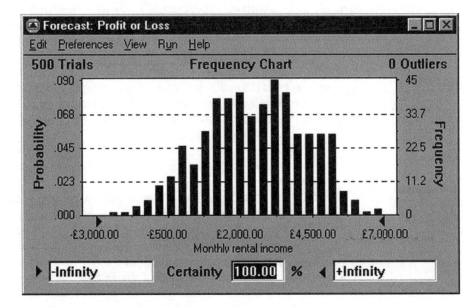

Fig 6.12 An example of simulation output from Crystal Ball

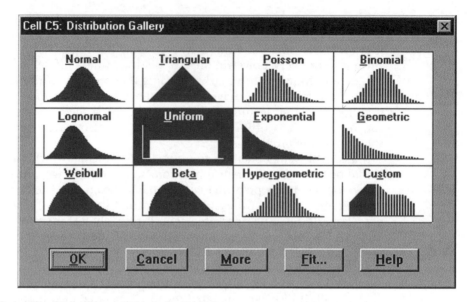

Fig 6.13 Probability distributions available in Crystal Ball

Another area where the spreadsheet random number generator will prove useful is in the application of bootstrap and small sample reuse techniques. Often, it is much more straightforward to carry out such an analysis using a spreadsheet package than to attempt to navigate the option jungle of a more powerful data analysis package.

6.7 Conclusion

The increasing popularity of spreadsheets in general, together with low prices and the fact that most new PCs are sold with bundled software that usually includes a spreadsheet package, suggests that virtually every computer user will have access to a spreadsheet on his or her desktop. The features of data display and analysis in particular make electronic spreadsheets in general an ideal tool for marketing research applications. However, it is often the ability to link the spreadsheet with a proprietary word processor and database that provides extra strength in that it allows clients to be given 'live' workbooks that they can interrogate at their leisure, whilst sitting at their own computers.

For Microsoft Excel in particular, the enhanced programming capability provided by Visual Basic will not only make more complex applications easier to develop but will also improve the links with other members of the Microsoft Office family.

The introduction of a mapping tool now brings geographical modelling and analysis onto every desktop. Increasingly detailed mapping templates are being developed together with more economically priced datasets. It should soon be possible to carry out much of the geodemographic work on a spreadsheet that is currently being processed by packages such as TACTICIAN and MapInfo.

It is not only professional marketers and marketing researchers who will find the features offered by modern spreadsheets to be increasingly appealing. Business schools are already finding that the user friendliness of the best spreadsheets are encouraging less confident students to attempt more ambitious forms of data analysis. Spreadsheets in general, and Microsoft Excel in particular, seem destined to play an increasingly important role in future marketing research applications.

REFERENCES

1. Hirst, M. (1994), 'End user computing', in Hooley, G. J. and Hussey, M. K. (eds), *Qualitative Methods in Marketing*, Academic Press, London, pp.221–46.

2. Hussey, M. K. and Hooley, G. J. (1995), *Quantitative Methods in Marketing: A Pan-European Study*, ESRC End of Award Report (R-000-23-3869).

3. Berger, A. (1997), 'How to support your sales force with competitive intelligence', *Computer Intelligence Review*, vol. 7, 4, pp.81–3.

4. Carpenter, P. (1995), 'Customer lifetime value: do the math', *Marketing Computing*, vol. 15, 1, pp.18–19.

5. Ozimek, J. (1993), *Targeting for Success*, McGraw Hill, Maidenhead.

6. Hacker, R. C. (1995), 'The road to high ticket sales', *Target Marketing*, vol. 18, 4, pp.24–5.

7. Davirs, M. (1994), 'The interactive evolution', *Journal of Business Strategy*, vol. 15, 4, pp.52–9.

8. Gorski, D. and Ingram, J. (1993), *The Price Waterhouse Sales and Marketing Software Handbook 1993*, second edition, Pitman Publishing, London.

9. Ville, de B. (1995), 'Pivot Tables qualify Excel as a serious marketing research tool … almost!', *Marketing Research*, vol. 7, 1, pp.50–4.

10. Neuford, J. L. (1997), *Learning Business Statistics with Microsoft Excel*, Prentice Hall, New Jersey; Liengme, B. V. (1997), *A Guide to Microsoft Excel: For Scientists and Engineers*, Arnold, London; Middleton, M. R. (1995), *Data Analysis Using Excel 5.0*, Duxbery Press, Belmont, California.

11. Bedient, J. B. (1989), *Marketing Decision Making: Using Lotus 1-2-3*, South Western Publishing Company, Cincinnati, Ohio.

12. Lilien, G. L. (1993), *Marketing Management: Analytic Exercises for Spreadsheets*, second edition, Boyd and Fraser, Danvers, Massachusetts.

SPREADSHEET EXERCISE

For most of us, the question of how we got our family name is fairly straightforward. Our parents gave it to us at birth – in the same way that their parents and their parents' parents had passed the name down through the generations.

First names, however, are a different matter. There is some flexibility of choice. So, here is the exercise. Carry out a short survey (say 100 people), who can be friends, relations, colleagues or even chance acquaintances (clearly a convenience sample), and ask just three questions: their first name(s), their gender and birth year. Now enter your data into the spreadsheet of your choice. By using the spreadsheet functions to order, filter and organise your data, can you say anything about the relationship between first names and age?

Note: Some marketing research providers use the fact that certain first names tend to be fashionable at different times in order to segment their clients' customers.

QUESTIONS

1. They say that a picture (chart) is worth a thousand words. The following data represents regional sales for two sports retailers, Kneelocker and Sportscamp. Use your spreadsheet to produce as many charts of the data as possible. Six would be a reasonable number.

Annual sales by region

Region	Kneelocker (%)	Sportscamp (%)
North	40	12
South	8	38
East	30	28
West	22	22

2. A company is considering introducing a 'cash-back' offer in its chain of retail outlets. Before proceeding it decides to carry out an experiment or 'trial' of the cash-back facility in eight representative stores. The results of the experiment in terms of increased percentage of revenue are given below both for the trial group of stores and a similar control group of stores.

Increased percentage of revenue

Trial group	Control group
8.6	2.6
11.4	8.5
12.5	9.9
17.4	6.7
18.6	4.4
10.4	6.4
11.5	7.7
19.1	10.6

Use the data analysis tests on your spreadsheet to investigate whether or not there is a significant difference between the experimental and control groups. (*Hint*: If you are using Excel then the function Ttest may be of help.)

3. (More difficult) Referring back to the presentation evaluation example (Figure 6.1), if the cost of the presentation is changed to £24K, the probability of winning the contract to 0.4 and the value of the contract to £200K, is it sensible for the agency to 'pitch' for the contract? (You may assume that the profit probabilities for successful contracts remain the same.)

7 Segmenting markets

Having gone through the principles and practices of marketing research from quantitative and qualitative approaches to the stages of how markets are explored, samples designed, data collected, statistically analysed and presented, the marketing research process now moves on to how markets are segmented.

> By knowing the principles and techniques of market segmentation organisations derive a better understanding of their customers – what they want to buy, how they buy, where and when they buy, and from whom they buy.

Segmentation studies seek to help organisations to understand the attitudes, motivations and behaviour of customers and to design product and service offerings for sought-after customers. Having spent much time and resources on their research designs, market researchers need to ensure that the messages about the products of their research to the selected target markets are less general and more specifically tailored to the selected or sought-after customer groups for their clients. Segmentation studies aid in the creation of their clients' marketing strategies or sub-strategies, such as identifying the correct promotion or price appeals to obtain the desired customer responses.

This chapter focuses on the segmentation variables and research techniques used to analyse the behaviour of established and likely, potential users in the selected product markets.

7.1 Why segment?

To 'segment' is to divide into parts. In marketing, to segment is to separate from a population the individual units, which are then classified into homogenous groups according to chosen characteristics. Market segmentation involves the classification of consumer types, in essence, the deliberate putting of birds of a feather in a flock together.

In marketing research, it is necessary to identify the relevant characteristics of market segments or groups of consumers so that the assessment of their demand, consumption patterns and buying potential for certain types of products and services can be arrived at. The customer does not usually know that he or she has been put in a homogenous group. Segmentation is, therefore, a supplier-based strategy.

The marketing research strategy aims to:

1. Locate a new opportunity, a 'gap' in customer needs which is unfulfilled or only partly fulfilled in a market.
2. Position a brand or brands strategically to compete with other competitors' brands so that the client's brand is favourably placed within the product field.

A market researcher is likely to approach design of a segmentation study from one of two angles:

1. Collection and analysis of data relating to the habits, attitudes and needs of consumers in domestic markets with a view to sorting them into homogenous groups differentiated by their lifestyles and buyer behaviour – **a consumer typology**.
2. Collection and analysis of data relating to the particular branded or unbranded products and services available in the market by focusing on how these are perceived by consumers (domestic markets) or customers (organisational markets) – **a product and service typology**.

By adopting the research process for (1), a producer, wholesaler or retailer aims to meet the requirements of those consumers whose wants are not being satisfied. In concentrating marketing effort on them as a particular segment of a market a manufacturer or retailer can expect to create loyalty sufficiently strong to counteract the appeal of competitors' brands. By consistently focusing effort on a target segment, a satisfactory relationship between marketing costs and sales revenue can be achieved. Research funds are laid out with maximum cost effectiveness when a targeted segment and its wants have been established.

The intention of (2) is to sort the brands into groups of those with similar attributes as perceived by purchasers so that a market researcher can identify the appeal or unique selling proposition (USP) for a product, for the purpose of product differentiation. Advertising messages and images can then be developed to appeal to the target segment.

It is necessary to develop a product or service to which both consumers and distributors/retailers respond. Advertising has a 'pull' effect in drawing consumers into the retail outlets to buy the products. Retailers will try to maximise their sales by making their products attractive to their consumers, the 'push' effect.

Figure 7.1 illustrates the way in which research inputs feature in the development of segmentation, targeting and positioning strategies for clients seeking to

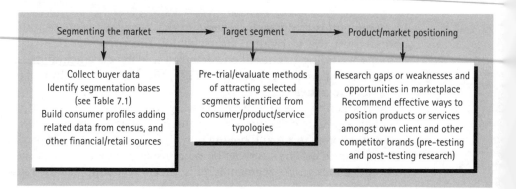

Segmenting the market ⟶ Target segment ⟶ Product/market positioning

| Collect buyer data Identify segmentation bases (see Table 7.1) Build consumer profiles adding related data from census, and other financial/retail sources | Pre-trial/evaluate methods of attracting selected segments identified from consumer/product/service typologies | Research gaps or weaknesses and opportunities in marketplace Recommend effective ways to position products or services amongst own client and other competitor brands (pre-testing and post-testing research) |

Fig 7.1 Research inputs into market segmentation strategies

establish new product and service launches in the marketplace or to optimise on their performances to gain more sales and market share.

A market research study to investigate a segment can work to a definitive brief specifying both of the following:

- the kind of people to be asked to discuss ideas about a product, e.g. for concept testing, and to take part in experiments to help determine final choices. Those selected will be put in consumer panels (see Section 2.8.3);

- the criteria to be used in the design of concept tests and experiments, and in the interpretation of results. For example, identifying the measures and conditions for pre-testing the stand-out effects of a new pack design, or post-testing advertisement recall of respondents after an advertising campaign under laboratory-type conditions.

7.2 Segmentation variables

In the search for a target segment we consider the ways in which purchasers in the market vary. These variables are summarised in Table 7.1.

7.2.1 Variables used in consumer and organisational markets

These fall into two broad categories:

1. Variables which are descriptive, e.g. geographic, cultural and demographic. These are related to factual evidence and the circumstances in which people live.
2. Variables which are explanatory, e.g. changes in social behaviour and psychographics.

These variables are explained in the following sections.

Density of population

The market research planning needs to be related to the infrastructural contexts to which it is applied. The contexts could be the work and lifestyle of the segmented population linked to the economic infrastructure. The infrastructures of London and Paris, for example, are quite different from any provincial city because there are higher concentrations of people within the capital cities who have more spending power related to their higher wage earnings, the intensity in the pace of lifestyles and spending patterns.

Industrialised regions with good employment records also tend to have higher population densities where there are good telecommunications and physical infrastructures in place, such as transport links by air, rail, sea and road to receive supplies and get goods to markets. Support industries such as banks, insurance firms, shops and fast food chains locate their branch outlets closer to their organisational customers, thereby adding to the population density and the demand for the construction of more buildings and roads.

Table 7.1 Segmentation variables

Variables used in domestic markets	Variables used in organisational (including industrial) markets
Culture Similarities and differences in social culture: ethnicity, language, social norms and customs	**Culture** Similarities and differences in business culture: ethnicity, language, business etiquette and dress
Geographic Physical and climatic variations Postcode divisions	**Geographic** Physical and climatic variations Standard Industrial Classification codes (SIC) Postcode divisions
Density of population City conurbation, suburb, village	**Density and proximity within geographic divisions** Numbers of industrial and service firms Nature of industry (heavy to light industries)
Demographic Age, gender, income, terminal education age (TEA), occupation, religion, race, nationality, family lifecycle, family size	**Demographic** Type of industries to seek out for sales Company size and location
Behaviour in the product field Usage rate (heavy, medium, light purchasers) Readiness to buy (brand loyalists or switchers) Low involvement or high involvement in decision-making processes (impulse or careful buyers) Product benefits sought (key benefits or differentiation sought, e.g. most effective cleaning product, best price) Special purchase occasions and significance (e.g. symbolic – celebrations, birthdays)	**Purchasing approaches** Usage rate (heavy, medium, light purchasers) Purchasing policies (loyal users or looking for best quotes/tenders) Decision-making units and relationships (number and type of personnel involved, e.g. buyers, gatekeepers, deciders, influencers, users) Product benefits sought (key benefits or differentiation sought, e.g. premium qualities, best price discounts) Attitudes to seller's products and sales representatives (enthusiastic or hostile, negative or positive, desirous or indifferent)
Psychographic Attitudes to products and suppliers (enthusiastic, indifferent to hostile) Social class and perceived social standing (working, middle and upper classes) First and last to buy (innovators, early and late adopters, laggards) Personality types (opinion leaders, dictators or democrats, high or low achievers, believers and strivers) Reference groups (direct 'face-to-face' and indirect influencers of the purchasers, such as parents and teachers) Peer groups (sub-groups with features of equality determining behavioural norms influencing modes of behaviour)	**Situational factors** Potential for large or small sized orders Emphasis on quick delivery and service Need for training in the use of the product Need for specialised applications (e.g. purchasing specialised electronic components or precision engineered parts to be put in the manufacture of a complete machine by an original equipment manufacturer (OEM)) Urgency in product need (e.g. need for a new model to fulfil immediate production schedules) Organisational structure (e.g. number of subsidiaries and their buying groups) Reputation of buying organisation, activity and product output

Cultural and geographical

Both in home and overseas markets, **cultural** and **geographical** variables are often related together. In an advanced and wealthy economy, regional differences become blurred as a result of increased mobility and communications brought about by modern advances in transport and telecommunications. Despite this, cultural differences brought about by different language, religion, race and social behaviour remain significant considerations in understanding the markets and marketing environments of countries. For example, ethnic groups can be geographically concentrated and culturally distinct and will, therefore, represent different market segments for food, toiletries, cosmetics, air travel and packaged holidays. When operating in a foreign market, companies may also find that their indigenous employees and business partners there require observation of national customs and business etiquette.

Demographic

Age is an important discriminator in many consumer markets. It is a useful check on the representativeness of samples, for the age distribution of the population is well documented. Two methods of establishing a respondent's age are in common use, by a straight question – 'What was your age last birthday?' or by means of a show card with age brackets. As with income, this may reduce reluctance to answer the question. However, there may well be respondents over the age of 16 attending 'day release' or part-time vocational courses, or mature students returning to higher education within a sample. So supplementary questions on education and training can be necessary.

Terminal education age (TEA) relates to when a person left school and relates to the qualifications received. School or university leaving ages and examinations passed have gained in significance as segmentation variables. The standard TEA question is 'How old were you when you finished your full-time education?'

As with **religion** and **race**, **gender** or the sex of the respondent are commonly asked questions, as on employee questionnaires. Questionnaires give a range of boxes and respondents can place a simple tick in the relevant ones. Gender is asked as 'male' or 'female' on printed questionnaires. For many it is a very easy one to answer by a simple 'tick'. In this respect questionnaires have not really changed, not even to accommodate the minority who might not find it easy to answer. One segment, though, in the past decade has been receiving increasing attention. The 'gay market' has had more attention from manufacturers and advertisers who have sought to increase their sales to this segment.

Income, and more especially disposable income, is a common classification variable used. To overcome the reluctance of respondents to give the information, they are asked to point to a figure on a show card, or a questionnaire on a computer monitor. For researchers, the main difficulty is in establishing what disposable incomes are, as those interviewed would consider the details of questions such as:

> 'Which of these comes closest to your total take-home income, from all sources, that is after deducting income tax, national insurance, pension schemes and so on?'
>
> SHOW CARD

> '...and what about mortgage, and commercial insurance repayments, that are you currently paying?'

to be their own private business. Unless the respondents have willingly contracted into an arrangement such as being on a consumer panel and keying in information or keeping panel diaries so that market researchers can have their information on a regular basis, personal information will be harder to obtain. It is, of course, necessary to keep the annual, monthly and weekly lists of earnings up to date. In many surveys the data, for example for diaries, relates to buying for a family by the housewife. Here, definition of income is further complicated by the fact that family income often derives from more than one wage packet. A full accurate investigation requires a whole questionnaire with documented cross-checks.

With or without marriage, the family remains a basic social unit in many countries. Demand for many products and services is related to the stage reached in the **family life cycle** and their **life stages**. These stages are commonly defined in a lifestyle classification as:

Young	Young single, no children	Young couple, youngest child under six	Young couple, youngest child six or +	Older couple, with children 18+ at home	Older couple, no children at home	Older single

This life stage classification uses the occupational database or employment in the family as well as the family's size and composition (number of occupants, age, sex, ethnic grouping) to increase the marketing relevance of this segmentation variable.

Behaviour in the product field and purchasing approaches

There is a wealth of data that can be collected about people's behaviour in the product field and organisational purchasing approaches as these include regular purchases.

Given adequate data, users of products and services can be divided into 'heavy', 'medium' and 'light' user categories according to amount bought and frequency of buying. This kind of analysis is best based on trend data derived from consumer panels, whether the data is recorded in diaries or by means of regular audits. Apart from the 'heavy', 'medium' and 'light' buyers it is also possible to sort the individuals on panels into 'loyalists' and 'switchers' according to how their buying moves between brands. The data about all these buying-behaviour groups can be added to and described in geographic and demographic terms within the contexts of where they work and live.

The **product benefit** approach to segmentation focuses on product or brand use but introduces psychological variables into the segmentation study. Consumers are grouped according to the principal benefit they seek when they make buying decisions.

Michael Thomas commented on benefit segmentation thus:

The goal of benefit segmentation is to find a group of people all seeking the same benefits from a product. Each segment is identified by the benefits being sought. It is not unusual for various segments to share individual benefits. The major factor is the amount of importance each segment places on each benefit.[1]

The 'benefit' approach to segmentation is particularly relevant to market planning for existing brands. It effectively describes, and begins to explain the branded product field as it is. Haley's analysis takes note of segmentation variables other than benefit sought, as Table 7.2 shows, but the criterion for segmentation is the principal benefit sought. As Haley pointed out,

> the benefits which people are seeking in consuming a given product are the basic reasons for the existence of true market segments,[2]

but consumers do not always find it easy to define the benefits they seek or to give true answers.

Haley used the example of toothpaste producers to show the benefit segmentation approach in launching new brands with perceived benefits, such as Crest toothpaste by Procter & Gamble. This built on the prevention of tooth decay with its anti-cavity protection for a unique selling proposition. Table 7.2 reproduces Russell Haley's benefit segmentation of the toothpaste market. Haley pioneered the 'principal benefit' idea and this is now a classic example.

Psychographic

Psychographics or lifestyle classification are used in market research because they contribute valued insights into the way people are motivated to behave. As explanatory variables the segmentation variables considered so far are important

Table 7.2 Russell Haley's benefit segmentation of the toothpaste market

Segment name	The sensory segment	The sociables	The worriers	The independent segment
Principal benefit sought: product	Flavour, appearance of teeth	Brightness, prevention	Decay	Price
Demographic strengths	Children	Teens, young people	Large families	Men
Special behavioural characteristics	Users of spearmint flavoured toothpaste	Smokers	Heavy users	Heavy users
Brands disproportionately favoured	Colgate, Stripe	Macleans plus White Ultra Brite	Crest	Brands on sale (i.e. on offer)
Personality characteristics	High self-involvement	High sociability	High hypochondriasis	High autonomy
Lifestyle characteristics	Hedonistic	Active	Conservative	Value-oriented

Source: Haley, R.I. (1968), 'Benefit segmentation: a decision-oriented research tool', *Journal of Marketing*, July, pp. 30–5.

for 'measurability' and 'accessibility'. They help to define the size of segments and how best to reach them through the media. All these variables are, however, descriptive: they do not explain behaviour. We can observe associations between the demographic variables and those relating to behaviour in the product field in order to infer reasons for the behaviour of consumers.

In a segmentation study, attitude statements forming the inventory (or battery) of scales can be elicited from group discussions, depth interviews or Kelly's 'personal construct' interviews. As a general rule the statements are put to consumers in the form of either Likert-type, or semantic differential scales (see Chapter 5), depending on whether the segmentation study is designed to classify consumers or to group products according to the ways in which consumers perceive them. For example, respondents would be asked to express their attitudes towards:

- a relevant activity, i.e. leisure, feeding the family, housekeeping, shaving, insuring against risks;

- types of products, brands, services which are available for carrying out the stated activity, i.e. which were the ones that were known about, and of those used, which performed best for the stated activity or activities.

A segmentation study will necessarily include questions of a demographic and product-use nature as well as the attitude battery. The range of questions will depend on how far it is intended to explore the lifestyles of those in the market.

A company embarking on a segmentation study is likely to have a good deal of descriptive data on file and to know what kinds of consumers to invite to group discussions or depth interviews. Taped recordings are transcribed, consumer statements sorted into groups according to topic, and attitude scales constructed. There may be 60 to 100 attitude statements on a questionnaire.

The occupation-based system of classification of social class (or social grade) remains a much used standard for both market and social research. The system in common use is that used in the continuous random-sampling procedure followed for the National Readership Survey (NRS). The class categories derived from this are summarised in Box 7.1. The NRS classification is further explained in Chapter 13, Section 13.6.3. However, see Chapter 13, Section 13.6.4 for the UK government's new proposed changes in the UK classifications.

Perceived social standing is closely related to the class to which people feel they belong. Some may have no patience with the notion of class which promotes class divisions – the 'them and us' syndrome – while others may seek to emulate those they perceive to be in a higher class with, therefore, higher social standing than themselves.

Procedures developed and tested by anthropologists, sociologists and, more particularly, psychologists might be applied to the segmentation of consumer markets, for example:

- dividing the population into innovators (2.5%), early adopters (13.5%), early majority (34%), late majority (34%) and late adopters (16%) following the 'diffusion of innovations' theory;

- establishing the kinds of individuals with whom consumers seek to identify themselves following the 'reference group' theory;

Box 7.1 Classification of social class

Social grade	Social status	Chief income earner's (CIE's) occupation
A	Upper middle class	Higher managerial, administrative or professional
B	Middle class	Intermediate managerial, administrative or professional
C	Lower middle class	Supervisory, clerical, junior administrative or professional
C2	Skilled working class	Skilled manual workers
D	Working class	Semi-skilled and unskilled manual workers
E	Those at lower levels of subsistence	State pensioners, widows, casual and lowest-grade earners

The social grade of an informant is normally based on the occupation of the chief income earner of his or her household; if the CIE is retired it is based on the CIE's former occupation. Where there is no such occupation, or information about it is unobtainable, the assessment of social grade is based on environmental factors such as the type of dwelling, the amenities in the home, the presence of domestic help, and so on. Income level is not used to define social grade.

Prior to July 1992, social grade was based on the head of household or, if the head of household was not in full-time employment, or was retired, widowed or a pensioner with an income of not more than the equivalent of the basic pension obtaining at the time of interview, then the social grade of the informant was based on the occupation of the chief wage earner (CWE) of his or her household.

Source: National Readership Surveys Ltd (1994), London.

- using psychologists' standardised personality inventories, i.e. standard lists of attitude and behaviour questions designed to sort individuals into homogenous personality groups.

To summarise, geographical locations, cultural characteristics, demographic distribution of population and behaviour of customers are all of importance to organisations in locating and estimating market potential for their products and services, whether or not these are in domestic or overseas markets. The ideas and applications for the geodemographic systems used in consumer markets can be applied to organisational markets. However, because of the smaller number of organisations compared with the billions of consumers in the world and the fact that organisational markets can be practically segmented by type of activity and productive output, the segmentation variables taken, such as the geographical location and size of the organisation, e.g. its share capitalisation, sales turnover and number of employees to be included will differ.

Market researchers concentrate on the details of the structure, composition and behavioural characteristics of decision-making units since these have immediate impact for market segmentation purposes in understanding the nature of demand and how, when and why buying decisions are made by profit or not-for-profit organisations within the specific market segments.

7.3 Geodemographic systems

Geodemographic systems relate population characteristics to the geographical distribution of population and the 1991 UK national census provides a rich database. CACI's ACORN classification system uses data allowed to be accessed from the 1991 census database to build its 54 ACORN types. CACI has as many as 79 different data items, carefully screened from some 9,000 items produced by the census authorities for each of the 150,000 small geographical areas covering Britain, incorporated in the ACORN classification.[3]

This means that all the significant factors – such as age, sex, marital status, occupation, economic position, education, home ownership and car ownership – are covered to give a very full and comprehensive picture of socio-economic status.

The purpose behind the range and detail offered in geodemographic analysis is to enable marketers to target those people from the classification database who are most likely to use their goods and services and avoid those people who are least likely users. For example, households in the CACI: F 'striving' category have much lower disposable incomes compared with the wealthy achievers in the A 'thriving' category. The 'strivers' are classified into social class C2 to DE grades, whilst the 'thrivers' are socially graded from AB to ABC1.

The competing systems, such as those from CACI (ACORN), Experian (MOSAIC), PinPoint (FINPIN) and CDMS (SuperProfiles) all relate population characteristics as revealed in the census to the enumeration districts from which the data is recorded. Statistical data reduces this mass of information to meaningful clusters. These systems vary in the census data and other variables fed into their computer programs, in the statistical procedures used to cluster them, in the number of residential population types emerging from the statistical treatment and in the descriptions attached to these types.

An example of a British geodemographic system, EuroMOSAIC, in Table 7.3 shows the distribution of consumer types within ten lifestyle categories (elite suburb to vacation/retirement) across nine European countries. A consistent segmentation

Table 7.3 EuroMOSAIC: lifestyle categories and consumer types EuroMOSAIC: national percentages

	Great Britain %	Netherlands %	Germany %	Spain %	Ireland %	Sweden %	Belgium %	Northern Ireland %	Italy %
1 Elite suburb	11.7	6.1	16.0	5.1	7.4	7.2	17.4	14.8	4.5
2 Average areas	15.8	13.4	20.9	6.6	27.4	19.4	18.9	14.3	14.3
3 Luxury flats	5.3	8.1	6.9	8.8	1.9	3.1	6.6	0.9	6.1
4 Low income inner city	8.6	12.2	8.4	4.9	7.5	6.8	2.3	4.3	7.9
5 Hi rise social housing	5.5	11.5	2.8	7.3	0	8.4	0	1.9	3.4
6 Industrial communities	19.4	12.2	13.0	12.4	4.9	11.9	17.0	10.8	14.6
7 Dynamic families	14.3	14.0	8.6	12.1	9.3	9.8	9.5	5.7	15.3
8 Low income families	8.2	5.1	4.5	11.5	12.1	7.1	13.4	16.4	8.0
9 Rural/agricultural	5.5	13.6	13.7	21.4	27.1	18.6	7.9	26.8	17.9
10 Vacation/retirement	5.9	3.9	6.1	9.7	4.2	7.9	4.5	4.3	7.3

Source: Evans, N. and Webber, R. (1995), *The Marketing Research Process* by Crimp, M. and Wright, L. Prentice Hall, p. 254.

system extending across the European markets can provide a means of identifying similarities and differences between them with regard to products and services.

Geographical, cultural and demographic variables are necessarily used to locate and delimit the social-psychological groups derived from attitudinal lifestyle and life stage studies. Most segmentation approaches involve the multivariate computer analysis of data.

7.4 Piloting a questionnaire and factor analysis

With a limited number of attitude statements it would be possible to establish associations between consumer responses by drawing up a correlation matrix, but it would clearly be difficult to 'read' a 60 × 60 correlation matrix (scale batteries can run to more than 60 items). We therefore need the means to deal with the interrelationship of many variables quickly by using the computer. Statistical techniques which simultaneously examine the relationships between many variables are known as multivariate statistical procedures.

Provided it is done on an adequate scale (say 200 calls) the pilot test gives us the opportunity to use the multivariate technique called factor analysis to reduce the battery of attitude statements to a small number of factors each made up of a group of highly correlated scales representing a particular dimension of the overall attitude. In the following example four factors were found to account for most of the variability shown in the answers of respondents to questions about their savings.

Exploratory stage: Depth interviews generated a list of some 25 attitude statements.

Pilot stage: These statements were put to 130 members of the public in the form of scales, and weights were attached to their responses.

Factor analysis: Multivariate analysis of the scores derived from the responses of the sample to individual statements yielded four factors. Each of these factors represents a different dimension of the overall attitude towards saving:

Factor 1 Temperamental difficulty in saving (e.g. 'I have never been able to save')
Factor 2 Sense of solidity (e.g. 'If you've got a bit of money saved you are not so likely to be pushed around')
Factor 3 Concern with independence (e.g. 'I hate to feel I might have to ask someone for financial help')
Factor 4 Feeling of financial security (e.g. 'I feel it's unlikely I shall have any financial emergencies in the near future')

Let us consider Factor 1 more closely. There is found to be an association with five attitude statements compared with four for Factors 2 and 3 and three for Factor 4.

Factor 1
(a) I have never been able to save.
(b) Unless you have some specific reason to save, it's better to spend and enjoy it.
(c) I believe in enjoying my money now and letting the future take care of itself.
(d) I don't feel it's necessary to save just now.
(e) I can't help spending all I earn.

7.5 Cluster analysis

The objective of a survey using cluster analysis is to locate homogeneous clusters of consumers, or of products as perceived by consumers.

The clusters must do two things:

1. Fulfil the three conditions for market segments of 'measurability, accessibility and substantiality'. Measurability means that the size of segments can be estimated or established. Accessibility infers that it should be possible to distribute and communicate to the target market segments. Substantiality means that the segments should be large enough with sufficient demand to generate the desired profits.

2. Be sufficiently distinct one from another to offer choices in marketing strategy and marketing mix to differentiate products for specific segments. With a large sample, say 1,500, the multivariate procedure of cluster analysis can be applied. While factor analysis examines correlations between variables across respondents, cluster analysis looks for correlations between respondents across the segmentation variables. The cluster characteristics will depend on the nature and range of the questions put to respondents. As with all survey work it is necessary to develop hypotheses before going into the field.

As an example, let us assume that we are clustering drinkers according to their use of, and attitudes towards, alcoholic drinks. Qualitative work at the exploratory stage may have suggested that there are at least four types of drinker: social, compulsive, restorative and self-compensating. Unless our questionnaire includes items which make it possible for respondents to reveal these proclivities, cluster analysis will neither prove, nor disprove, this hypothesis.

It would be helpful if the statistical procedure were to show a definitive association between the level of response to one particular attitude statement and membership of a particular cluster. In practice, it requires the responses recorded in answers to something like 12 statements to establish the membership of one of four or five psychographic clusters. If the psychographic questions produce psychographic types who show consistent results over time in terms of buying behaviour, or response to advertising campaigns, the reliability of the procedure used to type consumers is confirmed. Having determined attitude similarities, the groups can then be analysed against demographics, media and brands to produce an overall 'perspective'.

In consumer and organisational research cluster analysis is used to identify clusters or sets of neighbourhoods which are broadly similar. A wide range of socio-economic and demographic data can be overlaid on the cluster types. Descriptors of types of individuals are assigned to the names of each cluster type within a residential or industrial neighbourhood location. Descriptors are assigned in order to identify each cluster type for ease of reference, such as 'high achievers' or 'affluent greys' in ACORN's 'thriving' category. Different firms specialising in geodemographics produce different descriptors and categories.

There are advantages in classifying consumers using residential neighbourhoods, i.e. by type and geographical location of dwelling. Not all organisations are like the large financial institutions which hold vast stores of individual customer data. In contrast some organisations, such as very small firms or those who have not been in business for long, may hold scant consumer records. However, particularly in developed countries, the existence of a system of postcodes can facilitate the classification of consumers. A name and an address can immediately be added to a mailing list, a quick and inexpensive method when compared with a market research study with respondents. Since the locations of addresses can be pinpointed on a map, geodemographic companies are able to carry out mapping and modelling functions. As each postcode is grid-referenced the spatial distribution of geodemographic types in any given area can be mapped. The data is analysed to find the distribution of the different neighbourhood types. By matching customer profiles with neighbourhood profiles it is then possible to calculate the potential size of a market in a given area.

Take, for example, a large retail store chain wishing to set up a new store in a new location. The geodemographic firm commissioned to carry out the study would match the information of existing types of customers who already shop at other outlets belonging to the retail store concerned with the neighbourhood clusters around the proposed new store location to arrive at a spatial distribution of potential customers. By joining together the information from its existing database, such as social values and racial make-up, the retail store could then have a programme of marketing activities devised to draw customers into its store.

7.6 RI natural grouping

A technique used by Research International (RI) is presented in Figure 7.2. Respondents are given various stimuli, e.g. cards with brand names or photos of products, which they separate into groups of similar items, repeating the procedure until there is no clear differentiation between the last product sub-groups. In Figure 7.2 product cards A to O are shown.

As illustrated in the figure, faced with 15 different products (A–O) respondents can divide those with the closest similarities into two main groups, in this case ('a b g h l

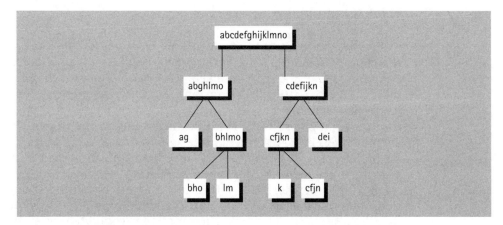

Fig 7.2 Developing attributes or product groups
Source: Research International (1994), Position Paper 1.

m o' and 'c d e f i j k n'. Respondents' comments on why and how an allocation into groups is made are recorded at each split. Further sub-divisions occur until the respondents can no longer discriminate between the final sub-groups of varying sizes.[4]

Brands are seen by consumers to be much the same; product positioning on brand mapping methods can help consumers to isolate or discriminate on key aspects between brands. It is possible to move brands apart so that perceived differences are maximised, price, packaging and advertising being brought into play with, possibly, product modification and a complete relaunch. If consumer perceptions of the deal carry conviction, the position of the ideal brand may suggest ways in which an existing brand might be modified in formulation and/or presentation.

7.7 Usage and attitude studies

Research methods for usage and attitude studies generally include qualitative orientations, e.g. focus group discussions, in-depth interviews, consumer diaries, observation studies and quantifiable results for analysis derived from rating scales, scoring and rank preferences by consumers.

Beliefs about products, e.g. brand awareness and the needs of consumers built around product use, purchase size and frequency, loyalty, prices paid, and so on, are examined in terms of the attitudinal and demographic characteristics of consumers. Respondents (as consumers) contribute to the research effort by making their preferences known through discriminating on product attributes. Product typologies on groups can be built around product characteristics with similar attributes which are deemed to be 'successful'.

Usage and attitude studies require:

1. Detailed coverage of products or brands to enable important differences between products or between brands to be identified.
2. Briefing respondents so that they understand the product or brand attributes on which they are to rate them.

7.7.1 Brand mapping

At the pilot stage attitude statements are more commonly put to respondents in the form of semantic differentials than as Likert-type scales. As in consumer typing, results of the pilot are likely to be factor analysed in order to extract the most influential attitude dimensions and to reduce the criterion variables to a manageable number.

At the survey stage the main difference comes in the way in which the results are presented. In place of descriptions of consumer types we can focus attention on brand maps. It is easy to visualise brand positioning based on consumer response to one semantic differential scale.

Let us assume there is a soft-drinks market containing seven brands, A–G. Consumers have been asked to rate these brands on a seven-point scale running from 'refreshing' to 'cloying'. A mean score is computed for each brand and the positions are plotted on the continuum, refreshing to cloying. If no two brands scored equally on this dimension we might get a result like this:

refreshing   A F   E G D   B C   *cloying*

If we had asked consumers to rate their ideal brand on the same dimension, the result might have been as follows:

refreshing   I   AF   E G D   B C   *cloying*

the scores for the seven named brands representing their distance from the ideal. When questions related to specific attributes are asked about the ideal brand as well as about available brands, the respondent's answers are more meaningful than when a general question is asked about 'your ideal soft drink'. It is also a simple matter to plot responses to two semantic differentials assuming 'economical to use' and 'extravagant to use' for the dimensions, see Figure 7.3.

Let us assume that F and E are two brands marketed by the same company, and that strategic planning decisions are being based on responses to these two semantic differential scales. There is a clear case for repositioning one of these two brands which consumers perceive as much the same. The repositioning might be achieved by making one brand more economical than the other, say by moving F closer to I, the ideal. A more 'value-for-money' image could be attached to the brand by modifying the formulation, changing the type of container used, or altering the advertising campaign (a relaunch if all three measures were taken).

Figure 7.3 shows that brand A is in a strong position because of its closeness to the ideal as perceived by consumers. B scores on 'economical to use' but is seen to be 'cloying'.

In some product fields 'extravagance' can be a plus quality but perhaps not for soft drinks. Theoretically, there is a gap in this market for a cloying rather than a refreshing product which tends to be extravagant in use; but it will be a long way from the ideal. The gap is a 'non-starter' and in some circumstances this may in itself be a significant finding. In evaluating responses to attitude statements, it is necessary to take account of the fact that some attributes will count far more with individual respondents than others.

When collecting data about consumers' perceptions of products, services or brands it is essential to establish the consumer's demographic characteristics and product experience. This is because of the following factors.

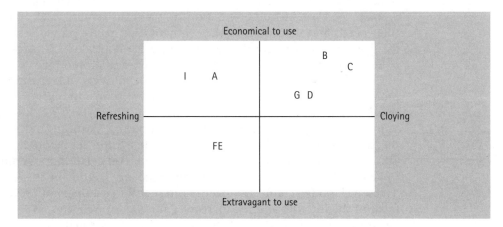

Fig 7.3 Brand positioning

- The perceptual map of ABC1 consumers may differ from that of C2DE consumers.
- The perceptions of 'loyal' users of a brand may well differ from those of 'switchers'.
- Demographic and user groups may vary significantly in their perceptions of the ideal.
- Knowledge of the demographic characteristics of target consumers is essential for media planning.

It is possible to chart the position of brands, taking account of the interaction between all the criterion variables, and for the map to show the following:

- whether a company's existing brands are competing with each other;
- whether there is a gap in the market waiting to be filled.

7.8 Conclusion

Segmentation in marketing terminology invariably involves some form of classification or categorisation of target markets. (Please refer to Chapter 13 for the NRS and proposed new government classifications on social class and occupation, respectively). This means that customers with homogenous characteristics are classed as one group or another so that marketers can target their product and service offerings specifically to the people within these targeted groups who have some shared common characteristics. These shared within-group common characteristics exist because marketers identified them as such, typically in terms of where people live and work, similarities in age, gender, lifestyle and buying patterns, employment status, income earned, social class and even educational background and religious affiliations.

A segmentation study carries the application of the marketing concept an important step forward. The outcome of the segmentation study is a strategic plan focused on the declared needs of a target in the market which has been carefully defined. This applies whether the study is made with the object of initiating a new product or of improving the positioning of one or more brands already in the product field. Data collected needs to include both research approaches (consumer typology and product differentiation) to yield the required data about consumers, their needs and perceptions. The segmentation study provides the blueprint for the development or improvement of a brand, the product, as perceived by buyers, to be an integrated mixture of packaging, price and promotion.

Through mass media channels marketers can devise advertising messages and promotional incentives to appeal to particular groups. In mass markets this makes sense because of mass media advertising and the costs of reaching people on an individual basis. However, with falling computing hardware and software costs in the past two decades the computer, as the television set before it, has become an affordable consumable item in domestic markets. The home computer can be linked to the Internet (some large retailers, e.g. Dixons in the UK, offering the 'Freeserve', no-fee connection to the Internet for customers in 1998). The development of the Internet and the increasing number of web sites, as seen in Chapter 2, has increased the scope for firms to reach their selected customers through the electronic medium. Moreover, the computer's propensity to handle complex calculations and large inputs of data has enabled marketers to construct and access customer databases so that 'profiling' can be undertaken in order to build a picture of the type(s) of customers sought. Database-driven marketing using transactional data (the why, how, when and what of customer goods and income transactions with sellers) overlaid with the multitude of geodemographic profile data is looked at in detail in the following chapter.

Chapter 8 on 'the new biographics', with its explanations of the ways in which firms use geodemographic data, including CACI (ACORN classifications), Experian (MOSAIC clusters) and Claritas (PRIZM life-stage, income and age indicators), puts into context the intensity with which consumer data is used to put across messages and to market products. Having researched the products and the markets, organisations now need to understand their customer base, i.e. what their customers in organisational markets and their consumers in domestic markets want and buy, before framing the messages and images to attract them to their product offerings.

REFERENCES

1. Thomas, M. (1988), 'Market segmentation', *The Quarterly Review of Marketing*, Autumn.

2. Haley, R.E. (1968), 'Benefit segmentation: a decision-oriented research tool', *Journal of Marketing*, July, pp.30–5.

3. CACI Ltd (1998), 'Acorn'; and (1998), 'Marketing systems', vol. 1, no 1.

4. Research International (1994), *Usage and Attitude Studies*, Position Paper 1.

FURTHER READING

1. Green, P. and Krieger, A. (1993), 'A simple approach to target market advertising strategy', *JMRS*, vol. 35, no. 2, April, pp. 161–70.

2. *MRS Researchplus*, (1997), 'Geodemographics: the people map', May.

QUESTIONS

1. (a) How would you segment the market when seeking to locate an opportunity to introduce one of the following new or modified products to consumers:
   (i) a new snack food range;
   (ii) packaged holidays;
   (iii) pet care accessories;
   (iv) car accessories?
   (b) How would you collect and process the required data?
   (c) To apply the results of your segmentation study and to demonstrate understanding of your target market, what marketing communications would you use in order to sell your product to this market segment?

2. (a) In what ways does the application of multivariate statistical treatment of data collected in segmentation studies further the development of marketing plans?
   (b) How might the data be treated and to what end should this be used in marketing?
3. Does the use of statistical techniques mentioned in the chapter:
   (a) diminish the scope for using human judgement, or
   (b) enhance it?
   Discuss.
4. Discuss the extent of the contribution to segmentation studies made by the developments in information technology.

8 Marketing research and the new biographics

Martin Evans

8.1 Introduction

Marketing research will never be the same again. Until the early 1980s the emphasis was on anonymised research approaches. Now marketing researchers are facing up to their greatest moral dilemma. The marketing industry is 'going direct'. This means that the marketer wants to know who is a good prospect for their targeting and they want to know as specifically as possible – and this includes names and addresses. Whereas in earlier days typical market analysis might be based on a sample survey of 1,000 adults nationally perhaps accompanied by a few group discussions, the new world that the marketer is forcing the market researcher to join is one of personalised database construction and analysis. This chapter addresses the move toward personalised research and the ethical concerns it raises for the market researcher.

8.2 Personalised research: the drivers

Back in the 1970s there were predictions that markets were moving to a greater degree of self-expression, individualism and 'inner direction'.[1] The Henley Centre discussed household behaviour as being 'cellular' rather than 'nuclear' – households were beginning to do things together less and less and beginning to behave more independently – families were not eating together as often, having TV and sound systems in their 'own' rooms. Research reported by Publicis[2] suggests that from 1973 to 1989 there had been a shift in 'motivators' from functional and rational factors (40–27% of the population) and 'outer directedness' (static at 35%) to more 'inner directedness' (25–38% of the population). The concept of post-modernism also includes a greater individualism, pluralism, and even fragmentation.[3] Perhaps a current trend which develops this theme is **tribalism**[4] which overcomes the problem of being too socially 'isolated' as a result of individualism because it allows individualistic behaviour among kindred spirits – and different forms of such affiliation in different social circumstances. Thus we still see a fragmentation of the market and the same individual can have multiple roles. Fragmented markets require more targeted marketing which in turn is informed by individualised information about customers.

In parallel with this, marketing researchers have recognised that the traditional research profiling variables, demographics, lack explanatory depth and are too broad for current targeting requirements. Also, in one study, it was found that of 400 respondents to earlier surveys who were re-interviewed to confirm their social grade, 41% had been allocated to the wrong group and this is an indication of instability of the system.[5] The typical market profiling according to age, gender and social grade saw, in the 1980s, parallel profiles in psychographic and geodemographic terms. Indeed, the rise of psychographics and geodemographics have added to demographics' decline because of their potential abilities to understand target customers in great detail, even individually, and to be able to target them equally specifically.

8.3 Geodemographics: the first catalyst?

It is a proposition of this chapter that one of the more significant events in moving from generalised customer profiles to more individualised approaches was the commercial availability of the census and the development of geodemographics from it. From the 1981 UK census, some 40 census variables were cluster analysed and the emerging clusters of households led to the creation of 39 neighbourhood types in the first geodemographic system in the UK (ACORN – A Classification Of Residential Neighbourhoods, developed by CACI). CACI was previously known as 'Californian Analysis Centre, Inc.', then as 'Consolidated Analysis Centre, Inc.' Compare this with one of the leading alternatives of the time – social grade – which classifies the entire population into just six groups on the basis of one variable (occupation of the chief income earner in the household). Whereas these profiles are often based on sample surveys of 1,000, the marketing industry now had access to a census of 56 million. Names and addresses cannot be revealed from the census, but the statistics for enumeration districts can. Such data can be linked with the postcode database (there is one postcode for approximately 15 households), and with the electoral register (another database) it is possible to identify individual households and their characteristics. One of the current debates (at the time of writing) is between the Data Protection Registrar's position that the electoral roll was not collated for marketing purposes and should not therefore be used in this way, and on the other hand the marketing industry which argues for freedom in its use. Clearly, without the electoral roll it would be difficult to identify individual households from census data. One study suggests that a ban on using electoral roll data could cost advertisers £55 million per year because 'the cost of not having access to the electoral roll would be five pence per (mail) pack'.[6] The Data Protection Registrar is concerned that some people may disenfranchise themselves by not registering for fear of being over-targeted by marketers. Although the electoral roll is 'rarely used as a list in itself, it is used as the base for virtually every targeting tool'[7] – and geodemographics started this process. The Data Protection Registrar[8] has submitted to the Constitutional and Community Policy Directorate of the Home Office that:

> the existing arrangements whereby the register is sold without restriction for non electoral purposes should be discontinued ... Individuals' details should not be sold unless they have signified agreement ... Individuals should have a choice over the sale of their data for ... particularly the compilation of direct marketing lists.

The first geodemographic system, ACORN, now consists of 54 different neighbourhood types, some of which are outlined in Table 8.1.

Table 8.1 ACORN profiles based on 1991 census

Categories	Population %	Group		Types	
A Thriving	19.7	1	Wealthy achievers in suburban areas	1.1	Wealthy suburbs, large detached houses
				1.2	Villages with wealthy commuters
				1.3	Mature, affluent home-owning areas
				1.4	Affluent suburbs, older families
				1.5	Mature, well-off suburbs
		2	Affluent greys in rural communities	2.6	Agricultural villages, home-based workers
				2.7	Holiday retreats, older people, home-based workers
		3	Prosperous pensioners in retirement areas	3.8	Home-owning areas, well-off older residents
				3.9	Private flats, elderly people
B Expanding	11.6	4	Affluent executives in family areas	4.10	Affluent working families with mortgages
				4.11	Affluent working couples with mortgages, new homes
				4.12	Transient workforces, living at their place of work
		5	Well-off workers in family areas	5.13	Home-owning family areas
				5.14	Home-owning family areas, older children
				5.15	Home-owning family areas, younger children
C Rising	7.5	6	Affluent urbanites in town and city areas	6.16	Well-off town and city areas
				6.17	Flats and mortgages, singles and young working couples
				6.18	Furnished flats and bedsits, younger single people
		7	Prosperous professionals in metropolitan areas	7.19	Apartments, young professional singles and couples
				7.20	Gentrified multi-ethnic areas
		8	Better-off executives in inner city areas	8.21	Prosperous enclaves, highly qualified executives
				8.22	Academic centres, students and young professionals
				8.23	Affluent city centre areas, tenements and flats
				8.24	Partially gentrified multi-ethnic areas
				8.25	Converted flats and bedsits, single people
D Settling	24.1	9	Comfortable middle agers, mature home-owning areas	9.26	Mature established home-owning areas
				9.27	Rural areas, mixed occupations
				9.28	Established home-owning areas
				9.29	Home-owning areas, council tenants, retired people

Table 8.1 Continued

Categories	Population %	Group		Types	
		10	Skilled workers, home-owning areas	10.30	Established home-owning areas, skilled workers
				10.31	Home-owners in older properties, younger workers
				10.32	Home-owning areas with skilled workers
E Aspiring	13.7	11	New home-owners, mature communities	11.33	Council areas, some new home owners
				11.34	Mature home-owning areas, skilled workers
				11.35	Low-rise estates, older workers, new home owners
		12	White collar workers, better-off multi-ethnic areas	12.36	Home-owning multi-ethnic areas, young families
				12.37	Multi-occupied town centres, mixed occupations
				12.38	Multi-ethnic areas, white collar workers
F Striving	22.7	13	Older people, less prosperous areas	13.39	Home owners, small council flats, single pensioners
				13.40	Council areas, older people, health problems
		14	Council estate residents, better-off homes	14.41	Better-off council areas, new home owners
				14.42	Council areas young families, some new home owners
				14.43	Council areas young families, many lone parents
				14.44	Multi-occupied terraces, multi-ethnic areas
				14.45	Low-rise council housing, less well-off families
				14.46	Council areas, residents with health problems
		15	Council estate residents, high unemployment	15.47	Estates with high unemployment
				15.48	Council flats, elderly people, health problems
				15.49	Council flats, very high unemployment, singles
		16	Council estate residents, greatest hardship	16.50	Council areas, high unemployment, lone parents
				16.51	Council flats, greatest hardship, many lone parents
		17	People in multi-ethnic, low-income areas	17.52	Multi-ethnic, large families, overcrowding
				17.53	Multi-ethnic, severe unemployment, lone parents
				17.54	Multi-ethnic, high unemployment, overcrowding

Source: CACI

Census statistics
Source: OPCS

Socio-economic data
Housing
Household and age

Demographic data
Source: Electoral registers

Age
Household composition
Population movement

Financial data
Source: Lord Chancellor's Office
          Companies House
Retail data
Housing data
Source: Land registry
Vehicle information
Source: DVLA

County court judgments
Directors
Accessibility
House price data

Fig 8.1 MOSAIC's data sources
Source: Experian

In terms of marketing research, there is now a full geodemographic analysis of the Target Group Index (TGI) which is an annual report in 34 volumes of buyer profiles in most product-markets and based on samples of over 20,000. From this, each geodemographic category's interest in the product concerned can be determined. In fact the TGI sample design is now based on geodemographic categories and so sample design is another research application of geodemographics. In addition, the National Readership Survey is similarly analysed by geodemographics and this can provide readership profiles for media selection purposes.

There are 'me-toos' of the original ACORN system. Richard Webber, who created ACORN, set up one of the competitors after he left CACI to join a similar agency, CCN (now called Experian, following the link with the American company of that name) and developed MOSAIC which analyses the census data in conjunction with a variety of data sources including CCJs, Electoral Roll and Royal Mail data. Figure 8.1 summarises the sources of MOSAIC's data and demonstrates that although the census still provides the motherload there is a fusion of data taking place to provide ever more sophisticated profiling methods.

The basic rationale behind geodemographics is that 'birds of a feather flock together', making neighbourhoods relatively homogenous. An easy criticism in riposte is that 'I am not like my neighbour'. However, geodemographics have proved to be reasonably robust overall.

Table 8.2 summarises some of the descriptors of ACORN, while Table 8.3 provides a detailed profile of ACORN Type 22.

Table 8.2 ACORN descriptors

Category and label	Description
Category A Group 1 Wealthy achievers, suburban areas	The majority of people in this group live in a large detached house and have access to two or more cars. They are typically well-educated professional people, the corporate managers in their middle age, enjoying the fruits of their labour. These are the consumers with the money and the space to enjoy very comfortable lifestyles.

Table 8.2 Continued

Category and label	Description
Category A Group 2 Affluent greys, rural communities	This group covers Britain's better-off farming communities – residents here are 12 times more likely than average to be involved in agriculture. Many are self-employed and work long hours. The very high incidence of visitors and households which are not the main residence show that these areas also include many holiday homes.
Category A Group 3 Prosperous pensioners, retirement areas	The better-off senior citizens in society are to be found in Group 3. Living in flats, detached houses or bungalows, these are old folk who can enjoy their retirement in pensioned comfort after their professional or executive careers. They are likely to own their home outright, so they have the disposable income to enjoy themselves.
Category B Group 4 Affluent executives, family areas	These are the well-qualified business people, successfully juggling jobs and families. There are lots of working women in this group. With mortgages, young children and often two or more cars to support, these busy people need their incomes but aren't having too hard a time making ends meet. They are likely to have large, modern detached houses and generally enjoy a good standard of living.
Category B Group 5 Well-off workers, family areas	In a wide range of well-paid occupations, people in Group 5 are likely to be in couples, often with children aged 0–14. Both Mum and Dad are working hard to pay off the mortgage on their detached or, more probably, semi-detached home. While they are not as highly qualified as people in Group 4, they still have an agreeable lifestyle, often with more than two cars per household.
Category C Group 6 Affluent urbanites, town and city areas	These are the young couples or single people starting out in life, a few years and a couple of kids behind the people in Group 4! They tend to live in flats, terraced houses or bedsits. There are quite a number of students in this group. Car ownership is average, reflecting the urban setting.
Category C Group 7 Prosperous professionals, metropolitan areas	People in Group 7 share many characteristics with Group 6. However, they live in more cosmopolitan areas with a high ethnic mix. They take the train or underground to the office each day, working long hours in fairly senior roles and making the most of their high qualifications.
Category C Group 8 Better-off executives, inner-city areas	These are well-qualified people, over a third of whom are single with no dependants. The age profile here is younger than for Groups 6 and 7 and there are many more students and other characteristics of academic centres. This group also has a relatively high proportion of professionals and executives and shares many of the cosmopolitan features of Group 7.
Category D Group 9 Comfortable middle agers, mature home-owning areas	Mr and Mrs Average are to be found in these areas – they are close to the national 'norm' on just about every key characteristic. Living in a detached or semi-detached house with at least one car, likely to be an older married couple, Group 9 represents middle-of-the-road Britain. They are not particularly well-off but have few problems with unemployment or health.

Category D Group 10 Skilled workers, home-owning areas	People in this group are likely to be found in manufacturing areas, working in skilled occupations. They tend to live in terraced homes and are more likely to be couples with children aged 0–14. Most are home-owners and the majority are buying with a mortgage. Although not quite as comfortable as Group 9 – car ownership is lower – people in these areas are also around the midpoint on the social ladder.
Category E Group 11 New home owners, mature communities	These areas are characterised by people who have bought up their semi-detached or terraced council houses. They are likely to be older couples, often pensioners. Those still at work tend to be involved in craft or machine-related occupations. Unemployment is only slightly above the national average.
Category E Group 12 White collar workers, better-off, multi- ethnic areas	The relatively high incidence of people from diverse ethnic groups – especially Afro-Caribbean and Indian – characterises these multi-ethnic family areas. Accommodation tends to be either terraced houses or flats. Unemployment is slightly higher than in Group 11, but overall living conditions are reasonable.
Category F Group 13 Older people, less prosperous areas	These are the areas of older couples aged 55+ who find the going quite tough. The incidence of limiting long-term illness is high. The majority do not have a car. People are generally living in small terraced houses or purpose-built flats, typically from housing associations. Those still at work tend to be in manual or unskilled occupations; unemployment is above average.
Category F Group 14 Council estate residents, better-off homes	These areas are typified by young couples with young children. Housing tends to be council or housing association terraces, often with cramped living conditions, though families tend to be better off than those in other groups in this category. Unemployment is relatively high and there are many single parents.
Category F Group15 Council estate residents, high unemployment	Group 15 has a greater ethnic mix and higher unemployment than Group 14. This group has an older age profile and the highest incidence of limiting long-term illness – almost double the national average. People live mainly in purpose-built council flats. Car ownership is lower in these areas than anywhere else.
Category F Group 16 Council estate residents, greatest hardship	Two key features characterise this group: single parents and unemployment, both of which – at roughly three times the national average – are higher in this group than in any other. Overall, living conditions are extremely tough. There are lots of young and very young children, with large households in small council flats.
Category F Group 17 People in multi-ethnic, low-income areas	The greatest ethnic mix in Britain is found in this group, especially of Pakistani and Bangladeshi groups which account for over 40% of the population. Single parenting and unemployment are very high. Many people are living in extremely cramped conditions in unmodernised terraced housing or council flats. Whilst these areas are relatively poor, there is evidence to suggest small pockets of more affluent residents.

Table 8.3 Type 22 Academic centres, students and young professionals

Overview	These are predominantly student areas. In addition to students, there are people who work in higher education and young professionals. They are cosmopolitan areas located near universities. ACORN Type 22 neighbourhoods are found all over Britain, but the highest concentration is in Oxford.
Demographics	These areas have 80% more people than average in the 15–24 age group. There is also an above average level of 25–44 year olds, but below average representation of all other age groups. There are above average proportions of ethnic minorities – twice the national proportion of people from the Afro-Caribbean ethnic group, over three times the national proportion of people from the Asian ethnic group and, within this, over five times the national level of people from the Pakistani ethnic group. In terms of household structure, there are 2.2 times the average proportion of single non-pensioner households.
Socio-economic profile	The socio-economic profile of ACORN Type 22 is dominated by education. Almost 47% of the adult population are students based in these neighbourhoods in term time. The non-student population is also highly educated, with three times the average proportion of people with degrees. The proportions of women, both with and without children, who work are below average. The level of professionals is over twice the average.
Housing	The housing structure of ACORN Type 22 is a mix of terraced homes (37% more than average), purpose-built flats (twice the national average proportion), converted flats (2.7 times more than average) and bedsits (5.2 times more than average). The key feature of the tenure profile is the level of furnished rented accommodation – almost seven times more than average. The proportion of households sharing amenities is three times greater than average.
Food and drink	People living in ACORN Type 22 neighbourhoods are more than twice as likely as average to do their grocery shopping on foot, though less likely than average to do daily food shopping. The typical student diet is reflected in the range of foods purchased regularly. Consumption of frozen ready meals is high, though consumption of other frozen foods such as beefburgers is below average. Other popular products are brown sauce and ketchup, tinned steak, boxed chocolates and fruit juice. Beer consumption is extremely high, especially of bottled lager, but consumption of wines and spirits is only just above average.
Durables	Car ownership levels are low, reflecting the socio-economic profile of the population. Twice as many people as average walk to work. Although car ownership is very low, the car profile is biased towards new, large and expensive cars. Company car ownership is 75% lower than average. 66% more people than average are buying home computers and 83% more people are buying tumble dryers. Purchase rates for other household durables are extremely low.
Financial	The average income in these areas is very low, as might be expected given the large numbers of students. Almost a quarter of people earn less than £5,000 per annum, and only 3% earn over £30,000 per annum. Almost twice as many people as average are opening new current accounts but virtually no one is opening new savings accounts. Ownership of all financial products is very low except debit cards which are owned by 48% more people than average.
Media	The penetration of cable television in these neighbourhoods is 46% higher than average. The *Financial Times*, the *Guardian* and the *Independent* all have much higher than average readership levels. Amongst the Sunday newspapers, the *Observer* and the *Independent on Sunday* are read by 2–3 times more people here than average. Both ITV viewing and commercial radio listening are very light.

Leisure	The proportion of people taking holidays is average, but 82% more people than average take long holidays. 2.5 times more people than average go camping, and destinations outside Britain and Europe are 82% more popular than average. There is a very high propensity to visit pubs regularly. The proportion of people eating out regularly is slightly above average. Burger bars are popular, as are Chinese, Indian and Italian restaurants. Sports which have very high participation rates are running and training, cricket, tennis, cycling, squash, table tennis, skiing and climbing. Attendance at cinemas, theatres and art galleries is very high.
Attitudes	People here are less likely than average to be happy with their standard of living. They are much more likely than average to search for the lowest prices when shopping. They are over twice as likely as average to be vegetarian. They like to take holidays off the beaten track, but are happy to return to the same holiday destination.

Geodemographic systems are not restricted to the UK, and a number of similar systems around the world are listed in Table 8.4. In other European countries similar systems exist, for example under the names: Geo Market profile and Omnidata. Several geodemographic companies now operate throughout many European countries, such as Experian (with its MOSAIC brand). See Figure 8.2 for an example of how MOSAIC profiles other European cities.

Table 8.4 Geodemographic systems around the world

	Vendor
USA	
• PRIZM	Claritas
• Cluster plus	Donnelly
• Niches	Polk
• ACORN	CACI
Canada	
• Cluster	Compusearchs
UK	
• MOSAIC	Experian
• ACORN	CACI
• Superprofiles	Claritas (former CDMS)
• Define	Infolink
• Cameo (formerly Neighbours & Prospects)	EuroDirect
Ireland	
• MOSAIC	Experian
Spain	
• Regio	Bertlesmann
• MOSAIC Iberia	Experian/PDM
Belgium	
• MOSAIC	Sopres

Table 8.4 Continued

	Vendor
Netherlands	
• MOSAIC	Experian
• GEO	Geomarktprofiel
Finland	
• ACORN	Gallup/Post Office
• Experian MarknadsAnalys	Experian
Australia	
• Pinpoint	Experian
South Africa	
• MOSAIC Marketing	Experian
Norway	
• MOSAIC	Experian/Norsk Micromosaic
New Zealand	
• Pinpoint	Experian
Italy	
• MOSAIC	Experian/SEAT
Greece	
• MOSAIC	Experian/Mellan Technologies
Germany	
• MOSAIC	Experian/Microm/Tell Sell
France	
• MOSAIC	Experian/Group Adress
Sweden	
• MOSAIC	MarknadsAnalys
• MarknadsAnalys	Experian/DAD

Source: Experian.
1 Turnover band: 1<£1m p.a.; 2 = £1m–£5m p.a.; 3>£5m p.a.

Figure 8.3 profiles the Bristol area and Table 8.5 shows the penetration of stylish singles around Bristol. The marketing research implications of geodemographics are substantial. First, having identified these profiles, names and addresses can be produced for direct mailings of relevant target groups in relevant locations. Equally, a map of the penetration of student drinkers in the Bristol area can also be generated (Figure 8.4). This demonstrates the linking of data from more than just the census and electoral roll; in this, additionally, from the PAS survey on drinking patterns. This sort of analysis could be used for direct targeting within areas – via direct mail because the analysis can produce lists of names and addresses or through door drops. Yet another research application is in retail catchment area analysis, for example, for a car dealer (Figure 8.5) based on ACORN groups. The dealer can determine which groups are the best prospect and acquire names and addresses for direct mailings.

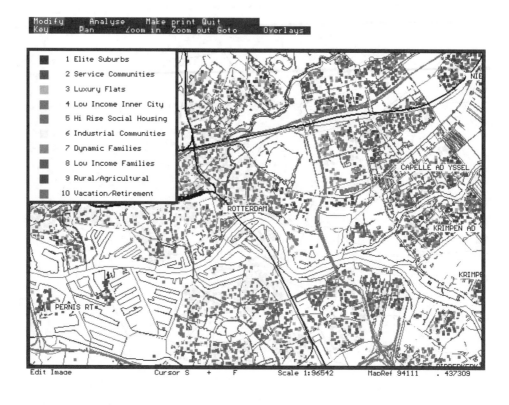

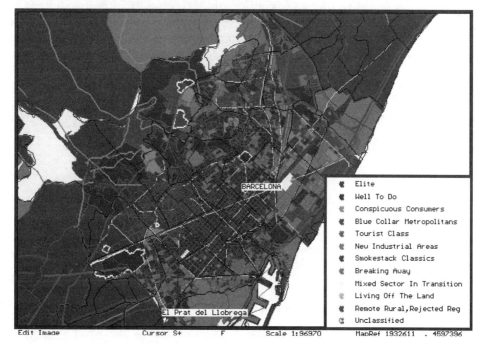

Fig 8.2 MOSAIC profiles of (a) Rotterdam and (b) Barcelona
Source: Experian.

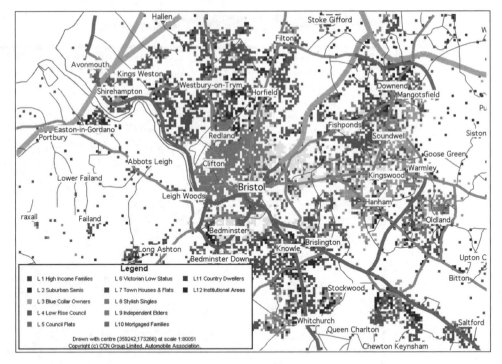

Fig 8.3 MOSAIC profile of Bristol
Source: Experian.

There have been other developments of the geodemographic principle but we need to discuss psychographics first and this is the theme of the next section. However, we can provide some of the proposals for the 2001 census which would affect geodemographics. First, it is interesting to note that the government has, for the first time, 'officially added commercial business to the list of users' of the census.[9] Second, new questions potentially relevant to the marketer and market researcher are proposed. Specifically, income (but the pre-census test only includes bands up to £25,000), religion (options include: Christian, Hindu, Jewish, Islam/Muslim, Sikh and Buddhist), whether there is provision of unpaid personal care, size of employer's organisation, length of time out of work if unemployed, and sexuality of partner.[10]

Table 8.5 Stylish singles in Bristol

References	Stylish singles	Target %	Total household estimate 1996	Base %	Penetration	Index
BS 8 2 Chantry Road, Bristol	3142	8.12	3147	0.81	0.9984	997
BS 8 1 Buckingham Pal, Clifton, Bristol	1780	4.60	1845	0.48	0.9648	963
BS 6 6 Cotham, Bristol	4917	12.70	5157	1.33	0.9535	952
BS 1 4 Colston Avenue, Bristol	228	0.59	242	0.06	0.9421	941
BS 8 4 Hotwells, Bristol	3393	8.77	3660	0.95	0.9270	926
BS 1 1 Baldwin Street, Bristol	162	0.42	183	0.05	0.8852	884
BS 6 5 Cheltenham Road, Bristol	3758	9.71	4433	1.15	0.8477	846
BS 1 5 Park Row, Bristol	549	1.42	681	0.18	0.8062	805
BA 1 2 James Street, Bath	2047	5.29	3093	0.80	0.6618	661
BS 6 7 Westbury Park, Bristol	2407	6.22	3716	0.96	0.6477	647
BS 8 3 Clifton, Abbots Leigh, Bristol	1450	3.75	2487	0.64	0.5830	582
BS 2 8 Jamaica Street, Bristol	1368	3.53	2583	0.67	0.5296	529
BA 1 5 Sion Hill, Bath	1209	3.12	2337	0.60	0.5173	517
BS 7 8 Redland, Bristol	2039	5.27	3991	1.03	0.5109	510
BS 1 6 Redcliffe Way, Bristol	757	1.96	1780	0.46	0.4253	425
BA 1 1 Avon Street, Bath	429	1.11	1011	0.26	0.4243	424
BA 2 4 Beechen Cliff, Bath	951	2.46	2611	0.68	0.3642	364
BA 1 6 Larkhall, Bath	1181	3.05	3604	0.93	0.3277	327
BS 7 9 Down Road, Bristol	1761	4.55	5674	1.47	0.3104	310
BS 3 1 Coronation Road, Bristol	897	2.32	3682	0.95	0.2436	243
BA 1 3 Newbridge, Bath	610	1.58	2653	0.69	0.2299	230
BS 1 3 Broadmead, Bristol	76	0.20	387	0.10	0.1964	196
BA 2 3 South Twerton, Bath	565	1.46	3291	0.85	0.1717	171
BA 2 6 Claverton, Bath	466	1.20	2958	0.77	0.1575	157
BS16 3 Speedwell, Bristol	400	1.03	2834	0.73	0.1411	141

Source: Experian

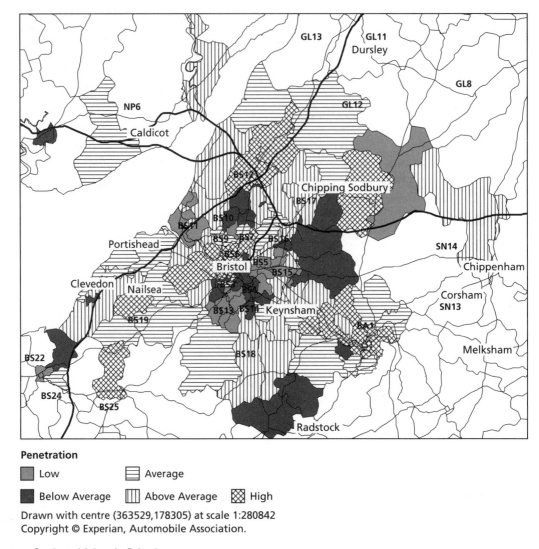

Penetration

▨ Low	▤ Average	
■ Below Average	▥ Above Average	▩ High

Drawn with centre (363529,178305) at scale 1:280842
Copyright © Experian, Automobile Association.

Fig 8.4 Student drinkers in Bristol

Source: Experian

ACORN application on car dealership (1981 categories)					
ACORN group	% of area	×	Model X index	=	Area sales potential
A	1.4	×	61	=	0.85
B	–	×	108	=	–
C	9.7	×	84	=	8.15
D	7.9	×	39	=	2.92
E	–	×	41	=	–
F	11.4	×	53	=	6.04
G	–	×	34	=	–
H	13.9	×	124	=	17.80
I	29.4	×	230	=	66.93
J	22.5	×	217	=	48.82
K	3.1	×	84	=	2.60
Total					154.11

If model X would be bought by 5% of the national population and the catchment area is 10,000, a sales potential of 10,000 × 5% = 500 would be expected. But the index here is 154.11, so for this catchment area the sales potential is 500 × 1.5411 = 770.

Fig 8.5 Catchment area analysis
Source: CACI

These questions could provide some additional data for marketing research, for example, income is a useful measure of potential disposable income, levels of personal help might be of interest to service providers and the questions about religion could be used to target individuals by church organisations – which are increasingly turning to marketing. The 1991 census included a controversial question about ethnic origin, which will probably be revised and extended for 2001 (SARs, 1999). Will the questions above prove equally controversial, such as sexuality of partner which would certainly help the market researcher whose brief is to analyse and identify the gay market, for example?

However extensive the census becomes, the major limitation of census data relates to the difficulties associated with updating information, particularly because in the UK the census is only carried out every ten years. Experian has reallocated approx 7% of postcodes and have six name changes in the MOSAIC typology, both as an update and to improve clarity of meaning. There are suggestions that annual updates might be based on survey research, especially of the 'lifestyle' type discussed in the next section.

Because geodemographics are based on census data, there is the corresponding criticism of those systems. In addition, as sophisticated as geodemographics are – certainly compared with the simplicity of age, gender and occupation (the main variables of the demographic alternative) the approach is essentially the same – that is, it 'profiles' people. It does not in itself explain why people behave as they do and neither does it provide individualised information on what people buy. These issues are, to some extent, addressed by other approaches, outlined in the sections below on psychographics, transactional data and biographics.

8.4 Psychographics

Although psychographic research covers analysis of personality, self-concept and lifestyle variables, the focus in this chapter is on the use of lifestyle research. This, originally, was based typically on the presentation to respondents of a series of statements (Likert scales). Figure 8.6 reproduces a short selection of the (246) lifestyle statements used in the TGI annual research programme.

This form of lifestyle research is concerned with investigating activities, interests and opinions and is sometimes referred to as AIO analysis. Such lifestyle data is then cluster analysed to produce groupings of respondents which are relatively homogenous and at the same time heterogeneous *between* clusters. Each cluster would then be allocated a somewhat glib title.

A UK lifestyle typology was named Taylor Nelson's Applied Futures and identified segments including 'The Belonger', 'The Survivor', 'The Experimentalist', 'The Conspicuous Consumer', 'The Social Resistor', 'The Self-Explorer' and 'The Aimless'. The Self-Explorer group was the fastest growing and further reinforces one of the propositions of this chapter, namely that some markets have become more orientated to self-expression and individualism.

This traditional form of lifestyle (AIO) segmentation provides useful insight into what makes people 'tick'. It is based upon traditional market research; administering Likert scaled statements to a sample of consumers. The data is anonymised and the resulting profiles are very useful for determining the style and mood of promotional messages, for example.

At this point, one of the key themes of this chapter is reinforced, namely that anonymised research is giving way to personalised database construction and analysis. This is because the more recent development in lifestyle research and segmentation is the 'lifestyle survey' which is conducted on a somewhat different basis. These surveys are designed by companies such as Claritas and Experian and essentially ask respondents to check those responses that apply – Figure 8.7 demonstrates some typical questions, some of which will be sponsored by specific companies.

I buy clothes for comfort, not for style.
Once I find a brand I like, I tend to stick to it.
I always buy British whenever I can.
I dress to please myself.
My family rarely sits down to a meal together at home.
I enjoy eating foreign food.
I like to do a lot when I am on holiday.

Fig 8.6 Examples of lifestyle statements

Please indicate your marital status
Single, married, divorced/separated, widowed:

What is your name and address:

What is your partner's full name:

Holidays:
How much are you likely to spend per person on your next main holiday:
up to £500 ☐ £501 – £999 ☐ £1000 – £1499 ☐ £1500 – £2000 ☐
£2000+ ☐

In which country are you likely to take your next main holiday: ________

In which month are you likely to take your main holiday: ________

Fig 8.7 Contemporary 'lifestyle' research

This reflects just a portion of typical current lifestyle surveys. Many more questions are included, covering claimed buying behaviour across many different product and service categories. Some questions will be sponsored by specific companies – for example a car insurance company might sponsor a question asking for the month in which the car insurance is renewed. Because these surveys are not anonymised, the data will be filed in a database by name and address of respondent and it is likely that the month prior to that respondent's renewal date, he or she will receive direct mailings soliciting defection to the sponsoring company.

Although the industry has claimed there is now a lifestyle census, the reality is somewhat different. Admittedly a large number of individuals (around 20 million in the UK) have responded, but the survey is, by definition, a self-selected sample and it is known that some respondents do not tell the whole truth in completing the questionnaire. The difference between the more traditional form of lifestyle segmentation and the current approach is that the former builds psychographic profiles of segments from relatively small datasets and expands these to generalise patterns within the larger population. The latter, however, has the ability to list names and addresses of those who claim to be interested in specific products, brands and services and it is this, of course, that the 'new marketing' values. It provides data on what respondents claim they buy but doesn't in itself reveal the same type of *affective* data on opinions and 'outlook on life' that can be derived from traditional AIO analysis.

8.5 Geolifestyle

Earlier, we paused the discussion of geodemographics pending coverage of psychographics. This was because although geodemographics traditionally relied upon the census as the main data source, there are now several variants available, some incorporating the lifestyle survey discussed above.

'Geolifestyle' research is an example. Here, databases are aggregated to unit post-code level and built around lifestyle survey data. Examples of geolifestyle are PRIZM, developed in the UK by Claritas. 'Lifestyle UK' by CACI is not postcoded, but operates at individual level, however, a newer product, 'PayCheck', an income model is postcode defined. There are a number of benefits associated with these new geolifestyle databases:[11]

- In contrast to census data which is collected every ten years, lifestyle data is collected continually. Thus, direct marketers can maintain up-to-date information on customers and prospects.

- Unlike the census, geolifestyle databases provide data on named individuals. Thus, they can assist in targeting of individuals for direct marketing offers. For example, a company selling dog food can target individuals who own dogs, as opposed to targeting neighbourhoods where people *are likely* to own dogs.

- Geolifestyle databases can be constructed at unit postcode levels, which are ten times smaller than census enumeration districts (EDs). Thus, the resulting neighbourhood profiles are far more precise.

- Individuals can be asked to provide additional information relating to personal interests and household income. Such data is not available from the census because it is designed for public service planners not consumer marketers.

- However, geolifestyle databases provide less information than the census, and furthermore are not legally compulsory. In contrast, the census is compulsory and every household responds at the same time.

As a result, 'it is still too early to say whether the new "geolifestyle" approach is superior to the conventional geodemographic route' (Leventhal, 1995). In any case, the drawbacks outlined previously that lifestyle survey participants are self-selecting, and may not always be truthful, suggests that there may be some biases or distortions in geolifestyle databases generally, but the approach reflects experimentation with combining data sources in different ways which is currently widespread in the industry. For example, CACI is offering 'People UK' which is based on lifestyle data but incorporates geodemographics and provides profiles at individual level (not neighbourhood or even household level) which are initially life-stage profiled as shown in Table 8.6.

Table 8.6 People UK

Lifestage 1	Starting out
Silver spoons	Young people with affluent parents
Popcorn and pop music	Singles in low-value housing
Friends in flats	Young flat sharers
Urban multi-cultural	Mixed metropolitan singles
Lifestage 2	Young with toddlers
Legoland families	Prosperous marrieds with pre-school children
Caravans and fun fairs	Young families in mid-value homes
Struggling singles	Single parents on low incomes

Lifestage 3
On the right track
PC parents
School fetes
Car boot sales
Camping and cottages
Loan-loaded lifestyles
Satellites and scratchcards

Young families
Up-market executive families
Affluent liberal young families
Aspiring couples with young children
Traditional families with average incomes
Moderate incomes, outdoor pursuits
Low incomes and high loans
Poorer families without bank accounts

Lifestage 4
Telebanking townies
Solvent set
On the terraces
Pubs and pool

Singles/couples, no kids
City flat sharers with affluent active lifestyles
Financially aware middle-aged singles/couples
Blue collar singles
Poorer singles in deprived areas

Lifestage 5
Serious money
Affluent intelligentsia
Two-car suburbia
Conventional families
Cross-Channel weekenders
Gardens and pets
Neighbourhood watch
Staid at home
Tabloids and TV

Middle-aged families
Wealthy families in exclusive areas
Cultured well-off couples
Prosperous people with teenage children
Comfortable households with traditional values
Moderately well-off settled families
Established families in country areas
Average incomes, suburban semis
Families with teenage children in low-value semis
Lower income families with older children

Lifestage 6
Prosperous empty nesters
Young at heart
Cautious couples
Radio 2 fans
Urban elderly
Beer and bookies

Empty nesters
Older couples living in expensive houses
Older couples with active interests
Modest lifestyles and moderate means
Average incomes and traditional attitudes
Poorer couples in council housing
Low income families with teenage children

Lifestage 7
The golden years
Cultured living
Keeping up appearances
Put the kettle on
Counting the pennies
Just coping

Retired couples
Affluent couples
Retired couples with up-market leisure interests
Retirees in bungalows
Inactive retirees
Elderly couples in low-value housing
Impoverished elderly couples

Lifestage 8
Older affluent urbanites
Active pensioners
Theatre and travel
Songs of praise
Grey blues
Church and bingo
Meals on wheels

Older singles
Older metropolitans in expensive housing
Older people with active lifestyles
Elderly city dwellers with up-market interests
Charitable elderly singles
Pensioners living in very poor areas
Very old and poor singles
Poorest elderly in council flats

Source: CACI: People UK

8.6 Transactional data: the second catalyst?

Retailers, such as Tesco, Safeway and Sainsbury, are capturing transactional data at point of sale via loyalty card schemes. By early 1999 Tesco had analysed their customer database and identified 80,000 different segments – each of which were targeted differently. The company analysing the Tesco data is DunnHumby and Clive Humby describes the interrogation of data and states that it is not worth including 'everything'.[12] There is always the danger of 'paralysis by analysis'! Humby goes on to suggest that 'it is not the detailed transaction data that is of interest, but patterns in transactions, such as an increasing balance over time of the range of products purchased'. He also highlights the problem that the industry has over a lack of staff to fill the IT-marketing gap.

If geodemographics were a significant catalyst in marketing research from the early 1980s, **transactional** data is now providing yet more dramatic impetus. As an example of transactional data, an inspection of a resulting retail loyalty scheme database revealed, for a certain 'Mrs Brown', her address and a variety of behavioural information, including: she shops once per week, usually on a Friday, has a baby (because she buys nappies), spends £90 per week on average and usually buys two bottles of gin every week. By knowing what individual consumers buy, the retailer might be able to target them with relevant offers whilst the consumer saves

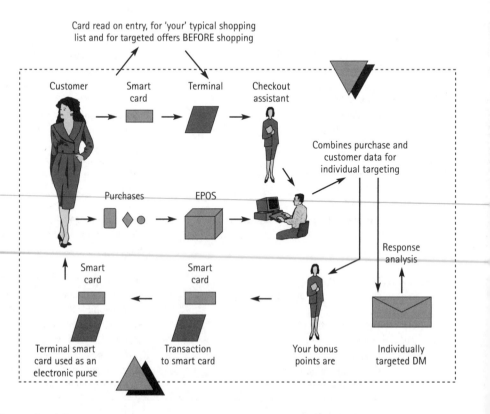

Fig 8.8 Transactional data

money in the process. If a 'relationship' develops, the retailer is moving from the more expensive 'acquisition' to the much cheaper 'retention' of consumers – advocated by several writers in times of low industry growth. Figure 8.8 summarises how transactional data can be collected, stored, analysed and used for subsequent personalised targeting.

8.7 Data fusion: the biographics era?

Now that transactional data is at the heart of many databases, overlaid with a multitude of profile data, we are perhaps moving into the era of **biographics** – the fusion of profile and transaction data. Figure 8.9 shows some of the typical sources of data for fusion into biographical profiles. Indeed, 'data matching is the key because it bridges sources' and provides the ability to match names, addresses, purchasing behaviour, and lifestyles all together.

Data fusion is the linking of data between databases, and a data warehouse is the merged database. Data warehousing is the process of creating one large collection of data in a single location. Typically, this requires gathering and storing data from multiple sources which then becomes the single focal point for all types of data analysis. The data warehouse allows fast queries on potentially any data attribute it contains. 'The data warehouse ... can be defined as a system that collects data from various applications throughout an organisation, integrates that data, stores it and then exploits it to deliver information throughout the organisation'.[13] This definition by the director of marketing at the SAS Institute – one of the world's largest software companies – shows that it goes beyond the marketing function and is an integrator of a variety of business functions.

Data fusion occurs on two levels. First, on an industry level – census data, geodemographics and lifestyle data build up a broad picture of the population – ideal for segmentation research. Second, at the individual company level, matching this data to credit history, actual purchasing behaviour and media response can potentially describe individual consumers' lives.

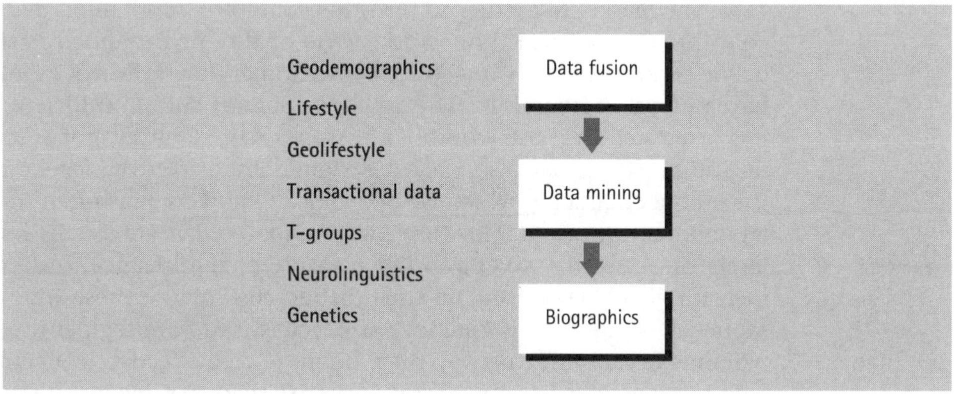

Geodemographics	Data fusion
Lifestyle	
Geolifestyle	
Transactional data	Data mining
T-groups	
Neurolinguistics	
Genetics	Biographics

Fig 8.9 Biographics and data fusion

Often it is very useful to be able to model, geographically, what the database information tells us. The key to this is address and postcode because from this there are geographical information systems (GIS) which allow any linked database to produce map overlays. Another application of GIS linked data is in the citing of posters for direct response advertising, based on the profile of the neighbourhood or even the profile of 'through' traffic. A related approach is the calculation drive times as isochrones (the distance one can drive in a given time along roads).

Another research approach is to fuse a GIS database with a biographic database to target as specifically as a newspaper round. This is usually around 150-200 households and by linking transactional data with lifestyle, geodemographics and panel data, a very accurate picture of individual buying patterns emerges. The newspaper round – or milk round – can be used for door drops or direct mail as well as for local catchment area analysis. This has been formalised by Unigate which has advertised a door-step delivery service based on MOSAIC geodemographic profiles at local level. In addition to product delivery they offer a delivery service for samples and vouchers and a delivery and collection service for questionnaires.

A different sort of data fusion is also taking place – there is clear evidence of a trend towards the creation of strategic alliances between non-competing companies based on sharing data. For example, an insurance company has a ten-year agreement with motor companies, a vehicle breakdown service and a satellite TV company. There is clearly synergy to be had between these if data is shared, with respect to complementary business (for 'cross selling') and for advertising purposes. Unilever, Kimberley Clark, Cadbury and Bass have joined to form the Consumer Needs Consortium which aims to reduce research and database costs. 'It is difficult to make the numbers work on expensive database building and direct marketing strategies, which provide the framework for ventures such as direct shopping, when you are churning out low purchase price items'.[14] An issue that is likely to be raised in the future is how to assess which companies should join such partnerships – corporate culture will be as important as product-market synergy. If some form of unified loyalty scheme is offered, customers will have to be researched on the basis of the total amalgam of the grouping rather than a single 'brand'.

The market researcher and analyst now recognises that the emphasis on the sample survey is something of the past. The present – and future – is in the collection of personalised data for database compilation and in the subsequent data fusing and data mining of layered databases.

For the market researcher to turn this data into 'information' requires a variety of conceptual analytical frameworks. One of the most popular is the 'recency, frequency and monetary value' (RFM) of customer orders. Recency – just knowing they have purchased from us in the past – is important but not sufficient; we are probably less interested in those who bought from us in 1984 but not since. Frequency – a one-off purchase may also make a customer less attractive (depending, of course, on the product-market in which we operate). So knowing how often they buy from us is an important measure. Monetary value – small orders are usually less attractive than larger ones, so this is yet another measure of significance. Indeed, marketers are increasingly concentrating on their 'better' customers – those who have the highest monetary value (and frequency) of purchase, and are segmenting on the basis of 'volume' because in this way they are more cost effective, concentrating on those who bring greater returns. Vilfredo Pareto's theory of income distribution has been transferred and borrowed by direct marketers to support the proposition that 80% of sales come from just 20% of customers – in many markets the ratio can be even more polarised (95:5 is not uncommon). Tesco has introduced segmentation based on this, via research which leads to 'gold', 'silver' and 'bronze' levels of purchasing (and hence loyalty card variants).[15] However, might the less privileged become disaffected when they realise that others are being presented with the 'better' offers? It has even been suggested from within the industry that alienated customers might see this as something 'Orwellian in nature'.[16] RFM analysis clearly, by the nature of the variables involved, means that transactional data must be tracked by the database – actual purchase history is needed.

In addition to leading to the identification of volume segments and best prospects, the RFM information also contributes to the calculation of 'lifetime value'. 'Lifetime' is perhaps a little of an overstatement – it doesn't mean the lifetime of the customer, but rather a designated period of time during which they are a customer of your organisation. Sometimes we might only use a 'lifetime' period of three years. It would probably be better to refer to 'longtime' value analysis but whatever period is relevant, the concept of what that customer is worth to the organisation in sales and profit terms over a period of time is becoming a critical marketing research concept.

Other dimensions of 'the new research' revolve around data mining, which is a 'process of extracting hidden or previously unknown, comprehensible and actionable information from large databases'.[17] From this there are two approaches that data mining can adopt. The first is *verification-driven*; 'extracting information to validate an hypothesis postulated by a user' (ibid.). The second approach refers to the digging around in databases in a relatively unstructured way with the aim of discovering links between customer behaviour and almost any variable that might potentially be useful. This second approach is *discovery driven*: 'identifying and extracting hidden, previously unknown information ... [to] scour the data for patterns which do not come naturally to the analysts' set of views or ideas' (ibid.). There is a parallel with market research versus environmental scanning, because the former focuses on specific problems and the latter has a wider-ranging brief to identify anything in the marketing environment which might have a relevant impact upon the marketing operation.

Marketing researchers are investigating a variety of **modelling** approaches, and some have tried a variety of unusual or unexpected areas in which to mine. For example, some have examined consumers' individual biorhythms and star signs as predictors of their purchasing patterns.[18]

Another approach is to investigate different information processing styles, some of which might be based on gender because, neurolinguistically, male and female brains have been found to process information differently.[19] Perhaps the ultimate research base is genetics and the financial services sector is already adding this to their layering of data to fuse and mine. More ethical concerns are clearly raised by this development.

A number of dedicated tools are available to the market researcher for analysing databases. One such 'product' is VIPER – software developed by Brann Software. This tool allows very fast linking and analysis of different databases. This fuses different databases and a 'query' on, say, a lifestyle database, linked with a, geodemographic database and, a geographical information system (GIS) might be: select those (name and address) who claim to be readers of *Cosmopolitan*, like gardening, drink above average quantities of beer and live in the south west.

The graphical printout of the model combines data from all of the databases interrogated and shows in both topographical form where these people live, and in tabular form the actual names and addresses of the individuals concerned. VIPER is not the only database interrogator on the market but it does reflect the sort of capability that is now available. The speed with which the analysis is completed is indeed impressive – and all on a standard desktop PC.

As a summary of this section, I would suggest that transactional data, fused with profiling data, will produce the new biographics and that this will be the basis of much marketing research over the next few years. It will also provide the overwhelming source of data for marketing analysis – and indeed will be the motherload of all marketing information in the new century.

8.8 The future

Although the shift of emphasis will be towards biographic research, there will always be a need for qualitative research, for sample surveys, observation, experimentation and all the other forms of research discussed in this book. An illustration will make the point: with colleagues, in 1997 I conducted some market research into consumer attitudes towards direct marketing and in interviews, some of the older women in particular declared that they received substantial quantities of direct mail on behalf of charities.[20] They also said that this was not 'junk mail' because it was of interest to them – the matching of 'causes' with their own interests was very accurate. They were so moved by the direct mailing that they felt it important to donate – and they did just this. As far as the marketer is concerned this 'response' reinforces the donors' status on the database and they will be targeted again – and probably by related charities who are likely to share lists.

The point which I feel is important is that in qualitative research the women went on to say that they were barely able to afford to donate, but felt they 'had to' and were almost in tears over the issue. The reaction of the marketing industry was 'but it worked' – such reliance on mechanistic experimentation at the expense of more insightful research is submitted here as being an issue that the industry would do well to address. Although this targeting might 'work' in the short term, what problems might be being stored up for the future – not only when the 'targets' decide enough is enough and refuse to donate any more and bin all subsequent mailings – but also if they merely spread ill will about the charities' direct marketing approach?

One future issue, then, is that as marketing moves more and more towards the direct approach and research is forced ever more to databased approaches there is a real danger that experimentation might displace more qualitative methods. Experimentation which relies on behavioural response rather than attitudinal measures. Much database data, such as transactional and profiling data, provides valuable information on who is buying what, when, how and where, but it is qualitative market research that can get beneath the surface even further and discover the reasons 'why' behaviour is as it is.[21] Research amongst direct marketers reveals an emphasis on 'testing' (experimentation) with, in relative terms, little qualitative input.[22]

Indeed, there is evidence that this is being recognised as some marketers are linking their databases with more traditional market research data. In this way, for example, consumer panels are linked with geodemographic or lifestyle databases. The 'T' means that 'horizontally' database data provides tremendous breadth of data over millions of consumers but the 'vertical', from market research (e.g. panels), provides greater depth of information over a period of time (because panels are 'continuous' data sources). Figure 8.10 summarises the characteristics of the T-Group.[23]

It has been from such research that the claimed levels of purchasing in lifestyle surveys have sometimes been found to be extremely over- or under-represented in actual buying behaviour. One version of linking panel data with lifestyle databases is the SMARTbase system developed by Taylor Nelson/Calyx, the former running a number of different consumer panels and the latter, lifestyle surveys.[24]

This chapter opened with reference to ethical concerns about the move toward personalised research. One issue that I had in mind was raised by Fletcher and Peters[25] with respect to the use of market research data for personalised selling. The main problem is one of using marketing research data for selling purposes (selling under the guise of research, or SUGGING). The 'catch-22' was alluded to in the opening sections of the chapter: on the one hand many market segments want to be treated as individuals. On the other hand, for this to be a reality, marketing researchers need to provide marketers with relevant personalised data on individuals. Even if marketers do not use the personal details for immediate selling, they are keen to develop databases of personal information – 'DUGGING' (data under the guise of research). The Market Research Society has long outlawed this practice but has now compromised over the issue by having dual codes of conduct for the two 'reasons' for data collection. These issues are well explored by Fletcher and Peters (ibid.) and their research revealed practitioners to be reasonably comfortable with the situation. Researchers and sellers were keen to make clear to their informants the purpose to which personal details might be put. However Fletcher and Peters show that privacy issues are highly relevant here and have not been resolved. As it stands at present, however, the MRS Code[26] overcomes the conflict

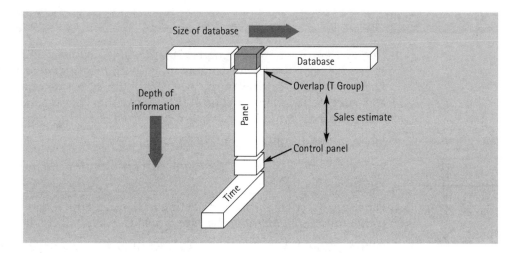

Fig 8.10 T-Groups

with the phrase: 'members shall only use the term *confidential survey research* to describe projects which are based upon respondent anonymity and do not involve the divulgence of names or personal details of informants to others except for research purposes'. The new code excludes, from its 'confidential research' principles, the collecting of personal data for sales or promotional approaches to the informant and for the compilation of databases which will be used for canvassing and fund-raising. In such circumstances the data collector should not claim to be involved in a confidential survey and should make this clear to the informant.

In a variety of empirical research studies[27] consumers have expressed concerns over the lack of privacy of their personal details and the privacy issue clearly needs constant vigilance. I would suggest that this will be an issue for the future as well as for the present.

8.11 Conclusion

This chapter has discussed some of the reasons for the growth in personalised marketing research – market fragmentation, database advances and the recognition by marketers of the need for their marketing to be better targeted. *Geodemographics* provided the first revolution in market profiling because they raised the stakes from sample surveys of 1,000 based on very few profiling characteristics (age, gender, occupation) to the census of 56 million based on 60 census variables and a variety of overlaying factors.

The future will be dominated by *transactional* data, overlaid by geodemographic, lifestyle and other *profiling* data, via *data fusion*, producing databases of *biographical* information for understanding, analysing and targeting individual customers (whose own buying behaviour has become increasingly individualistic) and is moving us to *mass customisation*. This raises a variety of ethical issues concerning the acquisition and use of personal data and the marketing and marketing research industries must continue to research and address the privacy issue.

REFERENCES

1. Henley Centre for Forecasting (1978), *Planning Consumer Markets and Leisure Futures*; Henley Centre for Forecasting (1992), *Presentation to Market Research Society*, 5 March, Bristol; Shay, P.A. (1978), 'Consumer revolution is coming', *Marketing*, September; MINTEL (1981), *Market Intelligence Special Report on the Teenage Market*.

2. Block, R. (1992), *Sales talk*, BBC Radio 4, January.

3. van Raaij, W. F. (1993), 'Postmodern consumption', *Journal of Economic Psychology*, 14, pp.541–63.

4. Patterson, M. (1998), 'Direct marketing in postmodernity: neo-tribes and direct communications', *Marketing Intelligence and Planning*, vol. 16, no. 1, pp.68–74.

5. O'Brien, S. and Ford, R. (1988), 'Can we at last say goodbye to social class?', *Journal of the Market Research Society*, 30, pp.289–332.

6. Denny, N. (1999), 'Electoral roll data ban could cost users £55m', *Marketing*, 18 March, p.12.

7. Masters, A. (1999), quoted in Denny, N. (1999), 'Electoral roll data ban could cost users £55m', *Marketing*, 18 March p.12.

8. Data Protection Registrar (1999), 'Commercial access to the electoral register', *MRScene*, March, p.3.

9. Exon, M. (1999), 'Count on a new Census for income and religion', *Precision Marketing*, 15 March, p.17.

10. ibid; *SARs Newsletter* (1999), Special Issue: 'The 2001 Census White Paper', No. 13, March, pp.2–3.

11. Leventhal, B. (1995), 'Evaluation of geodemographic classifications', *Journal of Targeting, Measurement and Analysis for Marketing*, 4(2), pp.173–83; Gorski, D. (1995), 'Systems for geodemographic and lifestyle analysis and targeting', *Journal of Targeting, Measurement and Analysis for Marketing*, 3(4), pp.372–80.

12. Humby, C. (1996a), 'Opening the information warehouse', *Marketing*, 18 Sept., pp.34–7; Humby, C. (1996b), 'Digging for information', *Marketing*, 21 Nov., pp.41–2.

13. Read, G. (1997), 'The future of data warehousing', *Business and Technology*, Feb., p.64.

14. Richards, A. (1998), 'Can unity beat the retailers?', *Marketing*, Feb., p.18.

15. Beenstock, S. (1999), 'Supermarkets entice the "ultra" customer', *Marketing*, 15 April, p. 15.

16. Wright, B. (1999), as reported in Beenstock, S. (1999), 'Supermarkets entice the "ultra" customer', *Marketing*, 15 April, p.15.

17. Antonio, T. (1997), 'Drilling or mining? Handling and analysis of data between now and the year 2000', *Marketing and Research Today*, May, pp.115–20.

18. Mitchell, V. W. and Haggett, S. (1997), 'Sun-sign astrology in market segmentation: an empirical investigation', *Journal of Consumer Marketing*, 14(2), pp.113–31.

19. Nairn, A. and Evans, M. (1999), 'Back to basics: reading, writing … and sex', *New Marketing Directions*, April.

20. Evans, M. (1997), 'Consumer reactions to supermarket loyalty schemes', *Journal of Database Marketing*.

21. Mouncey, P. (1997), IDM Symposium, 11 June, Transcription of Presentation.

22. Evans, M. and Middleton, S. (1998), 'Testing and research in direct mail: the agency perspective', *Journal of Database Marketing*, vol. 6, no. 2, pp.127–44.

23. Cowling, A. B. (1996), 'Big issues for the next five years: data fusion, reach the parts others don't', *IDM Symposium*, May.

24. Walker, J. (1996), 'SMART move but will it deliver the goods?', *Precision Marketing*, 6 May, pp.18–21.

25. Fletcher, K. and Peters, L. (1996), 'Issues in consumer information management', *Journal of the Market Research Society*, 38, 2, 145–60.

26. Market Research Society (1997), *Proposed Revised Code of Conduct*, London, p.3.

27. Evans, M., O'Malley, L. and Patterson, M. (1996), 'Direct mail and consumer response: an empirical study of consumer experiences of direct mail, *Journal of Database Marketing*, 3, 3, pp.250–61; Patterson, M., Evans, M. and O'Malley, L. (1996), 'The growth of direct marketing and consumer attitudinal response to the privacy issue, *Journal of Targeting, Measurement and Analysis for Marketing*, 4, 3, pp.201–13.

QUESTIONS

1   It is suggested that geodemographics and transactional data acted as major catalysts in changing marketing research. To what extent do you agree with this and why?

2   What are the issues involved with biographic research, from a market researcher's perspective, the consumers' perspective and a marketer's perspective?

3   Should marketing researchers have any moral concerns over DUGGING? Why is this?

4   'Testing' (experimentation) is more useful these days than qualitative research because the marketer can monitor actual response rates to different marketing approaches and this is what really matters. Discuss.

9 Research methodology and interpretation for developing a brand

The marketing research process has reached the point where data sources have been explored and sampling and segmentation have been conducted. We now need to look at how a product or service can be developed to meet the needs that the research has uncovered. This chapter considers the research methods used to specify the ingredients and the brand as a whole and how these are best packaged and priced, together with the application of advertising research to the development of the brand image.

Pricing research is presented and discussed towards the end of this chapter. Case study 9.1 gives a highly relevant and in-depth discussion of the *Pricesensitivitymeter* (PSM) approach by M. Mattinen.

9.1 What's in a brand?

A branded product or service consists of a whole bundle of benefits which goes further than the core benefit itself. If the core benefit is the fact that a product does the job of cleaning, as in toothpaste, a whole array of added benefits could then be included. Tangible benefits could be the good taste of the toothpaste or its competitive price compared with other brands on the market, and so on. Intangible and symbolic benefits could be the feeling of freshness or the perception of one's improved attractiveness to other people.

The ingredients in a brand constitute:

> The product itself, the packaging, the brand name, the promotion, the advertising and the overall presentation ... branding consists then, of the development and maintenance of sets of product attributes and values which are coherent, appropriate, distinctive, protectable and appealing to consumers ... Advertising is a narrower function within marketing which is concerned with the use of media to inform and stimulate consumers that products or services, branded or otherwise, are available for them to purchase.[1]

Our concern in this chapter is to examine how brands can be developed using marketing research processes when promising market segments have been located.

9.2 The validity of qualitative methods

During recent years great emphasis has been placed on the usefulness and validity of qualitative methods when new branded products or services are being developed. In essence, the findings from good qualitative research should have a truth that goes beyond the research context to a truth founded in the world. There are strong contributions from the sociological and psychological disciplines.

For example, the contribution of 'social constructionism' to research has been seen as broadly resting on:

> several key philosophical assumptions concerning the constitution of social life through language and discourse. Significant themes include the semiotic and illocutionary character of human discourse, the drive for ethnomethodological integrity in social research and the focus on the mutual construction of meaning as the main unit of analysis.[2]

In brief, social constructionists seek to engage their research subjects in a way which allows them to express and preserve the quality of their experiences, not merely as products of cognitive processing, but as constructions involving 'their active selection, suppression and purposiveness'. As an example, 'creativity' in advertising campaigns is a byword for excellence. To articulate a client's brief involves personal contacts and much thought and discussions to creatively turn the brief into a strong, strategically directed and distinctive campaign which fulfils client objectives and which exceeds expectations if the campaign proves to be a winning one.

There are those who contend that richer ideas and more meaningful decisions derive from a carefully designed programme of group discussions, extended individual interviews and other qualitative techniques than from a meticulously designed series of controlled experiments to which statistical tests can be applied.

In qualitative work findings are derived from the experience, perceptions and abilities of a small number of target consumers, say four groups of eight individuals, or 30 extended interviews, or a mix of the two. The setting of quotas for the recruitment of these individuals is clearly critical. So are the methods used to stimulate and focus discussion, the stimulus material, the role of the moderator or interviewer and the way in which consumer behaviour and opinions are recorded and presented, as discussed in Chapters 2 and 3.

9.3 Selection of participants

If a segmentation study has been carried out, the demographics, behaviour in the product field and lifestyle of those in the market of interest can be modelled, the characteristics of a potential target group defined and a quota representative of this group set. This applies to both qualitative and quantitative sampling as commonly practised.

In a qualitative research design the setting of the quota for participants' recruitment is especially important. Indeed it is generally agreed that the validity of qualitative research rests substantially on highly purposive sampling. Qualitative research is characterised by small samples.[3]

The respondent's experience in the use of the product concerned is important when quotas are set, whether for qualitative or for experimental work. Research[4] has shown that how the product is used can have a marked effect on choice, as shown in the example in Table 9.1. The three brands were considered to be very similar by the whole sample, but to be different when the sample was broken down by the way in which the respondents used the spirit. The 40% (3.02) who took the spirit neat preferred C, which had originally been the least preferred overall.

Table 9.1 Preference of spirits and relationship to use with a mixer or not

Brand	Total	Mixer	Neat
A	2.86	3.12	2.62
B	2.86	2.84	2.88
C	2.91	2.68	3.02

Source: Callingham, 1988.

9.4 Threats to validity

Validity is a genuine reflection of attitudes, behaviour or characteristics. It has been explained thus:

> A measure (such as a question, series of questions or test) is considered valid if it is thought to measure the concept or property which it claims to measure.[5]

Validity also depends on the right recruitment of respondents. Suitable subjects are recruited by interviewers, who are generally required to find quota members who have not been contaminated by previous group experience. It is not easy to locate suitable participants when working to a quota which may represent only 5% of the total population, while meeting standards set by associations, such as ESOMAR or the UK Association of Qualitative Research Practitioners (AQRP).

It is important that results can be validated if the competences of the researcher are to be respected. Research outcomes can be affected by the following historical, maturation, instrument and testing or learning aspects.

History

Outside events can affect the dependent variable during the course of the experiment. Clearly, the longer an experiment goes on the greater the risk of history contaminating the results.

Let us assume that we have designed an experiment to test the effect on sales of brand X paint in a home-decorating campaign. If there was a prolonged strike of public transport workers and no buses were running in the test area during the course of the experiment and if this strike meant that more workers stayed at home, the results of the experiment might be deceptively encouraging. The enforced 'leisure' of more people from the working population in an area would have an effect of stimulating home decorating. In this situation, increased sales would not be attributable to the campaign and the experimental results would be spurious.

Maturation

This effect relates to changes of the test subjects in the course of the experiment. They may, for example, get tired.

If we were comparing the effects of two sales training programmes we might find that test subjects 'played back' what they had learnt better at the beginning of the day than at the end. If we were aiming to compare two training methods, and failed to arrange that both groups contained comparable proportions of 'fresh' and 'stale' subjects, the results might then be spurious.

Instrument effect

As might be expected, this relates to inconsistent or faulty instruments and in experimentation the instrument is often a questionnaire administered by an interviewer. Mechanical instruments are also used, for example the tachistoscopes, psychogalvanometers and projectors which feature in experiments described in this chapter and in Chapter 10.

Continuing with the sales training example, we might expect the training officer to suffer fatigue too, so that the questionnaire is administered less effectively towards the end of the day.

Testing or learning effect

This is particularly relevant to company image, public relations and advertising research.

Let us assume that we have been commissioned to create a campaign to improve the image of a company in its employee catchment area. We decide to do a 'before' and 'after' test. We ask a sample of local people what they know about the kind of work the company offers, the amenities it provides and so forth, then we run the campaign and go back at a later date to see what effect the campaign has had on the experimental group's view of the company.

We cannot attribute greater awareness and changed opinions to the campaign because the respondents' attention would have been drawn to the company and its activities by the first call. What they learn at the first call may stimulate the sample to pay more attention to the campaign than they would otherwise have done, and to pick up information about the company which might otherwise have passed over their heads.

For this reason we either use an 'after-only' with control design when testing communications (see below) or we take the 'before' measurement with one group and the 'after' with another group matched to the first. In other words, matched samples are arrived at and used.

Selection of test subjects

This is not just a matter of ensuring that those who receive the experimental treatment represent the target for whom the product is designed. We also have to ensure that experimental and control groups are matched. (For the role of the control group see below.) Before designing an experiment it is necessary to know what demographic and product-use characteristics are critical. Experience in the product field often acts as an initial filter, for example, if we were developing a medicated bubble bath product, we would need to know whether the targeted consumers were bubble bath users or users of medicated bath products or both. Age and class might be critical demographic variables, but when it comes to setting quotas by age within class (or vice versa) as in an interrelated quota, it adds to the time needed to recruit and to the cost of the experiment. It is common practice to sort the test subjects into age and class strata, then to use a random process when assigning members from within these age and class strata to either the experimental or to the control group. If combinations of age and class are found to differ from the experimental to the control group, or from one experimental group to another, it is possible to standardise results by weighting, as in a disproportionate sample.

9.5 Control versus experimental groups

A control group is used in an experimental design to make it possible to discount the effect of unforeseen extraneous variables. The control group is matched to the experimental group. It is questioned, or observed, at the same time as the experimental group, but the control group does not receive the treatment, nor is it asked those questions which relate to the experimental group.

Control groups are not always used in marketing experiments. Decisions may be based on the responses of two or more matched experimental groups to alternative product formulations, pack designs or advertisements.

In comparative tests, especially in tests to decide product formulation, control may be exercised by setting a standard against which alternatives are assessed: for example, one group may be given the existing product and another the formulation which is thought to be an improvement on it with both products being wrapped and presented in the same way. In this case the control group receives a treatment but it is one against which the experimental treatment is judged. When two possible advertising treatments are shown to two matched groups we have a design based on two experimental groups.

However well designed an experiment may be, there is always a risk that an observed difference may be due to sampling error, and not to the effect of the treatment. The statistical procedures used to establish the significance of the differences observed are summarised in Appendix 3 at the end of this book. Unless subjects have been assigned to groups at random, or groups to treatments, these calculations should, strictly speaking, not be made.

9.6 Experimental designs in common use

The following designs form the bases of those in most common use. They help to concentrate ideas about experimental procedures. Experimental designs are explained further in Section 9.7.4 on lab versus field tests.

After–only without a control group

This is not a true experiment but it is not uncommon for an increase of sales, achieving more than targeted, to be attributed to some marketing tactic, such as a sales promotion or increased advertising, when other factors might have contributed. In other words, the collection of evidence has not been organised to validate the assumption nor has a hypothesis been tested. However, it is sometimes possible to guard against spurious results by asking questions – claimed awareness of an advertisement can be validated in this way.

After–only with control

Given that the experimental and control groups are well matched, that observations are made at the same time and that the environmental input is the same for both, we can use the control group to discount factors other than the treatment as contributing to the result shown by the experimental group.

Before–after

By observing the experimental group a suitable interval before and then after it receives the treatment we get a less ambiguous measurement than with an after-only design. However, where there is danger of the respondent learning from the pre-test an after-only design is to be preferred. But before-after with control makes it possible to allow for any continuation of the experimental result, as in the case of after-only with control.

Time series is an extended 'before-after' and it may be used with or without a control group (or area). In 'real-life' market tests it is common practice to take a number of observations before and after introduction of the new product, pack, price or advertising. The interval between observations is related to the rate at which the product is purchased by consumers, and the data is often derived from consumer panels. The repeat buying rate is an important factor in brand-share prediction.

With 'going' brands it is common practice to predict what would happen if the experimental treatment were not introduced, on the basis of the trend data collected 'before'. The effect of the experimental treatment, say a pack change, is then measured by comparing the 'actual after observations' with the 'after predictions'.

Cross–sectional

Different levels of treatment, such as different prices, levels of advertising and incentives to sales representatives, are applied to a number of matched groups at the same time. The main problem is matching the groups.

Randomised block

So far we have assumed that the only difference between groups is the kind of treatment they receive: in other words that, having matched groups on critical characteristics, the environmental effects will be the same for all groups. It may well be that previous research has alerted us to differences, for example of region or location, which may influence results. Blocking is stratification applied to experiments. Use of stratification to reduce sampling error in survey work is discussed in Chapter 4.

Let us assume that we need to measure the effect on sales of three pack designs. A supermarket chain has agreed to have the experiment staged in some of their branches. Previous research[6] has suggested that there may be regional differences in consumer reaction to the three packs.

Accordingly we do the following:

- Stratify by region, say the north, midlands and south parts of the country.
- Arrange for the test to be made in, say, three branches in each region.
- Use a random process to assign pack design to branch in each region as follows (T stands for treatment):

Region	Three branches in each region		
North	T1	T2	T3
Midlands	T1	T2	T3
South	T1	T2	T3

The product is put on sale in all three pack designs in each region. We are assuming that the supermarket branches do not have distinct regional characteristics. The statistical figurework (analysis of variance) is shown in Chapter 4 and Appendix 3. Briefly, the design makes it possible for us to isolate the between-regions source of error so that we are left with a smaller residual error to take account of when considering the between-treatments results. That is, the design is cost effective because we can use a smaller sample than would be the case if we had not 'blocked' (or stratified).

Latin square

The randomised block design illustrated above controls one extraneous variable. If the product was one which sold through more than one type of retail outlet, we might have decided to use a Latin square design. The Latin square is a cost-effective design which makes it possible to allow for two extraneous sources of variation, in our case region and type of retail outlet.

In the Latin square design it is conventional to think of the two extraneous sources of variation as forming the rows and columns of a table. Treatment effects are then assigned to cells in the table randomly, subject to the restriction that each treatment appears once only in each row and each column of the table. Consequently the number of rows, columns and treatments must be equal, a restriction not necessary in randomised block designs.

The finished design might look as follows:

Three regions, three types of retail outlet
(A, B, C) three treatments (T1, T2, T3)

Region	Type of retail outlet		
	A	B	C
North	T2	T3	T1
Midlands	T1	T2	T3
South	T3	T1	T2

The Latin square is an economical design for the measurement of main effects, in this case variation due to region and to type of retail outlet. Each treatment (in the case we have been considering, a pack design) is tested in each type of retail outlet and in each region. We can estimate error due to these two sources of variation using analysis of variance (see Appendix 3), but we are assuming that the treatment effects will not be contaminated by interaction between them. We allow for the effects individually but not where the one (test region) influences the other (retail outlet).

Factorial design

If it is necessary to take account of the interaction of variables, as opposed to measuring main effects, a factorial design is used. Anticipating product testing, let us assume we are developing a soft drink. We may expect that, in a taste test, there is likely to be interaction between the colour of the drink and the amount of sweetener in it: that the more acid the yellow of a lemon drink, the sourer the response to tastes.

Say we are experimenting with three variations of colour and three degrees of sweetness, then the factorial design would be as follows:

Sweetness		Colour	
	a	b	c
A	Aa	Ab	Ac
B	Ba	Bb	Bc
C	Ca	Cb	Cc

Every possible combination of colour and sweetness is allowed for in the design, which requires nine matched groups of testers. This can be an expensive design and we may find that we have not used a sufficiently large sample when it comes to considering the significance of results. If there is any doubt on this score the test should be replicated so that there are sufficient testers' judgements to warrant the drawing of firm conclusions. Replication may avoid the waste incurred when an unnecessarily large sample is drawn in the first instance, but it extends the time taken up by the test and there is always the possibility, of course, that time itself may affect results.

9.7 Pre-testing branded products and services

Market description may suggest the introduction of a new product or the modification of an existing one. Analysis of data about consumer behaviour and attitudes may yield tentative ideas, or hypotheses, about the kind of product required, the way in which it should be packaged and priced, and how it should be brought to the attention of potential consumers. It is then necessary to pre-test the whole brand, the finished version or part of the product, say the colour of a fruit cordial or the shape of its container, to minimise the risks of costly failures with a new product launch.

9.7.1 The whole and its parts

Before considering ways of testing hypotheses about the individual components mentioned above we have to recognise that, once the product is out on the market, consumer perception will be influenced by the interaction of the components, as well as by environmental factors such as the actions of competitors and distributors, not to mention the state of the world at the time.

Product formulation, packaging, pricing and communications are likely to be the subject of separate experiments on the way to 'real-life' testing in the market of the complete offering: first, on the grounds of cost, and second, to help assess the contribution made by constituent parts to the overall performance.

With regard to cost, even a small-scale test in the market makes notable demands on resources. The product must be available in sufficient quantity to meet demand and it has to be associated with properly finished packaging and advertising.

A product development programme will, therefore, include experiments specifically designed to aid decisions about formulation, packaging, price and communication, but it is likely also to include attempts to assess the interaction of these components.

The product concept may be introduced to the experimental group in the form of a rough advertisement before the product is tried and responses to the product both before and after actual trial are compared. Pack designs may be presented to testers along with designs for advertisements, while questions about selling price are likely to be asked at every stage. The fact that the whole may well be different from the sum of its parts has to be taken into account.

9.7.2 Having and trying out ideas

Most 'new' products or services derive from what is already available to consumers. The true innovation is rare indeed, and if successful, soon copied, as with the camcorder and compact disc products.

New product development (NPD) makes considerable demands on company resources. The modification of a going brand with a view to increasing its popularity or sustaining its life may make less demand on resources, but here there is the additional hazard of putting off existing supporters.

During the development stage, choices need to be made with confidence. To rely entirely on qualitative methods demands faith in the research supplier and understanding of the rigour with which qualitative methods may be applied.

It is easier for a marketing company to have confidence in the experimental approach. The setting of quotas and the recruitment of those taking part are as critical to the design of experiments as for qualitative work. But if the standardised methods are duly followed it is possible to subject the results of experiments to statistical tests. For the decision-maker there is comfort in numbers.

Given an experimental approach the collection of data is less open to bias, and the results less open to mistakes of interpretation. On the other hand, the opportunity for a new product breakthrough may be missed; experimental data lacks the stimulus of qualitative findings when the brand presentation is being designed.

In order to design experiments it is necessary to have hypotheses to test! Qualitative research is a valuable source of hypothetical ideas and the two approaches to NPD may be combined with advantage.

9.7.3 The experimental approach

To arrive at any hypothesis which is both meaningful and relevant it is necessary to have to hand data about the consumers and products in the market. Detailed knowledge of the market makes the following more pertinent and thus effective:

- choice of hypothesis to be tested;
- decisions regarding the criteria to be used when measuring and analysing results of the experiment;

- control of environmental factors;
- selection of the subjects to take part in the experiment.

For an ongoing brand, or for a new brand in a familiar market, 'detailed knowledge of the market' is likely to be driven from previous product research and from monitoring of own competitors' achievements in the product field. Explaining 'the experiment as a system' can be shown as a useful introduction to the forces at work in an experiment (see Figure 9.1).[7] The experimental input is called the 'independent variable' and the output is called the 'dependent variable'. The environmental input is made up of extraneous variables, some of which can be foreseen, others not, i.e. some of which are controllable variables and others uncontrollable variables. The experimental input is the treatment applied to subjects whether this is one variable, such as sweetness, or a combination, such as sweetness plus colour in a soft drink.

So how can research aid innovation? In the first instance by supplying background knowledge, and it clearly helps if that background knowledge is the result of thoughtful, rather than mechanistic, description of consumer habits and attitudes. Research can usefully 'try the idea out' in concept tests. A trade-off approach in which the respondent is asked to choose between a series of options can be applied. The technique is based on the concept that obtaining a desired product quality, say efficiency, will require the consumer to sacrifice – trade-off – some other desired quality, say gentleness. This use of the multivariate approach has, of course, been stimulated by the speed with which a long list of trade-off choices can be processed. The respondents may find the questioning procedure less tedious when using a PC.

One research stage can lead to another, for example:

Market description ⟶ Definition of a target segment
Definition of a target segment ⟶ Hypothesising about its requirements
Formulation of hypotheses ⟶ Trying out of concepts
Trying out of concepts ⟶ A programme of experiments

Blackett and Denton[8] recommended the development of, 'ideas into products which in their formulation, packaging, branding and general appeal offer a unique selling proposition'. This point of difference should be familiar or recognisable to consumers, be needed or wanted by consumers, be true to its promise and be communicated in all presentations to consumers.

9.7.4 'Lab' versus 'field'

A carefully controlled experiment, conducted in laboratory-like conditions, yields results which are unambiguous. The experiment has internal validity. But the con-

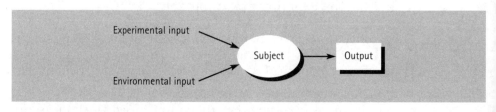

Fig 9.1 The experiment as a system

ditions in which the test is carried out are not those in which the product would normally be chosen or used and the lab-like experiment lacks external validity.

The field or market test, on the other hand, is conducted in a real-life context. The findings have external validity but they may well have been distorted by market influences or local happenings so that they are ambiguous and difficult to interpret. The more that is known about the forces at work in the market from descriptive work, the easier it is to control them or to allow for them when drawing conclusions. A comparison of laboratory and field product-testing procedures is shown in Table 9.2.

Companies which continuously engaged in product testing such as Heinz, Spillers and Unilever place products with panels of consumers. Demographic and product-use characteristics of panel members are recorded and the computer is programmed to retrieve experimental and control groups suitable for the test concerned. Test products are distributed by hand, or through the post, to panel members and the proportion returning the test questionnaire through the post is usually substantial (over 70%).

There is a risk that the panel members may learn from their testing experience and cease to be typical. But when the panel is a large one and the research supplier covers a wide range of product fields, it is possible to maintain the interest of panel members without running the risk of conditioning them. For control versus experimental groups, see Section 9.5.

In a monadic design the respondent experiences only one test product, whereas in a comparative test the respondent is given more than one product to try. The products may be given to the respondent simultaneously, or they may be given in sequence.

Comparison sharpens perception and so comparative tests are more sensitive than monadic ones, but the comparative procedure is further removed from real life than the monadic. In real life products are usually judged in the light of current or recent experience of a similar product. In a monadic test responses to the test product are similarly based on current or recent experience in the same product field, with the critical difference that the test product is likely to be in a plain package without the benefit of pack design and advertising support.

If the test programme is based on a series of paired comparison experiments, one test product can stand as a control throughout. The control product may be the market

Table 9.2 'Lab' versus 'field'

Laboratory	Field
Under controlled conditions (internal validity)	Under external environmental conditions (external validity)
Tested in-house (on company or agency premises)	Tested in-home (where product is used) or in test centres (where product is bought and viewed in shopping centres)
Trial, recording and observation of controlled versus experimental groups	Trial, recording and observation of target groups
Comparative or monadic tests	Monadic tests

leader or the leader in a particular market segment. If a product is being relaunched, the existing product is the control product. If a brand is being repositioned, it may be desirable to move closer to consumer perception of the 'ideal' brand.

Since, at the outset, all products are likely to be tested 'blind', the difference in dress and communication between the test product and a product actually on the market is obviated. If the same individuals make all the tests, sampling error is reduced, but we must ensure that learning from test experience does not contaminate the results.

It may be that there is no obvious control product and a number of possible product formulations are to be compared. This situation might arise if a range of prepared foods was being developed. In this case a 'round robin' would be an efficient design to choose, the products being 'rotated' round the respondents to try. For example:

Each respondent would be given four different fillings: A, B, C and D. The procedure would be to test:

A versus B	B versus C	C versus D
A versus C	A versus D	B versus D

If the tests were made by six matched groups of 50 from a sample of 300, each filling would be tried by 150 respondents.

In the blind test, products are judged on taste or performance. In the normal pack test, previous experience (packaging, price and advertising message) comes into play.

In a monadic test respondents deliver verdicts on a blind product in the light of their experience and knowledge of the product field. They are often asked what brand they use and are then encouraged to compare the test product with this brand. The test product has the advantage of being new and different, but the possible disadvantage of not being supported by pack design and advertising message.

9.8 Preference and discrimination

In most product tests a definite preference is being sought. It is hoped that new A will be preferred to old B, or that there will be a significant difference between the preference score of new A(1) and that of new A(2). But occasions arise when a product is established on the market and either substitution of another ingredient reduces production costs and so contributes to profit, or a source of supply is interrupted and an alternative source has to be found.

The substitute ingredient will not be used unless those concerned with the marketing of the product are satisfied that users will not notice the difference. Testers are reluctant to show lack of discrimination. Many are going to guess and there are two types of error to be avoided. If there is an observable difference, but the experiment does not reveal this, the position of an established brand may be undermined. If there is not an observable difference, and the results of the experiment suggest that this is a more likely happening, we pass up the opportunity to make a cost saving or to ensure supplies.

The triangular discrimination test, developed in the brewing industry, is one way of approaching this problem. There are two test products, new A and existing B. The sample is split in half. Each half is given three products to test: one gets triad AAB, the other ABB. The products are presented blind with ambiguous code numbers (A and B would certainly not be used).

The respondent is told that one product is different from the other two and is asked to find the different one. It is assumed that a third of the respondents will guess right and that the measure of discrimination is the percentage correctly picking the modified product, less 33.3%. If 40% picked correctly, the measure of discrimination would be [(40–33)/0.67]%, i.e. of the order of 10% instead of 7% because we have assumed that one-third of the testers will guess right.

Discrimination tests are not always triangular. Respondents may, for example, be told that, out of a group of five products, two are of one type and three of the other. This is a more severe, but perhaps rather intimidating, test of discrimination.

It follows that, as in real life, response to the product will be influenced by the way in which it is introduced. It is, of course, possible to try out more than one message and more than one pack design, not to mention price, together with a particular product formulation. The programme of tests could be rather expensive because testing or learning effects make it necessary to test each combination of elements on a separate sample, while results may be affected by the degree of finish of advertisements and packs. We return to the subject of concept testing in Chapter 10, where we focus on the procedures used to pre-test advertising messages.

The decision whether to test the components of the perceived product individually, or in combination, is a vexed one. A company such as General Foods draws on a considerable experience of product tests. By consistently following standard procedures a company accumulates normative data: it is able to compare pre-launch test results with post-launch performance and it is in a better position to construct pre-test models.

9.9 Pre-testing packs

9.9.1 Function, impact and image

Packaging, both 'inner' and 'outer', is a significant item in the costing of a product and packaging research is a wide-ranging subject involving studies carried out by R&D, production, distribution and the suppliers of packaging materials, as well as those commissioned by marketing among distributors and consumers.

We need to distinguish between tests to assess the functional efficiency of a pack, its visual impact at the point of sale and the image of the product conveyed by the packaging and its label.[9]

9.9.2 Functional testing

To give a product the best possible chance of success its pack must function well in the following conditions:

- on the production line;
- as bulked quantities travel along the distributive channel to the point of sale;
- at the point of sale after bulk has been broken;
- when being used by the consumer.

The pack has to protect the product from deterioration and from pilfering. It must stand up to handling and the shape should lend itself to efficient stacking, wrapping and palletisation. At the point of sale how the pack behaves compared with the competition is important. Does it 'hog' or take up too much shelf space, or fall over? When it reaches the consumer, ease of opening and of closing (if not used up at once), of dispensing the contents, together with being steady on its feet, are critical variables to be considered in experimental design.

The suitability of the materials used and of the method of construction are tested by R&D, production and by the suppliers of containers. Suppliers such as Metal Box, who make plastic as well as metal containers, are so close to the consumer market that it serves their purpose to carry out research among consumers as well as among manufacturers and distributors.

The supplier has to satisfy the manufacturer that their product will not deteriorate and that it will reach the point of sale in good order. Suppliers of packaging materials are particularly interested in consumer responses when introducing an innovation, such as the aerosol and the ring-top opener for cans. The innovation is likely to involve a considerable investment since the research findings help to persuade manufacturers to adopt the innovation, as well as improving it.

Distributors' complaints and the reports of sales representatives are the usual sources of information regarding the behaviour of the pack before it makes contact with the consumer at the point of sale. Here our concern is with the product as it presents itself to the consumer.

If the product is used up in one go, as with a can of beer, and the critical factor is ease of opening and dispensing, the experiment can be staged in a hall, mobile van or research centre, and the data is best collected by means of observation. Some consumers get fussed when faced with an unfamiliar method of opening or dispensing, and it is necessary to create a relaxed atmosphere. This is difficult to achieve if the tester's efforts are being closely watched and recorded by an observer, and a method used by Metal Box has much to commend it.

When a ring-top can-opening device was introduced as an alternative to the tear-off tag, consumers were invited into a mobile van to try one against the other. A hidden camera filmed the way in which the consumers approached and handled the cans.

The camera can also be used to record whether or not consumers read instructions, and whether one form of instruction appears to be easier to follow than another. Individuals vary in their dexterity, and with tests of functional efficiency there is a case for using a comparative design, with each respondent trying both types of opening, assuming there are two to be tried. It is probably sounder to allow for the learning effect by rotating the order in which packs are tried, than relying totally on samples being matched not only on product use and demographic criteria but also on how they are handled, but this is a matter of opinion.

If the product is used, closed and then reused, the experiment needs to be carried out where this goes on – kitchen, bathroom, garage, etc. – and data is likely to be collected by means of a questionnaire. In this context variations in dexterity are less critical, though still material. They are less critical because results will be based on how easy or difficult the respondent perceives the opening, closing and dispensing of the product rather than the observed behaviour.

To isolate the effect of function it is necessary to use plain packs as in a blind product test. If the opportunity is taken to test 'visuals' at the same time, response to visual effects may contaminate response to functional efficiency. On the other hand, we have to remember that when the product reaches the market, consumer response will be conditioned by the visuals.

9.9.3 Visual impact

As we all know, products have to speak for themselves at the point of sale. There is usually no one around to make the introduction. The term 'impact' is used here to mean 'stand-out' value. Tests of stand-out value are usually based on observation by means of the tachistoscope, or as in William Schlackman's 'find-time' procedure with a slide projector.[10]

The tachistoscope enables an image to be exposed for controlled lengths of time. Lengths of exposure likely to be used in a pack test are from 1/200 of a second up to 1/10. The respondent is either looking into a box-like instrument or a screen. After each exposure the respondent is asked what, if anything, was seen. This simple procedure is useful for comparing the visual impact of elements in a pack design, such as colour, brand name or message, but it does not stimulate the context in which the respondent is going to meet the pack.

A closer approach to reality is made under the following conditions:

- The respondent is shown the test pack along with two or three control packs, care being taken to simulate the size of the packs as they might 'loom up' on the shelf at the point of sale.

- After each timed exposure the respondent is asked to pick the three or four packs out from a display which reproduces the company in which the pack is likely to find itself on the self-service shelf.

In a test of this kind results can be contaminated by learning and it is advisable to use matched samples. If responses to the control products are of the same order for both samples, we are reassured that the samples are matched for acuity or representativeness, i.e. similar speed of perception and response, as well as on the more obvious criteria.

When designing experiments to measure visual impact it is necessary to take into account variations in sharpness of eyesight and the speed with which individuals respond to the image. They may, for example, be required to press a button as in the 'find-time' design described below. Organisations specialising in pack testing use standard acuity tests.

When recruiting for an experiment it would be time-consuming to take acuity into account as well as product use and weight and demographic characteristics. It may be necessary to weigh results when the acuity of matched samples is found to differ, but acuity is affected by age and familiarity with the product field, so matching on these variables may obviate the problem.

In the find-time procedure (Table 9.3) pioneered by William Schlackman[11] matched samples are used and the respondents are allowed to familiarise themselves with a test pack. They are told that this may or may not be present in the displays which will then be projected onto a screen.

- Some nine displays, typical of the product field at the point of sale, are photographed and the photographs are prepared for slide projection.
- In about six of the nine slides the test pack is among its competitors, in six different positions. It is absent from the other three slides.
- The slide remains on the screen until the respondent presses a button to signal that the test item has been found, or has not, as the case may be.
- The measure of stand-out value is the time taken to find the test pack when it is present. This is automatically recorded when the button is pressed.

Table 9.3 A 'find-time' experiment

Pack	Mean reaction time in seconds	t-test value	Significance level
V2	1.77		
P	1.59	1.99	not
V1	1.98		0.001
P	1.59	3.71	
V2	1.77		
V1	1.98	2.05	0.05

In this table results are compared for the three possible pairs. Clearly, neither of the new versions is an improvement on the current pack design.

*For statistical tests, see Appendix 3.

Source: Adapted from *The Newsletter of the BMRA*, No.1, July 1998, p8 and AMSO Annual Report 1997, p7.

9.9.4 Image of the product in the pack

The product has been designed to meet the requirements of a target group in the market. If a segmentation study has been made, the characteristics of the group, and the benefits wanted by it, are certainly known. The pack has to tell these consumers that it contains a product with the desired qualities. In a programme of image tests respondents are asked for their perceptions of the product in the pack before they have tried it. Box 9.1 describes a test carried out on members of a test panel in a test centre.

Box 9.1 An image test

At the test centre, panel members were asked what products they usually used for their main wash and for their light handwash. If they used a washing powder they were introduced to the experiment as follows:

'I am going to show you two different packs of washing powder called Coral. The manufacturer is considering two different versions of the product, and would like to know what housewives think about them.'

(The interviewer was instructed: SHOW FIRST PACK, THEN AN ALTERNATIVE AT EACH INTERVIEW.)

'I would like you to tell me what you think about the product in this packet by indicating where you think it would come on this scale. If you point to the largest box you strongly agree with the statement. If you point to the smallest box you think the statement applies very slightly to the product.' (There were seven sizes of the box.)

The respondent then rated each pack in turn on the following criteria without having tried the product:

- Suitable for all modern fabrics.
- Gets white nylon really white.
- Suitable for machine and handwash.
- Washes thoroughly but gently.
- Cares for delicate fabrics.
- Up to date.
- I would buy.

When a consumer meets a new product at the point of sale, the decision whether to try it is influenced by ideas about the product conveyed by its pack. Having carried out this concept test, the marketing company concerned might well have put the same questions to the test panel after actual trial. Comparison of the responses would show whether or not the product came up to expectation. If it exceeded expectation the pack design might need modification.

The pseudo-product test (see Box 9.2) is designed to measure what William Schlackman described as 'symbolic transference'. Influence of the labels on taste perceptions is further evidence of the importance of testing the whole as well as its parts.

Box 9.2 The pseudo-product test

Test items: 'A mild beverage', two labels L and M.

Design: Simultaneous comparison test: two bottles were 'placed' at the same time. Four days' trial were allowed.

Procedure: Respondents were asked to use one bottle first, then, on completion, the second. The order was rotated. Consumers were told the interviewer would be returning to ask them about their experience.

	L	M	DK	Total
Product found most acceptable	20	75	5	100
Product which was mild	25	65	10	100
Product most bitter	70	28	2	100

$n = 200$

Conclusion: label M moves the product more effectively in the direction of the marketing intention than does label L.

9.10 Testing the brand name

Companies may sometimes apply the company name to all their products, for example 'Heinz', or they may give each branded line a distinctive name, a practice pursued by firms such as Unilever and SmithKline Beecham.

Ideally, the brand name should convey or support the product concept. If the product has a unique selling proposition (USP) the brand name should, if possible, reiterate this: for example, 'Head and Shoulders' for an anti-dandruff shampoo. If the packaging and promotion are being designed to convey an emotional benefit in the context of a brand image, the name will be chosen to support the image, for instance calling a toothpaste 'Close-Up'.

Before brand names are tested for their power to communicate the nature of the brand, it is necessary to establish the following:

- the name is available for registration in the countries in which the brand is going to be marketed;
- the name has no dubious or unhelpful association in these countries;
- the name is easy to pronounce, read and remember.

Ease in pronouncing the name may be tested by asking consumers to read a short list of names, taking note of hesitations and of any variations in emphasis. A tape recorder makes it possible to play back responses.

The stand-out value of the name is likely to be tested as a component of the pack design, after the 'runners' have been reduced to a few, perhaps in a tachistoscopic or in a 'find-time' test (see Table 9.3).

The communicative power of the name is tested by establishing its associations in the minds of consumers. This is done in the folowing way:

1. In the first instance by means of 'free association', consumers being asked to say the first word, or thought, that comes into their head on hearing the name.
2. Then by asking consumers to associate kinds of products with the brand names as these are read out.
3. And/or by asking consumers to associate the brand names with product-attribute statements.

When designing research of this kind three factors need to be taken into account:

1. Respondents should be given a trial run before the critical names are put to them. This applies in particular to the free-association test.
2. The order in which names and/or statements are put to respondents should be rotated.
3. The time taken to respond must be recorded.

9.11 Testing the market for price

The price at which a product is offered to the market is influenced by many considerations. These include endogenous (internal) forces within the organisation and exogenous (external) forces in the marketplace.

The internal objectives of an organisation will include one or more of the following: return on investment; survival; growth; project maximisation; achievement of sales targets or increased sales volumes; defence, maintenance or exercise in market share; and market leadership. An organisation may also be concerned about its standards: interpretation; the provision of long-term employment and the staff development of its employees; its research and technological expertise; its reputation as a supplier of products and services; and its compliance with legal requirements, e.g. consumer protection acts.

Resource inputs, for example bought-in materials, equipment and skills, manu-facturing, transport and distribution, market research, marketing, selling, financial and administrative costs, are added considerations. All these internal considerations provide a 'feel' for an organisation of the price band in which it 'ought' to charge for a given product, particularly if it is a new product. There may be little room to manoeuvre if a product is already established in a fiercely competitive market. In this case, any product improvement or innovation will have to be presented to existing consumers as being significantly better than the old bundle of product attributes either to justify a rise in price or increased purchase at the old price.

However, what an organisation can charge for its product in the market depends on exogenous factors. For instance, what customers are prepared to pay and what product options are available from competitors.[12] Consumer perceptions of price associations with, for example, quality, value for money and image are also impor-tant constraints on the price that an organisation can charge.

Pricing research is, therefore, a very important area in marketing research. From the 'ideas' explanation stage of what product to produce, through the stages in the new product development process (screening, business analysis, market testing and commercialisation), soundings from the marketplace are taken. These soundings are usually in the form of intention to buy questions which are related to quoted and to competitive prices. It is common for competitive organisations, for example finan-cial services companies or car research companies, to use omnibus surveys. This has the advantages of bought-in market research expertise in a complex area and of pro-tecting the anonymity of the organisation commissioning the pricing research.

When the product goes on sale in a store test, or in a full market test, a credible verdict may be delivered depending on the length and sensitivity of the test.

The purpose of taking soundings on the way to a market test is as follows:

- To see what kind of price consumers associate with the product and how this varies between types of consumer.
- To try out the effect on price perception of changes in the product attributes, its packaging and advertising.

9.12 Pricing approaches

The willingness of consumers to buy at different prices can be used as a measure either of price elasticity in the brand field or of the value to the consumer of indi-vidual elements in the brand mix as, for example, packaging. Research International's approach to pricing,[13] illustrated in Figure 9.2, includes method-ological approaches to the problem of setting prices. The figure shows the relationship of pricing to the constituent product elements and to the whole (total) product.

Pricing research for the 'whole product' can take the monadic or the competitive form. Monadic pricing approaches vary from those which assess consumer responses to a range of manufacturers' prices to those where consumers themselves are asked to suggest appropriate prices for a given product. We will consider three monadic pricing approaches: TSP, Gabor and Granger, and PSM.

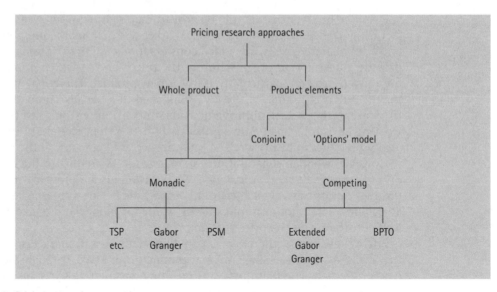

Fig 9.2 Pricing research
Source: Research International (1994), 'Pricing Research', Position Paper 10.

TSP (try, server, pay/purchase)

This is a simple approach which is based from 'definitely not buy' to 'definitely buy'. The TSP approach is an example of scalar methods used in the early days of pricing research. The possibility that consumers would try, serve and pay/purchase a food product at a given price could be measured by looking at the distributions of responses on the sale points.

Gabor and Granger

Instead of suggesting a price, a manufacturer may want to test different prices for a product. Gabor and Granger's buy-responses model (1965) uses price as an indicator of quality to measure consumers' likely purchase intentions.

The usual procedure is as follows:

- The range of consumer selling prices in the product field is recorded and not more than ten prices are chosen for testing.
- The respondent is shown the product, its pack or its advertising and is asked 'Would you buy X at ...?' The price first quoted will be near to the average for the product field. The other prices will be quoted at random so that upper and lower limits are not suggested to the respondent.
- The responses are summed for each price accepted by respondents and the acceptable prices are charted, as shown in Figure 9.3. Respondents are also asked prices last paid (for existing products) and here again the distribution is charted.

The idea of price as an indicator of quality has long been associated with durables and luxury goods. Methodological research has shown it to be relevant to fast-moving consumer goods. Too low a price is risky while a high price may be 'too dear'. The buy-response curve (Figure 9.3) shows the limits within which a selling price would not be a barrier to acceptance, while the shape of the curve shows

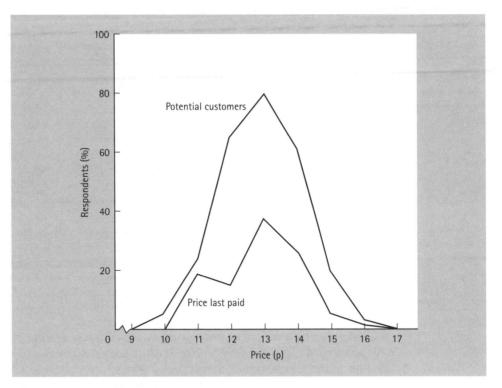

Fig 9.3 'Buy-response' and 'price-last-paid' curves
Source: Gabor, A. (1977), *Pricing: Principles and Practices*, London, Heinemann Educational Books.

where the most generally acceptable price is likely to fall. In addition, a comparison between the shape of the price-last-paid curve and the buy-response curve may indicate an opportunity. For example, in Figure 9.3 it would seem that brands priced at 12 pence, around 75 cents, do not enjoy their potential share. The tests are of the lab-type design taking no or little account of the competitive environment.

It is possible to use the buy-response method to compare the effect on consumer price perceptions of different product formulations, different packaging and different communications.

PSM (pricesensitivitymeasurement)

The pricesensitivitymeasurement approach is used in new product development, product line extension or product positioning research. Consumer perceptions of the most likely and acceptable prices for the new concept or product are sought with the objective of guiding a manufacturer in setting the optimum price. Each consumer would be asked at which point on the price scale a product was 'cheap', 'expensive', 'too cheap' and 'too expensive'.

Research International's development of PSM is shown in Figure 9.4. The area within the core acceptable range where the interesting curves meet is seen as the price range where most respondents think that the new product concept or brand is not cheap or expensive and not too cheap or too expensive.

'Intention to buy' is a measure of price acceptance where the objective is to answer the question: 'Are the considered price levels for a particular product going

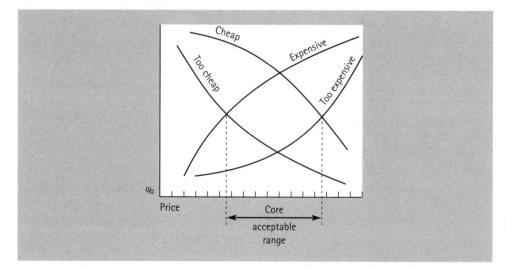

Fig 9.4 The PSM approach
Source: Research International (1994), 'Pricing Research', Position Paper 10.

to be accepted by a sufficient proportion of the consumer target group to make the new product viable?' However, price-acceptance research is distinguishable from price-importance research in that it seeks to measure the importance to the target consumer of different levels of price compared with different levels of other attributes, for example a range of car prices compared with a range of miles per litre/ maximum speeds/different lengths/numbers of seats/countries of origin.

The case study at the end of this chapter represents a research perspective from Finland and shows how the 'Pricesensitivitymeter' was developed in Holland and how a Finnish firm has applied it. Although this method has both practical applications and usefulness, as indicated, it has not before been presented in contemporary textbooks.

Having considered the three methods of pricing approach, TSP, Gabor and Granger, and PSM, the discussion now moves to a consideration of trade-offs.

9.12.1 Making trade-offs

Pricing research for this involves looking at how people make trade-offs in choosing among multi-attribute alternatives.

Conjoint

The conjoint or trade-off approach is employed to arrive at each respondent's preferred combination of product attributes. Presenting alternatives in pairs is the simplest form. However, the full concepts method may be preferable to those researchers who feel that the two-at-a-time (pair-wise) method to product attribute evaluation is less realistic.

In the pair-wise method, attributes are presented in pairs to each respondent, for example:

- taste versus colour
- taste versus size
- size versus colour
- and so on ...

Normally, the pairs are presented in 'grids' and each respondent undertakes a self-completion exercise by filling in a booklet containing such grids. The pairs are ranked in order of respondent's preferences. The task itself can become boring and repetitive and some researchers may prefer the 'full concepts' method.

Using the full concepts method, a number of combinations can be given as for size, colour and shape. For example, large or small (size), blue or yellow (colour), round or square (shape). Each respondent is asked either to rate all the possible combinations on scales or to rank them. Where there are 20 combinations or more, the task can become more complex for the respondent.

Take for instance, a large series of cards constructed with each card representing one of several possible mixes of attributes. The respondent is asked to order the cards from the most-liked combination to the least-liked. Care has to be taken to ensure that all possible combinations of attributes are represented by the cards. However, in a trade-off covering the multivariable relationships of all product attributes (instead of just price), the number of cards can become too large for one sorting operation. In this event, a preliminary sorting of cards can take place. That is, into 'definitely like', 'neither definitely like nor dislike', 'definitely dislike', followed by rankings within each of the three groups. This helps to concentrate the mind of a respondent.

Options model

Conjoint analysis lends itself to pricing research, for example in food products. However, the assessment of product attributes is not shown in relation to consumer budgets, an important consideration particularly where expensive consumer durables are concerned. The options model developed by Research International allows each respondent to build his or her own 'ideal' package, e.g. an audio/hi-fi system via computer-aided interviewing (CAI). The computer 'introduces' the respondent to up to 22 product features which the respondent can build onto the basic unit. Through analysis of all the 'ideal' packages built by the sample of respondents, the options model identifies an optimum durables package which would satisfy most potential consumers.

Pricing research approaches are now more 'predictive' than merely 'diagrammatic'. For example, if the objective is to predict actual brand share, the respondent taking part and the brands displayed should mirror the real market.

If the objective is to diagnose, say, brand-switching patterns, there is a case for drawing the sample of respondents from among those making frequent purchases in the product field and for excluding from the array of brands those which are bought infrequently (the trade-off price/response model gives useful insights into the elasticity of price changes). The predictive element is important in pricing research because the purchases psychology of consumers within a particular product or brand sector should mirror the real world as closely as possible.

9.13 Conclusion

Laboratory test conditions achieve internal validity but the conditions can, to varying extents, be unreal. It is therefore important to conduct experiments which also have external validity.

In practical terms the consumer is able to see the whole product formulation, packaging, plus price, plus the 'added value' of advertising, when it is presented as an entire package. It is, thus, possible to vary aspects, for example to devise a programme of experiments which seeks to show how various elements could be improved, such as price formulation and consumer interactions. Pre-testing consumer responses to pricing is one of the most complex areas in market research and requires both careful application in test design and attention to detail concerning purchase intentions within product sectors.

REFERENCES

1. Murphy, J. (ed) (1992), *Branding: A Key Marketing Tool*, Macmillan, p.3.

2. Hackley, C. (1998), 'Social constructionism and research in marketing', *Qualitative Market Research – An International Journal*, vol.1, no.3, pp.125–31.

3. Ruyter, K and Scholl, N. (1998), 'Positioning qualitative market research', *Qualitative Market Research – An International Journal*, vol. 1, no. 1, pp.7–14.

4. Callingham, M., (1988), 'The psychology of product testing and its relationship to objective scientific measures', *Journal of the Market Research Society*, vol. 30, no. 3 (July).

5. Marshall, G. (1994), *Concise Dictionary of Sociology*, Oxford University Press, p.26.

6. Cox, K. and Enis, B.N. (1973), *Experimentation for Marketing Decisions*, Intertext, Glasgow.

7. Kotler, (1997), *Marketing Management, Analysis, Planning and Control*, Prentice Hall, USA.

8. Kotler, (1994), *Marketing Management, Analysis, Planning and Control*, Prentice Hall, USA, pp.73-85.

9. Davies, M. and Wright, L. (1994), 'The importance of labelling examined in food marketing', *European Journal of Marketing*, vol.28, no.2, pp.57-67.

10. Schlackman, W. and Chittenden, D. (1988), 'Packaging research' in R.M. Worcester and J. Downham (eds) *Consumer Market Research Handbook*, Elsevier Press, Amsterdam, pp.513–36.

11. Ibid.

12. Doyle, P., Saunders, J. and Wright, L. (1989), 'A comparative study of US and Japanese marketing strategies in the British market', *International Journal of Research in Marketing*, 5(3), pp.171–84.

13. Research International (1994), 'Pricing Research', Position Paper 10.

QUESTIONS

1. Assume you are pre-testing an improved product for an established market. Make use of the list below to create experimental designs, measurement and testing.
   - What experimental designs would you advocate in the following circumstances?
   - How would you recruit the test subjects?
   - What treatment would you apply to the subjects?
   - How would you measure results?
   (a) Acceptability of a cooked breakfast cereal which, it is claimed, does not stick to the saucepan.
   (b) Response to an added low-sugar sweet for a confectionery line popular with junior schoolchildren.
   (c) Perceived effectiveness of a shampoo for cars with a protective ingredient which gives added shine.
   (d) Response to a range of selling prices for a new selection of gourmet foods.
   (e) Alternative packaging for a range of frozen desserts.

2. 'Whatever the difficulties of interpretation, research is only relevant if it attempts to stimulate the situation in the market.' Discuss this statement, focusing your answer on the pre-testing of a branded, fast-moving consumer product or service of your choice.

3. You have been asked to design an experiment to show which of the following two courses of action is more likely to increase the total of a bank's transactions with its customers (the bank has branches in major population centres throughout your country):
   (a) The offer of sales promotions incentives using discounts ranging from 10% to 25% for specific products, e.g. hi-fi equipment, computer games and clothes, on purchases at stated major retailing outlets.
   (b) Opening times to the public to be extended from 9am–4pm to 9am–6pm on weekdays and 9am–2pm at weekends.

   What experimental method would you use? How would you measure effects? How would you seek to achieve external validity?

'Pricesensitivitymeter': a practical tool for pricing research

Mikko Mattinen

Introduction

The 'Pricesensitivitymeter' (PSM) method was developed in Holland and has been presented by Peter van Westendorp (1976). The method has established its place in the marketing research industry although it has not been presented before in contemporary textbooks.

The main advantage of the PSM approach is its cost-effectiveness, simplicity and usability. The theoretical backbone of the approach lies in psychology and in pricing research methodology. The basis of the PSM approach is not scientifically robust because the reliability and the validity of this method have not been proven by testing. But practitioners have tested the approach in pricing projects and found it useful in decision-making.

Theoretical aspects of the PSM approach

van Westendorp names some theoretical aspects in the development of the PSM approach. The first two are related to psychology, while the third and the fourth are more connected to pricing research methodology.

1. **Absolute thresholds in price-perception.** Price can be compared to any other stimulus such as sound, vision or temperature. The absolute threshold of price-perception is comparable to any other stimulus because a stimulus must have a perceived minimum and a maximum level related to the range of acceptable prices.
2. **Differential thresholds in price-perception.** All stimuli must have an adequate level of change which can be perceived and measured. This is the basis for the differential threshold of the price.
3. **The theory of reasonable price.** There is a reasonable price for every product or service that the consumer is willing to pay.
4. **Relations between price-perception and quality.** For example, 'price' is a statement of 'quality', as Gabor (1988) and Granger have demonstrated.

These theoretical aspects are reasonable and acceptable for a pricing technique. The Gabor and Granger's buy-responses and price-last-paid technique can be used to study the relationship between price and quality of a product or a service. The PSM approach can also be used to study the same relationship, but it can answer many other questions. For example, it can be used to study:

- exact pricing points;
- range of prices;
- customers' reactions to different prices;
- acceptable pricing ranges;
- benchmarking the tested product or existing product's pricing to competitors' products' pricing;
- the relationship between estimated quantity of customers and possible volume of profits. Note that in this application you need information from the customer.

How to conduct a PSM survey?

The PSM approach involves four different questions. van Westendorp suggests the following:

1. At which price on this scale are you beginning to experience [THE NAME OF THE TESTED PRODUCT] as cheap? (The scale of prices should be from the highest price to the lowest price.)
2. At which price on this scale are you beginning to experience [THE NAME OF THE TESTED PRODUCT] as expensive? (This scale of prices should be from the lowest price to the highest price.)
3. At which price on this scale are you beginning to experience [THE NAME OF THE TESTED PRODUCT] as too expensive – so that you would never consider buying it yourself? (This scale should be from the lowest price to the highest.)
4. At which price on this scale are you beginning to experience [THE NAME OF THE TESTED PRODUCT] as too cheap – so that you say 'at this price the quality cannot be good'? (This scale of prices should be from the highest price to the lowest.)

There are many possible fieldwork methods which can be employed in collecting the PSM data, from paper and pencil to web survey. Essential in the design of the questionnaire is that the pricing scale should be wide enough so that the highest and the lowest prices are impossible for the respondent to accept. Another important issue is that some of the prices should appear to be possible in a real market situation, i.e. simulated market conditions. van Westendorp suggests that there should be 25–40 steps in the scale. This might be ideal, but in practice 15–25 steps are often adequate. The steps should not be too far apart, neither should the scale be too dense, because it may then appear trivial to the respondent and may lead to loss of respondents.

Analysis of the PSM data

The size of the sample is connected with the form of the scale, because the analysis of the PSM data is primarily based on graphical analysis. The distribution of data should resemble normal distribution. Practice has shown that a minimum size of sample for PSM data is 100–200 cases. One major problem in the graphical analysis of PSM is that the results of sub-sample analysis may be in conflict with the total sample if the size of the sample is too small. To be more exact, the results of the sub-samples do not form an arithmetical mean of the results of the total sample.

The processing of PSM data does not require vast effort, because the analysis is primarily based on cumulative distributions of the four questions. If the scales are in the order that has been suggested the data analyst does not have to do anything other than process the data and create graphical presentations of the results. van Westendorp points out that 'don't know' answers should be analysed in great detail, because they might indicate a general price-consciousness.

Example of PSM analysis

A Finnish marketing research company Market-Visio Ltd (which concentrates on analysing IT markets in the Nordic countries, the Baltic states and Russia) has used the PSM method for numerous client projects. Market-Visio researchers have used the approach to study pricing of services and durable goods. The following example is from a multiclient survey of price perception of personal computers (1997) in large Finnish com-

Continued

panies. The main target of the survey was to study the price and product elements of a PC. The survey was carried out by CATI and the size of the sample was 297 cases.

The key issue in the PSM approach is to interpret two exact pricing points and a pricing range. The indifference price (IDP) is calculated from the cumulative frequencies of cheap and expensive variables. The IDP is where the two curves cross, see Figure 9.5. In this example the indifference pricing point is 9,400 FIM. The result is that 70% (100 – 2×15%) of buyers would buy the studied PC with 9,400 FIM. The estimated number of buyers helps the product management and corporate business controllers to estimate the revenue of the studied product or service. This kind of information is vital to strategic planning. Figure 9.5 can also be used to study different pricing possibilities, for example if product management wants to examine different prices and estimate the demand.

The optimal pricing point (OPP) is where the curves of frequencies of too cheap and too expensive variables cross. The OPP for the PC is 8,450 FIM and with this price it will gain 90% of buyers. See Figure 9.6.

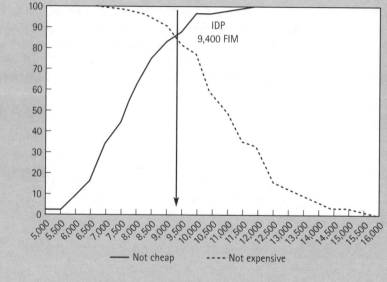

Fig 9.5

The range of acceptable prices gives to product management a clear vision of how the pricing of the product or the service should be managed. The range of acceptable prices here is 6,750–11,500 FIM. See Figure 9.7. We recommend that all the information should be gathered into one graphical presentation. This makes it understandable and easy to present.

Consumers are not able to name precise levels of cheapness, but that is not the case with an expensive price. Figure 9.8 illustrates consumers' price-consciousness. We can see that the gap between expensive and too expensive is quite small compared with the gap between cheap and too cheap. This means pricing of low-end products should be carefully analysed because there may be possibilities for numerous pricing strategies.

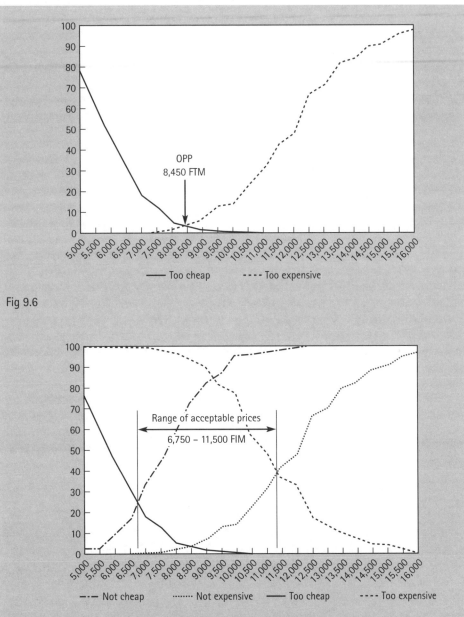

Fig 9.6

Fig 9.7

Benchmarking product pricing with PSM is a good approach to competitor intelligence. In Figure 9.9 we can see that with minor changes product X can be more attractive to buyers than product Y. Product X (10,500 FIM) is perceived to be expensive by 42% of buyers, but product Y is perceived to be expensive by 52% (11,000 FIM). If we lower product Y's price by 500 FIM and we get 10% more customers, this should lead to a higher revenue. This example illustrates that PSM is an appropriate tool for developing pricing strategies.

Continued

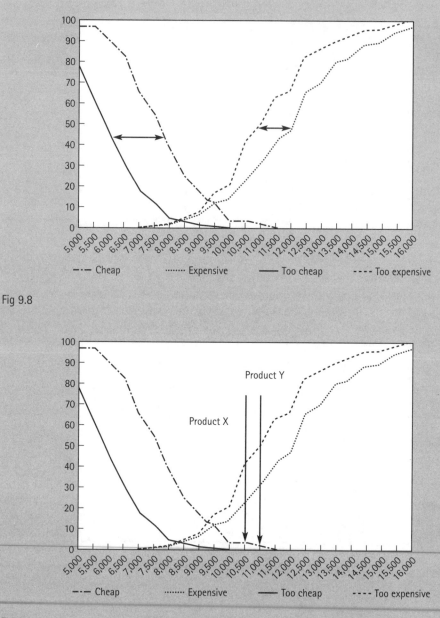

Fig 9.8

Fig 9.9

Future development of the PSM approach

The PSM approach should be developed into a more exact way of measuring price perception; there are a number of ways in which we can do this.

In the numerical analysis we could utilise multivariate analysis, for example, regression analysis, log-linear models or conjoint analysis could come in for examination. Regression analysis or log-linear models could be used to analyse what kind of effect the independent variables have on price. Conjoint analysis could be used to analyse the connection between price and other product elements at certain price levels.

Secondly, the PSM method should be tested as any other measure. The effect of the wording of the questions should be tested in order to find the most neutral way to conduct the measurement. The testing would give PSM exactness. Also the effect of different sample sizes should be tested to find out the optimal size of the sample. This would bring efficiency into the fieldwork and help costs.

Thirdly, the PSM method could be incorporated into qualitative methods to analyse the impression of different prices. This could be connected to the testing of the wording of the questions. For example, if the questions are as neutral as possible there should also be a way to measure the difference between 'cheap', 'too cheap', 'expensive' and 'too expensive'. The qualitative approach would give PSM depth.

Conclusion

The question of pricing is very important to all organisations that aim to make a profit. The PSM approach can be used to set a price for almost anything that can hold a label. It is a practical tool for pricing practitioners, but of course there can be many other fields than marketing research where the PSM method can be applied. Despite its practical usefulness, the development of this method seems to be sleeping like the Sleeping Beauty, although the PSM approach is a methodologically sound, economical and meaningful way of doing pricing research.

References

Gabor, A., (1988), *Pricing – Concepts and methods for effective marketing*, Gower, Cambridge.

van Westendorp, P.H. (1976), 'NSS-Pricesensitivitymeter (PSM) – A new approach to study consumer-perception of prices', ESOMAR.

10 Establishing the brand identity and pre-testing the whole

Uncertainty and risks are reduced through pricing research for a branded product that is being developed for the market, as explained in Chapter 9, and through the modelling process, described in Chapter 11. In this chapter we build upon the concepts by examining the process by which a promising target market or a niche segment can be developed to meet the needs of the market uncovered by the research processes so far. Branding – the product or service as perceived by consumers – is an important part of this and encompasses the creativity and vitality of the processes. Branding is a mixture of the intrinsic qualities (such as colour, taste, consistency) and the way in which these qualities are packaged and priced. Consumer perception is influenced by the way in which the brand is presented in advertisements. The case study of Halfords Motor Oils at the end this chapter shows how the largest UK retailer of car parts, cycles and accessories carried out successful market and advertising research to develop its own brand. Halfords has a presence in some of the major cities of northern Europe with its own store outlets.

This chapter also introduces the advertising, theory, objectives and tasks in the creative research programme. To complete the cycle of advertising research, Section 10.4.2 briefly looks ahead to the advertising research role after a campaign is launched. A discussion of how advertising works and a case study of Millward Brown's pre-testing for an advertising programme for Direct Line Insurance is presented at the end of Chapter 13.

The once hard and fast distinction between pre-testing and post-testing has been blurred. Greater confidence in the meaning of pre-test results, access to databanks and computer software plus disenchantment with the cost and necessary duration of the traditional test market have stimulated interest in research approaches designed to simulate the responses of the target segment before exposure to the market, which may well take the form of a rolling launch.

10.1 The creative research programme

Communications research is a large subject. Advertising is costly and mistakes will have longer than intended repercussions through the creation of an unfavourable brand image and bad publicity. Advertising budgets have to be justified,[1] and proposals should be made at the outset. Figure 10.1 sets the scene and summarises the stages in the development of an advertising campaign, relating these to the relevant chapters in this book.

The 1980s and 1990s saw an increasing emphasis on the role of the account planner in advertising agencies. The account planner creates a dialogue between the consumer and the process of creating advertisements.

The responsibility for setting advertising in its real-life context is what differentiates the account planner from, on the one hand, the market researcher, and, on the other, the account handler (or account executive). The market researcher is there to answer questions, the planner is there to ask them and to interpret the answers.

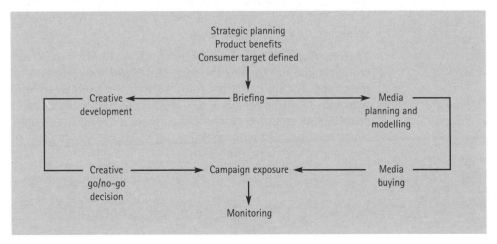

Fig 10.1 Stages in the development of an advertising campaign

The relationship between the message and the medium used to convey it is necessarily a close one, and the most cost-effective results are achieved when creative work and media planning proceed simultaneously and with joint consultation. If advertising objectives are agreed between client and agency at the outset, and if the creative task is defined at an early stage, there are defined standards for experimental and, finally, monitoring purposes.

10.2 Advertising objectives and creative tasks

We need to distinguish between marketing objectives, advertising objectives and creative tasks. The marketing objective is, in the last analysis, to improve the contribution to profit of a particular brand or to maintain its contribution for as long as possible. The profit contribution can be achieved by improving or maintaining sales value or, in the shorter term, by reducing marketing costs and this generally means the advertising appropriation.

The relationship between marketing objective, advertising objective and creative task can be illustrated by the following scenario:

- **The marketing objective** is to increase the market share of the brand by $x\%$. The client's promotional budget, which embraces trade deals and consumer promotions as well as the advertising appropriation, is related to this objective. A study of disaggregated panel data shows that, among those who buy the brand, there is a group of individuals who return to the brand time and again without being entirely loyal to it. The data describes the demographic characteristics of this group and indicates that the segment is sufficiently large to warrant further attention.

- **The advertising objective** is accordingly to stimulate the loyalty or to improve the repeat-purchase rate of a consumer target defined as, e.g., housewives with children at home who are working full- or part-time outside the home. The social class and age classification of the segment is known and this is important to media planning.

- **The creative task** may be determined by qualitative work, for example among women representative of the segment. Depth interviews or group discussions may suggest that, in this product field, the target consumer is anxious to maintain her home-making role in spite of the demands of outside work. The creative task might then be defined as supporting the domestic confidence of these hard-pressed women. There is, of course, more than one way of doing this in an advertising campaign.

10.3 Stages in the advertising research programme

The cycle of planning, creative development, decision and campaign exposure in Figure 10.2 illustrates the stages in the advertising research programme.

The role of planners in advertising agencies is to help ensure that the available data is effectively digested and to act as purveyors of the relevant and stimulating findings of research. The purveyor's role is especially important when it comes to briefing creative people. To do this effectively requires a rare combination of analytical and creative faculties. The advertising objective or objectives are defined at this stage and the creative group briefed.

Data considered for planning purposes can range from:

- a client's sales figures;
- trend data derived from subscription to consumer panels and/or retail audits;
- repeated attitude surveys tracking consumer responses to brands on the tests carried out during the development of the product;
- descriptive surveys including segmentation studies and qualitative work on file;
- media statistics, e.g. from BARB or MEAL (Media Expenditure Analysis Ltd).

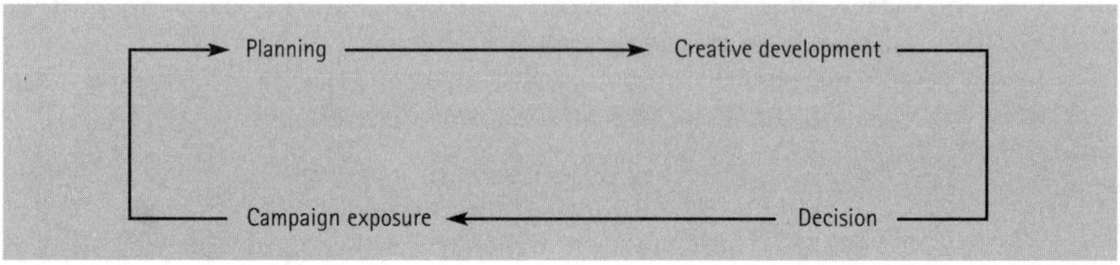

Fig 10.2 The creative programme

The study of consumer data in sufficient detail enables consumer groups or targets to be identified. Benefits to be conveyed to these groups are sharply defined when media and creative personnel in the advertising agency are briefed.

10.3.1 The development of creative ideas

When the creative task has been defined during the strategic planning stage, the creative group has been effectively briefed. At this early stage of creative development qualitative work is commonly used to try out ideas. A limited number of target consumers is shown creative ideas in an unfinished form. Such stimulus material is conveyed by, say, a sketched layout plus headline, or perhaps typed copy for print advertisements, or a storyboard or mocked-up video treatment for a television commercial. The degree of finish is a matter of judgement.

Stimulus material is a thing, article or item that is used to convey a product, pack or advertising to the consumers or to trigger their responses to a particular area of enquiry. Examples of stimulus materials in use are summarised in Table 10.1. This shows that the type of material chosen by research practitioners[2] to start a group discussion or an extended face-to-face interview is clearly going to influence the views expressed by participants. The choice of material, including the degree of finish, demands professional judgement based on experience and training in the behavioural sciences.

The material used will, of course, relate to the stage reached in the development of the product/service, from the initial concept or idea to the presentation of the brand in an advertisement. The concept may be introduced to those taking part as a simple statement on a board, with the eventual brand presentation as a photomatic.

Table 10.1 Stimulus material

Concept boards:	Single boards on which the product, pack or adverting ideas are expressed verbally and/or visually.
Storyboards:	Key frames for a commercial are drawn consecutively, like a comic strip. The script may be written underneath and/or played on a tape recorder with special sound effects.
Animatics:	Key frames for a commercial are drawn and then filmed on video with an accompanying sound track. The effect is of a somewhat jerky TV film, using drawn characters to represent live action.
Admatics:	A development of animatics, changing crudely animated storyboards into something nearly approaching the level of a finished commercial by using computer-generated and manipulated images.
Flip–overboards:	Key frames for a commercial are drawn as above but, to avoid the respondents reading ahead, they are exposed one by one by the interviewer in time to a taped sound track.
Narrative tapes:	An audio tape on which a voice artist narrates the dialogue, explains the action of the commercial and describes the characters. The tape may be accompanied by key visuals.
Photomatics:	A form of animatic using photographs instead of drawn key frames, thus showing the characters and scenes more realistically.

Three basic questions that are asked are:

1. 'What do consumers see when shown stimulus material?' Consumers evaluate all research stimuli as advertisements – most find it difficult to deal with concepts or ideas.
2. 'How "rough" or "real" should stimulus material be?' Consumers do not see 'rough ideas' when shown stimulus material – they see a finished execution.
3. 'How do consumers create meaning or decode stimulus material?' The material may convey an idea or message very different from the one intended, for example the Benetton advertisement featuring a dying man with AIDS in the early 1990s provoked media comment.

Stimulus material is used to provoke discussion in groups or in individual interviews. The discussion or interview is taped so that the creative group (who should in any case be involved in the research work) can play it back. In some agencies, videotape or one-way mirrors are used so that 'body language' may be observed by the creative staff.

No attempt is made to count heads. The numbers taking part in this qualitative work are sufficient to generate a good range of ideas and reactions, but not for statistical analysis.

Content of the tapes is analysed in terms of the following:

- Ideas about the product derived from the advertising stimulus, including ideas about the kind of people who might be expected to use the product.
- The extent to which those taking part associate themselves with the product and the context in which it is shown.
- Features ignored, which may indicate either that the message is unclear or that those present are disassociating themselves from this aspect.

As with product and price testing, definition of target and benefit(s) specifies the type of consumer to be involved in qualitative and experimental work, and what consumer perceptions of the product should be used as measures of advertising effectiveness.

Debate has for a long time centred on the validity of the measures used in pre-exposure testing, measures such as the recall of advertisements and their contents and expressed intention to buy the branded product. Once a pre-tested brand is out in the real world it is, of course, possible to compare actual performance with estimated performance: to establish the relationships between recall of advertisements in the pre-test and awareness of the advertising after exposure, between expressed intention to buy and actual sales, and to arrive at correction factors which enable predictions to be made with more confidence. The estimation of correction factors is, however, a difficult and expensive exercise.

It may be necessary to give statistical support to the agency proposal or to choose between more than one approach. What is now wanted is a quantified measurement of future performance in real conditions without incurring the cost of the complete marketing effort and before meeting competitors in the market.

10.3.2 Campaign exposure

Once the creative campaign is out and about in the media it becomes difficult to distinguish the effect of the creative work from that of the media selection. After exposure, advertising research is often used to see whether the opportunities to see/hear the creative message, offered by the media selected, are in fact being taken by the target consumers. Results of the recognition checks and campaign penetration studies (also considered in Chapters 13 and 14) are used to: (a) monitor performance and (b) refine future media scheduling, for the process is a circular one.

What we would like to be able to do at this stage is to relate the advertising costs to sales achievement. A simple cause-and-effect relationship between advertising and sales can be observed when response is direct, as in mail order. In most cases other marketing factors intervene. Has the sales force, perhaps aided by dealer incentives, been able to achieve not only distribution but stand-out value for the brand? What level of competitive activity is the campaign provoking? We discuss the research methods used to help answer questions such as these in Chapter 8.

In the meantime, the grey area is shrinking, with the increasing availability of disaggregated data – 'within person' and 'shop-by-shop' – and the associated development of computer programs which examine relationships between the brand and media consumption of individuals over time, while the availability of 'shop-to-shop' data will in due course make it easier to establish the effect of distributive, as opposed to advertising, tactics.

10.4 How advertising works

Ideas as to how advertising works influence the research methods used when advertisements are tested: it is now generally accepted that there can be no one all-embracing theory because advertising tasks are so varied.

The following illustrates two extreme cases.

1. In 'direct-response' advertising the goods are sold to the consumer in an advertisement and delivery is direct from the manufacturer or marketing company concerned on receipt of cash or credit card number. The Sunday newspapers carry many advertisements of this kind.
2. In 'corporate image advertising' the objective may be to protect profit growth from attack by political and social pressure groups; and the advertising task to keep the public informed about technological achievements of benefit to the community, e.g. the nuclear industry.

In the direct-response case (1), sales are substantially attributable to an advertisement in a particular medium, provided the print advertisement, television or radio commercial has a code attached to it, and the purchaser refers to the code.

In the corporate-image case (2), the effect of the campaign is likely to be measured by asking members of the public awareness and attitude questions in ad hoc surveys carried out at regular intervals, say once a year. By asking a standard core of questions in each survey it is possible to keep track of changes in the image of the enterprise held by the general public. In (1), advertising can be said to convert, and in (2), to reinforce. These two conceptions of the advertising task, conversion and reinforcement, are discussed next.

10.4.1 The early models

AIDA (attention, interest, desire and action) is one of the earliest models, which postulates a simple relationship between advertising and selling. Provided the advertising succeeds in attracting attention, arousing interest and stimulating desire, the result is a sale:

Attention ⟶ Interest ⟶ Desire ⟶ Action

ATR (awareness, trail and reinforcement) is a later model which recognises that not everyone is influenced by the strength of an advertising campaign and stresses the trial use of a product or service, and its reinforcement of the values of the brand.

Awareness ⟶ Trail ⟶ Reinforcement

Colley's DAGMAR model is more sophisticated in its approach, but the advertising process is still seen as one of step-by-step conversion.[3] DAGMAR stands for 'defining advertising goals for measured advertising results', the goals being to achieve the following in the consumer:

Awareness ⟶ Comprehension ⟶ Conviction ⟶ Action

Lavidge and Steiner's hierarchy-of-effects model[4] draws on the theory that an attitude embraces three elements of states – cognition (knowing), affect (evaluation) and conation (action) – but the advertising process is still seen as one in which, for the potential consumer, a change of attitude will precede a change in behaviour.

	Purchase	
Conation	↑	Conviction
		Preference
Affect		Liking
		Knowledge
Cognition		Awareness

The assumption that attitude change precedes change in behaviour ignores the implications of Festinger's theory of cognitive dissonance. Individuals aim to achieve consonance or harmony in their thinking and feeling. Choosing (as between products, brands and services) threatens a consumer with post-decisional dissonance (dissatisfaction after purchase). In other words, it is now generally accepted that a change in attitude may either precede or follow action: that the relationship may work in either direction.

Attitude ⟷ Behaviour

10.4.2 The reinforcement role

Dissonance theory suggests that advertising has a reinforcement role to play, for, by reassuring consumers that they have made a sensible choice, loyalty to a particular model or brand is reinforced. Rigorous examination of disaggregated panel data has shown that, in many product fields, 100% loyalty to a brand is rare indeed. On the other hand, choice is not haphazard.

Let us assume that a typical shopper's shortlist is of three brands: E, F and G. His or her habitual pattern of buying is more of E, than F and G. Our brand is G.

It would clearly improve our brand share if this shopper's buying of G is sufficiently frequent in relation to E and F to create a habitual buying pattern of G first followed by E, F, and then G again.

The advertising task would then be to reinforce the attraction of G and emphasise its attributes, including benefits over those of E and F, for those who already use the brand from time to time.

For established brands, sales increases represent only a small proportion of total sales in any one period and reinforcement of the status quo is essential to the maintenance of profit contribution. But consumers die, move out of the country or get too old for the product. Brands grow partly through attracting new buyers, partly through increased frequency of buying among existing users. The relative importance of these two roles, conversion and reinforcement, will depend on the nature of the market and the position of the brand in the market.

New users (converts) are essential to the baby food market. This is a field in which cognitive dissonance is particularly painful so reassurance to new users in numbers of mothers is necessary through reinforcing the brands and pointing out their advantages in advertising and sales promotions.

Finally there are, of course, situations in which advertising is used to defend a brand's position and the advertiser is satisfied if market share is maintained without any increase in advertising or other marketing costs.

10.4.3 The unique selling proposition and brand image

These two models were developed in New York advertising agencies in the early 1960s: the **unique selling proposition** (**USP**) by Rosser Reeves and the **brand image** concept by David Ogilvy. They are now considered in turn.

The unique selling proposition (1961)

In the rare case of a product with a unique, and desirable, attribute, definition of the USP is a straightforward matter.

However, integral differences between brands in a product field are often marginal and a USP is likely to be suggested by study of consumer habits and attitudes in the product field. To quote a classic example: use of toothpaste + fear of bad breath = 'the Colgate ring of confidence'.

The USP, once defined, must be adhered to in every communication about the brand. This is a behaviourist approach to 'how advertising works' and, as with Pavlov's dogs who came to dinner when a bell was rung, repetition is of the essence. Time is needed to condition the consumer to associate the proposition with the brand.

Brand image (1963)

David Ogilvy's concept of the 'brand image' has proved more fruitful in the development of creative advertising.

Consumers buy brands rather than products or services, and by developing a personality for the brand, as opposed to attaching a proposition to it, the brand is made more meaningful to the consumer and this added value strengthens loyalty. The consumer is treated as a rational being with conscious ends in view and a defined self-image.

Brand loyalty is strong when there is empathy between the brand's image and the consumer's self-image.

Recall and awareness are likely measures to use when assessing the effectiveness of a USP campaign, while attitude measurement and the tracking of changes in attitude over time are essential to brand image studies.

10.4.4 Fishbein and buying intention

Intention to buy (or **try**) questions are now accepted as valid indicators of consumer response to products and the advertising associated with them. The answers have been shown to have predictive value. As a result of Fishbein's work on attitude theory and measurement, investigations into consumer habits and attitudes often include questions relating to the act of purchase.[5]

Fishbein postulated that behavioural intention (BI) is the product of how we feel about the attitude towards the act (Aact). In this context the act is buying a brand – plus how we feel about society's attitude towards the act in general, a subjective norm (SN). In the formula given below, buying the brand (w_1) and trying the brand (w_2) are weights representing the strength of our wanting to carry out these acts taking into account the extent to which this might be modified by social considerations:

$$BI = Aactw_1 + SNw_2$$

Lintas and Research International have long made a practice of asking 'intention to buy' questions. The data has been systematically filed and where possible, correlated with actual purchase data. Experience has shown that 'intention to buy' scores indicate how far the total message effect adds up to a feeling of wanting to buy the brand, as opposed, for instance, to the enjoyment of an advertisement, and this feeling is related to subsequent sales.

10.5 Verbal measures

At the pre-test stage, i.e. before campaign exposure, the most commonly used measures of creative effectiveness are the following:

- recall, unaided and aided;
- attitude towards the product, branded or unbranded, and its likely users;
- intention to buy;

Questions relating to a respondent's habitual behaviour in the product field will often help to determine whether the respondent is a suitable participant in the test. They will also contribute to the interpretation of answers for recall, attitude and intention-to-buy questions.

The effects can be seen in the following:

- information conveyed to the respondent (usually measured by recall);
- the respondent's emotional response to the brand (measured by attitude questions);
- the strength of the respondent's desire for the brand (as indicated by intention-to-buy questions).

Figure 10.3 shows the effects of the hierarchical models with their cognitive, effective and conative components. There are two important differences which should also be noted:

1. We recognise that attitude change can be the *effect* as well as the *cause* of a change in behaviour, that it can be 'post' as well as 'pre'-action.

2. We distinguish between attitudes towards the brand of those who might potentially use it and attitudes of those who already use it and are again moving towards the act of purchasing or behavioural intention.

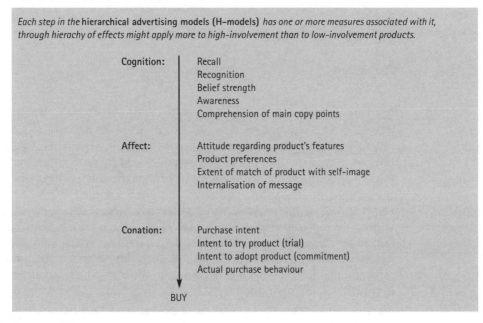

Each step in the **hierarchical advertising models (H-models)** *has one or more measures associated with it, through hierachy of effects might apply more to high-involvement than to low-involvement products.*

Cognition:	Recall Recognition Belief strength Awareness Comprehension of main copy points
Affect:	Attitude regarding product's features Product preferences Extent of match of product with self-image Internalisation of message
Conation:	Purchase intent Intent to try product (trial) Intent to adopt product (commitment) Actual purchase behaviour
	BUY

Fig 10.3 Elements in H-models

Once the campaign is out in the world **recognition** is an important measure. Recognition checks whether or not an advertisement has been noticed. This will, of course, depend on the effectiveness of the media planning and buying as well as on the creative impact.

Awareness, **campaign penetration** and **salience** are other terms used when discussing advertising research after campaign exposure (post-testing). Awareness covers a range of responses from mere recognition to unaided recall of the attributes the advertising seeks to associate with the brand. Campaign penetration and salience measures help to establish whether the opportunities to see, view or hear as offered in the media schedule are, in fact, being taken.

10.6 Testing before campaign exposure: three methodologies

Let us assume that the creative group has come up with two possible solutions to the creative task using the folder or reel test method to present two alternative test advertisements to selected respondents.

10.6.1 The folder or reel test: a lab-type experiment

The test material

This is in the form of two folders or videotape reels which are prepared containing a selection of advertisements. These advertisements will have to compete for the attention of the respondents and are likely to represent a variety of product fields. The two folders/reels are identical except for the test advertisements, assigned one to each and placed in the same position relative to the rest of the content. It is, of course, important that the test material should be of the same degree of finish as the rest of the content.

The design

Monadic Using two matched samples of 50–100 members of the target population.

Procedure The respondents are asked to go through one of the folders or to watch one of the tapes. They are then asked which advertisements they happen to have noticed. Given that the brand is an established one (as is often the case in advertising research) the test advertisement will not stand out as being of special interest to the interviewer. Once unaided recall has been recorded, a list of the brands in the test is shown to the respondent as a memory trigger. The respondent may be asked which was most liked and which was least liked, or which 'you would most like to talk about'. Procedures vary but essentially attention is gradually focused on the test advertisement and recall of its content. Recording of aided recall must of course be differentiated from unaided recall, and the order in which advertisements and product attributes are mentioned is likely to be significant as a measure of salience.

Measurement of results An after-only design based on two matched experimental groups (E_1) and (E_2) can be used, as shown:

Group	Treatment	Observation	Measurement
E_1	X_1	0_1	0_1 compared with 0_2 in a controlled context
E_2	X_2	0_2	0_2 in a controlled context

The basis for comparison is not likely to be limited to recall. Attitude and intention-to-buy questions may also be asked and behaviour in the product field will be taken into account.

10.6.2 Testing in the field before campaign exposure

If the brand is on sale it is possible to pre-test in the field by arranging for the run of a publication to be 'split', so that different areas receive issues with different advertisements, or by arranging for different transmitters to put out different commercials. Here again the context is controlled: same television programme, same publication, the independent variable being the advertisement.

Again the measures used to determine the relative effectiveness of the alternative advertising approaches are recall (unaided and aided), attitude questions, intention to buy (if not already doing so) in the light of experience to date in the product field.

The setting up of this kind of experiment is straightforward enough; publishers and independent television contractors offer standard packages as part of their own sales promotional activity.

The main procedural difficulties are the following:

- contacting suitable, i.e. target-group, respondents;
- matching experimental groups on critical product use and demographic criteria;
- making sure that respondents have in fact been exposed to the test material.

A question relating to editorial content of the issue, or in the case of television, about adjacent programmes, is the usual way of establishing that the responses recorded relate to the advertisements whose impact we are trying to assess. It is possible to use the media to test the effectiveness of a new advertising approach if the brand is 'ongoing' and in distribution. Were the media to be used to finalise advertising for a new brand it would be necessary to have produced the product in sufficient quantity, packed and priced to meet the demand created, and the competition would be alerted.

10.6.3 An 'after–only with control' example

When we pre-test the effect of communications we would like to be able to take a 'before' measurement and to base our conclusions on observation of the changes effected by the advertising material on the respondent's awareness, attitudes and intentions with regard to the brand. But we know that questions asked at the first interview are likely to influence responses at the second.

To validate a procedure which sidesteps this difficulty we can take two samples of about 100 target consumers matched on about two demographic characteristics and, where relevant, on some aspect of brand or product field usage. We then proceed as follows:

- The experimental group receives the advertising test material plus some other prompting stimulus such as a pack shot.

- The control group receives the other prompting stimulus without the advertising material.

- The two samples are questioned about the brand, and the added value of the advertising material is appraised by comparing the responses of the experimental group with those of the control group, e.g. 'considerable importance ...?' versus 'intention-to-buy' measures.

- The design is shown below, where X = advertising test material and Y = the other stimulus:

Group	Treatment	Observation	Measurement[*]
E	X + Y	0_1	$0_1 - 0_2$
C	Y	0_2	

[*] It is possible, of course, that some of the verbal measures used may not show a positive result for E, the experimental group, and that the overall result may not show value being added by the advertising.

In an 'after-only with control' design sampling error will be greater than it would be if both sets of measurements were taken on the same sample of respondents, as in a before-after design. In order to avoid the possible bias due to the learning effect, communications research relies very often on a comparison of responses from more than one group, whether these be two experimental groups, as in our previous first sample, or an experimental group with a control group. Matching of the groups is critical and it is advisable to ensure that test and control samples use the same interviewers in matched locations. When commercials are being tested, the location is likely to be a van, suitably equipped, or a hall.

10.7 Pre-testing with instruments

There is a good case for using mechanical means of observation when testing the stand-out effect of pack designs. For a time lab-type experiments using mechanical observation were fashionable in communications research, but the following considerations now count against the use of 'ironmongery' to measure advertising effects:

- Use of measuring devices such as the tachistoscope or psychogalvanometer restricts the venue for the experiment to a test centre or mobile van and adds to the cost of data collection, for the ironmongery is expensive and the procedure likely to be time consuming.

- Artificiality in the circumstances in the advertising material is exposed to the respondents reduces belief in the external validity of their responses.

- It is usual to ask questions in order to interpret the meaning of the physiological observations recorded by the instruments.

We are going to consider two devices: the **tachistoscope** and the **psychogalvanometer**. The tachistoscope is relevant to the testing of posters for stand-out value, and it could be claimed that the more speedily perceived of two advertisements has the better chance of being noticed in the press or during the commercial break on independent television channels. But, posters apart, experiments based on verbal measures are likely to produce richer and more actionable data for physiological aspects. It is always possible, of course, to combine the physiological and verbal procedures: to record the speed with which elements in the advertisement are perceived and then to ask the recall, attitude and intention questions.

As for the psychogalvanometer, the case for physiological measurements rests on doubts about the capacity of researchers to ask meaningful questions and of consumers to give true answers. Response to an advertising stimulus when attached to the psychogalvanometer or 'lie detector' is involuntary. Electrodes attached to the hands measure sweat levels. These are an autonomic indicator of emotional arousal, provided the temperature of the research centre, or van, is kept stable. Comparison of fluctuations with a base measurement will show how the respondent reacts to the development of a commercial, to the sight of a press advertisement or the sound of a radio commercial. The emotional responses are duly recorded but the nature of the responses, whether these are favourable or unfavourable, has to be elicited by means of questions.

10.8 Simulated test markets

Simulated test market tests have the following features:

- They have the advantage of speed, for both penetration and repeat buying are 'hothoused'.
- They provide for extensive diagnostic questioning.
- They depend on neither attitude measurement scores nor the availability of trend data.
- They can eliminate the need for much of the hitherto necessary separate testing of elements such as advertising, pack and product.

As an example, Research International's Sensor Model has simulated encounters with new brands at the point of sale:

- Respondents are recruited to central locations.
- Respondents are exposed to advertising.
- Respondents are taken to a simulated shop display including the new brand and its competitor.
- Respondents are given coupon money to spend on products in the display.
- Those who buy the test product are given it to use at home under natural conditions.
- After a suitable interval trialists are called on and asked brand preference questions.
- Prices are discussed using the 'trade-off' procedure.
- Respondents are given the opportunity to buy the test brand using their own money.

Sensor estimates market share. The model assumes that the size of the market (as revealed by shop audit, consumer panel or omnibus data) will remain much the same, but the marketing task in many cases is to establish a place for the brand in individual shopping baskets or purchasing repertoires and a measure of absolute volume sales is needed.

Modelling includes inputs such as availability, advertising, brand visibility, concept acceptability, product acceptability, frequency of purchasing and weight of purchasing. Predictive product testing provides estimates of sales volume at an early stage which can be validated, based on trial and adoption measures. The predictive value of RI models[6] depends on corporate experience in the market, the existence of trend data and the care with which preliminary research, such as the hall test, is designed and interpreted. Modelling techniques are discussed in more detail in Chapter 11.

Respondents can be conveniently tested in the following locations:

- in-hall, where there is greater interviewer control of product presentation and sample;
- in-home, where respondents can consume the product according to their normal daily routine;
- on-site, on business premises such as pubs, wine bars and working men's clubs.

10.9 Conclusion

In order to create effective advertising it is necessary to consider how advertising can work to further the marketing objective, and so to arrive at a definition of a specific advertising objective. Given an adequate advertising appropriation, successful achievement of the advertising objective depends on a combination of effective media planning and the capacity to create persuasive advertisements. Advertising is a substantial marketing cost, especially where branded consumer products are concerned. With considerable sums at stake advertisers are not, as a rule, happy to take creative work entirely on trust, while advertising agents, including their creative staff, seek reassurance that they are on the right lines. The usefulness of qualitative work is to stimulate creative thinking and to try out ideas.

The Halfords case study that follows contributes to the concepts and practical applications of the marketing research process at work.

REFERENCES

1. Ehrenberg A. Barnard N. and J. Scriven (1998), 'Justifying our advertising budgets: the weak and strong theories', Keynote presentation in *Proceedings of the 3rd Annual Conference of the Global Institute for Corporate and Marketing Communications*, Strathclyde University Graduate Business School, Scotland.

2. Gordon W. and R. Langmaid (1988), *Qualitative Research – A Practitioner's and Buyer's Guide*, Gower, London.

3. Colley R. (1961), *Advertising Goals for Measured Advertising Results*, Association of National Advertisers, New York.

4. Lavidge R. and C. Steiner (1961), 'A model for predictive measurements of advertising effectiveness', *Journal of Marketing*, Spring.

5. Fishbein M. (1967), *Readings: Attitude theory and measurement*, John Wiley, New York.

6. Research International (1994), Position Paper 5, p.10.

FURTHER READING

1. Macrae C. (1999), Special Issue on 'Brand Reality', Guest edited, *Journal of Marketing Management*, vol. 15, nos 1–3, pp.1–210.

2. *Market Leader*, the journal of the Marketing Society (1998), Issue no. 1, Spring.

QUESTIONS

1. 'In the advertising business we all know that the ultimate test of any advertising campaign is the sales result to which it contributes.' Does this statement imply that attempts to pre-test advertising campaigns are irrelevant?
2. 'Consumption decisions are a vital source of the culture of the time ... The individual uses consumption to say something about himself and his family and his locality.' Does this statement by an anthropologist answer the question, 'What makes advertising work?'
3. A marketing company, fearing 'me too' action by competitors, is hesitating to test-market a shampoo which includes an ingredient to improve hair 'rinsability' after shampooing. You have been asked to review and evaluate the method or methods whereby the impact of the total mix (formulation, package, price and communication) could be assessed without alerting the competition. Propose a suitable research design.

CASE STUDY 10.1

Halfords Motor Oils: Research and Own Brand Development[†]

Halfords is the largest UK retailer of car parts and accessories, cycles and cycle accessories. The company has steadily increased its commitment to own-brand products, recognising the Halfords brand as a key strategic cornerstone for the business. Continuous development and innovation in own-brand products has enhanced the brand credentials and leveraged company performance. In 1996/7 42% of Halfords' sales came from own-brand products.

In 1996 the company launched a highly successful range of own-brand motor oils, winning widespread praise and industry awards. The redesigned and repositioned range offered high technical quality, clear range segmentation, unique and customer-friendly packaging, competitive pricing and effective marketing communication. Research played an important role in the development of this new range, enabling Halfords to launch a product that not only met consumer needs but differentiated the company successfully from major competitors.

[†]Adapted by M Kirkup from Kirkup, M., Walley, P. and Temperley, J. (1999) in *Contemporary Cases in Retail Operations Management*, eds: B. Oldfield, R. Schmidt, I. Clarke, C. Hart and M. Kirkup.

Continued

Marketing objectives

In 1995 Halfords offered a range of motor oils that focused on the proprietary brands (Castrol, Duckhams and Mobil) alongside a limited own-brand offer. During that year a product range review was carried out by the buying team responsible for motor oils. Their review concluded that, while the own-brand range was achieving a 6% brand share and sales growth in line with the market, there were significant opportunities to increase sales and profit performance through redesign and repositioning. Although the market was highly competitive and price aggressive, the value of the market was increasing as a result of new product development and market segmentation introducing specialist lubricants to meet the needs of modern cars. The premium end of the market had therefore become more important and offered new opportunities. The team also felt there were opportunities to redesign the range to help consumers. Many consumers did not understand the difference between oil grades, or terms such as viscosity, and were therefore not buying the most appropriate oil for their cars. A repositioning of the range was also needed as, although the Halfords brand was perceived by consumers as offering value for money in terms of price and quality, it was not seen in the same quality league as the main proprietary brands.

Under the leadership of Chris Forman, buying controller for the Halfords Auto Business Centre, a major project was launched in 1995 to redesign and reposition the own-brand range of oils. The objective was to develop a serious alternative range to the brand leaders, increase oil sales, change the mix of oil sales towards premium products, and increase the share of own-brand oils against lower margin proprietary brands. The strategy to achieve these objectives had a number of elements. The Halfords brand offer was to be extended to include diesel and synthetic oil, and the oil quality was to be upgraded to match the leading proprietary brands. The main focus, however, was to design a container that provided significant added value benefits to consumers, improved consumer perceptions and understanding of the product, and innovative features that would exceed industry standards and differentiate the brand. Finally, an effective communication strategy was required to help consumers make an informed choice of oil grade and understand the benefits of Halfords oil.

Concept design

The project required a major team effort and took 12 months to complete. Within Halfords the project involved buyers, marketing experts and quality specialists. Externally the company required the assistance of design agencies, marketing research specialists, patent agents, oil suppliers, a container manufacturer, tool-makers, cap manufacturers, and plastics and label suppliers.

The Pentagram design agency took on the role of 'concept creators' – to design the structure and form of the new oil containers. The design objectives required that the new packaging should address consumer requirements and provide distinctive added value benefits that differentiated the range. The design had to achieve visual impact when on display, communicate effectively and demonstrate design flair and aesthetic appeal. The new range also had to reflect Halfords' brand values of quality, value for money, trust and confidence.

Pentagram's design process began with 'exploration': researching the oil market and competition, and brainstorming to explore the issues in oil packaging and the benefits sought by consumers, for example in handling, pouring and reducing spillage. Many existing competing oil containers were examined and the agency explored as many conceptual routes as possible to seek a novel solution. In generating ideas, consideration was given to style and aesthetics, handling and ergonomics, ease of filling for the oil company, ease of manufacture, ease of transporting, plus uniqueness and shelf-impact. Twelve designs were generated and the quality function deployment technique was used to evaluate the designs against 15 criteria. The three highest scoring designs were converted to solid models with preliminary graphics. Halfords did not choose the solution that scored the highest on Pentagram's analysis, but chose the most 'unique' design of the three to provide clear differentiation in the market.

The chosen design featured a handle on the front face of the can, with a deep undercut behind for ease of grip. The user could lower the spout much nearer to the engine before the oil began to pour – making pouring easier and reducing spillage. A 'visi-strip' was incorporated to indicate the oil level. There was debate over the choice of cap for the container and so two ideas were developed, a unique flip-cap and more conventional screw-cap. The Lippa Pearce agency developed graphics for the container, seeking to enhance the form and shape and provide labelling that would help consumers choose the oil grade most appropriate for their car. Different coloured containers were proposed for each grade of oil.

Concept testing

Consumer research played an important role in the product development process. A major research study was commissioned to Baughman Associates in May 1995. The research set out partly to examine aspects of consumer purchasing behaviour in the sector, but particularly to probe consumer reactions to the new design concepts and their needs and opportunities. The research method chosen was a series of seven extended focus groups. From previous research Halfords had identified that their auto business attracted three main customer types: 'car enthusiasts' (the grease monkey), 'driver-dabblers' and 'light users', and so two separate focus groups were held with each segment. Three groups were held in the north of the country and three in the south, all with male consumers. One all-female focus group was also held to consider whether female attitudes varied from male.

The research confirmed consumer perceptions of the main oil brands. In the north, Halfords was placed in the 'middle quality' band, below brands like Castrol and Duckhams but alongside own-brand oils sold by car accessory retailers such as Charlie Brown and Motor World. In the south, Halfords was placed alongside the lower quality supermarket and DIY brands. The research confirmed confusion and lack of understanding among consumers when purchasing motor oils (see Box 10.1).

Box 10.1 Examples of consumer attitudes to motor oils

'What type of oil do you usually buy?'

'Usually the cheapest.'
'The guy who services my car tells me to use 20/50 – I don't know much about oil apart from that.'
'I buy one of those synthetic oils – I probably pay more than I have to.'
'I've always bought Duckhams. I don't know which one – it costs about a tenner.'
'I use Esso. I wouldn't buy the one for £20 – the one in the middle is good enough for me.'
'I suppose the more expensive ones are purer.'
'I don't know much about oil so I use Castrol. It's been around for years so it must be good.'

Continued

The research found that factors influencing the choice of brand and grade included the degree of assurance the consumer needs, perceived quality (created by brand or retailer reputation), price and convenience. Premium oil users might be motivated by the age of their vehicle, a sense of responsibility to maintain a new or more expensive car, or through affection for their car. Middle quality oil users might be seeking adequate protection and reassurance but at a lower price. Lower quality oil users might select on price or convenience. The research suggested there was limited brand loyalty, and many of those few who did regularly buy a similar brand appeared to do it out of habit rather than a belief that their choice was superior or ideal for their car. However, the research observed that consumers are often loyal to a particular grade of oil – to ensure consistency in the type used – and would switch between brands depending on convenience and price on a given occasion.

The focus groups also evaluated various product segmentation systems used by oil manufacturer brands and their communication messages. These included the use of colour-coding for different oils, the segmentation of oils into 'type of car' categories, and also the use of chart-based engine-specific guides. Halfords' classification proposals were presented anonymously to the groups and were welcomed as 'short, sweet and to the point'. The proposed colour-coding scheme was seen as helpful to distinguish clearly between oil grades.

Consumers were presented with two block-models of the container – one with a flip-cap and one with a screw-cap. The container shape was described variously as 'modern', 'sculptured', 'expensive', 'different', 'impressive', 'eye catching', and 'quality'. Some consumers instantly appreciated the advantage of the shape for ease of pouring, even before handling the container. The flip-cap was well received – some consumers suggesting it might pour better – but there were concerns about leakage, spillage and how it could be reused for old oil. The consumers spontaneously noticed the visi-strip on the handle and noted it was in an ideal place. They liked the proposed green (premium) and silver (synthetic) container colours, and the metallic treatment was seen as enhancing the impression of quality. The proposed yellow for the Standard Plus Oil, however, was viewed as looking 'cheap'. One group of consumers in the south favoured a more traditional choice of colourway (white) for the main types of oil. The consumers welcomed the proposed label content on the container, but felt there was also a need for a strong 'quality' statement to emphasise the comparability with leading brands. The focus groups showed that the new packaging successfully moved Halfords Motor Oil up the hierarchy of brands. The consumers saw the new design moving Halfords to the top of the middle quality brands, and superior (in the north) to Charlie Brown and Motor World.

Following the focus groups, the buying team commissioned further research to identify a powerful quality statement, particularly as comparability was a key element in the Halfords brand positioning. Six alternative statements were developed for testing, and consumer interviews were held in a Halfords store to identify the most powerful phrases. The choice of statement also had to take into account legal requirements, and Halfords also consulted with their oil suppliers who marketed their own oil ranges. The company felt that a clear and effective quality statement was an important element in generating 'confidence' – Halfords was trying to maximise impact, minimise conflict and maximise consumer understanding.

The research findings helped Halfords and Pentagram refine the design of the new range of containers for manufacture, select the most appealing colour coding and graphics, and develop appropriate marketing communication strategies.

The launch success

Halfords wanted to improve the impact of oil displays in-store, promote additional sales opportunities through increased authority, communicate the chosen segmentation system and encourage trading up, as well as convey the unique product benefits of the new Halfords range. They wanted customers to appreciate that with a Halfords oil they could trade up to a higher grade but also save money. Acknowledging the research findings, the communication messages stressed that Halfords oil 'was just as good as the best on the market but offers better value for money than other leading brands', 'comes in unique bottles which make pouring easier and minimise spillage', and 'is easier to select the right oil'. External communication strategies focused particularly on exposure within carefully targeted motoring press. In-store merchandising included new graphics boards, and the colour-coded segmentation system developed for the packaging was mirrored in the presentation of stock to facilitate product selection for customers. In terms of pricing the team were able to lift price points as a result of the 'added value' injected through improved product quality and container design. The team did not consider test marketing would be appropriate. They opted for a national launch on a set date. Chris Forman felt the research had provided them with a good understanding of the customer, and they were confident about the product.

The new range was launched in spring 1996. The financial results underline its commercial success. One year later Halfords was reporting average product prices across the range up 12%, a 19% increase in sales volume, 44% increase in sales value and 54% increase in margin. Halfords' brand share in the UK motor oil market increased from 6% in 1996 to 12% in 1997.

Questions

1. What additional and/or alternative forms of research could Halfords have undertaken to support the launch strategy?
2. What further research might be helpful to the company 'after' the launch of the new range? What would the objectives of the research be, and what research methods would be appropriate?
3. Halfords will need to advise their suppliers of specific order quantities for each grade of oil, as well as forecast specific stock requirements for stores. What approach and techniques would you recommend?

11 Modelling techniques for product prediction and planning

Rory P Morgan

11.1 The role of market research in new product development

Market research has a key role in the new product development (NPD) process, partly in generating ideas and developing them, but primarily in reducing the risk or exposure to downside financial loss. The many hurdles that a new product must face include the following areas where market research techniques, appropriately applied, can significantly reduce this risk.

- **Accurate assessment of market demand**. Clearly, some internal estimate must be made of the potential for a new product or service, in order to justify the NPD exercise in the first place. This assessment should not only indicate the overall total demand, but also indicate the characteristics of potential triallists/adopters, plus any significant segmentation of the market in terms of users.

- **Obtaining a good product fit**. The product must be optimised to meet known demand, given the constraints of competition, production and cost. This may need to acknowledge some trade-offs in design/composition if targeted at specific user segments with a different needs profile from the population at large.

- **Identifying optimal positioning**. In most developed markets with existing competition, some consideration needs to be taken of these competitors. Generally speaking, the positioning of the new product or service will be defined in order to maximise some declared goal. For example, in a 'cloning' strategy, the aim would be to identify and mimic a target competitor, and develop a competing product that utilises some inherent benefit in order to develop a consumer proposition with a similar profile but with an advantage, e.g. through better distribution, pricing or branding equity (or, indeed, any of these in combination). Alternatively, a strategy of distinctiveness would lead to the development of a 'unique selling proposition', possibly resulting from an identified gap in the market. However, in either case, there is a need to estimate the likely source of business from other competitors (e.g. brand-switching patterns). This is particularly true when there is a need to minimise cannibalisation from one's own brands.

- **Payback and profitability**. Marketing is a commercial activity, and ultimately has the aim of generating profits. Hence, there is an overriding need to ensure that the stream of revenue resulting from sales of the new product will pay back the investment made in the required period, and has a good chance of sustaining profit levels in the foreseeable future. This invariably means making some estimate of the volume of sales, both in the period of growth (e.g. first and second years, in the case of many grocery products), and thereafter. The revenue resulting from these sales can be offset against known costs. The better the volume predictions, the more the risk is reduced.

Models using data derived from market research can be used to assist in all these areas. One feature of modern times is that the quantitative methods that have been developed have tended to become more and more specialised, and many of the better approaches use proprietary techniques developed by research agencies. It is likely that this process will continue, since even the largest marketing conglomerate finds it difficult to match the range of experience and case material available to agencies, who (in the largest companies) deal with hundreds of such exercises every year. And many of these are models in the sense that a variety of inputs both from survey research and from marketing are synthesised with the aim of making 'what if?' predictions. These are the predictive models. Others are more descriptive in nature.

The aim of this chapter is to provide an overview of the ways that market research models can assist the NPD process, from product inception to launch. It is highly selective, since there is already a vast number of marketing models in existence, ranging from highly theoretical (and possibly untested) to the highly practical (with years of experience and back data). I have therefore tended to concentrate on well-known services of proven stature, which are commonly available to marketing people. Even then, it is not exhaustive, but should serve to give a flavour of the area.

11.2 Sizing the potential

It is frequently thought that product forecasting takes place at the end of the NPD process, when a 'finished' product is available for production, and volume estimates are required. This is true, but often overlooked is the fact that the most critical forecasting exercise is (or should be) conducted right at the beginning. Some products must fail, despite high acceptance among actual users, simply because the number of users is insufficient to generate enough revenue to lead to profitability.

An initial assessment of demand (and, therefore, potential) is critical. Sometimes this is common sense – a new drug targeting migraine or asthma sufferers must take account of the simple number of such sufferers that exists. Other products, operating in fast-moving grocery areas, can make use of common patterns. The basis for a great number of marketing models was provided by Parfitt and Collins (1968), who postulated back in 1967 that brand share is a function of the penetration that is achieved (usually thought of as the proportion of product field buyers who have actually tried the test product), the repeat-purchasing rate (the proportion of triallists who buy again within a given time period), and the buying rate index (to take account of users of the test product using more or less than the average for the field).

Armed with this model, some preliminary 'scenario planning' is possible. For example, consider the following facts:

- In almost all product fields it is extremely rare for more than half of those who make a trial purchase to repeat purchase the product at all.
- Once the product has settled down, it is unusual for more than 15–20% of triallists to repeat purchase in any four-week period.
- Repeat buyers in most product fields purchase between 1.6 and 2.2 times per four-week period.
- New products very rarely have a higher purchase frequency than existing products.

Thus, if financial calculations suggest that 10 m units need to be sold in a year, we can estimate the region of trial levels required to support this. Good product performance might result in a repeat-purchase rate of 15%, with an average of 2 units per buyer in each four-week period of the year. Thus, if all 20 m households in Great Britain purchase (100% penetration, mind) 3 m (i.e. 15%) triallists would result in 78 m units sold in the year (3 m triallists × 2 units × 13 four-week periods). We should make a fortune!

So far so good. However, actual sales will depend on a number of other factors, of which actual penetration and physical distribution are the most significant. Penetration is certain to be much less than 100%. If the average penetration of the product field is 25%, and we are unlikely to get more than 50% distribution, then our new estimate would be 78 × 0.5 × 0.25 = 9.75 m units. Added to this the fact that we need to down-weight further, because we would not achieve 100% awareness or visibility of the product, and we are now well below our auction standard.

None of this, of course, takes account of any reaction from competitors that might occur. This could take the form of a price reduction, which would lessen the attractiveness to consumers of our own offer, unless we also reduced our price, with obvious implications on the bottom line. Alternatively, our competitors might react with a 'me-too' in a shorter time than we had envisaged, so that our product must now accept a share of the market.

The lesson to be drawn from this simple 'back of the envelope' modelling exercise is that all of these factors trade off with each other, so that even excellent products, operating in sectors with lowish penetration, find it difficult to achieve critical volume unless they can achieve compensating higher levels of distribution, communication, or reduced costs of manufacture.

In addition, there are occasions when the forecast will need to take account of longer-term changes in the market, and particularly when the expected life of a product might be measured in decades. Examples here would include changes in the birth rate (important for manufacturers of baby products), and the gradual ageing of the population. Equally, trends in the working status of women, disposable income, available leisure time (maybe resulting from the unemployment rate), health consciousness, etc., could be relevant.

Forecasting potential demand for consumer goods which have a longer purchase cycle (e.g. durables) offers different challenges, since repeat-purchase rates have less meaning.[1] This is also true for services, such as financial products. Commonly used methods here involve the synthesis of a number of different measures, some of which include formal models:

- **Industry consensus forecasts**. Many industries produce pooled estimates of the rate of growth (e.g. number of adults with bank accounts, satellite dishes, microwave ovens, and so on).

- **Econometric sales trend forecasts**. Statistical models can range from the very simple (moving averages) to the highly complex (Box-Jenkins forecasting). Much of this is conducted in-house, using commonly available statistical software, such as SPSS (Statistical Package for the Social Sciences). However, this is a very technical field, and the novice would be well advised to seek the services of specialised agencies.

- **Analogy with related fields**. Durables' manufacturers can determine the rates of penetration of analogous products. So a manufacturer of satellite dishes might be interested in the historical rates of growth of comparable products (such as video cassette recorders, camcorders, CD players, etc.).

In the case of durables, the notion of the 'park' can provide a basis for forecasting national demand. Here, we need to estimate the number of existing products currently in use (the park), the growth rate and the replacement rate. Given these, we can build a model which says (effectively) that demand for a product at any point in time is a function of the demand from initial buyers, and the demand for replacement at that time.

11.3 Innovation products

'Innovation' products, or those products that are so new and novel in conception that they have no obvious competition, are the most difficult of all to forecast. Indeed, identifying the need for them in the first place (the 'latent demand') can be fairly challenging. In many cases, classical market research involving concept testing can dramatically underestimate potential, simply because respondents cannot envisage the usefulness of the product – until, at least, they see it in use. Cellular phones are a good example of this, in their first few years of operation. Equally, it is said (apocryphally) that Sony Corporation pushed ahead with the development of the Walkman despite, and not because of, the market research.[2]

However, some basic principles do exist. The 'rate of diffusion' of a new idea (i.e. the cumulative sales) can be broken down as the combined effect of two distinct processes:

1. External influences – such as communication through the media, and advertising weight. On its own, the effect of these issues is proportional to the number of potential buyers who have not yet purchased. The effect is therefore logarithmic; it is reduced as the proportion of adopters increases.

2. Internal influences – such as the communication of buyers and potential buyers among themselves. This could be the result of word-of-mouth communication (e.g. recommendations), or simply the effect of products in use (e.g. cellular phones). On its own, the effect of these issues is proportional to the number of buyers to date, and is therefore exponential: its effect is enhanced as the proportion of adopters increases.

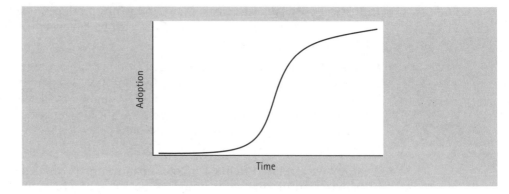

Fig 11.1 The S-shaped curve

The net result of these influences is the familiar S-shaped (sigmoid) curve, as shown in Figure 11.1. To quote Majahan and Peterson (1985):

> After the product is launched, only a few people buy. However, in subsequent time periods, an increasing number of adoptions per time period occur as the diffusion process begins to unfold more fully. Finally, the trajectory of the diffusion curve slows and begins to level off, ultimately reaching an upper asymptote, and the diffusion is complete.

Although the diffusion pattern of most innovations can be described in terms of a general S-shaped curve, the exact form of each curve, including the slope and the asymptote, may differ. For example, the slope may be very steep initially, indicating rapid diffusion, or it may be gradual, indicating relatively slow diffusion.

The shape of this curve can be modelled; both the logistic and Gompertz trends are popular here.

11.4 Meeting the demand

It almost goes without saying that any new product should, within the constraints of brand heritage, production and cost, meet the demands of its intended target customer base. This is particularly true of products that are intended to appeal to specific segments. The general rationale for segmented marketing is that by meeting a very specific set of needs, a price premium can be charged for the added value provided. For this reason, a segmentation approach based on needs is preferable.

Three situations commonly arise where there is an opportunity to develop products around changing needs :

1. Where a revolution in technology or production makes it possible suddenly to satisfy needs hitherto unmet or even unseen (e.g. pocket calculators, frozen foods, instant noodles, freeze-dried coffee, etc.). This can result in a situation known as a 'paradigm shift', where consumers are often initially unable to see the benefits to themselves, as referred to earlier. These sorts of products in effect generate their own demand (or hope to).

2. Where an advance in product delivery improves the way in which an existing need is met. Many products fit into this category, but a classic example would be disposable nappies. Note that 'need' in this instance can refer to a search for novelty, or fashion.

Another way to think of this is in terms of developing products to overcome problems. The research requirement here is to identify problems, and then quantify their importance and frequency of occurrence. Techniques such as problem detection studies[3] help to build a scatterplot of 'problems' as in Figure 11.2. This could be regarded as an example of a descriptive model, since the analysis suggests problem areas that offer the best opportunity, i.e. they occur frequently, and have the greatest impact, and therefore could be supposed to have the greatest benefit if they were put right.

3. Where the circumstances, behaviour or attitudes of consumers change, giving rise to new needs. Changes can result from fundamental trends such as in the increase of working mothers, changes in the patterns of family eating, or holidays taken abroad. Or, they could refer to more mercurial changes such as eating habits (snacking, meal times). Attitudinal topics might include health, environmentalism, and so on.

In situations where the new product is heavily dependent on patterns of behaviour (eg. snack products consumed in certain situations), it is important to the forecasting process to quantify the opportunities for use in the target population, since this will obviously have a direct bearing on the volume consumed. A classical approach here is to use panel diary data, or alternatively to use a sample of respondents asked to recall occasions of use, to build up an item-by-use matrix as shown in Figure 11.3. This is another descriptive model, where the relative frequency of occurrence of each of the cells in the matrix can then be used to indicate the potential of new products. In a sense, this is a form of forecasting demand.

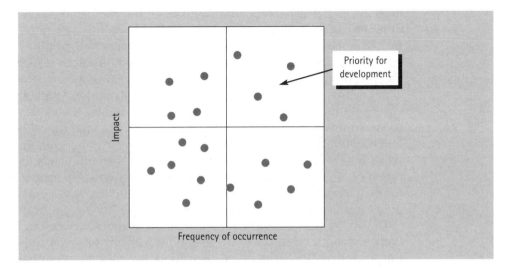

Fig 11.2 Scatterplot of 'problems'

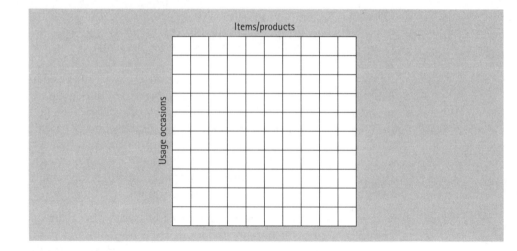

Fig 11.3 Items-by-use matrix

11.5 Conjoint analysis and discrete choice modelling

Another way to optimise products in terms of the way they meet core needs, while at the same time modelling market performance, is with the use of conjoint analysis, and associated techniques such as discrete choice modelling (DCM). These modelling techniques have become a very important method in the NPD armoury, since they can simultaneously quantify the importance of product features, identify segments of individuals who want different features, and model the likely market shares of potential product configurations.

In essence, a main-effects version of a statistical method is known as factorial testing. Conjoint analysis is known as a 'decompositional' method, since it proceeds by showing product configurations to respondents, and then asking for their degree of preference. From an analysis of all the configurations shown, the appeal or 'utility' of each of these constituent variables can be 'decomposed' and quantified. The method of administering these product configurations to respondents (and hence calculating from all the myriad combinations possible which is the best one to show next) can nowadays be done on a computer.

In practice, there is a risk of a 'combinatorial explosion'[4] with a large number of variables, and the practical limit is 12–20. Variables are expressed in terms of levels, so that a variable measuring, say, engine size might have levels of 1800 cc, 2000 cc and 2300 cc. Because of the nature of the exercise, conjoint analysis is best when used with relatively 'hard' features, and therefore lends itself to consumer durables, or services. While it can be used with grocery products (e.g. product forms, packaging, and so on) it is not best at handling 'softer' image-related attributes, for which other techniques are preferred.

The 'utility values' generated in a conjoint analysis exercise can be calculated for every variable level in the exercise, and individually for every respondent. There is not space here to consider their derivation, but they are commonly thought to be one of the most accurate and discriminating ways to measure the importance of product features. They can be used in three principal ways, described below, which are of great value in the new product development process (and, indeed, of general market studies).[5]

Discrete choice modelling is another variant on the conjoint principle, with the exception that the decision measured (and modelled) is that of *choice*, rather than *preference*. This is useful in situations where the assumption that the preference for brands should approximate to actual behaviour may not hold. It is a model that is analysed at the aggregate level, so that the data from each respondent is only a part of the total design (i.e. a single respondent will typically only answer a balanced subset of the total), which has the added benefit that interactions between variables (which are not accounted for in classical conjoint analysis) can be measured. This is, however, at the expense of restricting the number of variables to a smaller number than is typical in conjoint studies.

Sub-group analysis

In conjoint analysis, the utility values generated by every respondent for all attribute levels can be taken as a measure of 'importance' or desirability that they attach to these features. Therefore, we can analyse this data by groupings of individuals that we suppose, a priori, might differ in terms of what they consider to be important. For example, we can look at men versus women, northerners versus southerners, brand users versus non-users, in short any predefined group that we care to specify. Sub-groups can also be examined in discrete choice models, although care must be taken to ensure that these are statistically balanced due to the aggregate nature of the analysis.

Segmentation

At the same time, we can use statistical techniques such as cluster analysis to identify groupings of people who share the same notion of what they consider to be important in the product. In many respects this is the reverse of sub-group analysis since, having found groups of individuals, we then need to profile them by demographics, usership, etc., in order to find out who they are. Segments identified in this way have a very important significance in new product development, since they can be regarded as corresponding to primary need groups in the marketplace, and, therefore, offer an ideal mechanism for product development, since in principle we can easily see what the product form would be that would maximally satisfy them. The problem does not end here, since we would need to know if (and by how much) they would pay a price premium for the product. However, segmentation performed upon conjoint utilities is one of the classic ways of identifying product feature opportunities.

Simulating market shares

The real power of conjoint analysis can be seen in its ability to conduct simulation or 'what if?' modelling. One of the mathematical properties of computed utility values is that they can be used predictively to estimate the degree of preference that any individual would exhibit to any array of possible product configurations. Thus, we can estimate the likely appeal of a huge variety of possible product feature combinations – many more than we could possibly test through direct interviewing. Combined with cost data, we can therefore conduct an optimisation procedure that identifies a shortlist of product configurations that offer the best level of acceptance for the minimum cost of production.

This largely diagnostic principle has been taken further by the Locator[SM] model from Research International. This implements a fully predictive simulation model in which a variety of image positions/repositionings can be created, and the modelled changes in preference for brands used as the basis for product and communication planning. The power of this is examined next.

11.6 Optimising the positioning

In competitive markets, there is generally some need to explore the potential interactions that a new brand would have with existing brands following launch. This is partly done with the aim of controlling or targeting brand-switching behaviour in a desired direction.

Most NPD exercises will aim at developing a brand-positioning statement, around which the communication strategy will be developed. In many cases, the positioning will involve product performance issues. But increasingly, especially in western-style segmented markets, the positioning will incorporate softer motivational-type issues (for example, trust/reliability, sophistication, fashionability, age identification, and so on). The marketing arena can be thought of as a 'map' of product qualities, some hard and some soft, on which products are positioned.

In fact, quantitative mapping techniques can be used with brand-image data derived from survey research to create maps of this sort,[6] and these can be very useful in conceptualising the space, and analysing gaps in the market. However, on their own they are generally useless for the purposes of forecasting.

The big problem with these sorts of analyses is that they invariably do not take account of the underlying preferences that consumers may have, irrespective of the imagery that they have of brands. For example, I may think that Marlboro has a strong macho image, but this is irrelevant to my choice of cigarette brand if I do not find this property desirable. In fact, the brand manager of Marlboro may have a number of difficult choices. He or she may know exactly where to position the brand on a market map, but in which way should the communication message move – towards 'for real smokers', 'having special offers', 'pleasant tasting', 'suitable for all occasions', or what?

The clear message here is that in situations where the positioning involves non-functional issues (where the direction of benefit may be clearer), then image data of the current market on its own is a poor indicator of where to be. In many cases, it is simply a playback of past advertising history. This means that we need a good understanding of what drives preference in a market at any point in the NPD process.

What we are missing is some notion of what consumers find 'important'. For functional benefits, we can use conjoint analysis, and this is a useful way of giving some weight to product features. In markets where these play a large part (e.g. durables and some services) this is one way to proceed. However, this is much more difficult in those markets where non-functional and more emotive issues not only play a large part in the decision process, but are the very characteristics on which the market is defined.

In general, consumers' understanding of their own motivation is poor, and many purchasing decisions are at best semi-rational. Of course, we can always use our own 'common sense' about what is important, or even rely on qualitative evidence, but this is hardly using the principles of the systematic reduction of risk. In fact, a number of research models have been built to handle this problem. Generally speaking, the aim is to interview respondents and collect their images of brands in the market on a whole range of descriptors, using some form of scale. Like all scales, these should be unambiguous, related to preference, and discriminate between the brands rated. The modelling then consists of establishing a mathematical relationship between brand positions in this image space (similar to the mapping techniques discussed earlier), and the preference that respondents have for those brands.

Moreover, it is very difficult to approach this directly through survey research. Techniques such as conjoint analysis often work best when the variables under consideration are 'hard', i.e. deal with concrete functional benefits that can be easily described and categorised into levels. This is much more difficult to do when the variables (or some of them) are 'soft', i.e. image-rich topics that are dealing with psychosocial or emotional values. Although primarily tools for examining 'hard' product features, there is an emerging number of models which use the basic principles of conjoint analysis to investigate 'softer' issues – the IdeaMap system from Moskowitz-Jacobs, Inc. in the United States being one of these.

However, the tendency has been to develop specialised models for taking account of emotional variables to deal with:

- the typically larger number of emotional variables needed to take account of all the expressions of a brand;
- the fact that these variables resist easy categorisation into discrete levels;
- the fact that they are often inter-correlated, which violates a basic assumption of the conjoint model that the variables should be statistically independent.

The value of this is twofold :

- The process will generally give us some idea of how 'important' topics are (in the sense of influencing preference).

- The system can be used as a predictive 'what if' simulation model, in which the effects of changing image positions can be seen as directly affecting preference, and hence (putatively) market share.

It would be wrong to say that these sorts of models are specifically for the use of NPD, since they are increasingly being used to study current markets in an ongoing way. However, they fit into the NPD process in the following ways.

1. For exploring current markets and identifying promising positions relative to current brands (after all, most product launches are line extensions). In addition to 'modifying' existing brands, the ability exists in most of these models to 'create' new brands with specified properties, and determine what potential levels of preference share they might attract.

2. Used with concept testing, to measure the imagery generated by concepts, and incorporate this into a market model. This will indicate the relative strengths and weaknesses of the concept, and the potential for change.

3. Used with full market mix testing, often as part of the simulated test market (see below). The value here lies in providing a good actionable base for diagnosing any problems related to failures to gain acceptance, and providing a means of determining remedial action.

Image models are often used to investigate the relationships between psychosocial topics and brand preference. For example, the Perceptor model from Novaction identifies the dimensions that underlie a set of brand descriptors, and calculates their correlation with preference as an estimate of how 'influential' issues are in a market. This can be combined with the degree to which consumers perceive brands to perform on those characteristics, in order to obtain a 'quadrant analysis' that has strategic value, as shown in Figure 11.4.

There are a number of approaches here. In the early Sandpiper model,[7] respondents rated brands on image statements, on which they also indicated the position of their 'ideal' brand. In the modelling, summed distances from the ideal are taken as being inversely proportional to preference. Sandpiper models tend to be built from large exercises (5,000 respondents or more), and are run essentially as panel operations. A number of databases covering a number of product fields are maintained, and to which on-line access is offered.

In contrast, the Locator[SM] model[8] uses image data collected in the user's own study, and is presented very much as the modern way of analysing image data collected as part of the questionnaire. The process is also different, in that no 'ideal' data is collected, instead, respondents are asked for their brand preferences in addition to the image data, and the modelling therefore deals directly with imagery and preferences collected from the respondent. However, the model (which is very suitable for NPD exercises) operates in the same way, and can provide the user with a copy of their own model, running under Windows on their own PC.

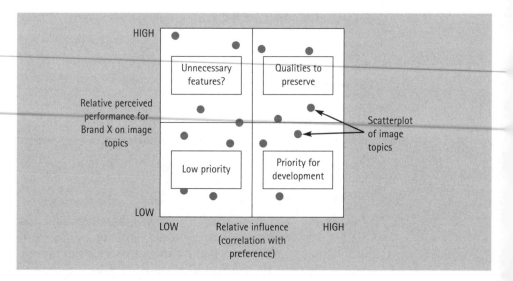

Fig 11.4 Quadrant analysis for Brand X

11.7 Optimising the range

Another area where modelling can help is in optimising a range of products designed to span a market (generally on a 'deluxe' to an 'economy' price scale). This is particularly applicable to durables, where a manufacturer would like to know what product profiles their 'high-end' and 'low-end' products should have to optimise appeal overall. This is frequently a tricky problem, since, for example, the best product would not necessarily have all the features that consumers prefer as it would then cost too much. So what features do we give up?

One way of solving this is by using the Options model.[9] In this, respondents are asked to complete a computer-administered task, in which they effectively build their own product from a list of costed components. So, for example, in an automotive exercise, the respondent would be told that the base car cost was £12,000, and he or she had the ability to add or take away a range of costed 'extras', which might include safety features, standard of interior trim, instruments, etc. When the respondent is happy with the final profile, and with the total cost of the package, the interview stops. The same process could occur with other product areas, eg. hi-fi equipment, cookers, and so on. It can even be used for service areas (e.g. hotel extras or package holidays).

This procedure leaves us with a database of choices from which we can build a simple but effective selection model. For example, suppose we want to examine two possible product profiles, one 'high-end', and the other 'low-end'. We know the ticket cost of these by adding up their features and adding this to the base cost. But who would buy what? We can tell this by examining our database of choices, and selecting the better 'fit' of each product for each respondent. For example, some respondents would rule out the more expensive option simply because the ticket price was higher than their own costed choice. Overall, we therefore know who would be likely to choose what. In some cases, they would choose nothing, if both prices exceed their minimum.

In fact, we can go further than this, since we can tell by how much the product they would be more likely to choose exceeds their maximum cost. In this way, we can conduct a series of simulations, exploring changes in product configuration, until we minimise this amount. In this way, choice models of this kind help us to optimise the product to meet the demand.

11.8 The 'go/no-go' decision: forecasting volume

As has been indicated earlier, the critical question preceding any launch decision will be 'Can I sell enough of the product to meet my profitability objectives?' The riskiest decision of all (but by no means uncommon in practice) is simply to trust to judgement and go ahead. However, it is worth restating that the function of market research is to reduce risk, and a wide range of models is available to do just that.

Historically, the first attempts to do this involved little research. Area test markets were used, which consisted of a limited sales effort in a localised geographical region where distribution and local media could be used. In the United States, with the ability to split cable television transmissions, different marketing support strategies could be simultaneously tested. However, they are becoming less frequently used, as they have a number of distinct disadvantages.

- They are costly.
- They require major production runs of product, and in-store merchandising.
- They are time consuming – competitors can counter-launch before they are over.
- They are difficult to organise (increasingly) through retail channels.
- They are not necessarily representative of other regions.
- They expose 'one's hand' at an early stage, and competitors can actually 'interfere'.
- Other methods offer good results, with fewer disadvantages.

Cut-down versions of this principle have also been used. For example, in store tests the product is sold through a limited number of outlets, and sales figures monitored. However, these suffer from similar problems, with the additional problem of accounting for matching stores carrying different marketing support strategies. Additionally, it is almost impossible to restrict media along store lines.

The pressure was on, therefore, to find acceptable substitutes, and it was this pressure that led to the development of simulated test markets, of which we can distinguish three main types:

1. **Mini-test markets**, in which a permanent consumer panel is serviced by an exclusive retail system, operated by the research agency. Here, purchasing is real.

2. **Laboratory test markets**, in which the choice situation is 'recreated' for potential purchasers with mock store shelving and product displays, including facings if required. Here, purchasing is semi-real, with respondents being given cash or tokens to exchange.

3. **Calibrated tests**, in which fully branded in-home product use tests are used to expose prospective purchasers to the advertising and the real product, and in which purchase-related questions are asked and assessed using empirically derived weights. Here, actual purchasing is seldom used.

Each of these then represents a trade-off between the *realism* of the task for respondents, and the *risk* to the manufacturer.

11.8.1 Mini–test markets

The controlled nature of these panel operations removed many of the problems associated with regional test markets. However, because the purchasing patterns of individual consumers could be monitored in a way that was not possible with simple sales testing, it was possible to distinguish two important diagnostic measures:

1. The proportion of potential buyers who bought the product at all in a given period (**penetration**).
2. The proportion of buyers who went on to buy again (**repeat purchasers**).

These became important diagnostic measures for manufacturers, because they indicated the source of any problems with the product. Thus, if the product's performance was the result of poor penetration, then more attention could be given to the concept, packaging and communication strategy. Alternatively, if poor levels of repeat purchasing were encountered, the problem lay at the door of the product itself in use. (It could also be both of these.)

In the early days, a problem that remained was that of the long period that a test took, since it was judged necessary to allow a considerable period before repeat-purchase rates stabilised in order to make an accurate prediction. A considerable amount of effort was made, therefore, to predict the final level of repeat purchasing from the early indications. From the work carried out in the 1960s (primarily by Parfitt and Collins on the Attwood consumer panel), a consistent model was developed to predict brand shares. In the event, however, these methods became sufficiently accurate for other ad hoc methods to be used to estimate the key parameters, with a high impact on reduced costs of the system, and shortened timings. Additionally, there was a growing need to obtain market potential feedback from earlier on in the NPD process, possibly single concepts only, and storyboards for advertising communication. With this, the mini-test markets fell into decline.

11.8.2 Laboratory test markets

The aim of these methods is to expose respondents to competitive market arrays, and to emulate a choice process in which they are commonly provided with actual money or tokens in which to purchase product.

A good early example of this can be seen with the Assessor model.[10] In this, respondents are invited to a simulated shop in a central location, in which the test product is displayed alongside the rest of the market. A constant sum preference (CSP) procedure is used to measure the shares of preference for established brands which they can see (alongside advertising, if required). They are then introduced to the test product (including advertising), stated at a given price, and given a coupon with a face value that would enable them to purchase any of the items on display. Then, irrespective of whether they choose the test brand, they are given it to be used in-home for a fixed trial period. After this, respondents are then re-interviewed, and their preferences measured again with CSP, except that this time the new product is included.

From this data, two models of choice (i.e. brand) share are constructed:

1. A preference model (derived from the constant sum preference).

2. A trial-repeat model, along the lines of Parfitt and Collins' approach (1968), which uses measures of trial and repeat purchase. Trial is measured by the observed number who chose the test product, but can also include estimates of sampling. This is qualified by input estimates of awareness and availability (distribution), which are assumed to be independent. Repeat purchase is measured by a Markov process, which is effectively the new brand's share of subsequent purchases in the category among triallists.

The two models are then compared. If they are consistent, all is well. If not, typically, the trial-repeat model is investigated, and the external inputs re-examined. Generally, sample sizes are chosen to result in 100 or so triallists, although this is difficult to predict in advance (actually, it is one of the reasons for doing the study).

The problem with these systems is that they are share-based, in that they assume a fixed market of known competition, and that the introduction of the new product will not affect the total size of the market. Volumes can therefore only be calculated by taking the total market, and calculating the appropriate fraction. This makes laboratory test markets (LTMs) difficult to use for innovation products, but also increasingly difficult to use where the nature of the competition is diffuse.

11.8.3 Calibrated tests

In contrast to LTMs, calibrated tests aim to predict volume, rather than share. As such they overcome many of the drawbacks of LTMs and are now, at least in the UK, the primary market prediction systems in use.

Historically, these are developments of the monadic concept-use product tests that used to be conducted as part of the optimising process in the NPD cycle. These tests are conducted in two stages: a *pre-trial* stage (in which the product in concept form is introduced to the respondent, often in a fixed location), and an in-home recall *post-trial* stage (in which reactions to the product in use are collected). For a full volume prediction, both stages are necessary, and this is normally what is meant by a full simulated test market (STM). However, if only the first stage is used, then a prediction can be made of potential levels of trial for a product, and most of the major systems have this as an option. In fact, there is an increasing tendency to encourage the use of STMs at an earlier point in the NPD process, rather than confirming a 'go/no-go' decision right at the end.

In this account of calibrated tests, I will refer to two systems: Bases[11] and MicroTest[SM],[12] since not only are these the principal systems currently in use in the UK, but they also represent quite different approaches. Both, however, aim to provide the following:

- sales forecasts in years 1 and 2, and the ongoing level thereafter;
- sales breakdown of levels of trial and repeat purchase (called 'adoption' in the MicroTest[SM] terminology).

Bases

The Bases system uses aggregated data, and is therefore a type of 'macro-model'. Respondents are selected according to some criteria, and then shown a concept board bearing a representation of the product, including price (the pack is not shown at this point). Purchase intentions are then obtained on five-point scales. Likely trial is subsequently computed by weighting the points in this scale, taking into account adjustments for the category penetration and rate of growth, and the seasonality. These adjustments are normative, i.e. they are empirically derived from past cases. External estimates of awareness and distribution are also used to compute trial levels.

After a period of trial, respondents are asked for their repurchase intention, plus other measures for value for money, and overall liking. These three scales are modelled to obtain a value of a first repeat rate, which is then converted using norms (possibly on a country basis) to a long-run weighted repeat-purchase measure.

To compute sales, the number of units purchased is needed, so the questionnaire also asks about the degree to which the new product will substitute for current products, and their purchasing frequency (which is also adjusted for over-claim using norms).

MicroTest^SM

The MicroTest^SM model works on a completely different principle. Instead of using macro aggregates of purchasing intention so that volumes are computed using averaged data, the modelling works at the individual level, so that the system is of a type known as a 'micro-model'. The advantages of this approach are threefold:

1. Modelling at the individual level (in essence, making a volume prediction for each person in the sample) makes no assumptions about the underlying distributions of the data, and can handle polarised reactions (e.g. where an 'average' score could result from a small number of people who like the product a lot, and a much larger number who are at best indifferent). In principle, it can never be any worse than macro-modelling, and is often much better. These techniques became available with the advent of cheap computing.

2. Individual predictions allow considerably better diagnostics, so that the profile of likely adopters can be established.

3. These systems place less reliance on norms for calibration, since as far as possible the central constructs are self-adjusting. This can be useful where norms are scanty (or do not exist for the product category, country or type of target market), or where they are old.

The fieldwork procedures are similar to those used by the Bases approach, although a wider variety of questions are used as inputs to the model. Central constructs of the MicroTest^SM approach are the following:

1. **Visibility** – or salience in the marketplace of the product, which is taken to be a function of the level of physical distribution achieved, the weight of advertising used (typically television ratings/gross rating points, and share of voice) and the 'heritage' of the brand. This last factor caters for the fact that products launched by major manufacturers, possibly under a house brand, have a higher impact on consumers than novel products with unknown antecedents. These inputs, some from the respondent and some from marketing, are integrated using a separate model.

2. **Trial** – which is modelled as being a function of the visibility achieved, but also in terms of the appeal of the concept. The key questionnaire inputs here are the attitude towards price, and the propensity to purchase ('buy' scale). Another issue taken into account is the innate experimentalism of the respondent, as measured by his or her claimed use of new products recently launched, as well as his or her perception of the 'risk' associated with purchasing in this product category.

3. **Adoption** – which is taken in this model to be a somewhat stricter definition than simple repeat purchase, since it refers to the probability of incorporating a product into a consumer's repertoire on a long-term basis, and not just the initial period of experimentalism. This is essentially the result of the degree to which the expectations created by the concept have been met in the product during test, as measured by 'pay' and 'buy' scales. At the same time, an adjustment

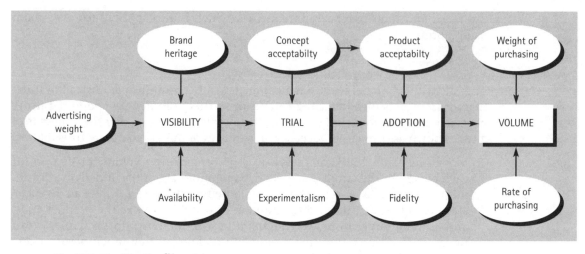

Fig 11.5 The MicroTest^{SM} model

is made for the respondent's innate *fidelity* towards new products, or for the degree to which they are not simply experimental 'gadflies' – always in search of the novel.

These concepts are integrated at the individual level, and the result is the computation of probabilities both of trial and adoption for the individual. However, before summing the results and projecting to the marketplace, they are adjusted by each person's *weight of purchase*, which in competitive markets is taken to be their frequency of purchase, and the average amount bought on those occasions.

The integration of these sub-models is shown in Figure 11.5.

All calibrated tests require marketing inputs, both for estimating trial levels, but also for projecting the results of the test to the market universe. Typically, marketing inputs would include:

Universe
- Market size, in terms of number of households or individuals
- Seasonality
- Regionality
- Category development

Marketing strategy
- Build of awareness (e.g. quarterly)
- Build of all commodity distribution (sterling) on a quarterly basis
- Promotional events
- Competitive activity
- Likely out of stock levels, if any

11.9 Handling price

It is a characteristic of calibrated tests that they operate in a monadic way – a single sample tests a single offering, and this must therefore include a single price. However, a common marketing conundrum is that we would really like to know how volume would vary with price – after all, it may be more profitable to go for a smaller brand share, but with bigger margins, particularly if production costs are constrained or non-linear. Strictly speaking, therefore, a number of test cells

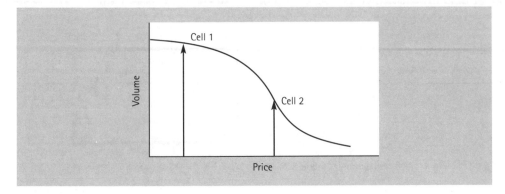

Fig 11.6 Brand/price trade-off demand curve

should be conducted if price itself is under investigation, but this could be a costly exercise. In order to avoid this, sometimes links are made with other models. One example of this is using the brand/price trade-off method, which can be used at the recall stage (post-trial). This system is useful insofar as it gives us a demand curve for price points. Using this system, and calibrating two end-points with test cells predicting volume, we can read off the likely volumes of intermediate price points, as shown in Figure 11.6.

11.10 Measuring brand equity

A significant number of new product launches are nowadays conducted as brand extensions, i.e. making use of an existing brand or marque, either used solus, or as a parent or 'umbrella' endorsement. In the current marketing environment this makes sense, not least because of the communication cost of generating a satisfactory level of awareness of a new brand. However, apart from this, it is often considered to be lower risk to capitalise on the heritage and trust associated with an established 'name', rather than build a new one from scratch.

This has led to a heightened interest in measuring the beneficial qualities imbued in brands, which can be summarised as their 'brand equities'. There are a number of approaches that can be taken here. One such, Brand Dynamics,[13] measures brand equity from the standpoint of marketplace performance, and envisages equity as a hierarchical pyramid of the proportions of potential consumers in a market that satisfy incremental criteria. The bigger the proportions higher up the pyramid, the more the predicted loyalty to the brand, as shown in Figure 11.7.

In this, a brand must first achieve a **presence** in the marketplace, in terms of awareness and salience. However, it must also achieve **relevance** to the consumer, by performing well (i.e. **performance**), and to achieve high levels of loyalty must achieve some sort of standout in terms of product benefit (i.e. **advantage**) that leads to the upper echelons of emotional commitment (i.e. **bonding**). The approach measures the brand, and its competitors, on these criteria.

In contrast, the Equity Engine[SM14] defines the nature of branding in terms of the emotional relationships that are engendered with consumers, taking the view that

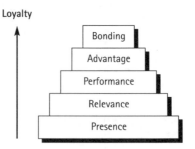

Fig 11.7 Brand dynamics model

much of marketplace performance is associated with physical factors such as advertising weight and distribution that have only an indirect connection with the core values associated with brand values. This model postulates that the 'value' that consumers attach to a product is a trade-off between the intrinsic benefits recognised (the 'equity') and the price paid. The equity can be broken down into two components: the value deriving from the product's performance in a *functional* or physical sense, and the *emotional* value derived from the branding. Moreover, while the functional benefits will always vary according to the category involved (automobiles are evaluated on different functional criteria from frozen vegetables), the emotional ones are not – and a fixed construct is used to evaluate three key basic emotional themes that operate for brands in all categories:

1. The **authority** of the brand, in terms of its heritage, trustworthiness, innovation, and so on.
2. The **identification** that the consumer personally has with the brand's core values, as represented by its personality, the sense of nostalgia it evokes, and so on.
3. The **approval** – the perception that the use/purchase of the brand will achieve a result that is likely to meet a person's perceived needs in a social sense.

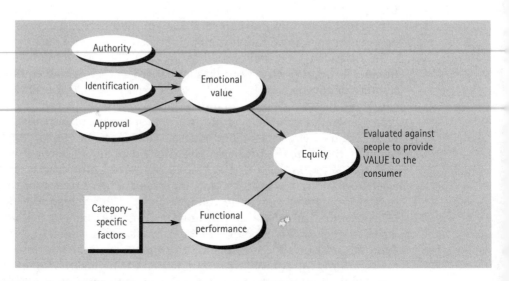

Fig 11.8 The Equity Engine[SM] model

These three dimensions can be measured for brands, giving them a unique 'foot print'. The full model, as shown in Figure 11.8, can be used to derive the relative contributions of the elements, so that it may be found that, in one category, the strength of a brand is mainly dependent on emotional factors, whereas the opposite might be true in another category.

11.11 Conclusion

One word of warning with all NPD models. Nearly all simulated test market systems are described in terms of a single, new product being launched in a well-developed market. Life is more complicated than that, and a majority of recent NPD launches in the UK has involved range extensions, line extensions or even relaunches of existing products. These can be coped with by STMs, but they normally require some amendment for particular situations. Equally, there are important differences in the way that 'difficult' markets are modelled – for example, the universe of mothers for baby products is a constantly moving one!

How reliable are the results? In many cases, subsequent validation (where possible) has shown them to be surprisingly accurate: 80% of tests plus or minus 20%. The overall conclusion, therefore, is that compared with the other costs involved in NPD, the reduction in risk is well worth the effort.

NOTES

1 Except at the extreme. For example, the average purchase cycle of white-goods is around eight years.
2 Surely an example of poor market research!
3 Originally developed by the advertising agency BBDO.
4 So said because the number of possible combinations rises exponentially when the number of variables increases – hence 'explosion'.
5 At least, configurations made up from the features studied in the exercise.
6 Multi-dimensional scaling, and correspondence analysis, are examples of this sort of map.
7 Developed by Frost International.
8 Developed by Research International.
9 Developed by Research International in 1990.
10 Developed by Management Decision Services.
11 Developed by Burke Marketing Research Inc.
12 Developed by Research International.
13 Developed by Millward Brown.
14 Developed by Research International.

REFERENCES AND FURTHER READING

Davis, J. (1986), 'Market testing and experimentation' in R. Worcester and J. Downham (eds) *Consumer Marketing Research Handbook*, third revised edition, ESOMAR/North-Holland, Amsterdam.

Majahan, V. and Peterson, R. (1985), 'Models for innovation diffusion', *Sage University Paper Series on Quantitative Applications in the Social Sciences*, 07-048, Sage Publications, Beverly Hills and London.

Morgan, R. (1987), 'Brand/price trade-off – where we stand now', EMAC/ESOMAR Symposium on Macro and Micro Modelling, Tutzing, October.

Morgan, R. (1990), 'Modelling: conjoint analysis', in R. Birn, P. Hague and P. Vangelder (eds) *A Handbook of Market Research Techniques*, Kogan Page, London.

Parfitt, J. H. and Collins, B. J. K. (1968), 'The use of consumer panels for brand share prediction', *Journal of Marketing Research*, vol. 5, no. 2.

Wind, Y., Majahan, V. and Cardozo, R. (1984) *New Product Forecasting*, D C Heath, Lexington, MA.

QUESTIONS

1. Products, from consumer durables to industrial goods, can span their markets in terms of price ranging from economy to premium high prices. Discuss the areas where modelling could help in optimising their product appeals.
2. What important elements need to be taken into account in measuring brand equity? How would the knowledge of brand equity make a contribution to the improvement of the new product development process?

12 Business-to-business research

Research among business people and professionals

Ken Clarke

12.1 The similarities and the differences between consumer and business research

The first question that will spring to the reader's mind is why the subject of business research merits a chapter all of its own. After all, does business research not use the same techniques and approaches which are described elsewhere in this book? Is not business research, therefore, simply the sensible application of approaches and methodologies used in consumer research to the particular environment of research amongst business organisations, marketing companies and similar bodies which cannot be described as consumers?

In a sense these questions have some justification. It is inescapable that business research must apply the same principles and methodological approaches as are used in consumer research: for example, concern for representativeness in sampling, careful questioning, objectivity in reporting. Yet the fact remains that there are enough points of difference and differences of such degree as to justify separate consideration of this area.

Before we go any further, though, let us be clear about the definition of the subject matter. For a number of different terms are often bandied about. Most commonly the area is known as business-to-business research, but there is also still a hangover from earlier days in talking about the subject as industrial marketing research. This last description is somewhat too narrow since it specifically refers to industrial marketing which in turn can be defined as the range of business and promotional activities which affect the movement of industrial products from the manufacturer to the industrial or commercial user. However, the opportunity for market research has widened out in recent years and reflects the changing pattern of business in the modern economy where services take a larger share of the gross national product than do the old manufacturing industries. In particular, the areas of finance, business services, health, leisure and travel, education and welfare, all make up this substantial service sector which is increasingly the focus of market research. For this reason some might prefer to refer to the whole area as organisational market research, but as we shall see shortly, there are problems even with this definition.

It is perhaps easier to start with a definition of what is not the subject matter of business-to-business research. Much of the rest of this book is concerned with consumer market research. The subject matter of this chapter is marketing research that is not concerned directly with consumers or members of the public acting as private individuals. Our concern here is with the behaviour, attitudes and opinions, needs and reactions of people acting in their career roles, whether as business people in commercial organisations, paid executives or volunteers in non-commercial organisations, or even as individuals within professions such as health and education.

The focus on people in their career roles helps to set the distinction with consumer research where the market researcher is interested in investigating people as individual members of the public or individual consumers. The same person who may be eligible for a consumer survey on attitudes to television programmes, for instance, may also be eligible for interview about decision-making criteria in their business or professional life. Of course, in the former role as individual consumer a respondent may be asked about issues which are relatively trivial: what brand of breakfast cereal one prefers is not a matter of great and painstaking consideration; nor are there great risks in making the wrong choice, since one can always put matters right by reverting to a known favourite brand at the next visit to the supermarket. In the career world the individual may well be concerned with matters of great importance involving investment of large sums of money or, in the medical profession, with matters of patient welfare and even of life and death. What motivates a person as an individual consumer is very different from what motivates that same person in their career role. Similarly, the scope of the impact which an individual may make in their professional or business capacity can be very much larger than they could ever make in a private capacity: an individual's decision about breakfast cereals is one amongst perhaps 20 million, whereas their decision about what major engineering equipment to purchase may be one amongst perhaps hundreds – or even just tens – which influence the shape of markets or the development of individual manufacturing suppliers.

Those with a traditional training in economics may well by this stage be starting to feel somewhat uneasy. They will be wondering what has happened to their traditional studies about the theory of the firm and how organisations behave in a rational world. They will be worrying that we have moved too quickly to a discussion of individuals and their motivations, and have left behind the role of organisations. There is of course a level at which information about organisations and markets is particularly valuable. The most obvious place is in the start of a programme of business research where we may want to use the collection of data in the form of desk research in order to provide a sound basis for planning and structuring a research programme, and to help understand the total business environment, companies' turnover and shares of market and the like. Business research is not unique in this regard, for many consumer research programmes will have a similar starting point.

Desk research into the sources of published data may be valuable and can be derived not only from published sources of data such as are made available by academic researchers, professional organisations and government departments, but also within companies' own accounting and sales records, annual reports and the like. The classical economist will also want to look at organisational behaviour and organisations' objectives, which can be briefly described as survival, profit and growth. Traditional economic models are based on an understanding of a rational environment in which decisions are made with these objectives as clear priorities. It is easy to understand that organisations must make profits if they are to survive, and it may be argued that the motivations of individuals play no part. It may also be argued that this is particularly true in large organisations where decision-making has to be ratified at various levels and generally arrived at through processes of formal or informal committee decisions. The determined rationalist in the classical economist mould will substantiate their argument by pointing to the fact that, when individuals are questioned about their motivations in business, they point to the importance of measurable data such as product quality, pricing, delivery, servicing and the like. These individuals, if asked specifically about elements of marketing, roundly deny that they are at all influenced by advertising, promotions, branding and other such fripperies.

The counter-argument is simply to think of what is most important to an individual in their career. Is it really the maximisation of profit for the organisation and the achievement of the overall corporate strategic objectives? Is not survival also the crucial issue for the individual; in other words, the protection of their career? Selfless pursuit of strategic objectives is difficult to maintain if the obvious outcome is the removal of the particular individual's career path – unless, of course, an escape route for the individual is built into this programme. Just as risk is at the heart of every business and organisational decision, so it is at the heart of every individual's considerations. Reassurance that the right decision has been made, that it is a safe decision, that it is beyond criticism, these are key benefits which are implicit in many marketing and selling tactics. It was not just the supreme confidence of the seller but an acute understanding of the needs of the target audience which lay behind that famous advertising slogan from some years ago: 'Nobody ever got fired for buying IBM'. The brand name was all the reassurance that a hesitant buyer could want. If things did go wrong subsequently, then the decision-maker could turn to senior management and point to the fact that he or she had, after all, bought what was universally recognised as the best. The management of risk is both a personal as well as a business objective. Talk to people in senior financial positions within organisations about their choice of financial advisers and bankers, and they will demand of these suppliers that they are clearly committed and seem to be in the same boat: 'They need to understand that if this boat goes down they are going down with me', is the way one finance director put it.

We come back then to the point made earlier about one of the key distinctions between business and consumer research, namely that in consumer purchasing situations there is normally little at risk beyond the relatively trivial amounts of money for a packet of cereal or whatever, together with the reassurance that if it was the wrong decision we can put that right in a matter of days.

The fact that the people we talk to and from whom we seek information in business and professional research are being interviewed in their career roles rather than as private individuals or as consumers has far-reaching implications for issues such as the basics of recruitment and winning the cooperation of these respondents, the methods adopted in interviewing, the type of interviewers to be used, the form of questioning, and so on.

Before going on to issues of interviewing, let us look at the issues involved in recruitment and winning cooperation. That brings us straight away to the issue of sampling and the problems of defining the 'universe' which is to be represented in any project.

12.2 Issues in sampling

12.2.1 Organisations

The problems of sampling in business research can be even more complex than those involved in consumer marketing research. The first complication arises from the fact that we have sampling at two different levels. The first requirement is to represent the types of organisations or businesses which are of direct interest to the sponsor of the research. Having defined those organisations, the next sampling issue is to define who within the organisations is best placed to meet the requirements of the research and to provide the information required in a comprehensive and reliable way.

Defining the universe is not in itself a straightforward task. Sometimes it can be relatively easy, since many research sponsors wish to conduct research amongst their own customers and customers of their major competitors. Customer lists provide the solution to the first part of that problem, and it is likely that the sponsor company also has lists of potential customers who are currently being supplied by their competitors. If those lists are not available, then the types of industry being supplied currently by the research sponsor provide an adequate framework. However, if the research objectives are spread more widely, it is not so obvious how the sample should be drawn. For example, we meet this problem in looking at the potential for new products or in evaluating how the brand franchise can be expanded into new areas.

A manufacturing company which makes fork-lift trucks may well know precisely the types of businesses which currently use fork-lift trucks and be able to identify who are the major buyers in the market. What might be more difficult to identify are the potential new customers for a range of vehicles which present a variation on existing designs. Transport, haulage, manufacturing and engineering companies all represent the current market for fork-lift trucks. One of the opportunities – and this is a purely hypothetical example – may lie in retailing where large pallets of products have to be moved around within warehouses and from warehouse to the inside of the retail store itself. Room for manoeuvre within the store is unlikely to be so free as it is in a large warehouse, and so the opportunity may lie for the provision of a smaller but powerful version of the fork-lift truck, particularly adapted to moving in small spaces and with slightly less cumbersome loads than a full pallet. This hypothetical example illustrates how carefully the opportunities and the potential research universe need to be considered and discussed between the researcher and the sponsor of the research.

The previous example keeps the problem within bounds, since it is addressed to just one type of product and its potential applications across industrial uses outside the current franchise. The problem becomes even more complicated if the issue is set at the corporate level. For example, an investment bank may wish to investigate how to expand its business. The universe of potential customers can be fairly clearly defined. Companies with less than a certain turnover are unlikely to need the services of a major investment bank. The scope of the bank's own activities and its need for large-scale business may also point in the direction of companies that operate on an international scale and that are therefore likely to need services such as currency exchange, interest rates and forward purchasing of currencies. However, investment banks have a very wide range of services, from these relatively straightforward operational issues to wider services such as mergers and acquisitions. The sampling problem therefore is to define in the first place what are the corporate services which the investment bank wishes to promote: these may include, for example, areas of special expertise and perhaps reputation, areas of new potential in the marketplace in general and wider geographical distribution. Only when the particular area of the research and the nature and scale of the opportunity is carefully defined can the sampling of organisations begin.

12.2.2 Individuals within organisations

This brings us to another point which the researcher needs to bear in mind, namely that decision-making powers and processes differ widely between larger organisations and smaller ones. In the smallest organisation the chief executive may well be the owner, senior partner or principal shareholder. The company is not so large as to have layers of management, and so key decisions come back to the chief executive's desk. In larger organisations there are more management levels, and it is more likely that there will be a committee structure, whether formally or informally, which helps to make the major decisions before being ratified by a senior manager or director of the organisation. The market researcher needs to bear these distinctions in mind in determining who shall be interviewed and how the approach to the company will be made in the first place. In most instances the search will be to identify and then interview the person who is responsible, solely or jointly with others, for making decisions about the services or products under investigation. This is more in line with the needs of a typical investigation than simply following job titles, which can be misleading. Of course, it is perfectly possible that the researcher, making his or her way into the organisation and seeking the decision-maker as defined immediately above, will be given false trails at the start, for example from the switchboard or from someone within the administration department. So the search for the appropriate person does not end after the first enquiry but continues through careful screening.

The researcher needs to make clear the subject matter of the investigation and to ask quite straightforwardly whether that falls within the authority and the job description of the person being interviewed. At senior levels this is not so necessary, but at middle-management levels it is vital in order to avoid the possible confusion that may arise from the misleading nature of a job title. For example, 'Accounts Manager' may be a senior executive in a finance department, a relative junior in a retail store looking after customer credit, or even a senior sales manager responsible for major business customers.

Before leaving the subject of sampling in large-scale business research we need to take into account the fact that there are many fewer buyers and decision-makers of products and services in organisational research than we find in consumer markets. For food products the consumer researcher needs to interview chief shoppers, formerly known as housewives, who are responsible for the main food purchasing within their household. There are literally millions of these in most countries and procedures of random or quota sampling can be followed, depending upon the particular nature of the task and the degree of statistical reliability that is required. In industrial, business and organisational research studies the total size of the universe is often limited. But this is not the only difference, since what characterises nearly all business markets is the fact that there is a heavy degree of concentration with a few very large businesses accounting for a very large share of the total market or total demand. There is then a long tail of smaller businesses which together account for only a relatively small proportion of demand. This is known as Pareto's law or the 80/20 rule.

This describes the surprisingly common structure in many markets, where 80% of turnover or demand is accounted for by just 20% of the total number of buyers or suppliers. If we were to take food retailing as an example, the major supermarket chains within the UK such as Tesco, Sainsbury, Asda, Safeway and the Co-op account for the majority of food purchasing; whereas there are thousands and thousands of small food retailers – grocers, greengrocers, fishmongers and butchers – which together account for only a minority of food purchasing these days. In many major business studies one of the crucial questions which needs to be asked at the outset is what part of the market is the focus of the investigation.

Many research sponsors will wish to have the very largest organisations omitted from the scope of the survey since they are extremely well known to the sponsor, have day-to-day contacts and indeed are intimately involved in each other's business. Going back to the food industry again, food manufacturing companies who supply to Marks & Spencer have traditionally had close relationships in which Marks & Spencer executives and food technologists are closely involved not only in production processes and quality standards but also in research and development of new products and range extensions. It is unlikely that any food manufacturer wishing to investigate the opportunities for their products would want an independent researcher to interview Marks & Spencer as part of the survey; they would prefer to talk to senior M & S managers direct. In some markets the decision to exclude the very largest businesses may encompass a number of large businesses, leaving small and medium enterprises (SMEs) as the chief target. In extreme cases it can be that the potential market is limited to a handful of very large businesses. In instances such as these the researcher will need to consider whether it is not their duty to tell the potential research buyer that they would be better advised taking each of the potential customers out for a very good lunch and establishing a close relationship in that way. Research is not always necessarily the best route to information-seeking.

In other markets where the spread of buying power is more even and across a large number of organisations, the decision will come down to who to exclude, who to include and what sampling effort is appropriate amongst those who are to be included. If a sample were to be drawn purely at random from within lists then by the laws of probability the process will generate a long list of companies making up the largest part of the sample although they are in fact just small organisations accounting for a small proportion of the market (the 80/20 rule). This would be wasteful of interviewing time, since each small organisation will take almost as much time and effort to contact and interview as each large organisation. Better to focus on the bigger organisations which account for a larger proportion of turnover and therefore to represent organisations in proportion to their turnover rather than to work in numerical incidence in the population at large. Sampling with probability proportional to turnover may be the most appropriate answer if lists are available of organisations identified by turnover or by size of business defined in some surrogate form such as number of employees.

12.2.3 Individuals outside organisations

In non-organisational work the size and nature of the organisation is clearly not an issue. However, the problem of identifying the appropriate individual can be relevant here, too. Let us take the example of the medical profession. In a practice of doctors or vets, it is likely that one particular member of the practice will be responsible for *ordering* drugs and equipment. This could today be the practice manager rather than a member of the medical staff. However, the key *decisions* are often made by the medical staff acting in committee; sometimes the decision lies at the final discretion of the senior partner in the practice who carries the responsibility for the overall business conduct and finances of the practice. This also provides a very practical example of why it is not safe to assume that there is one common pattern which will apply across all the units defined for sampling purposes, since it is not necessarily the case that the same purchasing decisions and processes will apply uniformly across all practices or within all business organisations.

Even when there is no intervening problem about sampling of organisations, careful thought needs to be given to the structure of the sample. In research on veterinary products, and particularly those for farm animals, the question immediately arises of whether we should interview vets or farmers or both. There is no one single correct answer which will apply in all projects. The solution will become clear only when we begin to think about the nature of the products under discussion. Some products have to be prescribed and administered by vets alone, while others can be administered by farmers. The interest of the vets is in the direction of their professional responsibilities and their desire to provide the best possible care for the animals in their charge. The same applies to the farmer, but in his or her case there is the added responsibility of the cost implications. And so a market may be defined into two categories of products which may demand different sampling approaches:

- products which can often be administered directly by the farmers themselves;
- products which are more powerful and can be administered only by the vet.

Careful consideration needs to be given to the most appropriate source of the information required. In many instances it may be judged that the vet is a perfectly adequate source of information about the opinions of farmer-clients since the vet will be well aware of how important cost is to the farmer as businessman/woman. Nevertheless, there can be situations where it would be important to interview the farmer – for instance, if there were issues surrounding the administration of drugs which regulations allow to be done by the farmers themselves.

What these examples serve to show is that there is no one single approach such as random sampling or quota sampling, techniques which are the common currency of textbook discussions of sampling issues. In business research, sampling needs to be the matter of most careful consideration in determining what shall be represented and who precisely shall be interviewed in order to arrive at the information and insight which is required by the end-user of the research.

12.3 Research methodology

Discussion of sampling issues brings us straight to one of the key methodological questions to be resolved in planning a new project, namely the scale of the research and the size of the sample to be employed. The business and professional researcher faces the same choice as the consumer researcher: between applying quantitative approaches for the sake of statistically reliable data, or using small-scale qualitative research for depth and insight when quantitative assessment is of lesser importance.

The criteria for the choice of qualitative or quantitative approaches in organisational research differ somewhat from those in consumer research. In consumer research quantitative techniques are appropriate when statistically reliable information is required about a population which is numerous and which may have a number of different characteristics. Going back to our food example, an investigation amongst chief shoppers would need to take into account the different requirements of people at different life stages and with different lifestyles as well as standard demographic differences such as age and social class. In consumer markets qualitative research is designed to provide depth and insight, subtlety of interpretation and – where appropriate – the generation of ideas and the development of an understanding of consumer language. The consumer researcher may well therefore advise the client that in order to meet the particular requirements of the research brief it is clearly advisable in one instance to use quantitative research since the reassurance of reliable statistics is crucial for a major decision, while in another instance qualitative research will be appropriate to uncover all the criteria which are relevant to consumers and the degree of importance which consumers attach to each of them. Qualitative research may be advisable as a precursor to the quantitative stage, in order to provide the list of attributes and image dimensions to be investigated as well as ensuring that the wording of the structured questionnaire is easily understood by respondents and adequately covers all the issues to be investigated.

12.4 Choosing a qualitative research approach

In business research the decision of whether to use quantitative or qualitative methods is based on additional criteria. One of the key issues is the size of the universe which is available. Here we come back to issues referred to earlier in the previous section. If the total population to be investigated is quite small or has a high degree of concentration in relatively few hands, then it is absolutely vital to glean as much information from the small population or the small subset of the population as is possible. Gleaning as much information as possible means ensuring that we get the interview with the most appropriate decision-maker and at the most senior level, and that we get from them as much information as we can. This would suggest that qualitative research is appropriate because a face-to-face interview lasting 45 minutes or more will give a full opportunity to explore all the issues. Another advantage of a more lengthy interview conducted face-to-face is that a rapport and a relaxed degree of confidence can be established between the interviewer and the interviewee, so that the respondent will talk more freely than they would, for example, in a more structured interview conducted remotely by telephone. We also need to bear in mind that at senior levels in management or in the professions respondents are generally unhappy to face a structured questionnaire: these are people who are used to expressing their opinions with authority and expect to have an opportunity to expand at length on their reasoning. As a result, they tend to view a structured interview as something of an insult, since it does not fully reflect the value of all that they have to say on the subjects under enquiry.

The qualitative, or perhaps we should more properly call it intensive, approach to interviewing also carries with it other advantages. Interviewing a small number of people at the top of their profession or their business organisation allows the researcher to obtain views from people who are probably the best informed about the market or about the professional subject. These are very much people who are experts in their area and can refer not only their own views but also those of their colleagues in other organisations or other parts of their profession. In the course of a relatively small number of interviews it is therefore possible to obtain a wide-ranging view of the subject. Of course, from time to time there will be differences of opinion expressed by different respondents, and there is no harm in challenging respondents with other points of view. Indeed, respondents often welcome a challenge of this kind, since it provides them with an opportunity to think through the arguments for and against the stance they have been taking

12.5 Choosing a quantitative research approach

Quantitative approaches are appropriate when there is a relatively large population to be surveyed, when there may be a wide diversity of opinion, perhaps reflecting different sizes of organisation or different specialities in a profession. Here the same arguments about the balance between qualitative and quantitative research as exist in consumer marketing research also apply to business research: what is the main aim of the survey – to explore in detail or to obtain a statistically reliable picture? To obtain a wide range of views or depth of insight into highly technical matters?

The question is not only one of depth of information versus quantitative assessment. One of the issues which is bound to affect the business and professional market researcher is that of the complexity and sometimes the sensitivity of the subjects which are to be covered. In highly technical areas such as finance, pharmaceuticals and electronics the issues to be explored can be very technical themselves and may not be readily susceptible to straightforward structured interviewing. The value of the research is likely to lie in getting behind the surface issues in order to understand deeper motivations and more complex matters. For example, in the more specialist areas of financial research the technicalities of the subject may be ones which are known to only a relatively small number of people. The subject could hardly be treated fully through a 20-minute telephone interview, nor could the experts involved be expected to be able to set down all the various issues and factors which influence them in their daily working lives within the straitjacket of this type of interview. In a face-to-face intensive interview on the other hand there is ample opportunity to explore the issues. In these highly technical areas the researcher can also use the actual technicality of the matter as a means of drawing out the respondent, simply by saying, 'I'm not sure I understood that fully. Could you explain it in more detail for me please?'

12.6 Choosing a qual–quant mixed approach

So far we have set the methodological issue as a straightforward choice between qualitative and quantitative approaches. There may be, however, opportunities to bring a combination of the two techniques together for greatest advantage in addressing the research issues. The problem with face-to-face interviews with difficult-to-reach audiences such as business and professional people is the sheer cost involved. The respondents are busy people and we are asking to interview them about their business and profession in their working time. Although appointments are made in the greatest faith, there will be emergencies and crises which may cause interviews to be aborted. Less expensive means of making the contact such as by telephone therefore have many attractions but suffer from the lack of depth, insight, subtlety and flexibility which can be afforded through the personal and face-to-face interview.

There are situations though where qualitative interviewing conducted over the telephone can be advantageous. These may be circumstances where, for example, the subject matter is not particularly sensitive or where it is not so vital for a confidential rapport to be established between respondent and interviewer. An example of this type of problem would be in testing new forms of advertising. The first approach to the respondents in investigating reactions to new advertising concepts may require careful probing and to be conducted in such a way as to allow the respondents to put their feelings in their own words and at some length. At the same time the research may call for a sizeable sample of people to be interviewed in order that the advertiser may have some degree of comfort in knowing that the possibility of adverse reactions to the new concepts has been fully measured. In situations such as this qualitative interviewing conducted by experienced qualitative interviewers over the phone may offer the best of both worlds.

We have now outlined a number of the crucial considerations which must be borne in mind by the researcher when choosing which is the most appropriate methodology to answer a particular problem. There are not only the issues of depth and richness of detail versus quantitative assessment but also complexity and sensitivity, the type of issue to be investigated, and of course the cost.

12.7 Detailed methodologies

12.7.1 Qualitative approach

The qualitative approach most commonly used in business and professional research is the individual interview. As with consumer market research the interview is based on an interview guide rather than a structured questionnaire. What is likely to make the business/professional interview different is the specialisation and complexity involved in the subject matter to be discussed. We need also to bear in mind that we are asking respondents to talk about their work and their career roles. The information we seek may often be sensitive in itself and respondents may be unwilling to divulge information or even on occasion to admit their own ignorance of some of the issues under discussion.

The interview therefore needs to be kept free-flowing, with a constant interchange of opinion, challenges thrown down on occasion with quotations from other people, and occasionally helped by the interviewer's expression of ignorance (whether real of feigned). Respondents participating in this type of work are generally articulate and happy to give their opinions at length. As the interview proceeds the initial defences against enquiry are lowered and respondents will tend to become more expansive and less guarded in their comments. At the mundane level, this is exemplified in discussions about advertising. The opening comment by most respondents is that they pay no attention to advertising and are certainly never persuaded by it. They refuse to accept that advertising could possibly influence them. However, as the interview proceeds, it is quite normal for respondents to say that they have favourite ads and to be able to describe these in some considerable detail. Once that defence is down, then the researcher can begin to explore detailed reactions to advertising in a way which would not have been possible 15 minutes earlier.

In one respect qualitative research is limited in business and professional work, namely the difficulty of employing group discussions. This is particularly true in business and rather less true in professions. Drawing together people from different competing organisations in business is rarely fruitful, because everybody is on their guard, distrustful of the others and unwilling to reveal anything which might be of advantage to others present. In professional work people are more used to participating in seminars and conferences. Indeed, the opportunity to share information and views in a group can often be welcomed by the participants, provided that the researcher carefully sets up the procedure to make it clear that this exchange will be possible and, indeed, to allow portions of the group discussions to be devoted to issues which lie strictly outside the area of interest to the research but which are matters of some importance to the respondents sitting round the table. The great disadvantage of group discussions, whether for professional or business people, is of course the sheer difficulty of organising very busy people to come together in one location; the costs therefore are that much greater.

In conducting qualitative research amongst specialist audiences of the kinds being described here, the question is sometimes raised as to whether the interviewers should be drawn from the business or profession in question or whether they should be professional market researchers even though amateurs in the topics under discussion. Fashions change in the market research industry. There was a time when interviewers were drawn from populations competent in the speciality under investigation even if they were not expert market researchers. While this can be of advantage in certain areas where the subject matter may be highly technical, there is the danger that the expert biochemist or electronics engineer is not necessarily a good market researcher. What may be particularly dangerous is that the expert may have their own very strong opinions which they bring to the research and which influence either the conduct of the interview or the subsequent reporting. There is a good argument for adopting the policy of using expert market researchers but ensuring that they are fully briefed on the subject under enquiry. We will return to this later when talking about planning a research project.

12.7.2 Quantitative approach

Some discussion of this issue has already occurred in earlier paragraphs where we have talked about the expense of face-to-face interviewing and particularly the difficulties of obtaining and maintaining appointments for interview. For this reason much quantitative large-scale research is conducted by telephone. The cost advantages are enormous. Of course issues of complexity, sensitivity, and so on have to be kept in mind when planning the research: even for a quantitative assessment face-to-face interviewing may be advisable if at all possible and economically viable. Fortunately respondents are willing to answer quite detailed questions by telephone and recognise that this is for themselves a very convenient way of meeting the request from the researcher. The structured interview which is not designed to explore sensitive and complex issues in great detail can nevertheless be useful in gathering a lot of market information and basic views of the population under investigation. An interview of this kind is likely to be limited to 15 minutes and perhaps 20 minutes at most before respondents begin to get fidgety and feel that they want to return to their normal work.

Limitations of time are important in considering the use of telephone research for business and professional studies. A further limitation is the difficulty of providing stimulus material in the form of advertising which may be under scrutiny, technical drawings, and the like. Careful preparation can get round some of these problems through prior recruitment of respondents, at which point they are asked to make an appointment for a later telephone interview so that in the meantime they may be sent the stimulus material under review. This has been found to work very well in advertising pre-testing, for example. Medical practitioners, even at senior levels within hospitals, have been extremely helpful in agreeing to this approach. There are some instances, though, where greater control may be required of the exposure of the stimulus material. It is of course impossible to control the order and amount of exposure when the respondent is sent all the stimulus material together in one package through the post. One of the approaches which is now coming into use is the Internet. This may have a number of advantages for the researcher. It certainly allows the materials themselves to be built into the structure of the questionnaire and therefore to be seen by the respondent only at the appropriate point in the interview. The approach used here is to pre-recruit respondents again and to ask them to receive an e-mail message which incorporates an icon onto which they can click and which will then take the respondent straight through to an Internet site which carries the questionnaire and the supporting material.

One particular advantage of this approach is that it allows the respondent to complete the questionnaire at a time to suit his or her convenience rather than having to abide by a fixed appointment. For people who are constantly interrupted in their day-to-day work by emergencies and crises this may be a particular benefit. One other element speaks in favour of the Internet, namely the ability of the respondent to move through a questionnaire very rapidly indeed, more rapidly in fact than in a telephone interview. Experience shows that an interview which would normally take half an hour to conduct by telephone can be quickly completed by the respondent in about half that time. A difficulty may arise if there are many open-ended questions which would require the respondent to type in an answer; the speed of interview would be slowed considerably. So far the major limitation on the use of the Internet for specialist research has been the availability of Internet access to the target audiences. In certain categories of work such as senior financial circles where people spend their days surrounded by screens and work constantly at their PCs, this is not a problem; but in smaller businesses access to the Internet is much more limited and would militate against obtaining a representative sample. Researchers are fortunate, for communications are changing rapidly these days. A recent report from a finance house shows that in the UK approximately two-thirds of SMEs now have access to the Internet. With many professions such as general practitioners, dentists and vets now linked to the Internet, and some of them even with their own web sites, the days are rapidly approaching when the Internet will provide the means of interviewing representative samples of most business and professional populations.

12.8 Planning the project

It cannot be said too strongly that planning is the essence of the successful completion of a market research project with business and professional people. Many of these issues have already been touched upon, namely determining the subject matter, the sampling, and the appropriate methodology. The planning must also take into account the nature of the subject matter and the need to brief the interviewers. Researchers should not be afraid of making the point to their clients that they will need extensive briefing and that the client must be willing to ensure that this is of a very high order if the project is to be successful. Equally researchers must show themselves to be willing to put in extra effort. The most extensive briefing may involve the reading of background books and days of detailed briefing about the nature of a client's operations, the international spread of the business, and the information already available to the client about the audience's requirements. Similarly the researcher who leads the project must be willing to put in a great deal of effort to brief all those who are going to be involved in conducting interviews. In a major international project this may mean producing video briefings to be sent to interviewers around the world so that they have a full opportunity to be briefed in detail, to see stimulus material and any promotional material which the client has prepared about the nature of their business.

Having received the brief and determined the appropriate methodology and the sampling, the next stage of planning is the setting-up of the interviews and the recruitment. Here we come back to the point made at the start of this chapter, that people are being interviewed in their career roles and will mostly need to be interviewed during their working hours. This means that respondents will need to be very carefully persuaded of the benefit of spending valuable time on something which they may easily regard as an unwelcome intrusion. It is important therefore that respondents feel that their time spent in the interview will ultimately be of some value to themselves and/or to their profession. For this reason it is necessary right at the start to make clear to the respondents the objectives of the research and how the information is going to be used. Similarly, respondents will need to know that their views will be treated in complete confidence and neither they nor their organisation will be named to the client subsequently. This means, therefore, that respondents need to receive in writing full information of this kind at the outset of the project. The letter which describes the project and gives the assurances of confidentiality should also make reference to codes of conduct which govern the research and its reporting, the bona fides of the research organisation and the nature of the subject matter which is to be covered. Only then can cooperation be sought via the initial recruitment. In conducting the recruitment it is highly advisable to employ specialist recruiters who have been trained and show a special aptitude for talking to people in senior business and professional positions and winning their confidence and cooperation. Flexibility must be promised to the respondents in making appointments for interview. With chief executives and chief financial officers it may be necessary to offer to conduct the interview in a car on the way to an airport, in a hotel where they happen to be staying on a business trip or wherever suits them.

One of the matters which troubles most respondents is the identity of the client to whom this information is going to be revealed. In some instances this will be immediately obvious from the nature of the enquiry itself, particularly if there are only one or two suppliers of the particular product or service. There is no point in being demure, and the researcher might as well reveal the name of the client right from the start (but only with the client's permission!). In most studies it is advantageous to keep the identity of the client unrevealed during the course of the interview since there is a danger that knowledge of the sponsor of the research may bias the responses which are given; respondents may feel that they will deliver one or two heartfelt messages, or that it would be unfair on a particular salesperson with whom they have good personal relations to complain about the quality of the product or background service. Nevertheless, it will usually be a sine qua non of obtaining cooperation that the client name should be revealed at least at the end of the interview. Client organisations are rarely opposed to this and recognise that it is necessary in most instances. The researcher may also use that final moment in the interview when they reveal the name of the client as a way of obtaining further information: 'What does this tell you about the client of ours, and how do you feel about them conducting this research?'

Nor should one overlook the benefits to be obtained from being known to have sponsored a serious piece of work which is designed to help the supplier improve the quality of product and service. The public relations benefit of conducting research should never be underestimated.

There is no doubt that senior professionals and business people are being called upon more and more to cooperate in market research surveys. Certain areas are very heavily researched; these include the medical profession, dentists, computer and management information systems management, senior financial officers, farmers, and senior marketing executives themselves. It is all the more important therefore to be considerate and thoughtful in the approach made to these people in seeking their cooperation. Incentives are often also advisable, particularly with such heavily researched audiences as these. The type of incentive needs to be considered extremely carefully. In business organisations it is often forbidden for any member of staff, no matter how senior, to receive any gifts at all. This is particularly the case within American headquartered businesses. It is often very persuasive to offer, as a mark of gratitude for cooperation, a contribution to a charity of the respondent's choice, and the more senior respondent the greater that contribution will need to be. When set against the other costs of the research even large incentives are a relatively small part of the total cost. Charity contributions should be separately itemised since they are often tax deductible.

Finally we come to what is probably the most important aspect in planning a research project of this kind, namely the final reporting. Right from the start the researcher needs to be clear about how the findings are going to be used by the research sponsor, whether representativeness is in itself the most crucial issue or whether insight into the needs and views of the target audience, their choice criteria and the like, are the crucial issues. The researcher needs to ask him or herself how firmly they will be able to stand by their conclusions and what they will be able to claim for them. Honesty is always the best policy and it is important not to lead the clients astray into thinking that they have a fully representative picture when in fact that might not be possible. Every effort needs to be made in the planning to ensure that the prime objectives are met. Methodologies need to be scrutinised with great care as to whether they will really deliver what is required. For example, the use of mail surveys in business and professional research tends to produce response rates which are worryingly low (what did all those non-respondents think?), while the quality of the information which comes back is limited by the need for respondents to write things out in their own hand rather than being given the opportunity to express themselves verbally. The problem of non-response in mail surveys is particularly acute, so that although at first sight they may appear a cost-efficient way of reaching a large audience, in practice the findings are often open to doubt.

12.9 The international dimension

In today's world it is increasingly common for major research sponsors to wish to have their research conducted in several different countries and often globally. Immediately the researcher's problems are multiplied by the number of countries involved and considerations of whether there are significant differences in matters such as structure of industry, openness to interviewing, acceptability of incentives, etc. which could affect the course of the work in each country. Some industries are already globalised. Listen to a merchant banker talking in Korea, describing the issues they face, the competition they must beat off, the techniques and services they must have available, and you could be listening to a banker in London or New York. Other industries are still localised, and individual country differences can be very important. Even in medicine where the pharmaceutical giants are global in their reach, the structure of health industries and health regulations are very different from one country to another. Patients suffering from a particular ailment or affliction in one country will be dealt with in entirely different ways and through different structures in another country – for example in one country through clinics, in another country through specialist nurses, in yet another country through general practitioners. Surprisingly, language differences are not so important here as in consumer markets since industries are increasingly organised on a global basis and since organisations need to be able to communicate internally using common terminology and to avoid misunderstandings through the use of different words. In many industries globalisation has gone so far as to make English the common language, so that it is possible to conduct interviews in many parts of the world in English even with people whose native language may be Chinese or Greek or in South America, Portuguese.

In the global village of today the use of the Internet as a means of interviewing and of coordinating projects will become increasingly beneficial to the market researcher. User-friendliness around the world is one of the key benefits of the Internet: a respondent may just click onto the language of their choice rather than be faced with their normal workday requirement to use English as a foreign language.

12.10 Conclusion

Business and professional research is very specialised. Although the techniques employed are those which are also used in consumer market research, the criteria for their use and the ways in which they are used are very different. The reasons for those differences have been explored at each of the crucial levels from planning through sampling to interviewing technique, to interviewer training and briefing, to respondent recruitment.

There are many ways in which business and professional research can be said to be more difficult than consumer research, because many of the problems which exist in business research do not exist on the consumer side, or not in such complex form. It is certainly true that business research often tends to be more expensive. We prevail upon people to give us their cooperation and to reveal much about themselves in their career roles. This is much more sensitive and much more demanding than asking the same people questions in their roles as private citizens and consumers. The researcher needs to be aware that far more goodwill is needed from respondents in giving information and providing an opportunity for interview. Therefore the researcher needs to make every effort to accommodate to the convenience of the respondent. The Internet is now offering new ways in which to access difficult-to-reach audiences at relatively low cost and in ways which suit respondents' convenience, language needs and competing demands on their time, while at the same time making it possible to research hitherto difficult areas such as advertising and promotional literature.

FURTHER READING

Blois, K. (1999), 'Relationships in business-to-business marketing – how is their value assessed?', *Marketing Intelligence and Planning*, vol. 17, no. 2, pp.91–9.

Cox, W. Jr and Dominguiz, L. (1979), 'The key issues and procedures of industrial marketing research', *Industrial Marketing Management*, 8, Jan., pp.81–93.

Deshpande, R. and Zaltman, G. (1987), 'A comparison of factors affecting the use of marketing information in consumer and industrial firms', *Journal of Marketing Research*, 242, Feb., p.114.

Gross, I. (1987), 'Why all of industry needs research', *Business Marketing*, 72, April, p.114.

Hutt, M. and Speh, T. (1998), *Business Marketing Management*, sixth edition, The Dryden Press.

QUESTIONS

1. What do you consider to be the main points of difference between the qualitative and quantitative approaches in research among business people and professionals? In what respects is the one able to complement the other in business-to-business research?
2. What means are available to get past the gatekeepers of business organisations? Having secured an interview with a senior executive how might it be possible to gain his/her cooperation, especially when the research might appear to be of little or no benefit to the executive concerned or to his/her firm?
3. A major US market research agency wishes to investigate the opportunity to enter the UK market for advertising research.

   Your brief is to put together a plan on how to investigate the size and nature of the UK market for advertising research. Provide notes on:
   (a) how the information is to be collected;
   (b) who is to be interviewed;
   (c) the type of questioning to be used;
   (d) the sampling frame.

   Your projected research will need to pay particular attention to the following issues:
   - definition of the major categories of advertising research and what techniques are currently used (note the balance between qualitative and quantitative approaches in advertising research;)
   - who the major suppliers are;
   - who commissions advertising research;
   - who pays for it and who, if anyone, uses it.

13 Marketing communications research

Media planning, monitoring and measuring

In growth terms international advertising is a phenomenal success and market research has been a cornerstone of this. From small beginnings at the turn of the twentieth century, the advertising industry has mushroomed into a multi-billion dollar global industry as the twenty-first century beckons. The UK buying agency, Zenith Media, has put global expenditure on advertising at US$303bn in 1999 and US$339bn in 2000.[1] The images and phrases produced by the advertising industry have helped to sell millions of products across the globe from large to small populations, from cities to remote villages.

13.1 Advertising and market research in changing markets

Advertising is a potent force. Advertisements are sent by individuals and agencies using the various forms of mass media in order to inform and to influence their audiences. The costs involved in producing and transmitting images and messages, the use of creative expertise and the proliferation of new media in the 1990s have led advertisers to develop their research skills in-house or to commission studies from external research agencies concerning the audiences at whom their advertising is to be aimed. For advertisers, research is an essential element in helping to prove the effectiveness of the advertising campaigns to their clients. Proving the effectiveness of advertising (in what ways has it worked and how well?) can be a complicated affair since there are many factors that influence people in choosing what and where they want to buy or not buy. Research is needed to test customer response prior to an advertising campaign and to track the response once a campaign has been running.

The Direct Line case study at the end of this chapter is based on the process of testing two separate campaigns from the designs of the initial advertisements, to their revisions and to the performances of the finished commercials. Advertisers differ in their use of quantitative and qualitative techniques for measuring customer responses, for example in measuring and forecasting the shifts in sales to the use of focus groups to illustrate shifting changes in attitudes. Millward Brown held the Direct Line account for the quantitative pre-testing, modelling and tracking of the advertising campaigns illustrated in the case study. The campaigns produced major results in establishing Direct Line as a leading brand and household name in the UK through its pioneering style of selling insurance direct to the public. The efforts were also successful in helping to set the fashionable precedence in direct selling of financial services to members of the public.

In simple terms, the advertising agency finds out from the client organisation what it wishes to convey to its target market and turns this into a commercial for the broadcast media (television, radio and cinema), artwork for the printed media (newspapers, magazines and outdoor posters), materials (novelty items, e.g. tee shirts and mugs) and direct communications (via direct mail, telephone and web sites on the Internet).

The research agency's job is to find out what the target audience is in terms of relevant products previously purchased, viewing habits for the various media, receptivity to advertising messages and to competitors' advertising, and which medium of communication is the best (value for money) in reaching this audience. Research and advertising need not necessarily be contracted out if companies have the people skills and resources to do the work in-house. Large companies, for example Dun and Bradstreet, through mergers and acquisitions, can consolidate their businesses in the related areas of advertising, supplying research and publishing.

Once the advertisements have been presented in test regions or in regional and national campaigns, research can be carried out to find out whether people have noticed the advertisements and acted on them. The pull of advertising is immediately recognised when there is a noticeable rise in the client's sales of the advertised product or service or in its market share for the relevant brand. Figure 13.1 shows a simplified model illustrating the integration of research into the cycle of activities for an advertising agency.

It should be noted that agencies would vary in their organisational structures. The figure illustrates how research can feed into the activities of a large advertising agency so that advertising campaigns can be planned, coordinated and executed. Media buyers will buy into the specialist services for the different types of marketing communications (e.g. advertising, publicity and public relations). Media

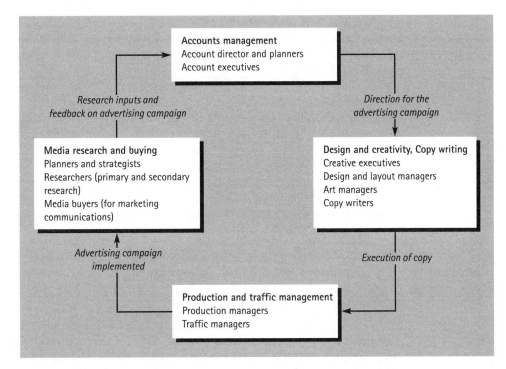

Fig 13.1 A typical agency model showing the integration of research in the agency's activities

researchers will conduct enquiries and check desk and field research information to feed into the planning activities. Media planners will advise the account directors on the effectiveness of advertising campaigns and what may or may not work. Winning the client accounts and handling the direction of the advertising campaign will be in the hands of the account management team. The media planners would need to know the advertising objectives as agreed between the client organisation and the market research supplier. Typically, the objectives include defining the target audience and reaching it by means of the most suitable and cost-effective type of media.

The sociodemographic characteristics of people within the market are of primary importance because most industry data is classified by sex, social grade, age, terminal education age, household size and employment or occupation of chief income earners. In the UK, geodemographic systems for market segmentation purposes can use the NRS (National Readership Survey) and MEAL (Media Analysis and Expenditure Ltd) data. To 'overlay' this data with owner and non-owner types of dwelling, regional groupings of neighbourhood types and lifestyle classifications, CACI's ACORN and Experian's MOSAIC can also be used. Research data relates products and services to brand choice and audience profiles in market segments, for example the British Market Research Bureau's Target Group Index (TGI), NOP's Financial Readership Survey and TN Sofrès' audience selection consumer omnibus survey 'Phonebus'.

A market segment is not viable unless it is accessible and in consumer markets this means accessible through the media. For media planning purposes it is necessary to translate psychographic and product-use classifications into demographic terms. Thus respondents' demographic and product use characteristics have to be recorded when collecting data about their wants, perceptions and attitudes, and this is what market researchers do to aid clients in their product and media planning. The information industry is a large and global one, A. C. Nielsen, for example, being one of the world's largest information organisations with total billings worldwide exceeding one billion US dollars.

The MEAL data on brand expenditure covers 475 product groups under 33 industry category headings. The impact that each brand achieves in advertisements on each one of six target audiences: housewives; housewives with children; men; adults; ABC1 adults; and adults aged 16–34, are calculated. Register-MEAL acts as an authoritative source of advertising expenditure and volume. As a guide to the size of coverage, its service report on advertising has over 500 individual press titles. Its reports contain expenditure and brand shares for terrestrial television, satellite television and radio. Its outdoor advertising expenditure reports are derived from research in partnership with the poster industry and cinema with major service contractors throughout the country.

13.1.1 Considerations in media planning

A brand may be more successful in, say, London, and south-east ITV areas, than in the north-west, Yorkshire or the north-east. This may be peculiar to the brand or it may apply to the product field as a whole. Given the variation in share by area the media planner needs to know whether the advertising objective is to be achieved by building on strength, counteracting weakness or by means of a judicious combination of the two. The decision will influence the allocation of the media appropriation as between areas and it may determine the choice of media category. Television and the regional press, together with radio, posters and cinema can be scheduled on a regional basis. Given a product or service with seasonal appeal the tactical decision 'from strength' or 'against weakness' still applies when allocating the appropriation. Should we concentrate expenditure in the high season or seek to extend demand by showing the product to be appropriate outside its season, for example by popularising ice cream as a year-round dessert?

If the product has a demonstrable benefit, use of the television medium is indicated. Television is a 'natural', for example, for the demonstration of gas appliances for cooking or heating. Television also 'glamorises' the process, as in the BBC's Master Chef's competition. On the other hand, television is less discriminating, for example, than print media, especially magazines which can be selected for the special interest, authority or ambience conveyed by their editorial content and presentation.

13.1.2 Determining the size of the appropriation

This is usually determined in advance of media planning, but in the rare cases where an unmodified 'objective and task' method is being used the media planner will play an important part in fixing the appropriation. Whether the appropriation is laid down or arrived at in consultation with the media planner, the criterion of success in media planning is the achievement of the optimum mix of:

Reach (or coverage) × Frequency × Length/Size

the last being influenced by creative considerations.

Data on how much the competition is spending and in what media it can be monitored is put together by subscribing to syndicated services, e.g. MEAL or the Media Register, or deduced for television from the BARB weekly reports. For a major advertiser the strategy is to plan a schedule which sidesteps the competition while offering effective reach, or coverage, of the target.

13.1.3 Conversion, reinforcement or both

This basic objective will affect how the appropriation is laid out over time. When a brand is launched, frequent appearances in the media, longer commercials and larger spaces may all be used to achieve conversion and penetration of the market in the shortest possible time so that the brand breaks even and makes a profit as soon as possible. With an established brand, reinforcement of existing usage may be more critical. There may also be cases for combining conversion with reinforcement by interspersing longer appearances with shorter ones. It all depends on where the brand stands in its life cycle, the size of the appropriation and the advertising task. One part of the task may be to ensure shelf space for the brand and increase its popularity with specific market segments.

13.1.4 Achieving cost–effectiveness and media changes

It will help us to appreciate the relevance of the audience research data if we consider what planning for cost-effectiveness involves before summarising the content of the reports and the methods used to collect the data. The task gets more formidable when we seek to take account of duplication between, say, television and print media, or between newspapers and magazines, or between the individual publications we are considering for a particular schedule. The National Readership Survey provides valuable input data about duplication as between the readers of different publications. The NRS information is collected from more than 300 newspapers and magazine titles and weight of viewing and listening to TV and radio. Access to teletext, subscription cable TV, satellite, cinema and use of Thomson Directories and Yellow Pages are found on the NRS 'Reference Source for Other Media'. This data indicates the intensity with which readers of specific newspapers and magazines also view television or listen to radio.

However, to achieve cost-effectiveness it is necessary to consider whether the opportunities being given to the target market to receive the advertising message are likely to be taken. The probabilities will, of course, vary as between the broad media categories and the specific publications and viewing times being considered.

Whether or not the opportunities to see (OTS) are effective and the message is received depends on the following:

- the frequency with which the advertisement appears;
- the period of time over which it appears;
- the frequency with which target readers see the issue of publication and view the advertisement;
- the creative impact achieved by the campaign.

If the creative work effectively conveys the product benefit, and if the media planning has been successfully focused on the target consumers in the market, we can expect selective perception to work in our favour.

13.1.5 Market and media weights

We may want to refine our estimate of effective coverage by taking account of the relative importance of groups in the target market. An organisation marketing baby food might well be particularly interested in reaching women aged 15–34. But older women sometimes have babies and, if experienced as mothers, they may influence the decisions of younger women. Here it would be reasonable to apply a weight of 1 to prime target, women aged 15–34, but to discount the value of the reading/viewing of older women by applying a weight of, say, 0.5 to the reading/viewing coverage recorded for them.

The chance of an advertising campaign attracting the attention of members of the target group is clearly influenced by the readership of the publications among members of the target group and, in the case of television, by their viewing habits. We can allow for the frequency with which respondents claim to read, view and listen when programming and can apply weights to this end.

As we shall see reading and viewing are ambiguous concepts in media research. Reading a publication can mean anything between reading it from beginning to end and glancing through it, while those recorded as viewing during our time slot may well miss our 30-second commercial.

We are on debatable ground when we attempt to weight media vehicles according to the probability that they will actually convey the message to the target group. In fact it is only worthwhile attempting to apply weights to take account of the probability of opportunities to see being taken if sound normative data is available.

If an advertiser is established in a particular field, if campaign penetration has been monitored regularly in terms of recognition or awareness levels achieved, and if it is possible to relate this achievement to individual media vehicles, then there might be a case for giving good carriers of the message preferential weights in the computer programming. Weighting for ambience and/or authority is even more debatable since the weights are determined by judgement, unless post-exposure campaign monitoring has yielded statistical data sufficiently robust to warrant this refinement. For the print media it might pay to run the computer program using market weights only and to use the resultant ranking of newspapers and magazines as a bargaining counter. If we are advertising to a middle-class ABC1 audience, we can ignore C2DE readers or viewers when relating coverage to cost.

Much work, therefore, goes into the monitoring and measurement of the effectiveness of advertising campaigns. The information derived with the aid of audience measurement research is intended to guide the media planners in their efficient purchases of media coverage from media sources.

13.2 Global advertising and the challenge of the new global media

Modern-day mass communications have enabled the larger agency advertising networks to offer to their multinational clients the reach to global audiences. There are economies of scale involved when a company uses a single agency to consolidate its purchasing power and its advertising campaigns, to streamline its decision-making and to grow its range of businesses on a global basis. Examples from 1998 include Pepsico, IBM, Procter & Gamble and Heinz.

Pepsico uses BBDO worldwide for media buying. Ogilvy & Mather Europe is handling IBM's worldwide advertising, with one campaign featuring nationalities in different countries: 'Solutions for a small planet' used in 47 countries and in 30 languages. British Airways' 'The world's favourite airline' campaign was devised by Saatchi & Saatchi before its breakup into Saatchi and Cordiant. This ran from the late 1980s into the 1990s and helped to create the stamp of a world-class image for BA. From the late 1990s, Leo Burnett has run all of Procter & Gamble's advertising for the entire Vidal Sassoon haircare brand as well as the Heinz advertising for ketchup worth an estimated £90m.

However, despite the growth of the global advertising industry, modern-day mass communications hold many problems. Markets have changed; for instance the fall of communism in the former Soviet Union, the destabilisation of the financial economies in many countries in the Far East with their impact overseas, the experiments with economic liberalisation in Russia and in China, political instability in the Balkans, political conflicts in parts of Africa, the Middle East and Latin America, the slowdown of economic growth in western Europe and the USA, have all added to the uncertainties and changes in people's purchasing habits and consumption. Market research continues to be an essential element to inform and to help advertisers plan their campaigns.

A big change which affects the way both advertising and research agencies conduct their businesses is the diversification between markets and the new media technologies. To keep up to date, agencies have set up, merged or taken part in acquisitions as the way forward in obtaining and building their expertise in the new information technologies, thereby offering to their clients their services across the conventional and new media.

The *Financial Times*[2] in 1998 reported on three surveys which showed the growing importance of the new media. The first survey by Forrester Research, a US technology market watcher, said that 'global internet advertising revenue could grow from $1.5bn this year to as much as $15.2bn in 2003'. The second by the Internet Advertising Bureau in New York found that 'online advertising revenue' had 'more than tripled in 1997 to a record $907m'. The third, a study in the UK by Fletcher Research, showed that in 1998 the total Internet advertising that year would be £15m and would rise to '£268m in 2001 as experimental new media campaigns become an increasing part of mainstream advertising'.

The challenges ahead for advertising and research agencies alike are the need to improve their creative ideas and research advice to clients; to keep on track with the developing technologies in the new media; and to find ways to handle the new media effectively as competing technologies continue to evolve and change. The goal of optimising a brand's potential and the vision of driving this forward in an integrated, coordinated way might prove to be a more difficult task given the advent of commercial terrestrial advertising, rising media costs and media fragmentation. These are further explained below.

13.3 Intermedia relationships and changes in industries

The 1990s saw dramatic changes bringing volatility in the broadcast and printed media. The number of independent radio franchises dramatically increased as did the number of radio stations. Newspaper and magazine paginations, colour supplements and on-the-run colour in the print media continued to grow. By the late 1990s there were well over 90 supplements with separate sections compared with ten in 1987. Taking newspapers and magazines together, there were over 7,000 diffferent regular publications in the UK available to advertisers.[3] Mergers and takeovers to form larger conglomerates in book publishing, newspapers, magazines and market research (e.g. acquisitions by Dun and Bradstreet) were reflected in the broadcast and television industry (for example the takeover of Central television by the Carlton group in 1994). Other changes included the replacement of the Independent Broadcasting Authority (IBA) and the Cable Authority in January 1991 by the Independent Television Commission (ITC). The ITC is a public body that licenses and regulates commercially funded television services provided in and from the UK. These include Channel 3 (ITV), Channel 4, Channel 5, public teletext and cable, local delivery and satellite services. By 1995 more than 30 new television channels had been set up. Franchises covered two-thirds of the UK population totalling around 14.2 million homes. One hundred and twenty-seven individual franchises were awarded with coverage varying in size from 10,000 to 500,000 homes.[4]

In October 1998, the British Sky Broadcasting Corporation (BSkyB) owned by Rupert Murdoch, with a worldwide newpaper and media communications network, introduced its digital television satellite service beaming programmes down from space for 140 channels. There were other rival digital broadcasters too, for example OnDigital with 30 channels, and the cable operators with 200 channels. For advertisers there will be the problems of integrating their advertising for the different television channels, let alone for the other forms of media. There will be opportunities for many creative approaches and greater reach globally. However, given that customers now have more choice and control over what they want to watch with the new pay channels, there is more media fragmentation. Advertisers might find that there might be a need to divert attention from mass- to micro-marketing as customers switch from channel to channel. The advent of the Internet on television will also mean that by buying the appropriate equipment, customers can download information from web sites and make their purchases from their living rooms without leaving their homes. This is a transformation from the traditional notion of advertising, that is 'pulling' people into shops where sales staff by personal selling would 'push' the products for people to purchase.

13.4 UK advertising expenditure

In 1995, UK advertisers spent £10.959m on advertising. Display advertising expenditure in the press, magazines, radio, television, direct mail and the cinema accounted for three-quarters of the total. The remainder was accounted for by company notices and announcements, job vacancies and small classified personal advertisements.

As the percentage breakdown in Table 13.1 shows, display advertising on television, in national newspapers and direct mail accounted for the largest individual sums. So it is not surprising that the advertising industry (advertisers, advertising agents and media owners) finance carefully designed and expensive research into the reading and viewing habits of the UK population.

Laser (representing Granada Television, London Weekend Television, Yorkshire Television, Tyne Tees Television and Border Television) has put its broadcast advertising revenue figures from January to March 1997 at a total expenditure of £29m.[5] Of this total, the percentage shares were: GMTV (1.5%); satellite and cable (4.5%), Channel 4 (20%) and the ITV regions with 15 other regional companies (75%).

Table 13.1 Advertising expenditure

	1998 display advertising (£m)[1]	1998 classified advertising (£m)[1]	1997 Adspend by media (US$m)[2]
Television	4,029	–	5,101.4
National press:			
National newspapers	1,351	441	
Consumer magazines	553	157	6,365.7[3]
Regional newspapers	826	1,563	
Business and professional journals	756	453	
Directories (including Yellow Pages)	–	780	
Press production costs	610	–	
Outdoor poster and transport	563	–	655.1
Radio	463	–	586.3
Cinema	97	–	117.9
Direct mail	1,666	–	

1. Adapted from The Advertising Association (1999) Advertising Statistics Yearbook, ATC Publications.
2. Adapted from NTC Publications (1999), Adspend Databank. Conversion rate: US$1 roughly equivalent to £$\frac{2}{3}$
3. Total for newspapers.

13.5 UK audience measurement research bodies

The main sources of above-the-line audience measurement research for television, press, radio and posters are:

- the Broadcasters' Audience Research Board Ltd (BARB) for television;
- the National Readership Surveys Ltd (NRS) for the press;
- the Radio Joint Audience Research Ltd (RAJAR) for radio;
- NOP Posters for 'outdoor site classification and audience research' (OSCAR, now known as POSTAR).

These sources are discussed below.

13.5.1 BARB objectives and structure

The independent television companies need to monitor audiences in order to sell time to advertisers and their agents, while the publicly accountable BBC needs audience figures when negotiating the licence fee on which it still depends. The audience ratings indicate the relative popularity of programmes and aid scheduling decisions. An important requirement of the 1977 Annan Committee on the future of broadcasting which preceded the setting up of BARB recommended a 'continued audience measurement system to remove arguments on whose audience size data was correct so that resources could be directed to research on audience reactions to programme content'. Previously, there had been different methods of data collection on audience measurement used by the BBC and ITV which had the inevitable consequence of producing different results, thus causing confusion.

The Broadcasters' Audience Research Board Ltd was formed as an executive management body in response to this in August 1980, and by 1981 a single system for TV audience research was set up with the BBC and the ITV Authority as joint shareholders. Shareholding has since been extended to other bodies. A director from each of the main subscriber groups: the Institute of Practitioners in Advertising (IPA), Channel 4, Channel 5, BSkyB (representing satellite broadcasters) and Flextech sits on the board of BARB in addition to the original BBC and ITV representation. The Incorporated Society of British Advertisers (ISBA) does not have a shareholding since it has not paid for one, the argument being, that since the advertising streams from its members pay for the industry it does not need to pay any more. The system now in place is intended to provide a database common to the shareholders and advertisers in reliability and acceptability in cost.

The *Economist* has put forward a different perspective. It has argued that the problem with British television was that it was 'still stuck with a regulatory structure designed for a bygone age ... the result was a non-commercial television industry ... it did not bother to develop an export market, nor in the main to invest in other parts of the business – which regulations discouraged it from doing. That is part of the reason why pay-television, the fastest growing bit of the business in Britain is dominated by BSkyB, a subsidiary of News Corporation which has grown out of the entrepreneurial Australian media business.'[6]

Under the BARB's chairmanship, a similarly representative body, the Technical Advisory Group, meets regularly to examine data quality and technical issues affecting its service. This service consists of the provision of information to broadcasters, advertising and media buying agencies and advertisers for the television industry. BARB employs a small staff and uses research suppliers on audience measurement research. Each week information is gathered about the numbers of people watching television and what programmes they watch. The research suppliers have the job of finding out who watches what and when. This helps the advertisers to plan when to show their commercials and how to select their audiences.

13.5.2 BARB's electronic audience measurement service

Tenders are invited from research suppliers for the BARB contract. The 1991–98 contract on audience measurement research was jointly shared by Audits of Great Britain (AGB), part of Taylor Nelson AGB Plc (prior to it being part of TN Sofrès Group) and RSMB Television Research Ltd. The division in responsibilities between TN AGB and RSMB and the method of metering for the BARB research are described in Box 13.1.

Box 13.1 Taylor Nelson 'Audience Measurement Research'

The 1991 BARB contract (which has been extended to December 2001) was awarded to two leading UK research contractors.

Taylor Nelson Sofrès (formerly AGB) is responsible for placing its meter equipment in the 4,500 BARB panel and processing the data collected. Its co-contractor, RSMB, is responsible for the Establishment Survey, panel home selection (chosen from the Establishment Survey) and ensuring that the structure of the panel closely represents that of the television-owning population.

The TV meter used in the current BARB contract is the AGB 4900 PeopleMeter. Each TV set within a panel home is metered and each has a handset that allows panel members to record their presence in the viewing room. A set-top meter display unit (MDU) registers when respondents press their buttons on the handsets. It also records the channel being viewed. This information is passed to a central meter in the home (central data storage unit or CDSU). This unit receives and stores the viewing statements from the TV sets in the panel home. The CDSU contains a modem and is linked to a telephone socket in the panel home. Overnight the TN computer dials up each BARB TV panel home and draws down details of any viewing since the last data collection from the CDSU between 1 am and 5 am.

This data is then processed and issued electronically to the industry by midday. Each day, TN calculates over 300 million separate audiences.

The PeopleMeter identifies video playback of recorded off-air programmes. It implants a 'fingerprint' onto the videotape when recording off-air is taking place. The fingerprint records the day/date/time and channel at one-second intervals. When the videotape is played back the PeopleMeter identifies that the video recorder is being used in playback mode and picks up the day/date/time/channel fingerprint from the recording. This fingerprint is used by the system to add playback viewing to the audience of the original broadcast (if played back within seven days). The industry uses these 'consolidated' (live plus timeshift viewing) ratings for all top programme rankings and for the audience delivery of commercial spots and schedules.

The PeopleMeter also allows BARB panel members to input the gender and age group of any guest viewers on the MDU via the handset. A new handset was introduced in 1999 allowing a greater number of guests to be entered (up to 99).

BARB will issue a tender specification for measurement requirements across the next contract period, starting from January 2002. The UK broadcast system will rapidly change over the coming decade as digital terrestrial and digital satellite TV services take over from the current analogue services. It is expected that the government will switch off analogue services around 2012. The new digital TV services will deliver many more channels. Viewers can expect to receive 150 or more, many of them subscription channels as well as opportunities to buy pay-per-view events.

New TV metering techniques will be used to measure which digital TV channel is being viewed. PictureMatching, a new technique developed by TN, involves matching samples of the picture displayed in the panel home with samples from all broadcast channels to identify the channel. This technique is currently being used in difficult to monitor homes including those with digital reception. Other new techniques that have been developed by TN include the use of special interfaces with digital set-top boxes to read which digital TV channel is being viewed.

For the 2002 contract, BARB shareholders have signalled their intention to make available special broadcast codes. These will allow meters to identify the digital or analogue TV channel being viewed. BARB hopes this will simplify TV metering and thereby save costs.

A growing problem with TV measurement in the digital TV age is the reporting of data from the BARB panel for very small TV channels. Whilst the bulk of viewing in a digital multi-channel home will usually be to a limited number of the more popular stations, the remaining viewing will be split across many small channels with low reach, or pay-per-view events and films. The media industry will need to consider what can be reported given the current panel sample size. The BARB system will not be able to deliver minute-by-minute published ratings for every channel on air as has been the case up to recent times. Very small channels may have to be content with estimates of monthly or even three-monthly reach and average daypart analysis.

Source: Roberts, B. (1999), TV Research UK, TN Sofrés Group

For audience measurement research it is vital to have the equipment to record the programmes being watched in the sampled households. Since there is no industry standard for satellite and cable feed through video recorders to connect into televisions sets, a problem created by the growth of satellite and cable viewing has been the neccessity to have different probes for each different type of device which householders have bought. So market research agencies involved with audience measurement research have needed to keep up with the technological developments in the field by finding or developing alternative methods of measuring. Monitoring of a home with, say, three television sets, two video recorders and two cable boxes, would require seven different probes, one for the tuner on each device. Taylor Nelson have developed their Picture Matching™ Technique to cope with this (see Box 13.1).[7] The system has the advantages of allowing new channels to be recognised, simpler in-home installations and the elimination of engineering visits to probe new satellite and cable boxes, thus ensuring better panel continuity by eliminating potential bias in the exclusion of panel members awaiting engineering visits.

13.5.3 Sample design

The sample design and data collection method used by Taylor Nelson Sofrès for BARB has three advantages:

1. Electronic observation is less susceptible to mistaken recording than 'day-after' recall.

2. Audience measurements are very soon available to those who need them.

3. When the same, or virtually the same, sample is being surveyed every day of the week the trend data is less susceptible to sampling variation than would be the case if a different sample were recruited in respect of each day's viewing.

The TN design, based on area panels of television homes, makes it possible to monitor the dynamics of television viewing using comparatively small samples, always provided that the panels are representative of the survey populations area by area and that panel membership remains reasonably loyal. The cost of the electronic methodology makes sample size a critical consideration.

Electronic metering, as explained in Box 13.1, means that it is possible to collect data from any number of television sets and video recorders in any one home with automatic feeding of the data each night into a central computer. This greatly enhances the speed of collection of data. Response rates from the panel are estimated by BARB[8] to be 98–99% which ensures a high degree of accuracy.

Metered records are combined with programme details and commercial broadcasts. Calculations are arrived at by computer in order to estimate audience size.

BARB subscribers can purchase the raw data from the meters (for re-analysing) or the calculations on audience statistics which show the number and percentage figures watching particular programmes and commercials.

BARB's Establishment Survey is based on a random sample of more than 43,000 interviews held through the year and structured according to postcode areas within the ITV regions.

The results of the Survey to determine television usage and ownership across the country are combined with census data. This enables a representative sample of houses in terms of viewing habits, television and video ownership, sociodemographics, etc. to be drawn up for the audience measurement panel. A ready pool of names and addresses is compiled in case there is a need to replace any household which drops out. The audience measurement panel consists of over 4,000 homes.

A nominal incentive payment is given to panel members in return for the provision of information to BARB. The Establishment Survey contributes to the making of marketing plans because it establishes regional variations in the viewing population, and 'the viewing population' is in effect 'the total population' since 98% of households have television. But its primary purpose is to give credence to the data derived from the viewing panels by defining the regions they represent and providing the pool of addresses. The area panels vary in size from 100 (Border) to 500 (Central) and 475 (London).

13.5.4 BARB specialist reports

BARB issues three specialist reports – the network report, the Astra report and the BBC report.

The 'green' weekly TV audience network report summarises live and time-shift data (audiences to programmes and audiences to time segments) for the main channels for subscribers to ITV companies, Channel 4, advertising agencies and their clients. The 'yellow' Astra satellite panel weekly TV audience report is for satellite broadcasters and summarises viewing statistics on homes which receive Astra channels by cable or dish aerial. The 'grey' BBC report includes time and time-shift data tailored to the needs of the BBC. A weekly press release 'The week's viewing in summary' gives hours of viewing to each channel (audience share) and the most popular programmes.

The BARB Audience Measurement Service is based on a considerable investment in the electronic collection and rapid processing of viewing data. In the past, output was largely paper-based with bulky weekly reports and data tapes. Data is now transmitted daily and electronically to BARB subscribers.

Data on audience measurement research is important to ITV companies in their drive for market share and profit. Advertisers buy opportunities for their campaigns to be seen on a particular ITV channel. However, there is no certainty that the audience recorded will be entirely present and watching when the advertisements are shown.

The introduction of the PeopleMeter has improved the quality of the data relating to the viewing of panel members, for with the push-button handset the presence of the individual viewer is electronically recorded as viewing takes place. Nevertheless, there is always the chance that a panel member will leave the room during a commercial break without pressing his or her button on the handset.

However, a set of display lights indicates to the family what data has been recorded and is used as a reminder device to ensure that the data is correct. Any attempt to establish actual, as opposed to potential, presence necessarily involves research studies designed to measure the impact of advertising campaigns using such measures as 'recognition' and 'awareness' in ad hoc studies, tracking studies or by subscription to media surveys.

13.5.6 BARB television opinion poll

The BBC's Broadcasting Research Department operates the television opinion panel for BARB. Electronic observation is a reliable method for counting viewers. The present system, operating from 1986, consists of a national panel of 3,000, on which Channel 4 and the ITV regions are represented according to population size and regional panels on which numbers are boosted to 500 for each region. The national panel completes a booklet once a week; the regional panel once every four weeks. Panellists sign on for a maximum of two years. The average response rate each week is 65% and, when recruiting, it is estimated that 100 letters will be required to generate 60 panel members. The panels are administered by post. Each respondent fills in two booklets – the Programme Diary and Viewpoint designed to cover seven days' programmes from Monday to Sunday.

For the Programme Diary, each respondent has to rate on a scale from one (least interesting or enjoyable) to six (most interesting or enjoyable). This information is used to calculate an appreciation index (AI) for each programme which is then compiled into a weekly Audience Appreciation Report. Viewpoint is based on finding out what the panel members think of various programmes and their booklet contains questions to be answered about any type of programme. In addition, a children's panel consisting of 1,000 respondents from the ages of four to 15 fill in similar pairs of booklets on networked children's programmes shown up to 9.00 pm.

The base for the television opinion panel has over 28,000 names and addresses derived from a sample of constituencies stratified by BBC and ITV region and by ACORN type. Within constituencies wards and streets are drawn with probability proportionate to size using a fixed interval from a random start, i.e. the sampling points are randomly located. Stratification by ACORN types obviates the need to set social-grade quotas. Age, sex and, for adults, working status are quota-controlled. In other words, the bank of addresses used for the television opinion panel is carefully drawn to be representative of the population – aged 12 and over.

The matrix described in Box 13.2 controls the national panel and each of the regional panels. There are in addition four marginal controls: sex, age, presence of

---

Box 13.2 Distribution of viewing hours

The names drawn within each area are distributed among an 18-cell matrix ($3 \times 3 \times 2$):

	Groups
Total weights of viewing (hours viewed per week)	=3
Channel preference (hours ITV/Channel 4 viewed out of 10)	=3
Social class (ABC1/C2DE)	=2

children and size of household. The panels are tightly controlled to ensure that they are representative of the viewing public so that they yield comparable data.

The appreciation index

For the Programme Diary, panellists are asked to watch as they would normally watch and to rate the programme watched. The attitude statement 'interesting and/or enjoyable' embraces two measures of appreciation and the statement is, on the face of it, asking two questions in one. The statement is flexible, because each panellist may be rating an information programme (in which case 'interesting' is particularly relevant) or an entertainment programme (when 'enjoyable' is a more suitable measure of appreciation). See Box 13.3.

Box 13.3 Audience appreciation

6 = Extremely interesting and/or enjoyable	5 = Very interesting and/or enjoyable	4 = Fairly interesting and/or enjoyable	3 = Neither one thing nor the other	2 = Not very interesting and/or enjoyable	1 = Not at all interesting and/or enjoyable

To sum the panellists' appreciation of a particular programme positions on the scale are scored as follows:

100	80	60	40	20	0

The appreciation index (AI) is calculated by dividing the total score for each programme by the total number of panellists reporting.

13.6 The NRS data

The National Readership Survey objective is as follows:

to provide the common currency of readership research data for newspapers and magazines, using methodology acceptable to both the publishers of print media and the buyers of space, to the highest standard in a way that is cost effective and sufficiently flexible to take account of change and the needs of users.[9]

The NRS data is derived from a meticulously designed probability sample representative of the adult population of Great Britain aged 15 and over. The fieldwork and analysis are subcontracted to Research Services Limited. The data is collected throughout the year and care is taken to timetable interviews so that seasonal and day-of-the-week fluctuations in the reading of newspapers and periodicals are represented in the results.

Computer-assisted personal interviewing was introduced from July 1992. Responses to questions on lap-top computers are transferred via modem to a central computer. This facilitates speed in field surveys and enables the NRS to report results within three weeks at the conclusion of the fieldwork.

When JICNARS, the Joint Industry Committee for National Readership Surveys, was abolished a new company, the National Readership Surveys Ltd was formed. The board of directors on NRS Ltd includes representatives from the Newspapers Publishers Association (NPA), the Periodical Publishers Association (PPA), the Institute of Practitioners in Advertising (IPA), the Incorporated Society of British Advertisers (ISBA) and the Association of Media Independents (AMI).

The sections that follow will first, consider the probability sampling procedure used to contact readers of newspapers and magazines; and second, describe questions on readership and look at readership panels.

13.6.1 Sampling procedure

The sampling procedure is described in detail in the NRS report, which is a useful source for anyone studying sample design. The NRS database is available on subscription through authorised computer bureaux, and monthly and half-yearly reports are published using moving averages for quarterly, half-yearly and annual bases.

The NRS data is based on a multistage stratified probability/random sample drawn from the postcode address file. The PAF is used as the sampling frame. The three-stage selection procedure is as follows:

1. 2,520 enumeration districts (EDs) are used as primary sampling units. Stratification of five categories of EDs is done according to ACORN type. The profile by ACORN types of the EDs drawn to represent the area in the samples is compared with the profile of all the EDs in the geographical group. Any imbalance is corrected. Each category is given differential weighting prior to point selection with booster samples for regional areas, Scotland and Wales.

2. Addresses are systematically drawn from each chosen ED, 28 addresses per point are selected with a reserve list of eight addresses in case any address replacement is needed.

3. From each address an individual is selected taking into account recent changes needed for tenement, institutional and multi-household addresses. A minimum of five calls has to be made to obtain a response from a selected address before abandonment. This is done to try to ensure that all adults as far as possible have a known chance of being included in the sample. Personal interviews with the selected individual for each household chosen are conducted.

Each monthly sample is balanced over time and replicates the annual sample.[10]

13.6.2 Readership questions and panels

Box 13.4 shows an example of questions on readership. Forty-five prompt cards containing six grouped titles are used and a total of 270 titles is measured. Weightings of results are used to estimate the numbers of readers from a total summary of 45.3 million adults.

A question on topic interest for magazine and newspaper readership research has been included to find out if people normally look at a list of topics when reading and looking at newspapers and magazines. Topics asked include:

UK/British news
European news and other foreign news
Sport
Cars/motoring
Food and drink, cooking
TV programmes
People, personalities and celebrities
Arts/books/music/theatre/
Entertainment listings
Film and video
Personal finance/investment
Business/company news
Travel and holidays

Property/houses for sale
Home ideas/furnishings/DIY
Gardening
Science/technology/computing
Medical/health and fitness
Fashion and clothes
Beauty and personal appearance
Relationships/emotional issues
Baby/childcare/parenting
Jobs/appointments
The environment
Women's pages generally

Box 13.4 Readership questions

1. Cards are sorted into 'any publication seen in the last year' and 'no publication seen in past year'. 'Not sure' cards are put onto the 'yes' pile.

   (Typescript side of card is used)

2. Informant rechecks 'no' cards.

3. 'Yes' cards are then dealt with one by one using the mini-masthead side of the prompt card. Each publication on the 'yes' card is coded 'yes' or 'no' for readership in the past year.

4. For each publication read in the past year the recency question is then asked, followed immediately by the frequency question. The questions below are those for all publications except daily newspapers, which have a special question to prompt for reading 'yesterday'.

   'When did you last read or look at any copy of ...?' (Apart from today.) The response (unprompted) is coded by the interviewer as:

   Past 7 days
   Past 2 weeks – fortnightly only
   Past 4 weeks
   Past 2 months – bi-monthly only
   Past 3 months
   Longer ago

   'And, looking at the scale on the card, which best describes how often you read or look at ...?'

   Almost always (at least 3 issues out of 4)

   Quite often (at least 1 issue out of 4)

   Only occasionally (less than 1 issue out of 4)

Source: The National Readership Survey (1994).

The questioning method has made it possible to record the penetration of a longer list of titles without increasing the length of the interview or decreasing response rates; it definitely reduces order effects and so improves data stability. But exactly what 'reading' means to different people is open to question. Relating 'reading' to issues with specific cover dates could be done using a panel, and reading occasions could be limited to those occurring in the home where the date could be confirmed. In a volatile highly competitive market it is useful to have data related to specific issues and to specific individuals over time, so that 'brand-switching' patterns could be extracted. In order to record the penetration of titles with modest circulations it would be necessary to set up and maintain a large panel. The cost advantage offered by the lower sampling error is more apparent than real. A solution may be to run panels for discrete periods in order to add richness to the standard data, or to monitor the effect on reading habits of a strike, promotion or new launch.

A stable print-media market, twice-a-year reporting and the size of the sample in any one month would yield data adequate for the needs of media planners. In reality, however, the print-media scene is a volatile one and the battle to maintain, let alone increase, circulations encourages the use of promotions, e.g. one-off offers, competitions and price cuts. Reading habits are in consequence disrupted. In addition, there has been a proliferation of titles to meet lifestyle interests and publications with quite modest circulations can be of importance to the media planner focusing on a closely defined target.

Average issue readership is especially in doubt where the less frequently published print media are concerned. Two kinds of error may occur: replicated readership issues of an earlier cover date being returned as read in the period, and parallel readership, more than one new reading occasion in an 'issued period' being treated as one. A record of specific-issue readership could be achieved using a readership panel. The panel could be required to record cover dates in their diaries, but there would still be doubt as to whether publications read outside the home have been correctly dated.

13.6.3 The NRS as a source of segmentation variables

The readership penetration tables in the NRS report include:

- readership among all adults;
- readership among chief income earners (previously 'heads of households');
- readership among men;
- readership among women;
- readership among housewives (female).

The social-grading system used by the NRS is a 'household' one. Prior to July 1992 the 'head of household' occupation determined the social grade of a given household. After this date, this was amended to 'chief income earner' to reflect the shift in the social-class profile of the population brought about by socio-economic changes. This redefinition was also seen as easier to administer for interviewers since it caused less confusion. The system gives a better up-market social-grade profile of the population in the UK (see Box 13.5). Social-grade classifications, so widely used in quota sampling, derive from NRS data. From the year 2000, a new system will be introduced (see Section 13.6.4 and Box 13.6).

Box 13.5 Change in social grade from 'head of household' to 'chief income earner'

I		NRS social grade % (All adults)	
Head of household (HOH) system		ABC1	C2DE
1960		31.3	68.7
1970		35.6	64.4
1980		38.5	61.5
1990		41.9	58.1
Chief income earner (CIE) system			
1993 (July–December)		47.3	52.7

II

Profile changes RSL (Research Services Ltd) estimates
Est. adults 15+ = 45,300,000

HoH/CIE definition

	'000	%	Index
A	1,300	2.9	100
B	6,800	15.0	100
C1	11,000	24.3	100
C2	12,300	27.2	100
D	7,900	17.4	100
E	6,000	13.2	100

CIE definition

A	1,400	3.1	108
B	7,600	16.8	112
C1	12,100	26.7	110
C2	11,200	24.7	91
D	7,400	16.3	94
E	5,600	12.4	94

Source: I. *The NRS Bulletin* (1994), no 31, 23 February, p.3.
II. *NRS Review* (1994), Issue 3, p.3.

In addition to establishing what kinds of people read individual newspapers and magazines and the numbers reading an average issue, the NRS questionnaire also has a number of questions about television viewing and radio listening. These questions probe the intensity of viewing/listening by channel or station and (for television) the equipment in use (number of sets, video recorder, remote control, video-disc player, teletext, access to subscription cable TV). The data on file makes it possible to correlate readership with listening and viewing. The TGI also has on file data about mixed-media habits. The NRS and the TGI data are of value for portraying longer-term trends when media plans are being made. Table 13.2 provides data from AIR (Average Issue Readership) in the last six months of 1998 using

Table 13.2 Selected examples from NRS AIR (Average Issue Readership) 1998

	Total	Sex		Social Grade		Age	
		Male	Female	ABC1	C2DE	15–44	45+
Unweighted sample	19,088	8,268	10,820	9,467	9,621	8,972	10,116
Est. population of 15+ (000s)	46,400	22,580	23,820	22,386	24,014	24,039	22,361
Daily newspapers							
The Sun	9,881	5,564	4,317	3,150	6,730	6,043	3,837
The Mirror/Record	8,169	4,414	3,755	2,723	5,445	4,102	4,066
Daily Mail	5,237	2,521	2,716	3,315	1,922	2,110	3,127
The Express	2,612	1,348	1,264	1,630	982	1,032	1,580
The Daily Telegraph	2,294	1,264	1,030	1,917	376	786	1,509
The Times	1,727	1,000	727	1,436	291	900	827
The Guardian	1,117	642	475	928	189	681	436
The Independent	690	406	284	561	129	393	297
The Financial Times	632	450	182	533	99	397	235
General monthly periodicals							
Skytv Guide	5,957	3,267	2,691	2,924	3,034	4,042	1,915
Reader's Digest	4,269	2,030	2,239	2,339	1,930	1,566	2,703
Cable Guide	3,182	1,643	1,539	1,492	1,690	2,420	762

Source: Adapted from the National Readership Surveys Ltd, *Latest Estimates of Average Issue Readership for Periods to August 1998.*

selected examples of daily newspapers and general monthly periodicals. The NRS lists are, of course, far more extensive.

13.6.4 New classifications

The UK government is introducing a new social classification (see Box 13.6) in its statistics in preparation for the next census from the year 2000. This reflects changes in the nature of work and employment conditions, for example the decline in manual labour and manufacturing. (From there being a million coal miners after the Second World War, there were only 10,000 in 1999.) Many women have entered the workforce and the number of self-employed has also risen.

As the *Financial Times* puts it:

The top social classes are now those that enjoy longer term salaried contracts with occupational pensions and other perks. They now make up 22% of the workforce, against 9% in 1984 – and 18% of women are now in the new social class one against 4% in 1984. The bottom social classes are those paid by time or piece-work with low job security and few fringe benefits. A new category has been created of the self-employed who work on their own account but are not classified as professionals.[11]

Box 13.6 Changing places: who's up and who's down

Up	Down
Old class II to new professional class 1	Old class III to new class 6

Company directors
Teachers
Social workers
Computer analysts
Airline pilots
Librarians
Personnel and industrial relations officers
Corporate bank managers and financial managers
Senior police officers
Senior local government officers

Shop assistants
Hairdressers
Plasterers
Cooks
Drivers
Welders
Supermarket checkout operators

Old classification

I. Professionals
II. Managerial and technical
III. Skilled non-manual
IV. Partly skilled
V. Unskilled

New classification

1. Higher managerial and professional
2. Lower managerial and professional
3. Intermediate
4. Small employers and own account workers
5. Lower supervisory, craft and related occupations
6. Semi-routine occupations
7. Routine occupations

Source: The Financial Times (1998), 'New class ranking marks changes in labour market', 1 December, p.14.

13.7 RAJAR

Radio, posters and cinema account for over 6% of total expenditure on display advertising. They are often used as local reminders of the national advertising message. The NRS questionnaire makes it possible to sort the population into categories according to the amount their respondents' claimed listening to radio, and the frequency with which they said they visited the cinema. Some of the data is included in the twice-yearly report. The data is available on the computer database, an important source of the support media.

Radio Joint Audience Research Ltd (RAJAR) was established in 1992 as a company jointly owned by the Association of Independent Radio Companies (AIRC) and the British Broadcasting Corporation (BBC). Its purpose is to operate a single audience measurement system for the radio industry comprising the BBC, UK licensed independent local radio (ILR) and commercial stations.[12] While the RAJAR board ratifies issues of policy and principles, its technical management committee (TMC) decides on technical and operational decisions. Representatives on these committees are drawn from the AIRC, the BBC and the associations in the advertising industry, as represented by the Institute of Practitioners in Advertising (IPA).

RAJAR publishes detailed summaries of its research design and methodology. It publishes details on sampling, fieldwork materials, data processing and weighting and predicted cumulative audiences. The sampling methodology and analysis are very useful for those interested in research design. Total survey areas are defined in terms of postcode sectors and the addresses of the participating household members are selected from the postcode address file. Box 13.7 gives the minimum adult sample sizes required for publication of each local service.

Box 13.7 Minimum adult sample sizes required for publication of each local service		
BBC:	All local services irrespective of population	650
Local commercial:		
	Population 8.0m and under 10m	2,470
	Population 6.0m and under 8.0m	1,820
	Population 4.0m and under 6.0m	1,170
	Population 1.75m and under 4.0m	1,040
	Population 1.0m and under 1.75m	910
	Population 0.3m and under 1.0m	650
	Population under 0.3m	650

Source: RAJAR (1998), *Service Overview*, August, p.4.

RAJAR's 'Service overview' and 'Code of practice' publications are carried out for the national BBC and commercial services, BBC National Regional Services Greater London Region (GLR) and independent local radio services with an adult population of 4 million plus.

The stations include all BBC networked radios (Radios 1, 2, 3, 4 and 5), BBC local/regional radio, all commercial radio, all national commercial radio (Atlantic 252, Classic FM and Virgin 1215), all local commercial and other listening radio. The 'Quarterly summary of radio listening' gives a breakdown of the population for each of these radio channels. Table 13.3 summarises the data provided for three of these groups as an example. Figures for 1994 have been retained to show the changes from 1998; the figures reflect a decline in radio listening in the 'all BBC' figures.

Data for this summary is collected from households. A 'contract' questionnaire is first administered at each household to check quota eligibility. A 'household' questionnaire is then used to collect the occupants' demographic details, including the number of radio sets and car radios owned. The RAJAR diary has two sections. The first is a self-completion questionnaire covering television viewing and newspaper readership, whilst the second records radio listening. On the covers are listings of radio services including the full titles, frequencies and brief descriptions of programme content. Informants are encouraged to write in the names of any other services not listed that they have listened to.

Incentives offered to informants include a free pen, a monthly prize draw for those who complete their booklets and a separate prize draw for those aged between 4 and 14 years.

To aid identification, the type of programme broadcast by each station, together with its position on the wave band, is included in the diary, which is small enough

Table 13.3 A quarterly summary of radio listening 1994–98

Adults aged 15 and over; UK population 47,652,000

	Weekly research '000	%	Average hours per head	per listener	Total hours '000	Share of listening %
All radio:						
1994	40,242	87	18.1	20.7	842,584	100.0
1998	40,642	84	17.8	21.0	845,854	100.0
All BBC:						
1994	29,256	63	9.4	15.1	440,737	52.3
1998	23,069	48	6.8	14.0	323,547	38.3
All commercial:						
1994	27,301	59	8.1	13.9	379,993	45.1
1998	27,975	59	8.8	15.1	421,704	49.9

Source: 1994 figures – RAJAR (1994), *Quarterly Summary of Radio Listening*, 10 January – 20 March.
1998 figures – RAJAR (1998), *Quarterly Summary of Radio Listening*, 20 June – 20 September.

to carry around in a pocket or handbag. Keeping the diary is simple enough (time-slots down the side, stations across the top) and marking off quarter-hours (or half-hours between midnight and 6 am). But keeping a diary does, of course, make listeners more conscious of their listening. It would be unreasonable to expect most listeners to keep a diary of their listening for more than a week so it is not possible to adopt the tactic used on consumer panels of ignoring entries until behaviour returns to normal. However, some are asked to carry on for another three weeks.

Twenty-four-hour recall, the method used by the BBC and by Radio Luxembourg is cheaper to apply and free from the risk of conditioning that is associated with keeping a diary. A sample of the general public is asked to recall its listening during the previous day and recall is aided by means of the programme. Whether or not recall is aided, the data is subject to the fallibility of the human memory and for most people listening is not a memorable activity.

Radio is still on the whole regarded as a purely tactical and local medium whose strength lies in its parochialism. It serves the following purposes:

- National advertisers can make local contact with their listening audiences, support local distributors and conduct local promotions.
- Local retailers and suppliers of services can advertise to their catchment areas.

Radio's coverage in the public domain is a wide one. It is a medium with loyal listeners who regularly tune into their favourite programmes. For advertisers, radio coverage is less expensive than television advertising, but messages for radio need to be simple, direct and creative and need to avoid annoyance to listeners. Increasingly, new advances in broadcasting technologies are being felt. Digital transmission appears to be the future for radio and television.

In 1995 Britain and Sweden were amongst the first countries to broadcast digital radio. The 23 June 1998 was the closing day for applications to the Radio Authority for Britain's first commercial franchise for digital radio.[13] In the autumn of 1998 Britain switched on digital television terrestrial broadcasts. In 1997 the

BBC sold its transmission system for £244m ($405m) and is paying for the digital radio transmission system it started building in 1995.

13.8 Development of OSCAR and POSTAR

In 1983 a census of all poster sites costing £700,000 was commissioned by the Outdoor Advertising Association (OAA) which represents the British poster industry. The research for the development of this important medium for an industry standard database was carried out by NOP Posters, formed as a merged operation between Associated Information Services and NOP Market Research in 1991.

The 120,000 OSCAR-assessed stationary roadside panels, or 90% of all poster sites, belong to members of the OAA. Since 1986, 10% of all poster sites have been reassessed each year. This data, based on observation, served to update OSCAR following its inception in 1981 to be based on 'individual site fieldwork'. Now OSCAR no longer exists and POSTAR, the new system, continues to provide, through statistical modelling, a gross audience estimate, pedestrian and vehicular – that is, the total possible audience passing the poster panel each week.

POSTAR[14] measures the 'likelihood to see' and provides accountability in audience research derived from a long and detailed checklist concerning:

- traffic counts;
- pedestrian counts;
- coverage calculations;
- dispersion over area;
- visibility adjusted impacts (VAIs) – likelihood to see;
- modelling – to predict impact of poster sites;
- data access via PC-based system.

From the early 1990s, the need to compete with new developments in the broadcast media (changes in television and radio audience systems) had led the industry to look for a stronger and more modern audience measurement system, and POSTAR was formed. POSTAR uses lasers to pinpont where people look when they pass a billboard. Each poster site in Britain has a rating to indicate how many eyes are likely to see it. See Box 13.8.

The OAA estimated that the outdoor advertising market in Britain was worth £500m in 1997 and equal with radio in growth at 14%.[15]

The poster market is a complex one. Many related factors influence the coverage estimated for any one campaign. On average poster campaigns run for two weeks at a time. People make return journeys, some travelling long distances. So in practice, people could pass similar posters from one campaign at least twice and therefore it can be expected that the reduction in cover from gross to impact would be limited.

The *Economist* has estimated that, the 'world outdoor advertising market – billboards, transport and "street furniture" (things like bus shelters and public toilets) – is worth about $18bn a year, just 6% of the world's spending on advertising'.[16] The cost of television advertising (a 30-second prime time TV slot in Britain costs over £60,000) has led advertisers to look at the outdoor medium, where an advertisement

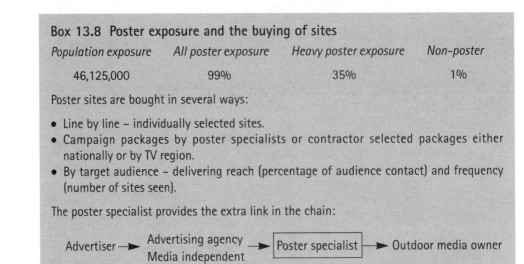

Box 13.8 Poster exposure and the buying of sites

Population exposure	All poster exposure	Heavy poster exposure	Non-poster
46,125,000	99%	35%	1%

Poster sites are bought in several ways:

- Line by line – individually selected sites.
- Campaign packages by poster specialists or contractor selected packages either nationally or by TV region.
- By target audience – delivering reach (percentage of audience contact) and frequency (number of sites seen).

The poster specialist provides the extra link in the chain:

Advertiser → Advertising agency / Media independent → Poster specialist → Outdoor media owner

Source: Adapted from the Outdoor Advertising Association (1999), *Outline Guide to the Outdoor Advertising Association.*

on a bus shelter for two weeks costs around £90. New designer bus shelters, kiosks with backlit displays and improvements in the plastic used for poster skins with colour and contrasts, have all helped to create a more modern image.

13.9 The cinema

Data relating to the number of cinema screens in the UK and the number of admissions to cinemas are published by the Department of Trade and Industry. The screen returns are published monthly, broken down into the Registrar General's standard regions. The Cinema Advertising Association (CAA) relies on NRS data for their published estimates relating to audiences and cinema-going (see Table 13.4). Cinema advertising accounts for only a fraction of advertising expenditure, 0.6% in 1991, but it is a useful medium for reaching the 15–24 age group. Advertising in general accounted for £69m in the same year.

By the 1970s television had become the most popular form of entertainment and this was followed by the introduction into the home of low cost computers for multimedia applications, video games and consoles – the Sony Playstation, Sega Dreamcast and Nintendo 64 – and the expansion of other forms of leisure, sport and entertainment facilities. As work and living standards improved generally in the UK, there was a corresponding rise in consumer disposable incomes, motorcar ownership and travel, all contributing to the greater variety of customer choice. Cinema audiences had declined to 54 million by 1985, but revived to 115 million by 1995 (see Table 13.4), helped by the large Hollywood blockbuster movies, such as *Jurassic Park* and *Titanic*. At the same time, the illegal copying of films, i.e. video piracy, has been felt in the UK and has led to a recession in other parts of the

Table 13.4 Cinema data: (a) audience composition and profile data, 1991; (b) display advertising in cinemas, 1995

(a)	Average audience profile	UK population profile %	Social standing	Average audience profile %	UK population profile %
Men	51	48	Class AB	26	18
Women	49	52	Class C1	32	24
Age 15–24	55	17	Class C2	22	27
Age 15-34	81	36	Class DE	20	31

Source: The Cinema Advertising Association (1991).

(b)

Advertising	£69m
Cinema screens	1,970 screens (some cinemas are multiscreen complexes)
Cinema audiences	115 million

Source for figures: The Advertising Association (1999), *Facts and Figures on Advertising Expenditure* and the Advertising Media, http://www.adassoc.org.uk/inform/in6.html.

world in cinema viewing, for example in Hong Kong in 1999 where the indigenous film industry suffered.

As bigger complexes like the UCI cinemas have been set up with multiscreens, so many local single-screen cinemas have closed. With nearly 2,000 screens nationally in the UK in 1995 the effects of cinema advertising have declined overall in media terms.

The CAA publishes reach and frequency estimates, broken down by ITV areas and by the socio-economic and media-usage characteristics of the population, based on the NRS data. Assumptions have to be made when coverage of a particular advertising campaign is estimated, for example the need to take into account the probability of individuals visiting a particular cinema or selection of cinemas. What is being shown in the cinemas has, of course, a critical effect on the size of the audience and therefore its exposure to any advertisements shown. Cinema attendance is taken to equate with opportunity-to-see the advertising.

Data from the CAA and the NRS allows better informed assumptions to be made when campain coverage is being estimated, because these bodies collect data relating to the profile of audiences for specific types of film and for specific films, as well as the cinema-going habits of respondents.

13.10 Monitoring media planning

In summary, the backbone of the monitoring system for media is provided by BARB, which monitors television buying very closely, and the NRS for the print media. In addition, advertising agencies and their clients buy into services which monitor their own and competitive expenditures across all media (e.g. MEAL and the Media Register), so that comparison of own costs with those of competitors is relatively straightforward. But allowance has to be made for the fact that rates are subject to offers and bargaining so that there is a margin of error around figures necessarily based on rate-card rates. Also, ambiguities inevitably arise when advertisements relate to more than one brand, or to more than one variety of a brand.

From the monitoring/planning point of view, two important questions need to be asked:

1. Are the opportunities to receive the message being taken?
2. Is media selection based on the demographic characteristics of buyers/users as closely on target (and therefore as cost-effective), as is desirable?

It is critical (in tracking studies) that sample designs, together with the asking of questions and recording of answers should be standardised. Core tracking questions should always be asked using the same words and be put to the respondent in the same order. Three of the intermediate measures used to monitor advertising effectiveness after campaign exposure concern recognition, brand salience and attitude change.

Recognition is more relevant to post- than to pre-testing. It attempts to measure whether the opportunity to see the advertisement has in fact been taken by the respondent. This depends, of course, on both the media selection and the creative work. In a recognition check the object is first and foremost to find out whether the respondent recognises the advertisement. It is not what is remembered about it or the respondent's **attitude change** after seeing the advertisement, but just whether the respondent happened to see it.

If the respondent knows the subject of the enquiry, he or she may oblige by recognising the advertisement. It is therefore necessary to use a procedure which either conceals the subject of interest or one which makes it easy for the respondent to say 'no'.

Brand salience measures are concerned with the impact achieved by the advertising. Once this has been established the aim is to reinforce its position *vis-à-vis* the competition in the potential consumer's mindset. Take the simple example in Box 13.9 where the objective could be to find out 'To what extent are the opportunities to see/hear/read actually making a real impact on the awareness of the target market?' 'Awareness' is affected by a number of factors, such as the creative presentation of the advertiser, as well as the amount of media spend and scheduling.

Box 13.9 Brand salience scores

'Please think about chocolate bars. Now tell me what products come into your mind.'

The respondent attempts to list the names of the chocolate bars, as many as he or she can think of.

The researcher records the names of the brands in the order in which they surface and ranks them. Let us assume that there are five brands mentioned. The first brand name mentioned could be scored out of, say, five possibles, i.e. scoring 5. The second would score 4, and so on.

Brand salience can be interpreted as a measure of the 'stand-out' effect in the consumer's mind achieved for the brand by the advertising campaign. In this case a consumer would be able to remember recent advertisements for chocolate bars and be able to name what he or she had seen or, perhaps, consumed.

Salience scores are aggregated for individual brands, e.g. for a company's own brand and for other competitors' brands. Mean scores are calculated by dividing the aggregates by the numbers in the sample. The mean scores used in conjunction with trend data (information accumulated over time) will indicate salience (the brand's standing relative to the competition over time).

Box 13.10 shows an example of how brand strength can be measured in relation to other factors, such as customer goodwill. The objective of this is to gain a greater understanding of customer attitudes (those who are loyal, those who are not and those who would not consider buying, i.e. the no-hopers). Advertisements can then be devised for the particular market segments with the aim of persuading or shifting buyer attitudes in favour of the advertised subject.

Box 13.10 Measuring the strength of a brand

A system used by the former Tracking Advertising and Brand Strength (TABS) agency was as follows. Answers to brand-usage questions were cross-analysed with the level of goodwill to obtain an indication of the strength of a brand. With large volumes of responses collected from large numbers of people, computer analysis would be utilised. The agency used to monitor advertising awareness and would then cross-check this with the television ratings recorded by BARB. For a more extensive account of TABS see the previous edition (1995) of this textbook.

In this example, buyers were asked to rate products on a self-completion questionnaire, on a scale of 1–100. Buyer categories were as follows:

For users and buyers

- Committed user – a current buyer, marking 77–99 scores at the top of the goodwill scale.
- Enthusiastic user – a current buyer marking less favourable scores of 66–33 on the 'for me, not for me' scale.
- Vulnerable user – a current buyer not particularly well disposed towards the brand scoring 0–22 on the goodwill scale.

For non-buyers

- A prospect – a current non-buyer though favourably disposed towards the brand scoring 33–99 on the goodwill scale.
- A no-hoper – a non-buyer with a low level of goodwill towards the brand scoring 0–22.

Attitude questions can take the following forms:

1. Association of a list of attributes with a list of brands, a simple checking-off operation, e.g. Persil ticked for whiteness.
2. A ranking of attributes, e.g. Persil first out of x brands for whiteness, the data being processed in the way described for salience scores.

3. A rating of attributes using either Likert or semantic differential scales, e.g. 'whiteness that shows'.

When collecting brand-image data it is, of course, advisable to establish what brand(s) the respondent is using, has used or is aware of. Attitude questions can be a component in a company's own 'usage and attitude' survey, carried out, say, once a year to add flesh to panel data. A company may also buy a subscription to a shared-cost syndicated service such as an omnibus survey. Trend data is collected from a series of tracking studies, consumer panels or retail audits.

Tracking studies are increasingly being used as inputs for market modelling whether these be pre-launch simulation models, models designed to diagnose mix-element effects as, for example, the contribution of advertising expenditure to brand share, or 'what if?' exercises set up to aid forward planning. Trend source data from consumer panels and retail audits represents considerable volumes of data which also include pre-launch claims and post-launch brand performance.

Economic and competitive pressures and rising costs, especially media costs, together with the existence of a wealth of expensive trend data and the computer facility to manipulate this data have encouraged companies to treat their stored data as a company asset.

13.11 Conclusion

The data sources reviewed in this chapter give a brief insight into the wealth of statistical data available to the media planner and the relationship between the media habits of consumers and brand consumption, e.g. from the TGI, Taylor Nelson Sofrès, BARB, NRS, RAJAR and the OAA. Media planning, buying and billing are integrated processes.

Television is the largest single advertising medium. The cost of advertising on television represents a considerable marketing investment for advertisers and it can be difficult to design an experimental test launch given the disparity of size between ITV areas with their variations in living standards, consumption habits and material practices and differences in the regional strengths and weaknesses of brands. Fortunately, for planning purposes, a large amount of marketing information is regularly published by the media organisations.

Readership statistics for newspapers and magazines are analysed on an ITV regional basis and there is much syndicated data relating to media consumption available (viewing, listening, hearing). In order to sell space to advertisers and to focus their editorial content, the provincial press also carries out its own research within its circulation areas.

Finally, advertising has been and continues to be a potent force in global markets in informing and persuading customers of the merits of the products and services offered by individuals and their organisations. Changes in the new global media environment, such as the impact of new technologies, have forced advertisers and researchers to adapt to new working methods.

REFERENCES

1. *Financial Times* (1998), 'The advertising industry', Survey, p.1.

2. ibid, p.2.

3. The Advertising Association (1999), *The Advertising Media*, Student Briefing no. 2, p.1, (http://www.adassoc.org.uk/inform/in2.html).

4. Independent Television Commission (1994), *Cable Satellite and Local Delivery in the UK*, Leaflet, p.3.

5. Laser (1999), *Market Trends*, Laser, London.

6. *Economist* (1998), 'Britain's media giants', 12 December, p.19.

7. TN Sofrès (1999), *PictureMatching*™ *Technique*, courtesy of B. Roberts.

8. BARB (1994), *Guide to the Broadcasters' Audience Research Board Ltd*, pp.1–6.

9. NRS (1994), The National Readership Survey, Appendix.

10. ibid, p.6.

11. *Financial Times* (1998), 'New class ranking marks changes in labour market', 1 December, p.14.

12. RAJAR (1998), *Service Overview*, August, fifth edition, p.1.

13. *Economist* (1998), 'Chris Smith's digital dare', 27 June, p.27.

14. NOP Posters Ltd (1994), *OSCAR: How Scores are Estimated*, p.1.

15. OAA (1999), *Outline Guide to the Outdoor Advertising Association*.

16. *Economist* (1998), 11–17 April, pp.69–70.

QUESTIONS

1. The *Economist* (23 August 1997, p.12) noted that 'two revolutions are under way ... First television is acquiring almost infinite channel capacity. As the technology of digital compression develops, the concept of the channel will become meaningless ... a second revolution is occurring in the amount that advertisers can learn about the customer'.
   (a) Explain the changes taking place in the global media environment.
   (b) Assess the impact on advertisers and market researchers of moving from mass marketing, by advertising on traditional television channels, to micro-marketing using the large amount of customer databases to pinpoint where the target groups of customers are likely to be.
2. Compare the pros and cons of the different types of media.
   (a) Explain why television advertising has continued to be the largest source of media expenditure by advertisers.
   (b) How exactly may 'readership' be defined?
3. A food manufacturer is planning the introduction of frozen pâtés and terrines under a 'farmhouse' label aimed entirely at the consumer market. The company

has a range of pies and sausages in national distribution. The board is divided between going for a national launch with the new, more up-market, range or a rolling launch in a test market region first. Anticipating competitive reaction, the board is, on the whole, in favour of a national launch.

The media planner at the advertising agency has been asked to recommend a media strategy, given an advertising appropriation of £950,000 (US$1,521,140) inclusive of production costs.

(a) What marketing information would the media planner need in order to formulate a cost-effective strategy?

(b) What research sources might he or she consult?

4. A company making dyes for the packaging industry has recently moved from the cutting of layouts by hand to the use of lasers, resulting in greater precision, a considerable saving in time and an urgent need for new business.

An agency with industrial experience has been appointed to advertise this high-tech development.

(a) What information would the advertising agency need in order to plan a media strategy?

(b) How might this data be collected?

Assume an appropriation of £350,000 (US$560,420).

CASE STUDY 13.1	Optimising advertising effectiveness for Direct Line: quantifying the major cost benefits of painstaking television pre-tests[†]

Stephen Ashman and Ken Clarke

Introduction

A new brand with unique price advantage, creating its own new sector of a big market through easily-monitored direct response, should have all the makings of an advertising success story. Indeed Direct Line Insurance is a big success. However, this article focuses mainly on how it went about making its advertising more effective than it would otherwise have been, through quantified pre-testing, modelling and 'real-life' tracking. The process of testing two separate campaigns is intimately discussed: the rough ads; then how these were revised; and how well the finished commercials, by comparison, performed. The improvements are claimed to have yielded media cost benefits of well into seven figures.

The cost of TV advertising productions and air-time is so large that it is important to ensure that an ad will be effective. It is not uncommon for an ad to cost half a million to produce and several more millions on showing it. Were similar sums being spent on new production equipment, then a whole series of capital propositions would be produced. Advertising budgets increasingly come under similar scrutiny.

Discriminating between good and bad in advertising calls for judgement rather than luck. But judgement, however well schooled and experienced is difficult to exercise, for those who need to judge are themselves so closely involved in the creating of the thing being judged. Apart from any issues of *amour-propre* and protective, parental feelings, the marketing person has one thing that the intended audience never has, the statement of advertising strategy. Ask all the right questions such as: 'Does the ad have one main

[†] This article was first published in *Admap* magazine in February 1994, pp.43–6. Reprinted with permission in the *Marketing Research Process*, 1995. *Admap* is produced by NTC Publications Ltd, Farm Road, Henley-on-Thames, Oxon. Tel. 01491 574671. With acknowledgements to the authors and to Mr Michael Waterstone, Chairman of NTC.

selling proposition?' 'Is that proposition unique to the brand, or is it expressed in a unique way?' and, with prior knowledge of the strategy, the answers become clearer and positive. The crucial problem is how to gauge how the ad will 'work' with those who are not privy to the strategy. No matter how hard we try, we can never wholly return to a state of ignorance, or successfully pretend that we do not know our aims. Executives called upon to decide about an ad not only cannot completely divorce themselves from prior knowledge; they are also more likely to see the ad successfully meeting its communication and selling objectives.

As the following case history illustrates, there may well be a feeling that we know all we need to know about our advertising and therefore have no need to test it with the public. In this instance, that would have been a disastrous mistake.

How advertisements work

So far, whenever we have talked about an ad 'working', we have used quotation marks; for the term needs definition. Since any company's natural objective is that advertising should help generate sales which would not otherwise have occurred, we define 'work' in terms of sales effectiveness.

Looked at from a negative point of view, it is safe to say that no ad is likely to be sales effective if nobody notices it or notices what it is advertising; if it fails to communicate anything to anybody; and if nobody likes it. Alongside impact, communication and enjoyability we need to add a 'market' variable, which may best be described as 'brand elasticity'. This variable is a function of market size and maturity, brand size and development, opportunity to respond, unit price, etc. The ad's chances of working will of course be enhanced the more money is spent on showing it. For new brands and markets, the opportunity for sales effects to occur are relatively large. On the other hand, in mature markets, long-established brands generally find it more difficult to make sales gains – although this is by no means impossible.

A brand's elasticity of response to advertising is a given, and outside the control of the producer of the ad. The choice of media is a financial consideration and a company has to decide at corporate management level what to spend money on and how much to spend. Of the three elements within the ad itself, two afford no great problem in research. Relevance of communications and the extent to which people understand it are not difficult to explore. Nor is enjoyability.

The third element is concerned with whether people notice the ad, and what it is for. What we wish to measure is an ad's efficiency in generating branded advertising associations – those messages and images from the advertising that spring to mind when we see the brand in a typical selling context, whether that be on the supermarket shelf, or in Yellow Pages. This efficiency in generating branded advertising association is often referred to as an Awareness Index; it is a measure of an ad's productivity; and is defined as a number of additional percentage points of claimed ad recall that would be generated by an additional 100 TVRs (television ratings).

Ad awareness and sales effectiveness

There is no simple relationship between sales and this measure of an ad's productivity. But, provided that there is a sales-effective message, low ad awareness is unlikely to be a good thing. The problem of establishing any relationship lies in the intervening stages between seller and buyer. Thus, having advertised the new wonder whitening powers of Zippo detergent, we find sales performance also being determined by Zippo's need to

Continued

stand on the shelf alongside competitors' brands and subject to comparison on price, promotion, packaging, etc.

However, in instances where there is no intervening retail environment, we find that a relationship does hold. This became clear in an earlier investigation in the 1980s, similarly concerning a financial market. In this instance, our client felt very unsure about our conclusion (from an advertising tracking study) that his second campaign seemed to be much less efficient than his first in generating branded advertising associations. The second campaign had an Awareness of four as against ten for the first. The client felt that sales had actually been 'fairly buoyant' during the second campaign and certainly nothing like so bad as our work on advertising suggested. We therefore conducted an econometric analysis of sales performance. 'Sales' were here defined as new openings of the type of account featured in the advertising.

This analysis shows (Figure 13.2) a good 'fit' between actual and model in the earlier period. Later, though, the modelled sales line becomes substantially higher that the actual, leaving a large negative discrepancy (Figure 13.3). The factors in the model could not be adjusted since they were measures of reality such as interest rates, unemployment levels and the like. Although the same could be said of advertising input in the forms of 'Adstocks' (Figure 13.4), this was not strictly true since it would assume that one Adstock was always of equal value to any other – in other words, that there could be no qualitative difference. This is plainly untrue.

We found that the sales model could be brought back into line with the actual sales if we downweighted the value of the Adstocks after the change in advertising campaigns. We needed to assume that the qualitative value of the second campaign's Adstocks was equivalent to only 40% of that in the first campaign. This brought the model back into line (Figure 13.5) and was consistent with the findings from the tracking study about the respective levels on the Awareness Index.

Direct Line

In the case of Direct Line Insurance, the method of operation helps to reduce the gap – the intervening stages – between advertising and effect. For Direct Line conducts its

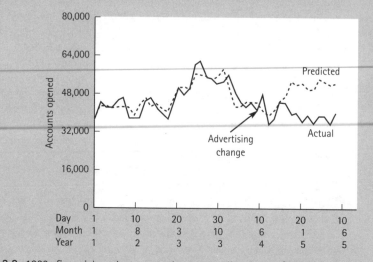

Fig 13.2 1980s financial product – actual versus predicted sales (if first campaign had continued unchanged)

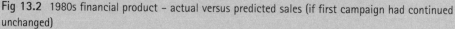

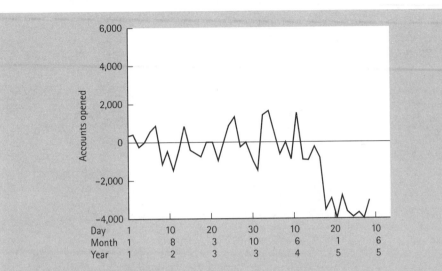

Fig 13.3 1980s financial product – unexplained variation in sales

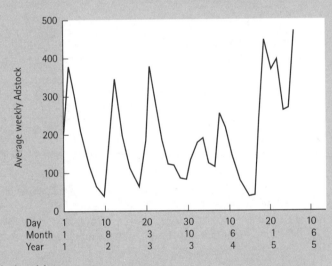

Fig 13.4 TV advertising

business with its customers over the phone – not in the form of direct selling, but by responding to calls from enquirers. The first response to an enquiry is the provision of an insurance quotation. These quotations are provided as the Direct Line operator keys the insurance details into a computer which calculates and displays the quote instantly – and stores the data for sales analysis. From the customer's viewpoint, seeking a quote is the initial expression of purchase interest. The subsequent decision to purchase or not is determined by the other classic marketing Ps – price, product, packaging, etc. Advertising is therefore the stimulus which prompts the enquirer to seek a quote. Quotes provide the measure – not actual sales in the form of insurance policies taken out. The trigger to enquire about a quotation is not by seeing the products in store; there is no retail environment and no immediate competitive contrast of price and content.

Continued

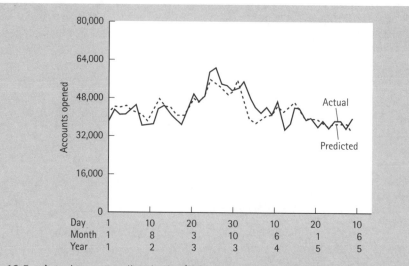

Fig 13.5   Actual versus predicted sales (if second campaign TVRs reduced by 60% in the prediction)

In other words, Direct Line is direct marketing driven and is not part of a broker-dominated distribution system. Since there is no middleman in the operation, premiums do not have to allow for commission payments. This has given the company a very compelling pricing platform – simply, 'cheaper insurance'.

Direct Line also enjoys another considerable advantage for its marketing operations – instant access to its customer-enquiry database of quotations. As the Direct Line operator also asks each enquirer how and where they heard of the company's name (and logs the information into the computer), it is possible to build up, day by day, a picture of how well different media are performing. In the press, for example, it has been possible to test different papers and different executions comprehensively – and to identify which would produce the most acceptable levels of response in terms both of absolute numbers and cost efficiency.

Millward Brown has been commissioned to use this database, and to conduct econometric analyses in order to establish the response per pound between different media for different categories of insurance. This econometric work has also been used to develop successful forecasting models.

Direct Line's advertising history

Direct Line began selling motor insurance in April 1985. It soon found that the most cost-effective format for advertising was bottom-of-the-page strip in national newspapers. Success prompted a number of competitors to emulate Direct Line's main selling features. Some of the competitors were traditional insurance companies. This meant that there was now a new category of 'direct insurers'. The competition helped to promote the general attractiveness of arranging insurance direct with the insurance company, while the entry of some long established names gave potential customers added assurance. However, all this helped to make for a much noisier, competitive market in which it would prove even more difficult for Direct Line to maintain share dominance. A new strategy was needed, designed to increase public awareness of Direct Line, its services and competitive advantages. As part of this new strategy it was decided that the brand and the product offer would best be advertised using the impact, reach and communication potential of television.

A new TV campaign

On 3 January 1990 a new motor insurance TV campaign broke in Scotland, the midlands, London and the south. The new ad had been thoroughly researched quantitatively via Millward Brown's recently introduced 'Link' TV pre-test system. The ad was tested in animatic form, so that there was opportunity and time to make changes if necessary – and before too much personal prestige had been invested in a finished film. It was as well that the pre-test was conducted.

This showed:

- Conclusions
  - The ad was found to be not very enjoyable.
  - There was only low brand prominence.
  - The focus of viewers' interest was on the little red phone which appeared in the ad as the endorsement of the idea that Direct Line came riding to the rescue of the harassed car insurer; but interest was low.
  - The key communication point – Direct Line's price competitiveness – did not come through clearly.

- Recommendations
  - The red phone as the main focus of attention and attraction needed a more prominent role, stronger personality and a closer identification with Direct Line.
  - The phone (and, by implication, Direct Line) needed to be more clearly positioned as the motorists' friend.
  - Restructuring of the audio and video elements was needed so that the message about competitive prices did not fight against strong visual distractions.
  - Responsibility comes from the imprimatur of the Royal Bank of Scotland; this needed strengthening.

Had the ad been left in its original form our prediction was for an Awareness Index of between one and two. That is, for each additional 100 TVRs put behind the ad, there would have been an extra one or two percentage points of claimed ad recall. Across the number of ads, which have been tested and then gone on to be shown on air in the same form, the correlation between prediction and actual outcome stands at 0.93. The ad was modified, though, in line with the recommendations, and in the event had a branded impact twice as high (Figure 13.6). The Awareness Index of four shown here comes within that brand of indices 3–5 where we find the majority of ads.

It is very satisfactory if not spectacular; an Awareness Index of two or less would have been cause for concern. This, of course, is not the only measure of an ad's effectiveness. In the pre-test, for instance, we had found that there was a real need to improve both communication and enjoyability.

Success: the demonstrable benefits

In the real-life situation the tracking study showed that the stronger role given to the phone in the finished ad made this branding device much stronger. For example, among those definitely recalling the Direct Line campaign, three-quarters specifically recalled the red telephone and its actions – jumping into the air, the bugle call, and so on. Similarly, when a series of statements about attitudes to the ad were put in front of people, we found in the tracking study that there was a strongly favourable balance; whereas in the pre-test the reverse had been true. The advertising had a number of demonstrable benefits

Continued

365

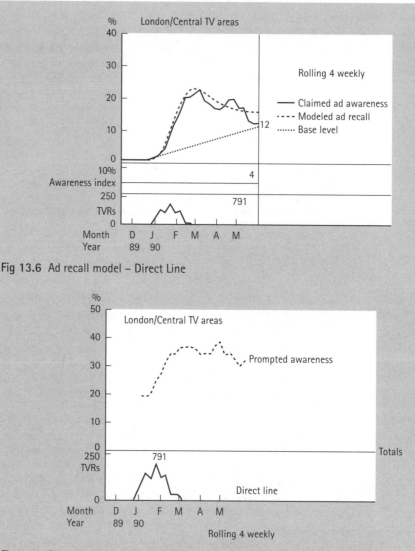

Fig 13.6 Ad recall model – Direct Line

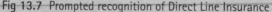

Fig 13.7 Prompted recognition of Direct Line Insurance

for Direct Line. One of the major effects looked for from the new strategy was an increase in public recognition of Direct Line and of the value in its services. In line with the strategy, prompted recognition of Direct Line rose markedly from the onset of the new campaign (Figure 13.7); while the reputation of the company and its services rose on a number of key dimensions (Figure 13.8). However, it was in its 'sales' effect that the ad was outstanding. Against a background of increasing competition, the underlying trend of Direct Line sales had been slightly downward. Once the new TV advertisements began, the trend rapidly turned upward: the much hoped for 'hockey stick syndrome' posited in many a brand manager's forward plans, yet so rarely eventualising (Figure 13.9). Had Direct Line not had the expertise of its research agency, Millward Brown, in the tracking study, the results might not have been so positive. It was estimated by the research agency that improved advertising gained Direct Line the equivalent of £5m of extra media expenditure.

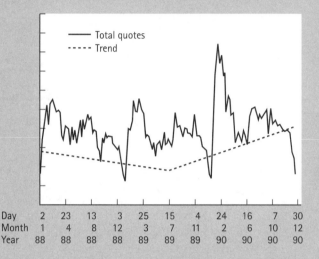

Index base 100 = Before advertising	
Becoming a popular choice for insurance	220
Good for people like me	170
Offer a high quality service	150

Fig 13.8 Direct Line – index of image shifts

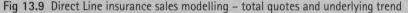

Fig 13.9 Direct Line insurance sales modelling – total quotes and underlying trend

The next opportunity: home insurance

The opportunity and the problem

In late 1988 Direct Line had also entered the market for home insurance. However, the press advertising policy which had initially proved so valuable for motor insurance was nothing like so successful in generating high volumes of sales of home insurance.

The reason for this relative lack of success was diagnosed as strong consumer inertia. This comes about from the control that mortgage lenders (primarily building societies) hold over sales and renewal of this kind of insurance. The mortgage lender naturally insists on insurance of the property. Thus most mortgage borrowers automatically take their insurance from their building society and automatically allow it to be renewed in subsequent years. There is no habit of shopping around as with motor insurance.

The need for advertising

Advertising for home insurance, therefore, had to do more than just announce Direct Line. That may have worked with motor insurance, but home insurance needed something else. In particular, the advertising would need to shake up people's beliefs and opinions, so that they would begin to think of shopping around.

Direct Line had something to shake people up all right: a saving of up to 20% off the annual premium paid via their building society (the cutting out of the middleman again).

Continued

Moreover, Direct Line had a proven format for this kind of advertising (albeit in the slightly different market of motor insurance):

- The buyers of house insurance, like the buyer of the new car in the ads previously tested, face a major problem – in this instance, the cost of the insurance on offer from the building society manager. Again, the little red telephone could come to the rescue with a saving of up to 20% of their previous premium.

- Within the advertising, the stronger role and clearer characterisation given to the little red phone in the earlier ad could be maintained, together with its friendly character as it once again it rode to the rescue.

Any need for new research?

To answer 'none' could be strongly defended. After all, the new advertising would have the same structure as the earlier ad. There was an adequate understanding of the basic cost problem facing the insurer. The Direct Line answer was clear, simple to grasp and strong – a saving of 20%. Furthermore, the mechanics of the ad, the desired characterisation of the red phone and its slightly 'cheeky chappie' appeal, had been learnt from the earlier ad testing and tracking.

Nor could the cost of testing the new ad be overlooked: some £9–10,000 for research and as much again, and possibly up to twice as much, on producing an animatic – a total cost of £20–30,000 plus extra time to be built into the planning and production schedule for the new campaign. In these circumstances many would have argued that there was little to be gained by further testing, and that we have by now learnt quite enough to judge advertising for home insurance. It was as well that the new home ad was put through a pre-test.

Pre-testing the new home ad

This ad, like its predecessor, did not rate well among the target audience on either enjoyability or on the scale of subjective assessment of brand prominence (Table 13.5). The only key rating on which the ad performed noticeably better than average was 'ease of understanding'. This, however, begs the important question of whether people actually understood the message correctly.

It had been concluded from the original motor insurance ad test that the phone must be given greater prominence, as the embodiment of the Direct Line service. Unfortunately, in the later animatic for home insurance, the red phone achieved even less prominence than it had in the earlier test (known as 'Showroom') – Table 13.6. The role of the red phone in the ad proved, in fact, to be the nub of the problem. This became clear when respondents were asked: 'Would you please tell me what was happening in the advertisement ... what was shown, what was said, the story being told and how it all fitted together?'

The verbatim reports of replies from people indicated that no less than 60% clearly misunderstood the message. Worse, they got the message completely the wrong way round. Rather than the telephone, people saw the principal character as the building society manager and thought that it was he – not the phone – who offered the cost saving. As a result, the identity and role of the little red phone became something of a mystery, indeed a source of irritation, being dismissed as 'silly', 'a gimmick' and the like.

It was recommended that the finished film needed crucially to identify the red phone as the main agent and provider of the solution. The sudden appearance of the phone inside

Table 13.5 Direct Line 'Dream Mortgage' – ratings summary

	Rating	Difference from average
Enjoyment	2.57	−0.62
Subjective 'attention getting'	2.72	0.05
Subjective brand prominence	2.71	−0.98
Ease of understanding	3.59	0.31

Table 13.6 Focus of the ad

'What is the main thing you will notice when you see the ad
repeatedly on television?'

	Home	'Show room'
Percentage mentioning phone	38	47

the building society office in the animatic was contributing to the audience's misconceptions. The telephone, therefore, needed to be seen clearly as coming to the rescue from outside the building; making its way to the side of the couple worried about the cost of home insurance; causing consternation to the building society manager, and finally as the agent removing worries and enabling the couple to get 'one up' on the manager.

These recommended modifications were put into effect in the finished film, which was itself put through a Link pre-test. Critically, it was found that the misunderstandings and misconceptions found with the animatic had been completely eradicated in the finished film.

The home insurance ad in real life
As with the earlier campaign, the start of the new home campaign saw a dramatic increase in prompted recognition of Direct Line (Figure 13.10). Similarly, claimed awareness of TV advertising showed a second spurt, some 50% of the target audience claiming to have seen advertising for Direct Line on TV recently – twice the peak level achieved with the earlier motor campaign for virtually the same level of TVRs.

Therefore the productivity of the second ad must have been considerably greater. This is confirmed by the Awareness Index. The earlier advertising was highly satisfactory, with an AI of four, but the new ad's AI of eight placed it as an unusually strong performer (Figure 13.11).

In passing we should also note that the vast majority of people (80%) found that the ad told them something of interest. This 'something' was the offer of a 20% saving, undercutting building societies, cheapest, and competitively priced. It is clear from the testing programme that had the ad stayed in its original form there would have been nothing like this communication success.

Sales effects
We suggested earlier that in the case of Direct Line there would be a more direct relationship between advertising efficiency and sales than would be the case with fmcg

Continued

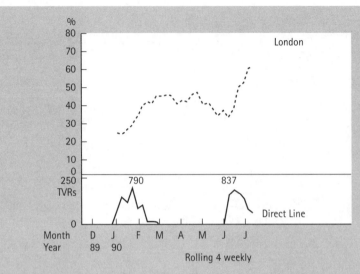

Fig 13.10 Prompted recognition of Direct Line

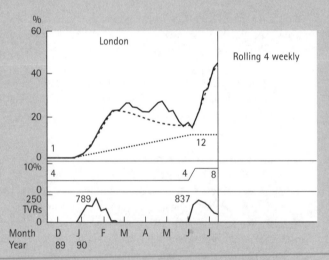

Fig 13.11 Direct Line modelled TV ad awareness

products. For one thing, there is a direct connection with the potential buyer and no intermediary such as a retailer or distributor. For another, the basic sales data is the quotation rather than a purchase which is influenced by the most crucial factor of price.

Thus when set side-by-side, we see how closely matched are the two key indicators of performance of the motor and house campaigns: sales uplift, and efficiency for the advertising as measured by the Awareness Index (Table 13.7).

We can also note the marked effect which TV advertising has had on the number of quotes requested. The econometric modelling had enabled us to say that TV advertising had added over 40% of motor quotes in those regions with advertising after allowing for longer-term trends (Figure 13.12).

Table 13.7 Sales uplift = ad efficiency

	Motor	Home
Sales uplift		
Index base 100 = year-on-year uplift in motor quotations after advertising	100	210
Ad efficiency		
Awareness index	4	8

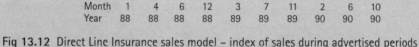

Day	2	23	13	3	25	15	4	24	16	14
Month	1	4	6	12	3	7	11	2	6	10
Year	88	88	88	88	89	89	89	90	90	90

Fig 13.12 Direct Line Insurance sales model – index of sales during advertised periods

Contribution of the research to sales and profitability

The acid test of the value of the pre-test research lies in the question: 'What would have happened if the original animatics had not been tested and had not been amended in the finished film?'

As a first step we would need to take the predicted value of the Awareness Indices as shown in the Link tests of the animatics. Then we would need to substitute the predicted value for the actual values in the ad recall mode (Figure 13.11 earlier). The tests on both animatics produced predictions for the Awareness Indices of between one and two.

Giving the advertisement the benefit of any doubt and adopting the high end of the range for our estimate, we have substituted the actual Awareness Indices of four and eight with a uniform Index of two for both campaigns. In order to bring back the modelled line of recall to fit with the actual, we have had to compensate for the loss of advertising efficiency by increasing the number of TVRs in the model. The resulting model is shown in Figure 13.3. Over the whole period, then, there would have needed to have been massively more TVRs to make up for poorer efficiency – 4,930 rather than 1,630.

Note that we have not made any allowance for the fact that the original animatic for home insurance caused great confusion in communication and some irritation over the role of the red phone: these would undoubtedly have further impaired the effectiveness

Continued

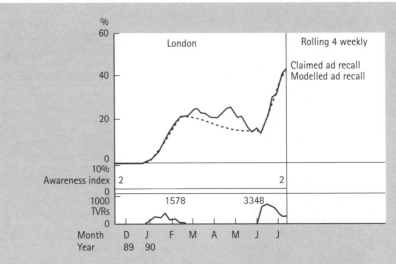

Fig 13.13 Ad recall model – Direct Line

of the advertising. Therefore the benefit of having improved the advertising was equivalent to at least some 3,300 TVRs in the first half of 1990. This may be translated through to a 'bottom line benefit' to Direct Line's profitability of some £5 million. Looked at the other way round, had the animatics not been improved, and extra money not been spent to compensate, fewer quotations would have been sought.

It can be said that these models indicate a loss of some tens of thousands on home insurance quotations, equivalent to a loss of two-thirds of business generated by the TV advertising.

Conclusions

1. Direct Line's first move into TV advertising in support of motor insurance would have been much less effective had it not been for the pre-testing of the ad.
2. At that point it would have been easy to say that the decision-maker's judgement had benefited from learning about consumer reactions: therefore, there would be no need to pre-test the next phase of the advertising for home insurance.
3. That would have left us showing a commercial which our target audience would not have readily associated with Direct Line, which would not have been readily understood – and indeed would have created confusion; and which would not have been enjoyable.
4. The loss to sales from having less efficient advertising would have been very large.
5. The value to Direct Line in having improved advertising was equivalent to £5 million of extra media expenditure.

Questions

1. The title takes account of the 'painstaking' work in television pre-testing. Clarify the major stages involved in the work undertaken in tracking and evaluating, from the pre-testing to the media campaigns. Assess the impact of the work in bringing the brand from that of low prominence (see section entitled 'A new TV campaign') to a successful and well-known household brand (see following section on 'Success').
2. Why is it difficult to measure advertising effectiveness? Propose and justify a survey methodology to determine the sample size for a television audience and the questions to be asked about advertising effectiveness.

14 Qualitative research

Mary Goodyear

Qualitative research is a diverse discipline; it consists of many different approaches to the solving of an increasingly large number of marketing problems.

14.1 What is qualitative research?

The versatility and informality of the qualitative approach is demonstrated in the several ways that it is defined in the marketing literature. See Box 14.1.

Box 14.1 Definitions of qualitative research

'Collection of data, usually by semi-structured or unstructured method from small samples in discursive verbal form. Analysis is by subjective summary, again in discursive form ... widely used, not only on account of the relative speed and cheapness of data collection, but also because of the relationships between all the variables which may be revealed.'

Baker, M.J. (ed.), *Macmillan Dictionary of Marketing and Advertising*

'A body of research techniques which can primarily be distinguished from quantitative methods because they do not attempt to make measurements. Instead they seek insights through a less structured, more flexible approach.'

Birn, Hague and Vangelder, *A Handbook of Market Research Techniques*

'Qualitative research is exploratory in nature and uses procedures such as in-depth interviews and focus group interviews to gain insights and develop creative advertising tactics.'

Toffler and Imber, *Dictionary of Marketing Terms*

'Qualitative research ... involves finding out what people think, and how they feel – or, at any rate, what they say they think and how they say they feel. This kind of information is subjective since it involves feelings and impressions, rather than numbers.'

Bellenger, Bernhardt and Goldstucker, *Qualitative Research in Marketing*, American Marketing Association

---

14.2 Differentiation of qualitative research from quantitative research

Despite this diversity, there are distinctive features about qualitative research in general which clearly differentiate it from the other survey discipline: quantitative research.

Both seek to understand and explain what is happening in the marketplace, but, whereas quantitative research uses *measurement and number*, qualitative research uses *description by words and pictures*.

Quantitative research is a science, with clearly defined parameters of what is good and what is unacceptable practice. Qualitative research tends to be more of a craft, where the quality of the findings is largely dependent on the skills of the individual researcher, and is often judged in terms of its utility for the client.

The difference between the two is most immediately seen in the difference between the type of reports that each produces. A typical quantitative report consists of numerical data and analysis and a brief commentary, whereas a qualitative report usually consists of a descriptively written account, often with consumer verbatims, and illustrations.

Underlying each is a different conceptual framework. **Quantitative research** is carried out within the framework of a scientific method, an approach that uses objectively agreed criteria and procedures to achieve results that have statistical reliability. It achieves this reliability through the use of large sample sizes, large enough to represent certain sectors of the population and usually involving hundreds or thousands of respondents. Standardised questionnaires are used to collect the data, which are then formally analysed and presented in a numerical format.

Qualitative research is focused on trying to represent the consumer and their world as accurately as possible, and in such a way that helps decision-makers in marketing or social policy.

The qualitative researcher acts as an interpreter between the consumer and the client. What this means in practice is that the qualitative researcher finds out about the consumer and the marketplace through some form of contact and then represents the consumer back in the client's world; in the advertising world it's known as 'bringing the consumer into the agency'.

There are various different ways of making that contact. Most of today's qualitative research involves face-to-face interviewing, either with individuals or groups of respondents. But the types of questions asked and the tasks employed (such as product sorting, collage building, role-playing, etc.) during those interviews vary from job to job, and can produce very different sorts of information. Observational techniques are also gaining in popularity, particularly participant observation, which allows the researcher to experience the consumer's world and, thereby, be able to represent it in a more empathetic and accurate way to the client. Data collection can also take place by the telephone (sometimes augmented by the fax for showing new materials) and, increasingly, by interviews and 'discussions' on the Internet.

The underlying discipline is not statistical method, but problem-solving through the use of a wide number of data-collection methods and the application of diverse conceptual frameworks. Moreover, in qualitative research the attitudinal stance is as important as the intellectual approach used. Quantitative research is constrained by the explicit discipline of statistics; qualitative research has to be more self-regulatory. Honesty and objectivity, at whatever cost, should guide the qualitative endeavour.

The primary goal of the qualitative researcher is to be honest in adhering to the formal contract set up between him or herself and the client, and the informal contract between researcher and respondent. (The Market Research Society of Great

Britain in their publication *Qualitative Research Guidelines* and their more general Code of Conduct are converting this informality into a more explicit code.)

The objectivity of the qualitative researcher is more difficult to achieve, many would say impossible; any qualitative study *must* be subjective, because the data collection and the analysis is determined by the researchers themselves, not by any explicit discipline. It is, after all, often described as 'a people business'. In theory, the researcher cannot remove his or her influence from the research. But in practice, qualitative researchers understand the problem and try, as far as is humanly possible, to separate out their own preferences and values from those of the respondents they are representing. Even more importantly, objectivity means to reality-test hypotheses and prejudices, and be prepared to modify or abandon 'favourite theories' in the face of the evidence of the data. The data must be evaluated in terms of their quality, but always respected. If they don't fit the preconceptions, then that misfit must be (1) acknowledged and (2) examined and resolved.

This 'representation' of the consumer can be purely descriptive (although inevitably it will be selective) with the researcher providing reportage of the data. The great bulk of qualitative research these days is of this type. It is of particular value in communications research (say, advertising creative development), where understanding the general marketing context (the environment in which people use the brand, the way they are behaving, what sort of language is used about the brand, etc.) helps advertisers communicate with their audience.

Or, the representation can not only describe the data but also analyse them, using secondary constructs taken from the social sciences (or in fact any established body of knowledge) in order to provide an understanding. It's important to note here that when qualitative methodologies were first being developed, there was a strong reliance on the social sciences for providing a conceptual framework.

As research markets matured, and the 'basics' about consumer behaviour were established and became widely known, so the body of knowledge generated by the research industry itself, contributed increasingly to the way the data were analysed. Few studies these days need to rediscover the basic dynamics of consumer behaviour (such as theories about motivation, psychoanalytic theory, cognitive dissonance, etc.). Much of this is already common knowledge taught in marketing schools. What is needed now is knowledge of these basic theories and familiarity with their applications within the marketing and research environment, such as the adoption process, the planning cycle, value studies, the different classifications of culture, and so on.

Moreover, many large client companies now have their own established body of knowledge about the behaviour of consumers in their own particular marketplace. It is common for the qualitative researcher to be asked to work within the client's constructs, for example, when working on needs-mapping or brand-positioning or assessing a global campaign.

Thus, it is rare these days for a qualitative researcher to be valued who works only with the theories from his or her degree subject. The primary need today is knowledge of consumer marketing, and an ability to work with its many constructs.

Nevertheless, many analytic – rather than just descriptive – researchers have qualifications and training in one particular social science, for example, psychology, sociology or anthropology, although few are conversant with the theories of more than one discipline. Thus, the client should have some awareness of what sort of information they need for a particular study before deciding which type of analytic researcher would be most appropriate. Some small companies specialise in a particular conceptual framework, but the majority tend to have multidisciplinary teams.

Although the information from (well-conducted) qualitative research can be said to be useful and even valid (see Section 14.4), it does not have statistical validity. The reasons for this are threefold:

1. The *method of sampling*, which in qualitative research is purposive rather than representative.
2. The *size of the sample*, which is usually (but not always) too small to provide statistical significance. Typically a project might consist of data from 30–40 people.
3. The approach to *data collection*, which in qualitative research is exploratory and non-directive, rather than pre-determined and standardised.

The quantitative interviewer works from a questionnaire, where the form of the questions, the sequence in which they are asked and, usually, the options in terms of what sort of answers can be given, are strictly predetermined.

The qualitative researcher uses an interviewer guide, which identifies which topics should be raised and roughly in what order. But the guide allows the researcher/interviewer to vary the way in which they ask their questions and to follow up on any relevant new topics introduced by the respondent.

Whereas the format of the quantitative interview is determined entirely in advance of fieldwork, the actual process of the qualitative interview is determined during fieldwork, by the interaction between interviewer and respondent.

Alan Hedges[1] describes the difference between quantitative and qualitative research as follows:

The strength of quantitative research is also its weakness – the questions and answers must be tightly controlled in form, and this inevitably limits the quality and richness of communication with respondents.

Qualitative research starts from the other end. It is informal and exploratory in nature – a series of loosely structured conversations with participants, either individually or in small groups. The aim is to throw as much light as possible on:

- The way people think, feel and behave
- Their images, values and attitudes
- The motivations behind their behaviour.

14.3 A brief history of qualitative research

There are four important aspects about the history of qualitative research:

- **Multi-disciplinary.** It has diversified from being an application of psychology, to include, in more recent years, many other theories and disciplines.

- **Growing diversity of application.** Whereas its use was once largely confined to fast-moving consumer goods marketing, it is now applied to the marketing of many different goods and services, and also in the non-commercial context of social research and public policy-making.

- **Global reach.** Although it started in the USA, there are now practitioners in nearly every country in the world, and many countries have caught up with, and some would say overtaken, the USA in terms of the sophistication of their approaches.

- **Consumer-driven.** In highly competitive marketplaces, methodologies are focused on recording what consumers *do*, rather than on what they *say they do*.

It is generally agreed that qualitative research was first practised in the USA. In the early days, motivational research, as it was then known, was introduced into the commercial world by a group of psychologists, concerned that marketers should appeal to their customers' emotions, as well as their rationality.

In only the second decade of the twentieth century, psychologists were proposing this thesis to a resistant audience of marketers.

> As early as 1912–13, the writer of this report, together with leading psychologists (such as Professor Hugh Muensterberg of Harvard, Profs. Woodworth, Hollingsworth, Pfoffenberger, etc., of Columbia, as well as a group of businessmen), organised the Economic Psychology Association and held a 3-day session at Columbia University, New York, in an effort to secure co-operation between psychologists and businessmen for psychological research in depth; but most businessmen proved to be still too confident in the old ways of selling; the old assumption that the consumer was merely a robot-like bowling-pin awaiting sufficient forceful impact of loud selling assertion, to be bowled over and buy. Businessmen resisted any subtleties or 'academic' study of this consumer and his emotions and motivations; the notion was deemed a 'long-hair' boon-doggling thing not worthy of the he-man, forceful, sales, go-getter's attention.[2]

The businessman's resistance to 'psychological research in depth' is still encountered today, in environments where the competition is not yet strong enough to force them to change their habits. Rational models of consumption are easier to understand and more comfortable to work with than theories that deal with emotions and brand intangibles – the very stuff that qualitative research is uniquely designed to provide.

Advertising agencies and pack designers have always been more open to qualitative research theory and more willing to use it to enhance their own creative abilities. They were aware, even when their clients were not, that their 'product' (communication and packaging) had to have a psychological appeal as well as functional utility.

Throughout the following decades a number of American researchers, many of them psychologists and sociologists, developed the science of motivational research, a mixture of both qualitative and quantitative methodologies, all of them designed to understand the motives that lie behind consumer behaviour, *why* people do what they do.

Motivational research was accelerated into the public arena in the 1950s with two men, Alfred Politz and Ernest Dichter. Their understanding of the importance of emotions in consumer marketing gave motivational research a high profile amongst businessmen. Their methods and their business success – Dichter's Institute for Motivational Research in Westchester County is said to have had a full-time staff of 62, which number included 45 qualified psychologists – aroused criticism as well as admirers. Many of Dichter's pronouncements were based on his own intuitive assessment of a situation, rather than on consumer data. Both men tended to be seen as highly creative, but not researchers as such. They were the first of a number of gurus who not only attracted enormous publicity but who also gave the application of psychology to marketing a dubious name in those early years.

> There had always been research – advertising and marketing men believed there was truth in numbers, but there had never been anything quite like this. Although Politz and Dichter fronted different schools of thought, both claimed star status, both brought with them the mystique of a German-educated scientist and both were, arguably, little more than snake oil salesmen.[3]

However, Dichter's 'in-depth' research techniques, based on Freudian theories of the power of unconscious motivations at influencing everyday behaviour, despite being seen by some as manipulative of the consumer, were inspired insights of great value to his clients. His understanding of the importance of emotions, even in making apparently 'rational' purchases, has helped set the qualitative agenda.

Simply put, Dichter's doctrine was that manufacturers needed to sell function and emotional security. In other words, for a product to succeed, two things were necessary: it had to work properly; and it had to appeal to feelings deep inside the psychological recesses of the human mind. 'Don't sell shoes,' Dichter advised a manufacturer of women's footwear, 'sell lovely feet'.[4]

General Mills were advised, in selling their cake mix packages, to make sure the housewife had something to do, such as add fresh eggs: wives would feel diminished and unhappy unless they were making a contribution (and would rationalise this as suspicion of the product).[5]

Vance Packard, in his book *The Hidden Persuader* published in 1957, brought the methods of 'depth researchers' to the public, arousing widespread concerns that the advertising and research business was brainwashing the public, all in the name of commerce. Meanwhile, Dichter had come across the Atlantic to open a motivational research office in London, an office that trained, either directly or indirectly, many of the first generation of motivational researchers in Britain.

By the mid-1960s, Dichter, to some extent, was discredited. His pronouncements were seen as opinion-based on a sample of one. Motivational research as a result was also discredited. However, the need to find out more about the customer through the open-ended questioning methods of the motivational researchers expanded rapidly with a flourishing consumer market. This expansion was helped considerably by the development of account planning departments in advertising agencies, a movement which started in London in the late 1960s and gained ground throughout the 1970s. The agencies' requirements, however, were not for independently-minded, and often controversial, gurus, but for researchers who could service their needs to help develop more effective advertising. Moreover, an increasing number of manufacturing companies were discovering that group discussions and in-depth interviews could give them quick and relatively cheap information about their markets, information that was also easier to understand than some of the statistically-based surveys. With the widening of the applications of this new type of research, the Politz/Dichter style of strategic 'motivational research' faded temporarily into insignificance.

With the change of emphasis, came a change of name. This new branch of the survey discipline gradually became known as 'qualitative research': generating information that complemented the numbers from quantitative research, providing an empirically-driven picture of the consumer and the marketplace, some of it drawing on psychology, but much of it simply descriptive.

In terms of status, then, qualitative research started off as the slightly unscrupulous relation within the research family: small sample sizes, open-ended questions and obviously high levels of personal interpretation by the researcher. It was not research as had been previously defined. This attitude changed over the years as the result of intelligent championing by a small group of practitioners, and also, inevitably, as qualitative research took a larger slice of the research cake. Whatever it lacked in perceived rigour, it obviously made up for in terms of utility.

In the 1970s, the continuing reaction against the 'excesses' of the pronouncements of the early qualitative gurus, plus a severe shortage of academically-qualified researchers to meet the demand, encouraged a journalistic, 'common sense', style to emerge. This formed the mainstream of qualitative research on both sides of the Atlantic for several years (and prevails still in the USA).

There were good and bad practitioners of the journalistic style; the bad paid no attention to the mechanics of the research process nor did they have any motivational insights into what makes consumers tick. The good practitioners may not have had much insight but they did place emphasis on research good practice. Attention was paid to such basics as sampling and recruitment, and to the best way to ask questions and explore the responses. Researchers were also expected to be able to substantiate their wilder claims by providing full transcripts of interviews, by quoting respondents in written reports and (in the USA) by allowing the client to view fieldwork. The whole process had started to become more transparent and more industrialised in its approach.

In this reactive process, some of the flair and creativity of the early practitioners was lost; it was no longer important to have psychological credentials, or to work with methods (such as projective techniques) borrowed from classical psychology. Even the name 'qualitative research' categorised it as an alternative to quantitative research, rather than as a stand-alone form of consultancy. The academic mindset went out of mainstream qualitative research in the USA and the UK, and was replaced by a new pragmatism and an orientation towards marketing. Other countries and regions, however, notably France, Italy, eastern Europe, India and South America amongst them, maintained their orientation towards the academic, in many cases because the qualitative sector was still in its infancy.

In the 1980s, economic expansion and the real start of global marketing helped develop research in general, including qualitative. As the qualitative marketplace got more competitive, psychology was once more playing a part. And, as well, other disciplines and types of specialisation began to flourish. For example, social anthropologists began to make their mark, responding to the ever-increasing demand for understanding foreign consumers and cultures.

And the growth in the volume of advertising stimulated a demand for communication studies, semiotics amongst them. This diversification was most strongly evident in Europe, where consumer markets were most crowded. In the USA, the rational model prevailed in marketing; consequently qualitative research in North America has tended to stay at the rational level with few attempts at incursions into the psychology of the consumer. Only in the late 1990s is this situation really changing.

At the time of writing, various observational methods are playing a more important role. This emphasis comes at a time when the consumer is believed to make many purchasing decisions as the result of the sales context and circumstances, and not as the result of a thought-through purchasing strategy. In these days of multifaceted consumers, portfolio purchasing and retailer power, the classic concept of brand loyalty, driven by habit and reinforced by advertising is out of date in many fmcg markets. Increasingly consumers do not know what they are going to buy, and may not even be able to recall what brand they purchased after the event. Post-modernist theory has provided the framework for the new, 'playful' world of collaboration between manufacturer, researcher and 'prosumer'. It is agreed to be better in these circumstances to see what people actually *do* in the marketplace, rather than rely on spoken reports.

Qualitative research in mature research markets commands about 20% of research revenue, but is considerably lower than that in less mature contexts. The discipline flourishes wherever the consumer goods arena is highly competitive and, therefore, where manufacturers need to find intangible, emotionally-based (as well as functionally-based) differentiation to give their brands competitive edge.

In developing countries, or in industry sectors where the manufacturer can still differentiate his product in terms of functional differences, advantage can be gained through promoting tangible benefits. Research must identify what functional benefits the consumer wants but it's not yet necessary to explore his or her emotional needs. And, therefore, there is no need for the more creative of research approaches in order to explore the consumer's psyche. In general, qualitative research has developed to meet the evolving needs of the marketer; a client say, in the agrochemical business, will not be able to use the emotional insights generated by creative qualitative research, whereas the brand manager in the highly competitive beer industry would be severely disadvantaged without it (see Figure 14.1).

Qualitative research has now become a legitimate information source for decision-makers in most areas of modem marketing. Its methodologies are now also commonly used in other areas of human activity, as well as commerce. The ubiquitous 'group discussion' or 'Focus group' has entered into the public domain and has become well established in social and political policy-making.

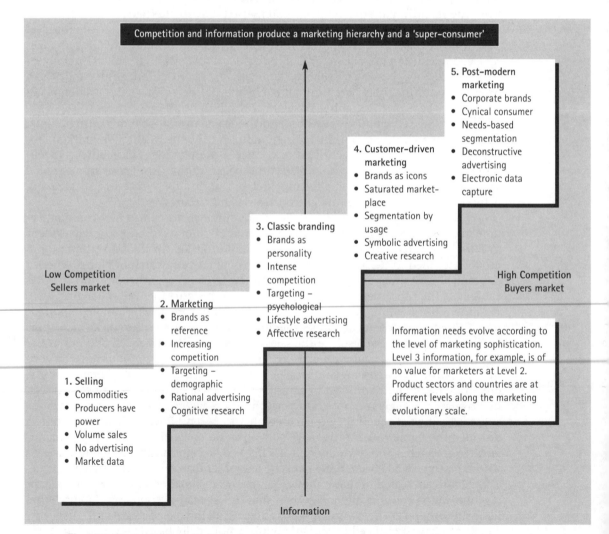

Fig 14.1 The marketing evolution

14.4 The problem of validity

Despite its obvious financial success, many people still harbour doubts about the discipline. The informality of qualitative research, the small unrepresentative samples and the obvious non-replicability of the whole process have led to questions about its utility and particularly its validity.

Some of the uncertainty about validity has arisen because of the confusion that can exist between validity and reliability. The **validity** of qualitative research lies in whether the information and the recommendations made by the researcher can be said to be sound, defensible and, perhaps most importantly, of use to the client. (See Box 14.2 for the five different types of validity.)

Box 14.2 Different types of validity

1. **Apparent or face validity** – when a research method produces the kind of information that is wanted or expected.
2. **Integral validity** – which refers to internal coherence, the fit between data and the findings.
3. **Instrumental validity** – the match between the research data and that generated by some alternative procedure.
4. **Theoretical validity** – the justification of research procedures in terms of established theory: psychological, anthropological, sociological, etc.
5. **Consultative validity** – validation of the data through consultation with those involved in the research process: respondents, clients, co-workers.

Source: Wendy Sykes, City Business School, London.

The **reliability** of research lies in whether or not the results can be extrapolated to the larger universe of consumers. Would the results from these group discussions, for example, be duplicated, were the project to be repeated? And can we say that the findings hold true for all people in the target group? The answer to both these questions is, no, not with any confidence.

The blurring of the difference in meaning between reliability and validity has led in the past to a certain amount of friction between the practitioners of both disciplines, specifically as to whether qualitative research was a legitimate marketing tool. And even today, there are few researchers who are expert in both types of research. There is usually a preference, perhaps even an intellectual predisposition, for either a numerical or a non-numerical approach.

However, the attitude towards the utility of qualitative research, at least in industrialised markets, has softened. It is now recognised that each type of research, qualitative and quantitative, has its own value and limitations. They are now recognised as complementary. Together they provide the full picture. Quantitative counts and measures; qualitative describes and explains.

In countries and in industry or service sectors where market research is not fully mature, there is still some uncertainty about the legitimacy of qualitative methods, especially as the whole process seems so strongly influenced (or 'biased' as some would say) by the researcher. Indeed it is true that in qualitative research the quality of a project is largely dependent on the expertise of the individual researcher. Whereas in quantitative research the different stages of the project work have to be handled by different people (which one researcher, for example, could interview a thousand consumers?), the qualitative researcher is personally responsible for most of the processes in their, much smaller, projects.

The quality of a project will largely depend on the qualitative researcher's personal skills at problem definition, in face-to-face interviewing and in the interpretation of what has been said or implied. Moreover, as the research industry has become more professional and sophisticated, so the quality of any research project is, increasingly, assessed by the way the results are presented, both orally and in writing.

14.5 What sorts of problems can qualitative research solve?

There are typically five main areas where qualitative research is used:

1. **Pre-piloting of quantitative questionnaires**. Qualitative studies are often run before a big quantitative study in order to identify issues and check out consumer language so that the resultant questionnaire is more relevant and meaningful for respondents.

2. **Exploring new market sectors, new countries or new ideas**. The open-ended, flexible, interactive qualitative research approach means that it is uniquely valuable in uncharted marketing territory to establish hypotheses about how that particular territory is structured.

   This kind of study is usually large in size and wide-ranging in scope. The output is often a benchmark study that is used as a reference for the commissioning client company. The study is usually designed with a particular conceptual framework in mind, whether anthropological, psychological or one from marketing theory. The choice is usually dependent on the background of the researcher, although sometimes it is implicit in the question. Thus, for example, a study about motivations should, ideally, involve some recognised motivational theory.

   Exploratory qualitative research provides information that can help answer the following sort of question:

   - What's the beer market like in Cambodia, and where could my brand fit in?
   - How do consumers perceive and structure the yoghurt market, and where is our brand within that structure?
   - What are men's attitudes towards the idea of a His n' Hers range of fragrances?
   - What are the motivations of people who give to charities for the Third World?
   - What scope is there for new hair-care products amongst Asians living in the UK?
   - What is the world of the teenager like in urban China?
   - What are our consumers like; how can we segment them?
   - How advertising literate is our target; what 'turns them on'?

3. **Diagnostic research and problem-solving**. There is a specific problem, in a known territory, that needs investigation in order that solutions can be found. The study is much more focused than exploratory work, in terms of sample, the scope of the questions and the reporting coverage. Reports are much smaller and the turnaround of the projects must faster.

   The researcher should know the product sector in order to be able to understand the nature of the problem. They should also have a good track record for problem-solving and lateral thinking. The choice of conceptual framework is largely determined by the client and the nature of the problem.

Diagnostic research deals with problems like the following:

- Why did we experience such a downturn of sales in the last quarter?
- How can we charge more for the brand?
- How should we reposition our brand in the new competitive environment?
- If we change the formula, what will be the reaction?
- Can we use the same communication in Jamaica as in Trinidad?
- What is our brand equity (non-financial) and how does it vary across our user segments?
- How can we reduce the dropout rate from our service?

4. **Evaluation**. Qualitative research is sometimes used as a quick check to see that a particular initiative is on target. Because the desired output is known, this research can be completed very quickly, with minimal reporting. It is also open to researcher abuse (providing the desired answer), lacks statistical reliability and is generally agreed to have limitations. But it helps with questions such as:

- Can we reduce these new product ideas to a more manageable number?
- Can we check out the changes we made to the ad?
- Does this ad concept meet our creative strategy objectives?
- Which of these four rough ads is the winner?
- Is this new packaging right for our new brand positioning?

5. **Creative development**. This consists of working with respondents in order to develop an idea for a new product or service or aspects of communication. It demands researchers who can empathise with their respondents and also understand their client's objectives and priorities. It can offer very fast turn-around work, with the results available almost at the end of fieldwork. It includes group discussions, 'workshops' and brain-storming sessions, and is collaborative in interviewing style.

It answers questions such as these:

- How can we best develop this ad?
- How can we develop a new product that meets consumer needs?
- How can we format our invoices for better customer understanding?
- How can we optimise our complaints service?
- Let's get some ideas for new products.

Qualitative research is not appropriate for projects where the client needs to know how many people think this way, or are likely to buy that product, etc. Qualitative explains why, and describes how; it provides understanding but not numbers.

14.6 What process is involved?

Typically, projects go through the following process: the research buyer contacts the research supplier with a marketing problem that they feel requires a qualitative approach. Unless this is a problem area that both buyer and supplier are very familiar with, in which case they can agree the details of the research by telephone or letter, there is often a face-to-face briefing session. The buyer explains what they see as the problem, the researcher listens and, in turn, asks for additional information that will help them understand if qualitative research is indeed what is required. If the buyer wants to know, for example, 'how many customers' or 'what proportion' or 'percentage' of the market their brand has – in other words, if they seem to want measurement of some kind – then it's not a problem that qualitative research can answer.

The interrogation process, challenging the buyer's assumptions, as well as learning about their brand and market sector, is a very important part of the briefing meeting. Even naive questions can help to identify the individual strands of the problem, and problem definition is the first step to understanding what kind of information is required.

Intelligent questioning at this stage should also find out how the research information is to be used, and by whom (their function within the company). What is going to be done as the result of the research? Knowing this helps the researcher orient their research, and the way the information is presented, with maximum utility. If, for example, information is required as to the nature of the brand image or personality and this is going to be used to brief the advertising agency, then it's important to provide information that speaks 'advertising language', that will stimulate the creative team as well as inform them. If, on the other hand, the information is going to be used by the head of sales, then a different perspective will be required, and probably a more pragmatic and commercial language.

Having learned all this, the researcher may then be asked to write a formal proposal, perhaps in competition with several other qualitative suppliers. This usually consists of the following structure, which illustrates well the process of many qualitative projects.

- **Background and problem definition**, which should demonstrate to the buyer that the researcher understands the problem and knows about their brand, its competitive environment and the market sector in general.

- The **research objectives**: what it's hoped will be achieved as the result of the research, and in broad terms, what will be done with those results.

- **Information required**. Here the researcher identifies more specifically exactly what information needs to be gathered in order that the research reaches its objectives.

- **Method**. What form will the data collection take (face-to-face interviews, telephone interviews, observation, etc.), what style of interviews will they be (group discussions, extended groups, individual interviews, etc.), how long and where, and in what kind of venue? Each of the suggestions made needs to be supported by some kind of rationale. For example, if the research project involved interviewing the managers of sports shops, the proposal might read:

  > We suggest individual interviews rather than group discussions because of the logistical problems involved in trying to bring sports shop managers together. Plus, we anticipate that they may have some anxiety about being outspoken in front of the potential 'competition', which could unnecessarily constrain the information obtained.

- **Creative hook**. Just as in advertising, there is often a creative aspect in good qualitative research. This takes the form of a special insight into the nature of the problem, which, in turn, helps define what technique, or form of questioning or special sampling requirement will provide the necessary data. See Box 14.3 for examples.

- **Topic guideline**. What topics are going to be covered, and in which order? The latter is sometimes a crucial issue. For example, suppose respondents were to be asked to assess a proposed design modification of an established brand in a product area where attitudes were very conservative. It would probably make sense to show the new modification *before* letting respondents refresh their memory of the current design. This would reveal if the modified packaging were even recognised as being new. It could be that consumers would *not* consciously register it as being different (although they might feel that the packaging was looking particularly attractive next time they went to buy). But if they were allowed to refresh their memories of the current packaging *before* seeing the new one, this might make them resistant to the change. This part of the proposal should also specify if the research approach is to involve any 'special', perhaps new, techniques. Here it would be customary to indicate whether any projective or facilitation techniques are to be used, and if so, what will be their benefit in terms of the information they generate. (See Box 14.4 for examples of projective techniques and when they are used.)

The information required and topic guideline parts of the proposal are where the problem-solving ability of the researcher is best displayed. Knowing (1) what information will solve the client's problem and (2) what kind of research approach will provide that information is at the core of all projects. This is where creativity and experience both play a major role. It should be noted here that the topic guideline is not quite the same as the interview or group discussion guide. The interview guide is the topic guide 'translated' into the actual questions and statements that the interviewer is going to use. These are expressed in consumer language, avoiding marketing terms (except where those are part of everyday speech). It would be inappropriate, for example, to ask respondents to 'Name brands in the competitive set of your preferred brand.' That question needs rewording as 'Which brands, of the same sort of category, could you buy as substitutes for your preferred brand?' Similarly, and most importantly, although much of qualitative research is about finding out 'why' the word 'why' is rarely used. (See Box 14.5) The interview guide would specify another question.

14.3 Creative hooks

1. How to get through the respondents' defence mechanisms

Bill Schlackman, former colleague of Dichter, is credited with this possibly apocryphal story about the creative hook in understanding consumers' attitudes towards lavatory cleaners. He asked his respondents not to clean their lavatories for two weeks before coming to the group discussion. That way they would be able to talk more vividly about the risk of germs, their anxieties about which might otherwise be suppressed by normal frequent cleaning routines.

Continued

2. How to avoid 'bargaining' with consumers over price

Many clients want to know how they can charge a higher price, but fear that respondents would not answer honestly if asked how much more they would pay.

Get them, instead, to talk about how the total mix could be improved in quality. The degree to which improvement is deemed necessary gives some indication of price elasticity. With elements of the mix identified as needing an upgrade, indicate where the opportunities lie for rationalising the higher price.

3. How to overcome prejudice

A product category has such a negative image that consumers won't even trial the product. One solution is to place the product without its usual packaging cues and find out if the product itself is acceptable, and how the consumer uses it and modifies it to suit their needs and preferences.

Then the marketer can start building the brand from 'the bottom up', maybe even ignoring reference to the product category itself.

4. Avoiding the Art Director response

Packaging research can end up with respondents playing art director and critiquing proposed new packs.

Pseudo-product testing can be useful. Respondents are presented with, say, the proposed new packaging and asked to guess 'from the look of it' in what way the product itself has been modified. Focusing on the product rather than the pack can indicate the pack design's communication values; aesthetic preferences can be explored later.

Box 14.4 Examples of projective techniques

- **Product sorting** – for understanding how consumers set up a 'structure' to a market, and which products and brands they see as competitive with the client's brand. This is useful in getting an early warning signal about possible threats to brand share, as well as learning about the key drivers and definitions of the market sector.

- **Anthropomorphising** – for understanding the feelings associated with a particular brand. Respondents are asked to spontaneously imagine and describe the brand as a person, an animal or a bird. They then do the same with competitive brands, and the differences are noted and discussed. The spontaneity of the process allows the unconscious associations with the brand(s) to surface in the choice of which kind of animal is chosen. It's important to ensure that the significance to the respondent(s) of what is chosen is thoroughly explored.

- **Picture-sorting and collage-building** – for facilitating the process of describing the associations that respondents have with a particular market sector or brand. Many people find it easier to access their feelings through the use of pictures than words. It's also much easier to respond to material that's provided, than try to create one's own picture.

  As always, it's important that respondents describe and analyse the pictures they choose. It shouldn't be assumed that everyone has the same response to visual stimuli; in fact they are more liable to be differently interpreted than words.

- **Completion exercise** – usually to understand brand values or personal motivations. Respondents are asked to complete a sentence or write a caption for a cartoon. Again, respondents find it easier to respond to something that is already half there, than have to create their own material entirely.

- **Role-playing** – often to establish the constructs that people use to defend their brand choice, and to assess how easily and in what way their defences may be lowered to enable brand switching.

- **Behaviour modification** – respondents are asked to change their behaviour between one interview and a reconvened session. Their experience helps identify areas of resistance to the client's brand, and how these might be overcome.

Box 14.5 The 'why' question

Although the job of the researcher is often to find out *why*, the word itself is rarely used. Reasons for this are:

- People may not know why, say, they prefer a certain brand; they may never have thought about their preference: if asked 'why?' they may, then, just say 'I don't know' or 'no particular reason' or 'I like it' – all of them of little value for the researcher.

- People may prefer not to give their reasons. For example, a particular brand name may be preferred because it has snob appeal; the respondent may decide this is socially unacceptable to give as an answer and revert to a general disclaimer such as, 'I don't know' or 'no particular reason', etc.

- People may resent the feeling of being interrogated, of being asked to explain themselves to the interviewer.

The best way to find out *why* is to ask respondents to describe their choice, as in 'How is the brand you prefer different?' and to then explain what value that difference has for their purposes, as in 'So how does the fact it's softer meet your particular requirements?'

These two aspects of *why* can be explored through question and answer, or through projective techniques as in picture-sorting to differentiate between two brands.

Interview guides written out in full are only really essential when the researcher is relatively inexperienced, or when research is being carried out by a team of different researchers (especially if from other companies and other countries). When there are several people working together, it's important to ensure a commonality of approach, otherwise the information returned will be too disparate for any kind of comparisons to be made. Many experienced researchers work from a topic guideline of key questions or issues, confident that they will know how to word the questions on the spot.

- **Sample**. The proposal should state how many people will be interviewed or observed, and what kind of people they are, specified in terms that are relevant to the problem in hand. This will probably include sociodemographics, and may also include attitude or lifestyle classification, and increasingly importantly, classification in terms of brand usage. The choice depends not only on the needs of the project, but also on the dynamics of the interview. For example, it could be that both men and women are users but that the culture precludes men and women being interviewed together. If the project is commissioned, then it will be important to specify very clearly, and agree with the client, all the recruitment criteria for obtaining the sample as defined.

- **Cost**. Costs of the same size qualitative project can vary enormously between suppliers, even for the same job. (See Box 14.6 for cost differences between proposals.) Because this is a competitive area of research, it's important for both the client and the supplier that the proposal spells out exactly what is being provided for the money. It's equally important to specify which executive(s) is going to work on the project, and what level of relevant experience they have had. Qualitative research is 'a people business', where experience really makes a difference to quality. It's also important to specify whether the cost of materials mentioned in the proposal, such as a selection of products for use to generate discussion about, say, packaging, has been included or is extra.

- **Timing**. The briefing meeting will usually have given very clear indications as to the timing constraints and whether the research must be completed 'by yesterday' or whether there will be time for a more considered approach. There are three time elements: time for recruitment, time for fieldwork and time for analysis and reporting. The actual time required to do the job well depends heavily on the type of problem. Advertising creative development, which rarely involves tape transcription or coding, can often be accomplished within a few days of being briefed. Strategic studies, and especially multi-country coordinated studies, need more time: a four-group strategic study typically taking between four and six weeks from briefing to the delivery of the written report.

Box 14.6 Comparing costs

Company A and Company B are both asked to quote for a four-group project in the fmcg sector.

Company A's price is slightly lower, enough for the client company to choose them, as they appear, on the surface, to be offering the same.

But the approach of the two companies, and their way of working is very different: Company A adopts the industrialised approach, of delegating and taking short cuts where possible.

Company B is more craft-oriented, where one senior researcher handles all stages of the project.

There is no way of knowing which company might do a better job, but there is a big difference in the amount of time that each devotes to the project.

It's important to understand these differences when comparing proposals.

Company A	Company B
Briefing meeting	Briefing meeting
1.25 hour groups	2.5 hour groups
No listening to tapes	Transcripts of tapes
Intuitive analysis is from memory	Coding and formal analysis
Formal debrief	Formal debrief
Five-page summary	Fifty-page report
Division of labour	Minimal division of labour
Senior researcher meets client, but junior or outworkers do everything else	Senior researcher meets client, moderates groups, analyses and writes reports
Total 20 executive hours	Total 90 executive hours

14.7 Fieldwork: the qualitative interview

14.7.1 The group discussion

Group discussions, usually known as **focus groups** in the USA, are the most frequently used form of data collection, and for many people typify the sector. Groups vary in the number of members (anything from 3–10 members is feasible) and duration (a minimum of one hour and a maximum of three or four hours is the norm for most projects) and very often in their ambience. Some groups are run as largely fact-finding exercises, with questions being asked that demand rational answers. Others, often longer in duration, are more emotional in content, with the research objective being to explore the motivations and psychological preferences of the group informants. These are referred to by a number of different names – extended groups, creative groups, analytic groups, etc. – names which imply that the process goes beyond the question-and-answer rationality of 'normal' groups.

Extended groups make use of various projective and facilitation techniques, largely borrowed from psychology, to explore the psychodynamics of consumer decision-making. These techniques help the researcher get behind the socially acceptable façade of consumer comments in order to reveal the less acceptable, unguarded truths of human behaviour. While the socialised man may rationalise, for example, his choice of a sports car in terms of fuel economy and being able to 'accelerate out of danger', creative questioning will reveal that underlying the socially acceptable reasons are the more compelling motives of self-assertion and display. The psychology of car choice is perhaps too well known a phenomenon to illustrate the real value of this type of qualitative research: surely, it could be argued, common sense alone will tell you that emotion drives purchasing in this area? Broadly speaking this is true. Ruthless introspection of one's own purchasing is often enough to set up strong hypotheses about the 'real' motives that underlie choice. Good qualitative researchers must be prepared to reveal and understand themselves before they explore others.

There are many different techniques in use (see Box 14.4) both for creating rapport amongst group members in order to facilitate the process of examining emotions, and for helping group members reveal their feelings about, and perceptions of, products and brands.

There has been a tendency in recent years, especially with the increase in the use of two-way mirrors, to use these creative techniques, not only to generate rich material, but also to provide entertainment for client observers behind the mirror. This has encouraged some research practitioners to create ever more visually interesting creative techniques in order to put on a good show and, sometimes, to show how well they can manipulate the consumers. It's probably superfluous to say here, that while these pyrotechnics may make good viewing, they don't necessarily illuminate the problem.

The real value of these creative qualitative techniques lies in the exploring of less familiar psychological territory, for example the motivations that drive farmers' choice of pesticide, or the emotional side of decision-making amongst business equipment purchasers. Creative questioning is also of inestimable value in establishing the values associated with different brands in the same product area. If all sports cars are about satisfying drivers' desires for self-assertion, then how can manufacturers differentiate their brands? Should they all link their cars with the imagery of self-assertion? The answer is that self-assertion is a threshold motivation, one that belongs to the whole product sector area. It is a necessary but not sufficient part of the image; each make of car must have as well another element to its identity, one that qualifies the main motivational drive. Thus, one could hypothesise that the self-assertion associated with, say, a Mercedes sports car is different from that of a Honda or Alfa-Romeo. Each has a different set of associations, partly as the result of being very different products, but also as the result of their individual histories, their different countries of origin and the imagery created by advertising.

These associations, often called the product 'intangibles', become increasingly important as markets mature. In mature, competitive markets, there are often minimal product differences, especially where there is shared technology. In these circumstances, the image associations or intangibles are the only point of differentiation. In modern industrialised societies consumers very often choose products on the basis of their brand *imagery*, rather than from any real sense of product functional advantage. Therefore, the management of that imagery (the '*intangibles*') plays a major role in modern marketing. Qualitative research's ability, through the use of creative data-collection techniques, to explore and understand the intangibles, is one of the reasons why it is valued in the sophisticated marketing environment.

14.7.2 Individual interviews

These are also known as **depth interviews**, or, sometimes, **one-on-one's** or **i.d.i.s**.

There are conceptual reasons for choosing these instead of the more common 'group'. For example, interviewing the individual is helpful when the subject is potentially too personal to be discussed amongst a group (contraception is often cited as one such subject), or when the objective is to obtain 'longitudinal' information, say an individual's history of purchasing in a particular area. Sometimes individual interviews are used when it's important to track the person's response untainted by the opinions of others, say, for example, how they respond to a press ad.

There are also operational reasons why individual interviews are used: for example, when the quota sample is very constrained and respondents are hard to find, let alone convene into groups. 'Difficult' samples are often interviewed in their home or place of work rather than expected to come to a central location. This usually adds extra, very useful understanding of the consumer and his or her world.

As well as in groups and individual interviews, consumers can also be interviewed in twosomes, often simultaneously. In some situations (such as taking holidays, for example, where it is suspected that there might be some disagreement over who plays which role in the joint decision-making) each respondent is first of all interviewed separately and then brought together for a further session, to reconcile any disparities.

There are practical reasons why group discussions provide the majority of qualitative data. First, groups are, on a per capita basis, cheaper than an equivalent number of respondents interviewed individually. Second, it's easier for clients to watch groups, which are more often held at a central location, and, as well, take less time.

And third, in many cultures, it is extremely difficult (and irrelevant) to isolate the individual, either physically or, more importantly, intellectually. In cultures described by Hofstede as Collective rather than Individualistic, the group or family unit often collaborates in making the decisions. The individual doesn't even necessarily have a strong viewpoint; he or she just copies the dominant member of their group. This kind of group-mindedness is common also amongst children and young teenagers in more individualistic cultures, and small friendship groups are often more productive than individual interviews, as they duplicate the purchasing environment.

14.7.3. The rules of interviewing

There are two elements to be learned about interviewing: first how to formulate the questions and second how to 'read' and react to the response.

Question formulation

There is plenty of literature available about the mechanics of qualitative interviewing; many of the rules of questionnaire interviews are relevant to the qualitative arena. As a good principle, it's best to have decided in advance on how the various research issues will be introduced to respondents. Moreover, the proper wording will help the questions to be more easily understood by respondents and be less liable to influence the way they are answered.

These basic rules need to be learned by new researchers at the beginning of their careers because they help to produce better, more 'transparent' data. They also inculcate an attitude of neutrality/objectivity in the interviewer and reinforce the value of logic in marketing problem-solving. There is a popular misconception of qualitative research as a purely intuitive business, where the researcher, through some wizardry and special insight into consumers, is able to achieve instant and dramatic knowledge. Although some may claim to work in this way – and may buyers beware of such claims – the great majority of conclusions derived from qualitative data are entirely the result of a logical process, be that covert or open for all to see.

Reading respondents

As well as the rules of question formulation, qualitative interviewing is about understanding the nature of the consumer response.

For example, group discussions demand some knowledge of the dynamics of small group behaviour. There are three aspects to this: the first is that all groups tend to go through certain stages, which arise from the adjustment that people need to make in revealing their ideas and their emotions in front of strangers. These stages have been reproduced as a mnemonic (see Box 14.7).

Box 14.7 The stages of a group discussion

When strangers get together and discuss, the session is described as usually going through these phases:

1. **Forming**: setting the scene, establishing rapport and ensuring that everyone feels included as a valid member of the group.
2. **Storming**: a jostling for position as respondents work out their roles, and in particular who is in control.
3. **Norming**: the settling-down period often heralded by a change in body language.
4. **Performing**: when the group acts together in a cooperative way. The most productive part of the interview.
5. **Mourning**: the summing-up, a chance for respondents to evaluate the content before leaving the group.

The second aspect of group dynamics, and also of the interaction between interviewer and respondent in individual interviews is role-playing. The same person in two different social circumstances will show a different part of his or her personality. For example, the moderate extrovert may become the silent observer if and as they encounter the *real* life and soul of the party. Similarly, in any long-standing partnership, the individuals within that partnership tend to polarise their personalities in order to find a non-competed-for psychological space. If one partner is generous, the other may find him or herself being the one who is 'sensible with money'. Or if one is concerned with punctuality, the other may find him or herself being categorised as being more relaxed about time.

Role-playing in small groups has been researched by a number of sociologists (such as Belben, Bales and Slater, etc.). Although their nomenclature differs, there is broad agreement that the roles vary in terms of assertiveness, sociability, reflection and withdrawal. Natural tendencies are modified within each group; the aggressive/assertive person, for example, often becoming more sociable if confronted with someone more assertive than themselves.

A third aspect of reading the response is body language and its interpretation. There are a number of books available on the interpretation of gross bodily and facial movements.

Understanding this language (which most of us do implicitly of our own culture) helps clarify what is happening between the various members of the group. It also enables the researcher to talk back to respondents through their own body language, and thereby exercise a degree of control whenever that might be necessary. 'Mirroring', for example, whereby the interviewer reproduces the posture and gesture of the respondent, helps facilitate rapport.

Within the last ten years or so there has also been interest in neuro-linguistic programming (NLP), specifically in the interpretation of small eye movements to understand how respondents process information. NLP theory says that noting the position of the eyes while the respondent is thinking can indicate which part of the brain, and, therefore, which function is being accessed for information. Thus, for example, it may be useful to learn whether a particular brand is recalled primarily through sight, or the aural or kinaesthetic sense, and how this compares with recall of a competitor brand.

Body language is also used by the researcher to add depth of interpretation to the response to the research issues, and particularly to stimulus material, such as advertising, new pack designs, and so on.

14.7.4 Other cultures

Much of the literature of marketing and research has been written from a western perspective, including the social dynamics of small groups.

Group discussions in other parts of the world often demand a slightly different style and approach to facilitate the process.

These differences can be learned through experience, through listening to local researchers when they comment on a centrally-controlled research design and through some recent publications on global research and advertising (see the Further reading list at the end of this chapter).

14.7.5 Recording the data

Most qualitative interviews are recorded, either on audio-tape or on both audio and video. The latter is preferable as it provides the all-important record of body language as well as the words that are spoken. Plus it's much easier to see exactly what happened during the interview, for example, which piece of stimulus material was used and when.

Video recordings are also more involving for the researcher to listen to, note and analyse later, and anything that can improve the likelihood that the data will be properly and rigorously scrutinised and thought about, is to be commended.

Where recording is impossible, either for practical reasons or because the respondent wishes not, then the only alternative is for the interviewer, or ideally a third person to take notes. In some countries, Brazil for example, it's common to use a stenographer, who sits in with the group and not only records every word but also allocates it to the right speaker.

Some researchers, on projects where they are very familiar with the market and the problem, may be tempted to eschew recording the data at all, relying instead on their own understanding of the information as they proceed, and on their memory of events at the end of fieldwork. This approach is usually feasible only on small sample projects, or where the problem is very narrowly focused, or where the outcome – perhaps the development of new advertising – is there at the end of the fieldwork, and needs no further thinking about or analysis. Most diagnostic or exploratory projects, and certainly all multi-country coordinated projects need data capture.

In addition to mechanised data recording, it's also useful if the researcher puts down his or her impressions and notes immediately after fieldwork. Those first thoughts emerging from the direct experience of the interview are often very reliable.

Pictorial information, in terms of collages made by respondents, or photographs taken during fieldwork, are also valuable records of the data, which can help interpretation and also bring the presentation of the results alive to those who could not observe it directly.

14.7.6 Other data collection methods

Observation

Observation of the consumer, rather than relying on respondents to remember and accurately recount their behaviour, is becoming more popular. In modern marketing contexts where the retail environment often dictates brand choice it's important to see what consumers do, rather than rely on what they say they do. The researcher literally watches his or her respondents, either covertly or after establishing some kind of relationship, and records what they do and how they do it. In between the two world wars, Mass Observation, under the directorship of Tom Harrison and Charles Madge, carried out many meticulous observations of ordinary everyday life, with their observers taking down detailed notes. With permission from respondents, much modern observation uses video cameras, in order to understand the logistics of specific aspects of product purchasing or usage.

Accompanied shopping

This approach allows a mix of observation and questioning.

The shopper's movements are noted, again, increasingly frequently on video. The interviewer intercedes with questions at relevant junctures throughout the process, asking for clarification or more information about decisions that are being made. This method is of particular utility in understanding how shoppers move around, interpret and use department stores and supermarkets.

Participant observation

This method tries even harder to get close to the respondent and avoid the inevitable 'Hawthorne effect', whereby the respondent modifies his or her behaviour simply because they are being observed.[6]

In participant observation, the researcher accompanies the respondents, whether to the shops, or to a bar or restaurant – any situation relevant for the client – and participates with them in the activity they undertake. While this offers a richer source of understanding of the life context in which certain decisions are made or products used, it is time-intensive and, therefore, expensive.

Non-participative observation

This avoids the observer effect by removing the observer from the action altogether, and by having the event recorded by the respondent. Thus, the respondent might be invited to record their 'Saturday night at the pub', perhaps with the help of a disposable camera. The pictures taken can then be evaluated as a relatively 'pure' record of proceedings, as seen and selected by the respondent. Their commentary and explanation of the photographs adds a further dimension of understanding. For projects with sophisticated and affluent respondents, video recordings can be substituted for photographs.

Mystery shopping

This is another qualitative approach, used to record the response of the retailer to a 'shopper' enquiry. The researcher here is masquerading as a genuine shopper, and evaluates the information and very often the style of response produced by the retail assistant.

There has been considerable anxiety about the ethics of such an approach, which lacks transparency between researcher and respondent about the interviewing process. The Code of Practice for ICC/ESOMAR and the Market Research Society has now produced a set of guidelines for such interviews.[7]

Computer-assisted interviewing

There has been some successful experimentation with the use of personal computers during group discussions to augment data collected through the spoken word. It has been found that when individuals can express themselves anonymously on certain key issues they are more outspoken. The mix of group and individual data would be of particular value on topics of a controversial nature, such as political and social issues, and where there could be great sensitivity or embarrassment, such as money or medical matters.

The Internet

Qualitative interviewing opportunities exist in discussion forums on the Internet, and software has been developed to facilitate the moderation of group discussions, including making possible the use of stimulus material such as rough ads or pack designs, etc.

There are many critics of the shortcomings of this method of data collection, such as: the lack of 'affect' resulting from the impersonality of the medium, the possibility that respondents might adopt false personae, and the limitation on sampling imposed by the skew toward the computer-literate. But as the technology which can mitigate some of the negative aspects is being developed, and as the number 'getting connected' spreads down into the mass market (well over 5% penetration of the UK population in 1996), the objections are dissolving.

If response rates continue to decline in urbanised societies, if samples continue to increase in complexity, and if international research continues to grow then it seems inevitable that Internet groups will be one of the main development areas of the qualitative research of the future.

A recent ESOMAR seminar about research on the Internet is a good starting point for learning more (*Proceedings of the World-wide Internet Seminar and Exhibition*, Paris, 1998, where Beasley and Chaplin, and Coates and Froggat gave papers specifically on qualitative research) and ESOMAR have also produced *Guidelines on Conducting Marketing and Opinion Research* using the Internet (1998).

14.8 Qualitative analysis

This aspect of qualitative research is rarely documented, partly because it is so huge and complex, and partly because it is often an intuitive business; even the researcher may not be fully aware of why they've come to certain conclusions.

The great majority of practitioners start their training by working with an experienced researcher, learning on the job. And most would agree that this process never stops. There seems to be an infinite amount to learn. There are as many different problems to be solved as there are projects.

There are two common fallacies connected with the analysis of qualitative projects: the first is that the researcher should, as far as possible, start a project with a mind free of ideas thereby being ready to receive and interpret consumer data. This is neither possible nor advisable. The process must start with hypotheses, as many and as refined as possible.

The second fallacy is that the analysis is a discrete process that starts after the fieldwork has been completed. In fact it starts right at the beginning of the project when the client first identifies the problem and invites a proposal.

14.8.1 How does the analytic process develop?

First, the most important aspect of qualitative analysis starts with *the definition of the client problem*, i.e.: 'What does he or she need to know, and why? Who is going to do what with the information? What information do they have already that can shed light onto the situation? What hypotheses do they have, both formal and informal, about the possible answer to their problem?'

The researcher's job is then to take this definition, and, together with his or her own hypotheses about the client's perception of the problem, use it to create a list of *information requirements*.

The third step is to translate the information requirements into *research data requirements*: 'What kind of methods should be used to get the kind of consumer data that will answer the client's needs? And from which sort of respondents?'

This diagnostic process is the most difficult and creative part of the whole qualitative process, requiring (ideally at least): knowledge of the client's business, knowledge of the client's marketing culture, some awareness of key trends affecting the market overall and a good working knowledge of which research methodologies will provide the required information.

Once the methodology and the overall process of the research has been agreed, then the fourth step is the *generation of hypotheses*, ideally by both client as well as researcher.

The qualitative process involves much introspection. If the study is about floor-cleaners, for example, then researchers find themselves thinking about their own attitudes towards floors, towards dirt, towards cleaners, about what Mum used, about what they use, etc. They will 'live' floor-cleaners for the duration of the project, and it's valuable that they do.

This step is often overlooked, largely because of lack of time, and sometimes because it is felt to be too intrusive. Surely the researcher should keep their ideas completely out of the way? Certainly the researcher should keep their own preferences and opinions separate from the data, but they must have some ideas that will be reality-tested by respondents. Qualitative researchers are impartial but not passive. And, the more that they have thought about the problem in advance, and the more ideas and conceptual frameworks they can bring to bear on the material, the more they will find in the data.

These four steps constitute the major part of the analysis. At the end of it, the competent researcher knows what the client needs and knows how to get that information. The rest is dependent on sound recruitment, effective interviewing, and dispassionate but involved evaluation of the data against the original hypotheses.

14.8.2 Some general approaches

That being said, there are some broad generalisations that can be made as to how the data organised for different types of enquiry: whether Exploratory, Diagnostic, Evaluative or Creative development.

For example, with *exploratory projects*, where the client needs to have a picture of a particular market or market sector, then the researcher's task is to amass and structure all the relevant information obtained from the research process. This may consist of information that has come from outside, as well as from within, the interviews, including information derived from observation or from reading as well as from what respondents said.

Typically, such an exercise may involve the following:

1. First of all the researcher may write down during and immediately after field-work as many hypotheses or ideas as he or she can remember while the data are fresh in the mind.

2. Then full transcripts are made of the recorded interviews.

3. A coding frame is set up, consisting of all the issues covered in the interview guide.

4. The researcher then proceeds to encode the contents of each transcript onto the framework, being careful to keep the information from different sub-samples in some way differentiated. The encoding process may be based on 'common sense', or it may involve the use of conceptual frameworks: theories and principles from, say, psychology, economics, anthropology, etc.

5. When all the transcripts have been entered onto the coding sheets, each issue is reviewed and assessed: 'What did people say? What did they mean? What similarities were there across the sample? Were there differences and what seem to be the reasons for those differences? What implications are there in all this for the client?'

Diagnostic projects already have a structure and, therefore, are more focused. They take less time but may need greater problem-solving skills.

Sometimes the solution to the problem emerges during fieldwork. For example, take the problem suggested earlier: 'How can we charge more for our brand?' It may become clear during fieldwork that the manufacturer will be able to charge more for the brand if the packaging is improved. While the product is performing well, the packaging is negatively compared with competitive brands. Once this idea is heard from a few interviews then the researcher must reality-test this hypothesis for the duration of the fieldwork. A good researcher will also explore in what way the current packaging is deficient (overall size or shape? closure problems? inappropriate material? wrong aesthetics for the brand or sector? etc.) Then, at the debriefing, he or she may be able to make some firm recommendations as to how to enhance the brand and help it to be worth more.

It must be said that such simplicity is very rare. Most projects consist of a whole bundle of problems and information needs, each of which may need a slightly different analytic approach.

Evaluative projects are easier to analyse, at least in theory. They consist of matching the data to the client's criteria for success or failure.

Thus, for example 'Does this rough ad meet our creative strategy objectives?' involves seeing that respondents' responses to the rough ad meet the client's communication objectives, and noting where there is any disparity. The common problem here is that few clients have firmly established criteria for success or failure. So the researcher may well find that they have to identify their own parameters and evaluate consumer response against these. Even so, the actual results tend to emerge throughout the fieldwork, and rarely require detailed transcription and coding.

Creative development is a collaborative process taking place between researcher and respondents, developing ideas for advertising or new products or services. There is information to be provided within a tight framework rather than problems to be solved. Accordingly, there is little analysis as such, except perhaps for a description of within-sample differences.

14.9 Conclusion: What is good practice?

Although qualitative research is not a rigorous and systematic science, it has its rules of good practice. These include:

- **Proper problem definition**: revealing an understanding of how consumer information can facilitate client decision-making.

- **Proper sampling**: recruiting and interviewing the agreed number of relevant respondents, unambiguously defined and honestly recruited.

- **Proper interviewing**: based on practical skills in terms of wording questions, and an understanding of the psychodynamics of the interviewing process.

- A **transparent analysis process**: being ready, willing and able to demonstrate how conclusions have been reached, including the use of any secondary constructs, such as theories from, for example, the social sciences.

Further details about the good practice of qualitative research can be found in the publications of MRS, the AQRP and ESOMAR. The publications also include ethical guidelines for the proper conduct of the relationship between researchers and respondent as well as between researcher and client.

Fifty years ago when qualitative research was just beginning to become established as a separate discipline, there was a good deal of suspicion about its status. It lacked the obvious rigour of approach and interpretation of quantitative research, and seemed, through its reliance on the personal skills and interpretation of the researcher, to be open to accusations of subjective bias at best, and charlatanism at worst.

These suspicions still prevail in less mature research markets or product sectors. Cultures which favour the technical and the rationalist viewpoint (such as, for example, the pharmaceutical business, or the financial services sector) prefer the apparent objectivity of statistics and numerically large samples as the basis for all their decision-making. However, with time, and especially with competition, the need for greater understanding of the consumer and their perspective, facilitates the acceptance of the qualitative mode of enquiry, with its emphasis on listening to the consumer.

In those early years much time and energy was spent by qualitative researchers proving that qualitative research was a legitimate and scientific marketing tool. More recently, it has focused less on trying to prove itself in the sense of being an objective science, and instead, has become much more concerned with providing a client service. It is a method of enquiry and investigation, which provides whatever kind of information has been agreed with the client.

Thus, a major factor in assessing research quality has been the degree to which the researcher has fulfilled their contract with the client. Has the research provided what was promised?

Then, just as importantly, although more difficult to determine, how useful is that information for the decision that is to be made? Utility is a key concept in perceptions of good practice in today's marketing environment. And although the researcher may feel that perhaps the information they provided has been good, the ultimate arbiters must be the decision-makers themselves. The best theories in the world are without value unless they have been understood, accepted and used. Hence the importance of the qualitative researcher being able to communicate his or her findings in an appealing and easily understood manner. Presenting the results with creativity and professionalism has become another important skill that the qualitative researcher needs to acquire.

With the inevitable increase in global marketing and the world-wide shift towards consumer-driven strategies, there is a growing need to understand the consumer. The future for qualitative research, therefore, looks good.

REFERENCES

1. Hedges, Alan (1998–9), *Introduction to the AQRP Directory*, AQRP.

2. Frederick, George (1996), *An Introduction to Motivation Research*, The Bell Press.

3. Robinson, Jeffrey, (1998), *The Manipulators*, Simon and Schuster, pp. 11–12.

4. ibid.

5. McDonald, Colin and King, Stephen, *Sampling the Universe*, NTC Publications.

6. *The Hawthorne Experiment*: classic wartime social experiment which found that factory workers changed their work practice simply because they were being observed.

7. *ICC/ESOMAR Code of Practice*: available from either the International Chambers of Commerce or the European Society for Opinion and Marketing Research. Updated each year.

FURTHER READING

Birn, R., Hayne P. and Vangelder, P. (1990), *A Handbook of Market Research Techniques*, Kogan Page, London.

Cowley, Don (ed.) (1991), *Understanding Brands*, Kogan Page.

De Mooij, M. (1992), *Culture and Organisations*, Prentice Hall.

Hankinson, G. and Cowking, P. (1996), *The Reality of Global Brands*, McGraw-Hill.

Hofstede, G. (1991), *Culture and Organisations*, McGraw Hill.

Gordon, Wendy and Langmaid, Roy (1988), *Qualitative Market Research: A Practitioner's and Buyer's Guide*, Gower.

Greenbaum, T. (1987), *The Practical Handbook and Guide to Focus Group Research*, Lexington Books, October.

Lannon, J. and Cooper, P. (1983), 'Humanistic advertising: a cultural perspective', *International Journal of Advertising*.

McDonald, C. and Vangelder, P. (1988), *ESOMAR Handbook of Market and Opinion Research*.

Trompenaars, F. (1993), *Riding the Waves of Culture*, Beasley, London.

Sherry, J.F. (ed.) (1995), *Contemporary Marketing and Consumer Behaviour: An anthropological source book*, Sage, California.

QUESTIONS

1. In what ways have historical processes influenced the development of qualitative research? What likely type of process would a typical qualitative project go through?
2. What are the differences between qualitative and quantitative research? Discuss the ways in which qualitative researchers could improve upon the reliability and validity of their research outcomes.
3. Write a report proposing a qualitative research method and justifying its adoption in the investigation of customer attitudes to one of the following:
   (a) a range of new designs for the covers of a new mobile phone;
   (b) a proposed imposition of high toll charges on motorists entering a city following the introduction of more pedestrian zones in the city centre.

15 The international marketing research process[†]

Caroline Noon

15.1 International marketing

Whereas articles over the past 10 to 15 years have talked of international opportunities and the move to globalisation, at the beginning of the twenty-first century 'globalisation' is clearly upon us and characterises most marketing activities.

International brands offer great potential rewards to companies involved in managing and marketing them. They can also create enormous challenges, sometimes entailing risk and significant investment, to make the brand successful in an increasingly competitive and international marketplace. International trade is a complex web of cultural and market differences, international regulation and commercial barriers and the job of navigating these hurdles often lies with the international marketing team.

These days there is little choice about participating in the world of international trade, even for a strictly national brand which may well need to develop defensive strategies against an invading foreign competitor. Companies are driven to increasing internationalism by a number of factors which are both complex and interrelated:

- A gradual erosion of competitive advantage that can be achieved by marketing brands in purely product performance terms – quality differences are often now so narrow that it is only the marketing and advertising communication that builds different imagery and equity for the brand.

- This is exacerbated by increasingly shorter product cycles – from design to production – and thus the possibility that competitors can react in a matter of months to any new development in product terms.

- There is a growing polarisation of brands – the mega players which offer global reach and economies of scale versus small local operators which have regional expertise and flexibility. This has the effect of squeezing medium size brands out of the market.

- Distribution channels and routes to market have become increasingly complex, and now the internet and e-commerce looks set to change the entire picture.

[†]Acknowledgements to Carol Coutts and Caroline Noon. This chapter has been updated by Caroline Noon, International Qualitative Research Director at The Research Business International (TRBI), based upon Chapter 3 in the fourth edition of this textbook by Carol Coutts, retired chairman of TRBI.

The research process is obviously driven by these developments:

- Brand equity and brand essence are extensively researched – leveraging a particular brand value or attribute is often the only point of differentiation with a competitor and forms the basis of the brand's whole communications platform. Creating global brands is a primary concern for many companies, with the benefits afforded by harmonisation of communications, advertising spend, marketing departments and even product name.

- International research is now rapid and pressured. Turnaround is faster and most marketing research companies now offer greater understanding of clients' issues and insight into moving the issues forward – the boundaries between research and brand/marketing consultancies are increasingly blurred.

- Client companies – or buyers of international research – also impact on research. Different multi-nationals have different structures, but the majority either centralise their market research function in one centre and conduct large, global projects or regionalise their research capacity and conduct research programmes that are more tailored to that region's needs. This determines the role and choice of research partners.

- The internet is creating new challenges for marketing research, whether as a subject for research or as a tool to actually conduct market research (for recruitment or interviewing on-line).

15.2 Communication

The environment in which all this activity is played out is also changing rapidly. The key change here is media: whereas once 'broadcast' media represented all the possible means of communicating with consumers there are now an enormous number of options that allow the marketer to talk to the whole market, individual target groups or individual consumers as required – 'narrowcast'. Whereas we have traditionally talked about above- and below-the-line communication, the explosion of media have made these terms obsolete.

The obvious changes here are

- The internet – allowing interaction with individual consumers'.

- Development of interactive TV – with the anticipated fusion of PC and TV the boundaries between advertising, direct mail and even market research could become blurred.

- Satellite broadcasting/pay per view channels allows fine choice of target audience.

- Sponsorship of events.

- Highly developed direct mail.

These changes have already, and will continue to profoundly affect opportunities for marketers to

- Develop a relationship with selected consumers.

- Deliver a specific message to groups or individuals within their current or potential target base.

This creates challenges for research in developing techniques and products that will allow measurements of the effectiveness of brand communications.

15.2.2 A relationship with consumers

With the proliferation in the media and increasing marketing, creating a dialogue with the consumer and building a relationship with them is now at the heart of marketing – communication with specific target groups rather than a general message for the whole marketplace.

Direct mail is now firmly established and is ever more refined in its ability to target mail shots as well as particular messages to key target groups. The advent of loyalty scheme cards has also given rise to affinity marketing – knowing more about a consumer's lifestyle to understand the choices that he or she is likely to make. This type of knowledge allows segmentation of customer types that enables a brand to address an appropriate message via relevant media to different groups. Clearly research has an important role in providing insight and data on behaviour and attitudes and needs to fuel this type of consumer understanding.

Relationships with consumers have also evolved remarkably in terms of the 'quality' of the interaction. Consumers generally are more sophisticated, more marketing literate and fully aware of the range of choices that they have. We now recognise that consumers often have a repertoire of brands, rather than making the assumption that they fit the profile of one type of consumer – a young, active woman who buys diet yoghurt may also be the indulgent, pampering partner who buys luxury mousse deserts for a treat on a Friday night. These various choices are often described as Need.States. An example of application of Need.States involvement with a brand or category is given below.

Need.States are the complex web of rational and, most often, emotional and subconscious triggers leading to a product choice. Importantly, they are a result of the situation the individual finds themselves in at a particular point in time, i.e. their own mood, attitude and feelings but also the dynamics around the circumstance or the shopping environment.

The need for this type of information has led to a raft of new research approaches and methods, focusing on techniques of 'being there' or ethnography which aim to document real behaviour and get as close to the 'moment of truth' as possible.

15.3 The rise of the strategic planner

The development of the brand planning function in advertising agencies bears witness to this change. Pioneered in the UK, the planner as a key member of an account team is now the norm in international agencies, where they act as 'the voice of the consumer' within the agency as well as taking responsibility for client strategy. The planner is also often the primary contact for the research within advertising.

15.4 The international consumer

Perhaps the most important evolution in the past few decades has been that of consumers themselves. Around the world there are often as many commonalities as there are differences between consumers – even between developed and emerging markets. The speed of development in eastern Europe, for example, has closed the gap between east and west in just a few years. What is certainly common is that all consumers face greater and more complex choices than ever before.

Nevertheless, to maximise the effectiveness of marketing and communication, it is necessary to understand what differences do exist. Differences are driven by:

- community (nationality/regionality)
- ethnicity
- culture
- language
- religion
- gender
- social class/economic situation.

While the 'international consumer' is often imagined to be the 'holy grail' of international marketing, in reality, he or she is affected by these demographic, ethnic and attitudinal differences which need to be understood to break through to the consumer. One thing that is emerging, particularly from developed markets, is increasing fragmentation and eclecticism – especially among younger consumers. Again, this represents challenges for the marketer, and researcher.

15.5 The market research industry

Market research itself has not stood still in this developing landscape. The industry is significantly more mature in developed markets, and leads the way in developing new techniques. However, as companies have become international and turned their attentions to new and emerging markets as well, so market research has developed. Whereas 20 years ago, conducting qualitative research required a lot of coaching for moderators and researchers, nowadays they are skilled practitioners; mirror facilities for groups, for instance, are available in most cities. Similarly in quantitative research, quality standards have been implemented from scratch, for example in China, where large, quantitative studies are possible. The industry itself is now a well-established part of marketing and, like advertising, takeovers and mergers dominate the industry headlines.

15.6 The role of international research

Aid to strategic planning

Good international research provides an understanding of different cultural environments and offers information and guidance to assess and pursue market opportunities. This has been described by John Pawle of Unilever plc as follows:

> The values of [qualitative] research to international business are threefold: first, to help identify and make best use of brand equity; secondly, to understand the social and cultural context of the different markets in which brands are operating: thirdly and as a result, to inform management of consumers' current and future needs. In short, to obtain consumer understanding, for the benefit of the company and its brands, in local, regional and global markets.

Consumer insight as well as market understanding has gained in importance and is essential nowadays for developing brand communication that is relevant and meaningful to the target audience. This is particularly important for advertising agencies, as outlined by the European planning director of Ogilvy & Mather in addressing international researchers:

> Very simply it's about insights, insights and more insights. Not ad research, it's too late. Not category research, but a better, deeper understanding of people's lives and ambitions. We have to challenge existing thinking and we need market researchers' help to do it.

Given that research is often as close to a crystal ball as most companies will ever get in anticipating the future for their market or their brand, it is normally an essential input to the marketing process. The information sought in the research process tends to fall into three main categories:

- extrapolating development from known market information/data;
- exploring concept ideas for consumer response to strategic or communication directions or product ideas;
- investigating markets for previously unearthed or unrecognisable behaviour and attitudes that provide the 'nugget' of an idea or strategic direction.

Increasingly, the role of the international researcher is to 'add value' or translate findings into actionable next steps for the international marketer. Research agencies are thus taking on more of a consultancy role.

The key about the consultancy approach is to provide an understanding of clients' marketing issues and needs and to provide answers that offer strategic thinking rather than a 'load of data' on various markets. This presents challenges and considerations for commissioning and conducting market research.

15.7 Commissioning and managing international research

The major differences in approach to international research management relate to two key aspects:

- Whether the project is coordinated centrally or handled separately in each country.

- Whether the project is managed primarily by the organisation's researchers or by the marketing team involved (experience suggests that international commissioning organisations do not necessarily appoint researchers to this role – the supplier's point of contact can sometimes be an international marketing or advertising manager or export director).

There are advantages and disadvantages inherent in each of these approaches which need to be tackled on a project-by-project basis. However, overall the key to developing good management of international research is to establish clear lines of communication from the outset.

15.8 An optimal approach to international research management

Perhaps the key recommendation to achieve optimal research management is to appoint the appropriate team *from the start*, involving all parties – users, client researchers and research suppliers – at both central and local levels. Lines of authority and communication should be clarified, ideally in a memo that is circulated to all concerned. A model of an ideal team structure is shown in Figure 15.1.

This model takes into account the need for all parties to communicate and consult with their internal and external partners. However, in the interests of avoiding anarchy, it restricts the lines of authority quite severely, while still recognising that

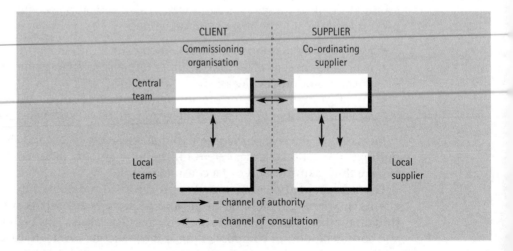

Fig 15.1 Model for an ideal international research management structure

degrees of autonomy among local operating companies can vary a lot. It is strongly recommended that diagonal lines of consultation or authority are not permitted! For organisations which have little or no formalised central management responsible for the project area, the recommendation is that one of the local groups should be voted to take on this function – again in the interests of communication efficiency.

15.9 Importance of comparability

What do marketing companies gain by having consumer information which can be evaluated for cross-country comparability as well as on an individual country basis?

Only with information which is genuinely comparable is it possible to:

- identify the relative size of business opportunities;
- assess the extent and nature of similarities between countries;
- understand the extent and nature of differences between countries;
- establish inter-country investment and marketing priorities;
- evaluate brand image and performance across countries on a consistent basis;
- develop international response to strategic questions (whether about brand positioning or advertising direction).

Comparability of information should in fact be welcomed not only by the globalists but also by the anti-globalists. If markets have latent similarities, comparable research should reveal them; but if markets really are different, there is no better way to demonstrate the fact than by revealing the differences in a comparable context.

So if we accept that comparability is generally reckoned to be 'a good thing' in international marketing circles, how do we go about achieving it? This question has no simple answer, and at the very least involves great difficulty and great cost – which sometimes makes you wonder, is it worth it? (One is reminded of the wisdom of a senior marketing man who said, 'You should never embark on a piece of market research if it is cheaper to make a mistake.')

But let us assume that some mistakes, especially in international marketing and advertising, can be prohibitively expensive to make, and that data comparability is judged to be of value.

15.10 Achieving comparability

15.10.1 Meaning of comparability

Comparability means finding differences and similarities between countries which are genuine, and not the result of differences in research techniques or interpretation.

Comparability rarely means the simultaneous application of the same sampling and questionnaire techniques in a number of countries, with the emergence weeks or months later of a neat set of tables with the countries at the top and a standard list of attributes down the side. Nor should it mean trying to iron out the nasty little differences between countries such as differences in language or social class divisions so as to achieve a perfect uniformity of data collection. If we could only get all respondents to speak English, or even Esperanto if only all countries had the same social and economic structure if only the sun would shine for exactly the same number of hours everywhere, all our problems would disappear.

To ignore these differences in the interests of spurious comparability is a cardinal sin – because it effectively takes a technique rather than a problem-oriented view of research and its application. Certain research requirements can arguably be tackled by using the same sample design and questionnaire in all countries, but frequently the imposition of a rigid research structure on a number of different countries may defeat the very objectives that the research is trying to achieve.

To achieve genuine comparability in international market research at the key stages of data collection and interpretation, two different principles must be kept in mind: the principles of **coordination** and **flexibility**.

15.10.2 Coordination

Coordination should mean not a rigid, unresponsive approach to all research matters, but rather a centralisation by one or other of the researchers involved of certain key functions, namely **planning**, **control** and **interpretation**.

International research projects can very easily founder through lack of a central coordinating function. If this function is not addressed, there is a very real danger of failing to maintain control and comparability through the planning and execution of a project, and ultimately failing to fulfil the client's original brief.

The best way to avoid these potential problems is to set up, for every project, one individual, or one small team, to take responsibility for the central management functions for the whole exercise. With this approach the original requirements of the research are far more likely to be kept in view than by handing on and spreading out responsibilities across disparate individuals and countries.

Similarly, any issues and problems which arise in the course of the project are known and dealt with by the coordinator, and not overlooked or ignored simply because they seemed unimportant to the local researchers involved.

Coordination not only ensures good control and direction of a project, it generally entails considerable economies of scale in both the planning and execution of international research when compared with a more loosely controlled approach on a country-by-country basis. A coordinated approach usually involves preparing only one major set of briefing documents, questionnaires, etc. rather than one set for each country. Processing and analysis of data, whether qualitative or quantitative, can also be more cost efficient when coordinated in one place by one small team of researchers, not to mention the greater comparability of interpretation which can also be achieved in this way.

15.10.3 Flexibility

Over-zealous coordination can sometimes lead to a lack of flexibility in international research. Despite the need for comparable information, markets are simply not the same. The principle of flexibility should therefore provide the counterpoint to the principle of coordination. It should involve paying close attention to local differences, and may well require the use of different techniques in the interests of achieving comparable results.

It is important to adopt a creative, pragmatic outlook in designing, conducting and interpreting international research, not to impose a Procrustean bed of standardised research techniques but to find out and decide on the best approach on a country-by-country basis.

In this context, it is always a good idea to seek the advice of local researchers before making commitments concerning objectives and plans. To achieve this, consultation of local research agencies should be made an integral part of the planning of the project.

Any silly ideas or misconceptions that may have arisen through lack of local knowledge will then get shot down in flames, and an improved, more soundly-based plan will finally get hammered out with the approval and support of all parties. This process also encourages the emergence of good ideas which can be used on the project from a wide range of researchers, not just those making up the central coordinating team.

In summary, careful application of the two principles of coordination and flexibility will go a long way towards achieving comparability, at both the data-collection stage and the interpretation stage. At the practical level, there is a need for both coordination and flexibility at all stages of research: planning, fieldwork, analysis and reporting.

15.11 Planning

15.11.1 Sensitivity to all the issues

Good planning is half the secret in international research, and it does help to have time to sort out the various requirements and constraints. The keynote is consultation, but the list below details the various ramifications, both large and small:

- obtain all relevant needs and viewpoints from research users;
- obtain agreement on research objectives and methods;
- obtain views and use experience of local colleagues/research agencies;
- clarify lines of communication, authority and reporting;
- ensure comparability of approach/methods/techniques;
- take care over all translation work involved;
- check out timetables and logistics with all concerned;
- check out costing (what is/is not included, exchange rate issues).

It is at the planning stage where local differences should be carefully considered. See Case study 15.1. Key areas of possible difference to check on should be:

- differences in actual and potential target groups;
- differences in ways in which products or services are used;
- differences in criteria for assessing products or services;
- differences in marketing conditions;

- differences in economic and social conditions;
- differences in cultural values;

and

- differences in market research facilities;
- differences in market research styles.

CASE STUDY 15.1

Product differences: beer – a hard or a soft drink?

In the UK, Germany and Scandinavia, beer is generally regarded as an alcoholic beverage and the factors underlying its consumption are similar to those underlying the consumption of other alcoholic beverages. In Greece, Spain or Italy beer is regarded as much more like a soft drink, such as Coca-Cola or orangeade. A survey designed to aid a beer manufacturer in the determination of their marketing strategy in Europe had to be designed to obtain information on behaviour and attitudes in relation to soft drinks in some countries and to alcoholic beverages in others. However, quite apart from the expense involved, there would be little point in obtaining information about both soft drinks and alcoholic beverages in all countries covered by the survey. Orangeade just does not compete with beer when it comes to a drinking session in an English pub, and very few Spaniards would consider beer as a serious alternative to whisky.

There are numerous examples of how the design of a multi-country survey can be affected by differences in attitude or behaviour patterns between one country and another. A German housewife, for instance, asked about her use of bar chocolate for cooking or in sandwiches would – to say the least – be somewhat surprised. However, in France cooking is an important use for bar chocolate, and in France and Italy it is quite common for children to be given a bar of chocolate between two slices of bread to eat during the school break.

Moreover, the criteria by which products are judged may differ considerably from one country to another. There is little point in asking about the suitability of a food product for snacks in Italy, particularly the south, since most Italians just do not eat between meals, but in northern Italy shorter lunch breaks are making inroads and just over the border in Austrian in many of the briefcases one sees carried around are bulging with an assortment of sandwiches, sausages, apfelstrudel and other delicacies.

Talking to whisk(e)y consumers means approaching older more sophisticated drinkers in northern Europe where the product is savoured in smaller intimate groups. In Thailand, on the other hand, the same brand will be drunk in a large social group with a bottle on the table in a club until it is finished. Researching this brand requires understanding of these different social contexts.

These examples indicate that it is possible to achieve genuine comparability in international market research if sufficient attention is paid to national differences at the early stages of planning and design.

15.11.2 Language and translation issues

Have you heard the story about the translator who was asked to render the phrase 'out of sight, out of mind' into Mandarin Chinese? When his version was back-translated, it came out as 'invisible, insane'! The dictionary defines 'translation' as: 'to turn from one language to another, preserving the meaning of the original', but sadly there are a good many cases in international research, not to mention marketing and advertising, where inanities of this kind occur.

International research involves a great deal of translating and translation-checking, from multi-language questionnaires and briefing documents through to reading or listening to foreign language group discussions and depth interviews, checking of concept material and delivering debriefs or reports in languages other than English. Even where English words are now used in foreign language advertising there are still differences in what that English word can actually mean.

Carrying out such translation work well is critical to the good conduct of international research. It is not just a question of sending things off to the nearest translation agency – the translator there will not have been party to the research objectives nor the development of the material, and cannot be expected to understand the cultural communication and research issues involved. This is one of the reasons why strong linguistic abilities are vital in international research.

Simply having good linguists in-house does not amount to an adequate system in itself. The ideal approach is to ask a 'native' speaker – usually someone working in the local supplier company – to make the first draft of translation. That person is selected to be familiar with research terminology – in both languages – and should be fully briefed on the background, the issues and any subtleties that must be respected or given careful attention. His or her translation is then back-translated by a member of the central project team, who is also familiar with those same issues.

In this way, any divergence from the original English version can be identified and further checked, corrected and resolved (see Case study 15.2). If necessary or requested, local staff of the client's organisation can also be asked to check on the appropriateness of the translation – particularly helpful when the subject matter is technical or a bit out of the ordinary run of normal vocabulary. It is not safe to rest easy until the final version of the document has been prepared and given a last once-over.

CASE STUDY 15.2

Preservatives or condoms?

In a recent study a client was planning the launch of a new soft drink brand in Europe – building on a very successful experience in the USA. The first stage of research concentrated on how to position the brand in Europe and various concepts were being considered. One key feature of the soft drink was that it was a natural product with no artificial preservatives. Preparing this for the Italian market, the agency in the UK had contracted a translator who had produced a literal rendition of 'no preservatives' in Italian. The Italian-speaking researcher reviewing the material prior to the research quickly spotted the obvious mistake – 'senza preservativi' actually means 'without condoms', probably not that meaningful or attractive positioning for a soft drinks consumer. In that instance, the researcher was able to avert a problem, however amusing.

And how about this for a cautionary tale – one from the annals of Guinness, thankfully years ago. A new Guinness TV ad had been prepared for use in a country in West Africa. The lingua franca was a language little known outside those parts, but the local ad agency there undertook to handle the translation and recording of the voice-over. No one at head office was able to check this local version, but it sounded great, with the word Guinness being mentioned recognisably in apparently appropriate places. Now it just so happened that someone was passing through head office at the time who did understand the local language – and apparently the back-translation showed that the text extolled the virtues, not only of Guinness, but also of a certain 'Ali's bazaar' in the local capital! Full marks for West African business enterprise, near-miss of egg on face for Guinness.

The moral is, as with most things in international research, not to take anything for granted; to check and back-check until you're quite sure of every last phrase and the Tower of Babel has been well and truly dismantled.

15.12 Fieldwork

15.12.1 Ground rules

Don't think of fieldwork as the time you can take a breather while you wait for the data to roll in. There are too many dangers – and too many opportunities – at this stage to be ignored (see Case study 15.3). Key aspects to watch out for are:

- Consider the value of piloting for quantitative work, and the roll-out or lead-country approach for qualitative.
- Specify clearly what is expected from local research agencies:
  - method agreed
  - form of data required
  - when and how delivered
  - involvement re analysis/reporting.
- Take opportunities to experience fieldwork at first-hand.
- Monitor progress and any problems.
- Keep copies of all data which is to be posted/couriered.

CASE STUDY 15.3

The fragrant Italians

A fragrance manufacturer wished to understand what types of fragrance were preferred by men in various European countries. Group discussions were undertaken in order to explore attitudes and perceptions in depth.

The researcher sent out to Italy from the central team experienced some dissonance in her observations. Although the Italian respondents waxed lyrical about their preference for subtle, delicate fragrances, her nose (she was sitting in the group discussion room) gave her strong contrary evidence – so much so that she almost passed out from the overpowering fragrances they were actually wearing.

Had she listened to tapes or read transcripts only, her conclusions would have been very different – hence the value of 'being there'.

15.13 Issues in qualitative research

How can comparability of data be applied to the unstructured nature of qualitative research? Differences in cultures and temperaments are obvious, even looking beyond the traditional stereotypical view of national characteristics, so that a group discussion in Paris or Madrid may give the appearance of no more than a mass of flailing arms to a Japanese moderator who is accustomed to the reserve and restraint of his or her typical respondents.

Often, these differences are more complex still than they appear on the surface. Even in markets where consumers are seemingly laying their innermost thoughts out on the table for all to view, such as in southern Europe their responses cannot necessarily be taken at face value. They may appear more animated and more candid, but deeper motivations often still remain hidden. Straightforward, direct questioning will freely reveal answers at rational or cognitive, and even to some extent emotional levels, yet can fail to uncover important issues relating to deeper motivations of which consumers may not themselves be fully conscious or which they may prefer not to reveal. At the other extreme, the more reserved natures of, say, the northern Europeans or south-east Asian consumers can mean that self-expression is more restrained, and the problem of social constraints and etiquette can elicit misleading response. These extremes of behavioural patterns also demand a means of accessing the more covert and emotional motivations at work in consumer habits and reaching beyond the inhibitions and social barriers.

Projective techniques are vital tools to the international researcher in helping to overcome these problems in that they offer a standardised, comparable means of reaching beneath surfaces which may be diverse and multifaceted. Different though these cultures may be, all respond well to the probing of the inner, unconscious world of the consumer which is achieved via projective techniques. The insight which this offers is often key to identifying a powerful motivation which lies hidden beneath apparent rational differences on the surface.

In the simplest of terms, projective techniques are games: games which reach beyond defences and social constraints, which give consumers the verbal and visual 'vocabulary' to help them access their deeper feelings and which create an environment in which they can express thoughts and feelings which they would not necessarily regard as part of their conscious views, or which at least give them 'permission' to express their views in a less direct way. A group of very smart, very rational German businessmen can often be transformed into a classroom of playful schoolboys when their imagination and creativity is unleashed via projective tasks such as collage-making or drawing. Examples of projective techniques are outlined in Chapter 14, Box 14.4.

Not all projective techniques are suitable for multi-country research. Clearly, it is preferable in centrally coordinated research that the techniques used should be of a central design, so that all moderators are working with the same set of tools. They need to be easy to administer and should require little or no adaptation to individual markets in order to ensure comparability. Techniques which 'travel' best are:

- **Brand mapping**, where respondents are presented with a variety of competitive brands and asked to group them into categories; a useful technique to understand how consumers view the market, to identify gaps, or to understand the positioning of a particular brand.

- **Word association**, a widely familiar technique presenting few problems applied internationally. Word association is useful in discovering brand imagery, product attributes and consumer vocabulary. It is quick and easy to administer on either a group or individual basis.

- **Personification**, a verbal technique with which most moderators are familiar. Respondents are asked to imagine brands as people and describe their appearance, personality, lifestyle, and so on. There are few problems in administering this technique (provided the group is suitably relaxed) but care has to be taken in interpretation. It is important, for example, to be aware of aspirational or non-aspirational descriptors which may differ from country to country. Driving a Golf GTI may denote a yuppie in the UK but a fairly ordinary chap in Germany; holidaying at Club Med may say something pretty good about a brand in the UK, but denote a rather more downmarket image in France.

- **Bubble drawings**, a technique whereby the respondent supplies the thoughts and feelings of an individual shown in a roughly drawn situation. Care must be taken internationally to ensure that the situation depicted is relevant. For example, a typical shopfront might differ from country to country or a drinking scenario would have to be shown as a pub in the UK but a bar elsewhere. In practice, however, these problems do not often arise since the drawings are very simple and adaptable.

- **Collages**, visual material in the form of picture boards made from scrap art. This kind of material works particularly well in multi-country research because (i) it provides a common body of projective stimuli, thereby producing comparable data for analysis, and (ii) it allows quick access to underlying thoughts and feelings since it provides respondents with a ready-made set of symbols and images to talk around and (iii) it bypasses translation problems.

Picture boards are particularly valuable in exploring user imagery and brand imagery. Each board shows a broad range of, say, people, lifestyles, occupations, environments, objects, usage occasions, or whatever is appropriate, which respondents can use to explain their feelings about a brand – why this kind of woman might be attracted to it, why this one would not, and so on. This gives us a great deal more depth, and furthermore will reveal common symbols or typologies across countries.

In designing picture boards for multi-country work, care must be taken to ensure that the final mix of images has sufficient relevance to all the countries concerned. There are many cases, even within Europe, where a particular symbol has different meanings, or the same value is represented in different ways.

Housing is an obvious problem area: house styles and their relative values differ greatly from country to country and it is usually necessary to produce specific country boards rather than one common board. Food is another area where thought must be given to ensure that relevant symbols are used: basic, everyday fare might need to be shown as meat-and-two-veg in the UK but as a plate of pasta in Italy and a dish of raw fish in Japan.

With careful advance planning, the incorporation of these kinds of projective materials and techniques into multi-country studies is easily achieved, and will give greater depth to the data without compromising comparability or control – surely a worthwhile benefit.

In the case of qualitative research projects involving group discussions, there appears to be some divergence of opinion on the relative merits of using local moderators versus moderators from the central team.

Arguably it is not a good idea for members of the central team, however fluent in the relevant languages, to conduct groups in other countries: unless they live as regular natives of the countries concerned they cannot hope to be tuned in to the latest issues, slang, TV programmes, etc. to the degree one would consider desirable. It does however help immensely in carrying through international projects involving group discussions for members of the central team who speak the relevant languages to brief the local moderators and attend the groups personally, guide and intervene if necessary, and to debrief the local moderator personally to ensure optimal fulfilment of the information brief.

15.14 Issues in quantitative research

Managing quantitative fieldwork internationally calls for much the same disciplines as for single-country projects. Careful briefing (whether in person or by phone/fax/e-mail) and close monitoring are even more important given the higher risks of misunderstanding and unforeseen circumstances.

Even the seemingly mechanical task of quantitative questionnaire coding requires extra care in international projects. Despite its unpromulgated role in the data-processing operation coding represents an important stage which demands meticulous attention to detail if it is to produce a valid and serviceable foundation to the research findings.

An international code frame clearly plays a vital role in establishing the basis for comparability and for highlighting country differences. Its significance should be acknowledged by assigning one or more multilingual research executives, forming part of the core team, to construct the frame, working from verbatim originals from each country. This approach is infinitely better than creating separate code-frames for each country: the latter will be maddeningly non-comparable and can serve only to reveal differences, not similarities.

A centrally formulated code frame takes full account of the survey objectives. At the same time, it accords equal weight to each country's responses whilst providing the flexibility needed for the range of emerging answers.

A piece of advertising researched quantitatively across Europe provides us with a simplistic example of the value of this. The ad in question elicited identical responses to one particular question from a large proportion of both French and German respondents. It was perceived by both to contain an abundance of information. However, to the rational German respondent, swayed by concrete facts and detail, this was a positive feature. To the Frenchman, whose responses are governed more frequently by emotions and influenced by more abstract forces, this was a positive turnoff! In this case therefore, two separate codes needed to be created.

15.15 Analysis, interpretation and reporting

15.15.1 A synthesised approach

All international research clients want to be able to compare findings from one market to another, and most also want a synthesis of findings in order to understand the broad patterns pertaining across markets as well as within them. It can be strongly argued (see Case study 15.4) that it is not possible to achieve a well-balanced or meaningful synthesis of findings if analysis is carried out separately in different countries by different researchers, however good those researchers may be as individuals.

CASE STUDY 15.4

The Freudian fur coat

A manufacturer of fur coats wished to understand women's motivations for purchase and ownership. It was felt that the subject required the involvement of the best qualitative researchers to be found in each country, and an identical brief was accordingly given to 12 separate chosen individuals, one based in each of the relevant countries.

When the 12 reports finally came in, the client found that most women, across all the countries in the study, seemed motivated primarily by factors involving status and fashion. However, it seemed that women in France were very different, since their main motives were to do with the Freudian, sexual connotations of fur.

The client was left wondering where the real difference lay – were the women of France so very different from their European counterparts or was it the French researcher who had the difference in outlook?

It is more appropriate to have the data analysis carried out by a central team of linguistic researchers using a common approach and framework for the task. In this way, comparisons between countries can be more closely weighed and evaluated, and similarities and differences can be seen in their full context. This is not to say that you should not ask local suppliers for their views and help in interpretation. Far from it. But in international research the whole makes up more than the sum of its parts and clients' requirements are best met by offering a fully integrated picture of findings from all markets rather than a disaggregated (and often non-comparable) series of local reports.

15.15.2 Harmonisation of data: summary of requirements

To summarise the needs at the stage of analysis and interpretation the international researcher should:

1. **Allow sufficient time for the process.** The author is only too aware of the time pressures inherent in international marketing programmes. But time must be scheduled carefully for fieldwork, analysis and reporting, taking account of the labyrinth of national holidays and organisational constraints.

2. **Insist on comparable approaches.** There will always be plenty of reasons why it is more appropriate/easier/cheaper/faster to have the research handled separately in each country. But the full value of international research projects cannot be realised unless comparability is achieved. Only then is it possible to discern the true nature and extent of similarities and differences across countries, and avoid bias to one country.

3. **Insist on a proper synthesis of findings**. Good international research does not consist only of a set of single-country reports, even if the research has been conducted on a comparable basis. Someone – ideally the coordinating research supplier – should prepare the data and reports in such a way that a valid picture of the whole is achieved rather than just the sum of its parts.

As a final, but vital element in the process, consider the best ways to approach presentation and reporting:

1. **Break the language barrier**. There is nothing more futile than a research presentation or report which cannot be understood by its potential users for reasons of language mismatch. There are several ways to tear down this particular wall: choose research suppliers who have good linguistic abilities, both spoken and written; arrange for translators for team members who would otherwise be cut off from the communication process; encourage presenters to be as clear as possible in their visual and verbal expression.

2. **Plan for relevant and creative reporting**. Depending on user needs, it should be decided in advance what kind of reporting is needed. Presentations and/or written reports? Separate country reports as well as overviews? Full teams at presentations or central and local groups separately? (There is no ideal in this respect – approaches need to be tailored to specific organisational and project requirements.) Plan for discussion time at presentations, and encourage research suppliers to make their presentations stimulating.

3. **Use the research process to achieve motivation and good teamwork**. When set against the typical background of cultural barriers, international research projects offer a significant opportunity to motivate the disparate groups involved. The discipline of planning, the experience of fieldwork and the sharing of information all bring the team together in a constructive and creative environment.

15.16 Conclusion

The world is now a very small place in terms of brands and marketing. Marketing and media companies need in-depth understanding of both the similarities and differences among countries if they are to develop their products and services successfully in an international world. Moreover, they need strong insights into the different consumers around the world if their messages and communication are to be as effectively constructed and targeted as possible in a very competitive climate.

International research, when it is conducted with professionalism and credibility, can make an important contribution to the process of international marketing by providing objective, comparable and constructive market information, and by helping clients to interpret and use it well.

REFERENCES AND FURTHER READING

Agnelli, U. (1990), 'Guidelines for the manager of the 1990s', *The International Management Development Review*, vol. 6, p. 59.

Barry, B. (1997), AQRP 1997 Trends Conference.

Building Successful Brands: The need for an integrated approach. ESOMAR conference, Prague, 26–9 October 1994 – various papers in particular sections – 'The perspective for brands', pp. 1–23; 'Organising for integration' pp. 265–93.

Burgaud, P.J. (1986), 'The research at the service of decision-making in collective build-up of the enterprise's project', 39th ESOMAR Congress 1986, pp. 599–619.

Hofstede, G. (1991), *Cultures and Organisations – Software of the Mind*, McGraw Hill.

Journal of the Market Research Society, vol. 39, January 1997, '50th anniversary of the Market Research Society: milestones in market research'.

Journal of the Market Research Society, vol. 41, no.1, January 1999, 'Qualitative Research for the 21st Century', Peter Cooper, guest ed.

Laborie, Jean-Louis (1989), 'What 1992 means for market research', Market Research Society Annual Conference, Brighton 1989.

Lachmann, U. (1988), '7, 8, 9 out! Could this be the future of market research in companies?', 41st ESOMAR Congress 1988, pp. 811–22.

Levitt, T. (1983), 'The Globalisation of Markets', *Harvard Business Review*, May/June.

Naeve, D. (1986), 'Integrating multi-country research into marketing strategy decisions – a case history', 39th ESOMAR Congress 1986, pp. 621–36.

Pawle, J. (1999), 'Mining the international consumer', *Journal of the Market Research Society*, vol. 41, no.1, January.

Potsch, L.E. and Limeira, T.M. (1986), 'The implications of the strategic-organisational dynamics of companies for the patterns of action of market research agencies', 39th ESOMAR Congress 1986, pp. 559–75.

Riley, N. and Leith, A. (1998) 'Understanding Need.States and their role in developing successful marketing strategies', *Journal of the Market Research Society*, vol. 40, no.1.

QUESTIONS

1. Discuss the importance of having comparability of techniques and interpretation in marketing research across national boundaries.
2. Why is 'recognisability' of the brands by consumers an important consideration in the standardisation of advertising messages? What aspects should marketing researchers be on the lookout for in the translation of advertising messages?
3. Discuss the impact of the technological changes that have facilitated the

growth of international marketing research.

4. Look for three examples of companies conducting businesses in globalising industries. For each of the companies take one of their well-known brands. Assess the appeals of the brands from a consumer viewpoint and discuss how the companies concerned have taken account of the views of consumers in the advertising of these brands.

Appendix 1
Access to secondary sources

Electronic desk research

This is increasingly via the Internet and on-line World Wide Web sources which are free or by subscription.

For example:

- Advertising Association (http://adassoc.org.uk/inform)
- ESOMAR (http://www.esomar.nl/esomar).

In the modern computerised world it is normal for desk researchers to use desktop or portable computers to gain access to secondary data. This was encouraged in the past by the proliferation of host bureaux, such as Prestel, Infoline, Data-Star, Dialogue and Textline, which made it possible for the researcher to consult a range of data sources through one supplier.

The information filed may be numeric, bibliographic or both:

- British Telcom's Prestel service is a file of some 200,000 pages of information on subjects ranging from accounts of companies to statistics on zinc production. Prestel is a numeric service.

- Pergamon Press's Infoline is a bibliographic service hosting abstracts of articles published in Dunn and Bradstreet, *Who Owns Whom* and Jordans on subjects such as chemical engineering, electronics, marketing.

- Data-Star hosts both numeric and bibliographic information.

- Textline from Finsbury Data Services abstracts articles from 80 British and European newspapers, plus journals such as *Marketing* and *Marketing Week*.

Many university libraries have on-line public access catalogue (OPAC) systems available at terminals in their libraries and via their campus networks. The outline OPAC system makes it easy to search for references to books and other library materials. The system features an action bar at the top of the screen, function key prompts at the foot, pull down menus and a series of window-like screens which overlap each other so that the information searched for on 'authors' and 'title(s)' appear on one screen.

Government statistical service

Government departments generate a wealth of statistical data critical to strategic planning. The Central Statistical Office databank offers 'regularly updated macro-economic and related statistical data in computer-readable form'. The data is available 'to host bureaux for incorporation in their client services' as well as to end-users.

Of particular interest to market researchers are the following:

- Statistics and Market Intelligence Library at the Department of Trade and Industry, 1 Victoria Street, London SW1H 0ET. Provides up-to-date and comprehensive trade statistics for all countries, and general statistical publications from all over the world.

- Office for National Statistics Reference Library at 1 Drummond Gate, London SW1Z 2QQ.

- Business Statistics Office, Cardiff Road, Newport, Gwent NPT 1XG.

There are numerous government publications, such as:

- *Annual Abstract of Statistics*
- *Business Monitor Surveys*
- *Census of Production, Census of Population*
- *Department of Employment Gazette*
- *Economic Trends, Financial Statistics*
- *Family Expenditure Surveys, General Household Survey*
- *Material Income and Expenditure Surveys*
- *Monthly Digest of Statistics, Regional Trends, Social Trends*
- *British Business and Monopolies Commission Reports*.

These are obtainable from HMSO bookstores. Further information on these publications is obtainable from the following:

- Central Statistical Office Press and Information Office, Room 65C/3, Great George Street, London SW1P 3AQ. (The CSO publishes *Government Statistics, A Brief Guide to Sources*, free of charge.

- Department of Trade and Industry, Ashdown House, 123 Victoria Street, London SW1E 6SW.

Also useful are the DTI's European Community Information; the DTI's Export Marketing Information Centre; the DTI's Business in Europe (for contacts and information on the single European market); the DTI's Export Intelligence at Prelink Ltd, Export House, 87a Wembley Hill Road, Wembley, Middlesex HA9 8BU. For expert help and publications, contact the nearest DTI regional office or DTI Export Publications, PO Box 55, Stratford-upon-Avon, Warwickshire CV37 9GE.

Other sources

- Association of British Chambers of Commerce (ABCC), 9 Tufton Street, London SW1P 3QB.
- British Standards Institute (BSI), Linford Way, Milton Keynes, Bucks.
- International Chamber of Commerce (ICC), 14–15 Belgrave Square, London SW1X 8PS.

- Office of the Data Protection Registrar, Springfield House, Water Lane, Wilmslow, Cheshire SK9 5AX.
- Independent Television Commission (ITC), 70 Brompton Road, London SW1.

Banks

The commercial banks, e.g. National Westminster, Barclays, HSBC and Lloyds TSB provide services through their international divisions for exporters or those wishing to research overseas markets. Guidelines and information for exporters vary between the banks.

Sources of marketing data

The 1999 *MRS Yearbook* and the *MRS Magazine* contain sources of marketing data including demographics and basic statistics, classification and lifestyle, products and services, retail trade trends, media and industry statistics, etc. See Appendix 4.

Shared-cost services and databanks feature in the *Yearbook*. Research suppliers, i.e. organisations and individuals in the UK, Republic of Ireland and overseas providing marketing research services are set out in the Glossary.

See also the Glossary of Abbreviations in the present book for the names of associations which have their own publications.

Appendix 2
The principles of analysis

John Bound

What is data analysis?

When quantitative data has been collected by marketing research methods, the data has to be analysed to turn it into information which will help in making marketing decisions. The data, which may be recorded on paper forms or in a computer file, has to be summarised so that its meaning may be understood. This is analysis.

This appendix treats both principles, which remain unchanged, and practice, which is changing rapidly. All sorts of analysis procedures may be carried out readily by a computer, and there are at the time of writing 200 program packages available in the UK for doing different parts or sorts of these tasks, using big or little computers.

The task of analysis needs a knowledge of techniques as well. For anyone who has not met the problem before, it is daunting to be confronted with a computer file containing already captured data or even a large pile of paper questionnaires. Marketers and planners are not usually called upon to do this, but may well be expected to analyse data sets set up ready for analysis by a particular interactive program. This is easy enough providing the user knows what is wanted. Even if a specialist analyst is employed, a knowledge of the possibilities of analysis is still necessary.

Our field here is an enquiry set up to answer a particular problem, or the ad hoc enquiry, as it is often called. More complicated enquiries, such as repeated enquiries over a period, can be reduced to the same principles.

What analysis is trying to do

The purpose of statistical analysis is to find patterns in data, and show them clearly in comparison with any previous expectations. There are thus two parts: the first is finding the patterns, and the second is seeing how well they fit any expectations. If certain patterns have been found before, then the easiest thing to do is straight away to see whether the new data is the same. To take a simple marketing research example: if it has previously been found that big dogs eat more of a test product than do small dogs, then we look to see if the same is true, and to what extent. To say whether any patterns we find are of practical interest we need to bring in other knowledge about the market: no automatic statistical test can do this.

The basic tool for statistical analysis is the table with rows and columns of figures. The table of this kind is one of mankind's great discoveries, enabling patterns to be readily seen and compared. Yet when a pattern is complex, involving many factors, it becomes hard to find it or to summarise it by tables. Then multivariate statistical methods may be used. These produce approximately correct mathematical or pictorial descriptions of complex data in terms of just a few factors. These methods also produce measures of how well the description works. Some of these procedures are mentioned below. The idea is simple: we replace a complicated explanation with a simpler one which is roughly correct, just as giving an average might make a statement which was more or less true about a lot of people, but perhaps not exactly correct about any one of them.

Techniques

General

There are some well-established routines for survey analysis. The main approach is the use of tabulations of various kinds, that is, counting the number of answers in various categories averaging any answers which are in the form of numbers, and then putting the resulting counts and averages into tables.

The usual path is to start with one-way, then to go on to two-way tables, and after that to many-way tables. After this the use of multivariate techniques may be considered. All these terms will be defined shortly. How far along this route to go depends on the objectives, the simplicity of the patterns revealed, and the amount of data.

When conclusions have been reached, suitably designed tables can then enable other people to understand both the conclusions and the way they have been derived. The tables for this are different from those we use in the initial search for patterns.

One–way tables

The first step is to produce these. A one-way table is a simple table which for a particular question or observation gives the number and percentage of the different answers. A set of these for all questions is sometimes called a 'code-book' or 'top-line results'. Table A2.1 is an example of how this may look for a single question. The figures in brackets are the percentages of respondents giving each answer.

Table A2.1 Q 21: Preference for new product

Base: all respondents	460 (100)
Prefer new	269 (58)
Prefer old	175 (38)
Don't know/ No preference	16 (3)

The heading refers to the question number and topic of the question on which the table is based. The base is the description and number of the respondents on which the table is based. Percentages to whole numbers are usual.

These results for all questions are often produced compactly by the computer in the form of a 'whole-count'; or 'hole-count', which is just what it was in the days of punched cards. Such a tabulation is a summary table showing the codes representing the possible answers across the top, and the questions down the side. The entries are then the number of times each answer code occurs for any question, handily with percentages. Some questions in the table may have multiple responses, so there is usually a 'Total responses' column. Another useful way to present these answers is to write in the percentages for each question onto a blank questionnaire, and some programs do this automatically.

For some enquiries these one-way figures give key results. In our example of a product test comparing two products, the key result might be the percentage preferring each, as shown in Table A2.1.

Two-way tables

Such one-way tables are seldom enough. The results need to be shown separately for sub-groups of the sample in the form of two-way tables.

Even in the product-test example above, we would clearly want to know what sort of people preferred each product, and would have collected data about this too. So we take our one-way table of 'Product preferred', and add two other columns, one headed perhaps 'Users of A', and the other 'Users of B'. So now we have a rectangular or two-way table that looks like Table A2.2.

Table A2.2 Q.21: Preference for test product according to usual brand

	Total	Use brand A	Use brand B
Base: All respondents	460 (100)	224 (100)	236 (100)
Prefer new	249 (54)	144 (64)	105 (44)
Prefer old	195 (42)	73 (33)	122 (52)
Don't know /no preference	16 (3)	7 (3)	9 (4)

These sub-group figures give a very different aspect to the figures for the total sample and a marketing decision is called for to decide whether the existing users of the brand or the users of a competitive brand are the more important in choosing the new formula. Quite a few existing users show little preference, so we shall want to look at the results for people who feel strongly, if we have thought to ask about this.

We conventionally show as 'base' a description of whatever group the table is based upon, and the sample size for this total and each sub-group.

In the body of the table we show both the numbers of responses and their percentage of the total sample size. Owing to rounding, the percentages do not always add tidily to 100. This happens in the 'Total' column of Table A2.2. People are used to this nowadays, and so it may be disregarded.

Sometimes we show the average of numerical answers, and perhaps the standard deviation or a standard error measuring the sampling precision, as well. The various sub-groups we put across the page, and the possible answers down the side. The typical survey computer printout, setting out side-by-side several sub-groupings or analysis breaks looks like Table A2.3 – useful for study, but not for communication results. In this example the number of people giving each response to a question asking them to rate something on a scale is given. Here the percentages have been shown with a percentage sign rather than in brackets. This is a matter of taste: numerous % signs on the whole look more untidy than brackets. The numerical score allotted to each response is shown in brackets next to it, and the mean or average of these scores is shown below.

However, the two-way table is only part of the story. We may well need more complex many-way tables.

Table A2.3 Q21: Test product preferred

| | | Total | Area | | | Age | | | Sex | |
			North	South	25 or under	26–40	Over 40	Male	Female
Total		72 100%	35 100%	37 100%	16 100%	9 100%	47 100%	36 100%	36 100%
Agree strongly	(5)	0 –	0 –	0 –	0 –	0 –	0 –	0 –	0 –
Agree	(4)	2 3%	2 6%	0 –	0 –	0 –	2 4%	0 –	2 6%
Neither	(3)	6 8%	0 –	6 16%	1 6%	1 11%	4 9%	4 11%	2 6%
Disagree	(2)	21 29%	13 37%	8 22%	7 44%	2 22%	12 26%	11 31%	10 28%
Disagree strongly	(1)	43 60%	20 57%	23 62%	8 50%	6 67%	29 62%	21 58%	22 61%
No answer		0	0	0	0	0	0	0	0
Mean score		1.54	1.54	1.54	1.56	1.44	1.55	1.53	1.56

Many-way tables

These tables come in sets. Each table is based upon only part of the sample. They are needed to see the patterns when there is interaction between analysis breaks.

Interaction arises if different parts of the sample, such as people in the town and in the country give different patterns of answers to a question. We then need a set of tables, one table for the town, and one for the country. From them we might perhaps see that people in the country with large families have different opinions from people in the country with small families, whereas in the town there is no difference between opinions according to size of families. Similarly, in the example, Table A2.3, the way in which preferences vary between users of brands is shown as different for people with strong preferences.

Such sets form a three-way, or three-dimensional table, but since paper has only two dimensions for printing, we have to make a set of tables. The third variable is sometimes called a filter variable. The number of tables in all the different possible sets escalates. In our example of a 20-question survey, there are 380 possible two-way tables, and 6,840 three-way sets. The problem of selection is obvious. But even this is not the end: the answers people give may vary in our example not only between town and country, but also this variation may itself be different in various parts of Britain.

So we need a four-way table, and even more multi-way tables as we find more complicated patterns. We may also derive new variables. For example, we might count the number of questions for which each respondent said 'don't know', and use this as a measure of involvement with the topic. This would enable yet more tables to be formed.

There are three things which stop this process going on indefinitely. The first is that we are willing to accept a simple explanation that fits roughly, but which everybody can understand. An exact but complicated explanation might well fit only data collected in exactly the same circumstances. We would like to think our answers had a chance of applying more widely, and the simple explanation may have a better chance of this.

The second reason is that the usefulness in marketing of complicated answers is limited. You usually just cannot sell a different product in each part of the country, or to people in the town against people in the country. If you can, then such knowledge may be useful.

The third reason is that we run out of sample size for the bases of the many-way tables. There may be only a handful or even none at all in some of the tables for sub-sub-groups of even the biggest sample survey. That is why the government conducts a Population Census of all the 60 million people in Britain: the results need to be broken down in great detail. In practice three-way tables are often as far as we go.

So there are a great many tables that can be produced, and we need a way to choose which to look at.

The selection of tables

For two-way tables we have to decide only the column headings. The side-headings for each line are the possible answers, or groupings of them. For many-way tables we have also to decide the filter or controlling variable for each value of which a separate table is to be produced.

Consider first two-way tables. The headings for the columns are sometimes called 'analysis breaks', 'independent variables' or 'predictor variables'. They may or may not vary from question to question: often a block of questions on the same topic will have the same breaks, and important predictor variables like age may be used for every question. A crude technique is to use the same group of analysis breaks for every question.

There are two ways of deciding which column headings to use. The better is to know already from other research or experience what sort of sub-groups are likely to vary. Age, sex and social class are most commonly found to make a difference between sub-groups. If you know the age, sex and social class of someone in Britain it is generally true that you can say much about what they buy, read and think. The advantage of this method is that if differences are not shown in the particular enquiry, that is a matter for comment. There is a snag: the possible predictor groupings may not be known, or some predictors may not have been discovered.

This leads to the second method, which is often used indiscriminately. This is to try out a large number of variables, and to see which of them makes a difference, perhaps deciding on this by some statistical significance test such as the chi-squared test. But 'hunting', as it is called, also has snags.

If you look at a lot of variables as potential analysis breaks, pure chance will make some of them appear important. There is no guarantee at all that any of the breaks you discover will apply to any other similar survey. What we are trying to do is to say something about the market in general, rather than to give an exact description of the particular sample. So if we come in with a theory then we can use our data to see if it is supported by the particular enquiry.

The use of significance tests also has technical problems: these tests do not theoretically apply if used repeatedly on different aspects of the same data, and most of them apply only to simple unrestricted probability samples which few market research surveys are. Having said this, we cannot deny that many people have used tests such as the chi-squared to find tables in which sub-groups vary and have found the results practically useful.

When we go beyond the two-way tables to three-way and many-way tables, it becomes quite impossible to produce more than a few out of the thousands which could be generated. Some theory is necessary to select which two-way tables to split further. A problem here is that a two-way table which shows no difference between sub-groups may show differences if such a table is produced separately for each sub-group of a third variable.

For instance, consumption of porridge varies little between homes with older and with younger adults Consumption also varies little between homes with children and homes without children. However, consumption varies a great deal between young homes with children and young homes without children. The three-way tabulation here is clearly essential to understand the market.

The selection of filter variables for many-way tables thus follows the same principles as for two-way tables. It has to be done with care to avoid producing too many tables.

We have not referred at all to graphical methods. These are of little use for understanding data based on counts of answers. On the other hand, a good chart can convey a particular point forcefully in presentation.

Table bases

Each table should show its base: that is, a description of the part or whole of the sample it covers, and the size of the sample. The size of each sub-group is also shown.

These bases vary because the table may be based upon only part of the data, and because the sub-groups analysed in the columns of tables may vary. As we said when discussing two-way tables, all tables based on samples should have this base or sample size shown for each sub-group, and also the size and description of the sample on which the table total is based. This sounds simple enough, but raises two other points which often cause confusion. They are weighting and multiple response.

Weighting

We describe this process in some detail because it is often mysterious, and can result in the apparent increase or decrease in sample sizes. Weighting is the process of giving some responses greater weight relative to others in totalling the numbers of responses to a question. It is done because, by accident or design, there are too many or too few of some types of respondent. When a table is weighted, each respondent is given an importance or weighting corresponding to the deficiency or over-representation of that type of respondent. Type of respondent is sometimes referred to as a 'cell', or entry in a table of sample or population composition.

It is only the relative importance of the weights that matters. If they are all for example doubled, the percentages calculated on the weighted responses will remain the same, although the total sample will appear twice the size. It is much less confusing if the usual practice of adjusting the weights so that they are relatively correct and also give the original total sample size is followed. Analysis programs normally do this.

Percentages are correctly worked out on this reweighted total even if it is different, but of course it is the original number of people that forms the 'unweighted base' and enables estimates to be made of the sampling variability of the figures in the table. Both types of base should therefore be shown if they differ. The effect of weighting is to increase sampling variability over that which would have resulted had the sample been structured exactly the same as the population from which it was drawn. This difference is normally small.

In the example in Table A2.2, the weighting might have been done to allow for the numbers of users of the two products in the market. In our table we analysed the responses of a sample consisting of 48.7% of users of A and 51.3% of users of B. We might know that in the market there are in fact slightly more users of A, say 55%, and only 45% of B. So we weight the results, giving the response of each user of A the value of 55/48.7 or 1.129 and the users of B a weight of 45/51.3 or 0.877.

The total sample of users of A is 224, and multiplied by 1.129 we get 253, as the weighted base. The 144 users of A preferring the new product multiplied by 1.129 become 163. When this is done for the categories of both groups of users, the results summed for the total sample and percentages calculated the result is as in

Table A2.4. Note that the percentages in the individual user groups remain unchanged, since each of the figures on which the percentages are calculated in a column are multiplied by the same factor. The percentages in the total column are however slightly different: on a weighted basis 55% prefer A, against 54% of the unweighted sample.

Table A2.4 Q.21: Preference for test product according to usual brand

	Total	Use brand A	Use brand B
Unweighted base:	460	224	236
Weighted base:	460 (100)	253 (100)	207 (100)
Prefer new	255 (55)	163 (64)	92 (44)
Prefer old	189 (41)	82 (32)	107 (52)
Don't know /no preference	16 (4)	8 (3)	8 (4)

The small difference from the unweighted figures in Table A2.2 is as usual: indeed, big differences would raise queries as to why the sample varied so much in structure from the population. The difference in structure may be intentional if, for example, it is wished to study one part of the population in greater detail than the rest, or if numerical data is being collected which is much more variable in some population groups than others. In the latter case, there are rules for calculating the optimum proportion of the sample to be taken from the more variable groups. When the sample is very differently structured from the population, then the weighted results are more different from the unweighted. It is often, though, surprising how little difference even large weights make.

Weighting is often more complicated where groups are subdivided: it may be known, for example, what proportion of the users of each of A and B are male and female, and males and females may be known to have differing preferences. Four weighting factors would then be calculated and applied. This process is limited by the detail of the knowledge available about the population, but several interlaced weighting categories are often used in large surveys.

It may be known what proportions of the overall population use A and B, and what proportions of the overall populations are male and or female, but this latter may not be known for the individual product user groups. These marginal weights can be used to estimate weights for the individual interlaced cells. This is easy enough for our example, but when many marginal weighting factors are used, estimation has to be carried out by computer programs for 'rim-weighting', which is one name for the process.

When the weight has been calculated for any group of respondents, it is recorded for each, and applied whatever analysis is performed using that respondent. However, any calculations of significance should properly be carried out using unweighted sample sizes.

Even if the weighting makes little difference, since it improves estimates at little effort now that the computer does the calculations, it should normally be carried out. The increase in the sampling error of the weighted sample described above is the cost of reducing the bias in the sample estimates. The sampling error of structured or stratified samples whether weighted or unweighted may be calculated, assuming the samples are statistically random, and is usually somewhat less than for an unstructured sample of the same size.

Note though that if samples are clustered, that is certain areas are chosen at random, and then respondents chosen within these areas, the sampling errors are increased, since people who live close together are generally more likely to be more alike than people who live further apart. Clustering is often done to reduce travelling costs in face-to-face interviewing.

Multiple response

Questions which have more than one simultaneously valid answer are known as multiple-response questions and require suitable software for recording and tabulation. The number of answers tabulated may exceed the number of respondents. The table may be based either on the number of respondents or the number of responses.

If we ask what newspaper was read yesterday, the answer may be to name none, one or several. If we want to know the number of people reading each paper, then the total of the numbers in each category will be greater than the total number of respondents, and the percentages add to more than a hundred. This may look odd, but is all right.

We might prefer to have the table based on the total number of newspapers read, so that the percentages would give the share of readership rather than readers. Similar considerations arise when people are asked their likes or dislikes about something, since they may have more than one.

Most software packages designed for marketing research surveys will readily handle these multiple-response questions, and tabulate them on whichever base is required. Not all analysis packages are designed to handle data in this form. If not, both questionnaire design and tabulation are made more complicated.

Multivariate analysis

When the methods of tabulation, starting with one-way tables, going on to two-way tables, and finally three- and more-way tables, have been fully explored we may turn to multivariate analysis. The techniques all provide a simplified explanation of the data which is more or less correct. The results may appear as mathematical descriptions or as graphic maps.

How do we know when this point has been reached? First, the bases for the tables we want to examine may be reduced to a handful of respondents or even none at all. Second, we may be tired of examining hundreds of tables, but believe relationships exist which we have not been able to find by using either our existing theory or by 'hunting'. Third, we may suspect that relationships are too complex to be presented by tables. If our trouble is sample size we should remember that multivariate analysis done on small samples will vary greatly in its results from sample to sample, just as will the results from tables with small bases.

Multivariate analysis is nowadays done by computer packages on personal computers as long as the data sets are not extremely large. These packages are easy to run with little knowledge of either computing systems or the statistical reasoning behind them. This does not matter very much (many people will disagree with this) if the results are taken as hypotheses, to be checked from other data gathered in other circumstances. Some understanding is required, though, if any useful insights are to be generated.

There is almost always a trade-off between the exactness of the explanation and its elaborateness. The simpler the explanation and the more it is consistent with, or based upon, what is already known, the more likely it is that we have found something which is of more general interest than giving an exact description of the particular data which we have by chance collected. Whenever we create a model from data, we should recall that there are innumerable other models we might have found which would fit nearly as well, or even better if we changed our criterion of what is a good fit.

There are two sorts of these techniques. The first is the analysis of dependence, when we know which variable or variables we want to predict given the others. The second is the analysis of interdependence, when we want to see how all the variables affect one another. This often takes the form of drawing a map to show how people, attitudes or brands stand in relation to one another, according to some criterion.

Analysis of dependence

Multiple regression is the commonest form, but has limited use in survey analysis. It predicts a number, such as the number of tea-bags purchased, given various other numbers, such as the number of children in a family, and the income per week.

The answer takes the form of an algebraic equation, from which it may be seen how important are the various predictors, and what would happen if they were changed in value in a particular instance. For survey data multiple regression has problems. The data is usually not just in the form of numbers which can be manipulated, but is the count of various categories. Very different results can often be produced by a slight change in technique.

Conjoint analysis takes the results of choices by respondents between hypothetical possibilities varying in a number of factors to estimate the relative importance of each of these factors.

Respondents might, for example, be asked whether they preferred a small car with medium acceleration or a large car with poor acceleration, and a series of similar questions. A deduction would then be made about the relative importance of size and acceleration. One problem of the technique is that it may need extensive questioning of each respondent, although programs have been developed to shorten later questions as data is successively entered on the keyboard. The appropriate questions are then presented on the screen at each stage.

Analysis of interdependence

If we have three observations about each of a number of entities such as people, or brands, or attitude scales, we may think of each entity as a point in three-dimensional space. We could construct a model with little balls on wires from which we could see the general relationships, grouping and outlying observations. If, though, we had more than three observations about each we should require many-dimensional space which we could not represent. However, mathematical procedures have been developed which do effectively the same thing.

Principal component analysis (PCA) is widely used. It constructs a number of factors which are weighted averages of the original measurements. A few of these factors, ignoring the rest, will often give a good description of the whole data set.

Sometimes it is called 'factor analysis', after a particular technique at one time popular. There are many variations of the method. PCA is often used with numerical responses from a sample of respondents to a series of attitude scales for each of a number of brands. The process produces uncorrelated factors, each of which is a weighted combination of a number of scales. As the factors are brought in they give an increasingly good explanation of the total pattern. The factors are then regarded as an underlying structure from which each of the scales is built up. Although there are as many factors as scales, only the first few factors are usually considered (there are rules of thumb for deciding which).

An example often quoted is that of measuring nearly rectangular parcels: if for each parcel the girth, diagonal of each side, and volume were recorded, PCA would show as major factors the underlying dimensions of length, breadth and height.

The technique has been criticised as showing little more than can be seen from looking at the correlations between each attitude scale. It is widely used as a method of reducing the number of attitude scales to be employed in further enquiries.

Cluster analysis seeks to put entities into groups on the basis of similarities on a number of measures. The number of groups, and the process of their formation (do you start with many groups and see what happens when some are amalgamated, or start with one group and split it successively?), are arbitrary. If the groups are distinct enough, the choice of method makes little difference, and subsequent analysis by group membership may be rewarding. The technique is applied to produce classification methods for databanks (such as the Target Group Index) appropriate for particular product fields rather than generally. Life-stage or lifestyle variables may be used as a basis for forming clusters.

A number of techniques under the heading of multidimensional scaling reduce data from many dimensions to an approximate representation to fewer, in practice, to two or three. These depend on measures of difference between the entities.

These measures may take many forms, such as the difference in the number of people saying a scale applies, whether a particular scale is thought to apply at all, or whether a particular brand is seen as having more of a characteristic than another. The resulting maps, which may include points not only for each brand, but also for scales and people, require interpretation, since the meaning of the dimensions on which they are plotted must be inferred from the positions of the entities, a somewhat circular process. Correspondence analysis is a form which takes categorical data, thus needing minimal assumptions about the form of the data.

Practical processing

The application of all these ideas in practice depends on the size of the job, the time available and the hard- and software. Specialised agencies will take data from the questionnaire stage and process it to specification, and can make many helpful suggestions. They cannot, of course, work without an analysis specification. Deriving this from knowledge of the objectives and methods of the enquiry is normally the job of the research executive concerned. An experienced analyst can take a questionnaire and a set of data and turn out what is usually required, but this is akin to asking the librarian to suggest a book to read. Particularly if the survey is large and complicated, the expertise of the professional analysts and the versatility of their equipment are often a good buy. They can work with great speed.

On the other hand, for small enquiries a personal computer or even a large flat surface can be an adequate tool. The researcher who analyses his or her own data comes to understand it in detail, and can explore it interactively. Whichever way analysis is done, it is necessary to know something about the practical considerations which the following section goes through.

Some survey data is still recorded on paper questionnaires in handwriting. The other possibilities are keying in on a PC (this method is normally used by telephone interviewers who type in the answers they hear on the phone, and described as CATI – Computer-Aided Telephone Interviewing) or into a lap-top PC (this method is often used by personal interviewers, and known as CAPI – Computer-Aided Personal Interviewing). Another method used on large surveys is a paper questionnaire on which marks are made to be read electronically (optical-mark recognition). Techniques for reading handwriting remain at the time of writing experimental.

The paper questionnaire requires a separate data-capture process if electronic processing is, as usual, to be used. Paper does, though, carry information beyond the words and figures it bears. All questionnaires on receipt should be examined one-by-one for completeness, consistency and the more elusive quality of meaningfulness. Whether there are major misunderstandings, if the document is carelessly completed, even facetious or fraudulent, may be seen by the human eye, particularly if a batch of documents from the same source is together. Rejection or correction of the data is then necessary. Personal editing is thus always needed, as well as the checks that may be made electronically.

Data capture or keying takes data from paper questionnaires to a computer. Some software is necessary to do this: many analysis packages provide a checking process. This sets up the recording so that only acceptable answers to a particular question will be read. For example, if adults are indicated at a particular point by the code 1, and non-adults by 2, any attempt to record any other code will be rejected. If multiple-response data is to be recorded, provision is made.

The layout of a paper questionnaire makes a great difference to the labour of data capture. If codes are clearly shown, preferably by being ringed, or clearly written in, with those answers which consist of numbers written in boxes, the work will be done faster and more accurately.

In the same way the detailed design of the questionnaire affects the work of the interviewer. The advantage of having the questionnaire on the screen as in CATI or CAPI is that data capture may be checked automatically, and routing to a question depending on the previous answer may be automatic. The data capture if manual may be checked. Some packages provide a verification procedure, in which some or all of the data may be rekeyed, and discrepancies shown up.

The data in a questionnaire may require coding. That is, the answers have to be put into numerical categories, when they have been received in words. This may be done by the interviewer, with the categories set out on the questionnaire, or later in the office. The categories may not be set until after the office has received the data. These will then be in the form of a summary in words of what a respondent said, the words themselves verbatim, if not too many, or a description of what was observed (if new packaging were being offered to respondents, interviewer might record, 'broke finger-nail'). Such material is not simple to record with a keyboard, so paper has an advantage. It typically arises as the answer to an open-ended question such as 'What makes this magazine article particularly interesting?' The process of setting the categories is known as 'making a coding frame'. Usually for an open-ended question for which responses are recorded more or less verbatim, the responses in a sample of the questionnaires are examined, and meaningful categories determined. Too many are confusing, but categories can be combined later, while creating new ones during the coding process means recoding questionnaires already processed. Not more than a dozen categories usually result. A separate frame has to be made and coding done for each open-ended question. Open-ended questions are therefore a costly form. If the verbatim answers have been keyed in at any stage, the process may be automated by specialist software, and codes allocated to responses accordingly.

If the codes are not inserted in this way, the next stage is to go through the questionnaires and write in or key in for each one at the answer to the particular question the number of the category. This is coding. Coding needs to be done carefully: it is easy to miss a category of mentions occurring only infrequently, but which is none the less important.

It is not necessary to have electronic equipment to analyse data. For a sample of a hundred or two, simple analysis may be done by a hand-count. This may be a preliminary operation to get top-line figures. The questionnaires are sorted into piles, each representing a combination of desired classifications. Thus if the data is to be analysed by three age groups and two sexes, there will be six piles. It is much easier if the same analysis breaks are used for every question. For each question in turn, the questionnaires are sorted into further piles, one for each answer. The piles are counted, the answers noted, and a check made that the total number of answers or respondents is correct.

An alternative is to work through each questionnaire in turn, putting a tick on a sheet in a box for the particular answer. Even more care is needed to get the totals correct. The totals have to be carefully written into tables and percentages worked out.

An intermediate method is to use a spreadsheet on a PC. This is suitable for small data sets where the answers consist mainly of numbers. These might be the answers to an industrial market research enquiry, where a limited number of respondents give estimates for various usage and market sizes. Such data can be incorporated in a spreadsheet. This enables ratios to be calculated for each respondent, and the original figures and the ratios compared between respondents by running the eye down the page. Totals and averages for all respondents may then be shown. Tabulation routines are available on many spreadsheets, but are tedious to use if many tables are required. The tables then normally need formatting so that they fit a report.

The one-way tables or whole-count will show any 'out-of-range' codes such as those denoting people aged 124, but not errors arising from the answers to two or more questions together. Programs are available to carry out logical checks to find such errors. When inconsistencies are found, they may be identified for querying and correction, or the data may be automatically modified. For example, if only those saying 'yes' in question 2 about whether they use the product are to be asked in question 8 what they think of it, the combination of the code representing 'no' in question 2 with any code except that for not applicable in question 8 shows an error.

An arbitrary correction may then be thought best, by changing the answer to question 8 to 'not applicable'. On the other hand, a detailed examination of the questionnaire and perhaps reference to the respondent may show where the error lies. Large surveys are open to hundreds of checks of this kind, and thousands of minor inconsistencies may be revealed. Automatic correction is then almost inevitable.

It is important to 'clean' the data. Not only is accuracy desirable, but discrepancies have a way of appearing in the finished tables in a prominent and embarrassing position. One of the great advantages of CAPI and CATI is that this process is not needed, since illogical answers cannot be entered if checks are set up on the entry procedure.

The use of computer packages

These are many. Some are menu-driven and others, the more powerful, require the preparation of computer files of instructions using some specialised language. They may provide a selection of data entry, data checking, data manipulation, tabulation in various forms, graphical presentation, calculation of summary statistics and tests of significance. They may further provide one or more modelling or multivariate techniques. The data-entry modules include some for CATI which assist in sample selection as well as data collection. As with all software, the more widely applicable and more flexible packages are more complex to use. Questionnaire layout facilities may also be provided, and question names and answer categories automatically linked to the analysis process. Providing these manually is a long job.

The Association for Survey Computing has in the past published a catalogue of numerous sets of software for statistical and survey analysis, and at the time of writing has put a new edition on the Web at www.assurcom.demon.co.uk.

The most complete service is provided by the specialist analysis houses referred to above. Many names appear in the Market Research Society *Research Buyer's Guide*. They will take questionnaires, code and key them, then produce tables to specification, doing all or part of these jobs as needed. They will apply multivariate techniques to the data as directed. Their staff can give valuable guidance in all this, but as always, executive involvement costs more. We emphasise the use of these agencies because the mechanics of the earlier stages of analysis are complicated and time-consuming for those who are not practised in their use.

Time spent this way is a diversion from the main purpose of marketers. For them, intelligent employment of specialists is likely to be an economy in both time and money. The specialists cannot work without a knowledge of the background, objects and methods of the enquiry, so they have to be directed by people who have some ideas of the problems and possibilities of analysis. There is, though, no reason why the individual researcher or student should not do it all, given time and access to equipment.

From the numerous packages, many of which are intended for specialist statistical purposes outside survey research, we have selected as examples two commonly met with, which illustrate some of the possibilities. This is not to say that they are the best.

SNAP (Mercator Computer Services Ltd, Bristol) is a Windows-based PC package. It does data entry, tabulation, with some statistical routines. As in all menu-driven programs the ease of initial use soon becomes tedious: there is, however, a batch option which enables large numbers of tables to be produced by entering a few commands.

SPSS (SPSS UK Ltd, Walton-on-Thames) is a suite available either for PCs or mainframes, capable of handling and manipulating large and complicated data sets. It has facilities for a wide range of modelling and multivariate techniques as well as summary statistics and numerous statistical tests. There are also extensive graphics capabilities.

The program, and others suitable for big enquiries, are driven by creating command files in a specialised language, described in a large manual needed to cover the numerous possibilities. SPSS is popular among social scientists, who use it for prolonged examination of their data sets. It can also be used more simply in a Windows mode.

Of the many other program packages some specialise in flexible tabulation, others in model building, some in time-series analysis, some in graphics display; some are designed to produce large volumes of repetitive output, some to generate tables one-by-one. Some link in input and output with others, while some store their data only in forms unintelligible to any other package. The choice is wide and costs vary widely. Type of machine is not normally a restriction with modern personal computers, although complicated operations on very large data sets may even nowadays mean a bigger machine.

The computer has made analysis both easier and more difficult. It can produce easily great volumes of tables: little is achieved, however, by transposing 250 questionnaires into 275 tables. Skilfully used, which is the difficult part, the computer can enable thorough and thoughtful study of data, and the eventual production of the few, rather differently appearing tables which will communicate effectively in a report. The way data becomes information needs understanding if marketers are to appreciate the potential and the limitations of their research.

References and further reading

Association for Survey Computing (1999), *Software for Statistical and Survey Analysis*, on www.ASC.org.uk

Ehrenberg, A. S. C. (1985), *A Primer in Data Reduction: Practical Guidance on Data Collection*, John Wiley, Chichester and New York. One of the few books which deal with the principles of tabulation for both investigation and reporting.

Hague, P. N. and Jackson, P. (1998), *Do Your Own Market Research*, third edition, Kogan Page, London. A discussion of analysis of wider application than the title suggests.

Hair, J., Tatham R., Anderson, R. and Black, W. (1998), *Multivariate Data Analysis*, fifth edition, Prentice Hall, London and New Jersey. A very general and practical approach to the use of multivariate analysis.

Market Research Society (1999), *The Research Buyers' Guide*, London.

Appendix 3
Statistical tests

E. John Davis

The null hypothesis

When dealing with the results of experiments or surveys carried out on samples of people, shops, or whatever, it is seldom possible to prove results. Instead, we usually attempt to assess which of two mutually exclusive hypotheses is more likely to be true on the basis of our observed results. The general forms of these two hypotheses and the symbols attached to them are:

H_0: the hypothesis that our results do not show any significant differences between population groups over whatever factors have been measured;

H_1: the hypothesis that differences shown in our results reflect real differences between population groups.

The first of these hypotheses, H_0, is known as the null hypothesis. If it is true it indicates that our results show nothing except chance differences between our measurements. If we can obtain sufficient evidence to refute this hypothesis with an acceptable level of confidence, then we are justified in accepting the alternative hypothesis H_1. In effect we begin by assuming that any difference between two sample measurements is not significant and is due to chance until we can find a good basis for rejecting this assumption. If we can reject the null hypothesis we say that our result is 'significant'.

Errors of the first and second kind

In addition to setting down our hypotheses, we need also to decide on the degree of risk we can accept of being wrong in taking a result as significant when it is not. For most market research purposes we work with a level of risk of 1 in 20 of being wrong, often referred to as the 95% limit or the 5% level of significance. In terms of the experiments discussed in Chapters 9 and 10, this means that we devise our experiments so that we can apply tests of significance such that if they indicate a real difference, this will be a correct evaluation 95 times out of 100. As we do not normally carry out our experiments often enough to be able to think in terms of being right on 95% of occasions we change the words slightly, and say that we have a 95% chance of being right. From this it follows that we have a 5% chance, or probability, of being wrong, and our tests are operating at the 5% or 0.05 level of significance.

The level of significance here indicates the level of risk of our being wrong in rejecting the null hypothesis when it is true, and thus of accepting our experimental difference as real when it is not. Being wrong in this way is known as a Type I Error.

There is a converse risk – that of failing to detect or to accept a positive experimental result because our experimental measurements are too crude. If, say, a change in some measure, such as consumption of some food product from 30 grams per head to 35 grams per head per day would show a profitable return on some marketing expenditure, then an experiment capable only of showing a change of 10 grams or more as significant will leave the company open to such a risk.

An opportunity to take profitable marketing action may be lost because an experiment is set up which is not powerful enough to measure results with the precision needed in the particular situation. Being wrong in this way is known as a Type II Error.

Two further elements which should be taken into account when assessing the levels of significance to be used are the size of the benefits expected if successful action is subsequently taken, and the penalties expected from taking a wrong decision. In situations such as the final stages of the development and launch of a new brand, the potential benefits and potential losses resulting from decisions based on the experimental results are high. This normally calls for the design of experiments giving high levels of precision and low risks of wrongly rejecting the null hypothesis – such as 1 chance in 100 (the 1% level), as opposed to the one chance in 20 (the 5% level). But such experiments are themselves costly, and should not be used in less risky situations where the costs would not be justified. Initial testing of ideas and products is often better undertaken based on the use of significance levels of 10% or more, simply because in the early stages of testing it is often unreasonable (and probably unprofitable) to insist on the more rigorous levels of significance appropriate to high-risk situations.

The problems then of interpreting the statistical results of experiments are by no means simple, nor confined merely to the use of prescribed formulae yielding magic numbers to be labelled 'significant' or 'not significant'. However, with these reservations the following statistical tests can be applied with care to a range of statistical results.

Differences between sample measurements

The range of uncertainty surrounding a measurement obtained from a sample is indicated by the 'standard error' of that measurement.

To calculate the standard error of a measurement, such as the mean price respondents say they would pay for a new product, their mean foot measurements, and so forth, we first calculate the arithmetic mean and use that as a basis for calculating the standard error. The standard error of a mean can then be calculated from this formula:

$$se_{m} = \sqrt{\frac{\Sigma(x - \bar{x})^2}{n^2}}$$

where n = sample size (assumed here to be at least 30);
x = each individual measurement taken in turn;
x = the mean of all values of x; and
Σ = indicates the values of $(x - \bar{x})^2$ added together.

When dealing with attributes such as whether a person smokes or not, whether they like the test product or whether they think they would buy the test product in preference to their usual brand, we can use a more simple version of this formula. In these cases we can put $x = 1$ whenever the respondent smokes, prefers, would buy, or whatever, and $x = 0$ if he or she does not. It is then easy to show that under these conditions the standard error of the percentage having the stated attribute can be calculated by the formula below:

$$se_p = \sqrt{\frac{p\,(100 - p)}{n}}$$

where p = the percentage scored 1 (preferably between 10% and 90%); and
       n = sample size (assumed to be at least 30).

When using proportions instead of percentages substitute $(1 - p)$ for $(100 - p)$ in the formula.

Testing experimental differences involving percentages

Experimental designs such as those used for rating new products (see Chapter 9) may involve monadic tests using independent matched samples each reporting on one variant, or comparative tests where the same sample of people report on two or more variants of the product. The procedures for testing the results vary, and are described separately.

Monadic results from independent samples

The hypotheses are:

H_0:   that any difference between readings p_1 and p_2 from two independent random samples of n_1 and n_2 respondents is the result of chance alone;

H_1:   that the difference between the readings must be attributed to the experimental conditions.

Note that these hypotheses do not stipulate any direction for any difference, i.e. whether p_1 or p_2 is the higher percentage. Hence a two-tailed test is used, and finding a significant difference in either direction would lead to the rejection of H_0.

First calculate p, the overall percentage given by combining both samples, on the assumption that they are both drawn from the same population. This is given by:

$$p = \frac{n_1 p_1 + n_2 p_2}{n_1 + n_2}$$

Then calculate the standard error of the difference $(p_1 - p_2)$:

$$se_d = \sqrt{p(100-p)\left[\frac{1}{n_1} + \frac{1}{n_2}\right]}$$

In the special case where $n_1 = n_2$:

$$p = \frac{p_1 + p_2}{2}$$

$$se_d = \sqrt{p(100-p) \cdot \frac{2}{n}}$$

Now calculate the absolute value of the test statistic, t, ignoring its sign, where t is defined as:

$$t = \frac{p_1 - p_2}{se_d}$$

If $t > 1.64$ the difference is significant at the 10% level; if $t \geq 1.96$ the difference is significant at the 5% level; and if $t \geq 2.58$ the difference is significant at the 1% level.

If a significant difference is found at the required level it suggests that the difference between the readings p_1 and p_2 is not simply due to chance, but reflects a real difference in preferences for the test items.

In some circumstances the direction of any difference is important, as in experiments with a new version of a product expected to be preferred by more people than the old. Here we are not testing whether there is a difference in *either* direction, but whether there is a difference in *one* direction only. In such cases a one-tailed test is used and rejection of H$_0$ only follows if the test is significant in the appropriate direction.

Assume that p_1 measures acceptance of the old product, and that p_2 measures acceptance of the new version when they have been tested on two independent samples. Then our hypotheses become the following:

H$_0$: that p_2 is no greater than p_1; and
H$_1$: that p_2 is greater than p_1.

We calculate se_p and t as before, but now we are only interested in t if p_2 exceeds p_1. The test is now concerned with only one tail of the distribution of error, and the values of t associated with different levels of significance are changed.

If $t \geq 1.29$ the one-way test is significant at the 10% level; if $t \geq 1.64$ the one-way test is significant at the 5% level; and if $t \geq 2.32$ the one-way test is significant at the 1% level.

Comparative readings from the same sample

If we measure preferences for A, B, C, etc. in the same sample, then there are problems of correlation. As p_a increases so p_b may well diminish, and vice versa. Now to establish whether any difference is significant we have to take account of correlation in our formula for se_p. Our hypotheses become the following:

H_0: there is no difference between the proportions p_a and p_b preferring A and B, measured within a single sample;

H_1: there is a difference between preferences for A and B.

Now the formula for the standard error of the difference becomes:

$$se_d = \sqrt{\frac{p_a\,(100 - p_a) + p_b\,(100 - p_b) + 2p_a p_b}{n}}$$

$$t = \frac{p_a - p_b}{se_d} \quad \text{as before,}$$

and the values of t apply as before for either one-tailed or two-tailed tests.

More complex tests of preference scores

Sometimes we wish to examine more complex situations, such as a preference test where the sample is broken down by some other attribute such as social class. Then the χ^2 or chi-squared test is a more useful way of proceeding.

Suppose we have the following results from a sample of 195 housewives who have each tested products X and Y and stated their preferences. Information on social class has also been collected from each respondent.

The results were as follows:

	ABC1	C2D	
Prefer X	55	45	100
Prefer Y	35	60	95
	90	105	195

A t-test on the overall split between preferences for X and Y has shown that this is not significant. It appears that there may be differences in preferences between social classes. While it would be possible to carry out a t-test for each class a χ^2 test is more powerful and economical. Here we have:

H_0: there is no difference between the pattern of preferences by social class;

H_1: the pattern of preferences differs between the two social classes.

If there is no difference between classes, then we would expect the same proportion of housewives in each class to prefer X, and the same proportion to prefer Y. The overall estimate of the preference of X is 100 out of 195. Applying this ratio to the 90 ABC1 housewives, we would expect 46.2 to prefer X, i.e., $100/195 \times 90$. Similarly we would expect $95/195 \times 90$ ABC1 housewives to prefer Y; $100/195 \times 105$ C2D housewives to prefer X, and $95/195 \times 105$ to prefer Y.

	Observed	Expected	O – E	(O – E)²	(O – E)²/E
X/ABC1	55	46.2	8.8	77.44	1.68
Y/ABC1	35	43.8	–8.8	77.44	1.77
X/C2D	45	53.8	–8.8	77.44	1.44
Y/C2D	60	51.2	8.8	77.44	1.51
	195	195.0	0		6.40

In fact, once we have calculated one of the four expected values in a 2 × 2 table such as this one, the other three values are fixed because of the need for columns and rows to add to their original totals. In technical terms we have only 'one degree of freedom' in such a table.

For each cell we now have an observed (O) and an expected (E) value. We then calculate $(O – E)^2/E$ and add.

We can now consult a table of values of χ^2 for our number of degrees of freedom and level of significance, and see whether our sample value exceeds the tabulated value or not. If it does, the differences are significant at that level.

	Degrees of freedom			
	1	2	3	4
10%	2.7	4.6	6.3	7.8
5%	3.8	6.0	7.8	9.5
1%	6.6	9.2	11.3	13.3

Some values of $\chi 2$

Comparing the calculated value of 6.40 with the table for one degree of freedom, the results are seen to be significant at the 5% level but not quite at the 1% level.

In general, when using χ^2:

- use frequencies, not percentages;
- cells should preferably contain five or more cases;
- degrees of freedom = (rows – 1) × (columns – 1), e.g. a table of two rows and three columns has (2 – 1) × (3 – 1) = 2 degrees of freedom.

Differences involving variables

The same general procedure is followed for comparing means of variables as for proportions. In these cases, for independent samples we calculate a pooled estimate of the *se* thus:

$$se_d = \sqrt{\frac{n_1}{n_2} \cdot se^2_{\bar{x}_1} + \frac{n_2}{n_1} \cdot se^2_{\bar{x}_2}} = \frac{n_1}{n_2} \cdot se^2_{x_1} + \frac{n_2}{n_1} \cdot se^2_{x_2}$$

$$t = \frac{\bar{x}_1 - \bar{x}_2}{se_d}$$

Null hypotheses and alternative hypotheses are set up as before, and the links between values of t and levels of significance for one-tailed and two-tailed tests are the same as for testing proportions.

Where pairs of readings are taken from the same sample, such as numbers of cigarettes smoked by individuals before and after an experiment or weights of slimmers before and after treatment, etc., the situation is most easily handled by calculating the difference, d, for each individual and $\bar{d}$, the average value of d. Then calculate se_d:

$$se_{\bar{d}} = \sqrt{\frac{\Sigma(d - \bar{d})^2}{n}}$$

Then our hypotheses become the following:

H_0: that the value of d is not significantly different from zero; and
H_1: that the observed differences are significant.

The tabulated values of t at different levels of significance and for one-tailed and for two-tailed tests apply as before.

For more complex situations 'analysis of variance' is used

Consider the experiment described in Section 9.6 with results in volume of sales by outlets in three areas, north, midlands and south, and with three pack designs or treatments on test.

	T1	T2	T3	Total	Average
			Shop sales in a pack test		
N	150	220	180	550	183.3
M	90	100	110	300	100
S	60	70	70	200	66.7
Total	300	390	360	1,050	
Average	100	130	120		116.7

The regional differences in sales are clearly seen, and on visual inspection they appear to be greater than the differences in sales between the experimental packs. It therefore becomes logical to try to separate the variation or 'variance' between treatments (pack designs in this case) from the variance between regions. Hence we undertake an analysis of variance.

Now the overall variance is given by:

$$s^2 = \frac{1}{n-1} \Sigma (x - \bar{x})^2$$

where n = number of cells in the analysis

x = the average sales level over all stores in all regions, namely

$$\bar{x} = \frac{1050}{9} = 116.67$$

Within the total variance some part will be due to the following:

- variations in sales between areas;
- variations in sales between pack designs;
- chance variations in sales between stores.

The statistic F is used to assess whether any observed differences in the variance contributions are significant, or probably due only to chance, and hypotheses H_0 and H_1 are set up as before.

The calculations necessary to analyse the overall variance from the experimental results into the parts due to each of these sources are as follows:

r = numbers of rows (areas)
t = number of treatments (packs)

Add up total sales and calculate average sales $(\bar{x})$.
For each area find total sales and average sales (rows) – $\bar{A}_i$.
For each pack find total sales and average sales (cols) – $\bar{P}_j$.

Calculate $\displaystyle\sum_1^r \sum_1^t (x_{ij} - \bar{x})^2$ = sum of squares, total (SST)

Calculate $\displaystyle r \sum_1^r (\bar{A}_i - \bar{x})^2$ = sum of squares, areas (SSA)

Calculate $\displaystyle t \sum_1^t (\bar{P}_j - \bar{x})^2$ = sum of squares, packs (SSP)

As a check on arithmetic one more figure may be calculated:

$$\sum_1^r \sum_1^t (x_{ij} - \bar{A}_i - \bar{P}_j + \bar{x})^2 = \text{error/residual sum of squares} = \text{(SSE)}$$

Calculate degrees of freedom (d.f.) as follows:

Total d.f.	= no. of areas × no. of treatments –1
	= $(r \times t) - 1$
Between areas d.f.	= no. of areas – 1
	= $(r - 1)$
Between treatments d.f.	= no. of treatments – 1
	= $(t - 1)$
Residual/error d.f.	= $(r - 1)(t - 1)$

Note that the degrees of freedom between areas + between treatments + residual = total degrees of freedom.

Then complete the following table:

Analysis of variance for random block design

Source of variance	Sum of squares	d.f.	Mean square	Value of F
Between packs	SSP	$t-1$	$MSP = SSP/(t-1)$	MSP/MSE
Between areas	SSA	$r-1$	$MSA = SSA/(r-1)$	MSA/MSE
Error/residual	SSE	$(r-1)(t-1)$	$MSE = SSE/(r-1)(t-1)$	
Total	SST	$rt-1$		

For the shop sales data from the pack test:

$r = \text{areas} = 3$

$t = \text{packs} = 3$

$$\sum_{1}^{r} \sum_{1}^{t} (x_{ij} - \bar{x})^2 = 24{,}400.0$$

$$r \sum_{1}^{t} (\bar{A}_i - \bar{x})^2 = 21{,}666.7$$

$$t \sum_{1}^{r} (\bar{P}_j - \bar{x})^2 = 1{,}400.0$$

$$\sum_{1}^{r} \sum_{1}^{t} (x_{ij} - \bar{A}_i - \bar{P} + \bar{x})^2 = 1{,}333.3$$

The table then becomes the following:

Source of variance	Sum of squares	d.f.	Mean square	Value of F
Areas	21,666.7	2	10833.3	32.5
Packs	1,400.0	2	700.0	2.1
Error	1,333.3	4	333.3	
Totals	24,400.0	8		

We can now consult tables of the values of F to test whether either of the F values is significant. We enter the tables with 2 d.f. for areas and 2 d.f. for packs (the numerators in the F ratios) and 4 d.f. for the mean square error (the denominator). In tables of the values of F the degrees of freedom for the numerator are denoted by v_1, and those for the denominator by v_2.

Using $v = 2$ and $v = 4$, the tables show the following significant values for F:

1% level $F = 18.00$
5% level $F = 6.94$
10% level $F = 4.32$
25% level $F = 2.00$

This result shows, as we suspected, that there are very strong area differences, with the between-areas value of F being significant well beyond the 1% level. The value of F for the packs however is only significant at the 25% level – that is, we could expect such observed differences in the sales of the different packs in one experiment in four, just by chance even if the packs had no differential effects on sales levels.

The action to be taken on this result would depend on other factors in the situation, such as the relative costs of the three packs, the time pressures for a decision, and so forth. Broadly we could do the following:

- adopt pack 3, accepting the low level of significance of the experimental result;
- continue with the existing pack (if there is one); or
- carry out further experiments to get a more specific indication of the effects of packs on sales.

Analysis of variance is such a widely used method of assessing the significance of experimental results that it is included in most computer statistical packages. The programs vary in detail, but the raw data is fed in as responses to promptings by the computer program, and the completed calculations printed out or displayed in a form similar to the table above. Some programs stop at the calculation of the F values, but others go on to indicate the associated levels of significance.

It is important to appreciate what calculations are taking place to produce the analysis of variance from a set of data, but seldom necessary to carry through the arithmetic by hand.

The facilities are also normally there for handling the calculations arising from more complex experiments quickly and accurately, for taking account of more factors, and for investigating possible interactions between levels of factors. At each stage of increasing complexity the calculations expand, but following the patterns shown above.

For example, the Latin square design discussed in Section 9.6 leads us to the table below.

The similarity in structure between the tables is seen, with the inclusion of an additional line in the Latin square results. The error/residual calculation is now

$$\sum_{1}^{t} \sum_{1}^{r} (x_{ij} - \bar{A}_i - \bar{P}_j - \bar{O}_k + 2\bar{x})^2$$

Analysis of variance for Latin square

Source of variance	Sum of squares	d.f.	Mean square	Value of F
Between packs	SSP	$t - 1$	$MSP = SSP/(t-1)$	MSP/MSE
Between areas	SSA	$t - 1$	$MSA = SSA/(t-1)$	MSA/MSE
Between outlets	SSO	$t - 1$	$MSO = SSO/(t-1)$	MSO/MSE
Error/residual	SSE	$(t-1)(t-2)$	$MSE = SSE/(t-1)(t-2)$	
	SST	$(t-1)^3$		

449

where   the $\bar{A}_i$s are the averages of the areas;

the $\bar{P}_j$ s are the averages of the packs; and

the $\bar{O}_k$s are the averages of the outlet types.

Worked example of the use of a Latin square

This example follows the design set out in Section 9.6, with three packs being tested in three outlet types in three areas. The sales figures are shown below.

Raw sales data from pack test

Region	Grocer	Type of retail outlet Chemist	CTN	Total	Average
North	122[2]	114[3]	139[1]	375	125
Midlands	108[1]	115[2]	104[3]	327	109
South	91[3]	110[1]	114[2]	315	105
Total	321	339	357	1,017	
Average	107	113	119		113

The indices against cell sales indicate the pack version used. To facilitate the calculation of the pack averages the figures may be rearranged thus:

				Total	Average
Pack 1 sales	139	108	110	357	119
Pack 2 sales	122	115	114	351	117
Pack 3 sales	114	104	91	309	103

It is now possible to calculate all the sums of squares required and to fit them into the analysis of variance table.

Source of variance	Sum of Squares	d.f.	Mean square	Value of F
Packs	456	2	228	25.3
Areas	672	2	336	37.3
Outlets	216	2	113	12.6
Error	18	2	9	–
Totals	1,362	8		

These values of F can be compared with the tabulated values of v_1 and v_2 both at two degrees of freedom:

at the 5% level $F = 19.0$
at the 1% level $F = 99.0$

Hence both pack figures and the area figures show significant differences at the 5% level.

The fact that the figures show significant variations by pack needs careful interpretation, and reference back to the averages by pack indicates that the variation arises from one pack performing less well than the other two. There is still doubt about which of the three packs may sell best – but some progress has been made in finding that one version sells less well than the other two.

FURTHER READING

Bagozzi, R. (1994), *Advanced Methods of Marketing Research*, Blackwell Publishers, USA.

Kinnear, T. and Taylor, I. (1991), *Marketing Research*: *An Applied Approach*, McGraw-Hill, USA.

Parasuraman, A. (1991), *Marketing Research*, Addison-Wesley, USA.

Tull, D. and Hawkins, D. (1990), *Marketing Research*: *Measurement and Method*, Macmillan Inc., USA.

Appendix 4
Market Research Society Publications

Research (monthly)
This was relaunched in October 1992 with a new title focusing on the news and issues of the market research industry with coverage of the Society's own activities. *Research* is a magazine which also carries the popular People pages with details about company and individual movements.

Calendar (monthly) is a supplement to *Research* with a full diary listing of forth-coming MRS and industry events, regional and social gatherings.

Journal of the Market Research Society (quarterly)
JMRS is a refereed journal. It includes papers and shorter notes concerning techni-cal advances and practical implications, appraisals of specific problem areas, correspondence and reviews about the wide field of marketing and social research.

Market Research Abstracts (bi-annually)
This covers all fields of marketing and advertising research as well as relevant papers in statistics, psychology and sociology. Started in 1963 it now has coverage of over 400 papers and articles abstracted each year from some 40 different English language journals. On-line search facilities are provided.

Field Newsheet (quarterly)
This has news, articles and practical advice of particular interest to interviewers.

Research Plus (10 times a year)
This publication, following the relaunch of *Research*, now focuses on a different indus-try sector each month, through a range of feature articles by leading practitioners.

Annuals

Market Research Society Yearbook
The *Yearbook* contains lists of members together with their affiliations. There are a few details about organisations and individuals providing market research services in the UK and Republic of Ireland. It also includes details of Society activities, ser-vices and useful addresses in the UK and overseas.

The *Orgs Book* is provided to members of the MRS with the *Code of Conduct*. It gives details of market research organisations in the UK and overseas.

International Directory of Market Research Organisations
The *International Directory*, published in more than ten editions, gives details of facilities of market research organisations in over 70 countries world-wide.

Other publications

Country Notes
These provide a basic guide to demographics, sampling methods, research procedures and sources of information in different countries. They are available in regional volumes as follows: Western Europe, Far East, North America, Eastern Europe and Latin America.

Dictionary of Market Research
The *Dictionary of Market Research* is a joint publication of the Market Research Society and the Incorporated Society of British Advertisers (ISBA).

Guide to Sources of Samples for Telephone Research
Thirty-three information sources are listed with full details about the type of data they provide.

Issues in Political Opinion Polling
The chapters cover the basic techniques of opinion polling, interviewing for opinion polls, the accuracy of opinion polls, bias and sample re-weighting, the publishing of poll findings, the electoral effects on opinion polls and a glossary of technical terms used in survey research.

Guide to the Practice of Market and Survey Research
The MRS has published this guide in order to explain to those outside the survey industry what market researchers do and what market and survey research in general are about.

Occupation Groupings: *a job dictionary*
An A–Z of common and not so common occupations by socio-economic gradings – a tool for the classification of respondents, especially for interviewers.

Recommended Papers for the Diploma of the Market Research Society
A comprehensive collection of papers covering all aspects of market research, including reprints from the *Journal of the Market Research Society* and its annual conference papers, ESOMAR conference and seminar proceedings, the *Journal of Marketing Consumer Research*, *Journal of Advertising Research* and *Journal of Marketing Research*.

Standardised questions
This publication was originally produced in July 1972 and again in October 1984. It examines the most commonly used methods of asking certain types of questions and of recording the answers.

Glossary of abbreviations

AA	Advertising Association
ABMRC	Association of British Market Research Companies
ACORN	A classification of residential neighbourhoods
AI	Appreciation Index
AIDA	Attention, interest, desire, action
AIO	Activities, interests and opinions
AIR	Average issue readership
AMA	American Marketing Association
AMSO	Association of Market Survey Organisations
AMTES	Area marketing test-evaluation system
AN	Article numbering
APG	Account Planning Group
API	Advertising-planning index
AQRP	Association of Qualitative Research Practitioners
AURA	Association of Users of Research Agencies
BARB	Broadcasters' Audience Research Board
BBC	British Broadcasting Corporation
BI	Behavioural intention
BMRA	British Market Research Association
BMRB	British Market Research Bureau
BPTO	Brand/price trade-off
BSB	British Satellite Broadcasting
BSO	Business Statistics Office
CAPI	Computer-assisted personal interviewing
CATI	Computer-assisted telephone interviewing
CAVIAR	Cinema and video industry audience-research
CCTV	Closed circuit television
CIE	Chief income earner
CRA	Cognitive response analysis
CRN	Classified residential neighbourhoods
CSO	Central Statistical Office
DAGMAR	Defining advertising goals for measured advertising results
DCM	Discrete choice modelling
DIY	Do-it-yourself
DK	Don't know
DMU	Decision-making unit
DSB	Direct Satellite Broadcasting
DTI	Department of Trade and Industry

EAN	European article numbering
EC	European Community
EDP	Electronic data processing
EML	Extended media list
EPOS	Electronic point-of-sale
ESOMAR	European Society for Opinion and Market Research
fmcg	Fast moving consumer goods
GIS	Geographical information system
GSS	Government Statistical Service
HOH	Head of household
ICC	International Chambers of Commerce
IDM	Institute of Direct Marketing
ILR	Independent local radio
IMF	International Monetary Fund
IPA	Institute of Practitioners in Advertising
IQCS	Interview Quality Control Scheme
ITC	Independent Television Commission
ITCA	Independent Television Companies Association
ITV	Independent Television
JMRS	*Journal of the Market Research Society*
LR	local radio
MEAL	Media Expenditure Analysis Ltd
MIS	Marketing information system
MLH	Minimum list heading
MORI	Market and Opinion Research International
mr	market research
MRDF	Market Research Development Fund
MRQSA	Market Research Quality Standards Association
MRS	Market Research Society
NBD/LSD	Negative binomial distribution/logarithmic series distribution
NOP	National Opinion Poll
NPD	New product development
NRS	National Readership Survey
ONS	Office for National Statistics
OPCS	Office of Population Censuses and Surveys
OR	Operational research
OSCAR	Outdoor site classification and audience research (now renamed POSTAR)
OTS	Opportunities to see

PAF	Postcode address file
PIN	Pinpoint Identified Neighbourhoods
POSTAR	Poster audience research
PPI	personal purchases index
PPS	probability proportionate to size
PSM	Pricesensitivitymeter
PSU	Primary sampling unit
RAJAR	Radio Joint Audience Research Ltd
R&D	research and development
RBI	Research Business International
RDF	Research Development Foundation (sponsored by the MRS)
RFM	Recency, frequency and monetary value
RI	Research International
RSGB	Research Services of Great Britain
RSL	Research Services Ltd
SCPR	Social and Community Planning Research (now renamed National Centre for Social Research)
SIC	standard industrial classification
SN	subjective norm
SPSS	Statistical Package for the Social Sciences
SRA	Social Research Association
TAT	thematic apperception test
TCA	television consumer audit
TCPI	toiletries and cosmetics purchasing index
TEA	terminal education age
TGI	Target Group Index
TN AGB	Taylor Nelson Audits of Great Britain, now part of TN Sofrès
TV	Television
TVR	Television rating
USP	Unique selling proposition
VCR	video cassette recorder
VDU	visual display unit
VIP	valued impressions per pound

Glossary of media terminology

Average issue readership (AIR) The number of people who claim to have read or looked at a publication in the last issue period, i.e. 'yesterday' in the case of *The Times*, or in the 'last week' in the case of *Woman's Weekly*.

Average listening hours The average number of hours listened to a radio station. Calculated by dividing total listening hours in a week by weekly reach (total number listening in a week).

Average OTS This is a measure of the frequency of exposure to an advertisement. If an audience is exposed to an advertisement on average three times each, then this is equivalent to an average OTS of 3.

Cost per hundred (CPH) The average cost of achieving 100 TVRs against a specified audience (see TVR).

Cost per thousand (CPT) Used with reference to a specific audience, cost per thousand is a measure of the average cost of reaching 1,000 members of this audience. For example, if a spot on ITV Carlton reaches 400,000 men and costs £4,000, then the cost per thousand men is £4,000 ÷ 400 = £10.

Cover (sometimes termed **reach** or **net coverage** The proportion of the audience having an opportunity to see the advertising one or more times. Usually measured as a percentage, but can be expressed in thousands.

Cumulative cover The increased cover resulting from taking space in more than one issue of a particular publication.

Effective reach (sometimes termed **effective cover**) The percentage of the target audience who have the opportunity to see the desired number of TV spots or hear radio spots or see press ads. For example, if it is desired that the target audience see between two and eight spots, then the effective reach of the schedule is the percentage with between two and eight OTS.

Equal impacts A strategy for regional allocation giving equal number of TVRs to all regions.

Frequency The average number of times the target audience has an opportunity to see the campaign measured in OTS (OTH for radio). Calculated as

> Frequency = gross OTS + net cover
>
> or = TVRs + net cover (for TV)

Gross rating points The total number of OTS achieved by a campaign expressed as a percentage of the universe. For TV this would be equivalent to total TVRs. For press, it would be the sum of individual AIRs. For example, a campaign achieving 70% cover at 4 OTS would yield 280 gross rating points.

Impacts (sometimes referred to as **gross impressions** or **messages**) These are the total number of separate occasions a commercial(s) is viewed by a specific audience, measured in thousands.

MPX (magazine-page exposure) MPX scores the number of times an average issue reader of a publication looks at an average page.

Net homes This describes the number of homes in a TV area, exclusive of overlap. (See TV overlap.)

POSTAR (poster advertising research) Formerly known as OSCAR (Outdoor site classification and audience research), POSTAR is the improved modern version which continues to provide classifications of outdoor site visibility/quality and traffic-past-site. Does not provide audience demographics research, but is used to measure numbers of people passing and how people see posters on outdoor sites, e.g. on buildings, bus shelters, billboards, etc.

OTH (opportunity to hear) The radio equivalent of OTS – the average number of times an audience is exposed to a radio commercial. 'Exposure' is defined as any listening within the clock quarter-hour.

OTS (opportunity to see) The opportunity to see a TV commercial or a press, cinema or poster advertisement, defined as follows:

Press: Read or looked at any issue (for at least two minutes) within the publication period, e.g. last week, for a weekly magazine.

Cinema: Measured in actual cinema admissions.

Posters: Traffic of people past the site

TV: Presence in room with set switched on at turn of clock minute to one channel, providing presence in room with set on is at least 15 consecutive seconds.

Page traffic The percentage of readers who 'look at' a specific page within a publication.

Pass-on readership (sometimes termed **secondary readership**) Readers of a publication other than the purchaser or his/her immediate household. For example, readership which takes place in a doctor's waiting room.

Penetration Refers to the proportion of a population who are reached by a medium.

Pre-empt A system of buying TV air-time similar in principle to an auction. The rate-card may consist of a range of many different rates. The buyer will select the rate desired to pay for a spot, but he/she can lose the spot if 'pre-empted' by another buyer subsequently paying more for that spot. Pre-emption can occur up to midday on the day of transmission.

Primary readership The first reader of a publication or all members of his/her household who read the publication.

Readers per copy (RPC) The average number of readers seeing each copy sold. Calculated as average issue readership ÷ circulation.

Timeshift Practice of recording programmes on VCRs and viewing later.

TV overlap TV overlap areas consist of districts falling within the boundaries of more than one TV area. For example, 18% of householders could be estimated as living in overlap areas.

TVR (television rating) Expressed in terms of a specific audience, e.g. adult TVRs, home TVRs, etc. For example, for a single TV spot 21 housewife TVRs means that 21% of all housewives were recorded as viewers of that spot. For more than one spot, TVRs represent the sum of individual spots. For example, a campaign of 20 spots, each of 15 TVRs is equivalent to 300 TVRs.

Glossary of sampling terms

Probability (random)

Disproportionate stratified random sample Where there is a marked variation in the sizes of the strata in a population, it is more efficient to use a variable sampling fraction. To calculate the sample estimates for the population as a whole, estimates driven from individual strata are weighted according to their relative size. A disproportionate sample is also used when the characteristic to be studied is markedly variable across the population, e.g. unemployment.

Multi-stage area sample The sample is drawn in more than one stage, usually after stratification by region and type of district. Three-stage drawing is quite common: first, constituencies; second, ward or polling districts; third, electors, using the register of electors as a sampling frame. This form of cluster sampling has more than two segmental stages of random sampling.

PPS With probability proportionate to size of population/electorate – used in multi-stage drawing and associated with the use of systematic interval. A range of numbers, equivalent to its population, is attached to each item on the list (e.g. each constituency, each polling district) before the draw is made. A number between one and the total population, divided by the number of sampling points, is drawn at random (or generated by computer). This indicates the starting point; the list of items is then systematically sampled, the probability of selection being proportionate to the size of each item.

Probability sample Each member of the population has a known (and non-zero) chance of being selected into the sample.

Proportionate stratified random sample A uniform sampling fraction is applied to all the strata, i.e. the proportion of n (the number in the sample) to N (the number in the population) is the same for all strata.

Sampling frame A specification of the population which allows for the identification of individual items. The frame should be completed, up to date and without duplication of items.

Simple cluster sample One stage over sampling in which the population is divided into clusters of units (sub-populations) from which a random sample of a few clusters can be chosen. All units in the chosen clusters can then be selected from a study.

Simple random sample All the population members are listed and numbered and the sample is drawn in one stage.

Stratification The population is divided into homogenous groups (strata) whose relative size is known. Strata must be mutually exclusive. A random sample is taken in each stratum.

Systematic sample The sampling interval is calculated (let $N/n = k$). The first member of the sample is drawn at random from a numbered list; k is added to the number of the randomly selected member. This identifies the second member and the procedure is repeated. (N = number of items in the population and n = number of items in the sample.)

Two-stage area sample Instead of selecting all units, a random selection of the chosen clusters are studied. This form of cluster sampling allows a wider and more representative examination of a geographic area.

Purposive (non-random)

Convenience sample Sample units are chosen according to what is conveniently available to the researcher.

Judgement sample A method of purposive sampling based on subjective judgement. Assumes the researcher is knowledgeable about the population in choosing the sample units.

Purposive sample A non-probability sampling method selection of sample members dependent on human judgement.

Quota sample A method of stratified sampling in which selection of sample members within each stratum is non-random. The population is divided into cells or segments subjectively on the basis of having certain control characteristics for each population cell; a quota of units is chosen based on the judgement of researchers. Sample units are selected for study to fill the quota in each cell.

Index